THE K.F.M. BRUCE LEE SOCIETY

A RETROSPECTIVE LOOK AT BRUCE LEE MANIA AND THE KUNG FU CRAZE OF THE 1970S

Compiled and Edited by
Carl Fox

PROMETHEAN PRESS™
Dallas   Vancouver

Published by Promethean Press™
A division of Promethean Multimedia, LLC
Dallas, TX
www.promethean-press.com

In association with

© 2021 Carl Fox
All Rights Reserved. No part of this book may be reproduced, scanned, or distributed in any printed or electronic form without permission.

Printed in the United States of America
ISBN 978-1-77331-003-9

For Caroline and George

Dedicated to my Dad, Kevin Fox, for supporting and assisting with my dreams and endeavours.

ACKNOWLEDGEMENTS

I would like to thank the following people:

Andrew Staton
For the many opportunities over the years, your guidance,
your wisdom, and your knowledge.

James Bishop
For your friendship, inspiration, and
editorial assistance during the production of this book.

Jason Hart
For your friendship and for supplying the missing three news sheets.
This book would never have been finished without your kind help.

Dean Routledge
For your friendship and putting up with our
Saturday night telephone conversations.

*For their contribution to this book with their stories, photos and knowledge,
I would also like to thank:*

John Little	**Martin Hughes**	**Matthew Robins**
John Overall	**Gary Kohatsu**	**Alison French**
Glynn Darbyshire	**Robert Lee**	**Gary Daniels**
Andrew Hadden	**Tony Lundberg**	**Mike Devereux**

*Most of all, for her hard work and dedication between 1976 and 1983,
I would also like to thank:*

Pam Hadden
Without you, this book would not exist.
Rest In Peace, Pam.

CREDITS

Original Newsletter Text & Layout Design: Pam Hadden
Editing and Book Layout & Design: Carl Fox
Additional Book Design and Copy Editing: James Bishop
Photograph Acknowlegements: Tony Lundberg, The Passionate Mind Institute,
Alamy, Gary Daniels, Carl Fox, Anne and Fred Hunt

Editor's Notes and Primary Research: Carl Fox
Additional Research: Andrew Staton, Jason Hart, & John Overall
Scanning Duties: George Kevin Fox
Cover Design: Carl Fox

The content contained herein is historical in nature and was originally published four decades ago. Please do not respond to any offers mentioned within this book or send any money through the post. This book is not affiliated with nor endorsed by the original Bruce Lee Society fan club. BRUCE LEE is a trademark of Bruce Lee Enterprises, LLC.

CONTENTS

Foreword	9
An Introduction	11
How To Use This Book	13
A Brief History of the Bruce Lee Society	15
The British Board of Film Censors vs. Bruce Lee	17
Issue #01 (September 1976)	29
Issue #02 (December 1976)	37
Issue #03 (March 1977)	49
Issue #04 (June 1977)	65
My Introduction to Bruce Lee by Glynn Darbyshire	79
Issue #05 (September 1977)	81
Issue #06 (December 1977)	95
Issue #07 (March 1978)	109
Issue #08 (June 1978)	125
Issue #09 (September 1978)	137
The Game of Death - An Interview with John Little	153
Issue #10 (December 1978)	159
An Interview with Gary Kohatsu	175
Issue #11 (March 1979)	179
Issue #12 (June 1979)	193
Issue #13 (September 1979)	209
The Great Voyage of Discovery: Pam Hadden in Hong Kong	219
Issue #14 (December 1979)	225
Issue #15 (March 1980)	237
Issue #16 (June 1980)	249
Issue #17 (September 1980)	261
Tony Lundberg Remembers the Bruce Lee Society	273
Issue #18 (December 1980)	277
Interview with Gary Daniels	291
Issue #19 (March 1981)	295
A Fan's Recollections by Martin Hughes	309
Issue #20 (June 1981)	311
Issue #21 (September 1981)	323
Issue #22 (December 1981)	337
Issue #23 (March 1982)	353
Issue #24 (June 1982)	375
Issue #25 (September 1982)	397
Issue #26 (December 1982)	417
Issue #27 (March 1983)	435
Issue #28 (June 1983)	453
Issue #29 (September 1983)	471
Issue #30 (December 1983)	491
Endings and Reflections	503
The Society, Pam Hadden & I by Tony Lundberg	506
Epilogue: *After the Bruce Lee Society*	511
Bruce Lee Society Membership	514
Bruce Lee Society Ephemera	521
Full QR Code Website Links	535

FOREWORD

When the Bruce Lee phenomenon broke internationally in the mid 1970s the United Kingdom led the way in publishing information and photos of the late superstar. Poster magazines such as *Kung Fu Monthly*, along with the various books put out by the same company, were highly anticipated, and (at least in Canada) anyone who had a contact in England was quickly sought out to establish a pipeline of Bruce Lee material flowing between the two countries.

The *Kung Fu Monthly* Bruce Lee Society was an offshoot of this and those who were fortunate enough to be members of it were the recipients of all the latest information, products and meetings of fellow fans of Lee. I had always thought that it was a society that was restricted exclusively to those who lived in the UK and, consequently, never sought membership in the fraternity. I believed then that I had simply missed out on all the material to which the Society members were entitled.

That was indeed the case until Carl Fox took on the massive task of compiling all of the material that appeared in those Bruce Lee Society newsletters and, in so doing, has constructed a time machine of sorts that allows us to travel back to a time when Bruce Lee, Kung Fu and Hong Kong Kung Fu movies were new, mysterious and fascinating. Carl has done a tremendous job on this book, and an even more remarkable job of preserving the history of Bruce Lee fandom in the UK.

- John Little

INTRODUCTION

Welcome and first of all, thank you for purchasing this book; It really means a lot to me.

My first interest in Bruce Lee began in 1986 around the age of seven, when I saw my cousin Glen watching *Enter the Dragon* on TV and from then on, I was hooked. My first Bruce Lee item which I can remember, was a blue t-shirt with a *Way of the Dragon* image on the front that my parents bought for me from one of those "Print Your Own T-Shirt" kiosks scattered around many of the British seaside towns.

Throughout the years, I collected various pieces of memorabilia and in 1998, after taking a website design course, I started my first website, "Dragon (UK)," which at the time was one of only few websites dedicated to Bruce Lee.

Whilst running the website, I got to know author James Bishop, who, at the time, was running another Bruce Lee website which was part of the "Everything About..." brand.

I met with James at the 2001 Dragon Expo convention in Las Vegas, where he introduced me to Andrew Staton, the head of the Bruce & Brandon Lee Association (BBLA) in the UK. After several discussions with Andrew, I was asked to write for the BBLA and design their website, as well as write for the magazines *Impact* and *Martial Arts Illustrated*, which I did for over fifteen years.

In 2002, I purchased a batch of Bruce Lee Society newsletters on eBay from Martin Hughes, a member whose name appears so often in the early issues. I flicked through the newsletters and thought nothing of them. As time passed, I flicked through them again and one day I realised that I was three issues short so every so often, I'd have a look for them online. More time passed, I had a family and one day while flicking through the newsletters again, I came to realise what a wonderful story they told. It wasn't a tell-all book about Bruce Lee that had been done so many times before, nor was it full of rare photographs. It was, instead, an honest representation of a time that we so often forget about in the internet age we live in. At that point I thought how great it would be to compile all of the newsletters into one complete volume for fans to have their own copies. Being little point to a project that I couldn't complete due to the missing issues, I reached out to my old friend Jason Hart to see if he could help with the three missing issues, which he duly sent through the post, and with doing so, this project began.

During the COVID-19 pandemic of 2020, I sat down and painstakingly scanned all 30 issues of the newsletters. The plan was to scan each page as an image and represent each newsletter as it originally appeared. However, with recent GDPR (General Data Protection Regulations), there could have been various implications with printing the addresses that were in the original newsletters, even though some were over 35 years old.

So I began the mammoth task of converting the newsletter images into text and saving each image as a separate file. That presented its own problems due some poor photocopying on the original newsletters, the non-uniform layout used throughout, spelling mistakes, etc. Eventually everything was converted, edited, reformatted, and spell-checked. **EDITOR'S NOTES** are included at the end of each newsletter, however, some corrections are made directly in the newsletters themselves. I've tried to include as much of the original material as I could, however seemingly pointless. Most typos have been corrected, although some have been left in for various reasons.

This isn't a "be-all and end-all" book about the Bruce Lee Society; it is merely a finger pointing to the moon.

If you were an original member of the Society, I hope that when you read this book, you'll be transported back in time for a fond and nostalgic walk down Memory Lane. Perhaps you were still at school or in your first serious relationship or just finding your way in the world and when you read these newsletters, they make you think of that time with fondness. If you're reading the newsletters for the first time, I really hope you enjoy the wonderful story contained in them.

Every single person in these newsletters had a story to tell; whether it was when they first saw Bruce Lee, or how they felt when Bruce jumped through the air on screen, or how Bruce Lee inspired them in some aspect of their life…

… this is for them.

Carl Fox
August 2020

A FEW NOTES ABOUT THE BOOK

I have tried to make the book as fascinating and interactive as I can, so here are a few notes that may assist you before you start.

The book is laid out in the format of one newsletter, followed by the "**EDITOR'S NOTES**," which comprise of anything that I felt could be explained a little clearer. It

is only basic research to give you an idea or introduction to the subject. You are free to do your own in-depth research at your own will.

Throughout the book, mostly in the "**EDITOR'S NOTES**" sections, you'll see odd-looking squares as shown here. These are QR Codes and feature a website address. To use the QR Codes, you will need a Smart Phone or Tablet using Android or iOS.

Head over to the App Store (iOS) or Google Play Store (Android) to download a QR Scanner App if you don't have one. There are many free ones available, though some may contain advertisements. Personally on Android, I use "QR & Barcode Scanner," a free App, which features a small banner advert at the bottom.

After you get your QR Code scanner, you're ready to go through the book. Upon encountering a QR Code, bring up your scanner app on your phone and scan it.

Once scanned, it will take you where the "**EDITOR'S NOTES**" state. The "Store" codes will take you to an online store where the item mentioned can be purchased. The "Video" codes will take you to watch a video clip, be it a trailer, documentary, interview, etc. The "Book" codes will lead you to download a PDF file of a some printed material. To view PDF files, you will need a PDF reader, many of which are available in The Apple App Store and Google Play Store. For PC and Mac, "Adobe Acrobat Reader" is available for free, as is the lighter free software "Foxit PDF Reader."

Happy Scanning!

Should you wish to do it the old fashioned way and enter each link manually, please head to page 535 for links to all videos, books and store items.

A BRIEF HISTORY OF THE BRUCE LEE SOCIETY

Kung Fu Monthly was an extremely profitable publication from its beginnings in the mid 1970s until its end in the mid 1980s, so much so that it was released in multiple countries and in multiple languages.

In the early days of *Kung Fu Monthly*, the only official Bruce Lee fan club in the UK was run by Rhona McVay. With her team of helpers and fully endorsed by Raymond Chow and Golden Harvest, Rhona enthusiastically ran The Official Bruce Lee Fan Club out of her London bedroom, replying to as many fans as she could. Letters to the fan club were varied; some fans wanted information about Bruce Lee and Kung Fu, while some fans started their letters with phrases such as, "Please don't laugh but I want to be as good as Bruce Lee."

In 1975, after returning from a Bruce Lee sight-seeing trip abroad, Rhona decided to close The Official Bruce Lee Fan Club, prompting Felix Dennis to pounce.

The Bruce Lee Secret Society was first featured in *Kung Fu Monthly* No. 20 from 1975, telling fans that, "*KFM* is planning to start its own Bruce Lee fan club!" and to "Hold on... don't write in yet. Full details in *KFM* No. 21."

It seemed that in No. 21, editor Felix Yen didn't have time to put full details together, instead opting for a full page advert on the back page stating that "full details will be in the next month's issue."

Kung Fu Monthly No. 22 boasted on the front cover, *"NOW OPEN! THE BRUCE LEE SECRET SOCIETY,"* with the back page of the magazine declaring:

> "Hi — it's Jenny Lee here and am I happy to be writing these few words! Thanks largely to a lot of persuasion from you, the KFM readers, I am delighted to announce the grand opening of the Bruce Lee Secret Society. Yes, your own Kung Fu Monthly is taking up the reins along with Pam Hadden and Carmella Rapa (who will be joint presidents of the club). They'll handle all the letter writing and day-to-day running of things. Good luck Pam and Carmella, I know you're going to need it! OK, I've said my piece so it's back to the mail for me. Over to you ..."

Thanks for the intro Jenny - we couldn't have done it better ourselves! Because we've got so much to tell you, I hope you'll forgive us if we itemise everything - that way well be able to squeeze more in.

1. On application you'll receive your membership card and a number, plus the fabulous Society Kit, containing your very own official certificate of membership (for framing), a Bruce Lee Secret Society badge and sticker, an autographed Bruce Lee picture and four incredible photos of the Little Dragon in action that we promise have never been published in the world before! All this plus news, views, facts and info - what a great package!
2. Then, once every three months, we'll post to you the quarterly Society news sheet - brim full of the latest chit-chat, letters, pen-pals, club offers and much more.

3. In every single issue of KFM you'll find your very own Bruce Lee Secret Society corner ... we'll be handling that!
4. All members will soon be able to get a discount on most KFM mail order offers.
5. On top of all that, there'll be lots of special Bruce Lee mail order products exclusively on offer to club members.
6. We are very sorry, but we have to point out that there is NO connection whatsoever between this and the previous Bruce Lee Fan Club. Regretfully therefore, we shall not be able to enter into any correspondence in regard to problems arising from its closure.
7. Sorry again! ... but we do really have to restrict membership to the United Kingdom only.
8. Finally, may we say here and now that we shall not be replying to letters that come without stamped addressed envelopes - you have been warned!

So there it is - what a great line-up and all for an subscription of only £2.95 - not bad eh?

Judging by the mail delude that comes in through Jenny's door, we think we have a fair idea of what we are letting ourselves in for — it's a good thing we're gluttons for punishment! But remember, if you've got any bright ideas on what you'd like to see in your club, don't hesitate to write ... we promise you ALL letters will be answered. And by the way, don't forget that's exactly what it is - your club. After all, what's a club without members?

The old Bruce Lee Fan Club apparently had around five thousand members when it closed, so let's see if we can double it — and keep open! DON'T DELAY! Just send your £2.95 to: The Bruce Lee Secret Society, Kung-Fu Monthly, 39 Goodge Street, London W1P 1FD. (Cheques/Postal orders made out to Kung-Fu Monthly please.) We'll get your Society Kit and membership card off to you as quickly as possibly. See you soon .

- Pam and Carmella

As you can see from the last paragraph, The Bruce Lee Secret Society was not the first Bruce lee fan club in the UK. That honour goes to the Bruce Lee Official Fan Club, run by Rhona McVay from 1974 to 1976. After the club was recognised as an official organisation by Producer Raymond Chow, letters poured in all over the world and some reports suggest there were as many as 22,000 members of the club by the time it folded in 1976. Whether that figure is true or not, it's a bit of a difference from the 5,000 mentioned just above.

There is a two-page interview with Rhona in *Kung Fu Monthly* No. 9, where she discusses the fan club and her Bruce Lee related pilgrimage to the United States. Footage of her being interviewed by the BBC was shown in their 1997 TV documentary *The Kung Fu Years*.

The Bruce Lee Society's membership numbers started at 1000. The earliest member I could find was member Eileen & Joey Green (different names appear throughout the newsletters) with number 1007, The very latest membership number I could find was number 3354 which belonged to Rajiv Gaikwar, who was the 2,254th member of The Bruce Lee Society.

THE BRITISH BOARD OF FILM CENSORS VS BRUCE LEE

Throughout the Bruce Lee Society news sheets, the censorship of martial arts films, especially those featuring Bruce Lee and the use of weapons, was a constant topic amongst fans. The purpose of this chapter is not to be the definitive guide to the censorship cuts but to assist you in understanding the cuts referred to as you read through the news letters contained in this book.

The nucleus of this article featured in a Bruce Lee 30th Anniversary Supplement from the UK magazine *Impact*.

It is with thanks to Hong Kong Legends and Warner Brothers, that since 2001, we have finally had all of Bruce Lee's films on DVD and Blu-ray, digitally remastered and fully uncut for the first time ever in the UK. Finally, UK fans can marvel at what the rest of the world have seen for years, Bruce Lee's most famous weapon - the nunchaku. The same cuts continued on home video formats, beginning with VHS and Betamax and continuing to DVD.

Even upon their official original cinema releases, the films were subject to cuts. The odd few prints were shown uncut, but the majority, in general, were subject to the censor's scissors.

Back in the days of the first VHS recorders, some of Bruce Lee's films did make it onto home video uncut, especially when they weren't required to be submitted to the British Board of Film Censors (BBFC) prior to release. Once the distributors were required to pass everything through Ferman & Co's system first, all hell broke loose with the fans, as evident in the Bruce Lee Society news sheets.

Throughout the Bruce Lee Society news sheets, the BBFC's Secretary, James Ferman, gets quite a lot of flack for the cuts. Having been appointed to the role in 1975, he was under tremendous public pressure to tighten up censorship by making cuts and a lot of fans firmly point the finger at him for doing so. But as is evident from this article, his predecessor Stephen Murphy had already started the ball rolling in October 1973 when he ordered the first cuts for *Enter the Dragon*'s original theatrical release.

Some cinema releases up to the early 1980s were completely uncut as some uncut prints managed to slip through the net, as mentioned by members in the news sheets and that is entirely possible.

THE BIG BOSS

The Big Boss was first submitted to the BBFC on 12th February 1974, where they ordered eight seconds of cuts in total, which included:

- Edits to the fight where Lee loses the medallion given to him by his mother
- Removal of shots of ice picks and knives being thrown into the bad guys' chests
- Trims made to several kicks and blows in the final fight

The approved running time for the film's 1974 theatrical release was 94 minutes 26 seconds.

The first home video release in April 1982 (VHS & Betamax) from Rank Video featured the Golden Harvest cartoon-style international poster on the front cover, with the rear cover featuring the synopsis inside a hand-drawn bamboo frame. Also on the rear cover and green-labelled cassette is the "X" certificate, a stated running time of 95 minutes and the catalogue number 74100700. The actual running time was 94 minutes 26 seconds, the same as the original cinema release. Rank Video released the film in a cardboard slip case first, before issuing a standard wraparound case later on.

Though not cut from the film due to UK censorship, several other scenes are still missing from the film, despite it being released uncut. Some of those missing scenes feature:

- Bruce Lee and James Tien jumping out of the way of a runaway cart in the first half of the film, just after they leave the gambling den.
- Nora Miao smiling at Lee from her refreshment cart which appeared in the 1971 trailer but didn't appear in the film.
- More graphic footage of the cousins' bodies being cut up in the ice factory.
- Spurting blood from the fight where Lee loses the medallion given to him by his mother.
- In the banquet scene where Lee gets drunk, alternative footage shows him imagining the young prostitute topless.
- Footage in a Super 8 trailer showing excessive blood pouring from James Tien's head during his fight with Tony Liu.
- When Bruce Lee sees James Tien's and the prostitute's heads in ice, the same Super 8 trailer mentioned above shows the blood-splattered face of someone else, too.
- Bruce Lee planting the saw through the head of the thug in the night time ice factory fight.
- The discovery of Bruce Lee's dead relatives after he returns home from the ice factory battle has been trimmed.
- A shot removed of Bruce Lee clenching his fist and shouting at the riverside.
- The entire scene of Lee's third and final visit to the prostitute is missing. Footage of this was in the 1971 trailer.
- Lee tasting his own blood in the final fight against the big boss at the end after being slashed across the abdomen.

Still photographs and footage of some of the scenes exist but not them all.

There are claims that the "Saw in the Head" scene was shown as part of the *KFM* Bruce Lee Festival at the Gaumont State Theatre in London on first December 1979.

KFM tried to acquire an English dubbed print of the film from EMI, who refused, wanting to keep them for their own re-release around the same time. Unperturbed, they approached Eddie Leahey at Golden Harvest's office in London and surprisingly, were given an uncut 35mm Mandarin print of the film, which some attendees say featured the infamous "Saw in the Head" scene.

Strangely, for each attendee who claims it was in the showing that day, there's one who says it wasn't. Even stranger, is the fact that there was no mention of it in *KFM* or the Society news sheets. In *Kung Fu Monthly No.* 53, it was stated that the version that they shown was showing signs of wear and wasn't in the best of conditions. There are rumours that a copy of the full uncut Mandarin print is in the hands of a private collector but as of 2020, that person has not been revealed.

For more information regarding the missing footage from The Big Boss, be sure to read Jason Hart's fantastic in-depth article at http://www.bruceleelives.co.uk/missingboss.html.

CUT HISTORY
As provided on the BBFC website as of 23/07/2020:

Date	Submitted Time	Passed Time	Cuts
12/02/74	Submitted Time 98m30s	Passed Time N/A	Cuts Yes[1]
14/04/86	Submitted Time 94m26s	Passed Time 94m26s	Cuts None
23/10/00	Submitted Time 95m58s	Passed Time 95m58s	Cuts None
16/11/00	Submitted Time 95m58s	Passed Time 95m58s	Cuts None
22/04/05	Submitted Time 94m26s	Passed Time 94m26s	Cuts None
22/04/05	Submitted Time N/A	Passed Time N/A	Cuts N/A[2]

[1] Running time in film format. No cut details available on the BBFC website. Other sources report 8 seconds of cuts.

[2] No details available for this entry though it was for the Medusa/Hong Kong Legends Platinum Edition release.

FIST OF FURY

Fist of Fury was first submitted to the BBFC on 22nd November 1972, where they ordered cuts to be made, but there are no official record of what those cuts were. According to some sources, they requested the removal of Lee kicking the boss in the throat before sending him crashing through the shoji screen at the end of the film.

With the slight cut, the approved running time for the film's theatrical release was 101 minutes 23 seconds, though even with that time, it would seem that the cut mentioned above is still included. On first August 1973, a company called Anglo EMI Distributors Ltd submitted the film again at a shorter running time of 85 minutes 32 seconds under its USA title *The Chinese Connection*, which was passed with no cuts.

There are also reports that an uncertified, full uncut version slipped out in 1976 without BBFC approval, which could have been the basis for reports of people seeing the full uncut version in cinemas in the late 70's and early 80's.

The first Home Video release in April 1982 (VHS & Betamax) from Rank Video featured the Golden Harvest cartoon-style international poster on the front cover, with the rear cover featuring the synopsis inside a hand-drawn bamboo frame. Also on the rear cover and green-labelled cassette is the 'X' certificate, a stated running time of 100 minutes and the catalogue number 74100710. The actual running time was 101 minutes 23 seconds, the same as the original cinema release, however, the scene involving Lee kicking the boss in the throat is intact. As with the *Big Boss* release, Rank Video released the film in a cardboard slip case first, before issuing a standard wraparound case later on.

CUT HISTORY
As provided on the BBFC website as of 23/07/2020:

Date	Submitted Time	Passed Time	Cuts
22/11/72	Submitted Time 105m38s	Passed Time N/A	Cuts Yes[1]
01/08/73	Submitted Time 85m32s	Passed Time 85m32s	Cuts None
14/04/86	Submitted Time 101m23s	Passed Time 98m32s	Cuts 2m51s
17/01/01	Submitted Time 101m54s	Passed Time 101m54s	Cuts None
31/01/01	Submitted Time 101m54s	Passed Time 101m54s	Cuts None
03/05/01	Submitted Time N/A	Passed Time N/A	Cuts N/A[2]

[1] Running time in film format. No cut details available on BBFC website. Other sources report slight cut to end fight scene.

[2] No details available for this entry though it was for the Medusa/Hong Kong Legends release.

WAY OF THE DRAGON

Way of the Dragon was first submitted to the BBFC on 15th February 1974, where they ordered approximately seven minutes of cuts, giving an approved running time for the film's theatrical release of around 87 minutes 21 seconds. According to the BBFC website, the details are the cuts are unavailable. However, it would appear that the cuts were to completely remove the double nunchaku scene, as well as making cuts to almost every fight sequence including:

- The removal of the "Dragon seeks path" and "Dragon whips his tail"
- sequence during Lee's first fight with the thugs
- Several blows to other thugs in the same fight are removed
- Cuts to the scene where Lee beats the gunman in the apartment
- Several cuts in the scene where the boss visits the restaurant for the first time and orders several of the waiters either beaten or pistol-whipped
- Lee beating several of the thugs with a bo staff in the courtyard at the back of

A RETROSPECTIVE LOOK AT BRUCE LEE MANIA & THE KUNG FU CRAZE OF THE 1970S

- the restaurant to be trimmed
- The complete removal of Lee using two pairs of nunchakus at once
- Cuts to the scene where Lee beats up the thugs in the boss' office
- Small cuts to where Whang In Sik and Chuck Norris' students fight each other
- Bob Wall's outdoor fight with the waiters to be edited
- Cuts to the fight between Bruce Lee and Bob Wall
- Edits to the fights between Whang In Sik, the waiter and Bruce Lee
- Footage cut of the fight between Bruce Lee and Chuck Norris

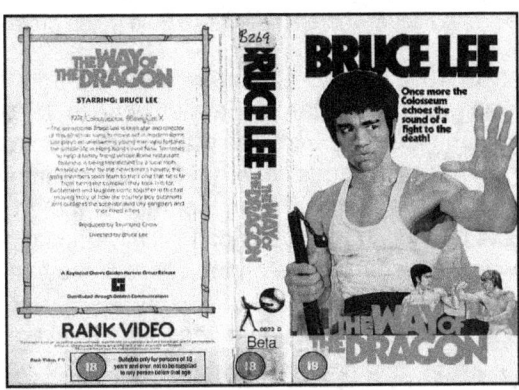

The first home video release in November 1982 (VHS & Betamax) from Rank Video featured the Golden Harvest cartoon-style international poster on the front cover, with the rear cover featuring the synopsis inside a hand-drawn bamboo frame. Also on the rear cover and green-labelled cassette is the "X" certificate, a stated running time of 88 minutes and the catalogue number 74100720. The actual running time was 87 minutes 21 seconds, the same as the original cinema release. As with the *Big Boss* and *Fist of Fury* releases, Rank Video released the film in a cardboard slip case first, before issuing a standard wraparound case later on.

CUT HISTORY
As provided on the BBFC website as of 23/07/2020:

Date	Submitted Time	Passed Time	Cuts
15/02/74	Submitted Time 98m31s	Passed Time N/A	Cuts Yes[1]
10/04/86	Submitted Time 87m21s	Passed Time 86m10s	Cuts 1m11s
18/05/01	Submitted Time 94m57s	Passed Time 94m57s	Cuts None
15/06/05	Submitted Time 86m9s	Passed Time 86m9s	Cuts None[2]
15/06/05	Submitted Time 95m0s	Passed Time 95m0s	Cuts None

[1] Running time in film format. No cut details available on BBFC website. Other sources report approximately seven minutes of cuts.
[2] The film was submitted twice on the same day. It appears that Medusa/Hong Kong Legends accidentally submitted a cut version in the first instance.

ENTER THE DRAGON

Upon submission on 23rd October 1973 for *Enter the Dragon's* theatrical release, the BBFC requested several scenes to be cut but the exact length of cuts is unknown as only the censor's notes are available.
The censor's notes dictated the cuts to be made were as follows:

- The day after Lee goes out for his first night time investigation, Han demands his guards are punished. The BBFC demanded the scenes where Bolo breaks

one guard's neck and another guard's spine to be removed plus the scene where their bloodied bodies are dragged away.
- In the Lee vs. O'Hara fight, the BBFC demanded cuts to remove footage showing Lee kicking O'Hara in the groin, O'Hara with the broken bottles and Lee stamping O'Hara to death.
- The fight with Han and Williams to be trimmed to removed excessive violence.
- In the underground sequence, the BBFC demanded the removal of the scene where Lee snaps the guard's (Jackie Chan's) neck.
- During Roper's final battle with Bolo, the BBFC demanded the removal of the scene where Roper kicks Bolo in the groin and leaves him to fall.

In 1975, Stephen Murphy resigned from his position as BBFC Secretary and was replaced by James Ferman, who in 1979, requested that *Enter the Dragon* be re-submitted for cuts to be made in addition to the ones already made in 1973.

The cuts requested in 1979 were to remove all sight of the nunchaku, not from just the film, but also from the trailers and promotional posters. It is entire plausible that the nunchaku poster ban initially only applied to cinema posters as the weapon was still clearly visible on the cover of the first few home video cassette releases.

It would appear that the ban was only applied to the home video covers from 1988, with the formation of the Video Packaging Review Committee (VPRC).

When released on Home Video in the early 1980s, *Enter the Dragon* was released in four different version, yet only one was fully uncut and it was actually longer than the original theatrical release, as you'll discover. All four versions featured the same artwork on the front cover (apart from the second rental release stating 'Rental' on the front cover and spine) of Bruce Lee holding his nunchakus aloft but varied slightly on the rear cover and cassette labels.

The first version, released in December 1980 (VHS and Betamax) was intended for rental use only. It was the only fully uncut version released in the UK on video until 2001, containing footage that wasn't even in the original theatrical release from January 1974. In the very early days of home video, distributors were not required to submit their releases for classification, hence why it was released with the footage that the BBFC demanded be cut from the original cinema release. This release was not certified anywhere and featured a full synopsis on the rear cover with cast details being listed on a separate black card inside the case. The cassette tape for this version featured a white front and bottom label. The running time for this release was 94 minutes 51 seconds, though as stated in the Bruce Lee Society news sheets, the rear cover and cassette incorrectly states a running time of 86 minutes. Warner Catalogue No. PEVN1006.

The next rental only version, released in 1982 (VHS and Betamax) was certified "X" (rear cover and cassette label) and featured a condensed half-and-half synopsis and cast list on the rear cover. This version featured "Rental" in red text in a blue box on the front cover and spine. The cassette tape for this version featured a blue front and bottom label. This was the first release of the movie to be released on home video after having a certificate from the BBFC. The cuts made, were the same ones requested in October 1973 to obtain a "X" certificate for the theatrical release. The actual running time for this release was 94 minutes 30 seconds, equating to 21 seconds of cuts from the original home video version. The rear cover states a running time of 96 minutes. Warner Catalogue No. WEV1006.

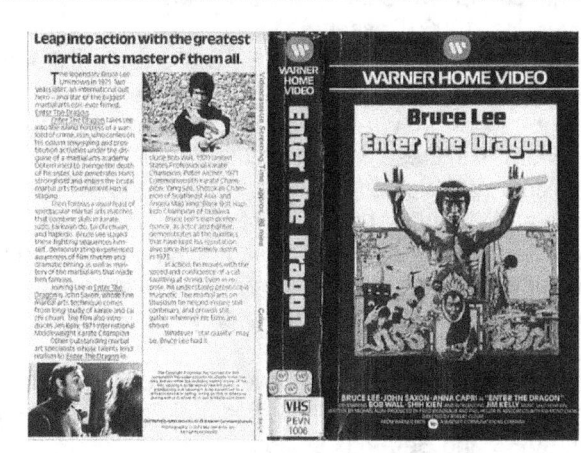

The first retail version, released a short time after its rental counterpart in 1982 (VHS and Betamax) was certified "18" (rear cover and cassette label). 1982 signalled a shift from the old "X" certificate to the new "18" one. This release featured the same condensed half-and-half synopsis and cast list on the rear cover as the rental version. The cassette tape for this version featured a white and blue (old oval style) WB logo-patterned front and bottom label, which stated a running time of 96 minutes. The rear cover stated a running time of 95 minutes. However, the official running time for this release was again, like its "X" certified rental counterpart, 94 minutes 30 seconds, having the same 21 seconds of cuts demanded for the theatrical and second rental releases. Warner Catalogue No. PEV1006.

The second retail version, released in 1984 (VHS) was the last to use the original artwork on the front cover and the first one to be released after the Video Recordings Act (VRA) 1984 was brought in. It was certified "18" on the rear cover only, as the cassette carried no certificate. It featured the exact same rear cover as the first retail release (condensed half-and-half synopsis and cast list) and stated a running time of 95  minutes. The front cassette label featured the more modern "shield-style" Warner Brothers logo used between 1984-1997, while omitting the bottom cassette label completely. The actual running time for this version was approximately one minute shorter than previous home video releases as the 1979 nunchaku related cuts would now have applied, due to the VRA. Also worth noting on this release was a hologram-type security sticker on the cassette. Early versions of the release featured the old oval logo on the security sticker, while later releases feature WHV. Warner Catalogue No. PEV1006 (Cover) No. 1006 (Cassette).

Warner Brothers re-submitted a pre-cut version film to the BBFC on 31st January 1988 for reclassification. The pre-cut submitted length was 94 minutes 27 seconds, which was almost the same cut version they released theatrically in 1974 and on home video in 1982. Not just content with these pre-made cuts, the BBFC demanded that the 1979 theatrical release cuts be repicated on video. The cuts made totalled a mammoth 1 minute 45 seconds and stated that every sight of the nunchaku should be removed from the film and the trailers. The Video Packaging Review Committee also came in force at this time, meaning that the video covers were also now subject to the same rules that applied to the cinema posters and promotional material from 1979.

It is interesting to note that the only uncut versions ever released in the United Kingdom with the original soundtrack and without the additional 25th Anniversary scenes, are the first ever 1980 VHS and Betamax editions.

Hopefully one day in the future, Warner Bros. would be kind enough to include that version in one of their releases, even if it's a direct transfer from the US Laserdisc in Standard Definition with Mono Sound. Those original VHS and Betamax tapes are getting hard to come by now. After all, the Criterion Collection have included it as part of their 2020 boxset released in the USA.

It has been extremely difficult to compile a 100% accurate list of cuts and reasons behind them for *Enter the Dragon*. This is because it was submitted several times; some submissions were recorded but some weren't. The 1973 submission is recorded but doesn't list the official passed running time and all we have is a case study on the BBFC website that states what cuts were ordered. The 1979 submission is not recorded at all on the BBFC website and is only mentioned in the same case study on the website.

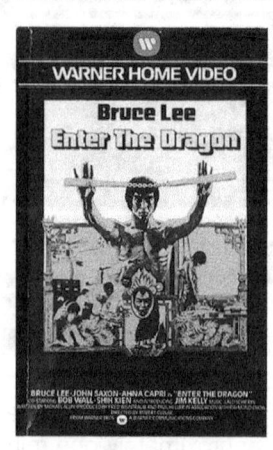  

CUT HISTORY
As provided on the BBFC website as of 23/07/2020:

23/10/73	Submitted Time 99m9s	Passed Time N/A	Cuts N/A[1]
31/01/88	Submitted Time 94m27s	Passed Time 94m41s	Cuts 1m45s
10/11/93	Submitted Time 194m57s	Passed Time 94m33s	Cuts 21s
26/01/96	Submitted Time 93m25s	Passed Time 93m25s	Cuts None
13/11/98	Submitted Time 96m58s	Passed Time 96m58s	Cuts None
31/07/01	Submitted Time 98m16s	Passed Time 98m16s	Cuts None

[1] Running time in film format. No cut details available on BBFC website but a case study on the website gives some notes.

GAME OF DEATH

Almost five years after Lee's death, *Game of Death* was first submitted to the BBFC on 26th April 1978, where they ordered 3 minutes 59 seconds of cuts, giving an approved running time for the film's theatrical release of 92 minutes 6 seconds. According to the BBFC website, the details of the cuts are unavailable, though it was the entire battle between Lee and Dan Inosanto that was removed.

The first Home Video release in December 1982 (VHS & Betamax) from Rank Video featured the Golden Harvest cartoon-style international poster on the front cover, with the rear cover featuring the synopsis inside a hand-drawn bamboo frame. Also on the rear cover and green-labelled cassette is the "X" certificate, a stated running time of 95 minutes and the catalogue number 74100730. The actual running time was 92 minutes 6 seconds, the same as the original cinema release. As with their other releases, Rank Video released the film in a cardboard slip case first, before issuing a standard wraparound case later on.

CUT HISTORY
As provided on the BBFC website as of 23/07/2020:

26/04/78	Submitted Time 92m49s	Passed Time N/A	Cuts Yes[1]
14/04/86	Submitted Time 92m6s	Passed Time 94m4s	Cuts 2s
28/08/01	Submitted Time 96m15s	Passed Time 96m15s	Cuts None
15/06/05	Submitted Time 92m6s	Passed Time 92m6s	Cuts None[2]
15/06/05	Submitted Time 96m15s	Passed Time 96m15s	Cuts None

[1] Running time in film format. No cut details available on BBFC website. Other sources report approximately four minutes of cuts, primarily the removal of the Lee/Inosanto fight.

IN SUMMARY

So there you have it. Looking back, it seems that *Fist of Fury* was really the only Bruce Lee film to generally avoid the censor's scissors and the logical explanation for that is down to when it was certified. When it was first submitted on 22nd November 1972, the Kung Fu craze in the UK hadn't even begun, with the film only being shown in small independent and Chinese cinemas. A little over twelve months later, *Enter the Dragon* was released and that's when it all kicked off. Within a few months of the film's release, *The Big Boss* and *Way of the Dragon* were rushed through to the censors to satisfy the demand of the fans but the negative press was already in full swing by that point, hence the heavy cuts to *Way of the Dragon*. A combination of growing public pressure on the BBFC, the Video Recordings Act 1984 and the Video Recording Packaging Committee all contributed to censorship issues over the years and it's important to note the years they became active in order to understand the possible reasons why certain restrictions were imposed at certain times but some weren't.

In the news sheets, members continually pointed out the seeming contradictory censorship differences that existed in the UK during the 1970's and 1980's, pointing out that you couldn't see Bruce Lee throwing a pair of nunchakus about but you could see someone getting butchered by a chainsaw in *The Texas Chainsaw Massacre*. The issue wasn't the violence; it was the ease in which the violence on screen could be replicated in the real world. The chances of a teenager running around the streets with a chainsaw were extremely slim compared to those of a teenager with a pair of homemade nunchakus. So I can sympathise with the BBFC at the time. However, the UK's brush with Kung Fu mania was well and truly over by the time Rank released their 1986 VHS tapes, and even more so when Warner Brothers released their VHS of *Enter the Dragon* in 1988, yet the BBFC ordered more cuts than they had done previously. Even *Kung Fu Monthly's* publisher Felix Dennis had realised the ship had sailed and abruptly ended the Bruce Lee Society and *Kung Fu Monthly*. Times had changed. Attitudes had changed. The only thing that hadn't changed was the BBFC, who were still a decade behind and would be so for more than a decade later.

The list of cuts mentioned here are not exhaustive but it will give you some information about them, which should assist you when reading the newsletters. It is extremely difficult to be 100% accurate as full records don't exist. This article was compiled from information gathered from several sources such as www.bbfc.co.uk, www.melonfarmers.co.uk, www.pre-cert.co.uk, www.movie-censorship.com, as well as several  publications including the Society newsletters, *Kung Fu Monthly,* and the actual video cassette tapes themselves. Scan the QR Code to see a thirty-two minute video called *Cutting Edge*, which focuses on the various cuts made to *Enter the Dragon* throughout the years.

There will be a difference in the running times of the original theatrical submissions stated here. This is because they were initially submitted in film format at 24fps (frames per second) and all subsequent submissions were in PAL format at 25fps. Due to the difference, the running time must be adjusted accordingly to give an accurate and relative running time.

The K.F.M.

A RETROSPECTIVE LOOK AT BRUCE LEE MANIA & THE KUNG FU CRAZE OF THE 1970S

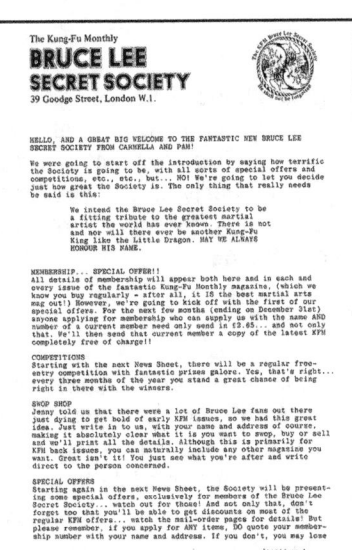

01
September 1976

HELLO, AND A GREAT BIG WELCOME TO THE FANTASTIC NEW BRUCE LEE SECRET SOCIETY FROM CARMELLA AND PAM!

We were going to start off the introduction by saying how terrific the Society is going to be, with all sorts of special offers and competitions, etc., etc., but... NO! We're going to let you decide just how great the Society is. The only thing that really needs be said is this:

We intend the Bruce Lee Secret Society to be a fitting tribute to the greatest martial artist the world has ever known. There is not and nor will there ever be another Kung Fu King like the Little Dragon. MAY WE ALWAYS HONOUR HIS NAME.

MEMBERSHIP... SPECIAL OFFER!!

All details of membership will appear both here and in each and every issue of the fantastic Kung Fu Monthly magazine, (which we know you buy regularly - after all, it IS the best martial arts magazine out!) However, we're going to kick off with the first of our special offers. For the next few months (ending on December 31st) anyone applying for membership who can supply us with the name AND number of a current member need only send in £2.65, and not only that, we'll then send that current member a copy of the latest *KFM* completely free of charge!!

COMPETITIONS

Starting with the next news sheet, there will be a regular free-entry competition with fantastic prizes galore. Yes, that's right; every three months of the year you stand a great chance of being right in there with the winners.

SWOP SHOP

Jenny told us that there were a lot of Bruce Lee fans out there just dying to get hold of early *KFM* issues, so we had this great idea. Just write in to us, with your name and address of course, making it absolutely clear what it is you want to swap, buy or sell and we'll print all the details. Although this is primarily for *KFM* back issues, you can naturally include any other magazine you want. Great isn't it! You just see what you're after and write direct to the person concerned.

SPECIAL OFFERS

Starting again in the next news sheet, the Society will be presenting some special offers, exclusively for members of the Bruce Lee Secret Society so watch out for those! And not only that - Don't forget too that you'll be able to get discounts on most of the regular *KFM* offers so watch the mail order pages for details! But please remember, if you apply for ANY items, DO quote your membership number with your name and address. If you don't, you may lose your reduction.

In fact, there are two golden rules:
1. Always enclose a stamped and addressed envelope when writing IF you are expecting a reply.
2. Always quote your membership number whenever you write for whatever reason.

BRUCE LEE - WORLD NEWS

Just a couple of items this issue.

Naturally with all the work involved in getting the show on the road there's not been a lot of time to tie up the latest news. In the months to come though, we aim to be bringing you all the latest and greatest in hot action AS it happens. And don't forget where you count here! Any little tasty morsel of news that you think the Society and its members ought to know about... just send it along and we'll print it! OK, now the round up.

Bruce Lee has a great club in America called the Dragon Fan Club and we've heard from them that a man named Norman Borine, who used to run a shop dealing in fantastic books and items on Bruce, is planning a week-long Little Dragon Commemoration for later this year. We hope to have more details of this in our next round-up.

We hear there are also plans to open a museum dedicated to Bruce in Los Angeles, with contributions from people all over the world. Wouldn't that be something! Again, we are keeping in touch and anything we find out we'll publish.

On the home front, we've made enquiries concerning the showing of Bruce's fabulous *Longstreet* series which featured some particularly good action shots of the master from a few years ago. We'll keep you posted on any results we get in.

We've also contacted the BBC concerning a documentary which they proposed making on the Little Dragon. As always, to try to find the right department of the BBC is a feat in itself. We were transferred to so many different extensions we nearly gave up. Finally, however, we made it to the right one and found to our dismay that the documentary is not in the pipeline at the moment. It seems that anything to do with Bruce has been put away for some future date (possibly after the release of *Game of Death*). We don't think that's good enough! Hopefully there'll be some way of stepping up the pressure and persuading these people that they must release something on him soon, to let the fans have a chance to see more of the master in action. After all, for younger members, it could be their ONLY chance. What beats us is the fact they can put programmes on television which are so outdated that most people aren't interested in them anyway and then have the nerve to say "by public demand." Okay, Mr. BBC, we're the public and we're demanding!

Finally a big word of thanks to all those readers of *KFM* who wrote in to Jenny to tell her that the elusive Robert Lee album IS very much available in Great Britain. For details of ordering just write to: The Martial Arts Supply Co., Box 119, Slough, Berkshire.

LETTERS

Obviously, having only just started the Society, the letters won't be rolling in for a week or two. However, rather than just leave it at that, we had a chat with Jenny from *KFM* and she's kindly agreed to let us answer some of the mail that she's received in the last few weeks.

Dear KFM,

Enclosed is a cutting from an American magazine (it's an advert from an "Elston Ransom of Jacksonville in Florida" offering for sale 8mm fight scenes from the four big Bruce Lee films). As you can imagine, my first reaction was WOW... Fancy viewing Bruce in action anytime I want!! But is this the case? As you are a magazine whose opinion I respect, what are your comments, if any, on this? Before I send for details or part with any hard earned cash, I was wondering what you might say about it. My first question was, "How did the person concerned obtain such film?" I would, if considered genuine and worthwhile, order a reel. I hope you print this, not only to answer my query, but also for other readers too, who may have seen the same advertisement and asked the same questions.

David D. Leeming, Rochdale

Dear David,

Our first reaction on seeing the clipping you sent in was, like yours, a very loud and joyous WOW! But, we have made some enquiries with a reliable source concerning this offer and we are now obliged to tell you it is almost certainly a very nasty 'con.' We are very, very glad you wrote in about this because apparently many people have sent money off to this gentleman and never even had a reply. Without doubt, Bruce would have been outraged at someone trying this despicable trick!

Please, everyone, wherever possible double check and then check again before sending money off to this sort of advertisement - you can always write to *KFM* or the Society if in doubt and you could so easily be just throwing your money down the drain!

Dear KFM,

You just wouldn't believe the arguments I have had at school with my friends over Bruce and" his films (especially 'Big Boss'). When Bruce jumps over the high fence to get to the evil Boss himself, my friends (who are supposed to be avid Bruce Lee followers) say he used a trampoline to get over. I insist though that he didn't. Please, please put me right.

John Reeves Meadows, Nottingham

Dear John,

Bruce did NOT use a trampoline in his films! Incredible as it seems, he did all the leaps, kicks and jumps without aids. In fact, as *KFM* pointed out not long ago, many of the Little Dragon's nunchaku scenes were actually SLOWED DOWN so as to make the superb action shots clearly visible to all! We have personally seen a Chinese actor do a six-foot backward somersault and to watch it is fantastic. Although unfortunately we have never seen Bruce perform other than on film, we know that with his skills he surpassed all others and simply had no need to resort to camera trickery.

O.K, that's about all we've got room for in this news sheet - the next one will be a bit bigger, hopefully! See you all again soon.

Pam and Carmella

BRUCE LEE SOCIETY COLUMN
KUNG FU MONTHLY NO. 23

Hi - and it's a big hello to you all from Pam and Carmella! We thought it wouldn't take long for the ball to start rolling and how right we were. Welcome therefore to all the first month's members. Judging by some of the letters we've already had back, there's no doubt that our choice of pictures, facts and info for the Society Kit, has struck a happy note amongst the fans - we've really got a good thing going! Not only that, you'll see if you look at the KFM mail order section, that the new reduced prices for Society members are now in operation. Please remember though to quote your membership number when ordering - otherwise you may miss the reduction.

The first tasty item of news is that we've just established very firm links with Dragon Club of Hollywood, USA. Gary Kohatsu who runs it has written us a very long and interesting letter about how things are Bruce Lee-wise in the States and that letter, plus our reply, will be published in full in the next Society news sheet. One point he did bring out though was this. Apparently someone over there is organising a Bruce Lee Memorial Exhibition and the exciting news is we are invited to send something along from Great Britain. We don't think there is all that much time to go, so how about all you Society members get writing in as quickly as possible with your ideas on what form the entry should take. Remember it has to be practical - six foot high statues of the Little Dragon are definitely out! The second Bruce Lee Secret Society news sheet will be out around Christmas time so we reckon we just have to include an extra something for the Xmas stocking! Because the idea is still a bit in the planning stage, we're not going to tell you what it's going to be until next month - you'll have to put your guessing caps on - all we will say is if you still haven't joined the Society, you'd better get your skates on; otherwise you'll be missing out!

Finally may we once again say a great big thank you to all the new members who have written back to us so quickly, offering everything from congratulations, advice and ideas to even the occasional criticism. You've no idea how much fun we have picking our way through the daily stack of mail -THAT is what makes it all worthwhile.

Sorry for running over it all again, but for all the *KFM* readers who missed the last issue - it's time to join the Bruce Lee Secret Society! You'll get a whole pile of goodies when you join, plus a regular news sheet sent directly to your home.

Don't delay - just send £2.95 to: The Bruce Lee Secret Society, *Kung Fu Monthly*, 39 Goodge Street, London, W1P 1FD.

See you all again next month!

BRUCE LEE SOCIETY COLUMN
KUNG FU MONTHLY NO. 24

Hello, it's Pam and Carmella here again...

Firstly - apology time! Due entirely to circumstances beyond our control, up to the time of writing, we haven't been able to include the sticker in the Society Kit. To put no finer point to it, the manufacturer let us down badly and we've had to take the job elsewhere. It's disgraceful, but there it is. Hopefully the delay should only be for a few weeks and I'm sure you'll be happy to bear with us.

Now the good news! The Bruce Lee Secret Society is proud to announce that three people have accepted honorary membership. They are: 1) Mr Tony Love of Cathay Films, 2) Mr Roy Byrne of Cathay Films and 3) Mr Eddy Pumer of Capital Radio (in London). We're delighted to welcome all three to the fold and look forward to a long and happy relationship. By the way, we'd love you to write and tell us of anyone YOU think should become an honorary member of the BLSS. We'll add the name(s) to the short list that we ourselves have already drawn up and as people accept, we'll be letting you know who they are.

Thank you for all the marvelous letters you've sent (and are still sending!) wishing us luck in running the club. As so often happens, not everything has gone as smoothly as we would have liked and there have been some delays in getting membership kits out. However, all that's in the past and now we've slipped into top gear, problems should be few and far between (we hope). Something that does help is CLEAR WRITING. It's awful having to guess at names and addresses - have we got it right or haven't we? So please use CAPITAL LETTERS if you think your writing may not be completely legible. Also try not to forget to include your first name. It's horribly formal to have to write to I. Smith or E. Jones and we don't even know if you're male or female!

Don't forget in the next news sheet we'll be including our first Swop Shop - so if there's anything you want to buy, swop or sell, write in quickly. There's a pen pals section too and of course both these columns are completely FREE to all Society members.

We've had so many enquiries about the Bruce Lee film soundtrack cassettes that we've decided to investigate the situation. So far we've discovered that of the Little Dragon's four major films, only the *Enter the Dragon* soundtrack has ever been released in the UK (and that itself is now deleted). Any other Bruce Lee film soundtracks you may have seen will be imported ones - probably from USA, Hong Kong or Tokyo. Anyway, these are the three places we intend to start our search, so keep your fingers crossed for us! Of course if any of you members have "inside information" PLEASE let us know.

Finally as a special gift to all Bruce Lee Secret Society members, with the next news sheet, we will be including a Society Christmas card, either for yourself to keep, or for you to send to someone else (further copies will be available at a reasonable price). We also expect to have one or two other mail order items available in time for December 25th, including (due to your enormous demand) club badges and stickers. On top of all that of course, in the next news sheet you'll find a competition, the swop shop and pen pals corner, plus all the usual news/views info and pictures. We both look forward to seeing you all again then!

Pam and Carmella

A RETROSPECTIVE LOOK AT BRUCE LEE MANIA & THE KUNG FU CRAZE OF THE 1970S

EDITOR'S NOTES

Norman Borine was a Bruce Lee fan, friend of the Lee family and the owner of the World of Bruce Lee Museum in Los Angeles. Opened on 20th July 1980 to 500 visitors including Lee's mother, plus another 100 visitors in the evening for a screening of *Enter the Dragon*, the Bruce Lee museum kept open its doors for over two decades.

Mr. Borine started out by running a shop in Hollywood Boulevard, when shortly after Bruce Lee's death, began selling poster and photographs of the late star. Even famous names began dropping by the store. Recalls Norman, "Chuck Norris dropped in to buy some photos of him fighting Bruce in *Way of the Dragon*, Gil Johnson (co-editor of *Tao of Jeet Kune Do*) was a regular visitor, Linda Lee saw us as she passed by then phoned us the next day." He and his wife expanded the business by taking out small mail order advertisements in American martial arts magazines such as *Fighting Stars* and *Inside Kung Fu*, before deciding to leave to Palm Springs to run a hotel.

Before leaving, Borine sold "The International Dragon Fan Club" to Gary Kohatsu (a name you will see printed many times as you read through these news sheets). Gary later informed Norman that he wasn't interested in continuing with the mail order business and offered Norman the chance to buy it from him, which he did, jumping at the chance to be "back home with Bruce Lee."

The World of Bruce Lee started out in a small suburb of Eagle Rock, California, where he became friends with Linda Lee and her attorney Adrian Marshall. Linda would later donate, from Brandon, a pair of black nunchakus that were handmade by Bruce.

Even Raymond Chow offered him work to help publicise the then-upcoming *Game of Death*, having an office right next door to the Golden Harvest chief. With the bits and pieces that were following him around, he says, "The office itself was taking on the appearance of a mini Bruce Lee museum!"

After the release of *Game of Death*, Norman concentrated his time on The World of Bruce Lee Museum and displaying the mass array of artefacts he'd acquired over the years. On occasion, he even took the museum on tour, showing some of his unique collection all over the world.

Among other things, the museum featured a 2,000 square foot photo gallery, as well as a roped-off area used for martial arts classes and seminars, which doubled as space for lectures of screenings of Bruce Lee's films. It truly was "The World of Bruce Lee."

Mentioned in this issue was an upcoming documentary being made by the BBC. Sadly, this never materialised. The BBC have never made a documentary exclusively about Bruce Lee but they have made several about the Kung Fu craze of the 1970's. These have included *The Kung Fu Years*, shown as part of BBC2's *Kung Fu Night* in 1997 and a short documentary titled, *Celebrity Relics: Bruce Lee's Nunchaku* shown in 2003 which featured footage filmed at a Bruce Lee Convention in Bradford in the same year. *The Kung Fu Years* also features a small interview with Bruce Lee Fan Club President Rhona McVay. Bruce Lee Society member Glynn Darbyshire recalls an extended version of this interview with Rhona appearing on "Looking For A Fight," a 1975 episode of the BBC series *Scene*, which is, at the time of writing, unavailable. As Glynn recalls, "'Looking for a Fight' was my introduction to Bruce Lee and martial arts."

 Before VHS and Betmax, the only way to watch movies at home, were on 8mm film and boy, were they expensive. "Super 8" as it was called, was launched in 1965 by Eastman Kodak and initially, each 50ft reel of film could hold 2.5 minutes of footage. Later advances allowed 200ft reels which allowed 10 minutes of footage. By the time the Bruce Lee Society was in full swing, Super 8 was available in 400ft reels, holding 20 minutes of footage.

 Most of the earlier Super 8 films were silent, with sound being provided from a separate cassette that the viewer would need to play at the same time of running the film projector. Later Super 8 films and projectors allowed simultaneous sound and video presentations.

As you read through the newsletters, you will notice the availability of these Super 8 films, either through the Swop Shop or in the General News/ Useful Addresses sections. Silent films would be exactly that, with sound on accompanying cassette or not at all and films with sound would have the audio strip running through the film itself.

 As you will notice, available Bruce Lee films usually came on 4 x 400ft reels (4 x 20 minutes) totalling 80 minutes, which means the films were cut to fit those 4 reels. The reason for trimming the films was probably down to cost. Selling prices circa 1978 were around £50 per reel so £200 per film. In 2019's prices, taking into account inflation etc, that would be £289 per reel or £1,156 per film. The average monthly wage in 1978 in the UK was around £300, making the cost of each film almost three weeks wages for the average worker. An expensive buy, even for the most keen Bruce Lee fan and only a dream for almost every teenage member.

It was only in 1980, with the advent of home video formats such as VHS and Betamax, that having your own copy of a Bruce Lee film to watch at home, would be an (almost) affordable reality.

02 December 1976

HI! AND A VERY WARM WELCOME TO THE SECOND QUARTERLY NEWS SHEET OF THE BRUCE LEE SECRET SOCIETY.

Firstly, may we say how fantastic the response has been to the club, and to apologise most sincerely to any of the fans who had to wait for delivery of their kits - where possible, we have replied personally and hopefully everyone has now received the Kit okay. If not, let us know - Please!

We were very upset about the delay, especially as we had worked so hard to get things going. And poor old *Kung Fu Monthly* have been inundated with OUR mail, as well as their own! You'll never know how glad we were to see all these 'teething problems' straightened out. So... without any further delay, let's launch into this issue!

GENERAL NEWS

As you all know, *Way of the Dragon* was out again in October/November on general release - and they have cut it YET AGAIN! It is incredible how a film such as this containing sheer artistry can be hacked to pieces while yet another third-rate Kung Fu movie can be left virtually intact - one where it is so obvious the stars (?) themselves are incapable of doing any of the moves and kicks without hours of practice and as much trick photography as can be managed. We do hope we can eventually get all Bruce's uncut films together and show them to the fans! This is our eventual aim - fingers crossed.

If any of you have been watching the *Water Margin* series (London, Tuesdays at 9.30 - BBC 2) you might be interested to know that the write up on this in the Radio Times described the star as being "much better looking than Bruce Lee" - of course, with that sort of remark we HAD to see it! Needless to say, we have now decided that the person who wrote the article is definitely in need of glasses! The series is okay... worth a peep, anyway.

Our friend in America - Gary Kohatsu, who runs the Dragon Fan Club - has been in contact with us again and you'll be hearing more about that later, in particular regarding our now very international Pen Pals section!

Courtesy of member No. 1061, Mike Devereux, we have heard that there is an L.P. out on the Sunset Record Label called *Great Action Film Themes* - number TCT 50366, which features a recording of *Fist of Fury* and *Enter the Dragon*... cost £2.00. However, he does say it's not the original soundtrack recording. So if you are interested, see your record dealer quickly! And thanks, Mike, for the tip.

We are tracing a contact for the original *Way of the Dragon* L.P. in Japan (and possibly some of Bruce's other films). Any news to follow.

We have just seen this snippet in *Karate and Oriental Arts* magazine (September/October issue). "Hong Kong releases sporadic news of Bruce Lee's unfinished film, *Game of Death*."

It will be interesting to see if the movie moguls can whip the fans into another frenzy or whether Lee's epics, like those of 007, simply tail off into the shadow heroes of yesterday!!! We fail to see the comparison with James Bond (with his ejector seats, bullet-proof windscreen shields, gold-covered girlfriends and the like) and we would suggest that the article writer looks us up in a few years to see whether Bruce's memory is still alive; that is if the writer is still in a position to matter.

SWOP SHOP

We have had a good response to the shop (considering the short notice that some of the fans received) which we now declare OPEN!

- Mike Devereux (No. 1061), Warrington, will exchange Popster No.23 (fantastic full-colour action-packed Poster of Bruce plus info.) and another colour poster of Bruce for *KFM* No.2.
- Rajinder Jutlla (No. 1380), Leeds, wants *KFM* No. 4.
- Gerald Rae (No.1498), Kincaidston, wants the full set of *KFM's* and the price required.
- C.R.N. Kellaway (No. 1296), St. Austell, wants *KFM's* 1 to 3. High price paid.
- Kay Drummond (No. 1195), Glenrothes, wants to exchange *Game of Death Collector's Edition* for a copy of *The Life and Tragic Death of Bruce Lee* by Linda Lee.
- William Luke (No. 1478), Whitfield, wants *KFM* No.3. Please state price required.
- Alexander Martin (No. 1023), Gowkthrapple, wants *KFM's* 1 and 2. Price, please.
- Tony Thompson (No. 1328), Ireleth, wants *KFM's* 1 to 7 inclusive. State price.
- Chris Morgan (No. 1051), Alsager, has for sale - *KFM's* 1 to 22 inc. three posters and other *KFM* goodies. £3.50
- Stephen Hatcher (No. 1191), Coldbrook, wants *KFM* No.2 in exchange for *Enter the Dragon* single.
- Derek Walton (No. 1433), Bury, wants *KFM* No.22.
- David Montagu (No. 1151), Ringfield, wants to swap *KFM's* 16 to 20 for *KFM's* 1 to 4 inc.
- Graham Jenkinson (No. 1381), Berry Brow, wants *KFM's* 1, 2 & 3 - will pay very high price for them.

SPECIAL OFFERS

In association with Cimac Martial Arts Ltd, we are delighted to have on special offer to Secret Society members only the following range of books and magazines:

BRUCE LEE'S NUNCHAKU IN ACTION... for the first time published. Many unseen photographs of Bruce Lee together with instructions on the Bruce Lee way to use the Nunchaku. A fantastic publication and a real collector's item. £1.45 (includes p&p)

BRUCE LEE HIS PRIVACY AND ANECDOTES... includes details of Bruce Lee's victory over a Thai boxing champion, how he planned to retire at 35, the secrets of Bruce's palm - and over 17 colour photographs. £1.45 (includes p&p)

BRUCE LEE: THE MAN ONLY I KNEW (by Linda Lee). This is Bruce Lee's true story. Follow his rise to fame and fortune, his training and fighting methods and share his deepest feelings in an intimate view of his life that only the wife who loved and understood him can give. With flick-through pages to bring Bruce back into action. £1.45 (includes p&p)

BRUCE LEE: 1940-1973. A collection of rare photographs in colour and black and white grace the candid accounts of the Little Dragon's life, his enthusiasm and his legendary ability as a martial artist. Beautifully produced with hardbound cover. £4.00 (includes p&p)

BRUCE LEE - FAREWELL MY FRIEND. Bruce Lee became the phenomenon of the entertainment world with the release of *Enter the Dragon*, but died just before the picture was released in 1973. This is a close friend's personal accolade of Bruce Lee in a new, specially bound edition for the collector. £3.75 (includes p&p)

PLUS... Few only!!! Bruce Lee medallions (there's really only a hundred left in stock!) Really heavy, solid cast pendants, imported direct from Hong Kong. £1.25 (includes p&p)

Please make out cheques and postal orders to *Kung Fu Monthly* AND ALSO MARK ON THE ENVELOPE THE NAME OF THE ITEM YOU WANT! Post off to: Secret Society Offers, 39 Goodge Street, London, W1P 1FD. Delivery should take about three weeks.

LETTERS

We have had so many letters pouring in, but here is a small selection:

Dear Pam and Carmella,

A nasty little film critic made some remarks about Bruce Lee... I quote: "Bruce Lee will not survive posthumously as a cult." He wrote this in early 1976, two and a half years after Bruce's death. I wrote a polite letter to him explaining his mistake and proving Bruce Lee's memory lives on. He answered it in a column and called him "Action Man." I sent another letter explaining Bruce wasn't a manufactured hero like Captain Marvel, Batman, etc. I proved again that Bruce's memory will always live on. No reply! Then he suggested Bruce was a forgotten hero! I sent another letter. He sent one back, insulted me and said I was the world's only Bruce Lee fan (well, suggested it anyway). Now I have sent another letter to him. The critic's address is, Ray Seaton, Express and Star, Queen Street, Wolverhampton, WV1 3BU.

Martin Hughes

Well, we had to write to Mr. Seaton and the letter went as follows:

Dear Mr. Seaton,

We have heard from one of the late Bruce Lee's many, many fans that you consider Bruce to be "a forgotten hero who will not survive posthumously as a cult." Taking into account the letters which arrive daily at *Kung Fu Monthly* concerning this artist and the thousands of members belonging to his ex-fan club (which incidentally closed due to pressure of work) we have now opened a brand new club in conjunction with *Kung Fu Monthly* to handle the needs of the fans of this well-loved artist. Of course, we do appreciate that there are people who do not concur with our views and that NO celebrity can possibly have a 100% following. However, we have to say that you do seem extremely mis-informed with regard to Bruce Lee's popularity. Also, surely someone in your position should not allow personal dislike of a star to dull your judgement as to that artist's abilities and undeniable popularity. We therefore cordially invite you to write to us outlining your point of view and perhaps explaining your apparently biased attitude towards a man who has contributed hours of pleasure and entertainment to his millions of fans the world over.

Ray Seaton replied...

Dear Pam and Carmella,

Thank you for your letter. You have been mis-informed. I have no personal dislike of Bruce Lee. I simply remarked in a cinema column that he was unlikely to survive as a cult as James Dean has, because he appealed to a certain section of cinema audiences at a given time. No doubt there will for long be a nostalgic devotion owing to his premature death, but I doubt if his films will become a genre as they lack the social or sociological context of Dean's and Brando's. I don't have to explain an apparently biased attitude, as you put it. For all I know you might be biased towards Errol Flynn, of whom I'm a "nostalgic devotee" but I wouldn't call you to task or ask you to explain your attitude. The fact that Bruce Lee has given countless (?) hours of pleasure and entertainment to millions of fans can be said of thousands of screen heroes since Laemmle created the first star of Florence Lawrence. Anyway, I shall be pleased to publicise your Fan Club when the next Bruce Lee [film] is showing in the West Midlands. I see that a programme of his has been booked at the oldest cinema in the country, The Haven at Stourport, which closes down on Sept. fourth. No connection of course!

Yours sincerely,

Ray Seaton

Any comments, fans???

Dear Pam & Carmella,

In an early edition of KFM, I read that Bruce Lee fights someone in Game of Death who uses a Filipino Martial Art called "Escrima." My fiancée is a Filipino, but she hasn't heard of this style, so could you print some more info on it?

John Rogers (No. 1009)

Dear John,

As you know, fighting arts have always been an integral part of the culturally and racially diversified society of the Philippines; these arts include empty-handed, stick, projectile and bladed-weapon techniques, many of which were brought to the country by early migrants. Bladed weapons abound, although each does not necessarily have an organised system of fighting skills but depends purely on the taste and requirements of the user. Although "Kali" signifies in general the use of various systems involving large-bladed weapons and knives, obviously individual schools/groups developed their own styles. Hence, "Escrima" came from "Bothoan," an ancient school in which the students learned fencing skills in addition to their academic pursuits.

Member No. 1150, Arthur Stone, is a keen martial arts fan and studies the basics of several arts, plus amateur boxing and wrestling. Here's part of his letter:

> I have training equipment all over the house. Even a punch bag in the toilet! So I can practise anywhere at anytime. I run five miles every morning at 4 a.m. (I'm a postman) and if anyone is up early enough, they may see me doing Jeet Kune Do footwork on my rounds! Another thing I've been working on to keep Bruce's memory alive is my own version of his life. Using a Super 8mm camera and my vast collection of Bruce Lee pictures from KFM and other sources I filmed and then edited them... adding a sound track. The result, titled Tribute to Bruce Lee runs for 30 minutes and tells his "Life to Death" story. I'm proud of it.

And so you should be, Arthur. That must have taken some effort... Well done!

COMPETITION!

Roll on the drums... As promised, here is the first Secret Society Competition, and we expect a full response to this. Get your pens out, brains working and gen up on the Little Dragon! The first five correct answers out of the bag will each receive a signed copy of *The Wisdom of Bruce Lee*... So here goes!

1. At the very end of Enter the Dragon, what was the name of the actor with whom Bruce fought?
2. What was the Frank Sinatra record played at Bruce's funeral?
3. What year did Yip Man, Bruce's Wing Chun instructor, die?

Put your answers on a postcard please (numbered 1,2 &3) and post off straight away to: Secret Society Competition No.1, *Kung Fu Monthly*, 39 Goodge Street, London W1P 1FD. All answers in by 27th December - winner's names and the correct answers to be published in February's *KFM*.

PEN PALS

Great news from our friend Gary Kohatsu of the Dragon Club of America. He has very kindly taken us up on our offer of an American/British pen pals section and to start off, he's given six red-hot Little Dragon fans in the USA for us to write to. What a marvellous opportunity for getting info from America - so come ON, British fans, don't let the side down. Let us have some names and addresses for America! You are all quick enough to write in to us - let's see some international link-ups.

Bill Miller, Columbus, Ohio, USA.
Rafael Cervantes, San Antonion, Texas, USA.
Jose Lopez, Chicago, Illinois, USA.
Butch Currier, , Michigan, USA.
Bill Wandler, Reseda, California, USA.
Carey Ishizuka, Waipahu, Hawaii, USA.

There are, Gary says, many, many more and we hope to include at least some of those in the next news sheet. Gary also says, "It's something that's been long overdue but I'm thrilled this opportunity will not pass us by again. I do hope your British fans will enjoy this as much as us Americans will."

THE BRUCE LEE MEMORIAL MAGAZINE OF POEMS AND DRAWINGS

How about this for an idea! We reckon it would be great for you all to send in an original poem/drawing on Bruce (and we DO mean original - no traced pictures, etc). We will then collect these together and at a future date, hopefully around the time of the next news sheet, we will produce a simple magazine, combining as many as possible of your entries as a Secret Society tribute to the Little Dragon! Everyone should have time to produce something by the end of January, so we'll make the closing date Jan 31st. Undoubtedly many of you will wish to take part - after all it will be something very special to keep, knowing you yourself had helped to produce it! ALL Society members will be entitled to a copy at cost price only - selected contributors will have theirs FREE.

We have had a couple of ideas as to what to send to the Bruce Lee Memorial to be held in America next year (a replica of the Society badge and the original nunchakus that Bruce used in *The Big Boss*) but we need more response than that. Is everybody asleep out there?

No, on second thoughts, judging by the mail that's been pouring in, that can't be true! And that by the way is just how we like it... keep on writing all those fantastic letters. If it takes a while for you to get a reply don't worry too much - we get there in the end! Unfortunately we have our own jobs to do in the day and so all Society work is done on evenings and weekends. In fact we were up until three and four in the morning getting the back-log of kits out to members! It is hard work, but we do it because we love and admire Bruce Lee enough to want to keep his fans in contact with each other through the medium of a club.

Finally, here's a late bit of news for you. Ron Stewart and Chris Izod who run the Classic Cinema in Westcliff have just staged their first Kung Fu "all-nighter," featuring in particular, *Fist of Fury*. It was a real shame we heard about it just too late to let everyone know it was coming. Never mind, the place was absolutely packed and such was the enthusiasm of everyone there, Ron assures me he'll be planning another one soon and we're going to make certain you hear about it.

Stand by for the next 1977 news sheet - we'll see you all then!

Pam and Carmella
(Joint Presidents of the Bruce Lee Secret Society)

EDITOR'S NOTES

  *The Water Margin* was a Japanese TV series that was shown on Japanese TV from 1973 to 1974, running for two series and based on the 1fourth century Chinese novel of the same name. It aired on UK TV from 1976 to 1978.

  In the Society news sheets, it's evident that Bruce Lee was idolised and some fans had a serious dislike for anything that didn't feature Bruce Lee. The most ardent fans even wrote angry and sometimes obsessive letters of objection to any writer saying an unkind word about their idol.

In the UK, *The Water Margin* was in general, respected and liked by the majority of Bruce Lee fans, as was the series *Monkey*.

You'll notice that towards the end of this issue, Pam mentions the "nunchakus in *The Big Boss*." As you'll no doubt be aware that no nunchakus sequence ever featured in *The Big Boss*. It was a mistake on Pam's part, which should have read *Fist of Fury* but Pam corrects the mistake in issue three. I left the mistake in this issue as I didn't want to remove Pam's correction in the next issue.

BRUCE LEE SOCIETY COLUMN
KUNG FU MONTHLY NO. 25

Hello there everyone. Pam and Carmella here again! There's lots of news about the fantastic Bruce Lee Secret Society for you this month.

First off, we're delighted to say that the final problem has been solved. Yes, the stickers have at last arrived and they'll be sent off to you along with the next news sheet. December 25th is drawing closer, so included in that package there'll be a special Christmas card signed by both of us PLUS a mail order sheet for ordering those late Xmas goodies.

The Swop Shop has really gone a bomb and between you and the two of us, there's at least one COMPLETE set of KFMs for sale at a very reasonable price. Jenny tells us that the demand for issues 1 to 3 of *KFM* seems to be increasing by the month so who is going to be the lucky Society member to get those? Other than that, there are lots of rare books and posters waiting to be swapped or sold around so the best of luck to everyone concerned. Of course, if YOU have something in mind you'd like to swap, sell or buy, please don't hesitate to let us know - we can put you in touch with the people who matter!

The pen pals section has been given a big boost in a very unexpected sort of way. Our old friend, Gary Kohatsu, of the Dragon Club in Hollywood, USA, reckons it's a good idea - and we agree with him - to start a little transatlantic communication between the faithful followers of Bruce Lee. So, what he's done is to round up the name and addresses of some of the hottest Little Dragon fans in America and sent them over to us. We simply CAN'T let him down after a gesture like that, so how about it? All details of where to write are in the next news sheet, so as soon as it pops through your door, get cracking with those pens!

What else have we got for you? Well, there are full details of the first ever Secret Society Competition with copies of *The Wisdom of Bruce Lee* to be given to the first five correct entries out of the hat. The questions (we hope) will make you think a little so stand by for a bit of brushing up in your Bruce Lee history books - it should be fun.

During a sudden brainstorm, we came up with the idea for a new sort of Society magazine. Without giving too much away here, the suggestion is that it be made up of contributions from Society members. Exactly what goes into it is largely a matter for YOU to decide - the only stipulation is that entries be connected in some way with Bruce so on with the thinking caps!

Finally, we are attempting on your behalf something which I think could make us pretty popular. Dotted around the country are many small Chinese cinema clubs. They show all sorts of Asian, and in particular, Kung Fu films and no doubt, many of you would love to have the chance to go along to one. Well, we're negotiating with someone right now to try and arrange just that - something special for Society members ONLY. Nothing has been agreed yet, but keep your fingers crossed ... you never know. See you all again next month

Pam and Carmella

BRUCE LEE SOCIETY COLUMN
KUNG FU MONTHLY NO. 26

Hello again, and a special welcome to all the many new members who have just joined our Society!

Firstly, a couple of people have written in to enroll without including an address. Their names are Mr. C. Cooper and Mr. M. Gray, so if both these gentlemen would quickly write back, we'll make sure their kits and news sheets are rushed off as soon as possible. (By the way, no cheating anybody - we DO know what areas they come from!) Finally for the problems section, we'd like Mr. L. Cumming who has recently left his address in Larkhall, Lanarkshire to contact us. His membership kit came back to us marked "moved away".

Arthur Stone (member No. 1150) has been keeping his eyes well peeled! Apparently Midlands TV screened The Wrecking Crew on the 27th October, starring Dean Martin as Matt Helm. At the end of the show when the titles came up, surprise surprise, who should be credited with arranging the fight scenes but Bruce Lee! Arthur wants to know if the Little Dragon worked on any other films in a similar capacity - does anyone have any ideas? Let us know if you have. It just goes to prove that the final few frames of a TV programme are definitely NOT the time to go putting the kettle on!

Lots of members have written in asking if there are any new posters available of Bruce. We must agree that, other than the great ones we get month by month in KFM, there's little else of interest around at the moment. Actually, some time ahead (when we get a bit richer!) we'd dearly love to bring out a special new poster for club members only. The trouble is, unless they're printed in absolutely enormous quantities, the price of each one can be very high indeed. Anyway, any members coming across something new, be sure to let us know where you got it and we'll make sure everyone has the address.

Late news - very shortly, the membership subscription to the Bruce Lee Secret Society will have to rise. We're sorry about this but hopefully everyone will understand that this has been simply forced upon us by rising prices. The moral is, if you're going to join, join now AND SAVE YOURSELF MONEY!

Finally, for all those who've written asking for a picture of the two of us, we're trying to arrange something around the time of the next News Sheet. We hope you know what you're letting yourselves in for!

Pam and Carmella

BRUCE LEE SOCIETY COLUMN
KUNG FU MONTHLY NO. 27

Hello, Pam and Carmella here - welcome to another Secret Society news page!

There are lots to tell you this month, but first off we want to put in huge, great letters, a very special THANK YOU to all the members who sent in Christmas cards to the two of us. We weren't actually expecting them and some were so ingenious we're thinking that one or two of them should go into the Secret Society magazine that's in the making.

Talking about the Society magazine, the response has been very good and there are lots of entries to choose from. Don't forget though that there's a few more weeks to go yet before we have to raise the "full-up" sign, so now the Christmas break is well and truly over, it's back on with the thinking caps. Remember, we're after just about anything that can be put into a magazine - things like poems, drawings, short essays and stories – whatever really crosses your mind, PROVIDED of course, it's about the Little Dragon!

News time, and we hear from member No. 1036, Marlene Condy, that she was recently able to buy the *Enter the Dragon* soundtrack through the John Menzies group of shops and newsagents. Their London office is at: 8 St. John's Lane, London EC1 so anyone interested in having a copy is recommended to try that address first. The number of the album is WEA Records Ltd K46275 ES2729 and its best that you quote that when ordering.

Okay, this is the part we haven't been looking forward to! Last issue we told you that the Secret Society would be increasing its cost of membership and, sad to say, that will be taking effect as from March 1st 1977. The new price is £3.25 and, fingers crossed, that's where it's going to stay for some time to come. Although costs seem to be rising almost by the week, we're going to try and make sure that Secret Society members get every single penny's worth of value out of the £3.25 that we can give them.

And now, the results of our first ever Bruce Lee Secret Society Competition. Firstly the answers: 1. Shih Kien, 2. *My Way*, 3. 1973. The first five correct postcards out of the hat were sent in by: Stephen Hatcher (1191), Kay Drummond (1195), Deborah Pledge (1301), James Hynes (1167), Hugh Lagan (1218). Well done! Your signed copies of *The Wisdom of Bruce Lee* should be reaching you in a few days. Watch out for the next competition in the March news sheet!

One final piece of late news. Our friend, Gary Kohatsu in America has written telling us that the international pen pals effort is starting to pay off handsomely. He is so pleased with your response to the names and addresses we printed in the last News Sheet that he's sent in another list of red hot USA Bruce Lee fans - to be printed in our March edition. Stand by for that! See you all again soon

Pam and Carmella

BRUCE LEE SOCIETY COLUMN
KUNG FU MONTHLY NO. 28

Hello, it's Pam and Carmella here and they've given us a really exciting job to do this month.

There we were, reading our pre-publication copies of *The Secret Art Of Bruce Lee*, when up came the *KFM* editor to tell us that we had twenty of them to give away! Put like that, how could we refuse? So, anyway, here goes and fingers crossed, we haven't forgotten anything! (Oh, in case you're wondering, there'll be lots of news, views, gossip and scandal again next month — honest!)

That's right, to celebrate this historic moment, the editor of *KFM* has agreed to donate 20 SIGNED AND NUMBERED copies of this sensational new book. All you have to do is write the answers to the following five questions (labeling them A, B, C, D and E) on a postcard ONLY PLEASE and NOT FORGETTING TO INCLUDE YOUR NAME, ADDRESS AND SECRET SOCIETY NUMBER!

A) MGM approached Bruce to co-star in a film with one of America's most famous pop singers. Who was he?

B) What year did Bruce take part in the famous Long Beach tournament?

C) Who took the film of Bruce performing at that tournament?

D) In *Fist of Fury*, what does Bruce disguise himself as to gain entrance into the Japanese club.

E) What was the name of the actor who played the son of the Big Boss?

Send your entries to: The BLSS Secret Art Competition, *Kung Fu Monthly*, 39 Goodge Street, London, W1P 1FD. Postcards to arrive not later than midday May 31st 1977. Answers arriving in letter form will not be considered. The senders of the first 20 correct entries to be drawn out of the mail sack by an executive of Cathay Films Ltd, are each guaranteed to receive a SIGNED AND NUMBERED COPY of *The Secret Art of Bruce Lee*. By the way, if you're not a member of the Secret Society but wish to take part in our fabulous competition, this time only, we will be accepting entries from non-members, PROVIDING SUCH ENTRIES ARE ACCOMPANIED BY A REQUEST FOR MEMBERSHIP. You may, in this case, send your postcard INSIDE your application letter to join the Secret Society.

What??? You STILL haven't joined the Bruce Lee Secret Society? Well, here's your chance to make amends AND catch up on all that's happening for Little Dragon fans everywhere. No true Bruce Lee fan would want to miss out on the opportunity to become part of the world's fastest growing Secret Society - so get in now!

Pam and Carmella

Pam Hadden's Son Remembers

Andrew Hadden, the son of Pam Hadden, recalls when Pam Hadden's love of Bruce Lee started and how it led to the creation of the Bruce Lee Society. "I think she originally became a Bruce Lee fan after seeing *Enter the Dragon*, on a date sort of thing," said Andrew. "I guess she admired the sort of the artistry and the skill and the speed of his martial arts. Felix Dennis used to do the poster magazines and latch on to every fad going. He started *Kung Fu Monthly* and I think my mum phoned up *Kung Fu Monthly*, spoke to them and asked about a fan club. It was around that time that she started going to the *Kung Fu Monthly* offices and to visit Eddy Pumer at Capital Radio. I think at the time she started going to the *Kung Fu Monthly* offices, Sting (former lead singer of The Police) might still have been working there but I'm not 100% sure. He used to work for Felix Dennis in the offices. He might have grunted at me once or twice when I was there. I remember going to *Kung Fu Monthly* and while my mum would be chatting away, I'd be sat next to piles of back issues of various magazines. I latched on to the old Oswald's books, the infamous Oz trial. I remember reading the magazines and I was allowed to take back issues and stuff home with me. I guess she got involved with *Kung Fu Monthly* because there was no fan club at the time and I think my mum wanted one. So the people at *Kung Fu Monthly* were like, 'Let's set one up and you can run it.' Her motivation for running the society was that it took on a life of its own and she ended up in a little circle of Bruce Lee enthusiasts, all kind of feeding each other's interest."

03
MARCH 1977

CHANGE OF ADDRESS! 14 RATHBONE PLACE, LONDON W1P IDE

HELLO! AND IT'S A GREAT BIG WELCOME TO THE THIRD QUARTERLY NEWS SHEET OF THE BRUCE LEE SECRET SOCIETY.

First off, the sad news is that Carmella has had to give up her joint president ship of the Society - due to the pressure of her full-time work. That's not to say of course that she won't be dropping by from time to time to help out, but I think anyway, now would be a great time to thank her for all the hard work and effort she's put into co-running the Secret Society. Setting up a club like this is never easy and I doubt we'd have got this far without her. That said, it's on with the news!

GENERAL NEWS

Firstly, yet again, an apology! Yes, I made a mistake in the last news sheet. That should please you all, eh?... but only two members caught me out, the rest of you didn't seem to notice it! Instead of putting *Fist of Fury* as the film from which Bruce's nunchakus had come, I put *Big Boss!* Can you believe it? I must have had a mental blackout. Anyway, forgiveness is craved!

Member 1232, Eric Holden, has informed us that Dan Inosanto, one of Bruce's number one pupils, might be coming to the U.K. soon; if he does, it's on the cards that he'll arrange some sort of Jeet Kune Do seminar. As soon as I find out when and where, I'll let you know. Talking about that, how's this for an interesting snippet. Some time ago in a local paper, *The Redditch Indicator*, a news piece appeared concerning the setting up of a Jeet Kune Do school by two young men who claimed they had been taught the art by Danny Inosanto when he visited here in 1972. Now, this news item caught the eye of "Cimac Man", Tim Ward, who knew full well that Dan had in fact never visited these shores. He also knew that the only British person qualified to teach JKD was Chris Nudds - a personal friend and pupil of Inosanto. Tim contacted the paper and asked them to investigate further. The result was almost comical. The two men, Peter Casterton (18) and Andrew Benton (17), when pressured, admitted the whole thing was a phoney. They'd never met Inosanto - never been taught JKD, but still had the nerve to claim that they'd studied all styles and were therefore qualified teachers. Not bad going for 17 and 18 year olds! Plans, however, for the school have now been abandoned. Apparently instead, they now intend to start up a Bruce Lee fan club!! Beware of fakes...

Eric Holden (1232) and Brian Cuffe (1048) think, and I agree, that it would be a good idea that Society members living close to one another should be able to get in touch. Let me know how you feel about this. Obviously, it would take a great deal of organisation from this end, but lists of members living in the same area could be drawn up with a little forethought. Any members not wanting their names and addresses passed on should let me know very soon, so I can honour their wishes; otherwise they may be on the lists! Anyway, let's see your response and whether you agree.

One thing I must mention - very many members are sending in questions, but are omitting to enclose an envelope with a stamp and their address on for a reply. Sorry, but I will have to clamp down and insist that ALL members send stamped and addressed envelopes. Those without simply won't get an answer.

Many thanks to all those members who have sent in poems and drawings to go in the special Society magazine. There's quite enough to be going on with now, so I'm calling a halt to entries as from receipt of this news sheet. All your works will be returned to contributors just as soon as the magazine is ready - with a free copy going of course to the authors of all entries selected.

Many members have enquired about the reissue of the "Kick" and "Dragon" posters put out some time ago by *KFM*. I'd be interested to know just how many of you would be keen to obtain further copies, so I can pass on the figures to *KFM*. Get writing, all of you... if the response is good, we may succeed!

Raymond Tidswell (1473) recently saw *Way of the Dragon* near his home and says that it had come round again because of many requests to the manager. So, if any of you are dying to see more of Bruce in action, why don't you follow Raymond's example and put requests in to your local cinemas? It seems some managers actually DO take notice of the public!

Courtesy of member 1056, Will Johnston, it seems that in Holland there is a film being shown called *Explosion of the Dragon* which is an amalgam of six episodes of the *Green Hornet*. I think this is probably the 20th Century-Fox film released in America in 1975 and I've written to our friend in Holland who runs the Dutch fan club to see if he can confirm this. If it's true, it might be worth sending a petition to 20th Century to have the picture shown here. Will also feels that a petition would be an idea, to be sent to the censors asking that *Game of Death* be left intact. Not a bad idea, Will, I'll see if I can work out a plan of action before the next news sheet.

Gary Kohatsu's Dragon Club in America is about to start a letter writing campaign

A RETROSPECTIVE LOOK AT BRUCE LEE MANIA & THE KUNG FU CRAZE OF THE 1970S

to Warner Bros, for them to complete the *Life and Legend of Bruce Lee* (which they were supposed to have released this year). Maybe it would be a good idea if we did the same, eh? Just drop us a line, saying you would like to see this released and we'll forward the letters to Gary. If you want some action, then get writing NOW!! Gary also tells us that the American Bruce Lee Commemoration Week (see news sheet No. 1) has now been postponed to this Summer. More info to come.

Finally for this issue, [we] noticed in another Kung Fu magazine... someone wrote to them asking why they weren't producing much on Bruce Lee any more. The magazine wrote, "Well, there isn't much more to tell, is there?" It depends where you're looking, I suppose - after all, *Kung Fu Monthly* seem to do alright!

USEFUL ADDRESSES

Sarah Hook of West Moors, Dorset will encase a photograph in Perspex as a paperweight. The picture must not measure more than would fit into a 3" circle. Delivery takes about 10 days and the price is £1.85 including postage. Write to her direct.

Fotopost Express, P.O. Box 100, Argyle Way, Stevenage, Herts will make a 2'6" by 1*8" poster from either a picture, photo, negative, slide, print, or even a magazine cutting. Black & White - £1.95... Colour - £4.95. Also from Dixons Photographers and most Westons Chemists.

THE BRUCE LEE SECRET SOCIETY MAIL ORDER PAGE

THE SECRET ART OF BRUCE LEE

Published by the editors of *Kung Fu Monthly*, this superb new book contains over a hundred new and never-before-seen pictures of Bruce Lee! Not only is it essential companion reading to the Tao, it also represents the finest value imaginable to all Bruce's true and loyal fans. Fantastic portrait shots and dynamic action sequences - it's all here and more! Don't delay for a second... rush your £3.75 cheques/postal orders to: *The Secret Art of Bruce Lee* Offer, 14 Rathbone Place, London W1P IDE.

BRUCE LEE'S FIGHTING METHOD
by M.Uyehara.

Another really useful new book for Bruce Lee fans, and in particular, students of Jeet Kune Do. There are many "street-scene" pictures of the master in action, plus easy to understand descriptions. Definitely another 'must' for the devoted followers of the late king of Kung Fu. Just send £4.20 (includes post and packing) to: *Bruce Lee's Fighting Method* Offer, 14 Rathbone Place, London W1P IDE.

JEET KUNE DO - THE ART AND PHILOSOPHY OF BRUCE LEE

by Danny Inosanto. The third of our trilogy of new Little Dragon books. What a blockbuster year it's been for fans of the Little Dragon - and Dan's offering makes a more than worthy addition to our mail order list for this issue. Personal anecdotes from a man who was a personal friend - not to mention star pupil of Bruce, plus, again, deep insight into the world of Jeet Kune Do. Probably no other living person is as qualified as Inosanto to write on the Little Dragon's legendary style and without doubt, this softback in another for the true collector. Send £8.55 right now to:

J.K.D - *The Art and Philosophy of Bruce Lee* Offer 14 Rathbone Place, London W1P IDE.

COMING SOON...CLUB T-SHIRTS...CLUB WRITING SETS...PILLOW SLIPS!

Stay glued on the Society page in *KFM* for more news!!

THE SWOP SHOP

If you have anything to swap, or wish to buy/sell in the martial arts line, let me know. Here's the latest batch...

- Guardsman William Luke 24164207 (1478), Waterloo Bks, requires *KFM* No.3. Price please.
- N. Allwood (1407) Harbourne, wants *KFM's* 1, 2 & 3.
- Arthur Crosthwaite (16740 wants to swap *Ballad of Bruce Lee* for nunchakus or shuriken.
- Tony Thompson (1328), Ireleth, wants the MAGAZINE (not book) called *Bruce Lee - King of Kung Fu,* published by N.E.L.
- Adam Davies (1494), Hereford, is offering £1.50 plus *KFM* 8, *Supersport* 6 (includes article on Bruce and *Enter* poster) for *KFM's* 1, 2, 3, 12 and 17.
- N. Lindsay (1690), Llanbryde, wants *KFM's* 1 and 22, B*ruce Lee Memorial Book,* and *Deadly Hands of Kung Fu.*
- George McFarlane (1645), Lochgelly, wants *KFM* No.1. Price please.
- Julian Midgley (1354), Perry Bar, wants magazine published by Tandem called *Bruce Lee - My Martial Arts Training Guide to Jeet Kune Do* by James Lee (no relation!)
- Paul Davies (1496), Walsall, wants to swap black karate suit for either black Kung Fu suit or a pair of ankle-tie Kung Fu trousers.
- Steven Willard (1156), Bexhill-on-Sea, will swap Bruce's Tao for *Legend of the 7 Golden Vampires* soundtrack + *Best of Bruce Lee* No.1 + *Cinema of Vengeance.*
- Mike Devereux (1061), Warrington, wants *Bruce Lee - My Martial Arts Training*

Guide to Jeet Kune Do by James Lee. High price paid.
- Ronald McVeigh (1772), Donaghadee, has cassette recorded - wishes to swop for Kung Fu boxing gloves.
- Miss Shane Phipps (1735), Chesterfield, wants to swap *Fist of Fury* poster for *Life and Tragic Death of Bruce Lee*.
- Michael Butler (1363), Uckington, wants to swap his *KFM's* 8, 11, 12, 13, 14 and 22 for numbers 1, 2 and 3.
- Mr. Paul Nayman (1680), Linthorpe, will swap *KFM's* 1,2,3 for 3 of: *Bruce Lee Scrapbook, Bruce Lee - King of Kung Fu,* N.E.L. *King of Kung Fu* magazine, *Kung-Fu Superstars, Kung Fu Fighters, Way* cinema poster, OR highest bidder.
- Mick Bargota (1322), Tipton, wants *KFM* 1. Price please.
- K. O'Neill (1663), Andersonstown, is selling brand new *Enter the Dragon* LP (originally cost £3.99). Snip at £3.50 inc p&p.

THE LETTERS

Dear Pam,

As I know both you and Jenny of KFM are true believers in Bruce Lee, you are the only ones I can turn to to get the load off my chest. What I want to ask is - can you believe that Bruce is still alive? I know that many people must have written to you saying that they believe he IS still alive and that you have written back assuring them that he is in fact dead. But you could never tell me or my friends that. I have had a lot of dreams recently, seeing Bruce walking on the streets and meeting people in secret, and I have found out that these dreams can come true. There must be thousands of fans out there willing to believe he is still alive, and if word got round people could write to me to tell me what they think. You could ask them where they think he's living, and why they think he left as he did.

Glynn Barker (1567), Sheffield.

Okay, members, anyone wishing to write DIRECT to Glynn on this, his address is above - so get writing.

Dear Pam & Carmella,

Thank you for the great Society kit. I was very pleased with it. You have created a unique club, and the support you get you deserve!

Gino Crane (1655)

Dear Pam,

Can you tell me what style of fighting Bolo (Yang Sze) and Roper (John Saxon) use in *Enter the Dragon?*

Arthur Crosthwaite (1674)

Dear Arthur,

Yang Sze - Shotokan champion of South East Asia and John Saxon - a master of Tai Chi Chuan.

Dear Pam & Carmella,

I have been a fan of Bruce's for three-and-a-half years now and I think he's just fantastic! What I'd like to know is if there is any chance of another "Bruce Lee Pilgrimage," or a visit to the great Master's graveside in Seattle?

Miss Molly Cullen (1749)

Dear Molly,

With regard to a Bruce Lee Pilgrimage, the difficulties involved are simply horrendous. However, if I can get something going, I'll let everyone know right away. Also I know that Linda Lee has moved Bruce from his grave at Lake View Cemetary, Seattle and I'm trying to find out exactly where he is now buried.

COMPETITION

One of our members, Al Briers, has sent in what he considers a good competition, and I agree. So, for all of you who said that the last one was too simple, maybe this will make you think a little!

1. In which film do we see a cat playing with a pebble?
2. Which film starts with a thunderstorm?
3. In *The Big Boss* Bruce fights off how many Alsatians?
4. Name two of Bruce's co-stars in *Way of the Dragon* who were NOT Oriental?
5. Who directed *Enter the Dragon*?
6. *Fist of Fury* was shot on location in Taiwan... true or false?
7. In which film did Bruce carry a bag of prawn crackers to his final battle?
8. *Enter the Dragon* was really made for either a) Mandarin audiences? b) The USA alone? or c) Western audiences?
9. Bruce uses 3 different weapons in *Way of the Dragon*. Name them.
10. In *Game of Death* the top floor of the pagoda is called what?

Put your answers on a postcard please, numbering the answers 1 to 10, and send off as soon as possible to: Secret Society Competition No.3, c/o *Kung Fu Monthly*, 14 Rathbone Place, London W1P 1DE - answers and winners to be published in the next news sheet!

In case you didn't see it in the *KFM* Society page, here are the winners to Secret Society Competition No. 1 (in issue No. 2):

Steven Hatcher (1191) James Hynes (1167) Debra Pledge (1301) Hugh Lagon (1218) Kay Drummond (1195).

The answers were: 1. Shih Kien, 2. My Way, 3. 1972.

PEN PALS

Thank you all you members who sent in requests for American pen pals. Your names and addresses have been passed on to Gary Kohatsu in America. With any luck you should be hearing something shortly. He promises even more people to write to for our next news sheet, but here anyway is his second batch!

- Jeff Rylott, New Brighton, Phillidelphia, U.S.A
- William Adkins, Valley City, Ohio, U.S.A
- Brian Lucey, Cypress, California, U.S.A.
- Tino Sosa, Fort Hood, Texas, U.S.A.
- Richard Bartelment, Chicago, Illinois, U.S.A.
- Jim Rosenbach, Fremont, Nebraska, U.S.A.
- Tom Vickers, Toledo, Ohio, U.S.A.
- Dirk Hobbs, Lindon, Indiana, U.S.A.
- Mario Veilleux, Beauce, South P.Q., Canada

Gary hopes these will keep you going until next time! And now... our own pen-pals - we've got quite a few!

THE BRUCE LEE SOCIETY

Keith Mandley (1013), Stoke-on-Trent, wants female Chinese pen pal aged between 15-18.

Kevin Walker (1019), East Dulwich, wants male/female aged 13-16 (he's 14). Interested in Bruce, art, karate, body building, stamp collecting.

James Wilson (1649), Crosshill, wants female Chinese pen pal aged 20-22 from Scotland or England

Brian Cuffe (1048), Wirral, wants someone nearby to partner him in the arts. Needs encouragement and enthusiasm from a person around the age of 18.

Kevin Houlihan (1739), Hanworth, wants pen pal - preferably girl - aged around 15.

Christopher Navas (1708), Torremolinos, Spain, wants male pen pal around 14.

Donald A. Ramirez, Columbus, Ohio, U.S.A., wants British pen pal/or abroad.

A GOOD IDEA!

Wanda Butts, who runs a fan club for Bruce in Florida, USA produces some terrific magazines of member's drawings and poems which she calls *Fangraphic*. So far she has done two and our friend Gary thinks it would be a great idea for us to pass on contributions for possible insertion into the next issue. She does not, obviously, guarantee that all items sent will be used; she has a pretty high standard. But if you want to send something to her let me have it (but PLEASE put the appropriate postage to America in your package - and if you want it returned by her, the appropriate number of international stamp coupons) and I'll make sure it gets off to her. State on your artwork/composition that you are a member of the Bruce Lee Secret Society in London and don't forget to give your membership number and address. Good luck!

LATE APOLOGY

Because of various difficulties (due to a very large extent to poor Post Office services around the Christmas period) it's come to my attention that many members were kept waiting far too long for the mail order items that appeared in the last news sheet. So far as I know, the backlog has now been cleared and everything should be working smoothly again. Please let me know if this is not the case!

FINAL TIT-BIT

I've written to a company who produce those terrific mirrors with pictures on to ask if they can do anything for us. If the price looks right I'll go ahead on that in the next news sheet!

Okay... that's it for the March edition of the Bruce Lee Secret Society news sheet. I hope you've liked it as much as you seem to have liked the previous issue - remember, your comments are ALWAYS appreciated. The special Society magazine of drawings and poems is on starting block now so watch out for news of it on the regular *KFM* Society page.

See you all soon!

Pam

EDITOR'S NOTES

The first thing you'll notice is that co-president Carmella Rapa quit her role and left the Bruce Lee Society.

Issue three contains the first mention of Will Johnston, who would go on to be a well known Bruce Lee historian, writing for The Bruce Lee Association (which became The Bruce & Brandon Lee Association), *Impact*, and *Martial Arts Illustrated*, in addition to being involved in numerous  book, video and DVD projects throughout the years and is regarded as one of the most respected authorities on Bruce Lee in the world. He also hosted the 1990 *Tracking the Dragon* Convention in London featuring *Enter the Dragon's* John Saxon, *Fist of Fury's* Bob Baker, and martial artist Howard Williams.

Speaking of John Saxon; as I write this, its two days on from the day news broke that the incomparable Roper had sadly passed away at the age of 83. I had

the most wonderful opportunity to interview John in Northampton on 17th May 2002. He was extremely kind, gracious and ever so keen to speak about his experiences of working with Bruce Lee and the filming of *Enter the Dragon*. I also had the experience of spending a weekend helping him out in 2005 at the martial arts show Seni, when he came over to promote his photo portfolio *Twelve Weeks In Hong Kong* which he did in collaboration with Red Lizard.

Gary Kohatsu is another name first appearing in issue three. As stated in the piece about Norman Borine at the end of issue one, Gary was responsible for The International Dragon Fan Club in the USA, which formed an official allegiance with The Bruce Lee Society in the UK. Check out the interview with Gary later in the book.

Another mistake mentioned by Pam was that Bruce had been moved from his grave in Seattle and his whereabouts were currently unknown. Bruce was never moved from his final resting place in Lake View Cemetery in Seattle and his son Brandon is buried beside him in a plot originally purchased for Linda.

BRUCE LEE SOCIETY COLUMN
KUNG FU MONTHLY NO. 29

Hello again, Pam here, and if you've read your news sheets, you'll know by now that Carmella has been forced to give up her joint presidency of the Secret Society due to the pressure of her daytime work. As I said in news sheet No. 3, it's very sad that she's had to make this decision but she does hope to be popping by now and again to help out when time permits. On behalf of all the members; thanks Carmella for all the invaluable work you've put in - we'll miss you.

Now, hands up all of you who answered the questions in last month's special Society competition No. 2? You know, the one with the 20 *Secret Art of Bruce Lee* books to be given away? Hmm, it really wasn't too difficult. By the way, don't get confused between that and the news sheet No. 3 competition - they ARE completely different! Actually, the No. 3 competition is much the harder of the two so I don't really expect to receive very many correct entries - but I'd love you all to prove me wrong!

Next up, quite a number of members have written in to me asking why *Kung Fu Monthly* doesn't print more posters from *The Big Boss*. Well firstly, let me assure you that your favourite martial arts magazine in no way thinks any the less of Bruce's first major film success. In fact the answer to your question is quite simple. For some reason, very few good quality "stills" were taken on the set while the film was originally being shot. Those that were have all been seen many times before and only very occasionally does something new come along. Perhaps rather than moan about it, we should instead, just be thankful that his other masterpieces received better coverage!

I've had a really exciting letter from members Martin Hughes (1695) and Mark Burns (1687). Lord knows the amount of work they've put into it but how about this for a labour of love. The two of them have collected a huge list of names and addresses of places where you can send off for Bruce Lee posters. What a great idea - it must have taken months of research to accomplish such a worthwhile task. Obviously this is something that just has to be shared with everyone else, so here's what I propose to do. Anyone wanting a copy of this list (and let's face it, who doesn't) just write in to me, ENCLOSING A STAMPED AND SELF ADDRESSED ENVELOPE PLEASE, and I'll see that one is popped in the post for you. By the way, many of the sources are in the States, so I strongly suggest that first of all, you just write asking for catalogues and prices. I wouldn't send money off straight away - unless you feel absolutely sure.

You'll all be glad to hear that I've made a start on separating members into areas. As you'll probably remember, the idea is for Secret Society people to be able to contact others who are living not too far away. I've often noticed while browsing through member's letters that two have come from the same town. I wouldn't mind betting though that neither knows of the other's existence! Well, here's everyone's chance to find out where their nearest Secret Society neighbour is. Once again I must insist that anyone writing in for information MUST INCLUDE A STAMPED/ADDRESSED ENVELOPE, oh, and by the way, don't expect a really quick reply. It's going to take a little while yet to fully complete the lists. Send your request to: BLSS Area Lists, 14

Rathbone Place, London W1.

See you all soon - Pam

BRUCE LEE SOCIETY COLUMN
KUNG FU MONTHLY NO. 30

Hello once again, Pam here, with some more tit-bits of news for all you Secret Society members.

First off, just a couple of reminders to you regarding the club itself. One or two of you seem a little confused about the subscription charge. As much as I'd love to make it £3.25 for life, I'm sorry to say it does have to be renewed annually! Even so, with prices the way they are, we have to keep our belts well buckled in this end. And the other thing is the special BLSS news sheet. Please don't expect one to arrive every month as it is in fact quarterly; in other words, you'll receive one every three months.

John Kemp (1729) writes to tell us that Jim Kelly appeared in *Shamus* with Burt Reynolds in 1973 and played a "heavy" called Grifter. Also, Chuck Norris was in *The Student Teacher*, made also in 1973. I've had word from Michael Moore of Co. Durham. He's just started an Angela Mao fan club and anyone wishing to add their support to that lovely lady of the martial arts should contact him. Talking of fan clubs, I've also had word for anyone interested, that the Steve McQueen club is at London SW16.

I'm sorry to hear that some of the problems regarding the non-arrival of club mail around Christmas time and just after, have still not been completely sorted out. If any of you are still awaiting books, etc. PLEASE let me know straight away. We're still not exactly sure what DID go wrong but we're working hard on putting things right. That over, I suggest you all start looking forward right away to the next BLSS news sheet. I've managed to work in a little extra surprise for everyone but I'm not telling you what it is here. Now that's got you thinking, hasn't it!

I've had a letter from Steven Walpole (1554) of Huddersfield. He'd like anyone who can help him find out the following information so write DIRECT please. He wants to know about Sonny Chiba who played Terry Surugy in *Blood of the Dragon* and *Kung Fu Street Fighter*. What style is he, what other films he's made, where and when born, is there a fan club, and so on. I hope somebody out there will be able to help you Steven.

A rather strange snippit comes in to me from Gary Green (1007). He says he was in London's "Chinatown" area and heard that *Game of Death* had been made into a documentary with guest stars James Coburn and Muhummad Ali, who talk about Bruce. I'm completely mystified. Does anyone have any idea what's going on? Gary Chedzoy (1032) writes to say that there's a Phillips LP out called *Flashpoint* (No. 638211) by the Ray Davies Orchestra. It features *Fist of Fury* and *The Big Boss* theme tunes, although I have a hunch they are the original Chinese versions rather than the ones we're used to in this country.

Sadly, two members have written in to say that the service we advertised in the last news sheet regarding the blowing up of cuttings into posters by Foto Post is now no longer operating. Does anyone know of a substitute we can advertise instead? Keith Milner (1541) has had a good idea. If you're interested in him making up a collage of some of your pictures and magazines (perhaps using some of the torn or creased material) just send him 60p (inc. handling) plus the pictures and wait around two weeks for the result. His address to write to is: Mastin Moor, Chesterfield.

See you again soon - Pam

BRUCE LEE SOCIETY COLUMN
KUNG FU MONTHLY NO. 31

It's Bruce Lee Secret Society time again and a big hello from me, Pam, to all you marvelous members.

Right away, I've got to tell you that the fabulous news is our own Secret Society magazine of pictures and poems will be ready in time for the next news sheet. Remember, all those of you with contributions included will be entitled to a free copy. All other members will be able to purchase a copy at cost price (sorry, you'll have to wait for news sheet No. 4. to find out the exact cost). Work, by the way, is now almost complete on news sheet No. 4 and I promise you it's going to be the best yet.

For anyone who is having difficulty obtaining a copy of the original *Enter the Dragon* soundtrack by Lalo Schifrin (Warner Bros. K46275-BS2727), I've managed to locate a shop who seem able to supply it in just a matter of days. I'm quite happy to place orders and mail LP's off to you, so any members interested, just send me £3.60 (to include post and packing) and I'll handle it for you (cheques and postal orders made out to *KFM*, please). Remember this is a very special Society service and for time reasons, I have to insist that it's open to Society members only.

Jerry Green (1007) has written to tell us about a great London shop called P.H. Crompton Ltd at 638 Fulham Road, London SW6. Apparently they stock a very reasonable list of kung-fu and Bruce Lee books, plus a good selection of Little Dragon posters. And talking of posters; so far as I know I've managed to mail all the "poster shop name and address" sheets that have been requested. However, I will repeat again that most of the sources are American. Anyone sending off money and then receiving nothing is going to find it very hard to do anything about it. Please, please write only to start with and ask for a brochure and price information. You may feel impatient now, but past experience has taught me the delay is worth it!

The other service I'm looking forward to providing is the area name and address sheets but its taking longer to do than I thought. In fact, it's really hard work so please don't blame me if the info is a bit of a time coming; it really shouldn't be long now. Michael Hodson (1755) has some useful information in particular for our Welsh readers. J. Lee of 52 St. Paul's Avenue, Barry 5, Glamorgan, has for sale some cheap and apparently good quality nunchakus. They measure 13" long and the natural wood finish costs £2.75 and the black finish, £3.00.

One last thing for this month. Over the time that the Society has been running, many members have sent in photographs of themselves to me. Some have been "action" shots, many have been ordinary portrait pictures. Well, I think it's a lovely idea and one that I'd like to see grow and grow. When I'm reading your letters and writing back to you there's nothing I like better than being able to SEE who I'm talking to, so how about it? As Jenny might say, let's hear those cameras a'clicking!

    Best wishes... Pam

BRUCE LEE SOCIETY COLUMN
KUNG FU MONTHLY NO. 32

    Hello again, Pam here with another knockout Secret Society page for all you thousand plus members.

    Did I say a thousand? YES I DID!! We've made it and if you want to find out who the lucky 1,000th member is, take a look inside your Society news sheet number 4. Sorry, by the way, that it's been a little later than I was hoping, but you've no idea how much I've had to do lately! There's been this *Kung Fu Monthly* Secret Society page to write, news sheet number 4, The *Member's Souvenir Magazine* to assemble and finally, the area lists I've been promising you. On top of all that, of course, there's been the usual pile of letters to answer too, so if I've been bit slow in replying to yours, now you know why! Don't worry though; I'm catching up slowly.

    Member, John Kemp, has informed me that a friend who is in the Elvis Presley Fan Club was with him one day when John bought a copy of *KFM*. The friend remarked, 'I can't see that magazine lasting for much longer' - it was *KFM* No. 3! John also tells me that he's got some great posters from "Dolans" and although he says he's had to wait a long time for them to come, he reckons it's been well worth it. For the address of the company, check out in our news sheet No. 4 as we've got all the details there.

    Apparently old monster magazines (such as *Modern Monsters* and *Castle of Frankenstein*) sometimes have articles in them on *Green Hornet* and on Bruce Lee in particular. I suggest everybody roots through old magazine and book shops whenever they get the chance. I expect there's quite a few of these rarities around, if we did but know it!

    By the way, a good place to write to for Little Dragon Cinema Posters, stills and press books is the following address: 34 Southwood Avenue, Bournemouth, BH6 3QB.

    Here are a few more goodies from members Martin Hughes and Mark Burns. They're the two nice people who gave us our fabulous poster list and to help keep the ball rolling, they've sent in a few more names.

1. A memorial poster of Bruce Lee is obtainable from PO Box 54338, Terminal Annexe, Los Angeles, California 90054,USA, for the sum of $2.50
2. A Jeet Kune Do technique poster from George Foon of 7011 Sunset Boulevard, Los Angeles, California 90028, USA for $1.00
3. And you can get a Bruce Lee t-shirt for £1.40 at Conray Publications and Enterprise Co., PO Box 2599, Kowloon Central, Hong Kong. Also, from the same address, there are Bruce Lee Kung Fu uniforms, small and medium for $19, large and extra large for $20 and Fist of Fury rubber nunchakus for $10.60.

A RETROSPECTIVE LOOK AT BRUCE LEE MANIA & THE KUNG FU CRAZE OF THE 1970S

Bruce Lee Society – 1st Year Triumph!

Though The Master Is Gone ...

THE BRUCE LEE SOCIETY

is guided by the teachings and philosophies he left us. They are our inspiration.

In just one short year, over 1,000 members have joined in helping perpetuate the memory of Bruce Lee, the Master. When they rejoin for the 2nd year, their great work will be recognised — in particular — by the receipt of a special commemorative Society Brooch, bearing the words, "THE BRUCE LEE SOCIETY – 2ND YEAR". We know this unique symbol will be worn with the humility, dignity and honour it deserves.

In addition, 2nd year members will also receive a new personal membership card and scroll, both coloured red and both inscribed "2nd Year". Finally, there'll be another great set of superb Bruce Lee in action pictures (one mounted and free-standing!).

If you have not as yet joined The Bruce Lee Society, then take a look at the treat you've got coming.
1. *A 1st year joining kit consisting of membership card, scroll, biography and fact sheet, the Official Society badge, stickers, action photos and an autographed pic of Bruce Lee.*
2. *The famous 3-Monthly News Sheet, sent DIRECT to your home.*
3. *A regular Society page, right here in every edition of Kung-Fu Monthly.*
4. *All your enquiries answered by our tireless President, Pam Hadden.*
5. *Competitions, special offers, the Swop Shop and lots, lots more.*

Amazing, and just think, whether you're joining up for the 1st or 2nd year, the price remains the same ... only £3.25.

Don't delay! Join now and help us make sure that the name of the Master, Bruce Lee, is not forgotten. Send your £3.25 subscription fee (cheques/postal orders made out to KFM) to:

The Bruce Lee Society
Subscriptions Dept
14 Rathbone Place
London W1P 1DE

Finally, please make it clear in your letter whether you are applying for your 1st or 2nd year of membership ... thank you.

To be honest, I'd be rather less than enthusiastic about sending large sums of money abroad for the latter items as it really can be so difficult if something goes wrong. I will leave it up to you take whatever precautions you can.

As you'll be able to see from news sheet No. 4, the *Society Souvenir* magazine of member's own contributions has finally been completed. Well, I won't say it wasn't a struggle. There was a lot to put in and not much space in which to get it all. Still, all's well that ends well! By the by, if in the future we decide to assemble a club souvenir magazine No. 2, could you all bear in mind the following points when it comes to submitting drawings and paintings? First, as the magazine itself will be in black and white, it usually helps a lot if the work you send us is also in black and white. Second, please try to use plain and not lined paper. Third, for the best possible results, try to use ink rather than pencil. If you really do prefer to use a pencil, please try to make sure it's a dark, that is, a hard one!

This month we've decided to put all the swaps into the news sheet, so there's none here in *KFM* this time - the same applies to the pen pals. Next issue, it's back to normal again! See you then... Pam

A RETROSPECTIVE LOOK AT BRUCE LEE MANIA & THE KUNG FU CRAZE OF THE 1970S

04 JUNE 1977

HELLO AND WELCOME TO THE FOURTH QUARTERLY NEWS SHEET! YOU CAN BET THERE'S GOING TO BE SOMETHING FOR EVERYONE, SO STANDBY AND HERE WE GO!

GENERAL NEWS

As I mentioned in *KFM*, the unfortunate news is that FOTOPOST EXPRESS (listed in the last news sheet) no longer do B&W copies from pictures, cuttings, etc., only colour. I am now seeking an alternative, so everybody, keep your eyes peeled. They can't have been the only people doing such work.

Now, can anyone help with member 1621, Paul Brosnan? He lives in Dublin and is desperate to know if there is a registered Kung Fu club nearby. Write to him direct, please, at Dublin, Ireland.

Michael Hodson (1755) tells us nunchakus can be obtained from J. Lee, 52 St. Paul's Avenue, Barry 5, Glamorgan, S.Wales. 13" long, in natural wood @ £2.75, black @ £3.00.

Also, a large selection of martial arts equipment is on sale at the North London Martial Arts Centre, 81 Broad Lane, London N.15.

Finally, equipment, magazines, posters and clothes are all at the A to Z Martial Arts & Book Centre, 3 Macclesfield St., London, W1.

If you're after Bruce Lee posters, why not try the local fairground, says David Anthony (1521)? He tells me he's been lucky that way a number of times.

I've been in touch with a company who make mirrors with printed images on with the idea of having one made of Bruce. We'd use his profile with the words "He Shall Not Be Forgotten." These can be got BUT the minimum order they will do is 500 -

which means that unless there's a good response we shan't be able to consider it! They would be unique - to the best of my knowledge, Bruce has never appeared on glass - so if you want something original and rare, now's the time! The size is 12 inches by 8 inches with plain, black wooded frame and the total cost would be in the region of £2.00 to £2.50. But don't send in money yet! First I need to check the response. Anyone interested, please send in a postcard with your name, address and number saying you'd like one. If I get lots of enquiries, I'll order the first 500.

Nigel Martin (1359) sent in the unusual snap of a car you can see here (number plate - LEE 111).

Anyone else seeing something as interesting as this, just "click" the camera and pop it in the post to me. It may get used in the next news sheet!

Now, although he may not know it himself yet, when he reads this, David Casey (2000) will find out he is our 1,000TH MEMBER! So, David, you can expect shortly to receive a very rare COMPLETE SET of *KFM's* as a prize!

I recently ordered and got back within a week, the *Enter the Dragon* LP from a local shop. So, if there are any of you out there still wanting it, write in to me, marking the envelope "*Enter* Record Offer" and enclosing £4.00 and I'll do the rest! Please - don't forget your name, address, membership number and allow three weeks for delivery.

Two new addresses for martial arts school information are: The Martial Arts Commission, 4 Deptford Bridge, London SE. 8 (01 691 3433) and The British Kung Fu Federation, 33 Kingfisher Drive, Ham, Surrey.

Would the member who sent me a fabulous pair of nunchakus, PLEASE TELL ME WHO THEY ARE!! I *think* I know who it is - but I don't want to go thanking the wrong person. Come on - own up!

John Kemp (1729) and Jeffrey Millington (1127) say Regent Films of PO Box 54, Blackpool, FY1 ISP, Lancs., are quite genuine when they offer trailers on Bruce's films. Write to them for lists.

Also, Mark Burns (1687) and Martin Hughes (1695), who produced the fabulous poster list, tell me Kung Fu Supplies Company, 188 Johnston Road, 7C Wanchi, Hong Kong, do Bruce trailers. There's a 15 min *Way of the Dragon* in colour -

Super 8, 400 ft long, with main plot/fight scenes and sound cassette to go with it. It costs U.S. $55.00 - again, I suggest you write first.

Martin Schell (1819) asks; Can I get some personal item of Bruce's to give as a prize? I'd say that was a tall order! He thinks too, that Don Maclean's record *Vincent* has words that could aptly describe Bruce - "This world was never meant for one as beautiful as you." Nice thought. He's a dab hand with the nunchakus and practises his own style called, (I quote) "Very Careful!!!"

Warning time... May I strongly suggest you order nothing whatsoever from Elston Ransom (Gary of the Dragon Fan Club in the US says the same thing). He is also behind CINEMA INC. of Daytona Beech, Florida and a fan club based in Jacksonville, Florida. He's a rip-off! Several members have already been caught for large sums of money.

And how about this.... Gary finishes off his letter to me with, "..one last comment, Pam. The movie *Bruce Lee - True Story* starring Bruce Li has been warmly welcomed in Los Angeles. I have seen the film, and despite its exploitive motives, I thought it to be highly entertaining and superbly choreographed and far superior to some of the other Lee exploitation films floating about." Well - all I can say is if Bruce Li has made a good film, that's something to see!

How's this for a comic tale? Nigel Martin (1359) owns a motor bike and has a crash helmet with "Bruce Lee" written across it. One day, at his insurance brokers, the man behind the counter asked, "Are you sure you've got an account with us, Mr. Lee?"

Finally, Mike Werowski (1686) sees Bruce as, "A great light and each of us as a part of that light. So that when we join together, we can again produce that great light that was Bruce Lee."

USEFUL ADDRESSES

Sent in by Eileen O'Connell (1563) - thanks Eileen.

a) The Cinema Bookshop, 13-14 Gt. Russell St., London WC1 - Film Stills
b) Treasures & Pleasures, 18 Newport Court, London WC2 - Film Stills
c) Cauldron Promotions, 98 Mill Lane, London NW.6 - Posters
d) Personality Posters, 9 Gorst Road, London NW.I - Posters
e) Big "0" Posters, 219 Eversleigh Road, London SW11 - Posters
f) Mantis Supply Co. PO BOX 3749, L.A. CA 90028, USA - Misc.
g) Gerald Lane, P/C Club, Russell Hill, Upton, Co. Cork – Books
h) Dolans Sports, 620 Fairview Ave, Neptune, NJ 07753, USA – Misc.
i) Rene Chateau, 38 Rue de Bassano, Paris 75008, France - Magazines
j) Larry Edmunds, Cinema Bookshop Inc, Hollywood, CA 90028, USA - Stills
k) Martial Arts Stationary, PO BOX 724, Largo, FL 33540, USA - Stationary

Eileen & Joey Green (1007) say Paul Crompton of 638, Fulham Road, London SW6 do Bruce Lee books, magazines, posters and Kung Fu equipment - and can recommend them.

THE BRUCE LEE SOCIETY

Angela Mao Fan Club - Michael Moore, 48 Coniston Cres, Watergate Estate, Crook, Co.Durham.

Official David Chiang Fan Club - Shiela Boardman, 8 Octavia Drive, Manchester M10 6NE.

Steve McQueen Fan Club - Steve Pepperrell, 38 Meadfoot Road, Streatham Vale, London SW16 5BL.

LETTERS

From Patrick Hennessy (1771), Dunlaoghaire, Dublin.

May I borrow space to query the bemusing attitude of the film censors towards violence on the screen. Recently I paid good money and time to see the inimitable Bruce Lee display his comprehensively brilliant fighting technique in Way [of the Dragon] *- which is re-issued consistently for the benefit of those who know Lee was the unbeatable genius of all time. However, there is less and less of the film each time, while elsewhere on view is* [Texas] Chainsaw Massacre, *with sex, sadism, witchcraft, assassination, rape and general violent horror. And if that lot is not enough, we can turn to TV and see the latest bombings or a boxing match to watch two fools drawing blood. Bruce Lee's films are cut unfairly as he was merely an impeccable exponent of a deadly sport, demonstrating the inexplicable potentiality of his magnificent ultimate domination of mind and body exclusive to him alone. For though millions will imitate, none will equal his feats, and his clear-cut performances put other films to shame and justifies only the complex minds of those who advocate publication of dirt compared to the authenticity of the late Bruce Lee.*

And so say all of us, Patrick! The censors seem incapable of telling violence from artistry these days. In fact, taking for instance *Hellfighters of the East* - at the end, it was a sheer massacre - but the censors let this go by. Yet Bruce in *Way of the Dragon* took on six opponents with the nunchaku, teased them, made faces at them and generally made the audiences laugh with him... and the censors thought it too violent! God alone knows how they can justify themselves...

Dear Pam,

Please send me the address of the American Bruce Lee Fan Club. By the way, you are always patting yourselves on the back in Kung Fu Monthly, *but I personally don't think you are all that fantastic in what you do for Bruce Lee fans. After all, it is your job to answer queries and dig up information on Bruce. I am afraid this letter is a bit rushed and I will elaborate on my opinions in a future letter to you.*

Joe Woods (1272), Shannon, Eire.

Actually Joe, sorry to correct you, but this isn't my "job." I run the club for you in my spare time and I have a full-time job to hold down at the same time. Anyway, comments on the letter are invited!

MAIL ORDER TIME FOLKS!

And first off, in the last issue I promised you we'd be starting the writing sets, so here we go.

To begin with, we're offering 30 sheets of Secret Society notepaper plus 20 envelopes. But this is only the start. Coming up very soon we should be getting some Bruce Lee pens and possibly a special stamp to go with it! If you've got any other ideas of additions to the kit... well, just let me know. For now though, the price of the paper and envelopes is just £1.25 (including handling). Remember, each sheet and envelope has the Secret Society emblem printed upon it!

Just send your £1.25 cheque/postal order (along with your name, address and membership number) to Secret Society Writing Sets Offer, 14 Rathbone Place, London W1P IDE. Please allow 4 weeks for delivery.

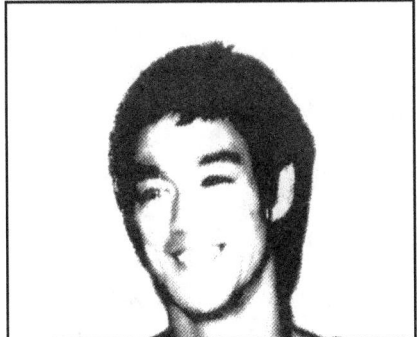

AND NOW... here is the moment many of you have been waiting for. Some time ago, *KFM* ran an offer for Bruce Lee PILLOW SLIPS, priced at £1.10 each. There were some left over - BUT NOT VERY MANY!! - and Society members are being offered the remainder at the knock-down price of just £0.75 each!!! Pleased be warned though, that a good many of them are "seconds," that is, they may have some imperfection. It's a case of first come, first served and I'll say again, there aren't many left. They are completely unavailable anywhere else in the world, so for all true Bruce Lee fans, this is a capital "M" must.

The demand when the offer first ran was absolutely huge and I've got no reason to suppose or believe it's going to be any different this time! Mail your 75p cheque or postal order (made out to *Kung Fu Monthly*, please) to: Society Pillow Slip Offer, 14 Rathbone Place, London W1P IDE. Once again may I ask that you allow at least four weeks for delivery.

COMPETITION RESULTS

The following lucky members won the last competition in the March news sheet. Richard Zincke (1874) of Doncaster, H. Craig (1728) of Ballymena, Paul Short (1164) of Sheffield, Richard Miller (1638) of Aberdeen, and John Watson (1933).

Correct answers were: 1) *Way of the Dragon,* 2) *Fist of Fury,* 3) Four Alsatians, 4) Chuck Norris and Bob Wall, 5) Robert Clouse, 6) False... *Fist* was shot in Hong Kong 7) The crackers were in *Big Boss,* 8) *Enter the Dragon* was made for Western audiences, 9) Nunchakus, Longsticks & Darts, and 10) Temple of the Unknown.

Each of the winners will be receiving a very rare copy of the original press handout for *Way of the Dragon* - courtesy of Cathay Films.

PEN PALS

It's pen pals time again, and once more, Gary has pulled some U.S.A. names out of the hat!

- Robert Mandoki, Hawthorne, California, U.S.A.
- Charles Webb, Ann, Virginia, U.S.A.
- Steve Chadwick, Loveland, Ohio, U.S.A.
- Patrick Nardone, Newark, New Jersey, U.S.A.
- Dorothy Sheenhan, Rochester, New York, U.S.A.
- Frederick James, Detroit, Michigan, U.S.A.
- David Rockling, Northbrook, Illinois, U.S.A.
- Pete Willis, Kingston, Ontario, Canada.
- Herb Woodall, Columbia, Ohio, U.S.A.
- Tim Young, Ellerslie, Aukland, New Zealand.
- Thomas Riza, Omaha, Nebraska, U.S.A.
- Allen Stewart, Cambridge, Mass, U.S.A.

Don't forget, if you'd like YOUR name/address to be sent along to Gary, just write and let me know!

And here's some more pen pal requests:

- Paul Rogers (1713), Castle Vale, Birmingham wants girl pen pal - 19/20 yrs who likes music, reading and sport. He's 21.
- Michael Adams (1573), Shephall wants Chinese/English female pen pal. He's 21, and has been learning Kung Fu for 2 years. Interests are Bruce Lee, Kung Fu, art and swimming.
- Joyce Tompkins (1410), Chells wants female pen pal aged 18/21, preferably Chinese, but any Bruce fanatic welcome. She's 20.
- Ian Milner (1891), Gedling, wants pen pal in UK aged 13/14 (he's 13). Photo please.
- Kevin Taylor (1885), Oldham, Lancs wants pen pal about 18yrs. Male/female, preferably Oriental.
- Paul Ruiz (1718), Hadleigh wants Chinese male/female pen pal 16/17 yrs.

SWOP SHOP

- John Kemp (1729), Bristol BS12 5EH has for sale to the highest bidder: 1) Set of five *Way of the Dragon* cinema stills and one B&W action still. 2) Copy of *KFM* No. 16. 3) Soundtrack of *The Big Boss*, *Fist of Fury*, and *Way of the Dragon* on cassettes - includes selection of music, dialogue and fights. 4) Book *Bruce Lee - Farewell My Friend*. He wants: American magazines such as *Black Belt*, *Best of Bruce Lee No.1*, and *Farewell to the Dragon*.
- Al Briers (1828), St. Helens wants mandarin work-jacket (40" chest or trousers

- 33"/34" for exchange or sale. He has for offer some super recordings of Bruce in *Way of the Dragon*, *Fist of Fury*, and *The Big Boss*. Also *Marlowe*, interviews and many other items.
- Julian Midgely (1354), Perry Bar, has all-colour posters Mirrors in *Enter the Dragon* (30 inch by 20 inch), Underground side-pose with nunchakus in *Enter the Dragon* (33 inch by 27 inch), artist's design original - Dragon behind with scars (38 inch by 27 inch) and a magic set No. 3 by "Airfix." Wants *My Martial Arts Training Guide* by James Lee and *KFM's* 1-4. High price paid.
- S.S. Green (1511), Rhostyllen wants *My Martial Arts Training Guide to Jeet Kune Do* by James Lee.
- Glynn Barker (1567), Sheffield wants 1) Two *Bruce Lee Scrapbooks* 2) *KFM's* 2, 16, 17, 19 and 24 and any rare illustrated books and magazines on Bruce 3) Also, original frame-sized photos of Bruce (not Society pictures or from Cimac please!) High prices paid. 4) Signed photo of Bruce - will buy or swap for something pretty expensive in exchange.
- Mark Burns (1687), Walsall has white Karate gi (med) to swap for Kung Fu trousers - *Way of the Dragon* style - or £6. Also seven different issues of *Black Belt*, five issues of *Karate Illustrated*, five issues of *Official Karate*, three issues of *Real Kung Fu*, one issue of *Samurai*, one issue of *Oriental Fighting Arts*, *Karate & Oriental Arts* 1968 issue, *Defensive Combat*, 13 Kung Fu paperbacks, *Step by Step Guide to Kung Fu*, two sets of nunchakus, *Live and Let Die* LP, and Bruce's films on tape - *The Big Boss*, *Fist of Fury*, and *Way of the Dragon*. He wants *Bruce Lee – King of Kung Fu* (New English Library), *Deadly Hands of Kung Fu* No. 7, *Clash* No.1 complete, *Fighting Stars* (any issues) *Kung Fu Superstars*, any Bruce Lee film posters and any rare Chinese magazines on Bruce. PHEW!!!
- Stephen Flynn, Glasgow has 21 *Dragon* magazines for sale. Offers please.
- Brian Rusk (1353), Bootle has *KFM's* 1-4 (2 sets), 4-14 (2 or more!) including special edition. Wants *Doc Savage* books.
- Michael Werkowski (1686), Chesterfield has *Beginner's Guide to Kung Fu* and issue 17 of *KFM* - both FREE to the first member to write to him!
- Ian Milner (1891), Gedling has record player and radio. Wants Kung Fu boxing gloves or book *Bruce Lee's Nunchaku's in Action*.
- A.Lindsay (1690), Llanbryde wants record of *Memory of Bruce Lee* by John and Rosalind, martial arts weapons for decoration, *Kung Fu Cinema of Vengence*, *KFM's* 5 and 6, *Best of Bruce Lee*, *Fighting Stars* magazines except Oct/Dec '74, *Kung Fu Superstars*, *Kung Fu Fighters*, all cinema posters, stills etc. of martial arts films, except of *Blood Money*.
- James Ruddy (1724), Greenock wants *KFM* No.1 Price please.
- Peter Barnacle (1598), London wants *KFM's* 1,2,3 and 4. Good price paid.
- Michael Adams (1573), Shephall has *Shorinji Kempo* by Doshin So. (originally cost, £10.75), *Secret Fighting Arts of the World* by John F. Gilby (cost £3.60). Offers please.
- A. Smyth (1931), Coleraine has three Bruce Lee books - *Studies on Jeet Kune Do*, *Nunchakus in Action*, and *Privacy and Anecdotes*. Also, *Dynamic Kicks*.

- Wants pair of Kung Fu ankle-tie trousers.
- Mr. C. Chedgzoy (2020), Abbeydale wants *KFM's* 1-4 inc. Price please.
- Mr. R.S,Richardson (1939), Stockport wants *KFM's* 1, 2 and 3 plus 2 Bruce Lee *Scrapbooks*.
- James McKeown (1976), Blackpool has *Dragons* 1, 2, 3, 5, 6,and 7. Will exchange for copy of *Best of Bruce Lee* No. 1 or any other American magazines.
- Mike Devereux (1061), Warrington wants *The Big Boss/Fist of Fury* cinema posters. Ultra-high price paid.
- Colin Sinfield, Kent has issues 1-13, 20-23 and 26 of *KFM*. Also *Super Kung Fu* album, the giant *Bruce Lee Scrapbook* and *Beginner's Guide to Kung Fu*. Also other publications.
- Anthony Clarke (1715), Carlisle wants *KFM's* 1, 2, and 3. Has to offer *Legend of Bruce Lee* by Alex Ben Block.
- Brian Beck (1890), Portadown wants poster magazine titled, *Kung Fu!* which states on front, "All you ever wanted to know about Bruce Lee - King of the Kung Fu movies!" (published by Top Sellers). Please state price.

Well, that's just got to be the biggest collection of swaps I've ever seen! Really, with the section getting to be so popular, I may just have to think about making it into a separate supplement. There's obviously a lot of collectors amongst you Secret Society people and to be honest, I can't blame you. Many of the early Bruce Lee books and magazines are starting to fetch really high prices - it's hard to get the first few *KFM's* for love or money! I hope I'm helping the best way I can by running this "Swop Shop."

If you can think of other ways of improving the service, just let me know. I notice, by the way, that there's a growing interest in American books and magazines. I'm making no promises, but there's just a chance that Gary over there with the *Dragon* club in Hollywood, may just be able to lend a hand. I'll be in touch with him again soon and I'll put it to him. Stand by for news of that! Lastly, could I suggest that, before sending your request into the Swop Shop, you just check through previous lists to make sure you're not asking for the impossible!

SECRET SOCIETY SOUVENIR ALBUM
OF MEMBERS' DRAWINGS AND POEMS

And now the time has come to tell you all about the SECRET SOCIETY SOUVENIR ALBUM OF MEMBERS' DRAWINGS AND POEMS. It's ready as of now, and as I promised, anyone who has contributed will receive a copy FREE OF CHARGE! It's turned out to be a real winner and I've got to say that the general level of work far exceeded my original expectations. So far as I'm concerned this album has got to be a real piece of Bruce Lee and Secret Society history. I'm absolutely sure that in years to come, this magazine will become a most sought after publication.

Take a look here at just one of the magnificent pages of the SECRET SOCIETY SOUVENIR ALBUM! Believe me, I'm not joking when I say how delighted I am with

A RETROSPECTIVE LOOK AT BRUCE LEE MANIA & THE KUNG FU CRAZE OF THE 1970S

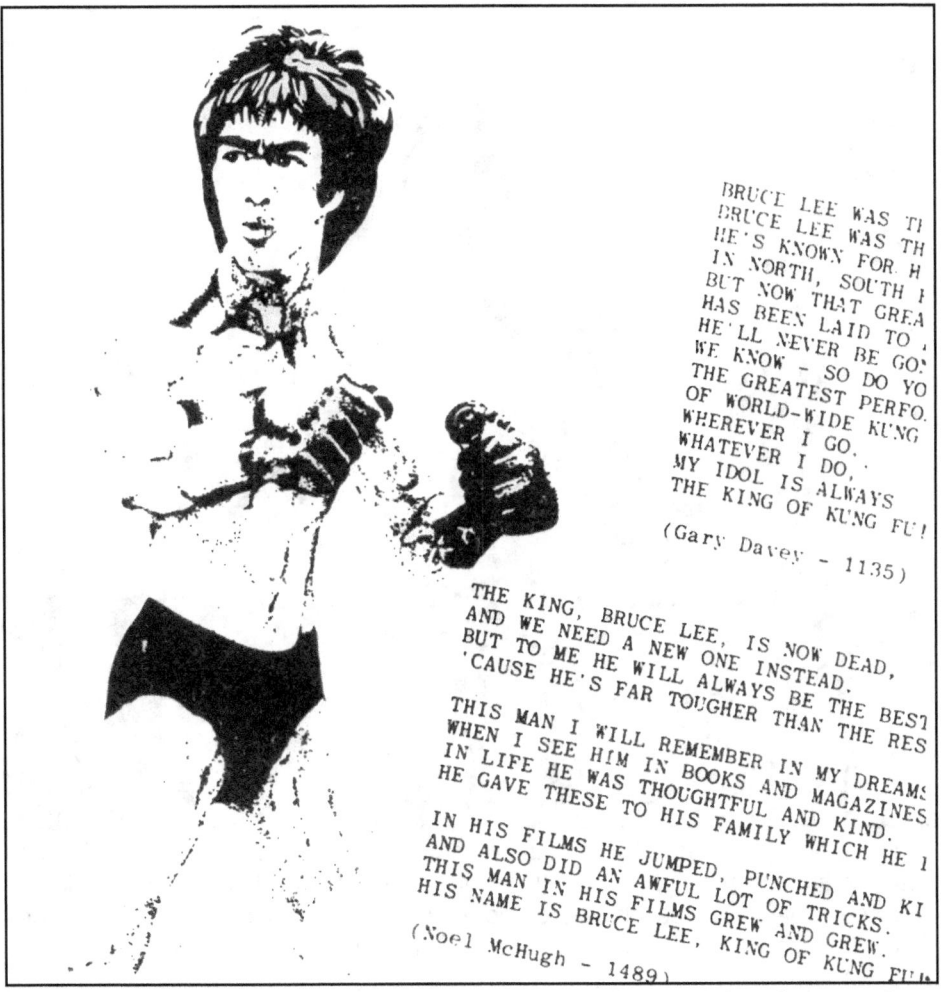

BRUCE LEE WAS T!
BRUCE LEE WAS TH
HE'S KNOWN FOR H
IN NORTH, SOUTH
BUT NOW THAT GREA
HAS BEEN LAID TO
HE'LL NEVER BE GO!
WE KNOW – SO DO YO
THE GREATEST PERFO.
OF WORLD-WIDE KUNG
WHEREVER I GO,
WHATEVER I DO,
MY IDOL IS ALWAYS
THE KING OF KUNG FU!

(Gary Davey – 1135)

THE KING, BRUCE LEE, IS NOW DEAD,
AND WE NEED A NEW ONE INSTEAD.
BUT TO ME HE WILL ALWAYS BE THE BEST
'CAUSE HE'S FAR TOUGHER THAN THE RES
THIS MAN I WILL REMEMBER IN MY DREAMS
WHEN I SEE HIM IN BOOKS AND MAGAZINES
IN LIFE HE WAS THOUGHTFUL AND KIND.
HE GAVE THESE TO HIS FAMILY WHICH HE I
IN HIS FILMS HE JUMPED, PUNCHED AND KI
AND ALSO DID AN AWFUL LOT OF TRICKS.
THIS MAN IN HIS FILMS GREW AND GREW.
HIS NAME IS BRUCE LEE, KING OF KUNG FU

(Noel McHugh – 1489)

the result of it all and I'm sure you will be too! Now, if you didn't in fact contribute to the pages, but still would like a copy of this historic work, the Society will be delighted to forward one to you at COST PRICE ONLY! And that means that I'm only going to be asking 50 pence (including postage), so please send your postal order as soon as possible to Society Album Offer, 14 Rathbone Place, London, W1P 1DE. Don't delay though. The time's not far off when we'll probably start work on Album No. 2 and then the first will become unavailable.

COMPETITION

The puzzle for this news sheet was sent in to us by John Rogers, member number 1009. It's an anagram or "Quizword" as he puts it. What you have to do is unscramble the anagram clues... in other words, rearrange the letters to form word/s closely connected with Bruce Lee and the world of Kung Fu. To set you off in the

off in the right direction, I'll give you the answer to the first clue. BIB SOGS, when changed around, spells BIG BOSS!! OK, off you go, and get those answers in for the next news sheet. Replies, please, to Secret Society Competition No. 4, 14 Rathbone Place, London W1P IDE. Check in news sheet No. 5 for the results!!

1. BIB SOGS
2. RAT BERKROBE
3. THREAT END GONER
4. FATE MADE HOG
5. NICK ROCSHUR
6. SERVED HANGOLT
7. IS TUFFY FOR
8. WEARLOM
9. WORD CHANMOY
10. DAY FORT HE WAGON
11. TRENTGLOSE

So there it is for the Bruce Lee Secret Society news sheet No. 4. I hope you all liked the "special free photograph" we've enclosed this time - it's another from the "never-before-seen" set featured in that great book, *The Secret Art of Bruce Lee!* FINALLY, DON'T FORGET ALL YOU MEMBERS WHO HAVE RECEIVED ALL FOUR NEWS SHEETS THAT YOUR SUBSCRIPTION RENEWAL FALLS DUE IN THREE MONTH'S TIME. DON'T FORGET TO SEND IT... OTHERWISE YOU'LL MISS THE NEXT NEWS SHEET! Love to you all – Pam

BRUCE LEE SOCIETY COLUMN
KUNG FU MONTHLY NO. 33

Once more it's a big hello from me, Pam, to all you members of the Bruce Lee Secret Society. It makes me really proud to think that every single one of you is dedicated to helping keep the name of the Little Dragon alive. And much more than that, don't forget the aim of this club is to see his ideas and his valuable philosophies on living are literally spread to the four corners of the globe. Let's have the memory of the master influencing the running of nations! It may sound over-hopeful of me to say that, but looking at the state of things right now, I reckon the world can do with all the help it can get.

As many of you may know, we have a sister Secret Society in the United States now and so far as I can make out, they're going great guns over there too! I've arranged for Stateside members to write and tell me if they want to correspond with their UK counterparts and I'm pretty sure many of them will want to do just that! So, what I'd like members this end to do, is write and tell me whether YOU want your name and address to be included on the list I'll be sending to all the USA enquirers. It's a great opportunity to get to know what's happening across the water and so far as I'm concerned, it's the first link in a chain I'd like to sec stretch right round the globe. UK members who want to be included on that list, please send me a POSTCARD saying so. Don't forget to include your name, address and Society number.

Member, M. Lockwood (2040) says that Magpie Records of Hop Market, Worcester have in stock an impressive collection of hard-to-get-hold-of LPs. For 15p they'll send you their complete brochure – featuring largely American, British and Italian product. Although we're not told for sure, it seems to me that the shop must be worth trying for Bruce Lee soundtrack material.

M. Hobson tells me about The Martial Arts Centre, 81 Broad Lane, Tottenham, London N15. Apparently they stock a number of Bruce Lee items including a t-shirt and photos so I'd say they are well worth checking out. Their terms are a full refund if not satisfied and they claim a "same day" despatch system.

I haven't had much response as yet on the Bruce Lee mirrors idea I mentioned in the last news sheet. As I said then, provided a good number of you write in and say you're interested, I'll go ahead with an order. If enquiries don't improve from the smallish number we've had so far, I'll have to knock the idea on the head. You have been warned!! And speaking of warnings; Following on what I said a few months ago, I am NOT replying to letters that arrive for me that DON'T include a stamped and addressed envelope. If you've written to me and as yet have had no reply, that may well be the reason why. I'm being really firm about this. Costs for everything are rising astronomically these days, so PLEASE help me in this small way.

See you again soon ... Pam

BRUCE LEE SOCIETY COLUMN
KUNG FU MONTHLY NO. 34

One year on and what a great event for the Society that's sweeping the world!

THE BRUCE LEE SOCIETY

And in line with our new-found maturity (as you can see above) I've decided now to call the club simply, THE BRUCE LEE SOCIETY.

Over the last year, the achievements of the Bruce Lee Society have been considerable. Who'd have believed to start with, that such a young club would be so soon, welcoming its 1,000th member! In addition, a sister Society has already been formed in the United States and many more are planned for the future. It really does look as though our dream of linking the countries of the world is starting to come true.

Another feather in our cap is the getting together of the club's first souvenir magazine. This, to me, has been very important, for it shows beyond any doubt, that the Society is acting as a society in the truest sense of the word. By that I mean it consists of members who LIKE and WANT to participate. The souvenir magazine is NOT mine; it belongs to everyone who took part in its making. I congratulate all of you.

For my part, I don't think there's a member who could claim that a letter to me hasn't been answered, where, of course, a stamped and addressed envelope has been enclosed! And while on that subject, I feel I must say, that although I love hearing from you, it would be really helpful if you restricted yourselves to asking just the main questions you want answered. I only have a certain amount of spare time in which to run the Society and everyone, after all, deserves a fair crack of the whip.

Another important thing I've been meaning to mention is if you have any queries on mail order goods, could you please address your letters direct to the KFM mail order department. I don't deal with that side of things and writing to me only delays solving your problem. For all you members about to send in your £3.25s to join up for another year in the Bruce Lee Society, I've got great news for you. After much hard thinking at this end, here's what the second-year members will receive: 1) More new and really great action photos of Bruce Lee; 2) A new membership card and scroll, both coloured red to signify your second year membership; 3) One free-standing, mounted action picture of Bruce Lee; 4) A superb, solid metal brooch/badge showing the Master's Yin/Yang sign and bearing the words, "Bruce Lee Society - Second Year". The badge will be unique to second-year members only and, subject to confirmation, the colours will be gold on black.

Back again next month... Pam

A RETROSPECTIVE LOOK AT BRUCE LEE MANIA & THE KUNG FU CRAZE OF THE 1970S

EDITOR'S NOTES

Mail order companies were prevalent in the 1970's and 1980's, and it wasn't difficult to fall foul to a rogue one, especially if they were non-domestic based. Reports upon reports of rips offs were rife. I'm sure that just about every Bruce Lee fan was left out of pocket at some point during their time, whether it was paying for goods and not receiving anything all or not receiving what was paid for. Sometimes it was outright fraud but sometimes it was just an oversight and underestimating demand, a company simply going out of business or an individual moving house.

In the modern age of the internet, transactions are a lot smoother. Occasionally things go wrong but companies such as eBay, PayPal and credit card companies are making it incredibly harder for fans to lose their money, largely thanks to the digital footprints that these transactions leave behind.

In the 1970's and 1980's payment was usually made by either cash, or money orders (international money orders for abroad). Even in the early days of eBay around 1998, my non-domestic eBay purchases would consist of sending exchanged cash from the local travel agency, by airmail post to eagerly wait for my goodies a few weeks later.

As you read through the newsletters, you'll see an increase in rip off companies emerging, all no doubt eager to ride the Kung Fu wave.

Issue four was the first mention of a Bruce Lee imitator, with the honour going to Bruce Li.

Bruce Li, born Ho Chung-tao was a Taiwanese actor originally began his film career as stuntman, going by the name James Ho, before acting in the film *Conspiracy*. After producers noticed his resemblance to the late Bruce Lee, Ho was given the name Bruce Li and hired to star in the Bruceploitation films *Goodbye Bruce Lee: His Last Game of Death*, *The Young Bruce Lee*, and *Bruce Lee: The Man The Myth*.

Some unscrupulous producers even credited him directly as "Bruce Lee" on their film posters in order to drive extra business by implying that the real Bruce Lee was starring in their films, as was the case for the film *Bruce Lee Against Supermen*. No internet and very little other reference material was available to fans at the time and many found themselves falling into the producers' traps time after time.

Other producers tried to dupe fans into believing that Li was Lee's chosen successor by making unofficial sequels to Lee's previous films *The Big Boss* and *Fist of Fury* or employing Lee's former co-stars such as Angela Mao and Dan Inosanto to appear with Li to add extra credibility and acceptance.

Li retired from acting at the age of 40 in 1990, having not had a major starring role for eight years. In a 1995 documentary, Li stated that he disliked the studios trying to turn him into a Bruce Lee imitator and even though he felt he could act like him, he could never have been him.

Throughout the news sheet, it is evident that there is sheer hatred for Li and his fellow imitators Dragon Lee, Bruce Lo, Bruce Liang, etc., but I think that view has generally softened over the years. There are those that still won't even watch a Bruce Li film but a lot of fans have seen those films or exactly what they were – damn fun Kung Fu movies that tried to quench an insatiable thirst for Chinese guys beating people up on screen.

BRUCE LI FILMOGRAPHY

Rickshaw Man (1974) (a.k.a. Rickshaw Driver, Shaolin Kung Fu)
Bruce Lee: A Dragon Story (1974)
Iron Man (1975)
Goodbye Bruce Lee: His Last Game of Death (1975)
Bruce Lee Against Supermen (1975)
Bruce Lee: The Man, The Myth (1976)
Exit the Dragon, Enter the Tiger (1976)
Enter the Panther (1976)
Bruce Lee's Secret (1976) (a.k.a. Bruce Lee's Deadly Kung Fu and *Story of the Dragon)*
The Ming Patriots (1977) (a.k.a. Revenge of the Patriots)
Bruce Li in New Guinea (1977)
Bruce Lee the Invincible (1977)
The Dragon Lives (1977)
Bruce Lee, We Miss You (1977) (a.k.a. Dragon Dies Hard)
Fist of Fury II (1977) (a.k.a. Chinese Connection 2 and *Fist of Fury Part II)*
Soul Brothers of Kung Fu (1978)
The Image of Bruce Lee (1978) (a.k.a. Storming Attacks)
Fists of Bruce Lee (1978)
Edge of Fury (1978)
Dynamo (1978)
Deadly Strike (1978) (a.k.a. Wanted! Bruce Li, Dead or Alive)
Bruce Li's Magnum Fist (1978)
Bruce Lee vs. the Iron Dragon (1978)
Return of the Tiger (1978)
Bruce Against Iron Hand (1979)
The Lama Avenger (1979) (a.k.a. The Three Avengers)
Fist of Fury III (1979) (a.k.a. Chinese Connection III)
The Iron Dragon Strikes Back (1979)
Blind Fist of Bruce (1979)
The Chinese Stuntman (1981)
Powerforce (1982)

MY INTRODUCTION TO BRUCE LEE
By Glynn Darbyshire
(Member 2885)

When I first got into Bruce Lee, it was around 1974 because I got beat up at school by a group of lads. I had to go out of the village to go to high school and there was this one tall lad and he started mouthing off at me. I was so tiny but I thought, "I'm not scared of you," so I called him back but he had his nine cronies around the corner and that was the start of me being beaten up nearly every day at school. Back then, the teachers didn't really care and neither did my parents to be honest. It was an awful time as I had nobody to turn to and when you're petrified to go to school, there's nowhere you can go because they were everywhere. It got to a point where I wouldn't go to school and various people had to get involved and eventually, I had to be tutored at home.

One lad called Alan was the only friend I had left as nobody else would dare talk to me. I remember being in the yard one day and Alan was walking down with the others. I thought, "What's happening?" I said, "Alan, what are you doing?" He said, "I've got to have a fight with you. If I don't fight you, they're going to beat me up. If you win me, they are going to beat you up but if you let me win you, they'll leave you alone." When the teacher came out, everyone dispersed and I ran all the way home. That was it; I was a nervous wreck so I wouldn't go back to school. A tutor came over to the house for six months. One day, I was watching the *Scene* school program which I watched every week. This particular episode was called "Looking For a Fight" and it started talking about how, in boxing clubs just recently, there had been a drop in attendance. The episode asked whether people were losing interest or had it something to do with films like this: *Bang! Bruce Lee fighting Chuck Norris!*

I was like, "Oh my god!" It was just this little guy on the screen. I'd never heard of Kung Fu before. I'd never even seen anybody kick anybody. There were a few bits where Bruce Lee is knocked down and I'm thinking, "Huh? He's losing!" but then it shows you ... and I was like, "Oh my God!" Then it went on to show footage of Rhona McVay who was running this fan club and from then one, it was just talking about Bruce Lee all the way through. I knew it was repeated the day after but in those days, there weren't any video recorders. I'd only got my cassette recorder so I set it up there and taped it. I wish I still had the actual cassette. When I taped it, I only wanted the Bruce Lee bit and I listened to it over and over and over – just his war cries.

It was literally two weeks later and someone asked me if I knew there was a new karate club that had opened and I was like, "Where? Where? Where?" "In the village at the welfare hall." Straight away, that was it. The guy who ran the club, Mick O'Hanlon, was only a blue belt but I went down, joined up and I think he ran it three times a week but I just absolutely loved it. I found out who his instructor was, who was a guy called Phil Milner so I went through to Dinnington and started training with him. I was training a minimum of five days a week, but mostly six days.

Around that time, I started buying martial arts magazines like *Black Belt, Combat,* and *Kung Fu Monthly* because I wanted to learn all I could about Bruce Lee. Back then in 1974, it was more exciting than it is now because there was no internet. You couldn't just click on a Bruce Lee video. I remember seeing *Marlowe* on TV for the first time and didn't know Bruce Lee was in it because there was no one to tell you what he'd been in. It was exciting because you'd never seen it before. Even the magazines were few and far between, and I remember travelling to different markets because they got magazines in from America and I couldn't wait for every weekend so that I could travel to Rotherham, Sheffield, Chesterfield and go to the market stalls that had them. The stall holders used to save me stuff with Bruce Lee on the covers.

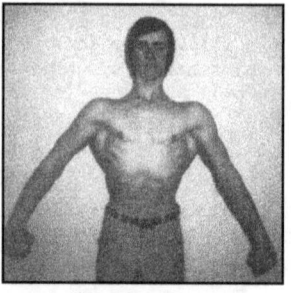

I was about 16 when *Fist of Fury* was showing at the local cinema. I saw the advertisement in the local paper and I was like, "Wow, *Fist of Fury* is on with *Amsterdam Kill*. I wasn't bothered about *Amsterdam Kill* though but it was the excitement. I wasn't old enough to see *Fist of Fury* but where I worked, I was a supervisor and I had a jacket that said "Supervisor" on it so I thought I'd put that on when I go and they'll think I'm old enough.

I travelled all over to see the films, getting the bus here and there. Nowadays, people just sit down on the sofa, press a button and everything is there for them but the excitement isn't there. Everyone from the Karate club back in the day, would go to Kung Fu All-Nighters at the cinema and you'd talk to people and have a conversation. Unlike now, where everything is typed over Messenger or something similar.

Even going to Birmingham to a little martial arts shop to buy a Japanese magazine or a pair of nunchakus was exciting. Now, you just go online, find what you want, click and three days later, it turns up at your door. The excitement isn't there anymore. I'd get the train down to London to visit this one shop that sold Bruce Lee stuff. You'd ring them up to see what they had in and then head down at the weekend.

At the time, there was no way to communicate with anybody about what you did. You could buy your magazines but there wasn't anywhere that you, as a fan,

could be featured. So when they set up the Bruce Lee Secret Society, all of a sudden, you could send a photo in and back then, everyone wanted to look like Bruce Lee. That was the only place you could send a photo in to show people that you did martial arts. It was the only place that you could write in to when you wanted to know something about Bruce Lee. There was no other way to communicate. You'd send a letter in, have it published but then you would have to wait until the next issue to see if anyone had replied. It was the excitement. Now, you have Facebook and people can reply straight away. I don't think the Society would work today for that reason. That excitement just isn't there anymore as you don't have to wait for things. Everything is instant.

Glynn Darbyshire
September 2020

05
SEPTEMBER 1977

HELLO EVERYONE... AFTER ALL THAT HOLIDAY LAZING-AROUND, NOW LET'S GET GOING ON BRUCE LEE SOCIETY NEWS SHEET NUMBER FIVE!

GENERAL NEWS

First off, many members have written in to say how shocked they were about the death of Elvis Presley, as indeed I was, being a very keen fan. As one person put it, Elvis was as good a singer as Bruce was a martial artist... and a very apt description, too. They are two originals who can never be replaced, and through their fans they will always live on!

Straight away, as many of you will have realized, the club is going to gradually drop the word "Secret" from its title. This, I feel, is very much in line with its more mature outlook. Therefore, from now on it will be called simply, The Bruce Lee Society.

M. Lockwood (2040) states that Magpie Records get copies of deleted or hard to find soundtracks - maybe they could help with Bruce Lee records? Worth a try, anyway. Their address is: Hopmarket, Worcester, Worcs. WR1 1UR. Telephone 0905 27267. They have a 24 hour answering service, so ring anytime.

A plea for help - on two counts!

Member John Stuart (1116) is really choked because somebody (and wouldn't I like to get my hands on him!) has broken into his home and stolen, among other things, every item he had on Bruce. I've sent off a couple of things to start his collection again - how about any of you members with spare copies of magazines and so on, sending something as well? Also, If you've anything to sell (he's got nothing left to swap!) let him know. His address is Aberdeen, Scotland.

Now, the second request. I always feel that anyone doing a service for charities should be given full support, so I'm asking on behalf of Shane Phipps (1735) for assistance in collecting used stamps. She does a terrific job of aiding Spina Bifida victims in this way. Send any stamps you might collect to Shane at Chesterfield, Derbyshire. Any other members out there who need help in similar ways, let me know!

I wonder how many members have the *Green Hornet* model car? I have and so has Michael Day (1701). And not only that, he has a *Green Hornet* annual, containing some pictures of Bruce and stories from *Green Hornet*. Quite a collector's item, I'd say. So, if you have any young nephews, brothers, etc, disposing of their car collections, keep an eye open. You might find a nice little model with Kato sitting in the front seat!

For those of you who have been caught by Elston Ransom in the USA and lost money, I might be getting an address from Gary in America where you can claim your refund. Don't get too excited, though, as Gary is not 100% certain how genuine it is. More on that soon.

Jeff Millington (1127) is thrilled with the trailer of *Fist of Fury* he has received from Regent Films (see previous news sheet - PO BOX 54, Blackpool FY1 ISP). You see Bruce disposing of the Japanese boss - in Jeff's words, "quite breathtaking!" Well, what Bruce Lee action isn't, eh?

David Carradine is to star in *The Silent Flute* reports David Scott (2057). He read this in *Movie World* magazine. Carradine, when asked about his "pet" project, said, "It's called *The Silent Flute*. I regard it as good a project as *Bound for Glory*. It deals with the martial arts and the late Bruce Lee. Jeff Cooper, who is the leading martial arts star in South America, will have a key role and I will portray the part originally written for Bruce Lee. Frankly, I think it will be the hottest thing I have ever done!" I have never been a great Carradine fan, nor has David, but we hope that he will do justice to the part, bearing in mind whose footsteps he has to follow in! What a pity it will not be Bruce taking the part.

WARNING!!! Member Graham Jenkinson (1381) says both he and several friends have written to C.P. Exports, Dept. RS-2533, 380 Madison Ave, New York, USA for a "Bruce Lee Explosive Power Package" and they have received nothing. I have sent a chase-up letter to the company on this score, but it looks like they may be rip-off artists. I'd suggest hold off sending anything to them. If it turns out okay, then I will let you know via either the Society page in *KFM* or a future news sheet. Thanks to Graham for mentioning this.

Spotted in Leigh-on-Sea, Essex, about 6/7 weeks ago - a young man wearing a Bruce Lee Society red & white sticker on his coat - wonder who that was??

Joe Woods (1272) (who wrote the rather critical remarks printed in the last news sheet) stirred up quite a few comments from various members by his remarks. I'm glad to say no-one agreed with Joe!! However, he has written to say that he wasn't really meaning to criticise the Society in particular. Anyway, under the circumstances, I shall not be printing any comments on his letter and will take the matter as closed! And he has kindly sent in the address of "Crazy Horse Corner," Georges Street, Dublin 2, Eire, (telephone 755228). There you can get pictures and negatives (B&W & Colour) blown up to 24 inch by 20 inch. He says he has not tried them himself yet, so write to them before sending any money.

Arthur Stone (1150) has what he believes may be the earliest mention of Bruce in an English paper. It is in the magazine, *TV Tornado*, dated February 1967, and the article concerns *The Green Hornet*. It says, "Kato, the Hornet's right-hand man, is played by Chinese newcomer Bruce Lee - a real-life black-belt Karate teacher! Bruce, whose father was a Chinese opera singer, had only a little previous acting experience - in Hong Kong." There's a drawing of the Green Hornet and Kato on the cover. Under Kato it says, "Kato - a master at Gung-Fu, advanced form of Karate and Ju Jitsu. He is Britt's houseboy and crime-fighting aide." Can anyone beat that for the earliest Bruce souvenir? Arthur is also very keen to have members get together with him in the making of a home movie on Bruce Lee and martial arts, and with this news sheet *[Editor's Note: reprinted below]* you will find an "open letter" to you all from Arthur about this. Write to him direct, please, not via the Society.

```
ARTHUR STONE, (1150)                              Burton on Trent
                        OPEN LETTER
Bruce Lee was famous as a martial artist and as a great film star. Now
that he is gone, many of us in our own small ways wish to pay tribute
to him. There are now over 1,100 members in the Bruce Lee Society. Some
are martial artists - some have other talents. Suppose we put those
talents together in one project? Bruce made movies... why don't we!
I suggest a home movie made somewhere on location, one week next
Summer. If anybody else is interested, please answer the following
questions: 1) Do you own/have access to a projector (sound/silent)?
2) Do you own a movie camera (sound/silent)? 3) Are your holidays next
Summer fixed or flexible?... if fixed, state when they are. 4) Do you
practise martial arts? 5) Have you any acting ability... or would you
like to try? It doesn't matter if you feel you can't help too much. The
idea is to have a week's holiday somewhere, get to know each other,
talk about Bruce, and to make a movie honouring Bruce's memory. People
not able to make it will still be able to buy the film. Those with
silent projectors will get a sound tape on cassette. If anyone has any
ideas, on anything else they wish to contribute, please write to me.
Story lines MUST be kept simple... not too many locations and prefer-
ably set in the countryside. Obviously we couldn't stage fight scenes
in a busy street! The best story ideas will be worked into the final
screenplay. All those interested, please contact me (if you want a
reply, DON'T forget to include a stamped and addressed envelope).
ARTHUR STONE.
```

David Atkinson (1776) has a part of the *Way of the Dragon* film where Bruce battles it out with Chuck Norris - which he obtained from his cousin in the USA. Anyone wanting the address to write to, contact David at Low Hill, Wolverhampton.

Nigel Martin (1359) says the chap running the Martial Arts Centre, 81 Broad Lane, London N15 is trying to get gloves like the one's Bruce wore in *Enter the Dragon*. Get writing members and then maybe he will chase up his suppliers for delivery! They also do t-shirts of Bruce with "Martial Arts Centre" on, as well as books, equipment, etc.

Back to photographs - Andy Hill (1443) states Broadway Photographers of 54a Broadway Market, London E8 (Telephone 01 249 4072) do B&W blow-ups from slides, photos, cuttings or artwork. Prices: 40" by 30" - £2.50, 60" by 40" - £7.50, 72" by 53" - £12.50, 30" by 20" - £2.25, 96" by 53" - £18.50 and 144" by 53" - £21.00 (WOW). Onto all these prices, you'll have to add 50p for postage and packing. Also colour from £6.00 plus p&p. Thanks, Andy - imagine a whole room done out in coloured Bruce Lee king-sized posters!!

Paul H. Crompton of 638 Fulham Road, London SW6 has some books you might find interesting, writes Richard Miller (1638). 1) *Bruce Lee Memorial* - volume of his life and rise to fame, with pictures... £2.75 plus 47p postage. 2) Various *Inside Kung Fu* magazines with articles on Bruce Lee... all priced at 55p each. 3) *Inside Kung Fu Yearbook* 1976 with articles, photos and centre poster of Lee... £1.35.

IMPORTANT NOTICE

Please, whatever you do, don't forget to send in those renewal slips. To help you remember, I've included those SAE envelopes, plus a taster of what you'll be getting for second-year membership. The special Society all-metal badge/brooch we've had designed is really beautiful and its black and gold colouring make it something you can be really proud to wear.

Secondly, and talking about SAE's, as from the receipt of this news sheet, unless members, when writing, enclose an envelope with their name, address and correct postage on, they WILL NOT be receiving a reply. I've mentioned this time and time again, and thankfully, most of you remember to do it. So come on, last warning, WITHOUT FAIL!! NO STAMP - NO REPLY.

MAIL ORDER PAGE

First off, don't forget to tell your friends that, up until December 31st, new members to the Society will be able to join up for ONLY £3.00. This bargain offer is only temporary, so get them to HURRY!!

Secondly, as advertised in *KFM*, there's a prize of a set of *KFM's* (starting issue 5) being offered to the first name out of the "hat" for RENEWING MEMBERS ONLY. Again the offer only lasts up until December 31st!!

MOST OF THEM HAVE NOW GONE... There are only a few PILLOW CASES LEFT and if you haven't got yours yet - you'd better be quick. Remember, they used to be £1.10 each in *KFM*, but now I'm offering them for only 75p each!!! Take advantage of this special Society offer. Mail your 75p cheques/postal orders (made out to *KFM*, please) to: Society Pillow Case Offer, 14 Rathbone Place, London W1P IDE. Please don't forget to allow four weeks for delivery.

SOCIETY WRITING SETS!

They're going like hot cakes, and no wonder! Don't forget, we're offering 30 sheets of writing paper, plus 20 envelopes for only £1.25. The design is tastefully coloured in two shades of green. When writing to fellow members, or even just friends, be proud to be a member of the Bruce Lee Society - use the official notepaper. Send your £1.25 (again, cheques/postal orders made out to *KFM*, please) to: Society Notepaper offer, 14 Rathbone Place, London W1P IDE.

As I mentioned last time, coming up pretty soon there should be Bruce Lee Society pens - to go with the writing sets. Stand by for more news on that in the coming months!

David Hare (1856) tells me Dolan's Sports, Dept. OK, 620 Fairview Avenue, Neptune, N.J 07753, USA do posters (send for catalogue).

The Cinema Attic, Dept TM, Box 5006, Philadelphia, Pa.19111, USA have *Farewell to the Dragon* Bruce Lee Memorial Book. Write for info.

There's a film club in Church Street, Portadown, Northern Ireland (by the Post Office) called the "Gateway Theatre," which recently showed *Enter the Dragon* uncut. He thinks maybe if members could send in requests to the manager, he might show other Bruce Lee films. Sometimes managers of cinemas can be quite helpful if approached in the right way - not with a pair of nunchakus and a war-like cry as you leap through the door!

More addresses from Mark Burns and Martin Hughes:

a) Strettons Studios of 29 Bradford Street, Walsall, Staffs (Telephone 28755) can do all Bruce's films (complete or separate reels) and photo enlargements (any size). Write for details.
b) New martial arts shop - "House of Han" in Walsall, Staffs (Telephone 611670).
c) Superstar Fanclub, Causeway Bay, Hong Kong - fee is $15HK per year.
d) Jerry Ohlinger's Movie Material Store, 120 West third Street, New York, NY 10012 - have 16mm colour sound trailers for *Enter the Dragon*, *The Big Boss*, *Fist of Fury*, and *The Green Hornet* and various stills, etc. Write for details.

Looks interesting. Thanks, Mark & Martin! And I loved their comments on Bruce Li. As you all know, he goes under many names, such as Nick Chung, Ho Chung Tao, Li Lung, Lee Roy Lung, and Lee Lung - and they added Lee missing Lung!!

Mike Devereux mentions a disco-pub in Chester called "Melanies" where they sell Lee Beer. The beer mats have "Lee for excellence" written on them!!

Regarding the area lists, I realize that members from 2033 onwards have not yet heard about it, and therefore have not had the opportunity to object at having their names & addresses passed to other members. Will members from 2033 NOT wishing to be included on the area list, PLEASE let me know immediately, so I can omit their names.

Finally, another useful address: Sports & Things, 272 Streatham High Road, London, SW16 (Telephone 01 769 0032). They do badges, martial arts books, equipment, clothing, swords, kendo armour, t-shirts, etc.

LETTERS

I was reading in the paper the other day about Jimmy Greaves wanting to get back into football. People were wondering if he'd still be up to it. They said he was slower, less fit and too old. Greaves is 37. In November, Bruce Lee would have been 37. Makes you think, doesn't it? How two people of the same ages and working in the same sort of exacting conditions can be classed so differently? Can you imagine people saying that Bruce was too old? Bruce made his four feature films in his early thirties - the time pro footballers are thinking of retirement. Perhaps they could learn a lesson from the Little Dragon!

Arthur Stone (1150)

Thanks for a great new sheet No. 4. I'm looking forward to No. 5. I have enclosed a picture of myself wearing the "Lee look." Everything you see comes from jumble sales and second-hand shops in Ryde and the whole lot cost less than £1.00. Any Bruce Lee fans can look like the Master with a bit of shop hunting. The jumper is Game of Death style, the rest Enter the Dragon style.

Cary Dean (1314)

Good idea, Cary - I'm a keen collector of old books and antiques as well. I often come across trousers suitable for training, plus punch-balls, weights and cycling machines at bazaars!

I must congratulate you on the superb BLSS and I am proud to be a member. Do you know the address of the film censors as I'd like to send them a letter. I was appalled at what I read about a new film where live pigs are hung from wires and gutted and where actors dressed in Nazi uniforms are seen "cavorting obscenely with the dying animals." The film had only 1' 37" cut and then got an "X" cert. How they can cut out great chunks of Bruce Lee artistry and then let this through, beats me.

Mark Salter (1972)

Me, too, Mark. For you, and anyone else wanting the address, it's The British Board of Film Censors, 3 Soho Square, London Wl.

Hi there! And I'm writing to tell you just how fantastic your drawings and poems magazine is. There are some really great contributions. Have you seen Tenant by Roman Polanski? Well, halfway through, a man and a woman enter a cinema and guess what film is showing? I'll tell you… it's Enter the Dragon! As you go in you see the poster. After a while the two start kissing and the camera goes onto the screen where Bruce is battling his way underground to the prisoners. I saw a part I haven't seen before where Bruce picks up a pair of nunchakus and starts swinging them around his neck. It was just fantastic!

Colm Quinn (1956)

Well, Colm, you must have seen some pretty badly cut films around your way.

Well, Colm, you must have seen some pretty badly cut films around your way. That bit's always been in the times I've seen *Enter the Dragon*. Thankfully, there now seem to be some much better prints going around, so anyone spotting a part they haven't seen before - like Colm - please let me know!

> After the first year of the Society, I would like to congratulate you on the marvellous job you've done in keeping the memory of Bruce alive. You will find enclosed the sum of £3.25 – I would like to enrol for a further year's membership.
>
> Andrew Southern (1577)

And welcome to the second year, Andrew! I'm delighted to say that many members are actually rejoining AHEAD of time. In fact, member Ray Wheaton hold the record... he rejoined five months early! All members between 1001 and 1627 please remember that your membership runs out between October/November!! If you don't hurry you might miss out on that fantastic second-year solid metal badge. For your convenience, I enclose a SAE.

SWOP SHOP

- Eric Holden (1232), Smethwick has *Jhoon Rhee Taekwondo* (5 vols), cost £3.25 ea (worth £16.25),. Will sell for ??? or swap for *Legend of Bruce Lee*, *KFM's* 1, 2, 3, and 5 and *KFM Scrapbook*.
- G.Hudson (1177), Wilmslow wants *Bruce Lee King of Kung Fu* magazine (N.E.L.), *Kung Fu Superstars*, *Kung Fu Fighters* No.1, any issues of old *Bruce Lee Club* magazines except No.2, *The Big Boss* cinema ad poster, *Clash Monthly* No. 1. Will exchange for *KFM* 1 & 3, *Bruce Lee Exposed* magazine, rare Chinese magazine and posters from Chinatown, *Enter the Dragon* LP.
- Al Briers (1828), St. Helens has *Enter the Dragon* LP, *Jaws* LP, and original soundtracks of all Lee films except *Enter the Dragon*. Will swap for *Best of Bruce Lee* No.1, *Bruce Lee Nunchakus in Action*, *Bruce Lee's Fighting Method*. Also wants *Secret Art* and *Chinese Boxing by the Master* (O'Hara Publications). Willing to swap a host of goodies - write.
- Miss Margaret Smith (1943), Clough has set of colour stills of all Bruce Lee films to swap for anything interesting. Also has cassettes (Japanese) of Bruce Lee films to swap.
- Paul Ashton (1717), Dundee has Bruce Lee Kung Fu team patch, pair of blue sweat bands, 2 Kung Fu annuals (TV), sheet of Chinese/English Kung Fu meanings, *Dragon* poster of Carter Wong (very good condition),, Motor bike jump poster (very good condition), Yin/Yang patch (good condition) and Kung Fu patch. Wants Safe-T-Chucks or similar, nunchaku case, *Enter the Dragon* cassette, Bruce Lee posters, Kung Fu film stills - as shown outside cinemas with credits. Send SAE when writing.
- Peter Willetts (1721), Bulwell has karate suit (large), plus brown belt. Wants *Enter the Dragon* LP and stills of Bruce Lee.
- Ian Hamilton (1213), Sunderland wants *Life & Tragic Death of Bruce Lee* by Linda Lee, *Bruce Lee Memorial Book*, *Best of Bruce Lee* No.1, *Bruce Lee Scrapbook*, *Farewell to the Dragon*, *Legend of Bruce Lee* poster magazine (Top Sell-

ers), soundtracks from all his films, any cinema posters, *Film Star* No.2, *King of Kung Fu* magazine and old *Monster* magazines with items on Bruce. Very high prices paid.
- David Willet (2048), Newark has *KFM* No.1. What offers?
- Mick Bargota (1322), Tipton has Bruce Lee bracelet (silvery) and a Bruce Lee keyring. Offers. It's first come, first served, so no reply means you've missed out. Also wants N.E.L. *Bruce Lee King of Kung Fu*.
- Paul Brosnan (1621), Dublin has *Judo* by Eric Dominy to sell (Judo basics).
- David Coe (1440), North Shields has *KFM's* 1-32, except No.3, *Black Belt* magazine, *Bruce Lee* No.2, *Kung Fu* magazine with Bruce Lee poster, *KFM Scrapbook*, *Popster* Bruce Lee fold out magazine, N.E.L. *Bruce Lee King of Kung Fu* magazine, *Bruce Lee His Privacy & Anecdotes*, *Bruce Lee Nunchakus in Action*, *The Big Boss* poster, two *Fist of Fury* Posters, *Enter the Dragon* poster, two Bruce Lee badges, *Farewell My Friend* softbound book and *Bruce Lee: The Man Only I Knew* by Linda Lee.
- Mike Devereux (1061), Warrington has a new octagonal three-sectional nunchakus (13" clubs, cord type). Wants *Fury* cinema poster. Also £10 offered for Bruce Lee *Chinese Gung-Fu Philosophical Art of Self Defence* in good condition. Has onecopy of *KFM's* 11 and 27 free to first person sending him the postage.
- Graham Jenkinson (1381), Berry Brow wants *Enter the Dragon* book by Mike Roote (Tandem).
- Chris Bowman (1445), Ipswich offers *Bruce Tegner's Complete Book of Aikido Holds and Locks* and two Bruce Lee nunchaku posters from *Enter the Dragon*. Wants *Bruce Lee: The Man Only I Knew* by Linda Lee and *Best of Bruce Lee* No. 2. Offers.
- Colin Lindell, Islington has original recordings of *Space 1999, Captain Scarlet,* and *Thunderbirds Story* plus *Joe 90* theme and all Barry Gray recordings in exchange for LP of *Thunderbirds* soundtrack with Thunderbird 1 on front cover or anything to do with *Space 1999* - books, models etc, OR £2 cash.
- Mark Burns (1687), Walsall has *Green Hornet* annual and two stills from *Cimac* to swap for anything on Bruce Lee or John Lennon. Write for info.

PEN PALS

- Crysia Zwiryk (1709), Bradford wants male, Jewish pen pal - 19/21 years.
- Dennis Cartwright (1565), Desford wants pen pals. He's a keep-fit fan, non-smoker/drinker, studies various arts, deep breathing, Tan Sien, fencing, unarmed combat, etc.
- Wesley Fleming (1935), Tasmania, Australia.

Sorry, Gary has missed the post with the American pen pals. I expect they'll arrive the minute this goes to press!

COMPETITION RESULTS

Here we go again. The five lucky members drawn out of the hat for the June news sheet competition were... T.McEniry (1497) of Swindon, Molly Cullen (1749) of Blackwood, Ralph Canswick (1189) of Leicester, Thomas Tong (1912) of Ilford and

and Robert Connelly (1202) of Preston.
And the answers were:

1) *The Big Boss,* 2) Robert Baker, 3) *Enter the Dragon,* 4) *Game of Death,* 5) Chuck Norris, 6) Golden Harvest, 7) *Fist of Fury,* 8) *Marlowe,* 9) Raymond Chow, 10) *Way of the Dragon, and* 11) *Longstreet.*

Each winner will be receiving a copy of *The Wisdom of Bruce Lee.*

THE SEPTEMBER COMPETITION

Ian Grant (1214) has sent in the competition below - and if any of you have tried to put a crossword together, you'll know how much work he's put into it! Anyway, as always, the first five members whose names are drawn out of the "hat" will be declared winners in the next news sheet. So get cracking. The response to the last competition was great – let's make the next one amazing!!

THE BRUCE LEE SOCIETY

Across
1) God may have the clue to this film (4) (2) (5)
7) ETEJ ____ OD (4)
8) Famous Fighting Sticks (8)
11) See 2 down
13) Yang ____ played Bolo (3)
15) The scarred villain in *Enter the Dragon* (5)
16) Bruce was one at JKD (6)
18) The type of snake used in *Enter the Dragon* (5)
19) Bruce was the Green ____'s side kick (6)

Down
2) Bruce's sister in *Enter* - also 11 across (6)
3) Drug handled by "Han" (5)
4) Bruce was a champion ____ in early days (6)
5) ____ Capri (4)
6) Part Bruce played in *Enter the Dragon* (3)
9) Bruce played ____ in 19 across (4)
10) Bruce's female co-star in *Way of the Dragon* (4) (4)
12) Shih Kien played ____ in *Enter the Dragon* (3)
13) Roper was played by John ____ (5)
14) A Dragon had to do this before he learnt the way (5)
17) ____ Wei director of *Boss* (2)

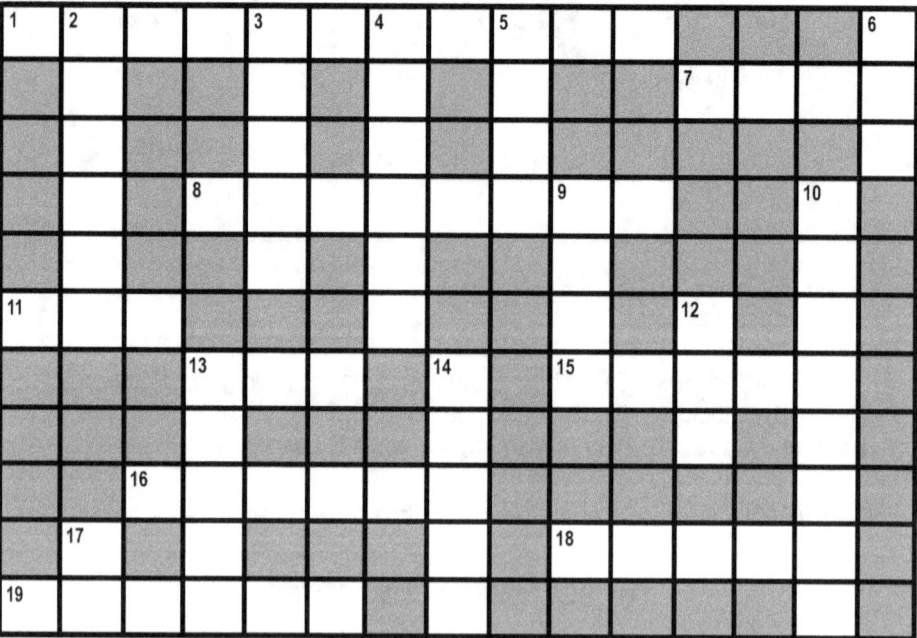

That's it for news sheet No. 5. See you soon!

Pam

BRUCE LEE SOCIETY COLUMN
KUNG FU MONTHLY NO. 35

A great big hello from me, Pam, to all you members of the *KFM* Bruce Lee Society.

First off, to celebrate the start of the second year of the club, I'm going to announce a similar offer to the one we ran last year around this time. Up to this Christmas, anybody joining the Bruce Lee Society for the first time can do so at the reduced rate of £3.00!! Remember, this bargain reduction can only last until December 31st so get your membership applications in quickly. Naturally, I can't reserve the special offers to new members alone so for renewing members only, on January 1st I shall be pulling one of your names from the hat. The lucky person will receive a set of *KFM's* (issues 5 to 35).

As December draws nearer, what I'm thinking about is not so much Christmas but the confirmation of the release date for *Game of Death*. At the time of going to press, the film company is still not letting on about anything, perhaps because they're organising a big advertising campaign. Anyway, I myself (plus the entire staff of *KFM*), will continue to keep hammering away at them to try and find out when the great day is going to be. Keep watching these pages! By the way, nothing back yet from Raymond Chow regarding the *KFM* petition, but Jenny's pretty confident we'll be hearing something soon!

As you'll see when you read the fifth news sheet, it looks like there's a growing number of rip-off mail order merchants around, many of whom (I'm sorry to say) seem to be in the States. Obviously it's much easier to deal with people who cheat you out of your money in this country than it is when the villain is somewhere abroad! There is no real hard and fast solution, other than to say just try to be cautious. That means sending for a brochure or price list BEFORE parting with the cash. Not many crooks will be bothered to go to the trouble of printing up lists (although I can think of one or two who HAVE!) so, generally, all you'll have lost is the price of a stamp. Normally speaking, try and base your decision on whether or not to part with money on the QUALITY of service apparently being offered. Tried and tested sources are, of course, the best.

Now this month, a great big reminder that for many of you, IT'S TIME TO RENEW YOUR SUBSCRIPTION. I've had a sneak preview of the great "Second Year" brooch we've had designed to celebrate a full years membership to all renewing members and it's absolutely amazing. It's totally in keeping with the "maturing image" of the Bruce Lee Society. If you've got any doubt at all about what's in it for YOU to join up with the world's most exclusive Society, then turn to the advertisement you'll find elsewhere in this *KFM*. The strength of the Bruce Lee Society rests with YOU the members. We count upon your dedication.

Finally, how about that News Sheet number 5?! I think I can honestly say we've never packed so much in before. A really GREAT new competition, lots more swaps, news to keep you drooling for hours, and what's more (at long last) a picture of yours truly! Yup, the camera finally caught up with me.

Back with you again next month. *Pam*

BRUCE LEE SOCIETY COLUMN
KUNG FU MONTHLY NO. 36

Hello, it's your very own president here once again with a really hot bit of news concerning film censorship.

Just before that though, word from Alan Mount (1109) on Bruce's appearances in the *Batman* series. Apparently many of the regions are showing episodes and Alan thought everyone would like to know which particular ones the Little Dragon appeared in. They are A "Piece of the Action" and "Batman's Satisfaction". As anyone who has caught these two will testify, it's fantastic seeing Bruce on TV. It's just a pity it's not more often, or come to that, not one of his feature films. Oh well, I suppose it will happen sometime. Meanwhile, all of you who haven't seen these particular *Batman* shows, now you've got the titles, how about writing to your local TV stations and asking when they're coming on?

Back on to the old question of censorship and how about this for a stupendous piece of news, sent in to us by John Rogers (1009)? I'm told that the Home Office has appointed a committee to look into the laws concerning violence, indecency and obscenity. Part of their work is to check up on how film censorship is arranged in the UK and the word is, the committee welcomes everybody's views. Well - do they now? I hardly think I need to spell out just exactly what I'd like to see you do sometime during the next few days. The address to send your comments is: Jon Davey, Committee on Obscenity and Film Censorship, Department 17, Home Office, Queen Anne's Gate, London SW1H 9AT. The sort of questions you might like to direct to Mr Davey are ones such as: What excuse can possibly be given for scissor-happy censors mutilating film footage of the world's finest latter-day kung-fu expert? Would they perhaps consider also banning film shots of Muhammed Ali actually knocking out his opponent? Why not just leave in the bits between rounds?!? When you consider the sheer, savage brutality - very often characterised by dreadful acting - that actually IS shown in cinemas these days, to me it is astounding that Little Dragon fans continue to be deprived of this rare Bruce Lee footage. Other countries, for example France, have left much of the Master's material untouched and I can't say I noticed any rioting in the streets when I was last there. So come on all you Society members - this is the moment we've all been waiting for. Mr Davey wants to know our feelings on film censorship so let's tell him about Bruce Lee!

Finally, a reminder again that for many of you, it's time to renew subscriptions to your favourite society. 1978 promises to be an even bigger year for us and I'm certain absolutely no one is going to want to miss out on the action. Don't forget, whether it's to join for the first time or whether you're renewing, the address remains the same. Just send along £3.25 to: The Bruce Lee Society, 14 Rathbone Place, London W1P 1DE. Welcome aboard!!

Pam Hadden - President of the Bruce Lee Society

EDITOR'S NOTES

On 16th August 1977, the King of Rock & Roll, Elvis Presley, passed away at his Graceland home in Memphis, Tennessee at the age of 42.

As well as an extremely successful singer, Presley was also an avid martial artist, studying Shotokan Karate under Tetsugio Murakami and later, Kenpo Karate under Bruce Lee's friend Ed Parker. After Parker introduced him to Hank Slomanski in Fort Campbell, Presley achieved his first Dan black belt on 21st July 1960.

Countless fake internet photographs exist of Bruce Lee posing with Elvis Presley but they never met in real life. The King of Kung Fu was obviously a fan of The King of Rock & Roll as Taky Kimura provided a certificate of authenticity and photograph of Bruce posing with Elvis' album *Blue Hawaii*. There was talk of the two doing a movie together in the early 1970's but it never came to fruition.

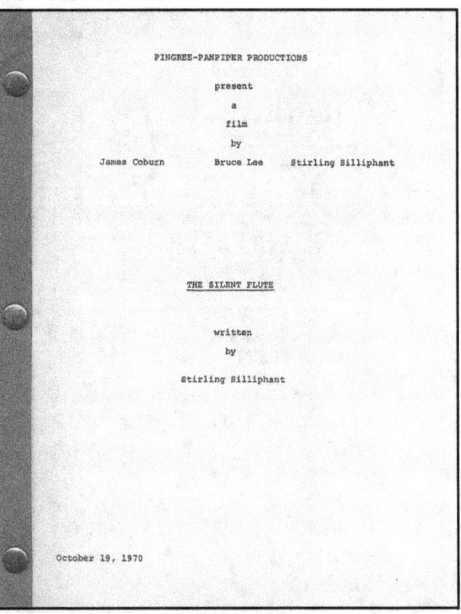

In 1969, Bruce Lee and his friends, actor James Coburn and producer Stirling Silliphant wrote the treatment for a film they would call, *The Silent Flute*. The premise of the film was that a martial arts seeker named Cord (to be played by Coburn) was after a book of enlightenment that would reveal all of life's answers. He had to pass a number of trials and was helped by an old blind man (to be played by Lee) who played a flute. Finally Cord would confront Zetan, the Keeper of the Book.

In February 1971, Lee, Coburn and Silliphant embarked on a location scouting trip to India but ran into unexpected problems, causing the project to be shelved.

In 1977, with the help of Stanley Mann, Stirling Silliphant wrote a script based on his, Lee's and Coburn's original story. Richard Moore jumped on board to direct with a cast of Jeff Cooper (taking Coburn's role of Cord) and Kung Fu's David Carradine (playing the flute player originally intended for Lee) plus a supporting cast including Christopher lee, Roddy McDowall and Eli Wallach. The film was released in 1978 to mixed reviews.

In Quentin Tarantino's 2004 martial arts epic *Kill Bill (Vol. 2)*, David Carradine's Bill is seen playing a flute similar to the one he played in *The Silent Flute* two-and-a-half decades earlier.

Included in issue five was loose slip of paper containing an open letter from member Arthur Stone. As you can see from the letter, he wanted to make a martial arts film with other Society members. Throughout the news sheets, you'll see how the project progresses and you'll see some surprising names pop up from time to time.

STOP!
AND LOOK AT WHAT YOU GET BY JOINING THE BRUCE LEE SECRET SOCIETY...

1. The unique Society *Badge* and *Sticker* – available ONLY to members. Plus photos, a biography and a fact sheet.
2. Your very own membership *Scroll*, tastefully designed for mounting and displaying.
3. A personal *Membership Card* – carry it with you always!
4. A superb THREE-MONTHLY *News Sheet* ... full of gossip, rumours, secrets, fan's comments, pix, pen-pals, competitions and much, much more.
5. A regular page in *Kung-Fu Monthly*, the world's greatest ever martial arts magazine – not to mention reductions on all the KFM mail order goods.
6. To cap it all, there's *Pam* and *Carmella* at the helm to see that EVERY SINGLE member's problem is solved and EVERY SINGLE question is answered – FANTASTIC!

NO OTHER FAN CLUB HAS EVER OFFERED AS MUCH... and yet, unbelievably, all this can be yours for ONLY £3.25. New members are always welcome so don't just think about it, MAKE SURE you join now – believe me, you'll never regret it!

Just send a £3.25 cheque or postal order to:
The Bruce Lee Secret Society
14 Rathbone Place
London W1P F1D

A RETROSPECTIVE LOOK AT BRUCE LEE MANIA & THE KUNG FU CRAZE OF THE 1970S

06
DECEMBER
1977

HI MEMBERS! WELCOME TO NEWS SHEET NUMBER SIX! FIRST OFF MAY I WISH YOU ALL A "MERRY CHRISTMAS AND HAPPY NEW YEAR."

GENERAL NEWS

To begin with, I'm going to ask you all for your help. Since producing the first Society magazine, I've learned from member John Kemp (1729) that his original picture (Society magazine page 14 - reproduced below of a *Game of Death* poster-type drawing has not reached him, and I can find no trace here. Somewhere out there, I'm hoping a member has received this by mistake. Perhaps you don't even know you've got it! Please have a good look for me (and for

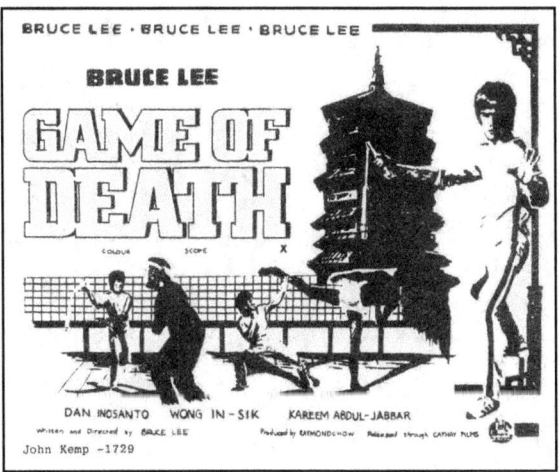

John). Anyone returning the picture to me will receive a crisp £5 note by return of post! The picture is coloured in browns, yellow and orange on a white background, if I remember correctly.

Anyone see the series, *The Man from Atlantis* recently on TV which starred Kareem Abdul Jabbar? Mike Devereux (1061) did, and he says Kareem played the part of an undersea dweller. Just to see what he's like, I shall keep my eyes open for this episode, as some areas get the series ahead of London. Mind you, if I miss Kareem, there's some consolation that the *Man from Atlantis* himself is quite watchable.

John Stuart (1116) wants to thank members who have been kind enough to help him get his Bruce Lee collection back together again after the original was stolen. He's had someshould be given full support, so I'm asking on behalf of Shane Phipps (1735) for assistance in really terrific items, and wishes to give special thanks to Paul Short (1164) who sent him some things he had never had before! John also says there is a strong rumour going around his way that *Enter* is to be shown on TV at Christmas. Has anyone read about this anywhere??

Great news is that, in response to tremendous demands, *KFM* are about to start selling back copy binders. At last we'll have a way of keeping all those rare issues in mint condition and naturally, this official binder will be going at a special discount to all Society members.

Please remember that issues 1, 2, 31, 32 and 33 are completely sold out. However, the good news is that all other issues are still available AND at non-ripoff prices

Single copies	£0.70 each
Any 10 back issues	£5.00
Any 20 back issues	£10.00
Any 30 back issues	£14.00
Any 40 back issues	£18.00
Any 50 back issues	£21.00

These are special new prices and they include handling. Society members, deduct 10% from the total value of your order.

Back Issue Binders

Back editions of KFM are VALUABLE — and will continue to grow in value over the years. Keep your set in mint condition with the help of official KFM Back Issue Binders — they cost **just £3.00 each (includes handling, Society members £2.70).**

By the way, does anyone know what Bruce's favourite colour was? I've been asked this by Kathy Parsons (1681) and I'm stumped! Anyone clued up, please let me know.

More good news... I've heard from Shiela Boardman who runs the David Chiang Fan Club that she is NOT now going to close. She is in contact with David direct and hopes, with his co-operation, to keep on going. There must be many David fans out there, so drop Shiela a line at Manchester, Lancs. I wish her all the luck.

Keep your eyes open for *Batman* episodes called "A Piece of the Action" and "Batman's Satisfaction." They feature the Green Hornet and Kato (Bruce, of course). Thanks for that, Alan Mount (1109).

There is a committee looking into film censorship in England and Wales, writes John Rogers (1009). The committee wants comments sent to them on the public's views on censorship, so now's the big time for all you members to tell them how you feel about the mutilation of Bruce's films - especially the nunchakus scenes from *Way of the Dragon*. Anyone who has seen these missing segments, and I know many of you have, will agree that they were absolutely out of this world. The people responsible for the censoring need censoring themselves! The address to write is: Jon Davey, Committee on Obscenity and Film Censorship, Dept. 17, Home Office, Queen Anne's Gate, London SW1H 9AT. And remember, POLITE letters please!!! If the censors receive aggressive and nasty letters, we'll just be playing into their hands. That could mean when *Game of Death* is released it could get a total massacring. The censor's view is that Bruce's films create violence - prove them wrong!

Talking of censorship, I've just been to see *Fist of Fury* again (showing with *Amsterdam Kill* over the country). I was delighted to see that the missing scenes have been replaced - in particular the graveyard scene with Bruce and his girl talking plus fight clips. Pure magic!

Cary Dean (1314) sent a cutting from the *Evening News* of Oct. 17th. It says that the 1,000 extras in *Game of Death*, Chinese and European, got so heated during filming that they actually came to genuine blows!! Extra security police were posted for re-shooting the scene which then continued without incident. Which only goes to prove that *Game of Death* is very much alive - in more ways then one!

While on the subject of *Game of Death*, Nigel Martin (1359) and Graham Jenkinson (1381) have both sent in cuttings about Bruce's great masterpiece. They say that the film is definitely finished after Robert Clouse, the Hollywood director, had managed to overcome script problems. Mr. Clouse (who also directed Bruce in box-office blockbuster *Enter the Dragon*) says the film will contain about 40 minutes of Bruce fighting, and describes them as ."..among the best made." Oh boy! I reckon the suspense will kill all of us off before *Game of Death* is released!!

Julius Fernandez (2065) of Ibadan, Nigeria, has very kindly offered to draw a picture of Bruce onto either the back of a postcard or photo and return to members. If you care to send him a couple of cards or pictures, plus 50p postal order and an envelope with your name and address on for return, he will do drawings and return to you without much delay by airmail. I have seen his work, and he is good. In fact, he sent me a letter through the post and the envelope was covered in Bruce pics. I bet the postman wondered what was going on! When sending P.O's please leave the addressee's name part blank.

Eric Holden (1232) tells me that most bodybuilders only achieve six "lumps" in their abdomen, whereas he read that Bruce had eight. Still, we all know that Bruce was unique, don't we, so the news isn't too surprising.

Member 1423 Richard McColl, sent me a picture of David Chiang, and says he got it from Shaw Brothers (H.K.) Ltd, at Lot 220, Clear Water Bay Road, Kowloon, Hong Kong. If you care to write, you may be lucky enough to get one too, he says. However, I would mention that Shiela who runs David's club got very little response from Shaws. Still, no harm in trying!

Robin Blades (1259) got some "Sports Cards" from Heron Books, and among the sports depicted was one on Karate, showing a picture of Bruce! It was titled "The James Dean of Martial Arts," and read, "The prodigious martial arts talents of Sensei Bruce Lee, professor, athlete and actor reduced the lack of understanding that often pits East against West." Investigations are going on to track these cards down.

Paul Wade (1836) is enquiring about *Hot Potato*, Jim Kelly's latest film. If anyone sees a release date over here for it, can they let me know?

Member John Black (1956) is pictured below with James Tien (*Fist of Fury* and *The Big Boss*) and Angela Miao from *Enter the Dragon*, taken when he was stationed in Hong Kong! Lucky John!!

Another member, Danny Wilde (1477) has sent in a picture of Linda Lee's mother, taken when she visited England some time back. Some really interesting pictures are turning up - keep 'em coming!

Regarding *The Silent Flute* mentioned in the last news sheet, it seems that David Carradine, who is now to appear in it, is now quite a keen Bruce fan - contrary to his former views! In a cutting sent in by Graham Jenkinson again, Carradine comments on his part in the film and how Bruce's most precious project has fallen into the hands of a man he has never met. Says David, "I feel almost possessed by the spirit of Bruce Lee. Seeing *Enter the Dragon* was the only passing I had with him, and I didn't see it until after he was dead. But I really feel possessed by him - it's weird. I saw the film and sat in the front row - I sneaked in, figuring it would be really freaky. But as I sat and watched it, I was just totally exhilarated. It was like seeing a religious experience." David, welcome to the club - you're hooked!!

Setudeh Nejad (1419) sent in an article from a youth magazine of Persia called *Javanun*. It's well known in Persia, America and Europe. Bruce is apparently very popular in Iran and they have all his films.

Time for a little poem now from John Scott (1559):

Born Nov. 27th 1940 in 'Frisco,
Died July 20th 1973 in Hong Kong,
A magnetic personality, studied philosophy,
The King of Kung Fu, highest paid actor ever.
A great man, no belt, no Dan,
Fight? He's shown he can!
He had to die - why now, why?
And now he's gone, there's one more to carry on.

Paul Brosnan (1621) states the comics *Eerie* and *Creepy* (American) were recently advertising taped radio episodes of *The Green Hornet*. He suggests you try and get hold of copies of the magazines and write to the firms concerned.

One of the most blatant rip-offs ever may be a new film coming out called the *Kentucky Fried Movie*. Paul Wade (1836) sent a cutting from *O.K.* magazine which says that actor Evan Kim is to star as "Mr. Loo" who fights and defeats the evil Dr. Klahn. The plot appears to be practically a direct copy of *Enter the Dragon* (note Klahn like Han) and a claw hand is even thrown in for the final fight scene!

For the assistance of many of you who are trying to find good Karate and Kung Fu clubs, the following are addresses to write to: British Kung Fu Federation, 33 Kingfisher Drive, Ham, Surrey and Martial Arts Commission, 4 Deptford Bridge, London SE8.

THE BRUCE LEE SOCIETY

MAIL ORDER TIME AGAIN!

And right away, don't forget to order YOUR set of Bruce Lee Society NOTEPAPER and ENVELOPES. For Just £1.25 you'll receive 30 sheets of exclusive headed paper plus 20 envelopes. How better to correspond with fellow Members of the Society? Stocks are running out fast, but there's still plenty there so get your order in quickly. Just send a cheque/postal order for £1.25 to: Society Stationary Offer, 14 Rathbone Place, London, WIP IDE. Please allow four weeks for delivery.

USEFUL ADDRESSES

J.C.Trophies, 8 Shakespeare Road, Shirley, Solihull, E.Midlands, B90 4RL - They do Bruce medallions on either neck-chain or as key-ring. 90p each or the two for £1.50 - all cheques/postal orders payable to J.C.Trophies.

Oriental World, 18 Swan Street, Manchester, Lancs - have many Bruce books/magazines including I notice, *Bruce Lee - Cinema of Vengeance* at £1.75 plus 20p p&p. There's a free Bruce calendar with all books whilst stocks last.

Jerry Ohlinger's Movie Material Store, 120 West third Street, New York, USA has 16mm colour film trailers from *Enter the Dragon, Fist of Fury, The Big Boss,* and *Green Hornet.* Write for lists.

Debonair Film Distributors Ltd, Coventry Cine Centre, Lower Ford Street, Coventry, CV1 5PW, Warks have Bruce and Van Williams in *Return of the Dragonfly* (a *Green Hornet* episode). Again, write for lists.

LETTERS

Dear Pam, just recently I discovered a great shop for Bruce Lee posters, stills and magazines - I've already bought the Big Boss *cinema poster, the original* Fist of Fury *and colour-set from* Way of the Dragon *and* Big Boss. *It's down the stairs in an antique shop in Shorts Gardens, London WC2. The nearest tube is Covent Garden.*

Gerald McNamara (1382)

Gerald, I can just see the invasion of members who are after rare cinema posters of Bruce, and the face of the poor shopkeeper when they walk in! Thanks for the info.

Dear Pam, when I went to London's West End recently, I found that H.M.V. Records had the Bruce Lee records in and were getting even more in a few weeks. I also found the original soundtrack to Man from Hong Kong *and it's terrific, with fight scenes too, like Bruce's records. I would recommend other members to get it.*

From Jeffrey Millington (1127)

AREA LISTS

It seems that the area lists I compiled have gone down well. For those of you not knowing what this is, it's a list of members in each area/town so you can write to people near by your home. All members up to 2032 have the list and those from 2033 to 2170 will now be receiving their list with this news sheet. Also, for all members up to 2032, to keep you up to date on this, I have enclosed a list of the new people to add to your existing list. Anyone whose number is over 2170 - will you let me know if you do not want your name passed on to other members in your area, please, as soon after receipt of this news sheet as possible. Then I can add the rest of the names to the March news sheet.

RENEWAL SLIPS

Members from 1628-1828 - your renewal falls due between now and the end of February. Of course, you can renew as early as you like and I will amend the records accordingly - you won't lose any time! If by chance some of you who have already renewed find a renewal notice with your news sheet, please ignore it.

PEN PALS

- Angela Davenport (2009), Northfield wants male/female pen pals anywhere aged between 18-21 (she's 18). Interested in Karate, Kung Fu, ice skating, writing, reggae. She's a computer operative.
- Ramesh Krishnaswamy (1987), Shuaiba, Kuwait wants pen pal around his age, 15 yrs. Likes martial arts, Bruce Lee, Angela Mao. reading, table tennis.
- Eric Holden (1232), Smethwick wants female pen pals between 18-21. He's 21.
- Steve Ziegler, Battle Creek, Michigan, USA is a member of our US sister club and wants to correspond and exchange info on Bruce Lee. He says there's lots of interest still over there so get writing members, and let our American counterparts see how active WE are.
- Tim Lawnorn, Indianapolis, Indiana, USA is a potential US member who wishes to hear from people here to exchange views, news, trades, etc.
- David Lussow, Forest Park, Illinois, USA wants pen pals everywhere! Very keen and his interests are Bruce Lee, Karate and Kung Fu.
- Mike Wilcox, Flagstaff, Arizona, USA is very interested in Bruce Lee and keen to link up with UK pen pals.

SWOP SHOP

- Keith Graham (1945), Edinburgh has big selection of magazines (eg, *Inside Kung Fu*) wants *KFM's* 2, 3, 5, 6, 7, 8, 10, 12, 13-16, 18, 20, 22, 23, 30 and 34. Write for list and state what you have.
- Michael Sanderson (1385), Washington has *KFM's* 5, 6, 8, 16-22, 25 and 29, *Dragon's* (Vol 2) 5, 7-12, 14, (Vol 3) 1-3, posters of *Way of the Dragon*, *Fist of Fury*, *Big Boss*, and three *Enter the Dragon*. Wants *KFM's* 1, 2, 3.
- Shane Phipps (1735), Chesterfield has 14" safety nunchakus in black polypropylene. Wants *Black Belt's* "Best of Bruce Lee No.1."
- Pete Broad (1799), Carlisle wants *KFM's* 1-4 and *Best of Bruce Lee No.1*. Will swap for new copy of Bruce Lee's *Tao of Jeet Kune Do*, *Studies on JKD*, two action pictures of Bruce and a poster showing badges of Karate clubs.

- Ronald Ramsay, West Calder has stacks of books and magazines on Bruce Lee and the martial arts. All very good condition. Write for lists.
- Andrew Barratt (1148), Lincoln has to sell: Black Kung Fu trousers & sash in very good condition - *Way of the Dragon* style, cost £9, take £6. *Beginner's Guide to Kung Fu* & *Kung Fu Exercise Book* - £1.50 each. Karate suit with JKD in Chinese on back - £5. *Hapkido, Korean Art of Self Defense* - £2.50, *Judo Grappling Techniques* - £2.50.
- William Longson (1947), Blackpool wants *KFM's* 1-3, *Best of Bruce Lee No. 1*, *My Martial Arts Training Guide to JKD*, *Combat's* 1-3, *Bruce Lee, King of Kung Fu*, *Clash* No. 1 complete, *Kung Fu Cinema of Vengeance,* and two *Bruce Lee Scrapbooks*. Has *Bruce Lee Nunchakus in Action, Bruce Lee Studies on JKD, Bruce Lee His Privacy & Anecdotes*, *KFM* 22, *Inside Kung Fu 1976 Year Book*, six *Starsky & Hutch* posters, *Starsky & Hutch Monthly* No. 2, *Shatter* No. 2, and two TV detective poster magazines plus other stuff, too.
- Kathryn Wray (2033), Codnor has *Bruce Lee 1940-73* in good condition (cover slightly damaged) and wants four early issues of *Dragon* excluding 8 and 12.
- Mr. E.R. Canham, Worksop has *Beginners Guide to Kung Fu, Kung Fu Teach Yourself* by Chee Soo, *The Martial Arts Articles on Kung Fu, Judo, Karate, Kendo, Aikido and Oriental Weaponry* by Jim Wilson, single of *Enter*. Wants *KFM's* 1-3, soundtrack of *Big Boss, Fist of Fury,* and *Way of the Dragon* - but not on Flashpoint or Great Action Themes records.
- Peter Ward (1446), Leicester has *Real Kung Fu* (Vol 1) Nos. 4, 6, 7, 9, 11, 12, *Combat* (Vol 1) No. 8, *Kung Fu & Karate Fighting* and monthly wall chart course No.1. Offers please.
- John R. Bell (1383), Ipswich has book called *Tai Chi* in new condition and will sell for £4 or swap for copy of *Secret Art* in very good condition (*Tai Chi* cost £6-£7 new).
- Mick Werkowski (1686), Chesterfield has reproduction samurai sword & wood scabbard in very good condition. Will exchange for Bruce Lee items or £10. Write please.

Finally, if I may, I'd like just this time to stick my nose into the Swop Shop! If any of you members have any Elvis Presley singles, old 78's or LP's, or EP's to sell, swap or whatever, please drop me a line (must be in perfect condition, though). I've only got a few of his albums and I'm aiming to collect the lot!

A RETROSPECTIVE LOOK AT BRUCE LEE MANIA & THE KUNG FU CRAZE OF THE 1970S

"I THOUGHT YOU SAID THOSE KUNG-FU OUTFITS WOULD KEEP THEM QUIET!"

COMPETITION RESULTS

The answers to the last comp were as follows:

ACROSS - 1. *Game of Death*. 7. Kune. 8. Nunchaku. 11. Mao. 13. Sze. 15. O'Hara. 16. Expert. 18. Cobra. 19. Hornet.
DOWN - 2. Angela. 3. Opium. 4. Dancer. 5. Ahna. 6. Lee. 9. Kato. 10. Nora Miao. 12. Han. 13. Saxon. 14. Enter. 17. Lo.

The lucky winners are: Fred Stuffin (1844) Soong Ken Ma (1040) Kate Feeney (1194) Angela French (1143) and John Rogers (1009). Stand by all of you for a FREE and BRAND NEW *KFM* Binder!!

THE NEW COMPETITION

The following comp was sent in by John Stuart (1116), with a couple of questions I've thrown in for luck. John and I reckon we should get some of you stumped so it's up to you to prove us wrong! Anyway, the first five correct answers out of the bag will be rewarded by five more of those great new *KFM* Binders, so don't delay, send in your answers to: Bruce Lee Society Comp No. 5, 14 Rathbone Place, London WIP IDE. Now Christmas is here there's no excuse at all for not entering. There'll be plenty of time to start thinking after eating the Xmas pud!

1. What was Bruce's shoe size?
2. Name the character Bruce played in *Marlowe*.
3. How many funerals did Bruce have?
4. In what film did Geoffrey Weeks star with Bruce?
5. Who did he play?
6. What weight was Bruce?
7. What kind of car did Bruce own?
8. What are the names of Bruce's two sisters?
9. Okay - what about his two brother's names?
10. What does Li Yuen Kam (Bruce's name at birth) mean in English?

Well, I can see you all now, dashing to your books and magazines on Bruce to find the answers. Good luck!!

One final, final thing... I know I'm always going on about it, but once again could I remind you that anyone writing in wanting a reply MUST enclose a stamped and addressed envelope. I have now stopped answering those without so anyone who hasn't yet had a letter back from me and who is expecting one, I expect that's the reason why. PLEASE DON'T FORGET.

That's all for now, folks... see you next time! Pam Hadden

BRUCE LEE SOCIETY COLUMN
KUNG FU MONTHLY NO. 37

Hello again, Pam here with all the latest news and views from members of the Bruce Lee Society.

First off, how about the newly cut version of *Fist of Fury* that's doing the rounds with *Amsterdam Kill?* Don't ask me how or why, but there's a lot more been left in this time around -particularly in the famed graveyard scene. It's all there, including the gruesome part where Bruce is chewing what looks to me suspiciously like roasted dog! Let's hope this less cut version is an omen for the future. Perhaps one day we'll actually be able to see the alley fight in *Way of the Dragon*; you never know. Perhaps, too, *Game of Death* may escape the itchy fingers of the scissor-happy censors.

For those of you who've only joined recently, I'd like to tell you about our area lists. What I've done is to separate members off into various areas of the country. Each area then has all the members in it printed up onto one sheet and everybody involved receives a copy. I reckon it's a great way of putting members in touch with one another. But, there may of course be some who don't wish to be included and I need to know who. This only applies to members whose membership number is over 2,000. Earlier people have already been checked.

Finally, how about those *KFM* binders we've got for you? Society members will have their usual mail order discount. If you're not yet a member of the world's greatest Bruce Lee Society, then NOW'S THE TIME TO JOIN! The cost is still only £3.25 and in return, there are news sheets, stickers, a membership card, photos, a badge and lots, lots more. Just drop me a line at the Bruce Lee Society, 14 Rathbone Place, London W1P IDE. . . and welcome to the club! Pam Hadden

BRUCE LEE SOCIETY COLUMN
KUNG FU MONTHLY NO. 38

Hi, Pam here again, as the great *Game of Death* release date draws ever-nearer, this month I'm writing an extra-special Society column, devoted almost entirely to the sensational up-coming film.

It isn't all good news, I'm afraid. The first rumour I've heard is that many of the press release photos might be "faked". In fact, it's even been suggested that some have been taken from *Enter the Dragon*, with the faces of the new stars inserted by photo-trickery. I sincerely hope this isn't the case. To start with, I can see no reason why it should be necessary.

By the way, it'll be interesting to keep an eye on the amount *Game* takes at the box office and to see how it compares eventually with *Enter the Dragon* and *Way of the Dragon*. The last time I saw any figures, *Way of the Dragon* had taken $27,000,000 and Enter the Dragon $25,000,000.

Back to *Game of Death* and it's time now for some hard facts! Apparently, the plot now concerns the rise of a young kung fu star called Billy Lo. Because of his rocket-like rise to fame (presumably mirroring Bruce's own phenomenal success),

Billy is approached by a crime syndicate who specialise in making fortunes out of actors and sportsmen. The syndicate chief wants to sign up Billy and his girlfriend, otherwise they say they'll wreck his career. The name of the evil boss is Dr. Land and the character is played by Dean Jagger. Other stars appearing are Gig Young, Colleen Camp, Hugh O'Brien and, yes you've guessed it, Bob Wall (you can't keep him away!). Also involved in the plot, we're promised, are a regiment of motorbiking soldiers.

According to our *KFM* editor, there is every chance that well be running a special "*Game of Death* is here" *KFM*, devoted entirely to the new film. With any luck at all, that might even be the next issue!

Talking of features in the pipe-line; another goodie to look forward to is a possible interview with Norman Borine, who is the man in America running the unique Bruce Lee "museum". That'll certainly be worth waiting for.

A word now about Society members whose annual subscription is up for renewal (check on your membership card if you're not certain when the date actually is). It really does help us this end if you can get your renewals in as early as possible.

And that's about it for this issue. Next month the Society report will be back to normal, so I'll see you all then - Pam

BRUCE LEE SOCIETY COLUMN
KUNG FU MONTHLY NO. 39

Hello again, everyone. This month I've left it to Jenny to spread the good news about *GAME OF DEATH*. Don't forget to read her full up-date on the storyline. So far as the Society is concerned, the new year has really blasted off successfully. Though it's pretty hard work for me, the area lists look like they're doing their job and putting members in touch with one another but let me know if you're having any difficulties.

Interesting news from Alex Buttigien (2199). He says he's heard a rumour that Madame Tussauds in London are having a wax model of Bruce made to put on display. It sounds fantastic and I'm checking it out.

Hot news from Jeff Millington (1127). He tells me that Regent Films, PO Box 54, Blackpool FY1 1SP, have just got in a new trailer of *The Big Boss*. It's in Super 8mm, runs to about 100' and it's in colour with sound. The price is £8.50 plus 25p p&p. Apparently it features Bruce's opening flying kick.

Derek Hamer (1944) has made his own Bruce Lee crosswords and puzzles book. He's really done it beautifully, with proper pages, pictures and so on. In fact, it's so nice, I'm thinking of trying to re-produce it for cost price only sale to all club members. More on that in the next news sheet.

Meanwhile though, how about all of you working out your own puzzles or competitions. Try and make them something out of the ordinary if you can. The winning ones I'll give a prize to and probably also feature in one of the news sheets to come.

Finally, let me remind you that subscriptions DO need to be renewed sometime! Check yours to see if the time is near. The price of joining OR renewing is still only £3.25 which just can't be bad. Don't forget, the address to write to is: The Bruce Lee Society, 14 Rathbone Place, London W1. - Pam

EDITOR'S NOTES

After *Game of Death*, Kareem Abdul-Jabbar acted in several films and TV shows, many whilst still playing basketball for the Los Angeles Lakers until his retirement in 1989 at the age of 42.

Born Ferdinand Lewis Alcindor Jr, he converted to Islam in 1971 and became Kareem Abdul-Jabbar. Whilst playing for the Milwaukee Bucks, Abdul-Jabbar met Bruce Lee and began taking private lessons in martial arts, for which Lee would charge up to US $1000 per hour ($6500 in 2019).

In 1972, Lee cast his friend and student in *Game of Death* as the guardian of the pagoda's top level. Abdul-Jabbar flew out to Hong Kong to film his fight scenes without the permission of the Milwaukee Bucks as he knew that they would never have allowed it in case of a potential injury, so everything was done on the quiet.

This was the first mention of the *Kung Fu Monthly* binders in the Society news sheets. Its surprising how seldom they come up for sale in modern times, considering how heavily advertised they were. The often fetch three-figure sums each when they do come up for sale. Each binder holds around 45 issues of *Kung Fu Monthly* so all 79 issues plus the magazine special fit quite nicely in two binders.

When the 1966 *Green Hornet* TV series is mentioned, some people tend to forget about the two "crossover" episodes with Batman. Episodes "A Piece of the Action" and "Batman's Satisfaction" were used to boost fledgling viewing figures for the *Green Hornet* and pitted Adam West's Batman and Burt Ward's Robin against Van Williams' Green Hornet and Bruce Lee's Kato.

In the episode, Kato and Robin fought to a draw; however the original script called for Kato to lose. Incensed by this, Bruce Lee threatened to walk out of filming, until the script was rewritten to an outcome to appease all parties.

Back in the 70's, a lot of Bruce Lee fans wanted to be just like him. They ate what he ate. They trained how he trained. They dressed how he dressed. So it wasn't uncommon to get questions asking if Bruce had many "lumps he had on his stomach" or what his diet consisted of etc. Very little information was out there at that time. These days, just picking up a phone and typing a few words into Google will give you an answer quicker than it took you just find a pen to write a letter in the Society days.

Jim Kelly went on to have a productive acting career after *Enter the Dragon* even if it was met with a mixed response. Starring in many martial arts themed Blaxploitation films such as *Black Belt Jones*, *Three the Hard Way*, *Hot Potato*, and *Black Samurai*, Kelly rarely appeared in movies after 1982's *One Down, Two To Go*.

Prior to filming *Enter the Dragon* in 1973, he was a professional tennis player and after his film career, he became a tennis coach, until his death from cancer in 2013, at the age of 67.

Before the 1966 *Green Hornet* TV series, there were three other incarnations of the character in the USA; a radio series and two movie serials.

The radio series, with Al Hodge voicing the titular hero, debuted on 31st January

1936 on Detroit radio station WXYZ, which also broadcast companion shows *The Lone Ranger* and *Challenge of the Yukon*. In April 1938, the station supplied the series to MBS (Mutual Broadcasting System), followed by NBC and eventually, from 1939-1950, to ABC. The series returned in 1952, and sponsored by Orange Crush for its brief run.

The Green Hornet was adapted into two movie serials, *The Green Hornet* in 1941 and *The Green Hornet Strikes Again!* in 1941.

In *The Green Hornet*, Gordon Jones played the title character but had his voiced dubbed by Al Hodge, the original radio show Hornet, whenever the mask was worn. In *The Green Hornet Strikes Again!*, Jones and Hodge were both replaced with Warren Hull. Charlie Chan's "Number One Son" Keye Luke, who later played Master Po opposite David Carradine in Kung Fu and provided the dubbing for Mr. Han's voice in *Enter the Dragon*, played the role of Kato in both serials. *The Green Hornet* ran for 13 chapters, while *The Green Hornet Strikes Again!* ran for 15 instalments.

VIDEO

The Kentucky Fried Movie is one of the funniest films of the 1970's and one of the greatest parodies of all time. With the Kung Fu boom and the Bruce Lee Look-alikes, it's easy to see why everyone jumped all over this movie in a bad way upon its release. The stills from the film looked like Evan Kim was trying to imitate Lee. The common themes of martial arts film made the genre a target for parody and *The Kentucky Fried Movie* did just that, through its segment "A Fistful of Yen."

VIDEO

STORE

A RETROSPECTIVE LOOK AT BRUCE LEE MANIA & THE KUNG FU CRAZE OF THE 1970S

07 MARCH 1978

HELLO MEMBERS! OFF AGAIN WITH ANOTHER NEWS SHEET (NUMBER SEVEN, IN FACT) AND I HOPE THAT, AS BEFORE, I CAN FIND A LITTLE SOMETHING FOR EVERYBODY!

GENERAL NEWS

First off, I'm happy to say the missing drawing (see news sheet #6) belonging to John Kemp (1729) has turned up... in Australia!! In error, it had been sent to Wesley Fleming (1935). He, thankfully, returned this much-travelled picture. John is overjoyed to have it back so thank you, Wesley.

Many members have been asking where they can get the Japanese double-LP and a single LP of *Enter the Dragon*. It has all the dialogue and it's a real collector's item. Thanks to Mike Devereux (1061), I can tell you that these records are obtainable from: Warner-Pioneer Corporation, 4-11-10, Roppongi, Minatoku, TOKYO, Japan. The cost for the double and single LP's is £23 (inc postage & packing) - BUT PLEASE - contact them first before sending any money to make sure they're in stock. I have them now myself and they are worth every penny. However, I would mention the single LP obviously contains part of *Enter the Dragon* only, whereas the double has everything.

I mentioned CP Exports of Madison Avenue, New York is a previous news sheet. They were not replying to letters and I warned not to send them money. Since then, I have also written and have had no reply. Therefore, I repeat, DO NOT SEND THEM MONEY... they are not reliable.

However, for really reliable service, I can confirm that Regent Films, PO Box 54, Blackpool, FY1 ISP cannot be beaten for their Bruce Lee film trailers. Write and check out the good selection. Jeffrey Millington (1127) says they now have a NEW *Big Boss* trailer in stock - approx 100,' Super 8mm colour/sound, price £8.50. It has the opening titles and shows Bruce's flying kick, along with other great sequences.

Still on trailers, Ian Hamilton (1213) tells me that Deranis Film Services, Film House, 171 Stourbridge Road, Dudley, W.Midlands have imported a *Big Boss* trailer from the States - colour/sound and priced at £6.75. Write for further details... BEFORE sending money!

I've had several enquiries about the gloves worn by Bruce in *Enter the Dragon*. Joseph Hartley (1543) says that A to Z Martial Arts & Books Centre, 3 Macclesfield Street, London WI now have them in stock, but at the high price of £39.85. Maybe they do have to pay import duty, but it still seems dear to me. I'd recommend readers interested shop around to see if they can be had any cheaper. Please let me know, anyone who has any luck.

Ann Hunt (1275) sent in the picture in this news sheet of ex-Monkee, Micky Dolenz - we both agree it does resemble the other picture shown of Bruce. (Anyone writing to ask who it is will be thumped!). Any other members finding a picture of a star who looks like Bruce, just send it in. (I bet you DON'T find any!).

Micky Dolenz and wife Trina

Members, please note, Stretton Studios of Walsall, Staffs do NOT in fact sell Bruce Lee films, as incorrectly reported in news sheet #5.

David Niedzailek (1021) tells me that Rafael A. Cervantes, San Antonio, Texas 78226, USA has a great selection of 8mm and 16mm trailers (*Way of the Dragon*, *Fist of Fury*, *Enter the Dragon*) as well as a film of Bruce as Kato from the *Green Hornet* and a behind the scenes of *Enter the Dragon* (Making of the film). They also do soundtrack cassettes. WRITE FIRST FOR DETAILS.

Andrew Aylett (2122) studies Kung Fu under Tony Yan-Kwai Leung. Tony is a keen Bruce Lee fan, and although I don't usually recommend clubs, anyone wishing to take up Kung Fu classes might like to try Tony's London School of Martial Arts at the Sobell Sports Centre, 40 Danbury Street, Islington, London N.I (01 359 7203).

As a bit of verification that *Game of Death* IS on the way, Martin Schell (1819) sends us a copy of a picture he saw in the cinema magazine, Screen International. Usually when magazines like this have such advertisements, the film isn't too far behind.

Gary Chedgzoy (1032) says that Oriental World, 18 Swan Street, Manchester have the best value going in books, etc on Bruce. The staff are friendly and helpful and the owner has an acquaintance who was a friend of Bruce. There's a picture of him on the *Way of the Dragon* set with Bruce, Chuck, Betty Ting Pei and Bob Wall. There are prints of this rare photo for sale at £1 plus 10p p&p and there's *Way of the Dragon* 8mm & colour at £32.70 plus 70p p&p (inc. the famed nunchaku scene).

Finally, Gary also mentions G. Tate, 4 Ebor Terrace, Hunslet Carr, Leeds 10, Yorkshire who will do an oil painting of the Master for £6.50 (size 18" by 14"). WRITE FIRST TO CHECK DETAILS!

So many members ask about Bruce's diet so I think now's the time to outline the details I do know. He liked health foods, and obviously Chinese food. He drank lots of protein drinks - made from protein powder - powered milk made up with ice water, eggs and their shells, vegetable oil, peanut flour and sometimes bananas. Even a touch of peanut butter occasionally. He had a favourite vegetable drink prepared in an electric juicer that contained carrots, celery and apples. He didn't drink coffee or tea (except the occasional Chinese tea), or eat goods if he thought they contained chemicals or preservatives. He drank orange juice, honey water and some Chinese herbs.

Sad to say, there is no truth in the rumour that Madame Tussaud's is planning a Bruce Lee wax model... some people have no taste!

It seems that Maltese members Alex Buttigieg (2199) and Ian Camilleri (1810) are getting together to form a Society offshoot to encourage new members. Good news. I hope they get plenty of members for us - and friends for themselves. Well done Ian and Alex.

Alan Mount (1109) writes urging members to bombard the censors with pleads not to cut *Game of Death*. He fears the worst after reading the following in Cinema '78. "Throughout the vastly popular *Pink Panther* series, Peter Sellers and Burt Kwouk engaged in a testing series of martial arts ambushes, which were good-natured and caused no problems; but in the new film, they resorted to chain sticks, a form of weaponry to which the censors have always been resolutely opposed because it is so lethal and easily improvised. Chain sticks are automatically disallowed in Kung Fu films and to pass them in the *Pink Panther Strikes Again* would have created a worrying precedent. It would not have been a question of upgrading the film to "A," rather in theory at least of refusing it a certificate at all. Therefore the scene was cut." As Alan says, the last part speaks for itself. Remember though that the censors have now let through the previously cut nunchaku scenes in *Way of the Dragon* so there is a chance that things have been relaxed a little. I can see no harm though in writing to ask that *Game of Death* be left alone.

Those who listen to Radio 1 in the mornings will have heard Noel Edmunds' current craze of getting listeners to write in with a sentence like: "I've had a nightmare - she said ho(a)rsely" (if you see what I'm getting at!). Well, Noel read out from one listener a line that went, "I love the hero of those Kung Fu films - she said brusquely (Bruce-k-Lee). Actually, it didn't sound too bad when read out on the radio. It looks kind of funny written down. (Wish I hadn't put it in now!)

Richard McColl (1423) is wanting to help with the Scottish side of the Society (and ANY help is a GREAT idea!) His address will be on the area lists, so what I suggest is, Scottish members contact him to arrange get-togethers and to form your own Society "extension." Perhaps you could even arrange trips out to meet members from other areas. If anything like that should happen, don't forget to let me know all about it... it's a must for the news sheet.

Richard also tells me that Cimac Martial Arts of 606 Stratford Road, Sparkhill, Birmingham have now got all the *Memorial Monthly Magazines* from 1 to 8 and also some new Bruce pictures.

John Hill (2109) tells me there's a good Chinese shop in Liverpool that sells nunchakus, Kung Fu slippers and trousers, punch bags and pads, wrist and ankle weights, leg exercisers and safety equipment. It's on the corner of Berry Street and Wood Street in the City Centre. Thanks for the info, John!

Further to Gerard McNamara's (1382) word on the shop in Shorts Gardens, London WC2 (below an antique shop), he now says he's now bought the original *Enter the Dragon* poster, plus stills and a large B&W picture of Bruce posing in a sun chair - apparently it's from Japan.

Gary Chedgzoy (1032) has got a felt-finished poster from Pepperwell Ltd of 784, High Road, London E11. It's £2 plus 15p p&p and comes from the States.

Also Oriental World (see earlier) have *Bruce Lee Flick Books* showing kick and nunchaku scenes from *Fist of Fury* for £1.50 plus 25p p&p.

Arthur Stone (1150) mentions that, apart from Kareem Abdul Jabbar appearing in the *Man from Atlantis* series, the December 24th episode also featured Ahna Capri (who played Han's attractive aide in *Enter the Dragon*). Also, the producer of *Atlantis* is Herman Miller, who took charge of many of the Carradine *Kung Fu* episodes.

Suresh Gandhi (1743), one of our Dutch members, recently saw on German TV a film entitled *The Yellow Men with the Flying Fists* - produced by Brian Trenchard-Smith, who also made *Man from Hong Kong*. Many extracts were shown from *The Big Boss* and *Fist of Fury* plus an interview with Raymond Chow, along with karate and Kung Fu demos being given. It sounds to me rather on the lines of the original *Man and Legend* Golden Harvest documentary.

The Bruce Lee JKD Club of Hong Kong has a new book called *Bruce Lee Revenges* says Julian Midgley (1354). It's magic and all about *Fist of Fury* on production and opening night in Hong Kong. They've also got a set of stickers - six sheets in all and flick books.

Several members have asked where to get plastic wallets for membership cards.

I'd suggest W.H.Smiths (and most other large stationers). The small ones sell for only around 7p.

Derek Hamer (1944) has send me a booklet full of crosswords and quizzes on Bruce, the martial arts and general knowledge. I reckon it's first class and I intend to arrange its sale to Society members at cost price only. Don't write in yet though as I'll tell you in the news sheet or *KFM* when it's ready. Thanks again to Derek as it's obvious he's put a terrific lot of work into its design and setting up!

SPECIAL MESSAGES

I've been asked by one of the members to place a special "personal message" in the news sheet, and this I'm pleased to do. If anyone else would like to pass on a birthday, good luck, or whatever message, just drop me a line. And you can thank member David Colville (1675) for the idea. He wants to pass on the following message to his girlfriend, Kathleen Feeney (1194):

"Kathleen Feeney, you're a beautiful person and I love you" - David.

(I think that's smashing...I'll bet there'll be some others coming soon!)

AREA LISTS

These are being sent to all members between the numbers 2171 and 2236 inclusive along with this news sheet. As I find it extremely difficult to cope with all the work I have (bearing in mind I run the Society in my spare time on evenings and weekends), I will not be sending out amendments lists where addresses have changed, and so on. If anyone (up to 2170) wants one, just send me a note plus stamped and addressed envelope and I'll post one off. Also, I will not be sending out names of new members, so again, if you want to know if there's any in your area, just drop me a line. ANY MEMBERS FROM 2237 ONWARDS NOT WANTING THEIR NAME PASSED ON TO OTHER MEMBERS, PLEASE LET ME KNOW STRAIGHT AWAY.

Another thing, although *KFM* kindly donate me the space for a column in the magazine, I do not work for them. Therefore, if you have any comments about the magazine in general, please write to them DIRECT. And it's worth remembering too that *KFM* handle ALL the Society mail order. If you do have any problems, please write to them (that is, other than for non-arrival of news sheets, membership kits and second-year kits). If you can all help me in that way, it'll give me that bit more time to devote to the Society proper - and do I need it!!

COMPETITION RESULTS

Answers to last December's competition are:

1) Size 7 shoe, 2) Winslow Wong, 3) Two - Hong Kong & Seattle, 4) *Enter the Dragon*, 5) Mr. Braithwaite, 6) 140 pounds, 7) Mercedes Benz/Porsche,

the Dragon, 5) Mr. Braithwaite, 6) 140 pounds, 7) Mercedes Benz/Porsche, 8) Phoebe and Agnes, 9) Peter and Robert, and 10) Li Yuen Kam - *Protector of San Francisco*.

The winners are: David Colville (1675), Fred Stuffin (1844), Ray Tidswell (1473), Mike Devereux (1061) and David Anthony (1521). They will each be receiving a free *Kung Fu Monthly Binder*.

THE NEW COMPETITION

This one was sent in (with thanks) by David C. King (1752). It's a little different from the usual, but it shouldn't prove too hard for the Kung Fu fanatics!

Below, you'll find 12 clues to words that fit ACROSS the diagram shown. Once you have managed to guess them all correctly, you'll find that one down spells out a phrase you'll all know rather well!. Once again, there'll be five winners and I'll be looking to see not only the one down quiz word, but also the correct answers to the 12 clues. Answers on a postcard please to: Society News Sheet 7 Comp, 14 Rathbone Place, London W1P IDE.

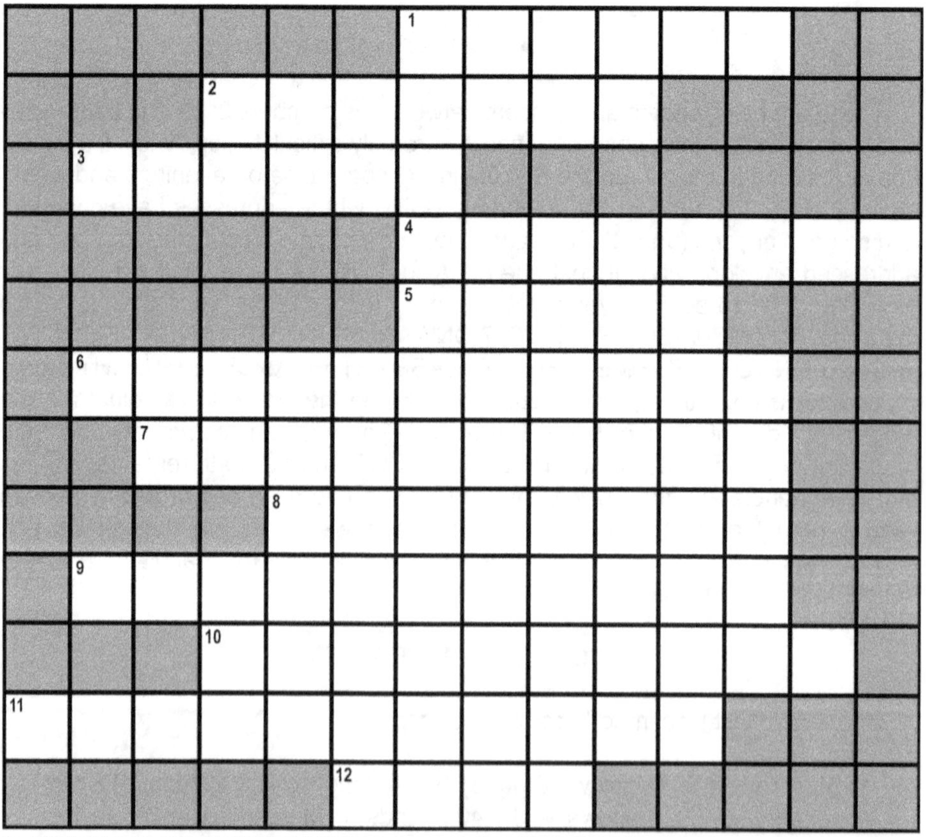

1. Chuck Norris was an expert in this field (6)
2. Bruce could even knock you down at this distance (3, 4)
3. Nobody was better at Wing Chun (3, 3)
4. The name of Bruce's mum (5, 3)
5. It was a deadly drug in *Enter the Dragon* (5)
6. Bruce's last and unfinished film (4, 2, 5)
7. "Way of the Intercepting Fist" (4, 4, 2)
8. He was the greatest (5, 3)
9. He had a hairy chest in *Way of the Dragon* (5, 6)
10. Where else did Bruce appear in a tracksuit? (10)
11. Bruce made this film very early on (5, 2, 1, 3)
12. The Master's fists were full of it (4)

RENEWAL SLIPS

Members from 1829 to 2021 - your membership falls due for renewal between March and the end of May... I look forward to seeing you all again next year.

LETTERS

> Dear Pam - enclosed is an article from our evening paper. It makes interesting reading about David Chiang. What he says about Bruce is, I think, in bad taste. Surely Bruce proved he did respect the martial arts and has Mr. Chiang never heard of Way of the Dragon or the other brilliant films? It's the easiest thing in the world to knock now that Bruce is gone.
>
> Richard Miller (1638)

I must say I agree with you, Richard, and for other members, this is part of what David said: "For years I was in Bruce Lee's shadow. Now Bruce is dead and I am alive. He was my friend, but I see no reason why I shouldn't be bigger than he was. (I wonder if David is talking about the size of his head?) Kung Fu as a film attraction has hardly started yet; Bruce Lee started to compromise when he became a celebrity. I have never done that. To me the arts are a venerable and respected way of life." (Oh really?... Funny he didn't mind compromising while Bruce was alive - as his "friend," he sure didn't have the guts to tell Bruce his true feelings!).

And there's more... "I am 10 times faster than anyone else and they know it. Only my friends wish to practise with me now. I can kill a man so easily with these hands that it sometimes frightens me. The reflexes have taken over. Most of all I'd like to make a really good film so everyone would know I'm not just a stuntman. Not even Bruce Lee succeeded in doing that."

Well, speaking for myself (and no doubt most of you) if it hadn't been for the fact that Bruce ALONE broke the East/West barriers to put Kung Fu and the martial arts on the map, I don't think there'd be many people in this part of the world who'd even heard of David Chiang!! However, if his skills compare in any way to his head-size, then he should be a knockout!

Dear Pam,

Recently I and four friends walked from Essex to London to see Fist of Fury *along with the* Amsterdam Kill. *When we reached the cinema we found there to be continuous showings of* Kill. *The manager said it was because many more older people would come out of nostalgia to see Mitchum. My question is, how has age got anything to do with it? We were going to see Bruce, partly for nostalgic reasons, especially as he is no longer alive (physically) whereas Mitchum is."*

Ray Tidswell (1473)

I can imagine just how you felt, Ray. I didn't think managers could do that without permission of the distributors. Try contacting EMI Film Distributors about it as maybe they weren't aware of the fact. Also tell the cinema concerned about what you intend to do.

And back again to your letter for some more bad news!

I was browsing through our local library and picked up Halliwell's Companion/ Film Guide. *Under the heading of "Lee," there was a picture of Bruce being used as publicity for martial arts equipment. Underneath it read (quote) "...that he was a diminutive Chinese of no real standing who rose out of obscurity for a short time with four films of varying quality and then died as quickly as he arrived." I don't know what to say!*

Nor do I, Ray, half these 'hack' writers don't know what they're talking about, so don't get too upset about it.

Dear Pam,

A friend will be going to Seattle for two weeks holiday this year and I have asked him to get plenty of pictures of Bruce's grave and to place flowers there on my behalf. Anyway, Pam, let me know if you'd like some of these photos. If you do, I'll send them on to you entirely free for your intense dedication to our great Master!"

Mick Werkowski - (1686)

Thank you, Mick. I'd be delighted to see the pictures. I could probably arrange for one or two to go into a future news sheet. Thanks for the kind offer.

THE TRAVELLERS

When Arthur Stone (1150) mentioned he wanted to produce a Society movie, we both knew it would take some doing. As a start, he put an advert in a news sheet and now, as a result of that, he and his co-producer, Glynn Barker (1567) are ready to begin. They ask me to print the following:

This coming July, in honour of the Master, Bruce Lee, the Society will be making the first British Kung Fu movie. Shot in the Lake District, the plot aims to be an extension of the Master's film career. It's set in China in the last century.

A group of martial artists called "The Travellers" help a village defend itself against bandits from the mountains. Tao, a young villager, falls in love with the bandit chief's daughter, and when her life is threatened, he reluctantly betrays his people. When he, in return, is betrayed he goes on the rampage, eventually meeting the bandit chief in a fight to the death, thereby restoring honour to his family name.

We're hoping that by around Christmas the film maybe available to members/ KFM readers.

Now, however, is your chance to appear. We need extras as travellers or bandits. Martial arts expertise is not necessary but helpful. Contact Glynn Barker, Greenhill, Sheffield (enclosing an SAE).

All the main parts are cast except for a leading lady who MUST be Oriental. Ladies, write direct to: Arthur Stone, Stapenhill, Burton-on-Trent.

For all members of the cast who have not yet found accommodation for Saturday July first, either contact The Tourist Information Centre, Town Hall, Barrow-in-Furness, Cumbria or try the following hotels and guest houses: Clarkes Arms Hotel - 25456, Duke of Edinburgh Hotel - 25447, Imperial Hotel - 21523, Victoria Park Hotel - 21159, White House Hotel - 25454, East Mount Private Hotel - 25242, Glen Garth Guest House - 25374, Lisdoonie Private Hotel - 27312, The Gables - 25497. .

Don't forget, if you are Chinese, or can look so when made up, please contact Arthur QUICKLY.

THE LEAD CHARACTERS

Glynn Barker   Paul Corrigan   Andy Hill   Arthur Stone

Paul Corrigan (1711) plays Ji Shin, leader of the villagers. Paul is 22, he teaches Shotokan Karate but is equally familiar with Wing Chun, White Crane and Siu Lum Kuen.

Arthur Stone plays Tao. Arthur is 23. He practises JKD, plus amateur boxing & wrestling... Wing Chun and Jun Fan.

Will Johnston (1056) plays Raku Mone, the mysterious and deadly bandit leader. Will is 19, he hopes to act full time and has already appeared in five films and four plays. He practises Jeet Kune Do.

Andy Hill (1443) plays Brother Mark. He practises Judo, Karate, Kung Fu and he's very good with the nunchakus.

Glynn Barker plays Brother John, leader of the Travellers. He's 18 and practises Jeet Kune Do, Preying Mantis, Hsing Kung Fu, Karate, stick fighting and the nunchaku.

Also taking part are M. Zamiteas (1696) as Tang Tsung and John Black (1956) as a Traveller. Pictures of these two appeared last news sheet.

SWOP SHOP

- Carl Jones (2121), St.Helens has various items on Bruce as well as other Kung Fu star (inc. magazines) to swap/sell. Contact for list.
- Miss S. Jolley (1330), Eccles has to sell: *Privacy & Anecdotes* paid £1.25, wants 70p, *Nunchaku in Action* - 70p, *Bruce Lee 1940-1973* - £2.95, *Secrets of Kung Fu* - 20p, *Farewell my Friend* - £3.50, *Game of Death Collectors Edition* - 20p, 16 *Dragon* magazines - 20p each, 24 posters (various prices), *Karate & Fighters Monthly* - 25p, *Life & Tragic Death* - 25p, *The Man Only I Knew* - 95p, *Kung Fu* magazine - 10p, *Kung Fu Master* - 10p, *Bruce Lee's Fighting Method* - £3.00 and 6 photos - 70p. All in very good condition. Write direct.
- Navrat Sihra (2157), Gillingham has to sell: Soundtrack to *Enter the Dragon* (music), two big pictures of Bruce, *Game of Death*, *KFM's* 1-7, 34 & 36, set of three Bruce Lee postcards, *Kung Fu* by Peter Nicholson, set of three large Bruce Lee posters, 12 Bruce Lee stickers, five big posters, *The Book of Kung Fu Fighters*, two *Giant Bruce Lee Scrapbooks* (KFM), *Kung Fu Superfighters*, around 300-400 magazine & newspaper cuttings (some rare, all on Bruce). He's asking for £45.00 for the whole collection.
- Andrea McLean (1029), Halifax has to sell: *KFM's* 29-32, *Book of Kung Fu* (KFM), *Best of Bruce Lee* No. 2, *Bruce Lee's Nunchaku in Action*, *Privacy & Anecdotes*, *Bruce Lee's Fighting Method*.
- Alex Buttigieg (2199), Msida, Malta wants to buy *KFM's* 1-11, 13-21 and 31. Contact him.
- Rajendra Chandarana (1927), Hemel Hempstead has Elvis single *All Shook Up-Heartbreak Hotel* to swap for *KFM's* 7 & 24. Can also record on tape *Elvis' 40 Greatest Hits* to swap for three *KFM's*. Write with numbers.
- Raghuir Kandola (1797), Gravesend wants to sell Bullworker for £10 or swap for *Bruce Lee's Fighting Method* books - Basic Training & Self-Defence. Write.
- Lee Percy (1072), Ilford has to swap: issues 1-5 of *Dragon*, *Legend of Bruce Lee* publicity poster magazine, *Game of Death* rip-off with *Goodbye Bruce Lee* film poster/advert sheet, *Tongfather* film poster (not very good condition), *Kung Fu & Karate Fighting* No.1, *Popster* No.26 on Kung Fu, *Kung Fu 75* No. 1. Wants KFM No.1, Bruce Tegner's book on Aikido, Ian Fleming's *For Your Eyes Only* (in very good condition please).
- Kieran O'Neill (1663), Andersonstown has to sell: *KFM's* 8-36, *Life & Tragic Death of Bruce Lee*, *Bruce Lee, King of Kung Fu*, *KFM Souvenir Album*. Wants £12 ono (inc. postage).
- Paul Short (1164), Sheffield has for sale/swap: *Bruce Lee Memorial Monthly* No. 2, *Way of the Dragon* and *Fist of Fury* press books, Bruce Lee still, *Enter the Dragon*, *The Big Boss*, and *Way of the Dragon* stills and few other film stills. Wants *Deadly Hands of Kung Fu* No.s 1, 2, 4, 5, 6, 8, 14 and any over 33 and anything on Bruce/martial arts.

A RETROSPECTIVE LOOK AT BRUCE LEE MANIA & THE KUNG FU CRAZE OF THE 1970S

- Andrew Aylett (2122), Bromley, has *Clash* magazine Vol. 1 No. 5, Bruce Tegner's Kung Fu & Tai Chi, *Dragon* Vol. 2 No.s 2-4. WANTS: *Way of the Dragon* soundtrack album in very good condition. Will pay good price if swaps not suitable.
- Miss Shane Phipps (1735), Brimington has sets of stills (B/W) from *Enter the Dragon* and four photos for £2.15 (some rare).
- M.J.Adams (1573), Melton Mowbray has to sell: *Bruce Lee - 1940-1973*, *Bruce Lee* by Alex Ben Block, *Life & Tragic Death*, *Secret Art* - signed & unsigned, *The Man Only I Knew*, *Bruce Lee Scrapbook* No. 1, *Bruce Lee King of Kung Fu*, *The Book of Kung Fu*, three Chinese magazines, *KFM's* No. 1-37, *Game of Death*, Bruce Lee Calendar 1977, *Tao of Jeet Kune Do*, *My Martial Arts Training Guide to Jeet Kune Do*, *Enter the Dragon*, *Privacy & Anecdotes*, three Bruce Lee Chinese magazines, *Best of Bruce Lee* No. 2, *Super Kung Fu*, numerous Bruce Lee photos, *20th Century Warriors*, *Wing-Chun Kung Fu*, *Shorinji Kempo*, 20 *Combat* magazines, 50 assorted Kung Fu magazines. Offers please.
- David Coe (1440), North Shields has *KFM's* 1-33, *Privacy & Anecdotes*, *Nunchakus in Action*, *The Man Only I Knew*, *Farewell my Friend*, *Kung Fu Magazine* No.1 , *Enter the Dragon* poster.
- David Moore (1783), Wakefield wants *KFM* 1 in very good condition (good price paid), Bruce Lee magazines or features on Bruce (British or foreign, but not *KFM*) and soft or hard-backed books on any martial arts. (Prices arranged through post).

PEN PALS

- Allan Macdonald (2134), Glenmavis-by-Airdrie wants female Chinese pen-pal, 16-17 years. He's 16 and interested in Bruce, Elvis and dancing. Photo please.
- Tom Wheeler (1904), Cardiff wants female pen pal, preferably Chinese but not too important - over 17 years old. He likes Bruce, Kung Fu, photography, ice-skating, chess and crosswords.
- Paul W. Kim (American Society Member), Camden, New Jersey USA would like British members to contact him.
- Anthony Leong (2238), Middlesbrough wants male/female pen pals from aged 15 onwards. Please contact.

And that's it folks! There's been a heck of a lot to say this month. See you again in June with lots more news of the world's greatest society. Pam

"COR, THATS A GREAT JUMP MATE!"

... "AND WATCH OUT FOR HIS LEFT HOOK"

BRUCE LEE SOCIETY COLUMN
KUNG FU MONTHLY NO. 40

Hi, I am here with some really hot Society news!

When member Arthur Stone (1150) told me some time ago that he wanted to produce a movie on kung fu, I knew he was going to be in for a tough time, especially as he wanted to rope in plenty of Society members. As I couldn't offer much in the way of organisational assistance, I instead placed an advert for the idea into a past news sheet. Well, I'm pleased to say the response has been very good.

Arthur and Glynn Barker (1567) are going to produce the first member's movie, to be entitled, *The Travellers*. It's going to be made in July this year and, naturally, it will be honouring our great Master, Bruce Lee. The film will be made on location in the Lake District and basically, the plot follows the direction in which Bruce was travelling. In fact, the plot is to be a logical extension of his film career. It's set in China in the last century. A group of martial artists called "The Travellers" help a village defend itself from a group of bandits in the mountains. Tao, a young villager, falls in love with the chief bandit's daughter and when her life is threatened, he reluctantly betrays his people. When he in return is betrayed, he goes on the rampage, eventually meeting the chief in a fight to the death. In so doing, he restores honour to his family name.

We're hoping that maybe we can make the film available to Society members/ *KFM* readers at a later date (probably around Christmas). But now is your big chance to appear in *The Travellers*. We need extras to appear as travelers or bandits. Martial arts expertise is not necessary, but helpful. If you're interested, please write to Glynn Barker in Sheffield. Also, please don't forget to enclose a stamped and addressed envelope. Finally, all the main parts are cast with the exception of a "leading lady" - who must be Oriental. Any interested ladies out there, please write direct to Arthur Stone at Stapenhill.

Wow, doesn't it sound great? See you next month with lots more news! - Pam

BRUCE LEE SOCIETY COLUMN
KUNG FU MONTHLY NO. 41

Hi everyone. This month's Society page is going to be a bit different this month! By now, you'll all have heard the awful news of what the censors are thinking of doing. I'm sure you'll all agree with me that it's an absolute disgrace. To remove THE major fight scene from *Game of Death* makes me feel like going around to their offices and chaining myself to the railings in protest!

Something has GOT to be done, AND FAST. You've already been asked to write direct to the film censors to register your total disapproval with what they're very likely going to do. Now what I want is for YOU to help me organise the quickest petition ever in the history of Great Britain. We got around 5,000 signatures together for Raymond Chow some while ago and I'd say we ought to be able to double that.

As you'll have already read, Raymond Chow is thinking of withdrawing the film completely, rather than see the best of the action sliced up. The only way to stop this is to act fast!

A RETROSPECTIVE LOOK AT BRUCE LEE MANIA & THE KUNG FU CRAZE OF THE 1970S

At Last The KFM BACK ISSUES BINDER

Keep your invaluable set of KFM back numbers in PERFECT condition by using the OFFICIAL KUNG-FU MONTHLY BINDER.

You'll see looking in the magazine, the usual price is £2.75. For Bruce Lee Society Members, however, the cost is ONLY £2.50!

Embossed with the words, 'Kung-Fu Monthly... the World's Finest Martial Arts Magazine', this smart black and gold binder will make a beautiful addition to your bookcase.

Send a £2.75 cheque/postal order (made out to KFM) to: KFM Binder Offer, 14 Rathbone Place, London W1P 1DE.

PS... don't forget that FOR A WHILE ONLY, each binder sold will contain a free copy of both KFM No.5 and 6.

Write the following onto a plain sheet of paper and try and get as many people as possible to sign their approval:

"I/we are shocked and astounded to hear of the British Board of Film Censor's decision to remove from *Game of Death*, the principal nunchaku battle scene. Bruce Lee was, and remains for many people, the greatest kung-fu artist the world has ever seen. It is outrageous that the last remaining footage containing his unique skills should be treated in such a barbarous fashion."

When you have got as many signatures as possible post them off to: GOD Censors Petition, *Kung Fu Monthly*, 14 Rathbone Place, London W1P 1DE.

Remember there is always a chance they will reverse their decision, but if, by the time this petition is collected, they haven't, I personally will deliver the signatures to their offices. No doubt many of the staff here at *KFM* will want to join me.

Lastly, may I apologise for the slightly late news sheet last time; it was entirely due to overwork! A timely reminder to anyone reading this who isn't a member of the Bruce Lee Society; JOIN UP NOW. There's no other club like it in the world and for all the good things you get - a badge, stickers, membership card, photos, regular News Sheets It's got to be amazing value at only £3.25 a year. Contact me, Pam Hadden at The Bruce Lee Society, 14 Rathbone Place, London, W1P 1DE. - Pam

BRUCE LEE SOCIETY COLUMN
KUNG FU MONTHLY NO. 42

Hi, Pam here again, with another installment of news for all you Society members. First off, of course, I have to thank you for putting together the already enormous petition response. I'm going to hold off delivering it up until the last possible second, in order to make the impact as big as possible.

Once we've cleared this particular demand. I'll give a bit of time for everybody to get their breath back, and then maybe have a go at getting *Longstreet* and *Green Hornet* on the TV, with another petition! I know its hard work, but I hope you agree with me that it's got to be worth it. Television companies tend to be quite influenced by such things - particularly as in this case, we've got the *Game of Death* event to offer as proof of Bruce's continued fame.

Patricia Davies (1834) has written in asking if I know of any shop in South East London that deals in Bruce items and/or sells Chinese clothes. Okay, can any of you London members help? For the life of me I can't think of anywhere, but I'm sure there must be something, somewhere.

Reminder time, anyone wanting to find details of any British martial arts schools, the people to contact are: The Martial Arts Commission, 4 Deptford Bridge, London SF8 (Tel. 01-691 3433). They'll be able to put you in touch with registered, reliable clubs.

Hot news, member Mr. T. Symons (2243) tells me that a Hong Kong magazine gives the names Chen Yao Po and Kim Tai Chung as TWO of the apparently many stand-ins used for Bruce in *Game of Death*. As you know, no names appear in the credits at all as the stand-ins say they don't want to be identified, though more likely, Raymond Chow doesn't want them to be identified.

For my full "biased/unbiased" comments on *Game of Death*, check out the next news sheet. I'm going to try to be fair, but factual. No punches are going to be pulled! I've seen the film twice now and believe me, there's plenty to talk about.

And that's about it for this month. Don't forget to enter our great new *Dragon Power* competition, and don't forget either, we've finally located some good *Game of Death* yellow suits and they're on offer to Society members at VERY reduced prices.

Last but not least, if you STILL aren't a member of the world's fastest-moving Society, then how about joining right now? It's still only £3.25 a year to belong and the address to write is: Pam Hadden, Bruce Lee Society, 14 Rathbone Place, London W1P 1DL. Bye for now . . . Pam

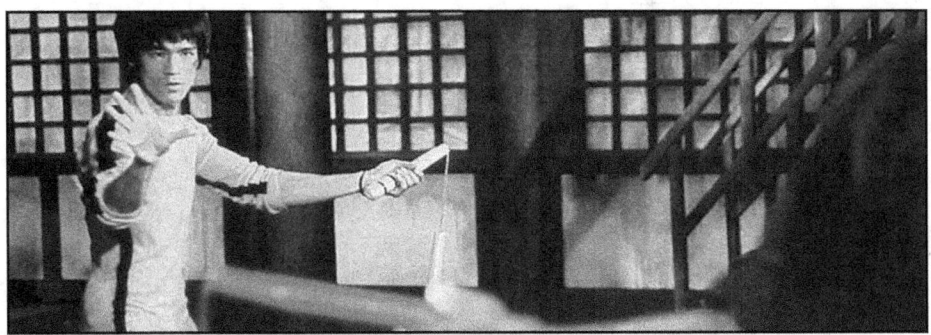

EDITOR'S NOTES

At the end of issue two, I touched upon Super 8 films. In issue seven, you have seen how the format is starting to become popular with some members but is still ridiculously expensive. Trailers are advertised at £6.75 and £8.50 each, which today, would equate to £39 and £49 respectively. It's a lot of money for a few minutes.

The *Enter the Dragon* style gloves mentioned were called Bong Sau gloves in some places and were mostly made entirely out of leather, making them quite expensive. The price quoted in this newsletter would have put it well beyond the reach of the average fan. The £39.85 cost would be an unbelievable £230 today.

The similarities between Micky Dolenz of The Monkees and Bruce Lee are uncanny in some photos, with some fans still being mistaken today. So it's very much understandable that people would have been caught out in the 70's.

The *Making of Enter the Dragon* 8mm and 16mm mentioned in issue seven would have been the Robin's Nest *On Location – Hong Kong* documentary that has appeared several times on DVD and Blu-ray releases of the film. At £18.50 (or £115 today) it was another expensive buy for the average Bruce Lee fan.

 *Game of Death* finally makes its first appearance in this newsletter and states that the film is almost due for release. This news must have sent hearts racing; for the first time in five years, a new Bruce Lee film will be on screen.

It took some time for Madame Tussauds to make a waxwork of Bruce Lee and they now have two. The first one, featuring Bruce Lee performing a flying kick from *Fist of Fury*, was unveiled in 2014 at Madam Tussauds Hong Kong while the second one, featuring him dressed in his yellow and black catsuit from *Game of Death* was unveiled in 2017 at Madam Tussauds Hollywood.

 The documentary *Yellow Men With The Flying Fists* shown on German TV is more than likely a 1974 Australian film called *Kung Fu Killers* directed by Brian Trenchard-Smith and featured Angela Mao, George Lazenby and Carter Wong, among others. Trenchard-Smith developed the contacts he made while filming the movie, to later make *The Man From Hong Kong* with Jimmy Wang Yu and George Lazenby.

The Society film is progressing and the makers have now released the title *The Travellers*, a rough synopsis, and some of the casting including Paul Corrigan, Arthur Stone, Glynn Barker, Mick Zamiteas and John Black and Will Johnston.

A RETROSPECTIVE LOOK AT BRUCE LEE MANIA & THE KUNG FU CRAZE OF THE 1970S

08
JUNE
1978

HELLO ONCE AGAIN! WELCOME TO OUR NEWS SHEET NUMBER EIGHT.

GAME OF DEATH

Through past news sheets I've tried continually to keep everybody informed on Bruce's last epic, ready for the time when "all would be revealed."

KFM themselves have covered the film in great depth - some really interesting reading too - so you can imagine how thrilled I was to accompany the magazine editor to an EMI preview. So, some weeks back, heart in mouth, I saw through the Master's film. On the way to the cinema the excitement mounted I had a feeling I was about to reach the top of a mountain, not knowing what was on the other side but expecting something fantastic.

I have to be honest... I was NOT overwhelmed. It was a good film - but not the Master's film.

The stand-ins did pretty well, but unfortunately Bruce's fight scenes were cut down to two only... with Danny Inosanto and Kareem Abdul Jabbar. Odd scenes from the Master's other films have also been popped in to fill things out. Even shots of his actual funeral have been used and fire has been added to the many rumours about his death by the insertion of sometimes unnecessary scenes. Raymond Chow, to my mind, has committed a gross error of judgment by leaving out fights and, I understand from a source in Hong Kong, "canning" them for future use. Whether he intends to use these for other Bruce Lee "epics," again adding more shots from previous films, plus dubious story content, remains to be seen.

But the saga continues... now the censors have entirely removed the Lee/Inosanto fight because it's all nunchaku fighting! And yet, they allow a similar scene to

santo fight because it's all nunchaku fighting! And yet, they allow a similar scene to be put back into *Way of the Dragon*. The situation is truly a disgrace. The censors seem to have a very convenient set of rules!

Game of Death is now left with only seven to eight minutes of new Bruce Lee action. But I'll say this, when the Little Dragon does come on the screen, even for the pitifully short time now left to him, he is, as always, pure perfection. How much more wonderful it would have been for the fans had Chow used all the footage of *Game of Death* to make this really the Master's last and greatest film.

Maybe I judge the film too harshly... maybe I expected too much. I leave it to all of you to go see the film - then let me know your feelings. Release date is 29th June.

In the meantime (as you'll see reading *KFM*) I'm collecting a petition to go to the censors about *Game of Death*. There's very little time, so try and get as many signatures as possible and sent them off immediately to *KFM*, Game Petition, 14 Rathbone Place, London W1P IDE. I will personally be handing them over to the censors. ACT NOW! and maybe they'll take some notice.

DISC TRIBUTE TO BRUCE

After seeing *Game of Death* and feeling that Raymond Chow/Robert Clouse had let the fans - and Bruce - very badly down (with the usual help of the censors), I really needed to know that somebody, somewhere thought enough about the Master to produce something that was a real, honest tribute to his memory. Well, it's happened! Personal friend and Honorary Society member, Eddy Pumer, put a fantastic idea to Henry Hadaway, managing director of Satril Records Ltd., for a new single to honour Bruce's name. They approached Warner Brothers and got permission to use the Little Dragon's actual voice and then, between the two of them, they put together a terrific record. It's a great disco sound - so it should appeal generally, too - and on top, there's Bruce's fabulous war cries and voice. No copies, no stand-ins, just "his Master's voice" coming over loud and strong! You'll hear him saying those famous words from *Enter the Dragon* - "You have offended my family and you have offended a Shaolin Temple." And if that weren't enough, take a listen to the B side. It contains twice as much talking and twice as many war cries... it also runs two minutes longer! The record will be released on June 16th, to begin with as a 12" single - a collector's item in its

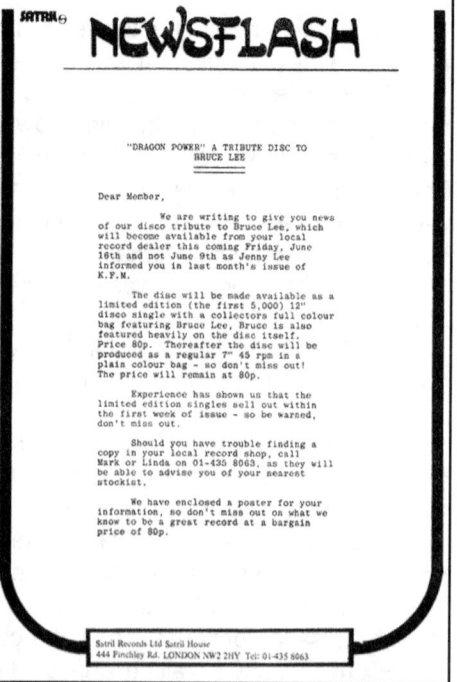

own right. There's a special sleeve with a picture of Bruce on it, plus a word from the Editor of *KFM*. Once those have sold out, the release will continue as a "45." Get to your nearest record dealer and make sure you get a copy of this unique record as it really IS knockout. At last, a true, honest-to-goodness tribute to the Little Dragon, and one to make the fans feel proud. Well done, Eddy, and thanks to Henry Hadaway for making the record available to the fans.

GENERAL NEWS

News on the Carradine version of Bruce's pet project, *Silent Flute*. Yael Shelach (2200) has written from Israel to say that *Flute* was filmed there - shooting started November 7th, 1977 and was completed by the end of December. Producers are Sandy Howard and Paul Maslansky and apart from Carradine, it stars Jeff Cooper, Roddy McDowall, Eli Wallach and Christopher Lee. Apparently Sandy Howard acquired the film rights three years ago. Jeff Cooper replaces Bruce's original choice of James Coburn. Check out the pictures that Yael has sent in to me. He also relates that, apart from Chinese New Year's being named after animals, so too are the hours of the day. As there are 24 hours in the day and only 12 animal signs in the Chinese horoscope, each animal represents two hours. Yael remembers reading that, not only was Bruce born in the year of the Dragon, but also the hour of the Dragon, too! That's really new information to me - that makes the Master's birth time between 7 and 9 in the morning.

Tim Stephens (1311) has sent in a photo of a picture he painted of Bruce when he was at school - and I think it's very good. Next to it you can see Tim doing a flying sidekick. I hope he managed to miss the poor photographer.

All of you who have seen *Saturday Night Fever* - couldn't have failed to have noticed that in one scene, John Travolta stands in his bedroom

before a large poster of Bruce from *Enter the Dragon* and poses in the identical trunks. I wonder if, in real life, John IS a Bruce Lee fan? Anyway, I must say I enjoyed *Fever* and John really IS a terrific dancer.

In the last news sheet, I mentioned *Enter the Dragon*-type sparring gloves being available from A to Z Martial Arts Centre at £39.85 (a price I felt to be ludicrous!). Well, Mark Salter (1792) tells me the North London Martial Arts Centre at 81 Broad

Lane, London N15 has the same gloves for £10.50 plus 50p handling. Some difference! They also have the Hong Kong style *GOD* tracksuits at around £11/£12 (not exact replicas though, if my memory serves me right).

Richard Miller (1638) says that Cimac Martial Arts at 606 Startford Road, Sparkhill, Birmingham Bll 4AP also have the gloves - at £19.95 plus £1 handling. I'd suggest writing to both the above companies. Thanks, Richard and Mark, for writing in.

Lots of members still write in about finding martial arts clubs in their areas. For information and advice on registered clubs, contact The Martial Arts Commission, 4 Deptford Bridge, London SE.8 (Telephone 01-691 3433).

If anyone has the current address of Member Eric Henderson (1940) please let me know. He lived in Blackburn, but his March news sheet came back marked "gone away."

Patricia Davies (1834) lives in Bromley and wonders if anyone knows of shops in the near vicinity that sell Chinese clothes. If you've got any ideas, contact Pat at Bromley, Kent.

Many members have inquired where to find the albums recently reviewed in *KFM*. Well, Magpie Records, Hopmarket Yard, Worcester WR1 1UR, have had *Way of the Dragon, The Big Boss, Fist of Fury,* and *Enter the Dragon* in stock - and they hope to have more. Drop them a line and check what they may be getting.

Also, Soundtrack & General, 406 Brockley Road, London SE4, have had *Way of the Dragon, Enter the Dragon* (Japanese double LP at £12.98 plus 55p handling) and, I believe, other soundtracks. Again, write directly.

Finally, HMV at 363 Oxford Street, London W1R 2BJ had *Way of the Dragon* and *The Big Boss* so drop them a line.

Carl Jones (2121) says Regent Films, PO Box 54, Blackpool FY1 ISP has an *Enter the Dragon* 200' film entitled *Location - Hong Kong - with Enter the Dragon*. It's colour and sound. Carl says it's absolutely terrific and costs £18.50 inc. handling. If you're going to order it, send a deposit of £1.50. It runs for about nine minutes and has shots of the crew filming the harbour/sampans scene, Bruce battling Han, Clouse/Bob Wall choreographing the O'Hara fight (with some of the fight shown), Saxon v Bolo (Yang Tse) Kelly v Peter Archer and Bruce coaching Yang Tse offset. Also the Angela Mao fight, Banquet scene rehearsal, Bruce choreographing the underground scene with Bruce and young Chinese dressed like possibly a stand-in. Sounds great. Carl has also sent for a film entitled *The Chinese Connection* (*Fist of Fury*), a trailer from Jerry Ohlingers Movie Store at 120 West third Street, New York,

Top: Tim Stephens' flying sidekick.
Bottom: The picture of Bruce that Tim painted while at school. It looks a pretty impressive work of art!

USA. They do Super 8 versions of their 16mm trailers. The price is $8.50, around £4/£5, which is a bargain.

Arthur Stone (1150) who's at present working on the Society film, writes to say that he's got the *Enter the Dragon* trailer from Regent and it's a knockout. He mentions several scenes, including one with Bruce reclining in a chair, with a grin on his face, watching Clouse show how he wants a scene tackled.

David Niedzailek (1021) also mentions the trailer and also a martial arts trailer of eight Kung Fu films (inc all the USA Bruce Lee trailers) that costs £32.50 - colour/sound. Another point he mentions is that they also do a trailer entitled *Bruce Lee, the Man and the Legend*. This is NOT of Bruce Lee but of Roy Lee Lung (or Bruce Li as he's otherwise known) - well known star of many rip offs.

Shane Phipps (1735) sent in a note to say that her Kung Fu instructor, Master Jeremy Yau, had a starring part in the TV series, *Gangsters*. Shane must be lucky to have his guidance.

Arthur Stone has also sent in the newspaper cutting shown here. It sounds potential rubbish, as usual! Once more, Bruce Li exploits Bruce Lee's death.

> The 'Enter The Dragon" series of films in which the legendary Bruce Lee displayed his mastery of the martial arts was commercially too hot for it to be buried alongside its hero.
>
> So "Exit The Dragon Enter The Tiger" (X) which comes to Screen Three at the Burton Odeon Film Centre next week, ensures that the series will live on.
>
> In fact rather than let Bruce Lee's death hamper the series "Enter The Tiger" exploits his death for its plot.
>
> Bruce Lee's friend David Lee (played by Bruce Li would you believe?) finds that his friend died in suspicious circumstances and, using the lessons of his friend and master, he determines to solve the mystery.
>
> This involves the new hero of the martial arts in the brutality and intrigue of Hong Kong's drug underworld.
>
> The action includes rape, torture and one scene in which the "Tiger" fights off no less than 20 of Hong Kong's meanest thugs.

Rajendra Chandarana (1927) has sent in details of a rather unusual door panel poster. It's a full size illustration of Bruce actually kicking through a door - amaze your friends! It measures 2200x860mms and comes in two, ready-pasted sections for £7.15 from Scandicor of Armdale Road, Feltham, Middlesex.

One further snippet, Oriental World at 18 Swan Street, Manchester have *Way of the Dragon* 8mm film and tape showing nunchakus scenes plus Bruce/Norris fight. They also have trailers from *The Big Boss* and *Enter the Dragon* with sound. Write direct to Oriental World. They also sell books, magazines and posters, etc.

COMPETITIONS

The answers to last news sheet's competition were as follows:

1) Karate, 2) One-Inch, 3) Yip Man, 4) Grace Lee, 5) Opium, 6) *Game of Death*, 7) Jeet Kune Do, 8) Bruce Lee, 9) Chuck Norris, 10) *Longstreet*, 11) *Birth of a Boy*, and 12) Fury.

And the winners (who will shortly be receiving a binder) were: Peter Love (1138), Pete Broad (1799), T.Stephens (1311), Keith Graham (1945) and Marlene Condy (1036).

THE NEW COMPETITION

As you all know, *Game of Death* is to be released on June 29th. Well, how about this? E.M.I, have offered 30 seats to Society members for a special preview to be held Sunday 25th June!!! Below, you will find a competition. The first 30 members to write in with the correct answers will be invited. Unfortunately this does eliminate our longest distance and foreign members, and that's a pity. I'd suggest that members who KNOW they CANNOT get to London, give the competition a miss this time. May I offer my very grateful thanks to E.M.I, for this great gesture. On with the competition! (sent in by Pete Broad - 1799).

1. Under what name was *Way of the Dragon* originally released in the USA?
2. Who played Parsons in *Enter the Dragon*?
3. What college did Bruce attend in Hong Kong?
4. What was the title of Bruce's first book (written in 1963)?
5. What was Bruce's father's full name?
6. What was the name of Bruce's great dane?
7. What did Bruce consider to be the "king" of exercises?
8. In what year did Bruce and Linda marry?

I'd say the last day for entries to arrive would be Monday 19th June so GET MOVING FAST! Send your answers ON A POSTCARD PLEASE to:- *KFM*, Society *Game of Death* Competition, 14 Rathbone Place, London W1P IDE.

CONGRATULATIONS

Member Graham Jenkinson and his wife have just become proud parents of a boy - to be called Lee. With that name, he can't go far wrong.

MEMBER'S PHOTOGRAPHS

I've had quite a few pictures of members, so from now on, I'm going to showing as many as possible in the news sheets.

AREA LISTS

Members numbered 2267 to 2302 will be receiving with this news sheet, the area list showing members of the Society living near them. Any members from 2302 on NOT wishing to have their name passed on to other members via a list, please write to let me know immediately so I can omit your names.

RENEWALS

Members from 2022 to 2084 - your membership falls due for renewal between June and the end of August. Don't forget to send in those subscriptions to get your fabulous second-year kit including the unique solid metal, gold and black enamel badge. Looks like it'll soon be time to start thinking about putting together the third year kit!

LETTERS

Dear Pam,

My friend here in South Africa is very willing to exchange stamps with overseas friends. Although he doesn't belong to the Society himself, he thinks he can help some of our club members. If anyone is interested, they can just send me their address and I will pass it on to him. And thank you for the kit - it really was a surprise.

Danis van der Merwe (2063)

Thank you Danis, and your friend, for the offer. I'm sure many members will be glad to take it up. The address to write is E. Transvaal, South Africa.

Dear Pam

I was very interested in the letter sent to you by member 1638, Richard Miller (re David Chiang's comments on Bruce). I have also got an article written on David over four years ago which is much like the one printed but somewhat twisted a bit. David did say, "Now that Bruce is dead I am ten times faster than anyone else." (Even the photographer admits he had to ask David to slow down for the photos). Also, David was asked how he thought he rated compared to Bruce. David's reply was, "Bruce was very beautiful," then he smiled and said, "But I am still alive." Also, David had already made a big name for himself in the East long before Bruce made Big Boss. *The only reason there are so few of David's films over here is that Shaw Brothers will not release them except to Shaw Theatres, which are mostly outside of the UK.*

Shiela Boardman (Official David Chiang Fan Club and Society Member 1763)

I've written back to Shiela to thank her for helping throw some light on the David article. Indeed, I told her I was expecting a letter from her, knowing she wouldn't let the letter go without comment! I don't dispute that David is a star in Hong Kong (and probably Japan, too), but only through Bruce was the East/West barrier bridged to the extent that everyone now has an interest in the Eastern film world. Bruce paved the way for others like David to follow. Shiela was also sad to inform me that her club is closing - due to her having been in hospital. I'm sure we all wish her a speedy recovery. I gather, too, that David will be coming to the UK later this year - more news on that when it comes. Also, Shiela has some stills/journals left which members might like to purchase. The journals are selling at 50p each. Anyone interested, write to Manchester. But no long letters please and don't forget to enclose a stamped and addressed envelope.

Dear Pam,

After the last news sheet, I thought it would be good if fans wrote about some of their more memorable Bruce Lee experiences. I can remember seeing Fist of Fury in London with a packed theatre who cheered, whistled and clapped whenever Lee appeared. I also went to see Marlowe, thinking that, as it was the second feature, everyone there had come to see the main film. But when Lee came on I heard people clap and shout, "There he is - that's Bruce Lee." An old Chinese man shouted Li Hsiou Lung and pointed at the picture on my T-Shirt. And only tonight in TV's Hong Kong Beat *the commentator referred to one H.K. village as,* "where Kung Fu and the spirit of Bruce Lee reigns supreme." So come on, let's hear about the good times! And what about the write up in TV Times about Marlowe that said, "Lee in fact steals the show" - not bad for a ten-minute performance!

Diane Webb (1073)

We all agree with your remarks, Diane. But I have to print the bad with the good - and quite often, as in your case, it prompts other members to write in and redress the balance. Actually, I can recall going to see *Marlowe*. The place was fairly packed, and after Bruce disappeared over the balcony my friends and I left. We were followed by nearly the whole cinema audience!

Dear Pam,

You may like to read some Game of Death *info from a Hong Kong magazine.* It said that over the last four years, ten scriptwriters have been used to complete Game of Death *and that 10 to 20 "shadow stars" were used to replace Bruce's body, expressions, actions, etc. One star is Chen Tao Po - he had no action scenes to do, he just stood quietly around. Another is Kim Tai Chung, aged 23 - an expert in Tae-Kwon-Do. He does do some action scenes. Neither actor wished their names to appear on the credits. Finally, Golden Harvest spent US$500,000 on the film.*

T.G.Symons (2243)

SWOP SHOP

- Mr. Sunil Sharma (2070), London has some 3" x 5" coloured stills from *Enter the Dragon* which he wishes to swap for other Lee stills/or sell. Send SAE for details with offers.
- Dave Goodwin (2025), Sheffield asks for any member having *The Ballad of Bruce Lee* LP (by Robert Lee) and the single of the theme from *The Water Margin*, please get in touch, with prices.
- David Coe (1440), North Shields has to sell (preferably in batch) three Bruce badges, *KFM's Game of Death*, an *Enter the Dragon* poster, *Bruce Lee, his Privacy & Anecdotes, Nunchakus in Action, KFM Scrapbook*, set of *KFM's* 1-30,

- total price, £8.00 the lot or nearest offer.
- Jeffrey Proctor (1815), Brierfield, has to offer, two 16 page scrapbooks (colour & B&W pictures), *Way of the Dragon, Fighting Stars, Deadly Hands of Kung Fu* No.s 4 and 14 (Bruce Lee), *KFM* No's 4-29, USA *KFM's* 2,5,6,8-10, *Karate Illustrated* (Bruce Lee), Chinese magazine on Bruce, *Best of Bruce Lee* No.2, hardbound *Bruce Lee 1940-1973, Bruce Lee, his Privacy & Anecdotes, Bruce Lee - King of Kung Fu*. All mint condition - offers?
- Miss Shane Phipps (1735), Chesterfield wants autographs of famous people, also wants *Best of Bruce Lee* No.1 and *Wisdom of Bruce Lee* and a signed copy of Danny Inosanto's book on Bruce.
- Al Briers (1828), St. Helens wants to sell, *Best of Bruce Lee* No.2, *Bruce Lee Tao* (soft) both in good condition. Also poster *Kung Fu* magazine (with Bruce and Chuck on cover in colour), a 10" x 8" glossy B&W from *Way of the Dragon*, cinema posters to *Chinese Vengeance* and *Chinese Connection*, soundtrack cassette to *Good, Bad & Ugly*, all soundtracks on cassette of Bruce's films including two hours of *Enter the Dragon* at £1.80 each. Dozens of Elvis recordings/interviews on cassette to swap for 1960/72 Elvis magazines. Pair hexagonal nunchakus with chain (medium weight) for articles on Clint Eastwood. Also wants *Elvis is Back* LP. Will pay/exchange for goods on Lee.
- Ralph Cansick (1189), Leicester has for swap, Bruce Lee films *Enter the Dragon, The Big Boss* - both for £10. *Way of the Dragon* for £25. Both sound and *Way of the Dragon* has the double nunchaku scene. He's interested in Japanese magazines.
- M.Nicolle (2278), St. Brelade, Jersey wants *Beginner's Guide to Kung Fu* - please contact.
- A.Delgoda (2105), Richmond wants to swap the following for anything on Elvis. *Bruce Lee King of Kung Fu* book, *KFM Super Kung Fu, KFM Scrapbook, KFM's* 25, 32, 37 (very good) 12, 11, 17, 3 (good) 8, 1 (fair). Write to arrange terms.
- Ian Hamilton (1213), Sunderland will swap *KFM's* 4-7, 9-11, 13-17, 21, 22, 25-27, 29-33 for the New English Library magazine *King of Kung Fu* or sell to highest bidder. Note - *KFM's* 5, 6, 7, 9, 10, 11 have ad removed from bottom of poster. Write sending SAE.
- Mr.K.Miller (1541), Chesterfield has for sale: *KFM's* 1-33 (£8 ono), *Tao of Jeet Kune Do* (£2), *Bruce Lee King of Kung Fu, Beginner's Guide to Kung Fu* and *Super Kung Fu*, 30p each, *The Holy Warrior Muhammed Ali* (40p) and he'll give away *Game of Death* to the first writer.
- Graham Jenkinson (1381), Huddersfield has for sale (preferably whole batch) *The Secret Art of Bruce Lee* - hardback (£3), *Bruce Lee King of Kung Fu* (£1), two sports magazines for 50p, 28 *KFM's* (not 1, 2 or 3. Also other magazines eg, *Fighting Stars* (incomplete), *Fighters Monthly* (featuring Bruce in *Fist of Fury*), *Fighting Arts, Bruce's Life and Death* in *American Marvel* magazine (£10 ono), two scrapbooks of cuttings from *KFM*/other magazines (£1 each), Bruce in poster from *Way of the Dragon* (nunchakus), (75p), press cuttings/photos by Linda Lee on Bruce in plastic folder (.35p), Will sell the lot for £16.50. Send SAE with 25p p&p for selected items or £1.25 if purchasing the lot.
- Paul Wade (1836), Hull has for sale, *Bruce Lee King of Kung Fu* book, *Legend of Bruce Lee* magazine, *Game of Death* magazine, *Inside Kung Fu Yearbook 1976* (with Lee articles), "Bruce Lee" *Fighting Stars* magazine, *KFM's* 33 & 34 and JKD magazines 1, 2, 4, 5, and 6. All for £7 plus 75p p&p. Also one pair of safety nunchakus - £1.50 inc p&p.

THE BRUCE LEE SOCIETY

- James ter Beek (2262), Leiden wants the soundtracks of all Bruce's films. Write with prices.
- Carl Jones (2121), St.Helens has stereo cassettes of *The Big Boss*, *Fist of Fury*, and *Way of the Dragon* (Japanese LP's) and *Enter the Dragon* music only. Will swap/sell. Also a B&W Super 8 movie (silent) called *Fists of Death* with Jimmy Wang Yu for sale/swap for other Super 8 film - what have you?

Left: Alex Bruce Buttigieg (2199) from Malta. Middle: Christopher Navas (1708) hailing from sunny Spain. Top Right: Another famous name, Mike Devereux (1061). Bottom Right: Eric Holden (1232), a dedicated Bruce Lee fan.

PEN PALS

- James ter Beek (2262), Leiden, Netherlands is 17, likes martial arts, Bruce Lee, weapon training, cinema, travel. Wants male/female pen pals 15 plus anywhere.
- Gary Anderson (2256), Bangor wants female Chinese pen pal who's interested in Lee. He studies Korean Art of Hi-Do Kuk Sool Won and likes physical fitness, basketball, fishing, hunting, writing short stories.
- H. Harry (2291), Durban, Natal, South Africa wants female Chinese pen pal. His interests are Bruce, pop music, Kung Fu - photo please.
- Mark Weeks (Non-Member), Bournemouth, has started a martial arts Pen Club and wants to hear from all boys/girls under 16 who are into the martial arts to exchange photos/letters, etc. Write to him direct.

Billy Holland sent the following list of names and addresses in. He says he's got

A RETROSPECTIVE LOOK AT BRUCE LEE MANIA & THE KUNG FU CRAZE OF THE 1970S

Billy Holland sent the following list of names and addresses in. He says he's got enough to write to already but he's promised them he'll try to get pen pals organised. Okay members, let's show what we can do!

- Wendy Kong, Perak, Malaysia - Chinese, aged 16
- Connie Liew, Sabah, East Malaysia - Buddist, age 19
- Estelitas Lee Oubiana, Manila, Philippines - Filipino
- Arlene Ang, Philippines - Filipino, age 22
- Juliano Chin, Sabah, East Malaysia - Chinese, age 18
- Josephine Fay, Sarawak, Malaysia - Chinese, age 18
- Charmine Ng, Jalan Ampang, Kuala Lumpur - Chinese, age 20
- Julie Tan, Manila, Philippines - Filipino
- Lesley Tan, Petaling Jaya, Malaysia - Chinese, age 20
- Daisy Aguilar, Manila, Philippines - Filipino, age 19
- Connie Chua, Sarawak, East Malaysia - Chinese, age 20
- Penny Tan Sai Tin, Sebesang Pesai, Malaysia - Malaysian
- Mr. Tarry Chyi, Pan-Chiao, Taiwan R.O.C. - Chinese, age 26

Well, I think that's about closed this sheet.

Don't forget the *Game of Death* petition to the censors and also, be quick to answer the new competition. I'll be back with the next news sheet in September - at the start of a third year with the Society!!!!! It really doesn't seem possible, but there it is. By the time I'm writing to you next, I expect most of you will have seen THE film. I'm sure I'll be getting a thousand or two letters about it as well!

Just time now for my usual reminder about joining the Society (if you happen to be reading this but happen NOT to be a member). The cost is still only £3.25 to join up with the world's greatest Society dedicated to the memory of Bruce Lee.

Bye for now... Pam

"BLIMEY, I WISH YOU'D WASH YOUR FEET!"

THE BRUCE LEE SOCIETY

EDITOR'S NOTES

Society President Pam Hadden accompanied *KFM* editor Felix Dennis to a special EMI preview screening of *Game of Death*. She mentions the Dan Inosanto and Kareem Abdul-Jabbar fights but states that the censors had cut the former from the film completely, leaving just seven or eight min- utes of Bruce Lee footage left in it. The cuts were in line with the BBFC's policy at the time, however, they would probably not have ordered the full fight sequence removed. It's completely plausible that the footage they did order to be removed, would have rendered the remaining footage incomprehensible. The version that Pam saw didn't include any footage of Bruce Lee fighting Ji Han Jae (Chi Hon Choi), the master of Hapkido but a review of another Society preview screening of the film in a later newsletter, the Ji Han Jae fight was included in the final release.

The *Dragon Power* single has been released on several formats over the years. Personally, I feels it sounds rather dated but if you still want to hear it again, here you go.

The *Silent Flute* is mentioned again, confirming that shooting  of the film commenced on 7th November 1978 and confirmed the  official casting of David Carradine, Eli Wallach and Jeff Cooper in the film. This is one of the perfect examples of how slowly word got around in pre-internet times. Every piece of information was effectively "drip fed" to the fans over a period of time.

A RETROSPECTIVE LOOK AT BRUCE LEE MANIA & THE KUNG FU CRAZE OF THE 1970S

09
SEPTEMBER 1978

WELCOME, EVERYBODY, TO NEWS SHEET NUMBER NINE - AND THE START OF THE THIRD YEAR OF THE BRUCE LEE SOCIETY.

GAME OF DEATH...THE LAST WORD!

First off, a few words of explanation regarding the competition I held last issue for the pre-release preview of *Game of Death*. You'll recall that 30 seats were available to us, but unfortunately, late delivery of news sheets meant I had to find another way of picking the lucky 30. Eventually I decided to send a brief letter to all members living in or around London - asking that they ring me at a particular time one evening if they wanted to go. As you can imagine, the phone went berserk! Anyway, on June 29 the big event actually happened. I was excited - if a little apprehensive - about meeting up with members, in fact we were all a bit subdued to start with. After seeing the film, however, all that soon changed!

Most members were utterly disgusted with the tragic censoring and many felt Raymond Chow and Robert Clouse should have used whatever footage there was on a documentary-type film of his life. In no way did anyone feel *Game of Death* to be a fitting tribute to the Little Dragon - especially with the changed storyline, the numerous flashbacks, the awful cardboard face-mask used in the dressing room scene, the repetitive kicking sequence in the changing room scene (with Bob Wall) and, sickest of all, the actual scenes from Bruce's Hong Kong funeral. The war cries of the stand-ins were described by some as more like alley-cats or air-raid sirens. Generally speaking, as a Kung Fu film it was not too bad. But this was supposed to be the Master's greatest and finest movie so what happened, Mr. Chow? Of course even among the bad there must be good, and that comes about 15 minutes from the end. Suddenly everything comes alive; stand-ins get forgotten and Bruce Lee rules. The Kareem fight is a knock-out. I was lucky enough to see the Inosanto battle before it got censored. Its replacement, the Master's confrontation with the Korean, Chi Hon Joi, I saw for the first time. I suppose you could compare *Game of Death* with *Marlowe* - both mediocre productions and neither worth a second look except when Bruce appears. After the film, several of us walked round London's Chinatown so it turned out a really nice day!

THE CENSORSHIP PETITION

There were nearly 4,000 signatures for *KFM's Game of Death* petition. Armed with these, plus a strongly worded letter, I arrived at the British Board of Film Censors' office in London's Soho Square. I half expected to be got rid of quickly, but to my surprise I was greeted more than courteously by Mr. Ferman, the secretary. My first point was regarding the reinstated *Way of the Dragon* sequences, to which, Mr. Ferman was surprised! He said that, to the best of his knowledge, nothing should have been put back at all. I said that, in my opinion, if the scenes HAD been replaced, then cutting similar shots from *Game of Death* was just ludicrous. I added too that there was nothing bloodthirsty or distasteful in any of Bruce's nunchaku fighting and it was pure artistry. Mr. Ferman checked the files and found no permission had been given for the *Way of the Dragon* reinstatement, leaving him feeling perturbed that illegal copies were being shown. I asked him not to look too hard! Why, I asked him, was the nunchaku scene in *Enter the Dragon* passed but the one in *Way of the Dragon*, censored. Apparently it was only after the release of *Enter the Dragon* (23rd October, 1973) that instances cropped up where kids started making their own weapons. (Mr. Ferman actually showed me a pair fashioned from stainless-steel, made by a ten-year-old schoolboy and they were lethal!) Therefore, public pressure for censorship didn't appear until after the release of *Enter the Dragon*. Luckily, it's not the policy of the censors to cut a film once it's been released. Actually, Mr. Ferman seemed quite interested in Bruce the artist. He professes great respect for his talents and emphasises there is nothing personal in the cutting of Bruce's films. I asked how films like *Hellfighters of the East* get through, with scalpings, stabbings with scissors and so on. Surely it would be far easier for someone to copy violent acts of that nature than for them to go to the trouble of making nunchakus? Mr. Ferman felt it would be impossible to remove all scenes with knives. I replied that censorship must be defeating its own object if some scenes are left in and others removed. Mr. Ferman agreed that was true but pointed out that if police, the authorities, and the public felt strongly about ANY particular type of scene, then censored it would have to be. He agreed too that Bruce Lee fans were suffering somewhat unfairly. Another point he brought up was that, even after reading my letter and checking all the signatures, there's no guarantee the Board would be able to effect changes, even if they wanted to. Their decisions can easily be overturned by local authorities. And apparently Bruce isn't the only star to be scissored, as in a recent Peter Sellers *Pink Panther* film, a nunchaku scene was removed prior to release. I paid my farewells to B.B.O.F.C. and thanked them for talking to me - Mr. Ferman has not a lot of spare time and rather a large quantity of letters from Society members to answer!

THE SOCIETY FILM
Arthur Stone, Will Johnston, Mick Zamiteas & Co.

Most members should know now about Arthur Stone's (1150) martial arts film project. Well, an awful lot of work went into casting, planning locations, arranging accomodation, adjusting holidays, etc and everything looked set. Unfortunately, human nature being what it is, several members decided to opt out at the last minute without letting anyone know. I'll refrain from passing comment, except that, let's hope the people concerned get the same treatment dished out to them one day. Anyway, undaunted, the remaining fifteen members carried on, but using a new storyline. The shooting took place around Barrow-in-Furness. There was persistent bad weather, forgotten lines, lack of film, missing batteries, lost film and so on but all in the end was completed. I'm looking forward to seeing the results from the cutting room. Arthur asks me to include the following statement:

> This summer the Society was going to make the first British-made movie, entitled The Travellers. Unfortunately we couldn't do the intended script, but after discussion, an alternative was decided on, which we think is a worthy substitute. There are some breathtaking martial arts action shots, an interesting storyline, plus fast-paced action running alongside.
> The synopsis is as follows: "Ken York and his friend, Walt, enjoy a well-deserved break from work. Walt buys a magazine and spots a picture of two gamblers, one of whom Ken recognises as the evil man who beat him up four years earlier. Ken goes looking for him and after tense confrontations, gets his chance. However, the gambler brings a mean-looking bunch of thugs with him. Can Ken and his newly acquired skills overcome the tremendous odds?"
> The cast is: Ken (Nick Giles), Walt (Will Johnston), Shimizu (Mick Zamiteas), Papa Byrne (Arthur), Dr. Takawa (Laura Bagguley), Jace (Andy Hill), Houseman (Gary Daniels), Hung (Hung Wan), Cordell (Paul Dean), Big Man (Glynn Barker), Girl in street (Rosa) and young boy (Norman Bagguley). Credits go to Arthur Stone (Producer), Will Johnston/Mick Zamiteas/Arthur Stone (Screenplay), Mick Zamiteas (Fight Arranger) and Will Johnston (Director).
> Finally, I would like to express my thanks to Mr. and Mrs. Johnston of Barrow for their gracious hospitality during filming. They helped make the project a very enjoyable experience, keeping cheerful while we cluttered up the home and generally got in the way. Mrs. Johnston gets my vote for Mother of the Year - thank you.

Thanks, Arthur, for that report and congratulations to everyone who finally took part for all your hard work, determination and for the fact you never gave up!

The Silent Flute

I was extremely lucky to be invited to a preview of this, the latest David Carradine film because, as you will probably know, it was originally the pet project of Bruce Lee. Written by Bruce and James Coburn, the movie starts with a tournament where head-strong Cord (Jeff Cooper taking Coburn's part) loses his final battle with Morthond, because of a foul blow. The winner has the chance to seek Zetan, the Keeper of the Book of Life. Various trials have to be tackled (parts of the film are much on the lines of a milder "Sinbad" fantasy, but all relevant to the storyline). Morthond loses his first encounter and asks the following Cord to continue towards Zetan. Cord meets with a blind man (David Carradine, in the part Bruce was to play) and is inspired by the man's highly developed senses as though blind, he seems to see everything and know all. Cord DOES reach Zetan and he does see the book. Do go see the film as I loved it and to my mind it's just the sort of thing Bruce was trying to do in his other films, but was unable to bring about.

Philosophy comes uppermost and it's a movie I shall enjoy seeing again. But don't expect the film to tell you everything as there are questions you'll have to answer for yourselves. Carradine handles the part well and something you may well be pleased about appears in the credits at the beginning, Bruce and James Coburn both get a "story by" credit - nice one! No one can take it away from the Little Dragon.

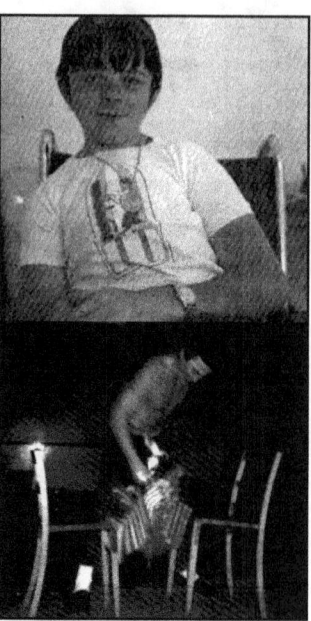

Top: Wesley Fleming (1935)
Bottom: Lee Squires (2315)

GENERAL NEWS

Space is precious this issue so I'll condense the news as much as possible. I mentioned last news sheet about *Enter the Dragon* gloves at the North London Martial Arts Centre being £10.50. However, I've since found out (Geoff Simmons - 1866) that they are in fact £26.50, and tracksuits £19.

Cimac at 606 Stratford Road, Sparkhill, Birmingham have the gloves at £23.95, rubber nunchakus at £8.95 and 2 superb posters of Bruce at £2.50 ea. Also there's *Memorial Monthly Magazines* at £1 ea. (John Hill - 2109).

Oriental World, 18 Swan Street, Manchester 4 and the Bruce Lee JKD Club of Hong Kong, Flat 9a, Sunny House, 268 Kings Road, North Point, Hong Kong have lots of stickers, *Memorial Magazines*, and other good magazines such as *The Immortal Dragon* and *Reminiscences of Bruce Lee*. Write to them for details. (Paul Short - 1164 and Michael Chow).

Stephen Whiteley (2202)

Ian Hamilton (1213) writes to confirm that Bruce Li's latest *Exit the Dragon, Enter the Tiger* is down to his usual standard. Apparently it's about him trying to find what happened to "his friend" Bruce Lee!!! Oh, no!

Jeff Millington (1127) says Regent Films have now the 400 foot colour/sound trailer with *The Big Boss, Fist of Fury, Way of the Dragon,* and *Enter the Dragon* on it - truly fantastic, he says. Also *The Big Boss* 400 foot colour/sound at £25.50.

Jeff also says that HMV Oxford St. have singles of all Bruce's film themes at about £2.50 ea.

Soundtrack & General is a name we've mentioned before. Well, I've been hearing from quite a few members that co-operation from this company seems thin on the ground - if not non-existent. The manager, Mike Jones, must have done pretty well from the business we've given him, yet I hear stories of him putting the phone down on enquiring members and handing out "rude remarks." They seem very keen to grab the money but less enthusiastic about giving good service. So, if you're wondering just where now to get those hard-to-come-by records of Bruce - DON'T WORRY! Member Eddy Pumer has the answer - he's recently informed me of a shop that not only has most, if not all, of the Little Dragon's recordings (including the singles mentioned above), they actually enjoy the hard work which Bruce Lee fans cause them! The company to contact is: Flyover Records, 15 Queen Carolyn Street, Hammersmith Broadway, London W.6 and the man to talk to is (he's going to love me for this) Lou Raynor. The telephone number is 01-748 1595. Thanks for the info, Eddy, let's hope we can continue to get the goods we need - plus service.

Martin Hughes (1687) informs me there was a comics convention in Birmingham and on May 27, the *Green Hornet* was shown.

Gary Stubbs (2186) says that Junequest Ltd., 748 High Road, London Ell 3AL have three Bruce, velvet-backed posters at £2 plus 15p p&p (UK postage). Picture codes are JQ BU 39/40/41.

Derek Hamer (1944) read that Bruce gave a lecture in 1969 on food and the martial arts. The write-up (in *Fighting Fit* by Malcolm Daniels) says: "Bruce, although having his own food concoctions, never ate any meats that were cooked but only ate them raw." As Derek said, he found this "rather hard to digest" (pardon the pun!) - thanks Derek.

Top: Al Briars (1828)
Bottom: Andy Hill (1443)

Mr. S.D. Collingwood (2241) would like members to know he has moved to: Salisbury, Rhodesia. He was in Portsmouth. I had a nice note from a non-member, Mr. M.

Taylor who sent me the picture reproduced here of Bruce's grave in Seattle. It's marvellous of him to have sent it and apparently, when he stood by the grave, he didn't know whether to laugh or cry. He was so happy to find what he had been looking for but then wondered to himself how the fittest man in the world could be lying there.

Rajendra Chandarana (1927) sent in a picture of Bruce idea for a door panel, priced at £7.15. It's certainly a novel idea.

LETTERS

Dear Pam,

I am a very new Bruce Lee Society Member - I think it's a good and interesting club. I enclose some copies of Danish adverts for films. Although he doesn't appear in any of the movies, they hope people will go and watch without realising it. I would like to obtain some of the British/other country's adverts of Bruce's films so can anyone help?

Heinrich Damsgaard (2125) from Denmark

Okay members, drop Heinrich a line (via me) and help him with his collection.

Dear Pam,

I was appalled at the censorship of Game of Death. I have great respect and admiration for Bruce, whose skills will never be equalled. What annoys me most, and I'm sure millions of others too, is that all the time and energy Bruce put into the footage and his devotion to see that all came out perfect is cut out by the censors. It makes me wonder if they know their jobs at all. Surely the argument is, if you don't wish to see it, then don't go and watch it. If people want to see Bruce's Kung Fu ability they should be allowed to do so.

Peter Thomas (1793)

I think we all agree with you, Peter and maybe someday soon, though, we'll be lucky enough to see all Bruce's film uncut.

Dear Pam,

I've got the record *Dragon Power* and I've never heard a record like it. It brings back memories of Bruce's films and it does have a great disco beat. When I first heard it I wanted to get up and act out what I'd seen Bruce do on the screen. When he talks, it's like he's in the room with me. His war cries send me crazy and I join in. I can remember first seeing *Fist of Fury* with my girlfriend and my stomach tightening with excitement as Bruce used his nunchakus. I nearly jumped out of my seat! It always gets us the same way, and no matter how many times I see him, it's always like the first time.

Andrew Clarke (2187)

MEMBER'S PICTURES

There are lots more photos of Society members in this issue... don't forget to keep sending them in. However, it's time for an apology to Wesley Fleming and Gary Chedgzoy whose photos appeared last time - but without captions (they fell off at the printers!). We'll be using stronger glue this time.

AREA LISTS

Members whose numbers run from 2085 to 2170 - remember your second year of membership is due for renewal between September and the end of November so send in early for you fabulous second-year kit. And members 1001 to 1627 - would you believe your THIRD year renewal is due at the same time? Just wait till you see the third year kit as there's some surprises!

SWOP SHOP

- Julian Midgley (1354), Perry Bar has for sale to the highest bidder (or swap for the *Best of Bruce Lee* No. 1) a copy of *My Martial Arts Training Guide to Jeet Kune Do* by James Lee.
- Michael Sanderson (1385), Washington, Tyne & Wear has posters (colour) from *Way of the Dragon*, *Fist of Fury*, and *Enter the Dragon* (2), also *Legend of*

- *Lee* colour cinema poster, 17" x 12" *Enter the Dragon* poster, B&W *Big Boss* poster, all pink *Big Boss* poster, *Enter the Dragon* cartoon poster. Also books *Legend of Bruce Lee* and *Bruce Lee, King of Kung Fu*, *KFM's* 5, 6, 8, 16-22 inc, 25, 27-30 inc, 32 & 40, *Dragons* 2, 7 and 12. Wants any old Elvis Presley singles and the *Book of Jeet Kune Do*.
- Roy Stannard (2314), Clapham wants *Dragon* magazines 1, 5, 6, 7, 9 and 10. Offering Vol 3, No.1 of *Dragon*, two B&W stills from *Enter the Dragon,* one B&W from *Way of the Dragon*, *Man from Atlantis* paperback (Death Scouts), plus £2.00.
- Rajendra Chandarana (1927), Hemel Hempstead wants members to contact him with any items on Bruce for sale or swap, to help his collection.
- Jeff Millington (1127), Islington asks that any member having the soundtrack record of the film *Sabata* starring Lee Van Clief, or can record it into cassette, please let Jeff know. He will either pay cash, or record the complete soundtrack with dialogue of *Enter* in exchange.
- Lee Squires (2315), Great Yarmouth has for sale, Kung Fu and Bruce Lee books and magazines. Also martial arts equipment for sale or swap. Please contact.
- Dale Bennett (2306), Walsgrave wants to buy the following: *Legend of Bruce Lee, Bruce Lee Memorial, Black Belt* No.1, featuring Bruce, *Deadly Hands of Kung Fu* Vol 1 No.28.
- Shane Phipps (1735), Chesterfield has *KFM's* 1-41 for sale, also blow-ups from *Enter the Dragon*. He can also produce prints from original picture of Bruce and John Saxon at the feast scene in *Enter* - 90p plus 10p post. (I've seen it, and it's good - Pam).
- Stephen Roberts (2290), Hull has *KFM's* 3-24 inc and 29. Also *Game of Death* special and *Clash* Vol. 1 numbers 1-6. Wants: pre-recorded cassettes, programmes, posters - anything to do with Deep Purple, Rush, or Rainbow.

"WHY CAN'T YOU WEAR THE PROPER UNIFORM LIKE EVERYONE ELSE?"

- Rick Edwards (1260), Coventry has plastic nunchakus at £1.25 each (2 pairs), karate, Kung Fu claw gripper at £2, *Bruce Lee Nunchakus in Action* - 60p, Japanese nunchaku poster - 75p, Dan Inosanto JKD wall chart - £1 each, *Hayward Mishioka Foot Throws* - £1.25, Howard Alexander, Quintin Chambers *Penjack-Silat* (hardback) - £2, *Doshinso Shorinji Kempo* (large hardback) - £7, *Bruce Lee's Fighting Methods*, Vols 1-4 at £2 each, *Tao of Jeet Kune Do* - £3. All the items are being offered at half their cost price.
- John Hill (2109), Liverpool wants to sell pair of rubber nunchakus for £6 (slight mark on the base of one stick).
- John Milne (2026), Glasgow wants Bruce Lee film posters, *Wisdom of Bruce Lee, Legend of Bruce Lee, Best of Bruce Lee* No.1, *Green Hornet Annual, Game of Death* film poster, *Cinema of Vengeance* by Verina Glassner, *Life and Tragic Death of Bruce Lee, Farewell to the Dragon*, the poster which was from *KFM* and was an artist's drawing of Bruce with a dragon around him, a picture of Bruce and the Green Hornet car. Has to offer: B&W picture of Bruce in *Way of the Dragon* and one from *Enter the Dragon, Exit the Dragon, Enter the Tiger* press books, *Black Belt* (August), *KFM's* 35 and 37, cassette recordings of *Way of the Dragon, Fist of Fury,* and *The Big Boss* soundtracks.
- Michael Hodson (1755), Birkenhead has to swap: 2two Billy Connolly stereo cassettes, *The Big Boss, Fist of Fury,* and *Way of the Dragon* press books (very rare) and Bruce Lee heavy medallion without a chain. Wants any 8mm Bruce film.

PEN PALS

- Carl Humpage (2326), Newcastle is aged 17, wants girl pen pal aged 16-18, interested in records and the martial arts.
- Alex Bruce Buttigieg (2199), Malta is after pen pals in the UK and from abroad. All who write will have their letters answered.
- Paul Kim, Franklin, USA would like any members to write to him. He's 15, Korean, and loves Bruce Lee, and in particular, watching *Enter the Dragon*.
- Alison Pickard (2299), Whitley Bay wants male pen pal about 17, who likes Bruce/disco dancing.
- Keith O'Hara (2076), Worcester wants Canadian/American male pen pal aged 12-24.

COMPETITION

As you already know, the last competition had to be abandoned (for reasons explained at the start of this news sheet). Here, however, is one for this issue and sent in by Mark Freeth (1081):

1. What year did Bruce enrol in St.Francis Xavier College?
2. Bruce Lee considered chopping wood with your hands an important martial arts training - true or false?
3. Who said of Bruce: "He didn't teach, he allowed you to. He would place you in a circumstance where you could evolve yourself."
4. What year was *Marlowe* made?
5. Who created the Green Hornet character?

  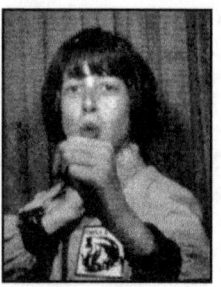 

Gary Daniels (2004)   Patrick Hennessy (1721)   Paul Brosnan (1621)   Richard McColl (1423)

Actually, there's one or two quite tough question there! Send your answers (on a postcard please) to: Society Competition No. 9, *KFM*, 14 Rathbone Place, London W1P IDE. Each winner will receive a 25" x 36" poster from *Game of Death*.

Well - that's it folks! Oh, in case any of you listen to Radio 4, did you hear my very brief (and I mean brief!) interview with Paul Hiney on the *Today* programme? It was at ten-to-eight one morning, some weeks back. I was praising up the record "Dragon Power," but I'm afraid my comments on *Game of Death* were not quite in the same category! Bye for now, see you in December ...Pam

(Oh, late P.S. - we've ten *KFM Scrapbooks* for competition prizes too! And, second thing, apologies but due to manufacture problems, the thirrd year kits are going to be a bit late).

BRUCE LEE SOCIETY COLUMN
KUNG FU MONTHLY NO. 43

Hi everyone, welcome back to the Bruce Lee Society news column.

First off, good news that not only is *KFM* giving away the 25 copies of *Dragon Power* by the JKD Band (last issue's competition), it looks like there'll be some more twelve inchers available for the September news sheet. Buy the way, I'm looking forward to hearing from you on your views of the record as I like it tremendously. It's quite cheered me up during the *Game of Death* problems!

As I recently reported, the Society film is now well on the way to being completed. About the time you read this, I'll be travelling up-country to meet the cast and film crew and, hopefully, to take some photographs. Providing they turn out okay, you'll be seeing the best of them in the next news sheet. It's really exciting that Britain's first real kung fu movie should be the brainchild of members of the Society.

I'm just getting overwhelmed with letters from members asking for details on where to buy copies of the various Bruce Lee albums that *KFM* has lately been reviewing. Please remember that in some cases, the LP's are quite rare so don't necessarily expect to be able to 'pop down the road' to your local shop and buy them.

Three addresses which I included in the last news sheet are worth repeating here: Soundtrack & General, 406 Brockley Road, London SE4; HMV, 363 Oxford Street, London W1R 2BJ; Magpie Records, Hopmarket Yard, Worcester WR1 1UR.

All these are certainly worth trying, but don't expect miracles as in many cases, they will only be able to order.

The petition response is looking very good. By the time you've read this I'll have delivered the results to the censor's office. I have to admit that I'm none too optimistic that they'll shift their ground, but you never know. At least they'll maybe just start to understand the upset, disappointment and wrath their action has incurred.

Something which I'd like to see happening soon is regional members organising local Bruce Lee events. I haven't finalised plans as yet, but the sort of things that come to mind are the hiring of films, collection displays, talks, and so on. There must be lots of other things you could do as well so how about writing in and giving me some ideas? Pam

BRUCE LEE SOCIETY COLUMN
KUNG FU MONTHLY NO. 44

Hi everyone, Pam here again with, this month, a report on the delivery of the *Game of Death* censorship petition.

On Thursday, July 13th, myself and photographer Rick Kemp, turned up on the doorstep of the British Board of Film Censors, armed with over three and a half thousand signatures. The bundle, plus several hundred words I'd written myself, were accepted most graciously by Mr. Ferman, Secretary of the Board.

We got to discussing the nunchaku battle in *Way of the Dragon* and Mr. Ferman made the point that, originally, the scene was included for general release. Apparently it was only after many complaints from the public, the police and local authorities, that the section was chopped out. It seems there were a number of instances of kids badly injuring themselves and those around them, with homemade varieties. I asked him why, therefore, the scene was now back in position. Mr. Ferman was surprised to hear the news! He said it must have been done without his knowledge and that any public showing of the reinstated battle was illegal!!! However, that said, Mr. Ferman admitted to being quite a fan of Bruce Lee and said he hated cutting anything out of the films.

I made the point that, if kids were mimicking Bruce in action by making and using nunchakus, surely that meant the "X" certificate system wasn't working? Why penalise serious fans of the Master because of a badly administered law? Furthermore, most of the public reaction took place some years ago, when Bruce had just died and the craze was still raging. Now, with a much more mature following, I can't see the same problem existing.

We also argued over where exactly the line should be drawn between violence that is acceptable and violence that is not. My feelings are very strong. How on earth can some of the more recent gory and bloody hackings, maimings and butcherings that all too frequently nauseate me when I go to the cinema, be acceptable? Yet a super-skilled display by the world's leading practitioner of an ancient weapon be unacceptable? I think he agreed that the whole business was very unfair indeed!

Mr. Ferman is putting the letter I gave him to the Board and the answer I receive will obviously be passed on as quickly as possible to you, the fans.

In the next news sheet, I'll include a much fuller account on the whole affair but let's just hope that, by then, the future for skilled, cinema martial action will be a good deal brighter!

Lastly, just take a look at the adverts page this month. The offer open for new members to the Society is absolutely stupendous! By the way, don't feel at all left out all you present members as there's something similar lined up for you in the next news sheet! *Pam*

BRUCE LEE SOCIETY COLUMN
KUNG FU MONTHLY NO. 45

Hello, Pam here again with this month's news and views on the world famous Bruce Lee Society!

To begin with, apologies all round to third-year members for the lateness in arrival of their new kit. I've tried to be ambitious and, unfortunately, we're paying the penalty in the amount of time it's taking. Hang on in is what I say!

Actually there's a good deal of re-working going on to make the various kits more standardised, and here's more or less what I'll be doing. The basis of it all will be special "Year Stickers" - which will follow the yin/yang design of the second-year brooches. Everyone, new members and old, will be receiving an updated version of the scroll, which will remain current all the time they're members of the Society, taking the place of any others they may have had. After each twelve-month period of membership, I'll be sending you the next year sticker to affix to the scroll in the area

From the collection of member Tony Lundbergh (2338)

shown. Easy, isn't it! And what's more, the new membership card you get sent on renewal each year will also carry the appropriate year sticker.

One particular aspect of the three-monthly news sheet that's growing in popularity is the "Member's Picture" section. Each issue now carries quite a few snap-shots, and it's great to see. Now, therefore, it would be a good moment to say a word or two about the sort of picture that will print the best. It needs to be clear and in focus and preferably with a fairly uncluttered background, such as a wall or the sky. Finally, and just as important, our design artist tells me that he definitely prefers to use black and white rather than colour. It's going to end up black and white eventually, so I suppose that makes sense!

After all the bad news, it's been refreshing to hear some good for a change. I'm talking about David Carradine's *Silent Flute* and, I've got to admit it, there was a time when David was my pet hate! Now I'm happy to say all is forgiven and in fact, he's really helped salvage the year of the *Game of Death* tragedy. After you've seen *The Silent Flute*, write and tell me if you feel the same way. How about sending in some local review? I've seen some good ones already.

That's about all I've time for this month. Remember, if you still haven't managed to find time to join our Bruce Lee Society, it's never too late. The subscription is still just £3.25 a year and the person to write to is me, Pam Hadden, at KFM, 14 Rathbone Place, London W1P 1DE.

See you next month! Pam

EDITOR'S NOTES

Thirty Society members embarked on a trip to see an early preview of Bruce Lee's final film *Game of Death* ahead of it's general release and they were extremely disappointed, with some being "utterly disgusted."

As reported in the previous issue, the censors demanded cuts to the Dan Inosanto fight and as the footage with just Bruce on his own and not holding nunchakus was minimal, the film company decided to completely cut the entire fight out. With the footage included in *Bruce Lee: A Warrior's Journey* and *Bruce Lee in G.O.D.*, both from 2001, its easy to see how little footage there is of Bruce without James Tien and Chieh Yuan or a pair of nunchaku in his hands. With the BBFC policy at the time, the only footage from that fight they would have allowed to be included would have been Bruce disarming Dan with the green bamboo cane and magically appearing on the next floor as all sight of the nunchakus would have had to be removed. So as not to cause confusion, the film makers removed the fight scene altogether but in its place, they put the fight with Ji Han Jae (Chi Hon Choi). It would take 23 years to finally see Bruce Lee's true vision for *Game of Death* via *Bruce Lee: A Warrior's Journey* and *Bruce Lee in G.O.D.*, and that true vision would only be a third of the completed film.

Some younger readers may not know of *Bruce Lee: A Warrior's Journey* and *Bruce Lee in G.O.D.* In 1999 whilst working for Media Asia, who at the time owned

the Bruce Lee titles after acquiring the company Golden Harvest, Bey Logan stumbled upon film cans containing original footage that Bruce Lee shot for *Game of Death* in 1972, just prior to shooting *Enter the Dragon*.
Logan approached then Bruce Lee Educational Foundation historian John Little, who, whilst sorting through and editing Bruce's papers into a series of books to form part of *The Bruce Lee Library*, happened across his original notes for *Game of Death*. John approached Warner Brothers, who green lit a project for American and Europe that would consist of a 60 minute documentary followed by 30 minutes of Lee's original footage, edited together according to his original notes which denoted the particular takes he intended to use in his final cut.  Even though Lee's notes stated which footage he would have used in the final cut of the film, that may have changed at a later date, had he lived. John therefore only cut the film according to how Lee would have cut it at the time he was working on it.

From Bruce's notes and photos, John was able to ascertain that the temple and pagoda Bruce was planning to use for the film was in Beopjusa (Popjusa) in South Korea. Armed with a film crew, John headed off to South Korea to make a short film of Lee's storyline to include in the documentary.

 Bruce Lee: A Warrior's Journey was released in 2001 and had its European Premiere at the "*Bruce Lee: A Warrior's Journey* Symposium" held by the Bruce & Brandon Lee Association at the National Media Museum in Bradford on 21st March of that year.

When John Little was making *Bruce Lee: A Warrior's Journey,* Media Asia also sold rights to the footage to the Japanese company Art Port Inc. for the Japanese market. Adopting a different approach to their film, director Toshikazu Okushi decided to create a docudrama which would feature a re-enactment of Bruce Lee's final year of his life, followed by a slightly different edit of the *Game of Death* footage. The reason for the different edit of the footage was that they had no notes to assist them in their editing of the film, so they had to take a guess at what he would have used. Due to not having the notes, they didn't know what the dialogue would have been. To obtain the dialogue, Art Port Inc. had  an individual attend the North America Premiere of *Bruce Lee: A Warrior's Journey* and secretly record the audio, to feed back to the film company so that they could complete their work. While the DVD is interesting, the actual footage they used ended up on the Hong Kong Legends' Platinum Edition DVD of *Game of Death*.

In this issue, Pam gave fans an insight into *The Silent Flute* after finally seeing it. It's the first time that Bruce Lee's philosophy is really mentioned in the newsletters and opened up fans' attitudes to a different side of their hero.

On the back page is a photo of a fourteen-year-old blond-haired boy named Gary Daniels (member 2004), who would later go on to become a professional kickboxer and successful action movie star. More about Gary later.

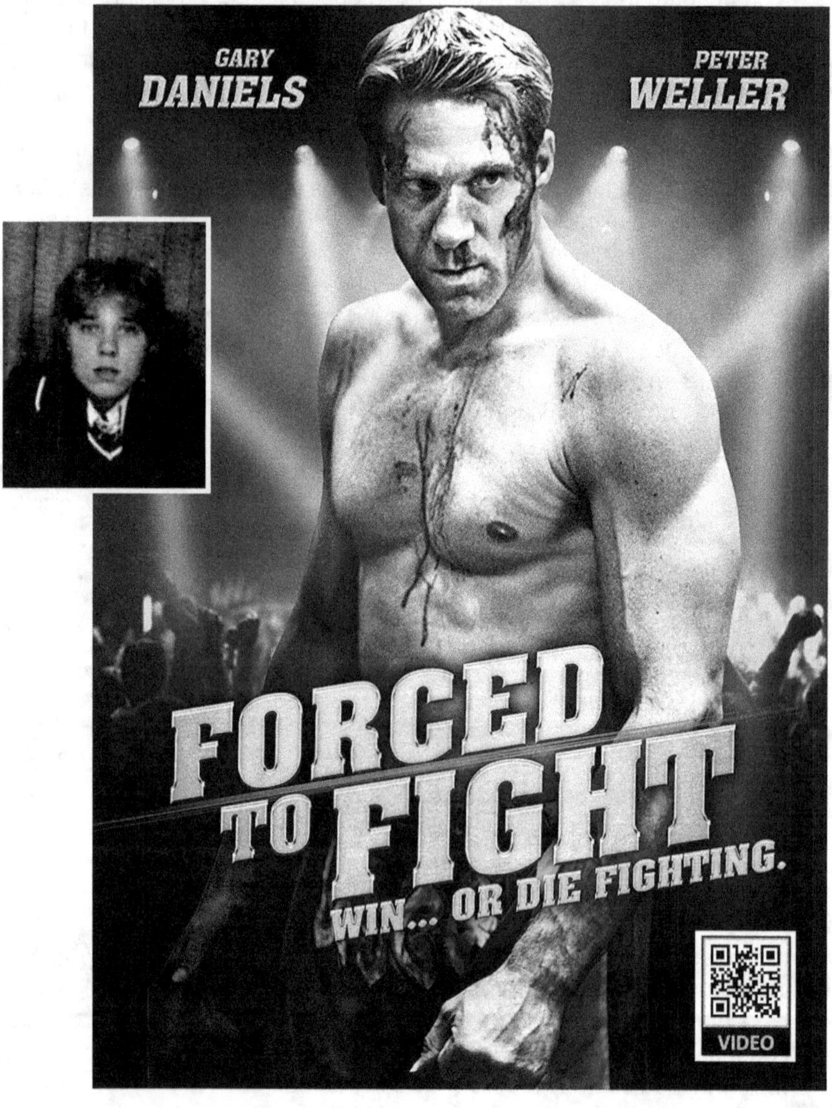

THE GAME OF DEATH
An Interview with John Little

John Little is a Canadian author and award-winning filmmaker. As well as writing several books on fitness, bodybuilding, and even a crime whodunnit, John was hired by the Bruce Lee Estate to compile and edit thousands of pages of notes into the highly regarded book series The Bruce Lee Library. *In addition to his written work, he has made several films including* Bruce Lee: A Warrior's Journey, Pursuit of the Dragon, *and the award-winning,* Bruce Lee: In His Own Words. *John's philosophical work on behalf of Bruce Lee was also documented in the 2020 film* Building the Bridge: The 2000 Bruce Lee Philosophy Lectures in Ireland.

How did you become a Bruce Lee fan?

I became a fan (slowly) after reading the first edition of *Fighting Stars* magazine, which had a special feature on *Enter the Dragon* and a profile on Lee in the issue. That stoked my furnace for wanting to see "his last film", which came to a local theater about three weeks after I read the issue. I saw the movie -- and went back and saw it repeatedly thereafter -- and that made me a fan to the point of obsession. My bedroom wall became a shrine to Lee, with posters covering every square inch.

John Little (right) with author James Bishop (left) during an interview with BBC Radio in September 2000. Courtesy of the Passionate Mind Institute.

At what point did you discover the philosophical side of Bruce?

In reading Linda's biography, which came out in 1974 or 1975, I believe. I bought it during a spare from high school and saw it on the shelf of a local variety store, took it home and devoured every page. She had included mostly his earlier philosophical writings (Tao, Yin-Yang), which represented my first exposure to such thought. I was fascinated by it.

Were you aware of the Kung Fu Monthly *magazines of the 70s?*

I was indeed. A friend of mine who was a big Bruce Lee fan and whose mother was English used to have copies of the poster magazine sent to him (along with certain of the books that Felix Dennis published on Bruce). I was amazed at the photos that appeared in the magazines (and of course the posters they unfolded into) and spent a lot of time at my friend's house pouring through them, even photocopying certain of the editions.

How did you originally obtain Felix Dennis' King of Kung Fu *book?*

It appeared one day on the shelf of a local bookstore (Cole's Bookstore, a franchise that usually could be located within most of the malls back in those days). I immediately purchased four copies of the book and read it repeatedly.

What did you think of Game of Death *when you first saw in in 78?*

I had mixed feelings the first time I saw *Game of Death* in 1978. I was hyper enthusiastic because it -- finally -- contained the never-before-seen footage from *The*

Game of Death that I (and millions of other fans) had long seen photos of and heard about. But there was something decidedly odd about it. It was almost a feeling that it was good to experience it (after attending several films such as *Goodbye Bruce Lee: His Last Game of Death* thinking that the footage would be included, only to find out that there was no footage of the real Bruce Lee at all in them), but perhaps it was the sign of a time that I had grown out of as there wasn't the same magic that attended the viewing of his other films. It seemed slower (even the fight scenes) and there were odd cuts in the editing of the film. Even then I could tell that they had used the same shot twice over (albeit zoomed in a bit). The intercutting of Bruce with other fight sequences with the look-alike also made me wonder if there simply had not been enough footage originally shot. I timed it many years later and (I think) the footage from the fight sequences featuring Bruce in that film totaled a little over nine minutes, but I had heard that he had shot 40 minutes that had then been edited and shown to certain of his colleagues. In short, I guess, I felt a bit disappointed.

When did you first become aware that the 1978 version bore no resemblance to Bruce Lee's original vision for the film?

Probably in reading the magazines from Hong Kong (or rather looking at the photos within them as I can't read Chinese), which featured photos of James Tien and Chieh Yuan, the latter of whom did not appear in the finished film and yet there were images of them with Bruce in certain sequences.

How did the footage and Bruce Lee's notes find each other?

John Little (left) gets a tour of the New Lodge area of Belfast with social worker Jim Deery (right) during a visit in 2000 to promote the philosophy of Bruce Lee. From the documentary Building the Bridge: The 2000 Bruce Lee Philosophy Lectures in Ireland. *Courtesy of the Passionate Mind Institute.*

I was tasked with moving all of Bruce's surviving materials (from his estate) from a storage locker to an office that Linda rented in Boise, Idaho. I purchased unassembled book cases and stocked all of his library books (according to topic) on the shelves, and moved in a few trunks of items (some clothing, some trophies, some equipment) and filing cabinets filled with papers that he had written or that he had collected, as well as several boxes of his writings, super 8 mm movie films, his old black and white backyard workout video tapes, etc. As I was trying to alphabetize and organize the papers, I came upon his scripts from his various films and discovered a file with all of his storyline and choreography notes (for the fight sequences he had shot) in amongst these papers.

I had tried to locate the footage in the mid 1990s once I found his script notes for the film. I took a flight to Hong Kong and set up an appointment with (I believe) Russell Cawthorne at Golden Harvest studios in an attempt to encourage the studio to locate it so that it might be restored in the manner that Bruce had originally envisioned. The fellow was polite but firm that it would be next to impossible to locate the footage as nobody at the studio was particularly nostalgic and, quite frankly, they didn't see any commercial possibility for the effort required to attempt to locate it. Then, in 1999, I was notified that Media Asia had found the footage (Bey Logan claimed to have found it but I believe it might have been sent over with a lot of other material that Media Asian had acquired from Golden Harvest) and they wanted to know if I would be interested in licencing it. It was found independent of the notes, of which only a few pages were released in the hope of stimulating interest in the search for the footage. The bulk of the notes remained in the filing cabinet and unknown to anyone but me and the estate at that time.

What gave you the idea of filming the storyline to The Game of Death *in Korea for* A Warrior's Journey?

Bruce Lee fans waiting in line to get an autograph from John Little at the Bruce and Brandon Lee Association's 2001 "Bruce Lee: A Warrior's Journey Symposium" in Bradford, West Yorkshire.

Bruce's script notes and photographs gave me the idea because a little research revealed that the photographs he had in his possession of the five-storey pagoda and giant Buddha statue were from a little village in South Korea. You can see that he had torn two pages from a (travel?) magazine out and pinned them on the corkboard wall of his office in Golden Harvest studios. Plus, when I read his script notes he mentioned that the location was Korea. All that existed were his notes for the concept of the story, some locations, some dialogue and the movement of he and the mercenaries upon the temple. All of the dialogue in the story line is verbatim from his script notes.

How was editing footage from The Game of Death *for* A Warrior's Journey? *What challenges did it present?*

No real challenges, as I was fortunate to be able to work directly from his original choreography writings, so I knew going into it what takes he wanted used, the sequence of shots and martial arts techniques and whatever dialogue he had written into the script. I suppose the only real challenge were the times in the footage when he had not written down the dialogue (such as when he yells out the window and another time when he is speaking to Dan Inosanto during their fight sequence). As he was speaking English to Dan, I even brought in my cousin who is deaf and a lip reader to try and decipher what he was saying, but she said she couldn't make it out. When he yelled out the window I had several Chinese friends attempt to read his lips and they unanimously concluded that he said the dialogue that ultimately went into the film.

A book written by John Little to accompany the Warrior's Journey *film.*

John Little (left) with Carl Fox (right) at the Bruce and Brandon Lee Association's 2001 "Bruce Lee: A Warrior's Journey Symposium" in Bradford, West Yorkshire.

I went off the script notes for the edits seen in the film. I actually brought the script notes with me to the studio as it was edited on DigiBeta, which looked like the console of the Starship Enterprise and was beyond my comprehension. The editing was done in Boise, while the foley was done in Los Angeles. I remember that we had a screening of the fight footage prior to the release of *A Warrior's Journey* at the seminar the Nucleus put on in San Francisco I believe. Evidently one of the people connected with Japan's *G.O.D.* release snuck a video camera into the screening in order to obtain the dialogue and certain of the edits for their version of the film -- or so I was told afterwards. It's interesting that nowhere in his notes are the names Betty Ting Pei or George Lazenby mentioned.

When I watch the film, what I noticed that clearly sets it apart from all other versions of the footage, is the uncorrected colours of the film.

Haha! Yes, I deliberately wanted the footage to be seen as it was; in the condition it was in when it was transferred from the original reels. I felt that adding something to it (as in colour correction or alteration) would make it less authentic. Same with the choice of music; it had to be similar to what might have been produced in that era (war cries too; I had to go through the films where he dubbed his own battle cries, check the technique he used a certain one with, the emotion of his character at the time, etc. Wherever possible I wanted it to be pure Bruce, as already by this point in time there were enough people asserting "how it should be done" into Bruce's legacy, when all the fans wanted was to see and hear Bruce without it being passed through anybody else's filter.

The Game of Death is very significant; not only because it was the last footage released but he was working in the film on the day that he died.

A RETROSPECTIVE LOOK AT BRUCE LEE MANIA & THE KUNG FU CRAZE OF THE 1970S

10 DECEMBER 1978

HI! TIME TO HIT OFF WITH THE 1978 CHRISTMAS NEWS SHEET...

AN APOLOGY

Firstly, I must apologise about the late arrival of the September news sheet. Due to various production difficulties and although written by the end of August, it didn't come ready for distribution until mid-October. Also, poor time-keeping by several manufacturers was the reason for the late arrival of the third year kits. By now though, all should be in order!

BRUCE LEE CONVENTION

Yes, you heard it right! To celebrate the Society entering its third year and also *KFM* reaching its 50th edition, plans are very much afoot for a May 1979 convention. Nothing's been finalised as yet and, as you can imagine, there's lots to be organised. Still it really would help if we could get some idea of how many fans would turn up. Obviously the success of such a venture depends very much upon just that... say, 200 for a minimum. So, no buts or maybes - could I have a clear-cut *yes* or *no* from as many of you as possible.

The cost of entry looks like it will fall in the region of £3 and attractions would probably include: two of Bruce's films, Chinese food, stalls selling magazines, books, equipment, films and records, a martial arts display, *live* Chinese music, competitions and a talk by a film company representative.

Those interested, would they please send me a card that says, "I would be interested in attending the Bruce Lee convention" - remember to include your name, membership number, and address. Check in *KFM* for details of buying tickets, etc. Also, remember if you live some way from London that a BR Weekend Return can work out reasonably cheap and the event will almost certainly be held on a Saturday. For now, though, bear in mind that all I want is a postcard telling me that you'd come. Mark it Bruce Lee Convention.

THE SILENT FLUTE

Following on my write-up in the September news sheet, I started wondering why we'd heard nothing more since its three-week showing in the West End of London. I rang the distributors and asked them why it had vanished from the scene. They told me it would soon be on general release and it was just waiting in the pipeline. I'll give it until January before I start shouting again!

GENERAL NEWS

Alan Mount (1109) tells me there's a major martial arts film star about to burst onto our screens. He's the American Karate Champion, Joe Lewis and his first film *Jaguar Lives* is scheduled for 1979. Word is that Joe is expected to hit the same heights as John Travolta. Alan seems convinced but I'll keep an open mind!

Gary Daniels (2004) wrote recently to the Mantis Supplies Co., in Los Angeles (in response to an advert), but received in reply a card which said: "We regret to inform you that we do not have any Bruce Lee items available. Due to legal restrictions from the Lee family, all Bruce Lee products have been discontinued." It seems that the legal net that's been threatening many organisations dealing in Bruce Lee material is starting to tighten but let's hope these restrictions are lifted soon, so that fans are able to continue their collections.

If anyone knows of shops in the area of Stretton, Derbyshire that sell items on Bruce, would they please inform: Lorraine Smith (2320) at Stretton. Contact direct, please. Lorraine also sent in a picture of a friend copying Bruce's *Enter the Dragon* stance as apparently, he's a big fan.

Will Johnson (1056)   Tim Stephens (1311)   Paul Das (2313)   Antwan Lombarts (2146)

Chris Cadman (2368) thinks that a competition to find the member with the best Bruce Lee collection would be fun. It would, although also very difficult to organise! However, why don't you meet with other members in your area and decide amongst you who has got the number one collection? Then, when you've decided, let me know the result (including a rough tally of the items). A photo of the winner, plus their collection, would make it even better. Maybe if I get enough response, we could hold some sort of national *final*.

Carl Jones (2121) wrote to, and received a reply from, Golden Harvest in Hong Kong. They told him that *Game of Death* ran for 106 minutes originally but that it was censored down to 94 minutes on release. I've heard news that Golden Harvest and EMI hope to reissue *The Big Boss* and *Way of the Dragon* before the end of 1978 so they're going to have to move fast!

Neil Devine (2325) tells me that on Radio 2 (200KHZ/1500M) they run a feature on Monday/Thursday nights at 10.00pm called *Star Sound*. The programme plays listeners requests and sometimes clips from films. He suggests that members write direct to: *Star Sound*, BBC, London W1A 4WW (postcards only), requesting a clip from one of Bruce's films. So come on, lets see the BBC snowed under with requests and maybe when they see how many people are interested, they might show something proper on TV. It's up to you.

Another address that Neil gives (for those living in and around the Newcastle-upon-Tyne area) is: Giles Squire Soundtrack, Metro Radio, Newcastle-Upon-Tyne, NE99 IBB. They have a soundtrack request programme on Monday nights at 10 o'clock. Write to them and tune in to 261MW/97VHF.

Andrew Staton (1670) says that Danny Inosanto has written a book on his Phillipino art called *Kali Training*.

James DeMile (one of Bruce's students) has written *Tao of Wing Chun Do* and *Bruce Lee's One-Inch and Three-Inch Punch*, describing how the Master used his close-quarter punches. These books would seem to be only available in the States but if anyone knows where to find them over here, please let me know.

Also, Bob Wall's *Who's Who in the Martial Arts* (published by Mantis) sounds interesting so anyone seeing copies, let me know.

I also gather from Andrew that Yip Man's sons have released a book with demonstrations by Yip Man and pictures. More info on that too, please.

Kate Feeney (1194) is looking for ladies Kung Fu slippers in her area. She lives at Glasgow.

If anyone can help her, contact direct. Michael Hodson (1755) tells me that recently he went to his local Birkenhead ABC cinema to see *Enter the Dragon* with *Death Race 2000*. They had some smashing *Game of Death* posters on sale for 75p and there's more coming. Michael also tells me that *Enter the Dragon* had to be retained for an extra week so that should shut-up the knockers!

Julian Midgley says he bought *Wisdom of Bruce Lee* from a shop called Nostalgia and Comics, 1 Hurst Street and 4-6 Hurst Street, Smallbrook, Ringway, City Centre, Birmingham 5, Warks.

There's a poster shop for Bruce pictures at Mail Order Promotions, 22 Moor Street, Queensway, Birmingham 4.

I hear too that the *Game of Death* LP is now available from Magpie Records, Hopmarket, Worcester.

Ian Hamilton (1213) and Carl Jones both say that Jerry Ohlinger's Movie Store at 120 West third St., New York, USA have Bruce's original *Green Hornet* screen test on film BUT, and you're going to hate me for this, only on 16mm. Some you lose, some you win!

Carl also says that Golden Harvest have given him the following running times for Bruce's films: *Big Boss* uncensored 104 minutes, UK release 98 minutes; *Fist of Fury* 104 minutes and 104 minutes; and *Way of the Dragon* 98½ minutes and 91 minutes. I honestly can't see where they get their *Fist of Fury* timings from, as after all, the censored love scene lasted five minutes! Carl also says that Golden Harvest use the same colour notepaper as the Society - fame at last!

William Longson (1947) has recently had a nameplate put on his house - it says "LEE NOVA" meaning new star. I rather like that! Perhaps I ought to put one outside my place saying "Bruce Lee" in Chinese. My neighbours already think I'm round the bend, so that should clinch it!

David Niedzailek (1021) gives the following address: Simonds, 28 Woodstock Road, London N.4. They do stills on Bruce, and also have the Japanese book import that's full right through with pictures. I already have a copy (some of the pictures are really unique). The price is £10. There's also a deluxe edition with different pictures (and quite incredible) costing £12. If you send Simmonds a 25p postal order plus large SAE they'll send you lists. Really, the Japanese books are two of the best I've ever seen.

Ian Hamilton (1213) sent in the advert shown here of Bruce Li's film, *Fist of Fury Part 2*. Ian feels the same way as most of us do about this so-called actor and the bit that gets us is the "new master" - who are they trying to kid? They either need psychiatric help or a visit to the opticians.

Mick Bargota (1522) was watching the programme *The Professionals* one night and was amazed to see in a scene set in a room with a dart-board, a picture of Bruce in a clip from *Way of the Dragon*. As different parts of the country are probably at different instalments I suggest keeping eyes peeled to catch it.

Some weeks back I saw *The Wrecking Crew* (a Matt Helm film starring Dean Martin), and in the credits at the beginning it said, "Fight/Karate Advisor, Bruce Lee." Actually it isn't quite true that I watched it. I caught the opening credits - then turned over as I'd seen all I wanted!

From Antwan Lombarts (2146)

In the last news sheet I included some adverts sent in by Heinrich Damsgard (2125) from Denmark. Now, Antwan Lombarts (2146) from Holland sends more. It's always great to have things come in from overseas.

I gather from Paul Marks (2346) and from other members that during a recent *World of Sport*, a clip from *Game of Death* was shown of Bruce fighting Jabbar. Paul tells me that Dickie Davis was talking with much respect for Bruce Lee but then they showed a clip of Bruce Li which was so far-fetched and embarrassing, even Dickie and the crew behind him were laughing. A very intelligent bunch of people!

Also, Neil Devine (2325) says that on *World of Sport* they showed a clip from *Silent Flute* and said that, far from Bruce's popularity dying down, it's on the increase!

Another foreign member, Hasan Karatas, sent in two snippets advertising *Flute*. Actually, now would be a good time for me to thank all you members for constantly sending in the information because it keeps the news sheet flowing.

Gino Crane (1978) has sent me quite a few pictures of Bruce over the months which I thought very good. Gino, like me, was a Presley admirer too so he's done a sort of two-in-one picture with El's head and Bruce's body!

From Ian Hamilton (1213)

Last news sheet we had a picture sent in by Malcolm Taylor (now joined, 2434) showing Bruce's grave. Now, one of our older members (in length of membership, not age!), Mike Devereux (1061) lends us a picture of the grave taken before the headstone was added. It's a pretty unusual picture and the two of them together make a rare "before and after" sequence.

Now to Keith Graham (1945) who tells me that "Sports Emporium" of 35 St. James Centre, Edinburgh, Scotland (Tel 031 556 3244) sells terrific martial arts equipment and Bruce Lee material as well.

Another good place to try, says John Latto (2196), is "Bruce's Record Shop" (that's a good start in itself!) at 46 High Street, Kirkclady, Fife, Scotland. They stock Bruce records and badges at 40p ea.

Mark Salter (1792) gives the following info for getting hold of nunchakus like those used in *Game of Death*. "Asian World of Martial Arts" at 4519 N.Broad St., Dept BBC6, Philadelphia, PA 19140, USA has them in stock at $12.95.

Joe Chiang (1044) tells me he has been having great difficulty getting any satisfaction from a certain P. Tobby of 34 Lindrop Street, Fulham, London SW.6. He warns not to send money under any circumstances! He also warns of Kung Fu Inc., PO Box 29164, Rio Piedras, Puerto Rico 00929, USA.

"ITS THE SAME EVERY-TIME HE WATCHES KUNG-FU ON THE TELEVISION!"

Paul Short (1164) says there's a *Game of Death* LP by John Barry which is music only (including that heard over the Inosanto fight sequence). The record has a free *Game of Death* poster, the number is YX- 7037 and it's distributed by TAM CAM. Contact Flyover Records at 15 Queen Carolyn Street, Hammersmith Broadway, London W.6 or Magpie Records at Hopmarket, Worcs. (The record gets a review in *KFM* 47). Well, that, I think, exhausts the general news so on to the next course!

SPECIAL MESSAGES

Three for this month but remember, any members wanting to pass on messages to friends, loved-ones, etc - this the place to do it!

Gary Daniels wishes to send his sincere thanks to Will Johnston, Arthur Stone, Mick Zamiteas and the rest of the cast of the Society movie. He thoroughly enjoyed meeting you all and looks forward to further link-ups in the future.

Andrew Aylett sends the following message to member, Margaret Smith: "Thanks a lot for the great things you're doing to make my Bruce Lee collection grow bigger all the time."

Lastly, Paul Shepherd has a special message for his girlfriend who, not being a Bruce fanatic, has obviously to put up with quite a lot! "Kim - thanks for putting up with me and Bruce. You're the best! Love, Paul."

no. 6700.
EURASIAN ROMANTIC a la Bruce Lee seeks attractive aware lady (26-30) for fruitful relationship. Newcastle upon Tyne area. Photo. Box no. 6699.

Sent in by Ian Hamilton (1213)

AREA LISTS

For those not already in the know, when I send out your second news sheet, you'll also receive a list of members living in and around your area so you can contact each other, and link up. Therefore if you come across a strange looking list of names and addresses, you know what to do with it (in the nicest possible way!).

RENEWALS

Members from No. 2171 to 2266 inclusive, remember your second-year membership falls due for renewal between December 1978 and the end of February, 1979. Get those applications off in time or you'll be missing a great kit. And third year members, you fall due for renewal in the same period numbers 1628 to 1828 inclusive). You'll find the third-year kit is amazing!

CHRISTMAS CARD/GENERAL CARD

Along with this news sheet you'll also be receiving a greetings card from the Society. If any of you would like to purchase these for general use throughout the year (to send to friends, and so on), write in and order them direct from *Kung Fu Monthly*, Society Card Offer, 14 Rathbone Place, London W1P IDE. They come with envelopes and cost £1 for 10.

LETTERS

Dear Pam,

I think there is something sad about Game of Death *and I feel there may be some sort of curse over it. Why, you may ask? Well, four people connected with it have died. First Bruce, then, last year, his original co-star, Chieh Yuan (who was to be his aide, along with James Tien) died in similar circumstances to Bruce, in his early thirties. Now we have the sad news that Gig Young and his wife Kim Schmidt (Gig playing Bruce's friend in* Game of Death *with Kim having a small, non-speaking part and also working as a technician), both are gone. What do you think about it, Pam?*

Carl Jones (2121).

Well, Carl, I must be truthful and say that when I read about Gig and his wife, my first thoughts were on a similar vein to your own as it did seem odd. I was especially interested about Chieh Yuan and that's something I'd like to know more about. Actually, jinxes on plays/films are not unknown. Some years back a play closed in London because of unusual happenings on stage and accidents, etc. Maybe it's all coincidence, but who knows?

Dear Pam,

I recently saw Game of Death *and what stood out immediately were the cat-like noises dubbed over both where Bruce and the doubles were fighting. Didn't Bruce make his own soundtrack? Overall, I thought it a good Kung Fu film that gradually got better, plot-wise, with more fighting power towards the end. I had difficulty, however, in adjusting to the lead character, Billy Lo because for some reason, I expected him to be called Bruce! However, as "one of Bruce Lee's greatest films" I think it was really just another excuse to use his name, however much they keep on splicing him in. A Bruce Lee film can only be of the Master himself.*

Author Unknown

The only film of Bruce's containing his own voice was *Enter the Dragon* - all Chinese films are dubbed, with the soundtrack not recorded at the time of filming. I suppose there must be a good reason for this, although it seems pretty pointless to me. Maybe it gives employment to out-of-work actors! So, as far as I'm concerned, it's far better hearing the original voices with the film, especially when it's Bruce's.

COMPETITIONS

Well, are you all asleep out there? Would you believe I only got back 13 competition answers to the September quiz!!! You should be ashamed of yourselves!

Anyway, the answers were: 1) 1956, 2) False, 3) James Coburn, 4) 1968, 5) Gene Trendle.

One thing, although Gene Trendle created the character of the Green Hornet, William Dozier did the TV series. There were only four, all-correct entries and I picked two of the remaining cards naming Dozier - but with the rest of the questions properly answered. The lucky winners, who'll be receiving a *Game of Death* poster are: John Kemp (1729), Gary Nash (2324), P. D. Booking (2206), Brett Morgan (1030), Gary Daniels (2004), and Marlene Condy (1036).

A RETROSPECTIVE LOOK AT BRUCE LEE MANIA & THE KUNG FU CRAZE OF THE 1970S

This news sheet competition should be a pretty easy one. In fact the ideas came from two members, Kay Drummond (1195), whose competition I'm using here and John Tandon (2092), whose entry I'll be using at a later date.

All you have to do is search the square to find the names listed and to show what I mean, I've already done three for you. All the words run in straight lines, either up or down, side to side, or corner to corner. Just circle the words when you find them, do a copy of the square (or cut it out) and send to the Bruce Lee Society at 14 Rathbone Place, London W1P IDE (and that's postcards only, please). The prize will be a 12" copy of the special edition, numbered, *Dragon Power* record.

1. 'Big Boss'
2. Bruce Lee
3. Brandon
4. 'Enter the Dragon'
5. 'Fist of Fury'
6. 'Game of Death'
7. 'Green Hornet'
8. Gung Fu
9. Hong Kong
10. Kato
11. Linda
12. 'Longstreet'
13. Nunchaku
14. Shannon
15. 'Way of the Dragon'
16. 'Marlowe'

SWOP-SHOP

- Keith Graham (1945), Edinburgh wants to buy LP soundtrack to *Way of the Dragon* - perfect condition, high price paid.
- Paul Wade (1836), Hull has for sale: *Dragon Power* record (special 12" edition), Enter the Dragon LP, *KFM's* 1, 4, 5, 6, 7, 13, 15, *Bruce Lee - Secret of JKD & Kung Fu*. Asking £8 inc p&p for the lot (all very good condition). Will sell separately - write.
- Michael Sanderson (1385), Washington has for sale *KFM's* 1-3, 5, 6, 8-10, 16-22, 25, 27-30, 32 and 40.
- Derek Crane (1064), Wirrel has for sale: *Way of the Dragon* super-eight film (400') running time 22 minutes and containing the double-nunchaku sequence and other cut footage - usual cost is £50, Derek wants £38 (colour and sound). He's also selling super 8/400'/24 minutes, non-stop fighting *Fist of Fury* - no sound, £27. Buy both films and you've saved £58!
- Paul Marks (2346), Burton-on-Trent has the following films for sale: Telygoons *Ascent of Everest* on 400' spool, Telygoons *Napolean's Piano*, 400' spool (both black & white/sound). Will swap for any Bruce Lee 8mm film - preferably *Enter the Dragon* or *Way of the Dragon* on 400' spool/sound. Also has three different *7th Voyage of Sinbad* B&W, silent, 200' spools and 2 x *Jason and the Argonauts*,

THE BRUCE LEE SOCIETY

200,' B&W, silent. Also Kung Fu film, *Fists of Death* (Wang Yu), 200' spool, B&W, silent. Also *Frankenstein Must Be Destroyed* on 200' spool, silent and B&W. Finally, *Curse of the Mummy's Tomb*, 200' B&W, silent. Swap for any one of Bruce Lee films on 400' spools, sound.

- Molly Cullen (1749), Blackwood wants copy of *Legend of Bruce Lee* by Alex Ben Block. Please write.
- William Black (2388), Glasgow wants tapes on Bruce's films/interviews, etc. Also copy of *My Martial Arts Training Guide* by James Lee.
- Dale Bennett (2306), Coventry wants the Bruce Lee mug (offered some years ago by *KFM*), *Black Belt Magazine - Best of Bruce Lee No. 1*, *Way of the Dragon* soundtrack, Bruce Lee calendar, *Life and Tragic Death of Bruce Lee* by Linda Lee (with pictures intact!).
- William Longson (1947), Blackpool urgently wants any items on Bruce as all his were stolen from his home recently. Write with items/prices.
- Colin Lindell (2352), London wants copy of TV theme to *The Incredible Hulk*. Alison Pickard (2299), Whitley Bay wants *My Martial Arts Training Guide to Jeet Kune Do*. Janet Ramsey, Colchester wants *The Life and Tragic Death of Bruce Lee* by Linda.
- Andrew Staton (1670), Leeds has many items for sale - write with SAE for list. Andrew wants cinema posters to *Fist of Fury, Enter the Dragon* in good condition and will pay £1.50 each.
- Jeffrey Proctor (1815), Brierfield has for sale: *KFM's* 4-29, *Privacy & Anecdotes*, *Dragon* Vol. 1 No. 13 & 14, Vol. 2 Nos. 1, 2, 3, 5, 6 and 8, *Defence & Combat* Aug. '75, *Official Karate* - June, Aug, Sept, Nov '75 and Jan '76, *Black Belt* '75-'76 - Feb, Sept, Nov, Feb, May, *Karate Illustrated* Sept '74, Dec '74, Jan '75, *Oriental Fighting Arts* June '75, *Martial Arts International* Vol. 1 No. 3, *Inside Kung Fu* Vol. 1 Nos. 9-12, Vol. 2 Nos. 1 & 2. All perfect or good condition. Cost £19 - will sell for £10 plus p&p.
- Colin Joelson (2377), Liverpool, wants tapes of Bruce's films/interviews etc., except English version of *Enter the Dragon*. Also wants colour stills of Bruce's films, and *Best of Bruce Lee No. 1*.
- Neil Devine (2325), South Shields wants *Bruce Lee - The Man Only I Knew* by Linda. Also wants *KFM's* 1-40 and offers £10, but must be in very good condition.
- Mr. C. Carruthers (1011), Carterton has the following for sale: *Bruce Lee, King of Kung Fu* - 60p, *Combat* No. 7, Vol. 4 on Bruce Lee - 20p, also No. 8 *Enter the Dragon* - 20p, *His Unknowns in Martial Arts* - 60p, Bruce Lee's *Game of Death* - 30p, *Fighters Monthly* Nos. 1, 2, 3 & 4 - 20p ea, *Exciting Cinema Kung Fu* (52 pages) - 25p, *Fighting Arts* Vol. 2 No. 2 on Bruce - 10p, *Combat* Vol. 1 No. 8 - 10p, *The 9th Annual Yearbook (Bruce Lee)* - 30p, *Clash* No. 1 1/3 & 1/2 - 10p ea, *Dragon* Vol. 3 No. 2 - 10p, *My Martial Arts Training Guide to JKD* - 30p, *Kung Fu '75* No. 1 on Bruce - 15p, several *Black Belts* at 10p ea, *Nunchakus in Action* - 60p, *Combat* Vol. 4 No. 6 - 20p, *The Pictorial Guide to the Martial Arts* - £1 (cost £2.25), *Official Karate* April/August '75 - 10p ea, *Black Belt* June '74 - 10p, *KFM's* 3-41 inc. at 13p ea. Send stamp with order.
- John Milne (2046), Glasgow wants the *Green Hornet* car (Corgi) desperately! - also the *The Green Hornet* annual.
- Hasan Karatas, Istanbul, Turkey has for sale: *Bruce Lee's Fighting Method Vol. 1* and *Wing Chun Kung Fu* by James Lee - would like to swap either for *Bruce Lee's Fighting Method Vol. 4* or sell for £3.50 ea. Also has *Tao of Jeet Kune Do* to swap for Danny Inosanto JKD book or sell for £3.50 (prices include p&p).

A RETROSPECTIVE LOOK AT BRUCE LEE MANIA & THE KUNG FU CRAZE OF THE 1970S

- Hugh Lagan (1218), Belfast, Northern Ireland wants all soundtracks & cinema posters of Bruce's films.
- Mr. R. Opie, Lanarks has to sell American film trailer (200') super 8 colour/sound featuring *Lightning Swords of Death, Triple Irons* (David Chiang), *Five Fingers of Death, Lady Kung Fu*. The film is new and cost £17.50 - will accept £10 from any member.
- Will Johnston (1056), Barrow-in-Furness has for TRADE ONLY (not selling): all fights from Bruce's films on 8mm (except beginning boxing from *Enter the Dragon* and Jabbar from *Game of Death*), stereo cassettes of Bruce in *Ironside* (1965), *Marlowe* (1969) and *Hong Kong Radio* (1971). Also all Lee films, 304 colour slides/prints (guaranteed unpublished) from all films except *Big Boss*, unique 1979 calendars (only five made), one set of glass mats depicting scenes from *Enter the Dragon* (only six made). Wants: Absolutely anything Japanese, Hawaiian, German, etc - in fact all countries - especially magazines. Write to Will - no SAE's needed.
- David Henderson (2462), Dundee wants all *KFM* books, plus also original film posters from *Way of the Dragon, Big Boss, Enter the Dragon, Legend of Bruce Lee*, etc. Needs *Best of Bruce Lee No. 1* and any other books on Bruce/Taoism - also press books on Bruce's films and collector's specials. Cash.
- Mr. P. Inglesfield (2424), Egremont wants urgently: Carmah Kendo trousers (very baggy, in black).
- Gerard McNamara (1382) Hammersmith has to sell, set of 5 16"x8" B&W prints of Bruce for £3 (any two for £1.50 (inc. p&p). Details of enlargement given if you send SAE (they're great, I've seen them - PAM).
- Paul Short (1164), Sheffield has a 12" *Dragon Power* single - offers? Also soundtrack to *Man from Hong Kong* - offers?
- Paul Marks (2346) Burton-on-Trent is looking for the poster of Bruce (from *Enter the Dragon*) - waist up, angle shot, holding nunchakus in front of him.

"I'LL BE GLAD WHEN YOUR DAD GETS OVER THE KUNG-FU CRAZE!"

- Paul Das (2313), Middlesbrough has for sale: *Dragon* posters 1, 2, 3, 8, *Popster* No. 23 (Kung Fu, Lee issue), *Memorial Monthly* magazines 8 & 9. Offers? - send SAE.
- Colin Linwell (2352), Islington has Bruce Lee items to swap for anything on Gerry Anderson (Thunderbirds, Star Trek, etc).

PEN PALS

Only two this time, probably, since I've sent out the Area Lists, members have had much less need of the section. At least it shows the Lists are working!

- John Richardson (2337), London wants to hear from anyone who is interested in the art of Jeet Kune Do.
- Paul Marks (2346), Burton-on-Trent wants male/female Chinese pen pals. His interests are Bruce, playing guitar, martial arts, music.

Okay, that's it for this issue. Late news, *Silent Flute* IS scheduled for general release - on December 10th. Great news!

Finally, DO have a really good Christmas... Pam

BRUCE LEE SOCIETY COLUMN
KUNG FU MONTHLY NO. 46

Hi everyone, Pam here with more word of the Bruce Lee Society.

The first thing I've got to mention is Carradine's *Silent Flute*. As many of you may know, it ran its premiere at London's Columbia cinema in Shaftesbury Avenue for three weeks, up to around mid-October before it promptly disappeared! At the time of writing this, the distributors are being very own and it's proving impossible to get word on dates for national release. I've no idea what might be holding things back but as soon as there's any news, I'll be sure to let you know.

Next I have to drag out an old chestnut that hasn't been mentioned for a while. Yes, it's SAE time again! Gradually more and more letters are starting to arrive without stamped and addressed envelopes. Please remember, if there's no SAE, you're not likely to get any reply.

There's been quite a bit of talk lately about the possibilities of arranging some sort of Bruce Lee convention. As Jenny mentions in "Kickback", probably the best way to organise it would be through the club. However, before going to an awful lot of trouble, I'd like to be sure that the interest is really there. Therefore, I'd like anyone interested to write in with their ideas such as where it should be held, whether it should be restricted to Society members only, and so on. Possibly a good date to hold it would be around four month's time to celebrate *KFM 50*!

Talking of meetings, as you'll probably recall, the area lists I worked out were specifically designed to enable members to meet each other and I even hoped that local enthusiasts might hold meetings together. So far I've not heard a peep that this is happening, so to help things on their way, anyone who would like to see this kind of thing happen, but who so far has been unable to make suitable arrangements, please write in telling me what the problems are and I'll help however I can.

Finally, some bits and pieces; If anyone knows of a shop in Derbyshire where members can buy Bruce Lee books and magazines, could they please write in and give me the address. Arthur Stone is still busy editing the Society film and if the convention idea comes off, let's hope it'll be ready for then. Lastly, I've still had no reply to my letter to the Censorship Board. It looks like it's time for me to send a reminder!

BRUCE LEE SOCIETY COLUMN
KUNG FU MONTHLY NO. 47

Hi. I'm here again with some stupendous word on the event everyone's been talking about; the coming Bruce Lee Society convention. Actually you'll see most of the information is in the big advertisement elsewhere this issue. What I want to say is just this. If all goes to plan, May 19th 1979 should turn out to be a momentous date for the UK fans of Bruce Lee. It's something I've often thought about doing but somehow it's taken a long time for me to actually pluck up the courage to make a start!

Okay, maybe it does sound a bit corny, but I say it again, the success of the convention will depend, not just on me or on you, but on everyone. All of us this end will do everything we can to make sure things run smoothly and all we can do now is await your interest and enthusiasm. Right now, I don't know whether there's going to be two or twenty thousand people wanting to come; the only thing I will say, is that, if you want to be sure of getting in, BOOK EARLY! There's no way at all that we'll be able to exceed the top figure of 400 people. Quite a few of the things we're not sure of, have obviously not appeared in the advertisement. One of the most exciting, and remember, this is NOT yet confirmed, is that we may be getting a copy of a film that's never (to my knowledge anyway) been seen in this country. It's a compilation of many of Bruce's childhood films and rare is not the word!

All of you will by now have received the December 1978 news sheet and I hope you find it a good read! Remember, the special member's Christmas card that went out with it is also available as a mail order item. They cost £1.00 for a bundle of ten (including envelopes) and should make pretty handy, all-purpose greeting cards for all Society members.

That's it for me this month; stand by for much more follow-up news on the convention! Pam

BRUCE LEE SOCIETY COLUMN
KUNG FU MONTHLY NO. 48

Hi. . . Pam here again! For ages now I've been wanting to organise some sort of Society book list. For the fans, finding out where to get hold of particular titles is often a time-consuming business and it would obviously be a good idea to bring as many as possible under "one umbrella". I'll be announcing more details soon, but perhaps in the meantime, anyone interested might like to drop me a POSTCARD ONLY please, listing the sort of selection you'd like to see.

Following on a brief mention in "Kickback" this month, Ian McNaughton (2445) writes in to tell us more on Golden Harvest's latest kung fu signing, Jackie Chan. Apparently he has a pretty good background in traditional acting and Golden Harvest are confidently going ahead with a movie aimed at the international market, entitled *The Fearless Hyena!* It's said by a spokesman that, although he has a long way to go before challenging the Master, he has the ambition to become a world star. Unfortunately, a critic describes him thus: a squat and muscular young man with a rubbery face that's dominated by a massive nose. Anyone for kung fu comedy?!

Now for something I don't like hearing about. Word comes from Graham Waggett (2602) that his local ABC cinema in Derby was recently seen advertising for its "Screen 2", Bruce Lee in *Fist of Fury Part 2*. If Graham's right, then I suggest that somebody gently reminds the management that it is in fact, Bruce Li who "stars" in the epic, before they get accused of ripping off the fans. Come to that, I wonder what EMI might think about any such false billing!

Lastly, thanks to so many of you for responding so well to my call for word on whether you'd attend a Bruce Lee convention. Now the day is actually drawing near, PLEASE make sure you come. For details, check the big ad that appears elsewhere in this issue. - Pam

EDITOR'S NOTES

Issue 10 marks the first mention of a possible Bruce Lee convention. At the time, no one knew what the turn out would be at such an event. As you'll read later in the book, they needn't have worried about the turn out.

At the time, no one really knew who Joe Lewis was; they may have known he was a martial artist and an actor but that's about it.

Joe Lewis was born in 1944 in North Carolina and at the age of 18, enlisted in the US Marine Corps, where from 1964, began studying Shorin-ryu Karate, earning his Black Belt in just seven months. After leaving the US Marine Corps in 1966, Lewis returned to the US and began competing  in martial arts tournaments, winning several. From 1967 to 1968, Lewis began training privately with Bruce Lee, who originally cast him as "Colt" in his 1972 film *Way of the Dragon* before being replaced with Chuck Norris, due to a disagreement between the two.

Reportedly, Lewis wasn't happy that his character would lose to Bruce's and felt it would have harmed the public's perception of him. He didn't see the on screen fight as "Tang Lung beating Colt"; he saw it as "Bruce Lee beating World Champion Joe Lewis."

Despite this, Lewis carved out a successful movie career for himself before his death in August 2012 at the age of 68.

Another first in this issue is the name Andrew Staton, a name synonymous with Bruce Lee in the UK. A regular contributor to the Society right up until it folded in 1983, an emotionally-drained Pam Hadden later chose Andrew Staton to carry on her good work of keeping Bruce Lee's memory alive.

Andrew Staton

As co-ordinator for The Bruce & Brandon Lee Association (formerly Bruce Lee Association), no one has done more to keep the memories of Bruce Lee and his son Brandon, alive in the UK. Andrew Staton has contributed in some way to every Bruce Lee videotape, DVD, Blu-ray, magazine, book, TV show, etc throughout the years, whether through research or acquiring footage and images to be officially released. Almost every Bruce Lee-related magazine supplement from *Impact* or *Martial Arts Illustrated* over the past 30 years bears his name.

An avid memorabilia collector, Staton is one of the most highly regarded and respected Bruce Lee historians in the world.

Up until a few years ago, Andrew organised, with the help of the Bruce & Brandon Lee Association staff, a Bruce Lee convention every year at the National Media Museum in Bradford, bring together fans from all over the country and show rare footage and uncut 35mm film prints on the big screen.

James DeMile was a student of Bruce Lee's from 1959 when they met at Edison Technical School shortly after Lee arrived in the United States and appeared in his 1963 book *Chinese Gung Fu: The Philosophical Art of Self Defense*. DeMile later released the book *Bruce Lee's 1 and 3 Inch Power Punch*, followed by an instructional VHS tape of the same name, released by martial arts company Hayashi. The VHS tape was out of print until 2008, when Hayashi collaborated with Eastern Edge to re-release it on DVD.

The timings of Bruce Lee's films, especially *Big Boss,* as quoted from Golden Harvest must be wrong. Even Hong Kong Legends' full uncut release in 2001 was 95 minutes 58 seconds (PAL) or 99 minutes 58 seconds (Film).

The Wrecking Crew isn't a Bruce Lee film as such because he didn't star in it but was hired to choreograph the fight scenes and Chuck Norris made his film debut in a small role. The film would mark actress Sharon Tate's final role before her violent murder at the hands of Charles Manson's followers.

In Quentin Tarantino's controversial 2019 film *Once Upon a Time in Hollywood*, Mike Moh portrays Lee on the set of *The Wrecking Crew*, having a fictitious fight with Brad Pitt's Cliff Booth.

Chieh Yuan was a Hong Kong actor and one of Bruce Lee's original co-stars in *Game of Death* where he played the foolish young fighter who accompanies Lee up the pagoda before being thrown down the stairs to his death by Kareem Abdul-Jabbar. Chieh Yuan passed away from cerebral edema in 1977, aged 32.

AN INTERVIEW WITH GARY KOHATSU
OF THE INTERNATIONAL DRAGON FAN CLUB

Gary Kohatsu is a professional photographer in the United States. In the 1970s, Kohatsu purchased the International Dragon Fan Club from "The World of Bruce Lee" curator Norman Borine and struck up a transatlantic partnership with the Bruce Lee Society. In 2019, Kohatsu retired as a photojournalism instructor at El Camino College in Torrance, California.

How did you get into Bruce Lee?

I was a regular viewer of the *Green Hornet* TV series back in the fall of '66. Kato's use of gung fu was revolutionary back then. This was during the cold war period and espionage was in vogue, so the martial arts was becoming more commonplace in film. But nothing compared to what Bruce Lee was doing, and on TV no less.
In 1973, when the influx of Chinese boxing films, such as *Five Fingers of Death* (*King Boxer*) and *Duel of the Iron Fist* (*The Duel* or *Duel of Fists*), were creating a buzz as the new action genre of cinema. I was already hooked on this stuff when Lee's films were released. It was a case of reuniting with a childhood hero.

How did you become aware of the Bruce Lee Society?

I became aware of the Bruce Lee Society through my association with Norman Borine's Dragon International Fan Club. Many British fans contacted me and eventually reached out with offers of trading BL material. And mentioned BLS. I was never a member of the Society.

A British friend (who I am still friends with on Facebook), Brian Harrison, was my main source of *Kung Fu Monthly* and *Dragon* magazines. Brian and I exchanged a lot of good material in the day.

Did you have any dealings with society president Pam Hadden and if so, what can you tell me about her?

No, I never had any contact with Pam. I only knew of her through *KFM* and English Bruce Lee fans. Well, actually, I did get a personal letter from Pam in early October 1976. I imagine that I wrote back. Or maybe she was answering my inquiry. Sadly, I don't recall the nature of the exchange.

Didn't you acquire the International Dragon Fan Club from Norman Borine? How did that come about?

Yes, I did purchase the club and mail-order business from Norman Borine. He and his wife Sandra operated a novelty shop (the Athena) on Hollywood Boulevard and I started patronizing his business for Bruce Lee magazines starting in 1974. Norman had a good source who imported Japanese publications on Bruce (from Roadshow, Haga and Screen), so I frequented his biz at least three times a month.

By late 1975 or early 1976, Norman and Sandra sold their shop and were moving to Palm Springs to operate the Tiki Palms Hotel. Norman, who didn't really know me well, inquired if I had interest in keeping the club alive. Of course, being young and adventurous, how could I resist.

Can you give me a brief history of the International Dragon Fan Club please?

Norman was a veteran Hollywood performer, a song-and-dance man decades earlier. I think he may have been a (background) dance performer in Hollywood musicals of the '30s and '40s. He loved the limelight.

He told me that a kid came into the Athena one day in offering to sell him a Lee poster (circa 1973) and started a dialogue about this fantastic Chinese action star, Bruce Lee. Norman was always fascinated by the drawing power of Hollywood icons, such as James Dean. He was unfamiliar with Bruce, his body of work and his previous TV performances in the U.S.

With *Enter the Dragon* playing locally, Norman said he checked out the film and became an instant fan. With Norman's background in sales and distribution, Norman found outlets to acquire posters and prints in bulk for the Athena.

That led Norman to starting a fan club/mail order business to reach a wider audience. He thought that the Hollywood connection was perfect for making the club and business viable. After securing a Hollywood mailbox, he started running ads in *Black Belt Magazine* and other Rainbow publications.

All of his posters, photos and fan club material were housed in an apartment in

Eagle Rock, California, which was about 20 miles from Hollywood. I took over the rent of the apartment through 1976 and part of 77.

In your opinion, what was the Bruce Lee scene like between 1976-1983?

There was a ton of fans, but the diehards had become more sophisticated in terms of seeking out memorabilia. Maybe a large part of that was because of making contact with other fans through organizations, such as the Bruce Lee Society.

This was also reflected in the material items they collected. The exposure to quality and diverse collectables (publications, photos) meant that fans were not settling for the simple (often seen) posters and photos that circulated between 1973 and 1975.

When I took over the Dragon Fan Club, members wanted to order a copy of the *Enter the Dragon* soundtrack. That was very difficult to order in bulk, but that item became a highly-sought-after collectable.

I would see out on soundtracks so fast, that I was always doubling up on orders. But I never could get enough albums to meet the demand.

There were a couple of versions of the *Enter* soundtrack; the better version I purchased in Little Tokyo, in the heart of downtown Los Angeles. This version I never offered through the fanclub.

In 1977, Norman Borine staged one of the first "Bruce Lee Museums." With the help of many of us local fans, Norman used a karate studio (operated by former Lee student, Pete Rosas). We merely decorated the studio with posters and photos. It was pretty spectacular for its time.

That museum open around Bruce's memorial — July 20, 1977. Ads were placed in *Black Belt Magazine* and *Fighting Stars* (both Rainbow Publications), and I was tasked with answering the influx of letters and inquiries about the week-long museum celebration.

Fans flew to Eagle Rock (where the museum was staged) for the event. It was amazing. The museum was even attended by Bruce's mom and brother, Grace and Robert; his widow, Linda, her attorney, Adrian Marshall, and students, including Dan Inosanto and Herb Jackson.

The museum was restaged in July 1978. By 1980, Norman and worked with Linda Lee to recreate a much larger and better produced Bruce Lee Museum in Hollywood, California. I was not a part of this latter project.

There was immense buzz about Bruce in 1979, with the release of the (first) *Game of Death*. At the premiere in Hollywood, Lee's family arrived — Brandon, Shannon, Linda.

Have you been to any conventions over the years? If so, which ones and what were your experiences of them?

No, I have not. The last convention that I attended was Norman's museum around 1980-81. The museum in Hollywood, in which he had a lot of sponsorship and the blessing of Linda and family.

What does Bruce Lee mean to you?

To me, the essence of Bruce Lee will always be from 1966 to his death in 1973. He opened a door. The years to follow were about embracing his legacy. Learning more about his life, his secrets.

I think Lee was a talent well before his time, and an individual with a particular and unique mindset. The kind of mindset that drive certain artists and athletes, such as Michael Jordan in basketball.

Bruce Lee's training was a mix of old-world dedication/philosophy and new-world evolution/preparation. He was like an Olympic athlete in his workouts and regimen. As he got older and wiser, he took his knowledge of martial arts and began applying it into a more reactive, animalistic (instinctive) combat that broke away from structure and repetition. But the magnetism was always there, as evident in his *Green Hornet* days.

Here we are, nearly 45 years from the start of the Bruce Lee Society. How do you feel the Bruce Lee scene has changed over the years?

The change I see of the Bruce Lee scene is division - those who grew up with him and those who discovered his legacy.

The fans who followed Lee during is breakout years as a small-and-big-screen star were part of that amazing journey in the late 1960s and early 1970s.

Those who were not part of that experience have a different perspective. It's probably the same with all icons/legends who have died before their time.

The level of experiences is what is different. Example: If you grew up when the Beatles broke out globally in 1964, is so much different that discovering the Fab Four in 1974, or later.

Lee was a phenomenon in the 1970s. He still is on a unique level. But the action-loving audiences became more sophisticated and knowledgeable from the 1980s to the present. Martial arts in the media became the norm, not the exception. New action stars have emerged. Fight choreography and filming techniques have evolved greatly. Bruce was highly responsible for the growth of martial arts utilized in action films since the 1970s.

Now generations have come and gone, and when millennials and those to follow look back at Lee, it's from the perspective of people who have been exposed to immense changes. The Jet Li, Steven Seagal, Jackie Chan, and Donny Yen's of the world have all made their mark. The quality of action in films has improved by leaps, but their time came after Lee's parting.

Today, many view Lee as a myth. They can see his videos and see performers who mimic his style, but there also tends to be a lot watered-down caricatures of the man.

There are those who assume he was an action star, not a real martial artist. Some see his antics as cartoonish, and even filmmakers like Quentin Tarantino (*Once Upon a Time in Hollywood*) create a fictional, buffoonish Lee.

11
MARCH 1979

HELLO, MEMBERS - IT'S TIME FOR THE 11TH SOCIETY NEWS SHEET (AND THE FIRST OF 1979!). A BIG "THANK YOU" TO EVERYONE WHO SENT ME A CHRISTMAS CARD. I TRUST, LIKE ME, YOU ALL HAD A GREAT TIME!!!

THE BRUCE LEE CONVENTION - MAY 12TH, 1979

Well, following the mention in the last news sheet, it seems the idea for a convention is a popular one, to say the least! Obviously there's a lot of detail to give about it, so what I've done, is give over a page of this Sheet as it'll contain all the info you need. One thing I must say, though, whether or not the whole thing is a success depends on YOU... and I mean that. Without the support of Bruce's truest fans, the event could be a rather hollow one so PLEASE don't let us down! Remember, if the Convention turns out the amazing day I think it will, it'll almost certainly become an annual event -and wouldn't that be a great tribute to Bruce - AND the Society. One other thing, non-members, brothers, sisters, mums, dads, etc, etc are ALL welcome, so nobody need miss out... see you on the 12th!

THE SILENT FLUTE

Although I mentioned a release date of the 10th December in the last news sheet, it seems *The Silent Flute* didn't get everywhere it should have done. In fact, South London where I live didn't see it at all! I'm extremely disappointed, and would like to hear from members (short notes only please, to which I won't be replying) in whose area it didn't get shown. Once I've heard from you, I'll be contacting the distributors to find out what's going on. As a tailpiece, but on the same sort of subject, I hear that

THE BRUCE LEE SOCIETY

Game of Death also missed out in a few places. I'm told it will be with those places soon.

GENERAL NEWS

Last news sheet, Andrew Staton (1670) asked about *Tao of Wing Chun Do* and *Bruce Lee's 1 and 3 Inch Punch*. Well I've heard from Mark Salter (1792), Paul Booking (2206), David Moore (1783), James ter Beek (2262) and Tony Boswell (2570) that these books are available from Paul H. Crompton Ltd., 638 Fulham Road, London SW6 and Oriental World, 18 Swan Street, Manchester 4, Lancs. The books by Yip Man's sons, also mentioned, are available from the North London Martial Arts Centre, 81 Broad Lane, London N15. Information is still needed however, on where to get *Kali Training* by Danny Inosanto.

Tony Boswell also mentioned that the magazine, *Karate & Oriental Arts* is publishing an article called "In the Steps of Bruce Lee" - starting from issue 76 (it's bi-monthly). He says, too, that the Yip Man books mentioned above which "reveal secret techniques practised by the late Bruce Lee" are available from: Yip Man Martial Arts Association, P.O. Box 139, Hadley, Mass 01035, USA – priced at $5.50. For our U.S. and Canadian members, this address may be better for writing to. Also, a request, Tony wants any books on Lau Kung Fu - write to him for info at: Bookham, Surrey.

James Sutherland tells me that copies of the 12" *Dragon Power* (with picture sleeve) can be bought from Adrian's, Shopping Hall, Wickford, Essex, England. Cost is £1.45, inc p&p.

Alex Bruce Buttigieg (2199) from Malta came across this in the movie magazine, *Big Screen*: "A Superior Court Judge in Hollywood has ordered Allied Artists and two other distributors to pay Bruce Lee's widow £8,000 for using Bruce Lee's name without permission. The court ruled that the name, likeness, lifestyle and character traits of the late Kung Fu star belong to the estate, which is administered by his wife, Linda Lee, who inherits over £1,000,000." So now we know why some of the companies to whom members have been writing have suddenly gone from the scene. If Linda IS taking legal action generally, as would appear, then many of the companies who make rip-off Bruce Lee pictures could be stopped dead in their tracks!

Alex also wrote to the magazine to ask when Bruce's films might be re-issued in Malta. They replied that *Game of Death* should be released soon and that they planned to organise a Bruce Lee Festival to coincide with the launch. Alex will tell us when as soon as he knows details.

James ter Beek (2262) from the Netherlands thinks that Society members should also consider joining the Bruce Lee JKD Club of Hong Kong, Flat 9A, Sunny House, 268 King's Road, North Point, Hong Kong. There's no accounting for taste, I suppose!!! (Didn't mean it, honest).

Paul Wade (1836) sent in some cuttings on *The Silent Flute* and Chuck Norris' latest film, *Good Guys Wear Black*. On the latter, the clip says that Norris could well be on the way to stardom - with a good supporting cast, he plays Major J.T. Booker, leader of the deadly Black Tigers. The unit is a U.S. Army commando team, stationed in Vietnam, whose brief is to rescue POW's from behind enemy lines. So good are they that an unwritten term in peace negotiations calls for their extinction. It sounds good so let's be hearing from members what they think of it, once it's been around.

Regarding *The Silent Flute,* Stirling Silliphant made the following comment: "Our hope is to portray an entirely different view of the fighting arts, much like the film *Easy Rider* did for motorcycling." If any member would like a photocopy of the complete write-up, just send me (Pam) a BIG stamped & addressed envelope, with a note saying *"Flute* Write-Up," and I'll post it off. There's far too much to include in this news sheet!

Paul Short (1164) tells me that Cimac Martial Arts, 606 Stratford Road, Sparkhill, Birmingham, Warks., England now have the *Game of Death Extract Edition* at £2.15 (inc p&p). It contains the complete outline of the story - with coloured pictures - and an interview with Robert Clouse.

Ann Fitzgerald (1090) says she was watching *Assignment* on BBC 2 and heard the announcer say regarding "the Hong Kong threat to Hollywood.".. "Those awful Kung Fu movies." They then showed an excerpt from one, and followed it by some words from Raymond Chow. During it, the announcer said that, "Bruce Lee was Chow's biggest money-spinner until his death in 1973." Ann says it's a good thing nothing nasty was said about Bruce - or they'd have got a nasty letter from her! (and me, for that matter!).

Change of subject... for members still wanting the full-colour stickers of Bruce, send £1.60 for a set of six sheets to Oriental World (see earlier for address).

Mr. I. McNorton (2445) tells me that Rane Records Ltd of 36 John Dalton Street, Manchester M2 6LE, England, have many of those hard-to-obtain cinema LPs. They also have *Game of Death* (music only) and Bruce "doubles" and all the soundtracks from Bruce's films. Price of a single is £11.99. For members in the Manchester area, it's worth a look-in.

Arthur Stone (1150) and Lorraine Smith (2320) both wrote saying they saw Billy Smart's Circus on Christmas Day - and were amazed and thrilled to hear that the music used during the trampoline act was the *Enter the Dragon* theme!

And talking of *Enter the Dragon,* Paul Wade (1836) writes to tell me that it's playing in his "local" for the eighth consecutive week!!

I've had several cuttings from members regarding the film *Jaguar Lives* that stars Joe Lewis - former World Karate Champion and acquaintance of Bruce. P. Inglesfield (2424) informs that *Jaguar Lives* is NOT a martial arts film, although Lewis does use his skills in it. There's cuttings this issue from Mike Devereux (1061) and Paul McKenna (2331) regarding the film.

The Bruce Lee JKD Club (see address earlier) are selling a *Game of Death* film that contains the Chi Hon Joi, Danny Inosanto and Jabbar fights. Its 200' feet long (colour) and costs $US28 (approx £14). They also offer *Fist of Fury* and *Enter the Dragon* (in two parts) at $US53 (about £26) each - 400'. Info comes courtesy of Carl Jones (2121).

Rick Edwards (1260) tells me that, apart from the Bruce Li rip-off, *Fist of Fury Part 2* (Enough said from me about that one!), there's also a new Nora Miao picture that follows on from Bruce's original masterpiece. Nora and two students leave Shanghai and start a new school. The star of the film steals a heavily-engraved casket from them, thinking the contents must be valuable - inside are the nunchakus from *Fist of Fury*. He returns them to Nora and they ask him to become a pupil but he refuses as he feels he's no fighter. However, being pushed around and tormented by the Japanese, he finally joins and learns all the techniques. Together they fight the Japanese (just like *Fist of Fury*) but, sorry to say, he also gets shot! Rick says he doesn't know the "hero's" name, but says he handles himself a lot better than Bruce Li (who said that shouldn't take much doing?!). I must say I'm looking forward to seeing the film myself. Comments from members who get to see it too are, of course, welcome.

Mr. A. Burns (2378) kindly sent in a cheque to the Society for £4.00 which are the proceeds of a raffle held among his friends (all Bruce fans, I gather!). Anyway, I've decided (with Mr. Burns' approval) to use it to buy items that will be given as prizes on Convention day.

David Dixon (1650) says that Magpie Records at Hopmarket, Worcester, WR1 1ER, Worcs, England has the double *Enter the Dragon* LP set and if you send them a stamped and addressed envelope, together with 15p, they'll post you their catalogue.

Member John Watson (1933) would like other members to contact him (those living within easy reach) for chats, etc. His address is London W11.

Finally, and I KNOW this is going to get to you!). Richard Miller (1638) wants you all to see the letter he wrote to *Sports Postbag*, Green Final, Lang Stracht, Mastrick, Aberdeen AB9 8AF, Scotland (after he read the previous week that a woman thought Muhammed Ali to be the greatest sportsman of all time, and never to be equalled). I don't know about you, but I think Richard's letter perfectly sensible and IN NO WAY does it deserve the stupid, immature remarks penned by the writer of *Sports Postbag* (who, in coward-like fashion, neglects to print his name. Now, of course I'm not trying to stir anything up, but just in case anyone should feel like writing to this twit (and naturally I wouldn't dream

KUNG FU KING WAS THE GREATEST

Richard Miller, 294 Hilton Drive, Aberdeen, will raise a few eyebrows with his nomination for the accolade of The Greatest—

I disagree with Muhammed Ali claiming this title. The man I regard as The Greatest is the late Bruce Lee, who, in my opinion, has no competition.

Although he died when only 32, he was the fittest man in the world and the greatest exponent of the martial arts of all time.

If Ali and Lee ever got into the ring together, I reckon Lee would have won within two rounds — yes, he was that good.

Lee did press-ups on a thumb and one finger with the other hand behind his back. He could knock a man, no matter his size, across a room with a punch from only three inches from the body.

There are thousands of styles in the martial arts, but Lee knew them all.

● I suppose you believe that Steve Austin can run at 80 m.p.h. as well . . .! Grow up — don't believe everything you see at the movies.

of encouraging you!) the address just happens to be above. And of course, the fact that I, anyway, shall be writing to this miserably ill-informed specimen (what's he doing handling a sports postbag?) should in no way influence your actions. Come on members, it's time to rid the world of such ignorance! The sad thing is that he's not the only one, which just shows how much work we've still got to do. Actually, I think it's time the Society started collecting gems like this for posterity. If any of you should come across similar nonsense, don't forget to at least send me a copy!

A RETROSPECTIVE LOOK AT BRUCE LEE MANIA & THE KUNG FU CRAZE OF THE 1970S

John Kemp - 1729

Kin Leong - friend of Lorraine Smith (2320) and David Rawson (2487)

Kate Feeney - 1194 / David Colville - 1675

Tim Stephens - 1311

Joe Lewis kicks out at a gun-toting villain in this scene

The former undefeated world heavyweight karate champion, Joe Lewis, in action for

JAGUAR LIVES

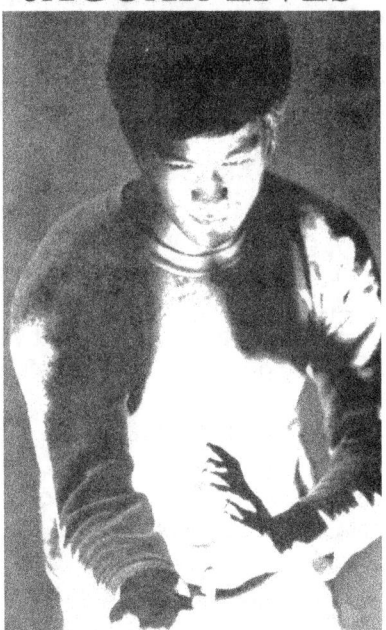

from GINO CRANE

DAN INOSANTO COURSE FOR J.K.D. IN U.K.?

We have had several bits of information from America recently. There is a possibility after the publicity given to him by *Fighters*, of Chris Kent coming over to England and starting a British Branch of the Filipino Kali Academy to teach both Escrima and J.K.D. This is a distinct possibility at the end of 1979 and of course your favourite magazine *Fighters* will be giving him every support possible. We have also heard that Dan Inosanto would be interested in completing an Escrima and J.K.D. Course in the U.K. next year. There would of course be considerable expense involved in paying for Dan Inosanto and at least two of his Senior Instructors to fly over to England and teach for a week. We are currently sponsoring this Event which would mean the probability of a five day residential course in England which would be limited in numbers. We have an approximate cost per student which would be in the region of £100-£120 for the five-day course. Bearing in mind the expenses involved in running such a Course we think that this would be a relatively small amount to pay for training under the man who was Bruce Lee's personal friend, assistant and Co-Developer of Jeet Kune-Do.

Clip from 'Fighters' (Lorraine Smith - 2320)

John Kemp - 1729

"HOPE YOU DONT MIND CHUM, BUT I LIKE TO BE ALONE WHEN IM DOING MY KUNG-FU TRAINING"

"THREE HOURS, SEVEN DAYS A WEEK KUNG-FU HE DOES, AND HE CATCHES COLD GETTING IN THE MILK!"

CONVENTION ASSISTANCE

This is a call to all far-away members (far away from London, that is). There may be quite a few of you who're not too sure about travelling down (or up!) to London on your own for the convention. Well, you all have area lists (or are receiving one with this sheet), so why not get together locally and make in a party? British Rail, in fact, offers quite reasonable party rates, and anyway, what better way to pass the time than chatting with a collection of fellow Bruce Lee buffs? With this in mind, member Paul McKenna is really very keen to come along to the great convention but he's only 15 and understandably apprehensive about making the journey alone. Therefore, anyone living near, or fairly near, Paul (he's at Pollok, Glasgow), PLEASE contact him as soon as you know that you'll definitely be coming too.

SPECIAL MESSAGES

Kate Feeney (1194) sends the following message to fellow member, David Colville (1675): "Davy - lots of love on your Birthday... from Kate" XXX (and, come to that, a happy birthday from all of us - and to all members with birthdays around this time).

AREA LISTS

For all those not already in the know, when I send out a second news sheet to members, they also receive a list of other members in and around their area, so that the fans can contact each other. What I'm trying to say is, when you get some odd sheet of paper arriving through the post, that's covered in lists of names and addresses - you know it's time to get writing, and hopefully, meeting.

RENEWALS

Members from 2267 to 2302 - remember your second-year renewal falls due between now and the end of May. And members 1829 to 2021 - your third-year renewal is due during this period, too!! I don't want any of you to miss out on the fabulous second and third-year kits or, for that matter, the Bruce Lee convention. Another thing is, although I think you'll agree that we've held our prices down pretty well over the last year or two, but it can't last for ever. Sooner or later we're going to have to think about a raise in price, so get those renewals (and first-year memberships!) in just as soon as possible.

LETTERS

Off we go with the latest batch of letters...

Dear Pam,

First off - I have to say 'it's about time' - why nobody thought of a convention earlier beats me! The idea is incredible. I have a well-deserved holiday coming up, so I shall definitely be there. Going on to Silent Flute, I was very pleased to read the excellent write-ups in KFM's 44 & 45, and I hope the film achieves all it sets out to do. It's a pity that Raymond Chow didn't hire someone like Stirling Silliphant to write Game of Death - maybe then we could have seen something to be proud of.

Arthur Stone (1150)

Yes, Arthur, I think that Chow let down all the fans (and Bruce) with the end product of Game of Death. And I congratulate David Carradine for doing a first-class job on The Silent Flute... I'm sure he played it exactly as Bruce would have wanted.

Pam,

Yesterday I saw Game of Death, and I didn't like it very much. Only the last 20 minutes were fantastic, when Bruce (the real one) ruled the screen. As always, he was fantastic! Over here, the film is uncensored, so the nunchaku scene with Bruce versus Danny Inosanto was left in. I really feel sorry for the British Society members because they missed one of the most beautiful fights Bruce ever made.

James ter Beek (2262)

James tells me the complete film is being sold (divided in four parts). Each will cost 149 Deutche Marks - available from: Budo-Artikel-Vertrieb Herbert Velk, Postfach 2107, D-6380 Bad Homburg v.d.h, W.Deutchland. Before sending money, I strongly suggest getting in touch first. Both James, and fellow-member Willem Uroegh (2213) are hoping to come to the convention. We look forward to welcoming them over!

Dear Pam,

I went to see the film, Revenge of the Pink Panther, with Peter Sellers, and was mad at the producers for the following: Peter Sellers' manservant (played by Burt Kwouk) is called in the film (wait for it) - Cato! And that resembles you-know who! Inspector Clouseau (Peter Sellers) and Cato are always doing Kung Fu sparring in a comic way, and to make things worse, they have a car called - "Silver Hornet" -a junk heap which always breaks up. Now that is an insult to the Master, and although I admit to enjoying the movie, these few things made me feel insulted as I admire the one and only great martial artist, Bruce Lee. However, I was happy to see Saturday Night Fever where John Travolta had the great Bruce Lee poster in his room!

Alex Bruce Buttigieg (2199) - from Malta

There's one thing, Alex - even though I was less than enamoured with this particular aspect of the Sellers movie, at least it was a fun film. On the other hand, Bruce Li's (which he expects us to take seriously) are an out-and-out insult in every respect. Anyway, at least with all the people using his name and, indirectly, advertising his greatness, Bruce Lee remains forever in the limelight!

THE BRUCE LEE SOCIETY

Dear Pam,

Referring to Paul Mark's comments on Bruce Li (last news sheet). I agree, as I fell about laughing at his antics. I must admit to seeing one of his films at the start of the Kung Fu "craze" and wondering what all the fuss was about. To show how bad the film was, I cannot even remember the title! Thank God that I saw the real Bruce Lee!

David Moore (1783)

I know one member, David (and I'm not going to give you his name) who actually saw a Bruce Li film and thought it was the Master! So he's got a nice surprise awaiting him at the convention, where we are showing the complete, uncensored version of *Way of the Dragon*!!!

COMPETITION

The winners of the December competition are: James ter Beek (2262); Laura Bagguley (2203), Geordie Nokes (1688), J.W.Cook (1339) and Alison French (1143). All of them will be each receiving a special, numbered edition of the 12" version of *Dragon Power!*

And now to the March competition - the results of which will be drawn at the May convention. The response to the last competition was excellent so I'm looking forward to seeing you all turn up trumps for this one!

1. Bruce played a "baddie" in the film, *Marlowe* - what was the name of the character he played?
2. When did Bruce's father die (the actual date)?
3. What was the name of the character Bruce played in *Way of the Dragon*?
4. When did Bruce first meet his friend, M. Uyehara?
5. Someone very close to Bruce became a scientific officer at the Royal Observatory in Hong Kong... who?

Now, for any true Bruce Lee fan, this shouldn't present many problems. Answers, please, on a POSTCARD ONLY to: The Bruce Lee Society, March Competition, 14 Rathbone Place, London W1P IDE. Oh, and by the way, as I promised in *KFM* recently, there'll be some rare *Bruce Lee Scrapbooks* that I'll be giving away as prizes!

LATE EXTRA

I've just had a note from member, David Colville, that his girlfriend, Kate Feeney (also a member) has had a bad accident and is in hospital (at the time of writing). On behalf of everyone, I wish her all the best and, Kate, here's a special message from David: Get well quickly and soon - I still love you very much - David XXX. I'd say that was the best tonic anyone could have.

A RETROSPECTIVE LOOK AT BRUCE LEE MANIA & THE KUNG FU CRAZE OF THE 1970S

The K.F.M. Bruce Lee Society presents

No, we can hardly believe it either! At last, KFM, Society President - Pam Hadden - plus friends are presenting the event we've been dreaming of all these years. We can't yet give the EXACT lo-down of the day's events, but here's a taster of the sort of thing we're planning:
1. The venue is the Acklam Hall, in London's Notting Hill Gate - the Convention will run approximately 10.30am to 5.00pm on Saturday, May 12th.
2. It looks like we'll have to set a ceiling on delegates of just 400. That means, to avoid disappointment, BOOK NOW!!!
3. By and large, entry will be by pre-paid ticket. However, there MAY be just a few tickets on sale at the door - BUT THERE'S NO GUARANTEE.

ATTRACTIONS...
* The moment everyone's been waiting for - come and view 'Way' - FREE OF ALL EUROPEAN CENSORSHIP! That's right, it'll include the legendary 'double nunchaku' sequence. What a monster scoop!
* Another fantastically rare reel of film... as described recently in KFM, catch a viewing of Bruce Lee as he makes his actual screen test for the 'Green Hornet' series.
* Collect as you enter the hall our unique Convention Kit - price included with your ticket. It'll contain, among other things, a rare 'Death' film brochure, plus a Commemorative Scroll
* You might like to visit our SWOP-SHOP CORNER. That's where fans will be able to barter and bargain to their hearts content. If you have anything to sell, swop of just give away, BRING IT WITH YOU!
* Among all the great stalls we expect to have lined up for you, don't forget to drop by the KFM stand. There'll be rare Bruce Lee books, back issues, special souvenir Convention T/Shirts, Drinking Mugs, Brooches, and much much more.
* On top of all that, we're arranging for a top-class martial arts display... food and drink will be on sale for most of the day... Master of Ceremonies will be our old friend (and ex-Cathay Films man), Roy Byrne... there'll be unusual, on-the-spot prizes, competitions, and who knows what else!!!

And that's the kind of line-up we're mid-way through assembling! But apart from anything else, it'll be the first-ever chance for Society members and fans to really get to meet each other on a truly National scale.

Come along and support THE BRUCE LEE CONVENTION - the entry is just £3.00 for Society Members, £3.25 for everyone else.

Send your cheque/postal order (made out to KFM) to: The Bruce Lee Convention, Kung-Fu Monthly, 14 Rathbone Place, London W1P 1DE.

A SPECIAL COMPETITION
We'll be making time on the day for a rather unusual competition. Anyone wanting to enter should accompany their ticket application with a statement on the subject - 'Why Bruce Lee was the greatest' - USING NOT MORE THAN 200 WORDS. The best ten of these will be picked out by Pam Hadden and the authors will be asked on the day of the CONVENTION to take the microphone and repeat their words to the fans present. The contender raising the biggest cheer will be adjudged the winner!

AVOID DISAPPOINTMENT - BOOK NOW FOR BRITAIN'S FIRST BRUCE LEE CONVENTION!

THE BRUCE LEE SOCIETY

SWOP SHOP

- David Nieldzailek (1021), Neath has the following to swap: super-8mm Bruce trailer *Fist of Fury/Enter the Dragon*, colour/sound - USA film, excellent quality. Wants *Life and Tragic Death of Bruce Lee* by Linda, *Clash* Nos. 1-6, *Kung Fu Fighters* Vol. 1, No. 1 "Lee Exposed" fold-out poster magazine, *Exciting Cinema* issues 1 & 2. Also wants copy of *Book of Kung Fu* by *KFM* and *Game of Death* poster.
- Richard Miller (1638), Aberdeen has to swap: *Shorinji Kempo* by Doshin So. Wants *Bruce Lee's Fighting Methods* Vols. 3 & 4.
- Carl Jones (2121), St.Helens wants anything on Bruce, particularly overseas, early British (1973/75) and Super-8mm material. Will trade for very good quality stereo cassettes of all Lee soundtrack records or fair price paid.
- Susan Davies, Solihull has for sale: *Game of Death* collector's edition - 25p, hardback, signed edition of *Secret Art of Bruce Lee* - £1.50 *Bruce Lee - 1940-1943* - £1, *Nunchakus in Action* - 35p, *King of Kung Fu* - 45p, *Enter the Dragon* colour poster - 45p, wooden nunchakus with metal chain - £2. All in very good condition.
- Margaret Smith (2565), London has lots of material to trade: colour slides from *Enter the Dragon, Way of the Dragon, Green Hornet,* and *Fist of Fury* plus screen photos from all Bruce's films, stills from *One Armed Boxer, Hand of Death* etc. To trade with anything on Bruce.
- Robert Walker (2565), Clydebank has to offer an Instant Polaroid EE Swinger camera/black & white pictures/brand new - wants any Bruce Lee LP in exchange.
- Paul McKenna (2331), Pollok has to swap, *Life and Tragic Death of Bruce Lee* by Linda, for any other Bruce book.
- Steven Robertson (2567), Queenslie, Glasgow wants the Kung Fu suit offered in early issues of *KFM* - size 4, for height 5' 7" to 5' 9."
- Sharon Hill (2360), Plymouth wants *Life and Tragic Death of Bruce Lee, The Man Only I Knew* by Linda Lee. Also *KFM* No. 1 and the Bruce Lee Treasure Kit offered in early *KFM's*.
- Munir Shaffi (2495), Oxford has for sale: Bruce *Fist of Fury* poster (holding nunchakus) - 26"x38" for 85p; *Bruce Lee: King of Kung Fu* for 70p; *KFM's* 28, 38, 39, 40, 42 and 44 - 30p each. All prices inc p&p.
- Yim Fai Lo (2149), Leeds wants to buy: *KFM Scrapbook*, Bruce calendar, *Kung Fu Superstars, Kung Fu Fighters,* Black Belt's *Best of Bruce Lee* Nos. 1 & 2, *Life and Tragic Death of Bruce Lee, Farewell to the Dragon, The Man Only I Knew, Enter the Dragon* by Mike Roote, *Kung Fu Cinema of Vengeance, Kung Fu Teach Yourself, Secrets of Kung Fu, Souvenir Album, Deadly Hands of Kung Fu, Best of Bruce Lee* (any).
- Mark Gardener (2340), Cheltenham wants: Bruce Lee's original film posters from *Way of the Dragon, Fist of Fury, Enter the Dragon, Game of Death* - will pay £1.60 each; also any Bruce information - good prices paid.
- James ter Beek (2262), Leiden, Netherlands wants tapes of any Bruce Lee interviews - please write with information of what sort of thing you have.
- Mohammed Afzal (2546), Midlothian wants *Beginner's Guide to Kung Fu* by *KFM*.
- Patrick Hennessey (1771), Dublin, Eire has for sale: 400' 8mm film from *Way of the Dragon* (colour/silent, but plus cassette). Cost £32, will sell for £22 or swap for any sound featurette of Bruce EXCEPT production trailer from *Enter the Dragon*.

PEN PALS

- Paul McKenna (2331), Pollok, Glasgow wants pen pals of around 15 years (his age); interests Kung Fu movies, martial arts and (of course) Bruce Lee.
- Jon Richardson (2337), London wants to hear from anyone who is interested in the art of Jeet Kune Do.
- Paul Marks (2346), Burton-on-Trent wants male/female Chinese pen pals. His interests are Bruce, playing guitar, Martial arts, music.

Well, that's about it for this issue of the Bruce Lee Society news sheet.

I look forward to seeing as many of you as possible at the convention - and don't forget, send off for those advance tickets (direct from *KFM*) just as soon as you can. We're going to have a terrific time... in fact, I just can't wait!!! Pam

BRUCE LEE SOCIETY COLUMN
KUNG FU MONTHLY NO. 49

Hi, Pam with you again, and one thing I'm not going to be mentioning is THAT convention! I'll have lots to say in next month's 50th issue tribute.

One idea that is worth outlining, though, is this one. For years now I've had request after request for the Society to arrange regular film shows, for us to hire out cinemas for the showing of Bruce's films (preferably not censored).

And it wouldn't have to stop at that. There are many other titles going around that, for one reason or another, fans of the Master would probably enjoy seeing; names such as David Chiang, Wang Yu and maybe even Bruce Le, spring immediately to mind. Considering the interest everybody demonstrated by coming to the convention, I'd say that those film events are now a very real possibility and without a doubt, the time has now come for us to check the availability of the movies concerned.

That's where YOU come in. I'd really appreciate as many members as possible sending me in postcards, listing the ones they'd most like to see. Obviously we'll be looking to show all the Bruce Lee material we can, so don't bother including the *Big Boss, Fist of Fury, Way of the Dragon, Enter the Dragon,* and *Game of Death* titles. Concentrate on lesser known material that you think is worthy of a place.

Changing the subject, I'm delighted to say that the book list I introduced in the last news sheet is quite a success. I had a feeling that bringing rare volumes under one roof (so to speak) might be a popular idea, but results have exceeded even MY cautious optimism. Keep letting me know of any new titles you think should be included! I can't promise that I'll be able to find all of the more items of Bruce Lee literature, but I'll certainly be trying as much as I can! And that's it for this month. Take care. Pam

BRUCE LEE SOCIETY COLUMN
KUNG FU MONTHLY NO. 50

It hardly needs me to say that, in terms of 50 issues of *Kung Fu Monthly*, the Bruce Lee Society is something of a newcomer. But that said, we are about to enter our fourth year and that, I feel, is no mean feat in itself.

People ask me, "What's to be gained by joining the Society, when much of the information we're after will appear in the magazine anyway?" That's an easy one to answer! Anyone who's ever been a member of an efficiently and enthusiastically run club or society will vouch for the difference. There is a strong sense of belonging and purpose too, and a feeling that YOU really do count in the things that matter. When a decision is taken or a step is made within the Society, there is every possibility that YOU could have been one of the voices behind it. Not only that, in some ways, *KFM* also caters for the more casual fan perhaps the newcomer who has yet to feel the full force and energy behind the Bruce Lee movement. Once that person experiences the need to become more actively involved, there's only one place to go looking - the Bruce Lee Society.

There's plenty of work to down to. High on our "urgent" list is to petition the TV stations to show the *Green Hornet* series. According to one information source, the reason we haven't yet seen it is that it's "too violent for kids viewing time and not adult enough for later in the evening." That's the sort of nonsense we're out to defeat. Then of course, there's the old chestnut of the ever-elusive Bruce Lee TV documentary. Maybe now there's been a successful convention, we'll be able to convince them the error of their forgetful ways.

There's also other lands to conquer! We've certainly got quite a few members from Europe and around the world, but nowhere near enough. I know that the Master's following is not just restricted to the British Isles and all that's missing is proper communication. It's a tough problem, but one I'll be working on.

I value the enthusiasm of every single member of the Bruce Lee Society and also the work they put into spreading the good word. There's nothing quite like fighting for something you know to be right as it's a great feeling. I hope every single fan who's a member now, will still be with us when *KFM* 100 comes along. I'll be there if you will. - Pam

BRUCE LEE SOCIETY COLUMN
KUNG FU MONTHLY NO. 50

Hello, it's Pam here with another column for members of the Bruce Lee Society.

This month, there's "news" to report. For some time now, we've been planning a Bruce Lee Festival for December 1st and everyone here has been looking forward to another really great day. Rank had kindly offered us an enormous and beautiful cinema in North London and so as far as we knew, securing the films was just going to be a formality. How wrong we were!

Our first request to EMI was met with point blank refusal as EMI/Warner now control Bruce's 35mm movies in this country and our second try, to the next-to-top man, was greeted with a, "Well, probably no; we're doing something around that time ourselves so we'll let you know in two months or so." Both he and I knew that, if a cinema was to disrupt its normal schedules, arrangements needed to be made there and then, not eight weeks later.

May I, through this column, remind EMI of one or two things? Firstly, it's largely been *Kung Fu Monthly* and the Society that have kept the Bruce Lee flag flying in this country. The fact that EMI can still fill their cinemas when showing Little Dragon films is largely down to the enthusiasm of the very people they are trying to slap in the face. Of course it isn't only *KFM* readers and Society members who pile into the theatres but we, however, are the pacemakers, the leaders of the movement.

Another thing is that EMI felt that such a showing might affect their own plans for re-releasing Bruce's films around the same time. Well, the most we could have crammed in would have been perhaps 1,500 fans; a flea-bite of a figure compared to the number EMI would attract on the national circuit. And not only that, the publicity surrounding such a great festival would almost certainly have helped BOOST box office receipts for any Lee films running at the same time; remember how the newspapers and TV took to the convention? Looked at from any direction, their decision is mean and self-defeating.

Want to know the good news? Despite the meanies at EMI, the Festival is ON!!!!!! Some very wonderful friends have come to the rescue with the offer of, and it's hard to believe it, the ORIGINAL, UNCENSORED CHINESE versions of *The Big Boss, Fist of Fury,* and *Way of the Dragon!* In celebration of this great victory, I hereby declare that forever more, the last week in November shall be known as BRUCE LEE WEEK. By an amazing stoke of fate, it will also of course coincide with the Master's birthday.

And how else could we have topped such a week than with the organising on the 7th day of the world's first-ever Bruce Lee Film Festival? Check elsewhere this issue for further details on what is bound to be another splendid event.

Society members, and for that matter, ALL other readers of *KFM*, BOOK TICKETS QUICKLY! I promised you a great Convention and you got it. This time I'm promising an amazing film festival so don't you dare miss out on it! - Pam

EDITOR'S NOTES

Upon it's UK cinema release, *The Silent Flute* received 51 seconds of cuts by the BBFC to remove footage of a Bo staff, a throwing star and a shot of a cow receiving a blow to it's neck. All home video releases all featured the same cuts, however, the cuts were waived for the 2008 DVD release.

The first *Kung Fu Monthly* Convention is formally announced to take place on Saturday 12th May 1979. Among the attractions to be shown are the full uncut version of *Way of the Dragon* (with double nunchakus scene) and Bruce Lee's original *Green Hornet* screen test. Had the showing of *Way of the Dragon* been in a cinema with a general screening, it would not have been shown uncut and would have had to be shown as the cut BBFC certified version. The reason that the uncut and uncertified version could be shown, was due to a loophole that stated that uncertified films could be shown at a private screening for club or society members only. There would have been attendees that weren't members of the Bruce Lee Society but were legally allowed to watch the film if the organisers "made" them members for the day, by using part of the ticket fee as a "membership fee." Whether they took money out for the "membership fee" is irrelevant, they just had to state that was happening. Its how the Bruce Lee Association, and later, the Bruce and Brandon Lee Association continued to show Bruce Lee films fully uncut on the big screen at conventions in Bradford, right up until the films were certified uncut by the BBFC in 2000. The same loophole could be used for under 18's to view an "18" film; as long as they were "members" of the club and had a parent or guardian present at the time, they would be let in by cinema staff.

The Green Hornet screen test mentioned wasn't actually filmed for *The Green Hornet*. It was filmed in 1965 for a proposed series called *Number One Son* which was part of the "Charlie Chan" franchise. It was only when the *Number One Son* project fell through, did the producers of *The Green Hornet* decide to cast Bruce Lee as "Kato." The 1965 screen test has been released on several UK DVDs over the past twenty years in varying quality but the best quality footage available is on the documentaries *Bruce Lee: The Immortal Dragon* and *Bruce Lee: The Lost Interview*.

HI EVERYONE - AND STRAIGHT INTO EDITION 12 OF THE SOCIETY NEWS SHEET.

THE BRUCE LEE CONVENTION - 1979

Yes, it's definitely now to be an annual event! The response was so overwhelming, that plans are even now under way for 1980. With fans journeying from Scotland, Wales, Ireland - not to mention Holland and Denmark - it's clear we'll be able to expand next year's convention into a monster-size event! Around 800 people actually got in on the magic day, though tragically, that meant over 300 fans being turned away. Inside, packed was not the word!

The books, records, novelties, t-shirts, mugs, records and martial arts equipment went like hot-cakes, while next door in the Swop Shop, many members were able to boost their collections and at the same time, make lots of new friends. The martial arts display was generally judged to be excellent, so thanks to Mr. Ooi for bringing along his very accomplished team.

Around 7.30 AM several Society members arrived by prior arrangement to help set up so special thanks to them, because without their assistance I don't think we'd have made it! Anyway, I gather they all enjoyed the experience. Inside the hall was a mass of Bruce Lee posters, plus an enormous black and white picture covering the back of the stage. Not everything went right by a long chalk. The slide projector proved uncooperative and winching up and down the screen turned out to be a mammoth task! The main film, *Way of the Dragon,* brought forth umpteen cameras which flashed away in the fight scenes, especially the double nunchaku sequence.

Actually, that's the only section I really got to see - shame there was so much work to do!

Afterwards lots of members told me that seeing *Way of the Dragon* uncut was in itself enough to make their journey worthwhile; judging by all the clapping and cheering that went on during the censored sections I think most people would agree with them. After the film we had the essay contest on "Why Bruce Lee was the greatest." Believe me that was a difficult one to judge, they were really all so good. Eventually we had a tie for first place. One of the winners being Will Johnston from Barrow, a name we know well. Hands up those who noticed his smart blue jumper, done specially to look like one of Bruce's. Congratulations too to the audience who gave a cracking response to all the competitors.

Japanese records and books, t-shirts, key rings, etc., were given out like wildfire and the later spot prizes (drawn from ticket numbers) sent many a member home with more items for his/her Bruce Lee collection. Then came another high point, a showing of the *Green Hornet* screen test. The start was nail-biting because every time the projector was started, the film snapped! Eventually, with no less than three people holding the giant spools, the rare, eight-minute snip took hold. It was a knockout! Shot when the Master was just 24, no one had ever seen anything like it. Every scene and camera angle captured his words, his mannerisms, his art and his skills. First time through we just sat and looked in amazement. A second showing was thrown open to the eager owners of cameras, for them to get snapping! The astonishing climax to the whole day was the unique, near unbelievable tape recording made just ten days before by James Coburn. To hear this tape was to understand their close relationship and James' deep admiration for the supreme talents of his friend. It really was a sincere and moving tribute to the Little Dragon. For an actor of his calibre to take the time to make this tape certainly proved how deeply he felt for his "brother" (as he called Bruce). At the end, James called for a minutes silence and, honestly, you could have heard a pin drop! It was a deeply moving scene as hundreds of people were stunned into revered silence by the words they had heard and the respect they held for Bruce.

We were drained, we were full of peace and we were all as one. It was a beautiful feeling. At this point I really must thank most sincerely, Eddy Pumer, for all his marvellous assistance in helping get the event off the ground and, in particular, for landing both the *The Green Hornet* screen test and the Coburn interview which was sensational stuff! Then thanks too should go to Roy Byrne (ex-Cathay Films and long-time friend) for carrying on the MC-ing in such an inimitable and carefree style, despite the many technical hitches. How he managed to withstand that heat in his very smart three-piece suit only he and his tailor will know! Also we mustn't forget *KFM's* Bruce Sawford who seemed to be in so many places at once, I thought he had twin brothers! Irene and Jane from "Sidekicks" were the true bastions behind the organisation, and Vic, Roger and Sally gave Stirling service on the *KFM* stand (sometimes the queue of potential customers stood nearly a dozen deep!). Congratulations must definitely go to Mr. Ooi for stage managing a superb martial arts demonstration (by members of his London club) under very testing conditions indeed.

A RETROSPECTIVE LOOK AT BRUCE LEE MANIA & THE KUNG FU CRAZE OF THE 1970S

Finally, a very special thank you to the Society members who turned up early to help with putting up posters, stalls, etc. That list includes Mike Devereux, Jeff Millington, John Watson, Peter Barnacle, Marlon and Elvis Whetton, David Rawson and Lorraine Smith, Dawn and Nigel Martin, Alison French, Ray Tidswell, John Milne and many others. With everyone pitching in, I think I can say that the first Bruce Lee convention was a great success. See you all again next year!

GENERAL NEWS

Members Colin Joelson, Paul Wade and Carl Jones have written in to say that the *Game of Death* Super-8 colour film they ordered and received from the Bruce Lee JKD Club of Hong Kong had to be returned, due to the exceptionally poor quality of the film. I believe that Regent Films have decided not to import it because of this quality problem. However, Paul does tell me he recently purchased a *Game of Death* 400 foot film from Miko Studios, Kennemstratweg 35, 1814 GB Alkmaar, Holland. They sell the film in four parts - each 400 foot reel costing £32. The quality is good. They also do 4 x 400 foot films of *Big Boss* and *Fist of Fury* and quite a few *Green Hornets*. Write to them for info, but if sending orders, pay by International Money Order only. Last thing, the *Game of Death* film has German dialogue! Colin Joelson (Kirkby, Liverpool) wants to know of any Wing Chun classes in Liverpool so can anyone help? Please write direct to Colin.

> ## Don't forget about Li
>
> I have been reading Combat Magazine since August, yet nothing has been mentioned about Bruce Li.
> I read in an article in Kung Fu monthly that Bruce Li is Bruce Lee's successor.
> I am a great admirer of Lee but on hearing so much on Li, most of it complimentary, I decided to see for myself and went to watch "Exit the Dragon, Enter the Tiger" and he is the next best to Bruce Lee.
> I am sure that I must express the wishes of many Combat readers to see Bruce Li in your magazine.
> Why not have Li on the Fighting Stars page?
>
> Kevan Cowley,
> Biddick,
> Washington,
> Tyne and Wear.

John Bell (our most regular news sheet cartoonist) tells me he recently saw a film entitled *It Lives Again*. During a scene where a woman goes into a cinema, we see on the screen - you've guessed it - Bruce, in *Enter the Dragon*. John tells me this was the best part of the film!

Member Graham Raggett sent me the cutting shown here. *Fist of Fury Part 2* (which of course stars Bruce Li and NOT the Master) is blatantly billed as starring Bruce Lee. I've already passed word on to Golden Harvest about this latest rip-off.

Check out too a new film that's going around in the States, *The Real Bruce Lee*. It positively guarantees the man himself, but co-stars Li and a certain Dragon Lee. It seems from my investigations (more on this in *KFM* 49) that the Little Dragon stuff comes mainly from *The Orphan,* one of his early childhood films.

That obviously makes it well worth a look, even though the advertising poster kinda gives the impression that there's latter-day Lee in there as well. That info, by the way, comes courtesy of Douglas W. Banks, a non-member, but still a Bruce fan.

Shahab Setudeh Nejad (member 1419 and who recently moved to Seattle, USA) wants fellow members to write to him with essays on why Bruce Lee was so famous, why he was so different from other martial artists and your ideas on how he became such a great name and legend in such a short time. Shahab is a devoted fan and he's trying to get together a survey on Bruce. He's willing to pay $5 per essay. He says there's very little news on the Little Dragon in Seattle (which is surprising). He's studying at Seattle University (yes, the actual one!) and apparently he wrote for his professor, an essay on Bruce and his philosophy. The professor was delighted and he admitted that he'd known very little about this aspect of Bruce Lee, thinking him only an actor (!). Shahab wants us to spread info on the Master, and with the help of his survey, he hopes to get a better insight into the problems. His address is: Seattle, Washington, USA.

Whilst on the subject of schools, member Yael Shelach from Israel has a pal in Hong Kong who's been telling him about the colleges Bruce attended there. La Salle College and St. Francis Xavier are both Catholic secondary schools, with a primary school attached to La Salle (which is a famous boys' school in Hong Kong). St. Francis Xavier is in the Yau Yast Juem district of Kowloon, close to Bruce's last home. I'm sure you'll all be interested in the letter reproduced here that's headed "Don't forget about Li." Member Paul Short sent in the cutting which he seems pretty disgusted with and he reckons Kevan Cowley is "seeing things"! Actually, I'd take one issue with Kevan saying that *KFM* had Li tipped as Lee's successor. That's news to me. Most of the words I've seen have been pretty uncomplimentary.

I expect many of you have seen *Marlowe* on TV of late as it seems to have been shown in most areas at one time or another. It's always worth watching, even for the short time that Bruce appears - Do you know that I've never seen it right through? I always switch off after the Little Dragon has gone over the balcony! By the way, if anyone knows where we can get *Marlowe* posters or stills, please let me know.

David Short (1854) wants urgently to buy a pair of nunchakus like those Bruce used in *Game of Death*. Can anyone help? If you can, write direct at Romford. He'd be most grateful.

Many of you will remember the record *In Memory of Bruce Lee* by John & Rosalind, which came out in 1974. Well, Richard Miller (1638) managed to obtain a copy recently from "Oldies Unlimited," 6/12 Stafford Street, St.George's, Telford, Shrops, TF2 9NQ, England. The record was released by Warner Brothers, No. K 16354.

Johnny Tandon (2092) thought a mention of his Karate club would be in order for anyone wishing to join up. It's The Wado Ryu Karate Club, Omagh, Co.Tyrone, N. Ireland.

Alexander Buttigieg (2199) from Malta wrote in to The Times paper about *Game of Death,* giving them a general run-down on the film and (craftily) a mention of the Society and its address! One point Alex raised with them was their mention of Kim Tai Jong as the "stand-in" for Bruce. Asking the paper where they'd got the info (as the name was supposedly being kept quiet), Mr. Emm J. Ellul said it was in *Monthly Film Bulletin* Vol. 45, June 1978, page 112.

Will the person who called on Cambridge member Don Clift (2172) sometime back in February, please contact him again. I gather you missed each other on that occasion. Don says you're welcome and asks you to come round about 6 PM some evening.

Mr. I. McNorton sent in a cutting telling about *Enter the new Bruce Lee*. It concerns an actor, Jackie Chan, who was a former Chinese Opera star whose last two martial arts epics have been blockbusters. His latest film, *The Fearless Hyena* (are they joking?) prompted a critic to write: "Most people believed Bruce Lee's mantle as Kung Fu King would be handed over to someone else one day. Few could have imagined, however, that it might be taken by a squat, muscular young man whose rubbery face is dominated by a massive nose." His career began at seven, with singing and acrobatics. His first film *Snake in the Eagle's Shadow* was (presumably) a blockbuster in Singapore, Malaysia and other Asian countries last year. He has directed *Hyena* and has signed up with Golden Harvest. Company Executive, Shen San, says they hope to make and release a worldwide film on Chan. He added cautiously: "Bruce Lee is an international celebrity; Jackie Chan has still to prove himself worldwide." Are we to be treated to yet another "martial arts epic," the sort that turns out so ludicrously infantile as to be an insult to the audience watching? We shall see.

Anyone watching the *Hazell* series recently, writes Ian Hamilton (1213), would have heard Hazell call a villain "Bruce Lee" - because he trained in the martial arts. I can't say I'm pleased with the man he called "Bruce," but still, a mention is a mention!

Now, members' assistance is required for a gentleman in London. This person purchased in 1968 a complete course of Malayan books on the art of Kung Fu by a famous exponent of the skills of wrestling. The books were advertised in a few magazines such as *Titbits* in 1968. The address was in Malaya and when our friend received his parcel it was, unluckily, destroyed in a fire! He has no more info than that, but maybe someone else who bought the books could help. If you can, write direct to at London.

I've heard from various sources, including members Gino Crane and Alan Mount that *The Silent Flute* has been re-titled *Circle of Iron* in the States. I can't personally understand the necessity for this. *The Silent Flute* is the best and only title for the film and no improvements can be made by changing it. Alan also says that receipts for *The Silent Flute* during its first three weeks were $111,027 and in Los Angeles, one cinema alone grossed $3,206 in a week. The film figures in the Top 50 movies of the week in the trade paper *Variety* and apparently in America, when a film achieves a degree of success, it then usually increases its box office potential. In fact, Alan feels that if *The Silent Flute* had opened in the States first, it would have done better here. The point is though, it's hardly been shown in the UK anyway!

Member David Moore points out the following similarities between Bruce and other big name stars: Charlie Chaplin who probably got into childhood acting because his father was a stage performer. He took parts he didn't like and he went to the States to make his fortune but constantly argued with a particular director and, eventually, he formed his own film studios. James Dean died before his last film was released. Elvis Presley was making a film about the martial arts when he died, though it's not clear whether the picture will be completed or not.

Graham Waggett (2602) saw an advert for a stretching device, and advertising it was Alex Kwon. He's billed as the number one kata champion who has been chosen to play the leading role in *Life and Legend of Bruce Lee*. Check out the clipping printed.

My Tribute to Bruce Lee - by John Milne:

> "At the Golden Harvest Studios in enters the Dragon, Bruce Lee, saying I am the Big Boss and I will show you the way of the Dragon. He began with his kicks of lightning and finished with his deadly fists of fury. But be was like a METEORITE passing across the sky... he did not know he was playing with the game of death."

Alex Kwon — The No. 1 Kata Champion has been chosen to play the leading role in 'The Life & Legend of Bruce Lee'.

MAIL ORDER SPECIAL

As all of you will soon be discovering, *KFM* 50 will have on very limited offer, most of the unique souvenirs that were on sale at the recent convention. However, I think it's only right (particularly in view of dwindling supplies) that Society members get first pickings. Obviously quite a few of you were unable, for one reason or another, to make it on the day, so I hope this helps make up a little for what you missed. Remember, most of these items will NEVER again be repeated once stocks have gone, and if past history is anything to go by, collectors will soon be hot on the trail and paying high prices! In some cases, there really are only very small quantities remaining, so move fast! We have:

- First Convention T-Shirts @ £2.25 (inc. p&p) - state large, medium or small.
- First Convention Mugs @ £2.16 (inc. p&p).
- First Convention Brooches @ 76p (inc. p&p).
- First Convention Scarves @ 54p (inc. p&p).
- Cassette of Bruce Lee's Last Interview @ ££3.60 (inc. p&p).

Note: All these prices include a 10% discount that is available to Society members ONLY. Send your cheque/postal order (made out to *Kung Fu Monthly*, please) to: Convention Offers, *Kung Fu Monthly*, 14 Rathbone Place, London W1P IDE.

SPECIAL MESSAGES

Congratulations to member John Milne and his wife, who recently had a happy addition to the family - named Robert Lee Milne! (need I say, after Bruce's brother). John's first baby was named after a member of the "Slade" pop group - Neville John Milne. It seems the newcomer is already turning on Bruce Lee actions and war cries (at just four years old!).

A message from myself to members Kate Feeney and Mr. Skipper. I hope you've both recovered from your respective accidents.

AREA LISTS

All members between numbers 2600 and 2685 will receive an area list with this sheet. It tells you the fans around your area that you can write to, contact or meet up with. Get cracking and organise your own mini-conventions!

RENEWALS

Members from 2303 through to 2377, your second-year renewal falls between now and the end of August. Members 2022 to 2084, your third-year renewal is due at the same time. Don't miss the next convention so get those renewals in fast!

LETTERS

Dear Pam,

I think it totally unfair to Raymond Chow that so many "so called" Bruce Lee fans have disliked Game of Death. *Have these complainers ever realised what a difficult task it must have been for Chow, when his number one man suddenly dies with the storyline and script stored in his head? If the double had not completed the movie through sheer hard work and determination, we'd never have known, let alone seen, the unique Bruce Lee ever again.*

Gillian Wood (2637)

Sorry, Gillian, I had to miss out much of your letter, but I think the fans will get the message! Actually, I disagree that Bruce died with the storyline in his head (not to mention the action sequences). The fights had largely been already recorded and in fact several still lie unused in Hong Kong. The main gist of the plot was also very well known to quite a few people. What fans (and I include myself) were particularly annoyed about was the lack of Bruce Lee fighting footage and the total change of story. There were quite enough action sequences available to keep to the origi-

"WHY DONT YOU KNOCK WHEN YOU COME HOME ?"

nal plot, while using a stand-in to fill in elsewhere.

Member Anne Fitzgerald wrote the following to the person in *Sports Postbag* who criticised Bruce (see last news sheet):

> I do not think you eligible to run a sports column, let alone make comments on someone you know nothing about. All I can say is, either you are an ill-informed specimen of the human race, or you are simply ignorant of this particular area of Kung Fu. Bruce Lee was the greatest exponent of Kung Fu the world has ever known, but Kung Fu is an ART first and can only be called a sport second. Perhaps you've not seen any of Bruce's movies but if you had, maybe you'd understand the grace, magic and pure artistry of it all.

COMPETITION

There are seven prizes for the last comp and these go to: Paul Bocking (2206), Richard Miller (1638), Michael Harris (1078), Paul Smith (1532), Gary Nash (2324), Carl Jones (2121) and Graeme Warwick (2619). They all receive a copy of *The Unbeatable Bruce Lee,* which is a fabulous new book that'll be available to fans soon. Answers were as follows: 1) Winslow Wong. 2) 9th February, 1965. 3) Tang Lung. 4) 1968. 5) Peter Lee (Bruce's brother). No space for a competition this issue. I'm planning on running them less frequently, but with much bigger prizes!

SWOP SHOP

- Wayne Jones (2230), London wants *KFM's* No. 1-4. Write to him with price or swap required.
- Paul Das (2313), Middlesbrough desperately needs *KFM's* No. 1 & 2. He'll pay up to £3.50 each in mint condition.
- Robert Chamberlain (2643), Monmouth has to swap *KFM's* 1 (2 copies), 3, 6 and 7 (1 copy of each) and he wants issues 10, 11, 12 and 13.
- Mr. W. Wilkinson (2561), Louth wants *KFM's* 1-4. Write with prices.
- Lorraine Smith (2320), Mickley wants info on where to obtain slides on Bruce. Any assistance appreciated. Write direct please.
- John Milne (2064), Glasgow has a *Fist of Fury* film poster, cassette copies of all Bruce soundtracks except *Way of the Dragon,* plus *Enter the Dragon* music only, *Ballad of Bruce Lee* LP by brother Robert. Wants in exchange, anything on the *Green Hornet* - especially the model Corgi car. Write with details.
- Colin Joelson (2377), Kirkby wants to know where to get the 8mm version of *Way of the Dragon* (inc. double nunchaku sequence) which was selling at Regent Films for £32.50. They're sold out at present. He also wants any taped interviews of Bruce, plus an original *Way of the Dragon* poster.
- Melanie Ogden (2319), Coton Fields has *Game of Death* film poster to swap for a *Close Encounters* film poster. Also *Dragon Power* poster to swap for *Close Encounters* fold-out poster magazine.
- David Thomas (2585), Stoke-on-Trent wants copy of *Best of Bruce Lee No. 1*. Will give in exchange the 12" *Dragon Power* record.
- Graeme Warwick (2619), Glasgow wants info on where to get *Green Hornet* items. First five people to write in with help or items will receive taped recordings

A RETROSPECTIVE LOOK AT BRUCE LEE MANIA & THE KUNG FU CRAZE OF THE 1970S

Paul Wade (1836)

John Milne (2046) & his son

D.G. Spence (2437)

2065 FERNANDEZ (NIGERIA)

John R Bell.

"I HATE IT WHEN THEY HAVE THESE KUNG-FU FILMS ON!"

JULIUS (2065) NIGERIA

of *Way of the Dragon* LP/*The Green Hornet* theme. Please, however, enclose a SAE. Also needs Bruce film posters/press books; *Best of Bruce Lee Nos. 1 and 2*, tapes of Lee interviews, JKD Club's *Bruce Lee Combats, Bruce Lee Memorial 1940-1973* book, *Secret Art of Bruce Lee, Bruce Lee in Action*, any foreign magazines/books on Bruce. He also has to swap: three singles - *Chinese Kung Fu* by Banzai, *Kung Fu* by Leval Thompson, *Ballad of Bruce Lee* by Robert Lee, two *Dragon Power* singles, photocopies of *Way of the Dragon* pressbooks, Chinese newspaper ad for *Enter the Dragon, Female Fugitive* Chinese film poster, all JKD Club books/posters.

- Kevin Stokes (2624), Newport wants *Bruce Lee's Nunchakus in Action* and *The Immortal Dragon*.
- David Niedzailek (1021), Neath has copy of *Enter the Dragon* film poster. Wants in exchange original of either *Fist of Fury, Way of the Dragon* or *Game of Death*.
- Graham Waggett (2602), Stenson Fields wants to know where to get an *Enter the Dragon* production trailer - other then from Regent films.
- David Leeming (1188), Rochdale has a medium size *Game of Death* tracksuit to swap for either *Best of Bruce Lee No. 1* (mint) or £10; or would consider Super-8 film trailer.
- T. Cape (2119), Gwent has to swap, *KFM's* 4, 5, 6, 10 & 11. Wants Nos. 2, 15, 17, 19, and 20.
- Christopher Morgan (1051), Stoke-on-Trent has colour/silent (but with cassette sound) film from *Way of the Dragon* - runs 15 mins. It contains double-nunchaku scenes and Bruce/ Norris fight. Cost £35 - selling (as new) for £25. His projector's packed up!
- Paul Wade (1836), Hull has to sell *Fist of Fury* Japanese LP for £6.50 inc p&p.
- Peter Jagger (2681), Birmingham wants *The Green Hornet* annual and original film posters from all Bruce's films.
- Mr.N.Kavanagh (2618), Kilmarnock says he can make brooches out of Society member's fave pictures. Any picture must be at least 8cms square. Badge will be back within a week of ordering. Prices: (exclusive of postage - send SAE), 1 to 5 badges @ 45p each, 5 to 10 badges @ 40p each, 10 and above @ 35p each.

PEN PALS

- Mr. G. A. Skipper (2344), Coventry wants Chinese pen pals, male/female (preferably female) aged about 18 (his age). His interests are Bruce and the martial arts - he does Shaolin Mok-Ka.
- Alan Cousins (2631), Leighton Buzzard wants female, Chinese pen pals. His interests are Bruce, martial arts, photography, motor cycling.
- Mr. S.Collingwood (2241), Rhodesia wants pen pals. He's aged 19, actor by profession, interested in Karate and Kung Fu (as well as Bruce!).
- Kevin Stokes (2624), Gwent wants Chinese/USA pen pal.

And that's all there's room for this news sheet. Once again, thanks to all you fans who came to the first convention... it was great! See you all again next year, along I hope with plenty of newcomers.

Lastly, don't forget to grab your copies of *KFM* 50; as you might have guessed, it's going to be the most sensational issue ever! Pam

BRUCE LEE SOCIETY COLUMN
KUNG FU MONTHLY NO. 52

BRUCE LEE WEEK - Nov 25th-Dec 1st.

Once more the Bruce Lee Society takes a vital step forward towards ultimate, worldwide recognition of the Master. *Kung Fu Monthly* was the first magazine of its kind anywhere and it remained true to its goal and survived when every one of the others fell by the wayside. The Bruce Lee Society, once formed, marshaled its forces and succeeded, where the rest just came and went. The Society organised the world's first Bruce Lee convention and so well was it received, others now try to copy it in almost every detail!

It's really rather flattering. The fame and charisma of the Master was enough to spawn a bumper crop of lookalikes and rip-offs but now it seems as though The Bruce Lee Society is getting the same treatment. As I say, I'm truly flattered.

What all this adds up to is SUCCESS. At last, the Bruce Lee movement is reaping rewards and that's largely down to all the years of hard work that you and all of us here have been putting in together. That others now see an opportunity to cash-in on it is proof enough that the job has been well done.

But for the Bruce Lee Society, enough is never enough, and to celebrate the next stage of our development, I've declared World Bruce Lee Week to run November 25th to December 1st. Every year I intend *KFM* and the Society to celebrate this unique event in the Bruce Lee calendar.

Of course there have to be objectives for each of the seven days, otherwise the week would ring very hollow indeed. Therefore, following now are my suggestions for the work to be carried out-during those celebrations.

Day 1 (Sunday 25th November) - A time of relaxation and meditation on the thoughts, sayings and words of the Master. Decide how YOU will live this week in a way Bruce would have approved.

Day 2 (Monday 26th November) - Time to start work on a campaign to spread the Master's word to as many people as possible. Contact local newspapers, radio and TV stations etc, to tell them of the seven-day celebration and to ask that they report the event in some way. Talk to them about your feelings for Bruce Lee and impress on them the size of the worldwide movement and the success of the Society.

Day 3 (Tuesday 27th November) - A very important day, of course, for it is time to celebrate his birthday. Perhaps consider what Bruce might have been doing now but be happy in the legacy He left with us. Essentially, however, it's a day of fun, and in that spirit it would be appropriate to hold a party, relaxed and informal.

Day 4 (Wednesday 28th November) - Let the real work begin! From today, until the end of the week, see how many new recruits you can find for the Society. Remember though, they must be interested in the aims of the Bruce Lee movement; a passing whim is not enough. Let me know how many new members YOU find; prizes will be offered to those who introduce five or more new faces.

Day 5 (Thursday 29th November) - Thursday is petitioning day. If there is something you'd like to see shown at your local cinema or on TV, or perhaps there's a film that hasn't yet been made, but you think should be, or maybe you just wish to protest about savage and senseless censorship. Whatever it is, this is the day to take action to let those in authority or command, know your view on their actions. Of course praise too, where praise is due.

Day 6 (Friday 30th November) - A day for tidying up loose ends. Your last chance to meditate on the implications of the world's first ever Bruce Lee Week, to introduce new members to the Society and to prepare yourself for the Bruce Lee Film Festival.

Day 7 (Saturday 1st December) - At last, the great day has arrived, the true culmination of a week's work and the finest possible way to bring to a close World Bruce Lee Week. Join hands with your brothers and sisters at the first Bruce Lee Film Festival.

You'll find all the details elsewhere in this issue of Kung-Fu Monthly. You can't afford to miss this, the seventh day of World Bruce Lee Week; celebrate along with us on a unique occasion.

We remember the legacy of the Master and once more, in the words of James Coburn, "the circle is rejoined."

- Pam

BRUCE LEE SOCIETY COLUMN
KUNG FU MONTHLY NO. 53

Thank you, thank you, thank you for coming along in such huge numbers to this country's second major Bruce Lee event of 1979; the first ever Bruce Lee Film Festival. It made a wonderful "last chapter" to my Hong Kong trip!

I think all those there will agree that this time the venue turned out to be near ideal because, size-wise, we filled Kilburn's massive State Theatre with only a few seats left to spare. That means over 1,700 fans piled in. You just don't know how relieved I am that NO ONE had to be turned away.

And I thought, too, that the projection work was excellently handled and the sound system, crystal clear. My congratulations to all the technicians concerned. Sadly, plans are afoot to convert the enormous auditorium into three screens, but if that gets delayed a while, I think we shall be looking no further for a site for the 1980 convention.

I hope everyone enjoyed the little tit-bits that were included at late notice; first it's James Coburn, then this time it's a greetings message from Robert Lee! Bruce Lee-wise, I must say I loved that snippet from *My Son Ah Chang* (I can't wait to see it in full at the next convention) and, of course, that very rare Golden Harvest tape that we played last of all, had to be the most fitting of finales.

Last, and definitely not least, I have to hand a warm vote of thanks to Eddy Pumer for his superb compeering work. Only he could have carried us over the one disappointment of the day; a chunk missing from *Fist of Fury*, presumably removed by a scissor-happy projectionist.

By the way, it's vital that I tell you the following disastrous news. Once the reels that we were showing wear out, and already they're looking somewhat "tired," I'm told there can NEVER be any replacements! That's not the case with the usual, English dialogue, censored version, just the uncut originals. Therefore, what we were showing is a slice of history that will quite soon disappear forever, which is a sad, indeed tragic fact. Take my advice and see them while you're still able to.

A quick change of subject. I've been thinking for a while about the possibility of having a bronze bust or statuette made of Bruce so recently I checked out some details. We can have a bust (life size) at a cost of around £200; a full-size statue (also lifesize) would set us back around £1,000/£1,500. So, what I want from ALL you members are suggestions on the siting of a Bruce Lee bust/statue and whether you would be willing to contribute the required amount. Please write to me via the Bruce Lee Society BUT ON A POSTCARD ONLY PLEASE.

Just time for a last minute "scoop". Most of you will know about that rarest of rare books; Bruce's own *Chinese Gung Fu*. Over the years, I've had hundreds of enquiries about it and now, exclusively for Society members, I've managed to get hold of some reprints. They're available DIRECT FROM ME so just send £4.50 inc postage (Outside Britain, add £1) to me at 14 Rathbone Place, London W1P 1DE. Please make cheques/PO's payable to Pam Hadden.

Lastly of course, a quick word on the one and only Bruce Lee Society. Our strength lies in our membership and not like most appreciation societies, a collection of half interested fans, the BLS can truly boast the most dedicated and active followers in the land. If YOU feel that YOUR enthusiasm fits the bill, then WE NEED YOU! Become a part of the great, worldwide Bruce Lee movement. Send a cheque or postal order for £3.25 (made out to KFM, please) to: Bruce Lee Society Subscriptions, 14 Rathbone Place, London W1P 1DE.

- Pam

BRUCE LEE SOCIETY COLUMN
KUNG FU MONTHLY NO. 54

Hello, fellow members of the Bruce Lee Society. Judging by the letters that have been piling in, it hardly needs me to tell you the sad, sad news. The British Board of Film Censors, the group of people who decide what's fit for us to see and what isn't, have finally brought *Enter the Dragon* and *Fist of Fury* into line with the rest of Bruce Lee's output by hacking out the nunchaku sequences! Intrigued as to why this should be happening so many years after the original release, we telephoned the Board's Mr. Ferman to see what he had to say.

"Mr. Ferman, we're approaching a decade of *Enter the Dragon* and *Fist of Fury*, why on earth chop them now?"

"*Enter the Dragon* and *Fist of Fury* are the only two films we've ever passed with chain stick sequences in as we didn't know what they were at the time! The films have now become standards; they go round time and again. Just like Douglas Fairbanks of the 20's and Errol Flynn of the 30's, Bruce Lee is the great action star of the 70's and his films will always be shown. The last time they went around, though, we had complaints about the appearance of chain sticks among kids in playgrounds, football matches and so on."

"Of course for a good part it will be the action that people will remember. Therefore does it not worry you that you're often chopping out the main fight scenes?"

"It never amounts to much material; three or four minutes is the most we've ever cut from a Bruce Lee film."

"Why though, have nunchakus been singled out when just about all other conventional weapons are apparently okay?"

"The chain stick is easily available, and having made it, there is no other use. A knife, for instance, has many other uses. And you've got to ask, too, why this country is not alone in its concern. Japan, for instance, has banned them completely. In Canada, chain sticks simply aren't allowed to be carried around without a permit as they're considered an offensive weapon. I personally think France's atitude is best; they say they don't mind having the weapon in films because they're not going to allow it anywhere in society."

"I'm not in any position to dispute with you how many people have been caught using nunchakus in an irresponsible way. However, it does seem to me that many of the films that pass the censor today are positively sickening in the effects they achieve. Don't you find this acceptance of what I call 'horror violence' far more worrying than anything Bruce Lee ever did? A good example, for instance, would be the slow motion, close-up of someone's brains being blown out that I saw recently."

"There are different kinds of violence. Some, like *The Deerstalker*, I agree is emotionally disturbing to watch. The problem with Bruce Lee films is that they're not emotionally disturbing to watch at all; they're bloody exciting and as I say, very easily imitated. What we've got to worry about is not the normal Bruce Lee fan; it's the abnormal Bruce Lee fan."

So there it is. It seems that emotionally disturbing violence is "okay", and that, as usual, the daft behaviour of the idiot few, is good enough excuse for the rest of us to miss out on what we love best. And as if all this isn't enough to worry about, try this for size. At present, there's a Williams Committee investigating for Parliament, amongst other things, the possibility of not allowing the private showing of unlicensed (i.e. uncensored) films. If that goes through in about a year's time, it would signal the end of the Bruce Lee Film Festival, at least as we know it. Stand by for a massive petition sometime in the future!

It's been several years now since we set the Bruce Lee Society subscription at £3.25 and unfortunately, the time is now set for a significant rise. As of April 1st the cost of a subscription will be £5.00 and although this may sound a lot, remember that we've been holding the price down while others have been increasing it as often as once a year.

If you want to beat the price rise, GET YOUR SUBCRIPTION IN NOW! £3.25's will be accepted up until the last day in March! The address to write is: 14 Rathbone Place, London W1P 1DE.

Thanks to KFM's Bruce Sawford for interviewing Mr. Ferman of the British Board of Film Censors. If you'd like to register your own protest, they're at 3 Soho Square, London W1.)

— Pam

EDITOR'S NOTES

 In the three months since the last issue, the first UK Bruce Lee convention had taken place and as is evident from the write up, it was a huge success.

The Real Bruce Lee was advertised as having just that; the real Bruce Lee! While it did contain the real Bruce Lee, it was limited to sepia-toned footage of four of his childhood films. The rest was made up of a highlights reel of imitator Bruce Li and feature film starring Korean imitator Dragon Lee in *Last Fist of Fury*. In a rare occurrence, the UK video release ran for 20 minutes longer than its US counterpart.

 Issue 12 marks the first mention of Jackie Chan. It's quite evident from the newsletters over the next couple of years that Jackie wasn't very well received to start with. I think that had to do with the abundance of imitators about, plus the fact that as soon as a new martial arts actor came along, the press and film companies were quick and happy to promote them with headlines such as "The New Superstar," "Better Than Bruce Lee" or "The Best Kung Fu Star Yet!"

As you carry on reading, once Chan finds his path, peoples' attitudes soften and eventually, he wins over an entire army of fans. *Bruce Lee: His Life and Legend* was an unmade biopic about the life of Bruce Lee, with a script written by *Enter the Dragon* director Robert Clouse. The research for the script ultimately because the nucleus for Clouse's 1988 book, *Bruce Lee: The Biography*.

COME VISIT US AT THE NEW KFM BACK ISSUES CENTRE!

Avoid postal delays and buy — on the spot — nearly all the Bruce Lee items advertised in this month's KFM Marketplace.

The Centre is at 14 Rathbone Place, London W1, and opening times are Monday to Friday, 10am to 6pm.

SEE YOU SOON!

WELCOME TO THE START OF THE FOURTH YEAR WITH THE SOCIETY - AND TO ALL THOSE MEMBERS JUST RECENTLY JOINED WHO MISSED THIS YEAR'S CONVENTION, PLANS ARE ALREADY WELL UNDER WAY FOR THE 1980 MAMMOTH EVENT - NOT TO MENTION THE BRUCE LEE FILM FESTIVAL ON DECEMBER 1ST! KEEP YOUR EYES GLUED TO FUTURE NEWS SHEETS AND ISSUES OF KFM.

GENERAL NEWS

First off, that news sheet "gremlin" struck again. All the convention offers that were advertised in the June news sheet went down well, except that we ended up without any scarves! In just about every edition, SOMETHING like this happens and I'm just beginning to wonder who the comic is who slips these in. What, I wonder, will it be this time? Seriously, apologies to anyone sending in for the scarves - all monies will of course be refunded. Next year we WILL be doing the scarves but this year we just got let down at the last minute.

Regarding the convention, just to let you know that I've written to James Coburn to thank him for the fabulous recording he made and to let him know how much we appreciated it. If I get any sort of reply, you can be sure that I'll let you know the contents!

Now, in case you haven't already heard about it, how about the up-coming Bruce Lee Film Festival? When EMI let us down in regards to lending us the films, I must say I thought it was all over. But no, some marvellous friends of ours have stepped into the breech and are lending us *Boss*, *Fist*, and *Way* - ALL COMPLETELY UN-CENSORED!!! Isn't that amazing? The great day will be December first and the venue is the Gaumont State Cinema, Kilburn High Road, London NW6. Tickets will cost £3.00 for Society members, and £3.50 for everyone else. I STRONGLY URGE YOU ALL TO BOOK AHEAD! There MAY be some available on the day, but I can't be sure. One thing I hate to think of is the sad faces of the fans who got to the Convention, only to find that it was sold out. It just isn't worth it. Check in *KFM* 51 for the latest information.

In line with the Festival, I'm declaring the week starting Sunday 25th of November to be WORLD BRUCE LEE WEEK. More on that in *KFM* 52, but the great thing is, that not only will the week end with the film festival, it will also, of course, include the date of Bruce's birth. With the convention every Summer and Bruce Lee Week every Winter, what better ways to celebrate the memory of the Master?

Ian Hamilton (1213) thinks (and I agree) that it would be a good idea to contact the makers of "Action Man" to see if they could do a model Bruce Lee, with all the equipment (nunchaku, clothes, etc). After all, they make the Bionic Man and Woman, so why not Bruce if the demand were big enough? That means I'm asking as many of you as possible to write to the makers - Palitoy Ltd., Coalville, Leicester, England - to enquire if it's possible. And it's no good everyone saying, "Why should I bother, when everyone else will do it." That way, nothing will get done. Maybe it's even worth getting some petitions done. Try asking them what sort of demand is necessary for them to take action. I'll be writing too, but just one person won't be enough so I need your support.

Ian also reports that Debonair Film Distributors Ltd., Coventry Cine Centre, Lower Ford Street, Coventry 5PW 1PW, England, have a 400 foot colour/silent *Game of Death* film that includes the censored Lee/Inosanto nunchaku fight, the Lee/Jabbar fight and end credits showing clips from *Big Boss, Fist of Fury* and *Way of the Dragon* - a great film priced at £32.50. They also do complete video-cassette tapes of (Bruce feature films) at £86.25.

Arthur Stone (1150) says that Regent Films, PO Box 54, Blackpool FY1 ISP are importing the German *Game of Death* reel (four reels for a complete film, each reel 400' long) - cost, £40 per reel. Arthur's been told the quality is excellent. All orders will be sent cash on delivery, so you don't pay until you get the goods.

For all of you who have written regarding Jerry Ohlinger's Movie Store, it's still at 120 West third Street, New York, N.Y. 10012, USA. Member John Kemp (1729) confirms this.

Robert Walker (2565) says Sports and Denim in Glasford Street, Glasgow, Scotland sells lots of Bruce books and martial arts gear so it's worth a visit.

In regards to information sent in (June Sheet) from Member Mr. I. McNorton on Jackie Chan (another proposed successor to Bruce), I've now got word from Derek Farrin that Jackie is a very talented artist and his film *Snake in the Eagle's Shadow* is better than *Enter the Dragon,* even though Derek says that Bruce is still the best! I wrote back and said it would take an awful lot to surpass *Enter the Dragon* - and in my eyes it can never be beaten for action and skill.

Peter Jagger (2681) is also a keen fan of Jackie, although he does not think his new film *New Fist of Fury* as a guideline to his talents - much he says, are *Half a Loaf of Kung Fu* (WHAT a title!!!), *Snake in Drunken Master*, and *Shaolin Woodenmen*. Well, I'll when leave it to members to decide when seeing these films - I'm afraid I can't give any opinion as I haven't yet seen Jackie. However a picture of him is reproduced of him here, for all to see.

Ian Hamilton informs me that in ITV's *Krypton Factor* (a general knowledge programme) one Friday in June, the question was asked, "Bruce Lee was an exponent of WHICH of the martial arts?" What a terrific plug, because those of you who know this programme will realise that it's taken very seriously indeed and watched by a very mixed audience. As if the plug wasn't enough (can there ever be enough?!), Phillip Bell (2506) sent in a cutting shown below that came from the *Sun* newspaper some weeks back. It seems like suddenly everyone's waking up to Bruce Lee!

Still on publicity, Ian Hamilton and Gino D'Ambrosio (1655) sent in a cutting (also reproduced here) from the *Daily Star*. The letter is from a John Wilks and I'm sure we all agree with his sentiments. Why don't as many of you as possible write to the *Daily Star*, just to let them know that there are more fans around like Mr. Wilks so support his letter. We shouldn't miss these opportunities to promote Bruce's name by giving as much publicity as possible to this sort of letter. Maybe eventually we'll get those long-awaited repeats of *Longstreet*, *Ironside*, etc. The more publicity, the more chance of success! Lastly from Ian, I hear that Iran have completely banned all Kung Fu films so fans there are really in for a hard time.

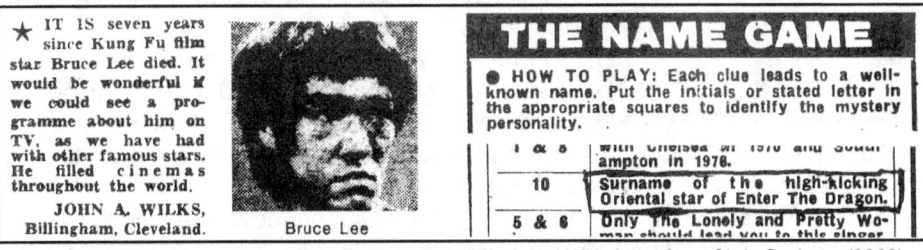

Picture Credits: "Name Game" from Philip Bell (2506); John Wilk's letter from Chris Cadman (2368).

David Moore (1783) read in *Official Karate* magazine that *The Silent Flute* been released in the States (through Avco Embassy) and re-titled *Circle of Iron* (as we've previously mentioned). However, we hear too, that consideration was also given to *Murder to the Fourth Degree* as a possible title but why an alteration is necessary is beyond me. Anyone wanting a copy of the book *Circle of Iron* (based on *The Silent Flute*)... it's released by Warner Books through the New English Library. The address for Warner Books is PO Box 690, New York, N.Y. 10019, USA. In the book itself it says that you can get any book published by Warners at this address, so it might be worth checking out on other Bruce Lee publications. David also says that Chuck Norris is making another film that's called *A Force of One*, with World Middle-Weight Champ, Bill "Super-Foot" Wallace. I must admit I never seem to spot his films locally

- which is a pity.

Heinrich Damsgaard (2125) sent me a cutting from a Danish magazine, which he translated in part for me. "Do you remember him? Bruce Lee - he lived in his dream, the dream to reach the top. He died at 32 - but then he already was a legend." The complete article gives a run-down on his life, but Heinrich says these are almost the only pictures he has seen on Bruce in Denmark - hence his request for assistance (see the Swop Shop).

Gary Nash (2324) asked me to listen to my *Enter the Dragon* soundtrack. He says that Parsons, when Bruce tricks him into the small boat, shouts and says: "Just get me out of this b......... boat! What's the matter with you kids? Come on, pull! Bruce, so help me, when I get out I'll 'ave you!" I listened, and although there's a lot of background noise, Gary could be right! What do other members think?

BRUCE LEE
1940-1973

I wonder how many of you saw the *Daily Mirror* some weeks back - talk about behind the times! They were advertising a new Bruce Lee film, starring Colleen Camp, called - you've guessed it - *Game of Death!!!* There were one or two errors in the text, too - when I rang the paper they passed me on to their "contact" who gave them the info - some press organisation. I pointed out to them that they were disgracefully out of date, but apparently they had got the info from the States. It seems that the film has only just been put out over there and *The Mirror*, not bothering to check the facts as they should have done, took it as a general release in this country! What a mess so enough said.

Enter the Dragon picture (left) sent by Philip Gibbs.

Just a quickie back on the Debonair Films mentioned earlier this news sheet, Rick Edwards (1260) tells me that this company does many, many Bruce trailers. Why not write to them for details? He has also sent in cuttings from *Fighters Monthly*.

Robert Walker (2565) went to see *Enter the Dragon* recently and was pleased to find that the supporting film, called *Master of the Flying Guillotine* and starring Jimmy Wang-Yu, was pretty good, and full of action. He suggests members see it if they can.

Referring back to the cutting included in the June news sheet, where *Fist of Fury Part II* was advertised as starring Bruce Lee (of course, it was rip-off artist, Bruce Li), Golden Harvest in London, when I contacted them, said they were going to be looking into the matter. I hope they find someone to "stamp on"! Phillip Bell also told me that the film has been showing at the ABC in Bradford - with the same outrageous billing. Apparently some of the fans, not knowing the real Bruce Lee, were yelling and screaming and saying how great Bruce Lee was! If only they were seeing the real thing!

Paul Wade (1836) reports that *Enter the Dragon* showed at his local cinema a while back and played on for six weeks! He also sent me in some cuttings - one being of a certain Ruben Morales, the latest contender (yes, yet another!) for Bruce's crown. *Official Karate* magazine (July 1979) says: "If given the opportunity, this young dynamo might make martial arts fans all over the world forget the late, great Kung Fu star." Haven't these magazines got anything better to do? Writer of the article, Mr. Bill Adams, certainly doesn't know Bruce Lee fans if he thinks they are so fickle-minded or that their feelings are so shallow that they can switch from one artist to another at random - on his, or anyone else's say so. I shall always be a Bruce Lee fan, first and foremost and a person as talented, persevering and determined as Bruce will never be forgotten, ever!

Alex Buttigieg (2199) send me in an article on *Game of Death* which contains the complete credit run-down for the film - production, editing, actors, etc. If anyone wants a copy so as to know who-did-what, and the storyline, then just send me a stamped and addressed envelope, asking for a copy of the piece.

David Niedzailek sent me in the cutting which shows an advert for Bruce Lee watches. I strongly suggest that interested members just write initially, to see if they're still available. Don't send any money until you get an answer.

Mark Hennessy, who writes on Bruce, seems to be very much a Bruce Lee fan. He says: "The trouble with articles about Bruce Lee is that nobody ever seems to look at him as a whole man (ever tried reading *KFM*, Mr. Hennessy?) Some take him as the serious practitioner of the martial arts, some as the film star - entertainer par excellence - a few have tried to probe the family side of the man. What does not seem to have happened is a realistic appraisal of all these three rolled into one PLUS the fact that although he was so Americanised and seemingly a modern man, he was Chinese. Therein lies, I think, the answer to everything Bruce did, thought and achieved (and he achieved a lot in those few precious years). A legend in his own lifetime, a man of achievement and yet a man greatly frustrated. But this is sure - if anyone brought a new broom to the cobwebby cupboards of martial arts thinking, then it was this man. And if any man can be named as responsible for causing the growth of all the arts through all the world, then it was this man. That has got to be a fitting epitaph." It's good to see someone applying a little thought before putting pen to paper.

Mark Tyler tells me that he's heard *Big Boss* and *Way of the Dragon* are to be released together, later this year which is great news, but it pales into insignificance beside the coming film festival!

Setudeh Nejad (1419), our Member in Seattle, says a Japanese Martial Arts friend told him Linda Lee is the Associate Professor of Sociology in the University of Washington. Also, on May 12th Setudah was in Los Angeles, and on a commercial TV station called K.T.L.A. at 6 PM, they showed a Kung Fu film called *Bruce Lee, The Man The Myth*. It appeared to have been the first of its kind to have been shown on TV there. Starring in it, was, of course, Bruce Li. (Pam here: What I find downright annoying is that TV companies, wherever they are, don't mind putting on stand-ins, but we never seem to get the real thing. Perhaps they just can't get them!

David Dixon (1650) wrote to say that the HMV shop, Trinity Street, Leed 1 (0532 35598) has several Japanese Bruce Lee records, and suggests members in the area contact them.

Ann Hunt (1275) sent the following little poem after the convention, which I found particularly appealing: "A special day, Another Year. A Loving thought, A silent tear. A little prayer to keep in touch with Bruce Lee, we love and miss so very much."

"If they had censored any more out of this film I'd have mistaken it for one of the adverts!"

SPECIAL REQUESTS

Mr. G. A. Skipper studied Wu Shu Kung Fu, also Wing Chun, and would like members in the Coventry area to take an interest in his art of Shaolin Mok-Ka. You can contact him at Coventry.

William Ross (2715) of Irvine wants members to contact him with a view to arranging film shows at the local cinemas, etc.

Mr. Anthony J. Latty of Penzance wants to organise the showing of films at a local cinema, which he's already been told that it's possible so he'd like members to write to him. He also wants to start his own club in the area. Again, could you write to him direct please.

Colin Joelson (2377) of Kirkby wants members to contact him too. Time to get out those dusty old pens and notepads and to get cracking! I expect to hear of several film shows taking place around the country.

A RETROSPECTIVE LOOK AT BRUCE LEE MANIA & THE KUNG FU CRAZE OF THE 1970S

Raj Sahni (2692) has a request, which I'm afraid I just haven't got the time to handle. Will any members who are able to, please write to him at Wolverhampton to give details of Bruce's complete work outs (ie warm-ups, how many sit-ups, press-ups, how long it took him, etc). Basically, anything about his training methods that's NOT been published in *KFM's*, *Memorial Monthly's*, JKD Magazines, *Tao*, or *Fighting Methods*. His thanks in advance.

LETTERS

Only room for one letter this month, and I make no apologies for reprinting the words of CARY DEAN that Jenny included in *KFM* 50 Kickback. Anyone reading this will, I know, feel as moved as I was when I first picked it up. A copy, by the way, has been sent to James Coburn - along with my "thank you" letter.

> Dear Pam,
>
> I must write down my feelings about Saturday's convention, before my sides split. I'd say not one of the many fans could deny walking away from it with a lump in their throats and tears in their eyes. I know I did after hearing James Coburn's thoughts and fond memories of Bruce Lee (I wish I had the same memories). Just by listening to James talk you could tell, like all of us, how he carries a burning admiration for the Little Dragon. In fact for me, the last 15 minutes of the convention were like hearing for the first time that Bruce had died that morning... that's how much it moved me. I am still on the crest of that unbreakable wave; I have felt a power within me ever since leaving and I can't remember feeling so low - and then so high - on anything in my life. Most of us arrived as strangers and left as friends - all because of two words, Bruce Lee. Well done all of you on a 100% success and I look forward to 1980's mammoth convention. The word must be spreading like a forest fire with a hundred mile an hour wind behind. If all the water on the Earth tipped at once, it could not douse the light burning in the middle of Bruce Lee's universe of fans!
>
> Cary Dean (1314)

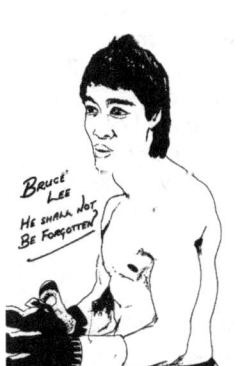

Picture Credits (Left to Right): Left - *Andrew Waite (2720)*, Centre - *Martin Schell (1819)*, Right - *Martin Schell (1819)*.

AN APOLOGY

Reading through the last news sheet, I noticed that member Yael Shelach (who is a very nice lady from Israel) was referred to as "he." I write to Yael often - and my apologies to her - but somehow or other the printers seem to love to change things around! Also, whenever I type the name "Sheila" it always seems to be changed around to "Shiela" so apologies to Sheila Boardman for that!

SPECIAL MESSAGES

Dawn and Nigel - thanks for a really smashing weekend - see you soon. Pam. One last, important thing:

Member, A. M. Burns (2378) held a raffle at work of Bruce Lee items, and managed to take £4 - which he kindly donated to the Society. As I was unable to use it at the Convention, I thought the best thing was to dip my hand into my list of member cards to select a lucky winner which turns out to be Jasdip Singh (2322). Thanks again to Mr. Burns for his nice contribution.

Paul McKenna (2331)

SWOP SHOP

- Munir Shafi (2495), Oxford wants the following for the prices quoted: *Bruce Lee in Action* - £2.50, *My Martial Arts Training Guide to Jeet Kune Do* - £1.00, *KFM Scrapbook* - £2.00, any Bruce "fighting" film trailer - £7-£9. Write direct with details.
- David Henderson (2462), Dundee has for sale to the highest bidder: *KFM Game of Death - Collectors Edition*, two *Popster* magazines (foldout posters of Bruce), 'Who Killed Bruce Lee?,' *The Secret Art of Bruce Lee, The Unbeatable Bruce Lee, KFM's Bruce Lee, King of Kung Fu, Kung Fu* special issue booklet, *KFM* hardback *Secret Art of Bruce Lee,* hardback copy of *Bruce Lee, 1940-1973,* Bruce Lee JKD magazines 1-12 complete, *Black Belt's Best of Bruce Lee No. 2, The Immortal Dragon, Bruce Lee Revenges, Reminiscence of Bruce Lee, The Fighting Spirit, Game of Death, His Unknowns in Martial Arts Learning, Secret of JKD & Kung Fu, Studies in JKD, His Privacy and Anecdotes, Nunchakus in Action,* Bruce Lee stickers - six sheets, *Flick* books, *1 and 3" Power Punch* - everything must go!
- Carl Jones (2121), St.Helens has large collection of Bruce material for sale - low prices (but buyer pays postage): Contact Carl for lists.
- Robert Walker (2565), Clydebank has for swapping Dolphin skateboard, skatepads and Kangol skate helmet, pair of black Kung Fu trousers. Wants in exchange, rubber nunchakus and any four books on Bruce or *KFM's* 47, 48, 49, 50. Has basic karate book for exchange for any book investigating Bruce's death.

- Martyn Lewis (2287), Gwent has for sale at £3.25 each, stereo cassettes of original soundtrack recording of *Way of the Dragon*.
- Heinrich Damsgaard (2125), Thisted, Denmark wants urgently to obtain books, magazines, pictures on Bruce. Write direct for details.
- Mr. P. Christakis, Clapton has various "doubles" of *KFM* magazines. Contact for details.
- Michael Roakes (2670), Burnley wants to swap *Enter the Dragon* LP for books on Bruce.
- Mark Tyler (2673), London has spare *Game of Death* cinema poster to swap for a good condition *Enter the Dragon* poster. Also for swap/sale: Double LP *Bruce Lee - Big Special* containing best of *Big Boss, Fist of Fury, Way of the Dragon,* and *Enter the Dragon* music (selling as has collected five main albums of all music)- in excellent condition, and selling for £9.50 (normally this sells in HMV for £15.95 - Pam). Wants *Big Boss, Fist of Fury, Enter the Dragon* still sets.
- Andrew Waite (2720), Bradford wants urgently: *KFM's* 1, 2, 3. Offered: £5 postal order and 27 issues of *KFM*, numbers are: 5, 6, 7, 10-18 inc, 22, 23, 25-35 inc, and 37, 38.
- William Ross (2715), Ayrshire wants Bruce posters, magazines, books (preferably not recent issues as these mostly bought already), also wants *KFM* Nos 1,2 and 4. Also offers free of charge to first person writing, *KFM's* 5 and 6.
- Paul Wade (1836), Hull wants urgently *Best of Bruce Lee No. 1* (Black Belt magazine).
- Stephen Pore, Gosport has for swap: *KFM's* 1-38 inc, plus very large amount of posters, books, stills, etc on Bruce. Wants original film soundtracks by composer Ennio Morricone such as 'Violent City' and 'Scilian Clan,' etc. Contact with details.

PEN PALS

- Michael Roakes (2670), Burnley wants female, Chinese pen pal, aged 16-17. He is 17, interested in martial arts, Bruce, cycling and reading.
- Mr. G.A. Skipper (2344),Bell Green wants male/female pen pals aged about 18 - he is 18. Interests: Bruce, martial arts, and Shaolin Mok-Ka Kung Fu.
- Robert Walker (2565), Clydebank wants pen pals interested, as he is, in Bruce, martial arts, Kung Fu movies.
- Mrs Tricia Irvine, Manchester wants boy/girl pen pal between 18-21 who (like Tricia) admires Bruce, martial arts, Kung Fu and *Blondie*.

And that's the lot for this, our lucky 13th news sheet! Back with you again for the Christmas '79 edition, but before that, remember, I'm looking forward to actually meeting as many of you as possible at the Bruce Lee Film Festival on December first. I'll be there if you will! Pam

LATE EXTRA!!!

As some members will already know, I've just been able to make the journey of a lifetime to Hong Kong! The 10 short days I had just were not enough, but even so, you'd hardly believe the experiences I managed to cram in chats with Bruce's brother, Robert, for one!. Keep an eye open in *KFM* 52 for the full, fantastic story.

Second thing is I'm afraid I shall be indisposed from Sept 12th to Oct 12th. Keep sending in the news, swaps, etc, but I'd appreciate it if you could hold back the chatty letters that need replying to. If you really can't wait that long, then member Derek Hamer of Willenhall will be doing his best to ably deputise during that month. Pam

EDITOR'S NOTES

The Bruce Lee Film Festival advertisement mentioned that EMI were lending *Kung Fu Monthly* the uncut dubbed film prints to show at the film festival but they backed out at the last minute as they wanted to keep them for their own re-release around the same time. Frantically, they approached Eddie Leahey at Golden Harvest's office in London and surprisingly, were given uncut 35mm Mandarin prints of the films. As I mentioned earlier in the book, some attendees of the film festival claimed *The Big Boss* contained the infamous "saw in the head" scene but for each attendee who claims it was shown that day, there's another that says it wasn't. Unfortunately, as that there was no mention of it in *KFM* or the Society news sheets, its one fan's word against another's.

Jimmy Wang Yu was one of the biggest stars of Hong Kong cinema in the 1970's, starring in classics such as *One-Armed Boxer*, *The Chinese Boxer*, *One-Armed Swordsman*, *The Man from Hong Kong* (with George Lazenby) and *Master of the Flying Guillotine*. In the late 1970's, as his career was beginning to take off, Jackie Chan had issues with trying to cancel what he  felt was an unfair contract with *Fist of Fury* director Lo Wei, who as you'll later discover was arrested in Hong Kong for Triad connections. Jimmy Wang Yu, having Triad connections himself, "persuaded" Lo Wei to release Chan from his contract, which he duly did.

Double bill showing of Bruce Lee films and martial arts films were popular in the 1970's, especially late night showings. The film companies would even have "Quad" posters made for the showings. Double bills in the UK featured *The Big Boss* & *Way of the Dragon*, *The Dragon Lives* & *Enter the Dragon*, *The Octagon* & *Tae Kwon Do Strikes in Paris*, *The Black Dragon* & *The Stranger from Canton* and *One Armed Boxer* & *The Sky Hawk*.

Wondering how Pam Hadden's pilgrimage to Hong Kong went and don't have KFM 52? The following is the report of her experience from *KFM* 53.

A RETROSPECTIVE LOOK AT BRUCE LEE MANIA & THE KUNG FU CRAZE OF THE 1970S

THE GREAT VOYAGE OF DISCOVERY
PAM HADDEN IN HONG KONG

"On the 9th August, 1979, Pam Hadden — president of the Bruce Lee Society — set out on a trip that she had been planning to make for years; the destination was Hong Kong! What happened to her while she was there - the people she met — is detailed right here in one, sensational, double-feature report. It's a very personalised account, for the words pour direct from her own pen, and for readers who are unable to embark on that momentous journey for themselves (and let's face it, that means MOST of us!) well, I guarantee Pam's ultra-descriptive account of her pilgrimage to that holiest of lands will serve as the finest of substitutes. KFM *brings you — literally — the journey of Pam Hadden's lifetime!*

"Hong Kong!"
I suppose that for any fan of the Master, next to "Bruce Lee," those are two of the most magical and inspiring words imaginable, for there lays the true roots of the legend that was the Little Dragon. For nearly six years I'd been planning the trip, so you can imagine my feelings as I climbed on board the plane at Heathrow. Not only was I very apprehensive, it was somehow as though I was walking in a dream.

If I needed reassurance that I was awake, well it wasn't long in coming as the plane got grounded at Frankfurt with engine trouble for four hours! At long last, though, we were on our way again with only stops at Bahrain, Bombay and Bangkok before final touchdown at Hong Kong.

After what seemed like an eternity, the Captain announced he'd be landing in about 10 minutes and as butterflies came and went, I glued myself to the window to await the first glimpse of the airport or harbour.

At last, the wheels touched down and even before we'd stopped rolling, I was first up and heading down the aisle for the exit. If I'd had an ejector seat, I'd have been out even sooner! Walking down the steps, I was suddenly near to tears as there was no question of it being anywhere else. Somehow I seemed to recognise the bustle, the chattering and the skyline that reminded of a miniature New York.

My "base" was the YMCA on Waterloo Road in Kowloon. I decided on that area because that was where there would be most that related to Bruce. I was close by a large main thoroughfare called Nathan Road and I spent many hours just strolling along it taking in the atmosphere. Strange fruits, exciting aromas, people carving away at skilful designs; all was perfect and intriguing, except the heat! It was during the monsoon season and most of the time, the perspiration just poured off me. It wasn't long before I learnt that it was a mistake to rush around in my usual British fashion!

But it was time to turn my attentions to my quest; the search for the memory of Bruce had begun! To start with, results were a little discouraging. Of course everyone knew the name "Bruce Lee," but apart from a poster and a book in Chinese, shops-wise there didn't seem to be a lot to add to my collection. I must admit to being disappointed but wouldn't you? At last, on Wednesday 15th August, things really got mining.

I met Mr. Robert A. Burton, Vice President of International Distribution at Golden Harvest. The company had already been informed by their London office that I was dropping by on a visit and over lunch at the Peninsular Hotel, we chatted generally about Bruce and Hong Kong. Mr. Burton is American and he's worked for Golden Harvest for 2½ years out of the 15 years that he's been out there. The meal in fact was superb, as was Mr. Burton's company. I felt at ease as soon as I met him and was eagerly looking forward to a visit to those famous studios.

We drove down Hammer Hill Road, and as we entered the gates, I started to feel again, that stirring of emotion that had affected me all the way over during the flight. I thought the buildings to be just large warehouse type wooden structures, approached by a dirt track. However, although to some extent this description is right, one thing omitted is the new and luxurious block of offices nearby.

Mr. Burton was called to the phone so he suggested I just carry on walking around taking pictures — until he was free again. The only proviso was that I didn't trip over cameras or get caught up in some Kung Fu film! I'd heard that new Golden Harvest protégé, Jackie Chan (tipped to replace Bruce Lee) was filming there and I was promised a meeting with him during one of the breaks. Meanwhile. I just strolled around, thinking to myself, "I wonder if Bruce Lee stood here" or, "I wonder what buildings Bruce filmed in?"

Wandering around between scenery and buildings, I was astounded at the simplicity of it all as it seemed unbelievable that it was here that a good part of Bruce Lee's films were made! I returned to the offices and fleetingly saw Raymond Chow. He was very busy — we smiled — and he carried on upstairs. As I stood talking to Raymond's secretary, Betty Kwong, a man came in and immediately I was struck by his nice smile and lively personality. Surprise, surprise, it was Jackie Chan himself and believe you me, the "rubber-faced, flat-nosed" description is more than a little unjust. Sure he doesn't have Bruce's good looks (how many people do!) but Jackie comes over as a sort of Chinese Charles Bronson. And there's no real attempt at billing him as some sort of Bruce replacement as he's more of a comedy actor, and anyway, his style of fighting is quite different.

Later, Mr. Burton took me round to see Bruce Lee's old dressing room, but as fate would have it, the door was locked; Jackie, the present occupier, was out shooting and he had the key with him. Ah well, you can't win them all! And on our travels we came across a street scene set, specially designed for Jackie's new film and I noticed that every bit of space seemed to be used to advantage. Mr. Burton pointed out that, although the studios were not as spectacular as near rivals Shaw Brothers, Golden Harvest didn't suffer the same overheads as Shaw's as they didn't keep a regular payroll of actors, but rather they employ them as and when needed. Presumably Golden Harvest's object is quality rather than quantity.

Back in his office, Robert Burton put me right on a certain question that's been cropping up for years; the change of coffin mystery that dates back to the time Bruce's body was being flown back to Seattle from Hong Kong. Various papers at the time reported that the casket had been opened and tampered with — speculation was rife that he had been prematurely buried.

In fact, I was told the casket had been damaged in transit. Also, because of pressure changes, apparently things can happen to bodies in flight. Unfortunately, because it was necessary to change the casket for Bruce's burial in the States, all sorts of rumours started up about somebody being buried in the Master's place.

Director of International Advertising and Public Relations Russell Cawthorne entered the conversation (by the way, a final credit to his name is that he also played the part of a doctor in *Game of Death*). I asked what had happened to Bruce's old training equipment and was told that much had been given away to the Little Dragon's old Hong Kong school (I'm waiting for a reply right now to discover whether we might be able to borrow some at a later date). Mr. Cawthorne has also promised to try and find anything else Bruce might have owned.

David Chan and Russell Cawthorne

Both Robert Burton and Russell Cawthorne seemed impressed at the functioning of *Kung Fu Monthly* and the Society and they expressed themselves keen to assist in any way possible. Making a good start, they sprang one little surprise; a quick phone call to the *Hong Kong Standard* and an interview was fixed up for me on the following day, with a Mr. Ken McKenzie! Generally very "wary" of such things, I went along with it and ended up pleasantly surprised. Not only was Mr. McKenzie completely "for" Bruce Lee, he also gave us a write-up measuring 18" by 4" and he missed nothing! Not to be misquoted and not to have one's words twisted around to make the story better came almost as a shock.

But enough, for the time being of Golden Harvest; I had a mini tour to start on and also a VERY important person to meet!

It was time to begin my investigations in earnest! I'd luckily already met up with a "safe" and very charming escort at the hotel, and as he had some time to spare, he happily agreed to help me on my whistle-stop, fact-finding tour of Hong Kong. The first destination, we decided, should be Bruce's old home, so, armed with camera and car, off we set. On the way, we passed by Queen Elizabeth Hospital so we briefly stopped at the ambulance bay to see if the vehicle which took Bruce there (number A43) was anywhere around. I couldn't see it, so I made do instead with taking some pictures of the casualty door and the driveway, etc. I thought once or twice about actually going inside, but I decided that might easily annoy someone — and foul up the whole thing. For the same reason, Happy Valley Cemetery (shown in *Enter the Dragon*) was also off bounds.

One more stop on the way to Bruce's house and that was at Betty Ting Pei's apartment and the place where Bruce was taken ill. I found some discrepancy about the number, so I took pictures of three separate blocks as it's better to be safe than sorry!

Up to that time, I'd tried to put an awful thought out of my head but now I couldn't avoid it any longer. Driving towards Bruce's old house in Cumberland Road, the rumour I'd heard kept coming back to me, that the place was now being used as a "house of ill repute," somewhere for "gentlemen" to take their lady friends for an hour or two. I didn't want to believe it, but as we drew up outside, my worst fears were confirmed. It took me a minute or two to fight back the tears that I could feel welling up. How could his house be used for such a thing? Eventually I told myself, well, whatever it's being used for now, it was Bruce's home and that's all that matters.

I left the car and approached the doorman. "Was this Bruce Lee's house?" I asked him. He told me, yes, did I like him? "Like him? Oh yes I like him!" I asked if he minded me taking some pictures and he happily agreed for me to carry on. I took shots of the house, the garden, the entrance - but what I'd have given to have gone inside. My escort friend saw how upset I was and when I told him how much I would have liked to have been able to look around the place, he soon got me laughing again by saying with a big grin, "It could be arranged quite easily!" (if you get his meaning). As we drove away, I wondered to myself just what Bruce would have thought about it all.

Part two of my search was — you've guessed it — to try and track down Bruce's brother, Robert. My friend came to the rescue. He suggested I contact Hong Kong TVB and try their Public Relations Officer, Miss Betty Young. Betty agreed to contact Robert and then call me back. This she did, and the unbelievable message was that Robert would be phoning me at the hotel shortly! It just didn't seem real and I simply couldn't convince myself that he would actually call me.

Suddenly the phone rang and I fell over the furniture rushing for the telephone. Trying to sound composed I came out with a very original greeting, "Hello?" A soft, American-Chinese accent asked, "Is that Pam Hadden? This is Robert Lee." *POW! ZAM!* Fighting for composure, I gurgled agreement that I'd meet him in the lobby of the hotel at 7.30pm — and the call was over.

I was there by 7.10, and feeling VERY emotional. Here I was, about to meet

Bruce's brother, a man who I admired as a singer in his own right. I remember thinking as I waited, about specific tracks on Robert's albums — ones that were very special to me. It helped stave off the panic!

All at once I saw a good-looking guy walk through the door wearing a smart cream suit, white shirt and cream tie — even minus the beard, I knew it was Robert. Other people in the hotel recognised him immediately but he came over to me and asked, "Pam?" We shook hands and one lovely smile later, I was instantly aware that I was in the presence of the Lee charm.

Robert put me at my ease immediately and asked about the Society. We chatted generally and I discovered that he married his wife, Sylvia, on December 18th, 1977 — in the States. She's a singer and actress who works under the name of Sum Sum. He also confirmed that his mother was living permanently in Los Angeles, with sisters Phoebe and Agnes, and that brother Peter was now Assistant Director at the Hong Kong Observatory.

The conversation changed tack and I asked about the Long Beach Tournament Film and did he know of its whereabouts? Robert confirmed (as we'd all suspected) that the only copy was in the hands of Ed Parker and his feeling was that Ed would only let go of it if he was sure it wasn't going to be used for commercial gain. Obviously therefore, he might relent for a convention (I'm looking into this right now).

I asked Robert what sort of questions he usually gets asked. "Everything under the sun. It's surprising what they can think up!!" I agreed and gave as an example, one of the questions a fan had once asked me, "Did Bruce wear pyjamas?" Robert gave his charming smile, and in reply to that questioner, I am now able to say in all truth that yes he did!

Robert Lee

Robert is extremely proud of his brother and it shows all the time. He told me that his mother, Grace, had now finished the book she's been writing, called *The Untold Story* and she might soon be going to countries like Japan to promote it. He confirmed, too, that Linda had not remarried and that Brandon (now 14 and very much the young gentleman) is often seen escorting his mother around. Robert also mentioned that Brandon is now quite like Bruce in looks and also that he IS continuing to study the arts under Danny Inosanto. Asked if he thought Brandon might follow in his father's footsteps, Robert is inclined to feel that there is a strong possibility.

I decided it was time to pop a controversial question: I asked him, "Robert, what did you think of *Game of Death*?" "I didn't like it" — he replied, "Except when Bruce appeared," he added, smiling. I asked whether he thought Bruce would have been disappointed had he seen it. "He would have hated it as it wasn't what he had in mind at all."

I changed the subject and asked, "Did you ever meet James Coburn?" "Yes, several times," replied Robert. "He's a nice guy. Bruce and I used to go to James' place a lot." (Robert lived in the States for 10 years and spent a good deal of time with Bruce and his friends.) And was James Coburn really Bruce's best friend? "Oh yes, definitely, they got on great together."

That settled, I decided to ask about one or two of the other questions that crop up regularly. I sprang a difficult one, "Was Bruce a bully when he was a boy?" Robert hesitated. "Come on — honestly!" He smiled that charming smile: "Well — yes. Often he'd fight twice a day." I said that I presumed it was fighting that prompted him to take up the martial arts — at the age of 13. "Yes, he went to Yip Man and other instructors and picked up everything he could." I had to ask, "Did Bruce actually attend Yip Man's funeral?" Robert replied very much in the affirmative. And how about the story of the sweat gland removal — was it true? Robert laughed and replied: "No, it wasn't."

And what about his own career? Were there just the two LPs, *Ballad of Bruce Lee* and *The Boat Song*? Robert confirmed that so far that was all, adding though that a new one was on the way. I asked him about the track, "Parting," on *Ballad of Bruce Lee* — it's credited to both Robert and Bruce, so who did what? "It was a joint effort really. Bruce wrote the poem and I did the music arrangement." Another question the fans are always putting to me, and one I had to pass along — did Bruce smoke or drink? Robert replied that, generally speaking, he did neither. However, shortly before his death, when visiting him one day, Bruce asked Robert for a drink of wine. Robert was surprised; "What! You — drink wine?" It was that unusual!

Lastly I asked another of those questions that crop up time and again. "Can you say anything about the electrical equipment that Bruce is supposed to have trained with? Robert confirmed that his brother had indeed used such a piece of equipment. Apparently you are supposed to start with it tuned to No. 1 and then to progress to the maximum position — No. 8. But Bruce didn't start at the bottom: "He went straight in at No. 8 — that's how he trained."

Robert had to leave as he was due to see his wife's show that evening. I thanked him sincerely for his kindness in talking to me for so long and for answering some fairly direct questions. All I can say about the man is that he really is a devoted fan of his brother. His pride when he talks about him shows clearly through. Also, on occasions, I caught a little of Bruce in the way he smiled and looked, and he has all the openness, charm and hospitality of the Chinese people. I keep my fingers crossed that everyone will be able to see him later this year because there's just a chance that he'll be able to make it over for the next convention!

My last hours in Hong Kong brought home to me all that had happened in those few, short days. I went to the top of the Sheraton Hotel and looked across the harbour at the boats, and further away, the peak stretching up into a dark sky. Even though all dreams have to end sometime, one thing I can say; seeing Hong Kong, Golden Harvest and Bruce's home was reward enough, but meeting Robert as well made me feel as though I'd put out my hand to reach the moon, only to come back with the stars as well!"

A RETROSPECTIVE LOOK AT BRUCE LEE MANIA & THE KUNG FU CRAZE OF THE 1970S

14
December
1979

HI, AND A HUGE WELCOME FROM ME, PAM, TO THIS THE FOURTEENTH (AND CHRISTMAS) EDITION OF THE BRUCE LEE SOCIETY NEWS SHEET!

GENERAL NEWS

For the information of new members, I was lucky enough to go over to Hong Kong in August and, amongst other amazing things, I met Robert, Bruce's famous, guitar playing brother; what a climax to my trip! I visited Golden Harvest and met several old friends and all in all, it really was the holiday of a lifetime. I intend going back there again, very soon.

An important little appeal to all members from me - following my operation and hospitalisation in September/October. I have to take things fairly easy for a while, so please, have a heart, no lengthy letters that need answering. Renewals and snippets of info not requiring acknowledgements are fine. I promise to be back on form soon... THANKS.

Suresh Gandhi (1743) has offered to do black ink drawings (on the lines of two of the examples of his work featured in the news sheet of your favourite photo - or whatever - of Bruce Lee. He does the drawing on 12" x 9" art paper. The cost is £1.00 plus 25p p&p per job and, judging by what I've seen, it's money well spent. His address is Eindhoven, Holland.

No doubt many of you now know of the book written by Bruce's mother that's called *The Untold Story*. It's a first-class paperback that contains rare and never-before-seen pictures of Bruce, plus anecdotes from his family on his early childhood. I hope soon to get hold of some copies especially for members but more on that soon!

Rick Edwards (1260) tells me of a book entitled *Those Who Died Young* which features such people as John Kennedy, Martin Luther King, various pop stars and (you've guessed it) Bruce! The cost is £3.95 and if you want to grab a copy you can easily order one from any branch of W. H. Smith. Rick says it's well worth the money and I hope mine comes soon.

Rick also tells me that he heard on a Radio 1 programme (Tuesday September fourth, *Personal Call* - introduced by Ed Stewart) someone called Mr. Ferman talking about Bruce Lee. Now Mr. Ferman, who I met and talked to some 18 months ago, is the Chairman of the British Board of Film Censors and what Rick didn't know was that fellow-member, Alan Mount (1109) was one of the lucky people to have a call accepted by the programme, where he tackled Mr. Ferman on various points! Apparently Mr. Ferman considers Bruce a true artist, calling him "astonishing" and likened his style of action film to those classic Douglas Fairbanks swashbucklers of the silent days. He said that Bruce was very commercial and that he expected to see more films containing footage from his movies as time goes by. Mr. Ferman said: "I am a great fan of Bruce - he was a true artist and if it was up to me alone, all of his films would be left completely intact!" Well done, Alan, for getting onto the programme.

Rick also says he saw *Tiger Strikes Back*, featuring Bruce Li, and that he enjoyed it, saying he feels Li has improved of late. Well, I suppose I ought to suppress the thought that, because really, he couldn't have got much worse.

I heard from Maria Fernandes (2751) that Columbia Pictures are petitioning the Hollywood Chamber of Commerce to place the name of Bruce Lee by one of the famous stars embedded in the sidewalks of Hollywood Boulevard - indeed Linda was apparently the first person to sign the petition. NOW, a suggestion which I expect EACH AND EVERY ONE OF YOU to take up. Collect together as many names and address as you possibly can and send them to me via the usual address - but in an envelope marked "Hollywood Petition." I shall be sending them all off to the Chamber of Commerce (via Linda's lawyers), along with a written statement of support. PLEASE, just names and addresses - no letters; and get them to me within two weeks of your receiving this news sheet. That means that you've gotta work FAST!

Back with Rick again - he tells me there's a new TV series being made in the States called *The Brown Hornet*; it stars Bill Crosby of TV's *I Spy* fame - along with Robert Culp. Can you believe THAT. Anyone finding out more information, I'd be VERY interested to hear it! Surely it has to be a comic series?

Also according to Rick, some time ago a magazine did an article on one Eric Lee (his own name!) who has many awards and who is called "King of Kata." He was asked if he would ever consider doing a *Bruce Lee Story* type of film (apparently he doesn't look too unlike the Little Dragon). Eric replied that that he could not take on such a responsibility because: "No matter how good, or how much I tried, I would still disappoint his fans. You might find someone looking like Bruce, and fighting like him, but it would still not work because Bruce had a special charm, grace and dignity that made him a once-off artist." Rick and Eric Law feel that Jackie Chan (the new Golden Harvest protégé) has great talent, and that his films are worth watching - especially *Shaolin Woodenmen*.

Alan Mount says that Raymond Chow and Fred Weintraub/Robert Clouse of the *Enter the Dragon* team are reassembling in January 1980 to feature Jackie in his first American film - provisionally entitled *Battlecreek Brawl*. Alan feels (and I must say I agree) that Clouse's best film was *Enter the Dragon,* but even that cannot really be classed as a hit thanks to his "directorial" talents because, let's face it, it was much more Bruce's star quality, etc! However, having met Jackie in Hong Kong, I'm inclined to like him. He in no way classes himself as a contender for the Bruce crown as his films are quite comic, and I found him an unpretentious, natural and friendly person. Let's hope he stays that way!

David and Lorraine Rawson (2487/2320) went to see some wrestling a little while back and met the guy named "Kung Fu" after his performance. They asked him to sign his picture "To a Bruce Lee fan." He replied that he could not do that. When asked why not, he said he couldn't put his name under Bruce's because Bruce was much too good. What a nice compliment. Also David and Lorraine went to Blackpool and had one of those headlines printed where you put what you fancy onto a newspaper headline. Theirs read, "David and Lorraine to star with Bruce Lee!" The cheeky pair!

Kathryn Wray (2033) sends me a clip announcing that British Caledonian Airways are planning a bargain-fare of £100 for the trip to Hong Kong (£200 return), which is not bad (although still pretty high for many members, I suspect). Anyway, it seems that the Hong Kong fare may fall even further in the near future, so let's all keep our eyes peeled.

Patrick Hennessy (1771) saw an article in *The Evening Press* stating that, "Muhammed Ali would have beaten them all." This prompted Patrick to write in to their paper asking if they considered Ali would have lasted the distance with "The late and incomparable Bruce Lee, who was capable of switching to Queensbury Rules, since he gave up boxing and karate to teach the world comprehensive Kung Fu?" Patrick went on: "Many reckon that Lee's blistering speed, one-inch punch and inimitable tactics - plus superior precision, footwork and docile anticipation - would have left Ali floundering like a novice." Nice work, Patrick, that told them!

Philip Bell (2506) sends in a cutting about a football match that turned into a punch-up; it seems some bad feeling erupted into real fisticuffs! Anyway, the heading that amused Philip (and myself) was "The Fist of Fury"!! Similarly, Philip saw in *The Star* newspaper, a write-up on the arrival of the Chinese Football Team here as "Enter the Dragons"!!

USEFUL ADDRESSES

From Arthur Stone (1150), news that he has now received from Regent Films, P.O. Box 54, Blackpool FY1 ISP, the German version of *The Big Boss*. The quality is excellent and, of course, if you know the story, the German dialogue is no real bother. Arthur says though, that the factory fight, with the ranting and raving of a deep German voice, had him rolling on the floor!

More films info as David Niedailek (1021) tells me that Miko Studios have many Bruce films, where I believe may be where Regent get their copies. Anyway, Miko have *The Big Boss* on four reels and also *The Green Hornet*, so write for current prices to: Kennemwestraatweg 35, 1814 GB Alkmaar, Holland.

David has also given me the names of a few fan clubs for Bruce ... here are the addresses. Bruce Lee Nationwide Fan Club, 4424 Montebello Drive #106, Colorado Springs, Co.80918, U.S.A. A Club Bruce Lee, 18 Rue Theodore-Deck, 75015 PARIS, France. Bruce Lee Club, Postbus 13, 7230 Frameries, Belgium.

Paul Wade has sent me info on Miko too, and says that they have *Game of Death* on four reels - including the Inosanto fight, but not including the Chi Hon Joi match.

Paul also says that the *Official Karate* Yearbook (10th Anniversary) Fall 1979 has awarded Bruce the title "Martial Artist of the Decade." I expect there will be a mad rush by all of you to get a copy but all I hope is that you have more success than I have!

Back to films, Mark Tyler (2673) says that Mirage Films, "Delphi," The Street, Swallowfield, Reading RG7 IRE, Berks (phone: Reading 884273) have Bruce's German films available at £34 per reel, plus 50p postage - which works out cheaper than sending direct to Miko. It looks like you'll have to sort out what's best for yourselves!

For anyone who's still after *Enter the Dragon* type gloves, they're available from Oriental World at 18 Swan Street, Manchester at a cost of £22.50.

Any members who're looking for the soft-backed *Bruce Lee 1940-1973*, I hope to have copies for sale shortly. As you may know, it's out of print at the moment.

Lee Percy (1072) tells me that the A.C.E. Cinema, Barkingside, Ilford in Essex recently showed *Enter the Dragon* (some cinemas DO have taste). Well, he asked them to feature more Bruce films, so if YOU live around that area, why not back Lee up and drop a line to the manager. By the way, a useful address he sent: The film *Game of Death* can be got from Quality Products (Romford) Ltd., 43 Victoria Road, Romford, Essex (phone 01-702 8413).

How many of you, I wonder, collected the magazine, *Deadly Hands of Kung Fu*? This featured a comic-strip of Bruce's life, and some useful articles on him. If you have any of the copies missing (I do, for one!) then Simon Bulley suggests you try for them at "Dark They Were and Golden-Eyed," St. Anne's Court, Wardour Street, London W.1. Simon also recommends a comic called *Shang-Chi, Master of Kung Fu*, whose central character (being the son of Fu Manchu - and a Bruce Lee Lookalike) is drawn by Paul Gulacy. He reckons Paul to be the greatest martial-arts artist anywhere.

Anyone living near Brighton? Then I can tell you that the Classic Cinema, West End, Brighton, has a regular Kung Fu film night. Check with them to find out what's coming.

It's funny the way Bruce's name keeps cropping up in the most unlikely places. For instance, did you know there's a racehorse called "Bruce Lee" which ran recently at Windsor and Studley (info courtesy Graham Waggett - 2602 and David Dixon - 1650) Glad to see he was the favourite!

David also sent a cutting from his sister's comic, *Cheeky Weekly*.

Shaune Bridgwood (2688) says he recently read a kung fu book called *Dragon's Fists* where the hero, when faced by would-be killers asking what style he uses,

replies... "whatever style you want." The villains then retort... "we believe in the ways of the late Bruce Lee." Also in a *Hulk* annual, where a runaway car is rampaging the streets, a pedestrian says... "I don't know, but of Bruce Lee is at the wheel, I'm getting out of here"! Shaune also says that the editors of *Film Review* magazine report Bruce as the most talked-about name in the letters they get. They have, by back issues containing word on the Little Dragon - that's July 1978 and August 1975. If you want copies, write to: Old Court Place, Kensington High Street, London W.8.

Extra snippet for those living in the Norwich area - there's a shop called "Sneakers" that stocks Bruce records.

Something to gladden our hearts... David Moore (1783) sent in the *TV Times* clipping (21st-27th July edition) shown here. It quotes some fine words from Oliver Tobias. Robert Walker (2565) says there's a new Kung Fu series called *Young Kim* that is going to star Clint Eastwood. I gather Chuck Norris has been interviewed for a role. Robert also says he has joined a new karate club in his area, with all sorts of nice things - showers, video tapes, TV, lounge, bar, gym with punch bags, etc. If all that interests you, write to him at Clydebank, Scotland.

> "I've also been looking at the terrific action in the Bruce Lee movies and asking myself, 'Why can't we have more of that in the West?' I adore the swordplay and the leaping about and so, I believe, do kids of all ages.
>
> "To put dash and daring into *Arabian Adventure* I spent two months in a gymnasium with five stunt men. We rehearsed with swords and trampolines so that we could leap right over people's heads, Bruce Lee-style. (OLIVER TOBIAS)

John Black (1956) sent in the cutting shown here, taken from a Japanese newspaper. It shows fans from that country at a special service on the first anniversary of his death. I believe that Japan, the States and Hawaii all hold Bruce Lee "Days."

Tokyo fans pay homage to Bruce Lee

KUNG FU fans all over the world are paying homage to Hongkong's own superstar, Bruce Lee, on the first anniversary of his tragic death.

In Tokyo, more than 20,000 devoted fans of the Chinese actor gathered for a memorial service, and reruns of his movies.

The fans are pictured filing past a special altar, highlighted by a huge photograph of Lee.

Many of you will have seen the *George & Mildred* TV comedy show where George gets given a pair of black silk pyjamas, embossed with a gold dragon. She tells him that, "They'll make you look just like Bruce Lee!" Somehow I don't think so - still, a mention is a mention. In *Somebody is Watching Me*, the heroine, thinking there is a burglar in her flat, shouts out "I think it only fair to warn you that I was a student of the late Bruce Lee and studied under him for two years" Also, in BBC's *The Comedians*, a young and talented performer called Jonathan Pryce referred to Bruce in the play as "God."

Poems time. First of all from Shaune Bridgwood (I love this one!):

Float like a butterfly;
Sting like a bee;
The great smell of Brut
And a punch from Bruce Lee!"

And another (rather more sensitive one) from Ann Hunt:

B is for BRUCE - the one and only,
R is for REGRET that he's no longer with us.
U is for UNIQUE - there'll be no other.
C is for CAPTIVATING the hearts of millions.
E is for his exquisite body.
L is for the LOVE we feel for him.
E is for his EXPLOSIVE fists.
E is for his EXPLORATION of the Martial Arts.

Paul Short (1164) is looking for some help. He's compiling his own catalogue of Kung Fu films and needs to know the director/producer of all of the following: *Lightning Swords of Death, Fists of Vengeance, Mr. Hercules Against Karate, Deaf and Mute Heroine, Shanghai Lil & the Sun Luck Kid, Fist of Justice, Fist of Shaolin, Match of Dragon and Tiger, Master of Shaolin Kung Fu, Kung Fu Killers*, and *Revenge of the Dragon - Sister Streetfighter*. Write to Paul at Sheffield. Thanks from him, in advance.

John Milne (2046) let his son, Neville, enter a fancy dress competition as Bruce Lee, complete with black plimsolls, black trousers, white socks and with scars painted across his chest and face and a pair of safety nunchakus. He took third place (he'd have come first if I'd been judging!).

LETTERS

It would be impossible to print all the letters of congratulation I've had in about the convention. And, of course, the film festival is also getting its fair share of praise. Here, though, is one letter that I particularly liked.

Dear Pam,

Just writing in to express how I feel about being a member of the honorary Bruce Lee Society. I have to say it really is great to feel the magic of Bruce that is growing even greater throughout the world - among the fans who love and remember him most and not forgetting the devotion and widespread interest generated by the Society. And when the news broke of the Bruce Lee Convention, it was the biggest thing to happen concerning the great Master, and what a meaning it was to have for those who feel the burning spirit of the Little Dragon within them. The James Coburn tribute was spoken with truthfulness and a sense of loss - I know he carries the spirit of Bruce with him. The few words he spoke bring out how Bruce is to both his fans and those who knew him personally; how fortunate were those who touched a "nova" before it burned out. Though gone, he will never be forgotten, and so will never die.

Alan Appleton (2701)

Dear Pam,

I've enclosed a recent letter received from Yorkshire TV which was in answer to a letter I sent on behalf of the Bruce Lee Society, asking that they show The Green Hornet.

Philip Bell (2506)

And so, for everyone who hasn't yet realised the misguided people we have to deal with, here's the reply that YTV sent to Philip.

"Thank you for your letter and interest in our programmes. I am afraid that we do not have any plans to show the series Green Hornet as it is too violent for television. I am sorry we cannot be more obliging in this instance"

*C. Ledgrave (Viewers Correspondence)
Yorkshire Television, The Television Centre, Leeds LS3 US*

What an absolute load of rubbish! Since when has *The Green Hornet* been more violent than *Batman*, or numerous other things that've appeared on TV? For such a person to be in such a position, and to be so completely ignorant is almost beyond belief. Members, you've got C. Ledgrave's address so how about letting him/her know your feelings!!!

Lastly, a few very nicely chosen words from Tony Lundberg (2338)

Hello Little Dragon! Now the darkness is gone over your head and you are passed away, think about all these people who are crying now just because of you - you must be so proud! Bruce, why did you pass away without saying goodbye? Why? You were the world's greatest athlete, actor and Kung Fu fighter ever known! Hey, Bruce, I always wanted to tell you one thing... I will always remember what you taught me. Thank you Bruce. Now my heart trembles when I say "Goodbye, Little Dragon" - I hope I can see you again. Farewell, J.K.D.

SPECIAL MESSAGES

Stephen Hill (1104) wants to put this little message in for a very special young lady: "I'm sorry, Fiona; I love you. Please - let's try again. Love Steve."

Mr. Stephen Roberts (2290) has recently become a proud dad to baby James Lee. Congratulations to the family!

Congratulations due to Erik Larsen (2376) and his wife on the birth of their daughter.

Tricia Irvine (2610) wishes to pass on belated birthday wishes to her husband on his 21st last year.

Birthday wishes too, to Jeff Millington (1127) and Nigel Martin (1359).

RENEWALS

Members 2531 to 2599 inclusive, remember your second year membership falls due for renewal between now and the end of February. Members 2171 to 2266 inclusive, your third year renewals fall at the same time. The same also goes for fourth year renewals, numbers 1628 to 1828 inclusive.

One last thing before the Swaps... I thought I'd tell you of some "name definitions" that I came across; as you'll see, some are very apt indeed! BRUCE - positive, daring! ROBERT - winner over all. PETER - reliable, dependable, a rock. AGNES - pure, (no PHOEBE). GRACE - God's blessing. LINDA - beautiful, (no SHANNON). BRANDON - a fighter!

SWOP SHOP

- William Ross (2715), Irvine wants *Bruce Lee 1940-1973, Game of Death Collector's Edition, Bruce Lee Stars in Game of Death, Bruce Lee in Action, KFM*s 1, 2,

- 5, 6, Bruce Pendant, *Secret Art* (Collector's Edition and Standard Edition), Bruce Treasure Kit, *The Man Only I Knew*, *Legend of Bruce Lee*, *Art & Philosophy of Bruce Lee*. Write direct.
- John Rogers (1009), Basildon has for sale large selection of books nd magazines on Bruce (including *King of Kung Fu, Inedit, Bruce Lee Scrapbook*). Also colour stills from *The Big Boss, Fist of Fury, Way of the Dragon* and *Enter the Dragon,* plus many cuttings. Send SAE for list.
- Mark Tyler (2673) has for swap *Man From Hong Kong* poster and B&W stills set, *Kung Fu Cinema of Vengeance* (mint), *When Taekwondo Strikes* Chinese film poster, various other Chinese posters of Angela Mao, etc. Wants *Enter the Dragon* film poster plus set of stills.
- Mr. N.J. Savage, Bexleyheath has for sale Japanese original soundtracks *Way of the Dragon* & *Fist of Fury* (cost approx. £18). Sell £5 each or £9 both (inc p&p).
- William Luke (1478), London wants records or cassettes of *You Make It Move* by Dave Dee, *Rainbow Valley* by Love Affair, *I've Been A Bad, Bad Boy* by Paul Jones, *Where Are You Elvis* by Jenny Nicholas, *A Little Loving* by Fourmost, and *Listen to Me* by Hollies.
- Robert Walker (2565), Linnvale wants any members with Bruce records to sell/swap to contact him.
- Mr. K. Spicer (2699), Kent wants Bruce tapes, interviews etc, except one recently featured in *KFM*, in exchange for a black Kung Fu suit.
- Keith Emberton (2444), Wirral wants Bruce records - contact with info.
- Andrew Staton (1670), Leeds has for sale/swap: stills from *Marlowe, The Wrecking Crew*, also *Legend of Bruce Lee, The Bruce Lee Story* (Li, not Lee), plus other info on David Chiang, rare magazines, etc. Send SAE for list.
- Neil Devine (2325), Dyfed wants *The Man Only I Knew* by Linda - high price offered. Miss Linda Diver (2351), London wants *Secret Art of Bruce Lee*.
- Mr. G.Davis, Bradford has for sale *KFM*s 1-50 (except 22 & 23), *Legend of Bruce Lee, Life and Tragic Death of Bruce Lee, KFM*s *Game of Death, My Martial Arts Training Guide to JKD, Secret Art of Bruce Lee*.
- Paul Wade (1836), 5 Ada's Avenue, Ena Street, Boulevard, Hull, Yorks... FOR SALE: *Bruce Lee Combats* £1.15, *Fist of Fury* & *The Big Boss* LPs, £5.25 each (inc p&p) - all vgc.
- Paul Short (1164), Sheffield has for sale/swap: Japanese book on Bruce, *Memorial Monthly* No. 2, *KFM*s 5 & 6, *Secret of JKD and Kung Fu, Way of the Dragon* pressbook, five assorted Bruce Lee B&W stills, *His Unknown in Martial Arts Learning*.
- Rick Edwards (1260), Coventry has for sale/swap: super 8 sound & colour, 200' trailers of *Enter the Dragon, Way of the Dragon, Fist of Fury,* and *The Big Boss*. Cost £34, sell £22. Trailers of *Lightning Swords of Death, New One-Armed Swordsman, King Boxer, Hapkido*. Cost £28, sell £18 (200'), trailer (100') *Enter the Dragon*. Cost £9.50, sell £6. Trailer *The Big Boss* (100'). Cost £9.50, sell £6.
- Patrick Hennessy (1771), Dublin has for sale/swap: sound & colour trailers of *Enter the Dragon, The Big Boss* and *The Making of Enter the Dragon* and silent film of Coliseum battle from *Way of the Dragon*. All on 400' reel or can trade separate for other Bruce films (fights etc).
- David Niedzailek (1021), Neath wants original *Fist of Fury* cinema poster - will pay £5 for one in very good condition.
- Eric Law, Kuala Lumpur, Malaysia wants members to contact him with any books, etc they have to sell/swap.

PEN PALS

- Jayne Coupe (2599), Chesterfield wants male/female pen pal (age immaterial). She's 19, interested in Bruce, music (especially ELO, Floyd, Jefferson Starship and disco) and motorcycling on her bike. Any bikers out there liking Bruce - write to Jayne.
- Elvis Whetton (2599), London wants pen pals interested in home movie making, getting together with ideas and making various films, also accompanying him to movies, etc. Please ring or write (phone 01-XXX XXXX).
- Shaune Bridgwood (2688), Norwich wants pen pals of similar interests - Bruce, martial arts, reading and films. He's 14. Also, Bruce fans in the Norwich area, please contact re organising film shows or mini-Conventions. Great idea, Shaune.
- Graham Ellis (2728), Hinckley wants other Members to contact him with view to having local off-shoot of the Society, with possible film shows, bargain swap-shops and group outings. Another GREAT idea. Will Graham be forming Britain's first regional "chapter" of the BLS? All Members living locally, please write to him. If the move catches on, I'll take steps to make such "chapters" official in some way.

Back with you all again in March - Pam

EDITOR'S NOTES

In this issue, Pam started a petition to have Bruce Lee commemorated with a star on the Hollywood Walk of Fame but it wouldn't happen in the Society's lifetime and when it finally did happen, it had a tinge of sadness about it.

In 1993, twenty years after his death, Bruce Lee finally had a star placed in the Hollywood Walk of Fame at the premiere of his biopic *Dragon: The Bruce Lee Story* which starred Jason Scott Lee and Lauren Holly and directed but Rob Cohen. In attendance that day was Bruce's widow Linda, daughter Shannon, biopic director Rob Cohen and martial arts actor Jean-Claude Van Damme. One person notably missing was son Brandon, who had sadly passed away from an accidental gun shot wound a short while before, while making the film *The Crow*. So while the petition was victorious, that victory was bittersweet.

The Brown Hornet was originally an African-American version of *The Green Hornet* on a radio programme presented by now-disgraced actor Bill Cosby before transitioning to a TV animation. It featured as a cartoon-in-a-cartoon on Bill Cosby's

animated series *Fat Albert and the Cosby Kids* before having its own spin-off show from 1979 to 1984. It was produced by the animation company Filmation, who were responsible for many animated superhero TV series from 1963 to 1989. Their later notable series included classics such as *He-Man*, *She-Ra*, *Ghostbusters*, and *Bravestarr*.

Bruce Lee: The Untold Story by Grace Lee was published in April 1980. It is currently out of print but does come up quite regularly on Amazon for a reasonable price.

Dark They Were, and Golden Eyed was a science fiction book and comics store, located at 10 Berwick Street in London's Soho. Named after a short story by Ray Bradbury, it was the largest of its kind in Europe in the 1970s. Later, it moved to

St. Annes Court, off Wardour Street, Soho. Owner Derek "Bram" Stokes was, along with regular customer Nick Landau, one of the major players behind the annual British Comic Art Convention. The shop closed down in 1981. Landau and his partners at Titan Distribution later opened a rival shop, the popular Forbidden Planet.

The British World of Sport wrestler "Kung Fu" was the alter-ego of Northern Irish wrestler Eddie Hamill, who said, "I'd been wrestling for a few years, when I realised that I needed a gimmick to go farther in the business." He continued, "I thought of the name "Kung Fu" as that phrase

THE BRUCE LEE SOCIETY

WORLD BRUCE LEE WEEK

Tell the world of your commitment to Bruce Lee by taking advantage of these never-to-be repeated, celebratory offers

WORLD BRUCE LEE WEEK T-SHIRTS

The shirt features a specially designed, "universal" image that symbolises peace and unity throughout every country. Wear it with sincerity, wear it with pride.

Send a cheque or postal order for £2.95 (members £2.50) includes post & packing to:
WBLW T-Shirt Offer
KFM
14 Rathbone Place
London W1P 1DE

Please remember to state the size of shirt you require—small, medium or large.

WORLD BRUCE LEE WEEK BUTTON BADGE

Again, symbolising peace between nations, consider too proclaiming Bruce Lee's word by wearing this unique button badge memento. Measuring approximately 1" across and coloured black and yellow, the offer is one that cannot be re-run. Order yours quickly while stocks last

Send a cheque or postal order for 40p per badge (members 35p) or £1 for three (members 90p) includes post & packing.
WBLW Badge Offer
KFM
14 Rathbone Place
London W1P 1DE

SPECIAL PUBLICITY STICKERS

FREE Every person who buys both the T-Shirt and the Button Badge will receive ABSOLUTELY FREE, 10 World Bruce Lee Week Stickers

was just beginning to get very popular at the time, due to the Bruce Lee films. Also, I had done some martial arts before so I incorporated them into my bouts. I added the mask for a mask for an extra bit of mystery and it all seemed to fit into place." His manager wasn't too happy about the mask gimmick, insisting that only villains wore masks. Hamill disagreed, stating, "Batman wears a mask. Spiderman wears a mask. The Lone Ranger wears a mask. Do you want me to go on?" His manager still didn't think it was a good idea but let him run with it anyway. The popularity of Kung Fu at the time is what probably allowed him to win over the fans as they probably saw him as a masked Bruce Lee in the ring.

A RETROSPECTIVE LOOK AT BRUCE LEE MANIA & THE KUNG FU CRAZE OF THE 1970S

15 March 1980

HELLO EVERYONE! BEFORE I FRET GOING WITH THE FIFTEENTH SOCIETY NEWS SHEET, MAY I THANK SINCERELY ALL THE MEMBERS WHO SO KINDLY SENT ME CHRISTMAS CARDS (AND DOESN'T THAT SOUND A LONG TIME AGO!). ALTHOUGH I CAN'T THANK YOU PERSONALLY, I WOULD LIKE YOU TO KNOW THAT IT WAS MUCH APPRECIATED.

SENSATIONAL NEWS

A date has now been fixed for the SECOND BRUCE LEE CONVENTION!!! The follow-up to last year's amazing success will be held on July 19th and the venue will be the same as for last year's Film Festival - that's the Kilburn State Theatre, Kilburn High Road, London NW6.

CONFIRMED: We'll be showing the complete, uncensored *Game of Death*. Also *My Son Ah Chang*, starring Bruce Lee, the "kid" superstar! A famous martial arts entertainer and Bruce Lee impersonator will be re-running the famed Bruce/Chuck confrontation from *Way of the Dragon* (that I can't wait to see!)

UNCONFIRMED: A personal visit from Robert Lee!!! Yes, it's really on the cards. Also a travelling sideshow of Bruce Lee clothes and other personal items.

On top of all that, there'll be an even bigger display of stalls, stands and sideshows - so BOOK NOW TO AVOID DISAPPOINTMENT. Tickets are £4.50 to members, £5.00 non- members from: Convention tickets, *Kung Fu Monthly*, 14 Rathbone Place, London W1P IDE.

GENERAL NEWS

One of the biggest blows yet to the memory of Bruce has been struck (once more) by the British Board of Film Censors. As though their original massacring of the Master's films was not enough, they've now, after YEARS of public showings, cut out the nunchaku underground sequence from *Enter the Dragon* and also the fight with the guards. *Fist of Fury* and *Way of the Dragon* have also had major parts removed. Why? After all this time, what reasons can possibly justify such a savage attack on Bruce's films and his many fans, by this petty-minded authority? The Film Censors need to be kicked where it hurts and that means that, although *Kung Fu Monthly* and the Bruce Lee Society will do all they can to reverse this stupid decision, it now depends on YOU. All of you, write to Mr. Ferman, Secretary, British Board of Film Censors, Soho Square, London W1. Voice your opinion politely but firmly about this insane action, and ask them WHY? Get your friends, fellow- members and anyone who will help to write to Mr. Ferman. Also contact sports columns in papers, film magazines, martial arts magazines - anyone who looks worth a try. Drum up all the support you can against this latest, monstrous action. Don't leave it until tomorrow, the time for action is NOW! And don't think, "Oh well, at least we'll still be able to see the real thing at the Society Film Festivals," because if you read *KFM* 54, you'll find that a certain "Williams Committee" is thinking about putting a stop to that sort of thing too. What IS the world coming to?

> By LESLEY HARDIE
>
> CULT heroes like Bruce Lee and David Carradine gave the he-man glamour aspect to the Martial Arts back in the early 1970s.
>
> They turned Kung-Fu into deadly ballets in which countless opponents were violently dispatched.
>
> It is a source of intense irritation to serious followers that the Martial Arts thus acquired what they see as tawdry fringes.
>
> Real Kung-Fu experts avoid publicity, and attend private meetings in Chinese-only clubs...
>
> And exponents of the main Martial Arts currently practised in Scotland stress that under proper conditions, with properly trained instructors, to practise is less dangerous than going to watch a football match.

■ Bruce Lee's films, which still make thousands of people happy, raised the deadly, unarmed Oriental combat, Kung-Fu to a cult.
Lee's most famous film has to be "Enter the Dragon." He died aged 32, from injuries in a film fight scene.

Members Roy Braithwaite (2509) and Richard Miller (1638) sent me the snippets shown here - taken from an article by Lesley Hardie of the *Daily Record*, Andeston Quay, Glasgow G3 8DA, Scotland - so yet again we have an example of a prejudiced, misinformed man who not only puts Bruce in the same category as David Carradine, but also shows his ignorance by giving the Master's cause of death as "injuries in a film fight scene!" Perhaps one or two of you would like to drop him a line suggesting that next time he bothers to do some homework - it's not as though that sort of information is difficult to come by.

Our Maltese member, Alex Buttigieg (2199) says rip-off artist Bruce Li's film *Fist of Fury Part II* was showing at his local cinema. The normal time for a film to be held over is apparently seven days, but Alex reports that sanity ruled and it was removed after only three days! Alex also says that, if any members are visiting Malta, look him up - he'd be very pleased to see them. His address is Msida, Malta.

Sean Daly (2294) says (returning once more to the man we love to hate) that he recently saw Li starring in *The Dragon Lives*. His feelings are that, although the man has picked up some of the Lee mannerisms quite well, there's about as much resemblence to Bruce as Hilda Ogden is to Marilyn Monroe! (For the benefit of foreign members, Hilda is a dowdy, common, noisy little housewife in a regular British TV series). If you don't know who Marilyn was - heaven knows where you've been hiding!

Anthony King (2208) sent in a cutting about ruthless European flyweight champion, Charlie Magri, who came up against karate expert Anecito Vargas at the Royal Albert Hall in London - quote: "Not even the spirit of Kung Fu hero, Bruce Lee, could stop Magri last night - he slammed into Vargas who, attempting to fend him off, hooked his leg around the little Cockney in a perfect example of the Chinese martial arts; unluckily, after a smiling rebuke from the international referee, Vargas was battered unmercifully by Magri and ended up outside the ropes." Pity Bruce wasn't there to give Magri a little lesson!

Heinrich Damsgaard (2125) tells us that on Danish TV on January 12th, in the American series *Hollywood*, they showed a cut from *The Green Hornet*. GREAT! says Heinrich - let's have some more! I don't think anyone will argue with that.

Shahab Setudeh Nejad (1419) who moved to Seattle some time back from England, has sent in the cuttings shown here. One is a write-up on *A Force of One* with Chuck Norris (I've had mixed reports on this from members, varying from "first class" to a load of rubbish) and the other shows a team list of basketball players that features Kareem Abdul Jabbar of the Los Angeles Lakers.

Sonics 112, Lakers 110

LOS ANGELES (110)

	Min	fg	3-pt	ft	or	tr	a	pf	to	tp
Haywood	26	5-10	0-0	0-0	0	4	0	4	1	10
Wilkes	37	7-14	0-0	2-2	2	9	4	1	1	16
Abdul-Jabbar	38	9-15	0-0	5-5	3	7	4	2	3	23
E.Johnson	31	4-8	0-0	7-8	0	3	4	0	5	15
Nixon	34	9-13	1-1	2-5	0	4	5	5	5	21
Boone	22	5-8	0-0	0-0	1	3	2	2	1	10
Chones	17	2-5	0-0	3-4	1	4	3	6	0	7
Ford	11	1-2	0-0	0-0	0	1	0	2	1	2
Carr	15	3-4	0-0	0-0	1	3	1	3	2	6
Cooper	9	0-1	0-0	0-0	0	0	2	1	0	0
Totals		45-80	1-1	19-24	8	38	25	26	19	110

A FORCE OF ONE — Although he's a terrible actor with zero screen presence, world karate champion Chuck Norris appears to be the most likely heir to the late Bruce Lee's stardom. Ernest Tidyman's script follows the standard karate-movie formula — it's about a team of undercover agents investigating a narcotics ring — but the actors and production values are closier than usual. At Coliseum, Aurora, Renton, SeaTac Mall, Crossroads Cinemas and the Duwamish and Bel-Kirk drive-in. "PG" — Parental guidance advised, due to violence.

Setudeh has also sent along some other cuttings and one in particular is about Ruby Chow (in whose restaurant Bruce once worked). Apparently she was elected as chairwoman to the county council for 1979. The *Seattle Times*, dated 21st July, 1979, ran a lengthy article by Erik Lacitis on Bruce. Talking about the grave he says that ardent fans leave flowers there every week; in fact he says that one youth stayed there all day, and left the following framed message: "This is to let all of you know that there are still people who think of Bruce Lee not only as the King of Kung Fu and the best martial artist in the world, but the one who was responsible for the growth and popularity of martial arts - and this is why I can truly say that Bruce Lee was, and still is, the best martial arts artist in the world; he will always be an inspiration to us all." In my opinion that's one of the most fitting epitaphs I've ever seen. Also in the article, Linda says that neither she, nor many people, realised that his popularity was going to grow, grow, grow! "It's really been an amazing thing. I get lots of mail from people, but I don't answer any more - it's too time consuming." She rarely gives interviews: "I want to have a private life of my own and raise my children

"I SEE GEORGE HAS BEEN DOING HIS KUNG-FU AGAIN"

in the normal way; and I want to keep my memories of Bruce, of our husband-wife relationship, separate. I'd hate for it to become that all I could remember is that he was a superstar!"

Setudah, in addition, sent me in a list of "22 Greatest Moments in Seattle Movie History," that was printed in a newspaper. Number 14 says: "Kung Fu movie star Bruce Lee was buried in Lake View Pioneer Cemetery in 1973."

Variety Magazine voted *Game of Death* No. 28 from 50 in the USA's top rating films.

Maria Fernandes (2751), our Brazilian member, has also sent me a number of cuttings from her country. The following extract is a discussion between John Corcoran and Emil Farkas (other interview extracts will follow in later news sheets).

Q) Was Bruce the best martial artist in America?

A) The best is like "most beautiful" - it's in the eye ofnthe beholder. There is no question that Bruce was superb in all three levels of combat - physical, psychological and academic - and he certainly was the best known artist in the entire world. Whether on not he was the best in actual performance can only be answered by those who knew and trained with himc Since Bruce had no interest in competing in tournaments, there is no competitive yardstick by which to judge him. Nevertheless he was an advocate of full contact combat long before it became fashionable in America, and many of the karate champions came to him for instruction. *(Pam here - on the occasion that Bruce appeared at the Long Beach Tournament and gave a display, in 1964, he astounded all who saw him; and the fact that champions came to him for pointers and instruction proves who was better than whom!).*

Q) How did The Green Hornet originate?

A) From comic book heroes of the 1930's - William Dozier decided to transfer characters to TV on the heels of his success with *Batman*.

Q) How long did the series run?

A) From September 9, 1966, until March 17, 1967 (26 half-hour episodes in colour - reruns began in 1968). Several episodes were released as a feature film in the States *(Pam again - also in Holland and Denmark)*.

Q) What was the offer made to Bruce by Run Run Shaw in 1970?

A) He offered Bruce the standard Asian contract actor's wage of $575 per week!

After Lee's phenomenal success, Shaws said: "He was just another actor - who knew?" When Bruce was Kung Fu King in 1972, Shaw offered Bruce an estimated $5250,000 for a single film - Bruce demanded $400,00 - and Shaw accepted. Tragically, before a film was started, Bruce died.

Q) How did Bruce feel women should defend themselves when attacked?

A) Bruce had no illusions about their ability to defend themselves against an attacker, particularly one that's big and strong. "I advise any female learning gung-fu that, if ever attacked, to hit 'em in the groin, poke 'em in the eye, kick 'em in the shins or knee - and run like hell!" Thanks Setudeh and Maria for your time, trouble and great research.

Last news sheet I put in a contact address for Graham Ellis (2728) who wanted local members to contact him with a view to forming an off-shoot of the Society locally; both he and I were surprised - or maybe astounded is more the word - at the poor response he had to this. I think that, considering all the people reading this are Bruce Lee fans, they should be pleased to find someone wanting to arrange get-togethers, etc. with a view to furthering the name of Bruce! So come on all of you... give the TV and the football matches a break for a while and get in contact with Graham at Hinckley. He really does mean business 'cause he's already been advertising in the local press! He's also got the support of the local cinema managers so, if you get together, you could all be doing yourselves a favour!

Also I understand from Graham that Intervision video tape distributors are planning to release later this year (contract discussions now in progress) three Bruce Lee feature films (they're not saying which).

Ian Hamilton (1213) and Arthur Stone (1150) say Debonair Films at Lower Ford Street, Coventry CV1 5PW, W.Midlands, have on video *The Real Bruce Lee* - running time two hours, excellent quality & colour (it includes his past, earlier films, the opening of his first Kung Fu school, etc.) Unfortunately imitators are also shown on this video, with just half-an-hour of pure Bruce (which I gather is superb). Copies vary between £41.60 and £55.64, depending on the make of video cassette.

Also on video, *Fist of Fury* in colour at £60 and *Enter the Dragon* in colour at £60. They also do 8mm film, 400' colour/ silent *Game of Death,* trailers on *Enter the Dragon* and *The Big Boss*, 100' approx. and colour - at £9.20 each, *Fist of Fury* and *Enter the Dragon* trailers on one reel (along with other, non-Bruce, films at £19.55; 200' *Enter the Dragon* trailer at £19.70 and *Way of the Dragon* trailer, 400' spool, at £35; *The Big Boss* and *Fist of Fury,* 2x400' spool each film at £32.50 each (silent/colour)

Ian Fawcett and Mark Tyler (2673) give Miko Studios at Kennemerstraatweg 35, 1814 GB, Alkmaar, Holland, stating that each film of Bruce's can be bought on 4 x 72 minute reels at £34.50 each reel. Also they have two "Hornet" episodes available, each on a 400'reel at £34.50 (all colour/sound).

Graham Waggett (2602) says members can get Bruce records from Dixons, 6 The Strand Arcade, Derby (Telephone: Derby 43762).

Still on records, Tony Harrington (2607) gives Swanscombe Post Office (Record Section), High Street, Swanscombe, Kent (for people in the Greenhithe, Northfleet and Swanscombe area). Personal shoppers are preferred, but if anyone wants records who cannot get there, Tony is kindly offering to call on your behalf. His address is: Swanscombe.

David Niedzailek (1021) sent in the clip shown here. It may possibly be unobtainable now, but it's certainly worth writing to see if the *Game of Death* board game is still for sale!

Tiswas, the Saturday morning programme on TV had a clip from *Enter the Dragon* a little while back, says Simon Bulley (2738) and other members saw this too. It showed, however, only the Roper/Williams tournament scenes and Bruce, only in a single face shot! What a disappointment!! The presenter said the clip was in response to many requests for Kung Fu footage - I'm sure what the people actually wanted was Bruce Lee footage!

Barry Norman (Film '79) gave a mention: "Kung Fu came and went with Bruce Lee" - and a few still shots were popped in for good measure at the end of the programme.

Not again! - Weekly *Movie* magazine showed a small picture of Bruce with the caption: "Of course it's Bruce Lee; what was his first picture?" Answer given: *MARLOWE!!!* (it only gets worse!).

Here's another snippet - this time from Phillip Bell (2506) on karate expert, Evan Kim; the cutting is self-explanatory. The writer seems to think quite highly of Evan and although I personally can see a little of Bruce's facial expression, what's that I see around his middle... could it possibly be a roll of fat???

Heinrich Damsgaard (2126) in Denmark has just seen the release of *Green Hornet* in a full length feature film, new title translated being *Rage of the Dragon*. Maybe we'll get it over in Britain one day. Who knows? But we do seem to be getting awfully behind the Dutch, German and Danish film distributors in this country. The sense of adventure seems to have deserted us but Heinrich has kindly send me advertising material from the film and I've an address for the distributors. I promise I'll be chasing this one personally!!!

PICTURED ABOVE are the late Bruce Lee and his look-alike Taiwanese actor, Ho Tsung-Tao alias Bruce Lai.

Final cutting for this page; the most famous look-alike of them all - Bruce Li. Thanks to Martin Schell.

Both Graham Waggett and Colin Quinton (2708), among many others, sent cutting from *Combat* magazine that's shown here. You would have thought that a leading martial magazine

A RETROSPECTIVE LOOK AT BRUCE LEE MANIA & THE KUNG FU CRAZE OF THE 1970S

TOP: A rare picture of Bruce Lee and his wife. Was he the most skillful Martial Artist of all?

would by now know what Linda Lee looks like - or at least that they'd take the trouble to check their facts! If they can make mistakes like this on something that obvious, just imagine the errors that could be appearing in their written material!

LETTERS

More on the video mentioned earlier in this news sheet...

Dear Pam,

In Real Bruce Lee, *sadly only the first 30 minutes feature Bruce; the remaining 90 are hogged by Bruce Li and Dragon Lee. I must admit, though, that Dragon Lee was a surprise. When Li took off his shirt his body was ordinary. When Lee did, I was amazed. The guy has muscle and in fact possessed the only body I've ever seen to equal Bruce's. The war-cry is exactly the same as Bruce's, and the side profile is almost a dead ringer. Pity Robert (Clouse) didn't use him in* Game of Death. *I don't, though, see why these guys impersonate Bruce - the one-and-only. The Chinese movie industry booms thanks to one man, but they keep using cardboard replicas of him, instead of new faces. How much better to see some new talents coming from the East!*

Arthur Stone (1150)

Arthur goes on to mention *Monkey*, the TV series with Masaaki Sakai, which he enjoys. I've seen one episode and liked the comical originality and personality of Masaaki. He doesn't impersonate Bruce in any way, and what a refreshing change that is to see!

THE BRUCE LEE SOCIETY

Dear Pam,

Over the last couple of weeks, I've been noticing that quite a few "old friends" keep turning up in unusual places. Angela Mao Ying (ex Enter the Dragon*) was a regular in* Man from Atlantis *TV show; also Kareem Abdul Jabbar starred in an episode called "Giant" (surprise, surprise!) Colleen Camp appeared in* Apocalypse Now *as a Bunny Girl - quite a step down from Dragon lady to Bunny Girl!*

Simon Bulley (2738)

I always seem to miss these programmes, Simon. I'd love to see the *Batman* episodes with Kato in, too - but maybe we'll all be even luckier if the film is released here soon.

Dear Pam,

I've enclosed a letter I received from BBC TV after I wrote to Barry Norman of Film '79 *about showing clips from Bruce's films.*

Kevin Hobbs (1033)

Kevin got a standardised letter, but a personal little note at the bottom which said: "Your suggestions about Bruce Lee are borne in mind, but we generally only review current films in the programme - and I'm afraid he's not on our short-list for a *Hollywood Greats*. Well, all I can say is it's about time he was on the list! Why don't you all drop a letter to the BBC, Television Centre, Wood Lane, London W12 7RJ (addressed to Barry Brown) to remind him of the fact. Some strong pestering might just convince him that Bruce's fans are many, active and willing to put on the pressure when necessary!

Dear Pam,

I recently saw Kentucky Fried Movie *which basically is a series of sketches poking fun at films in general. A piece called* Fistful of Yen *consists almost entirely of* Enter the Dragon *mickey-taking! I think the more narrow-minded among Bruce's legion of fans will find it in bad taste which, in parts admittedly, it is. But I, personally, found it too funny to be offensive! Evan Kim plays Loo and he's a very good martial artist and copies Bruce's style very well - I recommend it highly.*

David Dixon (1650)

I've yet to see this film, but taking it for what it is, I expect I'll enjoy it too.

Dear Pam,

Did I ever tell you about an incident I had in school with an English teacher? Well, we were given an essay to write on "a person whom I admire." Well, she asked for it, so I gave her 65 pages - yes 65! - all about Bruce, starting from his birth right through

THE BRUCE LEE SOCIETY

his youth, marriage, etc. She refused to read any further than two pages - and I was sent to the headmistress for the impertinence of writing about a celebrity instead of my mum or a teacher, or the like! Ah well, you can't win, can you!

Kate Feeney (1194)

It amazes me that "teachers" (and I use the word advisedly), having discovered something that actually interests one of their pupils, so often haven't the sense to make use of it.

RENEWALS - AND SORRY, IT'S TIME FOR A PRICE RISE!

Members 2600 to 2697 - your second year membership falls due for renewal between now and the end of May; similarly, members 2267 to 2302 need to renew their third year at this time; fourth year members from 1829 to 2021 should also renew, I think everyone will agree that we've managed to hold down prices for a very long time indeed. Well, like everything else in this world, it couldn't last for ever. As of April 1st this year, I'm afraid everyone's annual sub will have to increase to £5.00. That's not the sort of news that I like handing out, so I shan't say any more - except that, as before, there should be no more increases for a long time to come!

LATE EXTRA

KFM and the Society are at present getting together as many addresses as possible for places where items on Bruce may be purchased; that's for Britain AND for the rest of the world. The idea is that our scope of mail order offers will be greatly increased - and the final list can also be given out free to all members.

SWOP SHOP

- Alison French (1143), Watford has *Dragon* magazines 2, 3, 5, 6, 8-10, 13; Vol 2, 1-9 inc. Will sell for £4.50 (inc. p&p) or swap.
- Ian Fawcett, Skelmersdale wants soundtracks of all Bruce's films, reel-to-reel, cassette, record all OK. Must be good quality & in English.
- Jorgen Muller (2886), Kastrup, Denmark wants urgently magazines, posters, soundtracks etc. to swap for German/Danish material.
- Maria Fernandes (2751), Sao Paulo, Brazil wants *Unbeatable Bruce Lee* & *Bruce Lee in Action*.
- Steve Palmer (2660), Luton, wants a book called *Kung Fu History, Technique and Philosophy*. He's very keen to have it - can anyone help?
- Suresh Gandhi (1021), Neath wants urgently a copy of *Enter the Dragon* in paperback.
- Raj Sahni (2692), Wolverhampton has for sale/swap: *Dragon Sounds Special*,

Original Soundtrack recording - Bruce Lee in *Fist of Fury*. Originally cost £9.90 each, but selling both for £14. Excellent condition. Swap for other Bruce items, except records.
- Mr. N. J. Savage (1024), Bexleyheath has for sale set of 51 *KFM* magazines. Also "Bruce Lee Last Interview" tape, *Power Training in Kung Fu & Karate, Beginner's Guide to Kung Fu*.
- William Ross (2715), Irvine wants *Bruce Lee - 1940-1973* book, *My Martial Arts Training Guide to JKD* magazine, *Legend of Bruce Lee* paperback.
- Anthony King (2208), Huddersfield wants rubber-type nunchakus, *Enter the Dragon* style - good price paid.

PEN PALS

- Karen Buttigieg, Msida, Malta wants English male pen pal, aged 18-23 years.
- Keith O'Hara Jnr (2076), Worcester... he's 14 years old, likes watching martial arts and studies Taekwondo. Great Elvis fan. Wants pen pals.
- Anthony King (2208), Huddersfield wants (preferably) Chinese girl pen pal, aged 15-17 years. Interests are Bruce, David Bowie and karate.

Well folks, that's about it this time! One last thing, though, have you ever looked closely at Dinsdale Landen, star of ITV's *Piggy in the Middle* comedy series? Although there's no resemblance to Bruce, some of his facial expressions look almost identical to the ones Bruce used while posing as a Japanese phone repair man - the glasses are almost identical! SEE YOU!!!

EDITOR'S NOTES

The *Kung Fu Monthly*'s Second Bruce Lee Convention was announced, confirming the date of 19th July, with showings of the uncut *Way of the Dragon* and Lee's childhood movie *My Son Ah Chang*.

Some of Bruce Lee's childhood movies have been released over the years, especially on VCD and DVD, mainly in China and Hong Kong. Many UK film companies are reluctant to buy the rights to them as there is limited commercial value in releasing them.

Born in 1920 in Seattle, Washington, Ruby Chow, along with her husband, opened the restaurant "Ruby Chow's" in 1948. Located at 1122 Jefferson Street in Seattle's First Hill neighbourhood, it was the first Chinese restaurant outside of Seattle's Chinatown. In 1959, when he first arrived in the US from Hong Kong, Chow employed a young Bruce Lee as one of her restaurant staff. Her first brush with politics was in 1962, when she had all of the Chinese restaurants print "It's wise to vote for Wing Luke" as their fortune cookies, in her bid to get Wing Chong Luke elected to the Seattle City Council, making him the first Asian-American to hold elected office in the state.

In 1973, Chow decided to run for the King County Council as a Democrat, serving

three terms as a Kings County councilwoman in Washington. She was the fist Asian-American elected to King County Council, an in 1985, she was a park named after her at the corner of South Albro Place and 13th Avenue South. She passed away in 2008, two days before her 88th birthday.

In the biopic *Dragon: The Bruce Lee Story*, released in 1993, Ruby Chow is portrayed by Nancy Kwan, who Bruce Lee trained for *The Wrecking Crew*, also serving as the film's fight choreographer.

The three films that UK distributors Intervision were going to release on home video probably included *The Real Bruce Lee*, *Bruce's Fingers*, and *Goodbye Bruce Lee*. Not one them was an actual Bruce Lee film as they all featured Bruce Lee imitators such as Bruce Li or Dragon Lee.

A RETROSPECTIVE LOOK AT BRUCE LEE MANIA & THE KUNG FU CRAZE OF THE 1970S

16
June
1980

HI EVERYONE - I CAN HARDLY BELIEVE IT, BUT THIS IS THE LAST NEWS SHEET OF THE FOURTH YEAR; WE'RE ACTUALLY ENTERING THE FIFTH YEAR OF THE BRUCE LEE SOCIETY! IT REALLY DOESN'T SEEM POSSIBLE, DOES IT? ANYWAY, HANG ON, IT'S TIME TO GET GOING!...

GENERAL NEWS

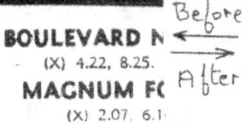

You'll find there're quite a few cuttings in this month's report - and one particularly interesting one was sent in by Andy Curtis (2759), who complained to the management of the Gemini Cinema that their advert in the local paper said "Bruce Lee starring in *Exit the Dragon, Enter the Tiger* (see picture). The efforts paid off because the next week the advert had been changed to show Bruce Li in the leading role (see second picture). It's good to see that some cinemas do take notice of the fans. I wish I could say the same about the censors!

This article was sent in by Mick Bargota (1322). Mick wonders if any one has any info about this film, *Iron Fisted Monk* - and what does "Return of Bruce Lee" mean? There's also *To Kill With Intrigue (Bruce Lee's Secret)*. Write in if you can help on any of these. Mick also mentions that in the TV programme *Not the Nine O'Clock News*, two men dressed in karate uniform demonstrated a few funny moves in front of some Bruce Lee posters. He says the camera moved in close enough to show some really good shots!

Philip Bell (2506) has put forward a suggestion that I think might be well worth taking up. His idea is an all-night Kung Fu spectacular in aid of the hospital building that Jimmy Saville is sponsoring for spinal cases. Well, let's get the convention out of the way and we can start thinking along those lines. If not an all-night spectacular, then some other way of raising money as it really is a worthwhile cause.

Philip also sent the cutting shown here. There are so many mentions of Bruce Lee these days it's impossible to know where the name is going to turn up next! Of course, one mention we could well have done without was the very sad affair you may have seen in the papers - where a bus driver went berserk and demolished a bus shelter, hit vans and cars, veered onto the pavement and hit a house, shouting "I am God - I am Bruce Lee." Publicity is great, but not that sort!

> FOUR years is a scandalous punishment for one fist of fury—whether or not it landed on target. Is a punch on the jaw 14st Dennis was a black-belt karate expert. When the attackers struck, Dennis hit back with a bit of Bruce Lee-style legwork. The bruised raiders
>
> Yesterday Poplar, East was awarded £75 cheque bravery by Office. A CHEQUE

Member Andrew Upton (2672) wants info on Chuck Norris, how many films, his style, fan club, etc. Any members similarly interested should write direct to Andrew at Birkenhead. Chuck was actually over here in May. He really is a very nice man and some of you indeed must have seen his appearance on TV's *Nationwide*. The good news is that *KFM* is publishing an exclusive interview with the star himself next month!

Alex Buttigieg (2199), our Maltese member, has been in touch with a Mr. Pace of K.R.S. Film Distributors - and he sent Alex a list of the top 20 box office films in Malta, with *Game of Death* being No. 10, *Fist of Fury* reissue No. 13, *Way of the Dragon* reissue No. 15, and *Enter the Dragon* reissue No. 17. Bruce's films, in order of 1980 popularity, turn out to be first *Game of Death,* second *Fist of Fury,* third *Way of the Dragon,* fourth *Enter the Dragon,* and fifth *Big Boss*. *Game of Death* is top because it's a new release. Alex asked Mr. Pace his personal view on Bruce as a person and his reply was, "A great master in all dimensions" - a most apt description.

One final point, during one week in Malta while *The Silent Flute* was showing, there were also films starring fellow actors James Coburn, James Franciscus and John Saxon. The Master had plenty of company!

Graham Ellis (2728) -

Mr Clink - manager of the Nuneaton "Ritz"

Mr Nicolls - manager of the Hinckley "Classic"

who has been advertising recently via the news sheets for fellow-members to contact him with a view to a local off-shoot of the Society - has sent in two pictures of local cinema managers who are co-operating with him in the endeavour. Again, this does show that people are approachable, if only one makes the necessary attempt. These worthy gentlemen are shown here.

Graham also wrote to the BBC about the Bruce tribute film and their reply, I'm afraid, was the standard one as there are no plans at present to show it. Now, by way of a little persuasion, you'll find at the convention a certain petition form and one that suggests that the BBC should change its mind. Please, DON'T forget to add your name to the list! Meanwhile, to get the ball rolling a little, how about dropping a line to Miss Maureen Stevens, Programme Correspondence Section, BBC, Broadcasting House, London W1A 1AA to tell her how and why you disagree with that out of touch policy. I'm sure she'll be pleased to hear from you!!!

Arthur Stone (1150) has sent in a small amendment to a snippet that appeared in the last news sheet. Another member had reported that he thought Angela Mao Ying had appeared in a *Man from Atlantis* episode; it turns out the lady in question was in fact Jean Marier Hon and not Angela - though Arthur says they do look quite similar. Thanks for putting us right!

Maria Fernandes (2751) has sent in a list published in *The Big Book of Karate* January 1980, by Sammy Kays. It shows 14 names (not necessarily in rank, but in popularity) voted by readers - and Bruce rated No. 1 spot!!! The others, in number order, were: Mike Wallace, George Dillman, Ed Parker, Robert Trias, Mike Foster, Chuck Norris, S. Henry Cho, Joe Corley, Jim Harrison, Joe Lewis, Jhoon Rhee, Allen Steen, and Steve Armstrong.

Kevin Stokes (2624) read in a USA magazine *Street Chopper*, that there are two Chinese men who do murals for the magazine and who also run a martial arts school called "Draggin Enterprises." The headline for the article was "Enter the Draggin" and a quote was: "When Draggin' first opened, the first two bikes to roll through the doors were twin Harley's built for Vic and his instructor Richard Bustillo. In order to be giving lessons to a black belt with 18 years experience, you can imagine what sort of credentials Rich must carry. Rich, along with his partner, Dan Inosanto, own the Filipino Academy in Torrance and both were close friends of Bruce Lee." (Slight misquotes there, but the basics of what they are saying get through - Pam.)

Lee Percy (1072) has an article and photo printed in his local paper concerning Bruce and the Society (shown here). He's certainly managed to get all of us a good write up - well done Lee!

Donald Clift (2172) wants help from

fellow members as he's very interested in Jeremy Yau's style of Kung Fu called "Lau Gar," but cannot find much on it. Anyone able to assist in any way, please write to Donald at Cambridge.

Shahab Setudeh Nejad (1419), a member who went off to live in the States, has sent me some more snippets of news. A quote from Taky Kimura on Bruce's death, "I firmly believe that Bruce worked himself to death. He was uncompromising. I was planning to tell him to slow down but he was so dedicated and I don't think he even knew how to slow down." Bruce's mother-in-law said, "Everything Bruce did, had to be perfect. In his films, if something didn't meet his standards, he'd do it over and over until it was right."

USEFUL ADDRESSES

On the 8mm film scene, Ian Hamilton (1213) thought that members would like to know Warner Brothers have just released a 400' colour/sound version of *Enter the Dragon* - mostly the fights (including the bottle scene) and also clips of the Roper/Williams battles. Quality is excellent and the cost is around £31.95. Check out good photographic stores or adverts in *Moviemaker* magazine for details.

Simon Bulley (2738) gives branches of Andy's Record Shop (in and around the Cambridge area) as good places for second-hand records. He recently bought a 12" copy of *Dragon Power* for 30p which is surely the bargain of the week!

Maria Fernandes is the representative of the Little Dragon Club International in Venezuela. She's very kindly made me an honorary member and for those of you wishing to join, the membership "fee" is two martial arts magazines sent to her, plus name and address and two small photos. In return you'll get a membership card. Her address is: Sao Paulo, Brazil. The club, if you wish to write direct, is at Av. Fraternidad No. 12-56, P.O. Box 16, El Tocuyo, Edo Lara, Republic of Venezuela.

Jorgen Muller (2886) says you can get all the JKD Club of Hong Kong books at around £3 each, plus other German books at around £2, plus four of Bruce's films (*Big Boss, Fist of Fury, Game of Death* and *Way of the Dragon*) - each movie in four parts and each part costing £38 (colour/sound/Super 8). Address: Budo-Artical-Vertrieb, Postfach 2107, D.6380 Bad Homburg, V.D.H. Germany.

THE CONVENTION

Many members have written to me as it seems confusion was rife on the date of the forthcoming convention. It seems that, after the announcement of our July 19th event (YES, it is still on!) many members started to receive advertisements for another convention, held in June. I'll leave you to draw your own conclusions as to the morals of the people concerned and would just add that quite a number of fans have said that they thought it unethical and certainly not something that a true Bruce Lee devotee would even consider doing.

I also happen to know that a good number of the fans who were sent this material had NEVER knowingly given their addresses to the businessmen concerned. I can only assume, therefore, that our Area Lists have somehow fallen into their hands. It really hurts to think that one of our members has deliberately helped these people. If they REALLY want to get involved in the Bruce Lee scene then let them get up off their backsides and do the work we have; the work that's enabled them to be able to cash-in of Britain's Little Dragon fans. I'd be interested to hear what Society members have to say about this state of affairs!

Anyway, to repeat, 19th July is the date for Britain's second official convention. I look forward to seeing you all there. If you thought the May '79 event was good, this is going to be a mindblower. Remember we've got Robert Lee coming, Ted Pollard and Dougie Robinson are re-enacting the Lee/Norris fight from *Way of the Dragon* - LIVE ON STAGE(!), there's *My Son Ah Chang* (a complete showing of Bruce in his first major starring role - at the age of nine), *Game of Death* - uncensored and in wide-screen 35mm for the first time in Britain, a Bruce Lee look-alike competition (see *KFM* 55 for details), on sale - Bruce's famous protein drink... and of course, much, much more. If you still haven't booked then you better move fast. The price to Society members is just £4.50 (BEFORE the day) and £5 to everyone else. On the door, it's a fixed price of £6. Order tickets from the usual address, 14 Rathbone Place, London WIP IDE.

CENSORSHIP

Many, many members have sent me copies of the letter they received from the film censors regarding the latest mutilation to Bruce's films. And I can tell you all now, they must have been receiving a heck of a lot of mail to have run off a standard letter - yes, everyone got the same reply!

Basically, they condone their latest cuts by stating that they have been made "where nunchakus and chainsticks are used or where excessive kicks or punches to the head or crotch are seen." They hasten to add "that we are not worried that genuine students of Kung Fu will use chainsticks, but they are a small part of the community. A far larger audience is continually being created as youngsters reach the age when they can see X-rated films and we have evidence that the weapons they see in these films can easily be copied and used." (Pam here - I cannot, will not, do not agree -it's far easier for them to pick up a knife, which is easily accessible, or a stick, or any other heavy/blunt instrument and attack someone - IF THEY ARE SO INCLINED. Such a person is NOT going to go to the trouble of searching for, or making, a pair of nunchakus.)

The censors say they have the support of the local authorities and the police, and that it's extremely unlikely the cuts will ever be restored. They also say that no Bruce Lee film has been cut by more than five minutes and some far less than this. Although I dispute these timings, hasn't it occurred to them just what to Bruce Lee fans these precious minutes contain?

Still with the censors, Mrs. Ann Jones (2782) recently went to see *Way of the Dragon* and found more cuts in the fight scenes. Quite rightly, she went to the Manager and asked for her money back - without result. So she wrote to Warner Brothers and, happily, they expressed some sympathy. Unhappily, there seems little they can do either. For those of you who haven't yet got a copy of the film censor's latest list of excuses, the address to write is: The British Board of Film Censors, 3 Soho Square, London WI. I might even suggest that you ring them on 01-437 2677... it's up to you!

SPECIAL MESSAGES

Alex Buttigieg (2199) in Malta wants to pass on a message to Ian Camilleri (1819) who was in Malta but is now in Wales. "Far is the distance between us, but our friendship will never part. May the Lord help you find the new and happier life you seek."

And a message to member John Milne (2046), his wife and family - on behalf of all of us. "Sincere condolences on the sad loss of your little son Robert, who died on 21st March. (The memory of the just is blessed)."

RECORDS NEWS

A very rare chance indeed for fans to purchase special re-press copies of Robert Lee's *Ballad of Bruce Lee* LP. The offer really is limited and I should add that each album is PERSONALLY SIGNED BY ROBERT! This is something I'm dealing with personally, so cheques/postal orders (for £4) made out to Pam Hadden please and sent to Pam Hadden Record Offer, 14 Rathbone Place, London WIP IDE. I'll also be throwing in a free and unusual photo of Bruce and Robert.

Secondly, a message from Satril Records. "We've had so many letters and enquiries from you about our tribute record to Bruce Lee that we have decided to re-release the single in early July. The 7" record, which heavily features the voice of Bruce plus combat sound effects, will be packaged in a (first 5000) limited edition colour picture sleeve and will have a different B side from the first time around. Called *Mellow Terrain*, it again features the voice of Bruce Lee. The price in record will be around 99p.

Those lucky enough to get the original 12" collectors picture sleeve need not worry about the exclusivity of their copy (some are being sold for £25 a throw these days!) ... we won't more of these. But if you're after a copy of the new version, move fast! Experience has shown that these limited sleeves usually sell out within weeks of issue. If you have difficulty in finding a copy, call Mark or Linda on 01-435 8063, and they'll advise you on your nearest stockist.

REQUEST FOR INFO

I've had letters from Stephen Readman (Hartlepool) and Mr. R M Carlyle (Windsor) for info on Bruce. Stephen wants photos, info for a book he is writing, which he says will be the best ever written on the Master. Mr. Carlyle is writing a documentary about Bruce's life, in the hope of interesting a TV station. He, too, needs help with the research. These sound like very worthwhile ventures, and there must be many of you out there who could really lend a hand. Don't just leave it to 'someone else.'.. pitch in!

RENEWALS

Members 2698 to 2737 - your second year membership falls due between now and the end of August; similarly, members 2303 to 2349 - your thirdrd year falls due at this time also. fourth year members from 2022 to 2084 should also renew.

LETTERS

Dear Pam,

I enclose the reply I received from the censors. I'm sad to say it looks like there is nothing we can do about the cutting. I think that their decision is completely unnecessary and totally unfair - people will not want to pay full price to see only 50% of a film, with hardly any fighting action in it. If some idiots think Bruce's art is brutal and disturbing, they should not go to see X-certificated movies and I for one am writing again to the Secretary of the Film Censors, Mr. Ferman, to plead with him to think again. P.S. Is his name "Ferman" or "Vermin" (the dirty rat!?!?!).

Andy Curtis (2759)

I've quoted bits of the standard letter already, and you know my feelings!! All we can hope is that private showings of films will not be affected, that would be the last straw.

Dear Pam,

I enclose a copy of the reply I received from Southern TV *when I wrote and asked them to show* The Green Hornet *and* Longstreet *on television.*

Shane James (2818)

Southern TV replied:

"Thank you for your letter. I am not aware that the comic strip you refer to - The Green Hornet - has yet been offered to ITV in this country, but I am passing your request for this and Longstreet to our Programme Planning Department. I regret I cannot give you any certainty that they will be able to either acquire or transmit these programmes in the immediate future."

Simon Theobalds
Head of Press and Public Relations
Southern Television Ltd
Southern Television Centre
Northam, Southampton S09 4YQ, Hants

Well, it sounds a little promising to me, so get out the pens and paper and start writing to Mr. Theobalds. If he gets enough requests, who knows?

THE BRUCE LEE SOCIETY

Dear Pam,

Elvis Presley, before his death, was making a martial arts film called New Gladiators *with World Karate Champion Bill "Superfoot" Wallace; there's 20/25 minutes of El "in the can," but at the moment there's some litigation and people are hanging onto the film until suitable monies are forthcoming for their efforts. The film really belongs to El and his estate - but it looks like it's going to end up another* Game of Death. *If El were alive, like Bruce he would have stood no nonsense; it would have been finished AND a good job would have been made of it!*

David Moore (1783)

I've always been a great El fan, and what I would have loved to have seen would have been Bruce and Elvis together in a martial arts movie. The charisma, sheer talent and magnetism of this pair would have blown the screens apart!

PEN PALS

Tony Lundberg (2338), Copenhagen, Denmark wants English/USA pen pals - his interests are Bruce, philosophy, martial arts, Jeet Kune Do and movies. Anyone can write, because he wants to hear from you all!!

Mr. James Flanagan (2824), Oldham wants female Chinese pen pal aged 16-19. He's 17 and interests are Bruce, martial arts, reading, body-building, running.

A RETROSPECTIVE LOOK AT BRUCE LEE MANIA & THE KUNG FU CRAZE OF THE 1970S

"SORRY DOC, I SHOULD HAVE TOLD YOU I'M A KUNG-FU EXPERT BEFORE YOU TRIED MY REFLEXES"

BRITT DO ME A FAVOUR AND FORGET THE GUN, YOU CAN'T BEAT A GOOD OLD DOUBLE TOP!

Cherrilyne Banks (2863)

Kung Fu Bruce Lee King of Kung Fu By Martin Coleman Society No. 2030

Tony Lundberg (2338)

Shane James (2828)

Pointing Finger

Glynn Derbyshire

THE WORK OF PAUL SMITH, GREAT BRUCE LEE SOCIETY NUMBER-1532.

SWOP SHOP

- Mark Salter (1792), Sheffield S13 8AZ has for sale 400'colour/sound trailer inc. 4 Bruce trailers *Fist of Fury, Big Boss, Enter the Dragon, Way of the Dragon* (containing much of the censored nunchaku scene) plus four non-Bruce trailers *Lightning Swords of Death, Lady Kung Fu, Triple Irons, Five Fingers of Death* - Super 8, £20. 200' Super 8 colour/sound *Fists of the Double K*, £8. 400' colour/sound Super 8 *Star Wars* - £15. All excellent condition.
- Carl Jones (2121), St. Helens has for sale or swap for Bruce Super 8 films/Sci-Fi etc (please state what) - assorted Bruce books/magazines, many rare! (e.g. *Bruce Lee Between Wing Chun and JKD* by Jesse Glover (£3.50); *Chinese Gung-Fu* by Bruce (reprint); *Inedito* (Spanish version of *Inedit*) - £4.50. Prices include postage, etc). Loads more to choose, send SAE for list with details of what you have.
- Graham Ellis (2728), Hinckley has for sale *Game of Death* tracksuit, medium size - worn once, perfect. £15.00.
- Mr. J McGeachy (2371), Glasgow has for sale or swap *Way of the Dragon* film which includes the nunchaku scene - not sound, but with cassette.
- Mr. N J Savage (1024), Bexleyheath has for sale *Fist of Fury* LP, set of 53 *KFM* magazines plus spares, and Bruce Lee Interview tape.
- Mr. Martin White, Cayton has for sale *KFM*s 1-23, 26-40 (except 39); *Beginners Guide to Kung Fu, Kung Fu* 75 No. 1, *KFM Bruce Lee Scrapbook*; *Enter the Dragon* album soundtrack; *Book of Kung Fu* (*KFM*); *Dragon* Nos. 2, 3, 9, 11, & 12; *Clash* No. 1, 2, *Kung Fu* (big Bruce poster magazine); *Karate* Nos. 63 & 64. Total value around £25 - nearest offer to £15 secures.
- Andy Curtiss (2759), Bath wants *KFM*s 1-2 and 31 on, will pay very high price if mint. Also has brand new *Dragon Sounds Special* LP (Bruce) - will swap for *Fist of Fury* or *Way of the Dragon* soundtrack in good condition or rubber *Enter the Dragon* type nunchakus.
- Mr. C Barwell, Stoke-on-Trent has for sale *KFM* 34-52; *Bruce Lee King of Kung Fu*; *Farewell My Friend*; one flick book - asking £11 for the lot.
- Miss C. Banks (2863), Nottingham wants *Bruce Lee: The Man Only I Knew* by Linda. David Evans (2026), Llandinam needs *KFM* 3. £5 offered, must be excellent condition.
- Tony Lundberg (2338), Copenhagen, Denmark wants to buy Bruce books, magazines, posters, records, tapes, badges, films. Will pay good price, write to him with details.
- David Moore (1783), Wakefield has many items (books, records, magazines, pictures on Bruce for sale, also other martial arts items, all very cheap. Write for list, including SAE. He wants: any Bruce Tegner martial arts weapons books; *Bruce Lee in Action*, *KFM*s 2 and 20, *Combat* magazines before Vol. 4 No. 5, *Fighting Arts* magazine before Vol. 3 No. 3, *Karate & Oriental Arts* before 70, any foreign magazines, film posters of *Big Boss, Fist of Fury, Way of the Dragon* and *Enter the Dragon*. All must be in good condition.

Well, that's it for this time! See you all at the convention on 19th July and I think most of you will understand if I leave you with this little quote from Shakespeare's *Henry V* - "In peace there's nothing so becomes a man as modest stillness and humility; but when the blast of war blows in our ears, then imitate the action of the tiger: stiffen the sinews, summon up the blood, disguise fair nature with hard-favoured rage!"

Please remember, by the way, we shall be starting off our BBC petition on the day. You'll find a poster and a bundle of forms in the theatre's foyer area. Please support it. If there's one thing I'd like to achieve in the near future, is the TV screening of the Bruce Lee documentary that's been collecting dust for so many years! See you - Pam

BRUCE LEE SOCIETY COLUMN
KUNG FU MONTHLY NO. 56

Hi, it's Pam here, and very happy to be slotting into the new page. A Bruce Lee news section is long overdue say!! Something that I'm less happy about (and that's putting it MILDLY) is the response to our Hollywood Boulevard Petition; I'm sorry to say this, but so far it's a disgrace! In the past, we've had signatures piling in for all manner of causes. Why not to have Bruce's name put alongside all the other 'greats' on the famous Hollywood Walk of Fame sidewalk? If you don't believe me, here are some figures. Since last Christmas I've had in a total of around 1000 names; the Convention itself contributed a pitiful 150/200.

In order to have Bruce's name put where it belongs, we need around 40.000 signatures, not 1000! From the figures I've had from the petition organizer, Norman Borine, for the first time ever, the Americans are actually way ahead of us in the collecting stakes. The Bruce Lee Society is now known worldwide to be THE Little Dragon Society so we CAN and MUST do better than this.

On this occasion, please collect from WHOEVER and WHEREVER you can. It's quantity we need and fast. Just head sheets "Hollywood Boulevard Petition", then post them off to me, Pam Hadden, c/o Hollywood Petition, *Kung Fu Monthly*, 14 Rathbone Place, London W1P 1DE. For maximum incentive, I've arranged with the *KFM* editor that the sender of the letter containing the most signatures will receive a FREE twelve-issue subscription to *KFM*. Come on everybody, let's make it happen!!!

Many of you will have noticed at the convention that we were selling Robert Lee's *Ballad of Bruce Lee* album. In fact, that album is now rather special. It's deleted from the normal lists, which means you won't be able to buy it in record shops anymore and each of the copies in our possession has been PERSONALLY SIGNED by the man himself, Robert Lee. Now that means they really are something of collector editions and although a great many were snapped up on the day, there are still just a few left. This is something I'm doing off my own bat so if you want a copy the price is £4.50 (UK), £5.00 (Europe) and £6.00 (Rest of the World). Please send orders direct to me, Pam Hadden, c/o 14 Rathbone Place, London W1P 1DE with all cheques and postal orders on this occasion to be made out to Pam Hadden, please.

Lastly for this month, the GREAT news is that plans are already well advanced for the event to end all Bruce Lee events. I'm not allowed to say any more than that, for reasons that we'd rather not have "certain people" pinching any more of our ideas. Just keep reading *KFM* and they'll keep you informed!

EDITOR'S NOTES

Actor Sammo Hung was virtually unknown in the UK 1980. Some fans would have recognised him as 'that guy at the beginning of *Enter the Dragon* but that would have been about it. *The Iron-Fisted Monk* was Hung's directorial debut. Released in 1977, with himself taking the lead role, with Chan Sing and Bruce Lee's former co-star James Tien in supporting roles, the film is now regarded as a classic by fans of the genre.

There is some confusion as to what the "Bruce Lee tribute film" mentioned throughout the newsletters could be. Some state it was the 1973 documentary *The Man and the Legend* or something the BBC was working on around that same time.

The Man and the Legend was the first Bruce Lee documentary ever made. Shortly after his star's death, Raymond Chow sent cameras around Bruce Lee's home to capture footage of how he lived. Hastily cut footage from Lee's feature films were added, together with footage from Lee's funeral and on 14th October 1973, a mere three months after his passing, it was released in Hong Kong. It was re-edited and updated in 1983 to become *Bruce Lee The Legend* but wouldn't be released in its original form in the UK until 1998.

The rumoured BBC tribute film idea must have been abandoned down the line as nothing ever came of it. They have done documentaries in recent years such as *The Kung Fu Years* in 1997 but nothing of any substance. It is said that in 1973, the BBC sent a camera crew out to Hong Kong to interview Bruce Lee on the set of *Enter the Dragon* and to get footage of the film being made. Where that film is and what condition it is likely to be in is anyone's guess.

The New Gladiators was a martial arts documentary project featuring Elvis Presley. Initially presented as an idea to Presley's Karate instructor and Bruce Lee's friend Ed Parker in 1974 by George Waite, Parker passed the project onto Presley, who liked the idea. After a meeting in Graceland, Presley wrote a $50,000 cheque to begin production on the film but after his death in 1977, the footage was stored in a truck in Hollywood garage, surrounded by other bits of memorabilia. In 2001, the footage was found, restored and released in 2002 by Isaac Florentine and Don Warrener of Rising Sun Productions. An extended version of the film was released in 2009 by Elvis Presley Enterprises.

A RETROSPECTIVE LOOK AT BRUCE LEE MANIA & THE KUNG FU CRAZE OF THE 1970S

17 September 1980

WELL, WE'RE OFF WITH THE FIFTH YEAR OF THE BRUCE LEE SOCIETY AND WHAT A VERY PROMISING YEAR IT LOOKS TO BE! READ ON FOR MORE ABOUT THAT.

THE SECOND OFFICIAL BRUCE LEE CONVENTION

It's hard to know where to start describing the events behind the scenes on the morning of this year's amazing official convention. People dashing here, there and everywhere; tables appearing out of thin air; posters, pictures and placards fixing themselves on walls as if by magic. It seemed impossible that, in only an hour or so's time, all would be ready for the Bruce Lee event of the year. Backstage, tension was rising as we ran through a quick rehearsal and, thank heavens, everything seemed to be okay. I was to look after the lighting and I was relieved to find that the man who actually understood the enormous bank of switches was able to make them do what I wanted. There was one problem... all of us behind the stage were going to be relying on the verbal cues of compare for the day, Tony Myatt - and unfortunately at the back of the stage we couldn't hear a word he was saying! A special loudspeaker was quickly plugged-up in the wings.

The show opened with a stunning slide sequence, devised and scripted by Eddy Pumer. Depicting a rapid journey through the life of Bruce Lee, it was accompanied by some fine music (including the very rousing *Fanfare for the Common Man*) and a storyline told by Tony Myatt. We moved straight on to the first of the feature films, and what a rarity it was! *My Son Ah Chang* is probably the only remaining legacy we have of Bruce's very young past and as such it just has to be essential viewing for every true fan. Admittedly there are times when it drags a bit - and where the Little

Dragon makes only a few appearances. But what's that compared with this marvellous slice of history. Actually, one or two people suggested that perhaps we should have just cut together the pieces that featured Bruce. I wonder what Eddy Leahy, the man from Golden Harvest who very kindly hired us the film, would have said about that!!! When the film ended, Tony Myatt rounded up the afternoon's events... then it was time for lunch.

The stands seemed very popular indeed and books, magazines, etc, etc were just disappearing like wildfire. Not only that, *KFM* Editor Bruce Sawford LOST his bet and we quickly sold all four gallons of Bruce Lee's protein drink (one of my rare ideas!) and, naturally, the special reprints of Robert Lee's *Ballad of Bruce Lee* album (signed personally by Robert) also changed hands at great speed (see Special Offers this month). And lunchtime was when I was able to meet and talk to the most members... obviously a very pleasant part of the day for me. Indeed, here would be a good place for me to thank all those who gave their time so generously in helping in so many ways on the day.

The afternoon began with the long anticipated re-stage of the Bruce/Chuck fight from *Way of the Dragon* with Ted Pollard and Dougie Robinson taking the stage honours. But we mustn't forget either a Mr. Norman Fisher who, at late notice was able to produce that super backdrop of the Coliseum... it looked splendid! And the fight was splendid too. To encouraging cheers and yells from the audience, they carried through the entire fight sequence and managed to achieve exactly the right dramatic effect. And believe me, it wasn't luck that brought that kind of perfection... more the result of hours and hours of practise and rehearsing. Obviously their intention was not to be another Bruce or Chuck - for that could never be! What they succeeded in doing was to reproduce, with the greatest of skill, the mood and flavour of the original confrontation. It was a job well done and they thoroughly deserved the applause they got.

Tony Myatt then arrived back on stage to make one of the most long-awaited introductions of the day for, of course, Robert Lee! As chance would have it, Tony and Robert had actually met before - some time ago in Hong Kong. That meant they were able to chat away about people and places and Bruce which was enthralling stuff for everyone. But for me it was fingernail chewing time because Robert was beginning to perform his songs. He started, I hit my first lighting cue at the right moment, and suddenly the tension drained away from me... it was going to be okay (could it be that Bruce himself was guiding and watching?) Well, needless to say in the end everything went off fine and, performance-wise, Robert was absolutely superb. He captivated everyone, and the amount of mail I've since received about the man has been just overwhelming,, Suffice to say that we shall undoubtedly be seeing more of Robert in the future! He opened with *Pointing Finger* and followed it by reading live a poem written by his brother - *Parting*. Then he went into *Ballad of Bruce Lee,* followed by *JKD* and ending with *The Boat Song.* Altogether a first-rate performance by a very talented young man — a "chip off the old block" one might even say! The applause he received at the end was resounding - and deserved.

It was time for "Questions and Answers" and this year the panel was most auspicious indeed for it included, in addition to myself, Bruce Sawford, Eddy Pumer and

"Professor" Will Johnston... that's right, Robert and, to deal with any fighting queries, Ted Pollard. Tony Myatt threw out the questions. It's hard to tell when you're actually up there, but it seemed to me to be a really interesting session. I gather, though, that we caused great hilarity with the microphone nearly always ending up in the hand of Robert - must to his amusement, too, I might add!

What can I say about the Bruce Lee Look-a-like contest that followed? Bruce Sawford who devised the idea was a worried man at the start of the day as we only had three contestants. His view was that people were too shy to take part... I felt that it might be members just knew they couldn't match a man of such talent and greatness. But the point of the competition was to be FUN and, thankfully, once the two or three brave ones had been up and done their bit, suddenly there was a deluge! Eventually we had 17 people enter!!! And it was very difficult to judge - what with nunchaku displays, press-ups, imitations, etc., etc. Robert was after some of Bruce's philosophical influence and so we tried to get competitors to say what influence the Little Dragon had had on their lives. Things really swung along well and the audience seemed as gripped as we were... who was going to do what next??? Gradually it dawned that we had stumbled on another, unexpected highlight to the show. Eventually, after making a very tough decision, member Frank Salmon was declared the winner and one of the joint winners of last year's essay competition, Alan l'Anson, was declared one of the runners-up.

Ted Pollard took the stage again for a quite remarkable nunchaku display - I must say it was good seeing the way the audience got behind him. Ted's another man who I'm sure we'll be seeing a lot of in the future. I don't want to make comparisons with anyone, but the way he handles the sticks with lightning speed and precision, accompanied by superb theatrical feeling... must make his performance one of the most professional and entertaining acts of its kind in the world. What's more, I can vouch for the fact that he is a very pleasant man who's totally dedicated to the principles for which Bruce stood.

Last to go before the tea break were three short film clips - two of which were known about already. They were "Behind the Scenes of *Enter the Dragon*" and the sensation of last year's convention, the Bruce Lee "Screen Test." The third item, however, was a real bolt from the blue - the trailer for the upcoming *Game of Death* follow-up, entitled *Game of Death 2*. Although a double features heavily in it, fans were treated to some never-before-seen movie shots of Bruce Lee - a real coup for the second official Bruce Lee convention!

After the second break, it was time for a showing of *Game of Death*, uncensored and in all its original glory. It was well worth it, for when we reached the part where Bruce proper arrived at what was the pagoda to begin his floor by floor battles, the atmosphere grew positively electric. But that was nothing to when he faced up to the usually censored Danny Inosanto. Cheers rang out as fans were at last able to see this great fight.

A great day finally came to an end with Tony Myatt giving the goodbyes from our end and, of course, the now traditional speech from James Coburn. Fans wended their way home safe in the knowledge that the legend of Bruce Lee remains safe in the UK - and I suspect having just witnessed the greatest Little Dragon event ever to be staged in Britain. All I can say is thanks to everyone involved - and to all the people who came. I reckon it was an historic occasion!

ASSISTANCE NEEDED

Please can anyone who knows of any Kung Fu clubs around the Hull area, pass the info on to Andrew Newington of 15 Cottesmore Road, Hessle, North Humberside, HU13 9JQ. He desperately wants to join one.

THE WORLD OF BRUCE LEE

As many of you - and all who attended the convention - will know, in June I met with Norman Borine, an authority on Bruce and friend of the Lee family, and also Richard Vinson, who runs the World of Bruce Lee Museum in Los Angeles. They do a fantastic job with the museum, and run film shows at weekends. They also have many rare items belonging to Bruce such as clothing, and so on. You could say that they are really the official "club" for Bruce in the States. And their aims are very similar to ours; to promote the name of Bruce and to spread the words of the Master throughout the world through his philosophy, his art and his memory. It made a lot of sense then to form an alliance, one which in the future could even transform into one big club or society. So, for the immediate future, it's been agreed that the World of Bruce Lee, *KFM* and the Bruce Lee Society shall work together with a view to organising Conventions worldwide, as well as other events too.

While I was over there recently I also had the pleasure of meeting with Grace Lee, a truly lovely lady and one who we expect to be appearing soon at a UK Convention. I also met with Danny Inosanto (who has just finished a two-volume book on his art - more on that soon) and he too is very keen to revisit our shores. All in all, the future looks very exciting for Bruce Lee fans.

GENERAL NEWS

Due to the late printing (again!) of the last news sheet, I was unable to do the tribute which I had planned - for sending flowers to Bruce's grave. So I'm just going to mention that next year I shall be making a collection so that the Society will be able to get its tribute over to the States in plenty of time. I shall be advertising this in every future March Sheet.

David Moore (1783) and Joseph Chiang (1044) were both annoyed (and rightly so) about articles they read in *Official Karate*. Frank Clark, American Kyokushinkai-style Karate, third Dan, shoots his (stupid) mouth off about Bruce in amazing fashion: "It will take a while before all that garbage - such as the Bruce Lee movies - gets cleaned from the air. It was that junk that made people think karate was little more than jumping in the air and screaming blue murder." He goes on to say: "People still believe that Bruce was the best in the world, but when he trained in Hawaii in Kyokushinai-Kan, he was trounced many times. The camera can create an illusion which is quite different from reality." Well, I expect like me you are all seething over this idiotic article. Remember though that this is the cheapest kind of self-publicity going, to knock some well-loved and famous figure and you'll hit the headlines. If he also happens to be dead, so much the better as he can't hit you back. Personally I think that's the reason for all this rubbish, but if this guy really thinks he's such an authority on Bruce - indeed, judging by his comments one might well conclude that he thinks himself an authority on just about everything - then perhaps he'd like to show us just how the arts are done. Let him make a film giving us this shining example of how the camera doesn't have to lie when it gets such a wonderful, self-opinionated little upstart as Frank Clark in front of it. I am the first to listen to constructive comments on Bruce or his films - indeed I'd be a complete idiot myself if I were to believe that everyone in the world liked Bruce Lee but when someone says something as ridiculous as the above, then it makes my blood boil. Bruce's art was his life - he dedicated himself to it and perfected every move. His leaps were spectacular, breathtaking, and unbelievable and thereby may hang the motive for these remarks (if plain self-advertisement isn't the answer). Because Bruce's moves were unbelievable - far more outrageous than anyone would be expected to perform - those that hadn't already see him would probably much prefer to believe it was all exaggeration; that way they don't have to try to match up to it themselves. So Mr. Clark, if you're so good, let's see YOU in action!

David Moore also mentions a book he's just read called *Martial Arts* by Michael Random, dealing with Japanese religious backgrounds and the arts. There are many sayings in this book from past Japanese Masters that could be connected to Bruce: "The Dragon is the symbol of untamed forces" and "One must always aim beyond one's target.".. Bruce was always pointing out the latter remark. And to balance Frank Clark's comments, here is another item from David (this time written by Speedy Otis) and taken from the *Official Karate Yearbook Magazine*. It reads: "The martial arts can change your life by giving you better health, confidence, self-awareness, etc. The prime example, I think, is still Bruce Lee, a man who literally remade himself through his studies. Those who have read any of Lee's books know that his physical abilities represented only the external portion of what was taking place within him. Through his training, Lee discovered certain truths about human nature and about himself which were reflected in his writings as well as his fighting. In short, what Lee found, and what more people are discovering, is that the separation between the martial arts and 'life' is artificial." He goes on to comment that he failed to enjoy *Game of Death*, because it contains only 15 minutes of Bruce and there's also that dreadful superimposing of Bruce's face onto a double (something we all agree with, I know). He says on Chuck Norris that his best film so far is *The Octagon*. Chuck himself believes his acting is improving and Otis remarks that, unlike so many others, he is not trying to emulate Bruce. Chuck himself says: "Bruce was Bruce and there will never be anyone like him." A nice tribute from a really nice guy.

Ian Fawcett (2918) sent a letter to his local paper, the *Wigan Reporter*, about censorship of Bruce's films - shown here. I also show a cutting sent in by Kevin Hobbs (1033) - the sort of thing I do NOT like seeing!

A FAN of martial arts film star Bruce Lee explained to Hereford city magistrates on Monday how Chinese fighting sticks were used.

Colin Antony Webb, aged 18, said the two foot-long sticks, held together by a short chain, were held by the chain and "waved about."

Webb claimed the homemade sticks were for use as ornaments. "I was going to hang them on the wall as I am a Bruce Lee fan. I collect pictures and posters of him," he said.

Webb, of Princess Avenue, College Estate admitted charges of possessing the fighting sticks, described as "Nung Chakau sticks," and a sheath knife – both offensive weapons – in a public place.

Insp Roger Wedlake said the defendant was seen "waving the sticks about" while sitting in a car in West Street on Saturday night. When he spoke to him a police officer noticed a knife with a five-inch blade, out of its sheath, also in the car.

Webb told him he realised the fighting sticks were weapons and that he had made them. The sheath knife was used for fishing.

Webb described himself as "a Bruce Lee fan," and claimed he intended to put the sticks, also described as "rice flails," on the wall for decoration. He had been swinging them about to remove wood dust as he was carving his initials on them.

Fining Webb a total of £40, Mr Paul Barnsley, chairman, pointed out that the offences were serious. "You could be fined £1,000 on each, or go to prison for three months," he said.

A plea against Bruce Lee censorship - written by Ian Fawcett (2918).

SIR — Please can I make this plea to the readers of the *Wigan Reporter*.

The British Board of film Censors are planning to censor yet again the already heavily censored Bruce Lee films.

Bruce Lee died tragically in 1973 after making only 4½ films.

The films coming under the axe are Enter The Dragon, The Way Of The Dragon, and Fist of Fury. The censor is cutting out the 'Nunchako' sequence from a fight scene in Enter The Dragon. Nunchaku's being a weapon which Bruce Lee used with incredible speed and skill, which he spent 20 years mastering. Fist Of Fury and Way Of The Dragon are also to have major parts removed.

Bruce Lee was the undisputed king of Kung-Fu and probably will never be equalled.

The brutal censoring is a big blow to the memory of Bruce Lee.

But Bruce Lee fans can help to get this decision reversed by voicing your opinion politely but firmly to the film censors.

The address is: Mr Firman, Secretary, British Board of Film Censors, Soho Square, London W1.

Every single letter will help.

Ian Fawcett
Stanley Road,
Upholland.

PS: A petition is even better!

ADDRESSES

Peter Jagger (1087) says that he bought a Super 8mm film, 400' (approx 20 minutes), colour/sound of *Enter the Dragon* - containing the Lee/O'Hara fight with bottle scene, underground scenes using nunchakus, plus the Lee/Kan fight. Excellent quality, he says, and it's obtainable from Cimac Martial Arts, 606 Stratford Road, Sparkhill, Birmingham, Warks. Andrew Upton (2672) gives the address of a shop in Birkenhead who do much the same items on Bruce as Cimac. Their address is Merseyside Martial Arts, 78 Westbourne Road, Birkenhead, Merseyside.

And David Moore reports that Karate & Oriental Arts (Paul H Crompton) at 638 Fulham Road, London SW6 have loads of Bruce material – *Untold Story*, *Bruce Lee in Action*, *Studies on JKD*, etc. Simon Bulley (2738) bought a poster of a painting by Lynn Smith (A2 size) from Nostalgia Bookshop, Cambridge Square, London W1, He says it's fabulous and well worth getting. Another place for films - Bryan Bath (2768) gives Quality Products Ltd, 42 Victoria Road, Romford RM3 7EB, Essex as having the same *Enter the Dragon* as Cimac are selling and also *The Big Boss* (2 x 400' reels @ £32.50 each), colour/sound and the same for *Fist of Fury* and *Game of Death*.

SPECIAL MESSAGES

Good wishes to Wesley Fleming - a very brave young man who, with many serious operations behind him, keeps cheerful despite it all. And also to Patrick Hennessy, who keeps his chin up and fights back.

LETTERS

Dear Pam,

I'm writing to tell you what I thought of the convention. I'm usually pretty eloquent, but really, words fail me. It was a truly wonderful event, and I'm sure loads of letters will pour in on its success. That opening sequence? Great - I loved the Fanfare for the Common Man *and the slide show that followed, especially the James Coburn/ Chuck Norris quotes, Could the sound system be improved as the soundtrack was blurred and too loud? Still, the best possible convention opening. Tony Myatt - a real professional compere who should definitely become a regular.* My Son Ah Chang... *well I think I'd have prefered to have had clips from all Bruce's films as this was really only for the completist.* Game of Death *- what can I say? We loved Bruce and hated the rest. Could you hear the cheers when the real thing appeared? I think the censored sequences could have been run twice, if possible.* On Location with Enter the Dragon *- a real surprise and I was delighted to see this rare bit of film; the same goes for the* Hornet *screentest. The* Game Of Death 2 *preview really had me on the edge of my seat with the* Enter the Dragon *clips that were included in it. The Look-a-like contest was really less imitation and more a display of how Bruce has influenced the lives of his many talented followers. Robert Lee - the high spot of the convention. He came across as a really nice guy, just as your Hong Kong report described him, and I found it particularly touching that he continually referred to Bruce as though he was still alive. One of Robert's most memorable quotes: "Bruce loves you and I love you too." I think we all admired his "no comment" when he refused to answer some idiot's question about how he believed his brother died. The Answer Panel - I don't know how you avoided becoming a sit-down comedienne all these years! You have a great line in dead- pan humour. But these panels could be more exciting if queries from the floor were allowed. Still, it was most entertaining to watch you all play "pass the microphone"!!*

Simon Bulley (2738)

Simon, thanks for the useful comments. Taking one or two of them, yes, I'm afraid we didn't have complete control over the sound level of the opening sequence although we got it sorted eventually. I totally agree re your feeling about Tony Myatt. I'm sure if we can get him away from his commitments at Capital Radio he'll come and work with us again in the future. Two reason for not taking questions from the floor for the Questions & Answers session - one, we were hoping to avoid the kind of insensitive question that we actually got (!) and two, in a building that size, only those in the audience with "megaphone" voices can easily be heard on stage. We had problems on that score last year and in a much smaller place.

> Dear Pam,
>
> I thought I'd give you a brief run-down on how I became interested in Bruce. When the martial arts boom was high in 1974, I thought Bruce Lee was balony (I choke on the words!). A friend showed me KFM 1 and I told him everything was FAKED with trampolines and false legs! (I've seen a psychiatrist since). As the months went on I was drummed left and right with Bruce Lee this and Bruce Lee that - so I decided to go and see for myself. I went to look at The Big Boss, my first "X" film - I was overwhelmed. What more can I say?
>
> Shaun Boland (2805)

> Dear Pam,
>
> I was reading about World Heavyweight full-contact karate champion, Benny Urquidez. He developed his own free-style of fighting from various arts he studied, and his philosophy is similar to Bruce's. It's also because of this fluid fighting and philosophy that people call him the next Bruce Lee. However Benny himself says: "That's nonsense. There is no next Bruce Lee. I had a tremendous respect for the man, but he was one of a kind. So am I - my goal is to become the best possible Benny that I can." He is planning a manual on full-contact karate, and if his future films go the way of his ring record, the film world could be in for a very big shock, very soon!
>
> David Moore (1783)

I can always admire artists who develop themselves in their own way and who, like Benny, respect other artists. We get too many of the other kind!

MAIL ORDER

Lots of you I'm sure have still not obtained a copy of the personally signed Robert Lee LP, *The Ballad of Bruce Lee*. I'm handling this direct and the cost is £4.50 including handling (Europe £5.50, rest of world £6.00), This is probably your last opportunity to own a copy of this rare album - Robert's own tribute to his brother - so make up your minds quickly. Cheques and postal orders to be made out to myself, Pam Hadden, please and the address to send orders is: Pam Hadden (LP Offer), 14 Rathbone Place, London W1P IDE. Also available from me is a black and white photo (signed by Robert) of himself standing looking up at Bruce as he soars overhead! It's definitely a very rare collector's item (size 10" x 8" approx) and the cost (including handling) is £1.20.

THE HOLLYWOOD PETITION

Hey! Come ON out there! You call yourselves FANS of Bruce, but where in the name of Heaven are the petitions I'm collecting for his name to be placed against a gold star on Hollywood Boulevard? I'm going to be honest - I'm actually ashamed at the results so far. Oh yes, the loyal fans have gone out of their way to help - as usual, but would you believe that the total so far is a pitiful 700!!!??? And that's from fans who say they "wish *KFM* and the Society would do something about arranging various petitions." Well, I try and so do *KFM*, so why don't YOU? Or are you quite satisfied to leave all the hard work to the minority - as usual? If this sounds as though I'm slightly annoyed - YOU'D BETTER BELIEVE IT! If I don't get a positive response from you all within a few weeks, it's the last petition I shall ever organise on behalf of the Society - and I mean it! If I don't get your support, how can we ever hope to achieve anything?

RENEWALS

Members 2738 to 2803 - your second-year membership falls due between now and the end of November. Similarly, members 2350 to 2487 - third-year renewal -and 2085 to 2170 - fourth-year renewal; also, we are now entering fifth-year renewals, so members 1001 to 1627 - you are now due!

SWOP SHOP

- John Robinson (2734), Darlaston has for sale/exchange: posters – *Snake in the Eagles Shadow* (Jackie Chan and Wong Chin Li), *Big Boss Part II* (Lo Lieh and Bruce Li). Wants *KFM's* 1 & 2.
- Phillip Lai (2694), Rotherham Wants *Enter the Dragon* double album or someone to record this for him. Also has large amount of Bruce material to swap. Mr. L. K. Stanley (3034), Sheldon wants issues 1 & 2 of *KFM*.
- Anthony Jackson (1530), Halewood has spare *KFM* No. 1 plus *Way of the Dragon* poster (black background/Chinese dragon/top half of Bruce). Write with offers.
- William Ross (2715), Irvine, wants *Bruce Lee Revenges, La Legende du Petit Dragon*, posters, newspapers on Bruce, *Black Belt's Best of Bruce Lee No. 1*.
- Ian Hamilton (1213), Sunderland has for sale 400' colour/silent *Fist of Fury* & *Enter the Dragon* films - cost £25 each, sell £10 each (poor quality, but good action).
- David Willett (2048), Newark has for sale: "Bong Sau" sparring gloves; *Takamiyama* (hardback) by Wheeler; Karate sparring gloves (closed finger); *Sumo* by Sargeant; *Dynamic Kicks* by Chong Lee; *Ninja* by Andrew Adams; *Kick Boxing Muay Thai* by Hardy Stockman; *Secrets of Shaolin Boxing* by Bryn Williams; *Bruce Lee and JKD* magazines Nos. 1-10; *Farewell My Friend* by Mito Uyehara. Write for prices.

PEN PALS

H. Harry, Durban, South Africa wants Japanese pen pal (female).

LATE NEWS

It is my very sad task to have to convey the news to you of the death of one of the Society's most regular contributors - member and cartoonist, John Bell. John passed away recently, following a period of prolonged illness and I on behalf of the Society have already written a letter of condolence to his mother. At this tragic time, it is perhaps not inappropriate to remember that, though battling against ill-health, he was able to continually keep his spirits raised and to enthusiastically supply us with many quite excellent cartoons. We shall all miss his presence - and his humour.

Well, that's about IT for this time! But just one final thing; many members have written in asking for the recipe for Bruce's protein drink. Well, here it is. I give the quantities I used, but I suggest you adjust them to your own personal taste. Half-pint iced water; one tablespoon of protein powder; one tablespoon of powdered milk (such as "five-pints"); half a teaspoon of vegetable oil (optional); one teaspoonful of peanut butter; half a banana; one-to-two eggs and shells. Mix the lot together in a blender but if too thick, either add more water or decrease ingredients. Enjoy yourselves!

Pam Hadden (Bruce Lee Society President)

BRUCE LEE SOCIETY COLUMN
KUNG FU MONTHLY NO. 57

I don't think anyone who attended the second Official Bruce Lee Convention, sadly the last that can ever be held at London's Gaumont State Theatre, could have realised how apprehensive we all were on the evening of the day before! Just think, the previous year's relatively straightforward event had been somewhat jinxed by problems and failures of various kinds. Let's face it, we're only amateurs at this game and now, here we were, about to attempt something far more complicated. I had to keep reminding myself that Bruce used to say, "If you want something, aim beyond it". Well, here we were, pretending to be the Lew Grades of the Little Dragon world! You can't aim much further than that.

In just about every department, we wanted the event to be unusual and interesting. For instance, delegates' first sight on entering the main door was a 12 foot by 8 foot "blow-up" of Bruce. Maybe it HAD taken our editor the best part of three hours to screw it together and suspend it safely, but it was worth it! And my idea of selling Bruce's protein drink proved another instant winner as all four gallons seemed to go in no time.

But it was inside the auditorium that we really saw some fireworks. The day kicked off with our own Eddy Pumer's superb slide sequence of the life of Bruce Lee, from babe in arms to the solemnity and tragedy of the funeral. All the while, we were treated to a commentary by Capital Radio's Tony Myatt, rare words from Chuck Norris and James Coburn, plus some absolutely sensational music. Well done Eddy, it was a gem of an opening.

My Son Ah Chang followed and although quite a few people decided not to stay the course, a good two-thirds stuck with it. Perhaps it was really something for "the completist." Even so, it would have been almost criminal for us to have passed up the chance of allowing what may well be the only screening in this country of Bruce Lee in full, nine-year-old glory.

Lunch followed, and tables previously laden down with Little Dragon produce of every kind, rapidly grew lighter as fans fought their way through for the bargains.

Back for the restart, it was time for the restaging of the Norris/Lee battle by Ted Pollard and Douggie Robinson. It must have been really difficult for them, coming onto a stage cold, to try and evoke a scene of such high emotional content. But great skill and hours of practice carried them through; the cheers of the audience confirmed that. I especially liked the part where "Bruce" walked away from the "body," only to return and lay the coat over; quite masterly.

And then came the moment we'd all been awaiting. On stage came Robert Lee, looking dapper and immaculate, to first of all be interviewed by our excellent compere of the day, Tony Myatt. It was an interesting chat, for they'd actually met in Hong Kong, many years before. But the songs were what we were awaiting and let down we certainly were NOT! *Pointing Finger* was followed by a live rendition of *Parting* (a poem written by Bruce). Then it was, *Ballad of Bruce Lee, JKD,* and finally, *The Boat Song.*

With the help of some preplanned lighting changes, excellently supervised by myself may I say, Robert turned in a performance that I don't think any of us are likely to forget; it was stunning.

Next up came Questions and Answers, one of the perennial favourites, and this year the line up could hardly have been more comprehensive. Anyone who was anyone was there on stage, though to be honest, poor Robert ended up answering the lion's share of the questions. The lookalike contest was a real slice of fine entertainment. The worries we'd had about it working were soon dispelled by Tony Myatt's slick and professional handling and altogether 17 fans clambered up with us to do their bit and all credit to them say I. I have a feeling, judging by audience reaction, the lookalike contest is here to stay.

Ted Pollard then returned to the stage for a quite amazing nunchaku display and at one point, he was even performing blindfolded! Ted really does possess a superb combination of martial arts skills that marries perfectly to the entertainer and dancer in him; years of experience and training have honed him into a quite exceptional performer.

Another surprise before the tea break was the third in our trilogy of 16mm shorts. Having seen behind the scenes of *Enter the Dragon* plus a re-run of last year's sensation, the Bruce Lee screen test, suddenly Eddy Pumer was introducing a clip that NO ONE was expecting; the trailer for *Game of Death 2!* It was a real scoop, but I'll say no more here as next month Eddy will be offering a complete feature on that very subject so stay tuned!

And finally, what else but *Game of Death* UNCENSORED? Fans sat politely through the build-up, priming themselves to explode as the action cut to the real Bruce Lee. It was a magic moment, but of course the highlight had to be the unusually unseen Inosanto/ Lee nunchaku duel. If you weren't there to witness it, sorry, but nothing less than a bookful of words would do it justice. All I can say is, if you get the chance again. GO!

And there it was for another year. All that remained were the timeless words of James Coburn to tie the knot on a day that, by some miracle or other, had actually run quite smoothly. Of course we're already working on 1981 and, if everything goes to plan, it should represent another quite remarkable jump ahead. It's going to be different, I promise you that. But that's how it should be. Bruce himself never liked to keep repeating things when there was always something new around the corner so we'll just follow his example!

- Pam

Convention Recollections with Robert Lee

Andrew Haddon, the son of Pam Hadden, remembers a few memorable dinners with his mother and Robert Lee during the convention: "We were once taken out for a luxury dinner by Robert Lee when he came over and that was huge. I think I was 16 at the time and we went to this posh restaurant in Kensington where I ordered lobster and it was a heaven. I thought, *'Wow!'* and I think that's the only time I've ever had it, actually. The only time I've ever had lobster and it was bought by Robert Lee. We also went out to a Chinese restaurant which was the only four-star Chinese restaurant in Europe or something. At the time, Robert was a star in his own right and when he went into the restaurant, all the waitresses were like, *'Whoo! Robert Lee!'* in Chinese or whatever and the waiters were all shaking his hand."

He also recalls some mischief on the part of the convention organisers. "I remember when Robert came over for the convention. "He was told it was a good idea to bring over a boat load of his LP records to sell at the convention. That was a malarkey. My mum thought there was a bit of skullduggery going on because, when he got to the convention, there was nowhere for him to sell the albums. No space set up or anything like that. My mum always had the idea that it was a bit of a fiddle and that a certain person hoped that he'd leave all these records behind so that he could then sell them on at a later date. That's what she thought anyway. She ended up trying to sell them herself through the newsletters on behalf of Robert and she sent the remaining ones back when the club finished. Strangely enough, but when I was clearing some stuff out recently, I actually found a box that didn't get sent back, so I have still got a box of *The Ballad of Bruce Lee* records."

TONY LUNDBERG REMEMBERS THE BRUCE LEE SOCIETY

Over the years, Tony Lundberg from Denmark, has been involved in over one hundred major Bruce Lee projects, beginning with writing articles when he was still in his teens. In 1980, Tony was personally invited by Pam Hadden, the then president of The Bruce Lee Society, to travel to England for the second Official Bruce Lee Convention to help out as an usher for the day. This is Tony's story...

I became aware of The Bruce Lee Secret Society and later, of president Pam Hadden through some Bruce Lee pen pals of mine, and began writing to her around 1977, when I was 14 or 15 years old. I would ask her about anything; about Bruce Lee, his family, new publications, other fan clubs etc.

The great thing about Pam was that she was so polite, sweet and humble and she answered my letters all the time. She knew so many things, and for me back then, she was a living dictionary and lexicon, when it came to knowing stuff about Bruce Lee and the whole movement around him.

She was so nice to me, and told me a lot of great stories over the years; about her Bruce Lee fan club, her work, and the relationship she had with Bruce Lee's family.

She talked about her goals for the future with the club etc, but also about her personal life. I once remember telling her that if she ever needed any kind of help, I would love to help her out by doing anything to keep Bruce Lee's name alive and to keep the Bruce Lee Society running. She told me that she really needed all the help she could get because it was mostly a one-person operation running the Bruce Lee fan club. Later she told me in confidence that she had a very hard time trusting people, because a lot of people close to her took advantage of kindness, her position, and her work.

So she needed someone she could trust and rely on. Shorty after that, I began working for her. She really wanted me to spread the word out about the fan club's existence, publicize upcoming Bruce Lee projects in England, and to keep her updated about the Bruce Lee news in Denmark, the Scandinavian countries, as well as wanting me to write articles, stories, quizzes and poems for the news sheets.

I wrote articles to the Danish and Nordic countries' newspapers, the Boards of British and Danish television, movie theatres, and companies for new information about Bruce Lee.

We spoke about making future projects together, such as a book project, a new convention, a possible Bruce Lee exhibition etc.

Pam invited me over to England to help out as a helper or an "usher" at the First Official Bruce Lee Convention and Film Festival in 1979, but unfortunately at that time, I could not make it, but to help her out, I did a lot of administration work for her, including writing to people, making advertisements, writing articles etc.

The following year, in 1980, I was once again asked to help out as an usher at the second Official Bruce Lee Convention in England, which I did, with great pride, joy and honour. I was only 17 years old at that time and I remember that she gave me the title, "My Little Bruce Lee Representative in Denmark." It's funny to think about that today.

When I made this trip to London, I remember being so excited because it the first time I would meet Pam face to face, which really meant a lot to me, not only as a person, but also as a huge Bruce Lee and Pam fan. I had so much respect and love for Pam, and for her dedication and work to keep Bruce Lee's name alive.

The trip over to England took over 24 hours on a bus back in the day. Driving through Germany in a full, hot and overcrowded bus with no air conditioning, screaming kids, and only two stops to stretch, pee, drink and eat, it was a nightmare. The trip back took even longer.

So when I finally arrived in England with my 15 year old Danish friend, I was so tired and exhausted, but felt great, happy and invincible, because I knew this trip would be a turning point for me, as an person, and as a Bruce Lee fan.

I remember wearing my blue Wrangler jacket which had a huge Bruce Lee patch on the back as well as over 20 Bruce Lee badges on it too, which was really trendy back then. Everyone was talking about my jacket and asking where I got the badges, which is funny to think about today because it's a different time and culture now.

As I got closer and closer to the theatre, I remember seeing a crowd of people which began freaking me out. Everyone was talking, shouting, play-fighting, yelling like Bruce Lee. Everyone was excited, just like me!

I saw this huge line in front of the theatre and knew that I had to skip the line so I could be on time because a lot of people were waiting for me inside.

So I had to push myself forward through the line towards the theatre as fast as possible but whilst doing so, people were getting angry at me, and started shouting at me to go back to the end of the line. So I had to tell them that I was there to help out at the convention. Some people started shouting, "Boo!" Some other people tried getting friendly with me, and thought they could show me the way in and come in for free. Funnily enough, they couldn't but I found my way in by myself eventually.

Making this trip, made me feel honored and proud because first of all, Pam had ac-

tually invited me over to help her out with setting up the convention and because I had been chosen from so many people, to help her out. To stand by her side and physically being able to help her and the staff out with setting up the Bruce Lee convention, was a milestone in my Bruce Lee career.

I remember a lot from that day. When I arrived at the theatre, everybody was running around between one another and couldn't find out what to do or how to do it. I remember just standing there in the middle of everything for a minute or so, just to inhale the atmosphere, while watching all these people running around like crazy ants.

I still remember the smell that was inside the theatre, which reminded me of a museum. I saw the Bruce Lee posters and this big sign saying, Kung Fu Monthly and thought, "Whoa!" After coming to my senses, I remember just grabbing the first person I saw and asked for Pam, but nobody knew where she was. So I grabbed the next one passerby, and asked her if she knew what I should do.

It was so overwhelming seeing all those Bruce Lee fans outside the theatre and coming together to keep Bruce Lee's name alive. As I stood inside with a badge on my chest saying "USHER," I remember feeling so proud and privileged to be a part of the team, and to be able to make a difference.

Eventually I met the staff at a meeting in the middle of the hall and it was so cool seeing Pam for the first time as it really meant the world to me.

My very first assignment of the day was to clear out all the cardboard boxes, from where all the books came in as they were laying all over. Next I was told to hold the ladder which Kung Fu Monthly owner and King of Kung Fu author Felix Dennis was standing on. He was taking care of all the light bulbs and setting up signs. We had a great time working together. He was so funny and a crazy kind of a guy. I really liked him. Later in the day, he gave me a copy of his book, which I still have, to thank me for helping me.

Another of my jobs was setting up all the Bruce Lee material in a straight line on the sales stand. Pam came over and told me that, for all my help and for coming all this way, I could take one piece of everything at the stand but I had a hard time doing so because I didn't want anything for my help. I did it because I felt honored doing it and that was enough for me. Later, she came over again, and asked me if I have taken the objects and I told her that I hadn't. She then turned around, went straight over to the sales stand, and told them to pack one piece of everything for me in plastic bags. So I got plenty of goodies that day. I felt so good, proud and very happy.

Before the doors opened, I took a lot of pictures of the staff and of the sales stand. I also got somebody to take a picture of me in an *Enter the Dragon* photo stand, where Bruce Lee was on. You had to put your head in the cut-out and you suddenly became Bruce Lee. It was quite funny.

Tony Lundberg (September 2020)

Once the event started, I met all the fans at the door, welcomed them, took their tickets and showed them the way in.

On the day, my best movie surprise was when I saw one of Bruce Lee's childhood movies called, *My Son Ah Chang,* in Mandarin. That was really a great experience. I spoke with a lot of great Bruce Lee fans from around the world, exchanging addresses and phone numbers for several new pen pals, who I wrote with for years to come.

During the interval, I was invited backstage with all these outstanding people such as Tony Myatt from Capital Radio, Eddy Pumer, Pamela Hadden, Robert Lee (Bruce Lee's little brother), *Kung Fu Monthly* editor Bruce Sawford, Will Johnston, Ted Pollard (the martial artist who did the nunchaku show), Felix Dennis, and Dougie Robinson (Martial Artist, who did the Bruce Lee and Chuck Norris fight, with Ted Pollard), and was blown away.

When the convention was over, I remember sweeping the floors with a broom and thinking about all the impressions I got and I suddenly felt Bruce Lee's presence around me. I remember feeling like I was about to cry, as I had just witnessed something great and something so outstanding, that it was just overwhelming me.

At the end of the day, Pam and I said our goodbyes, she told me that she was so proud of me for all the work and help I did for her, Bruce Lee and for the fan club. We also made an agreement that everything we talked about in private concerning the fan club, Bruce Lee's privacy, and his family, stayed between us and that is a promise I have kept for over 39 years. We kept on working together until she closed her fan club, and we still kept our friendship until the end of 1988, after which, I never heard from her again.

Photographs courtesy of Tony Lundberg

A RETROSPECTIVE LOOK AT BRUCE LEE MANIA & THE KUNG FU CRAZE OF THE 1970S

18 December 1980

FIRSTLY, OF COURSE, MAY I WISH EACH AND EVERY ONE OF YOU A GREAT CHRISTMAS! LET'S HOPE THAT 1981 WILL BRING ABOUT A CHANGE OF HEART WITH THE CENSORS, AND THAT THE BBC WILL UNPADLOCK THEIR WELL-GUARDED DOCUMENTARY ON BRUCE... YOU NEVER KNOW! TIME NOW TO GET INTO OUR 18TH NEWS SHEET.

HOLLYWOOD PETITION

Although, following my last appeal in the September report, I've had more petitions in, there are just not enough members participating; we MUST all pull together if we are to achieve anything, so please, do keep collecting and sending in the signatures. My thanks go to all those who actually have put their backs into it.

WORLD OF BRUCE LEE

I've recently returned from a week in Los Angeles where I spend a great deal of my time with Norman Borine and Richard Vinson of the World of Bruce Lee. The museum really is a marvellous tribute to Bruce - and has the official sanction of the Lee family. In fact, I know that Grace, Bruce's mother, whom I met again and had lunch with, feels very pleased with the whole project - understandably so, considering how tastefully and reverently the whole project has been handled. If any of you get to Los Angeles, do pay the place a visit... it's well worthwhile and there's lots of items on sale. And keep an eye open for the planned joint world convention - it could blow your minds!

GENERAL NEWS

Mark James (2880) thinks other members would like to know of his local cinema, which runs film shows every other Saturday night, around 11 pm. They show Bruce's films quite a lot, and the cinema in question is the Classic, Nottingham.

Peter Jagger (1087) belongs to another cinema club at the Gala Cinema, Bristol Street, Birmingham, Warks; recently he managed to see *Fist of Fury* uncut... not bad! I'm sure other members in the area will want to join as well.

David Moore (1738) and many other members have read the rather good article by Paul Philips (in *Music and Video Magazine*) titled "A Pack of Lee's." It takes the lid off the Bruce Lee doubles business and the associated - usually poor quality - films. He informs the uninitiated of the stars (Li Leong, Cheung Nick and Dragon Lee) and their films... for example, *Exit the Dragon, Enter the Tiger* which clearly states "See Bruce Lee choose his successor." Mr. Philips runs through similar examples of such nonsense and remarks on the inaccuracies, and clips taken from Bruce's early films. He recounts too Bruce's high status in the film world, and how producers like Carlo Ponti wanted to use him and how MGM were looking for some kind of link-up with Elvis Presley. Paul Philips also says that... "Had he lived, he would have ended up as the highest paid film star of all time. Warner Bros, had made him a stunning offer of US$100,000/year for the rest of his life if he would accept the lead in any one of five scripts on offer." WOW! David also says that the September 6-12 *TV Times* had an article on James Coburn, and Bruce got a mention as Coburn's great friend.

Simon Bulley (2738) saw a recent *Starsky & Hutch* episode featuring John Saxon (who thought he was a vampire!) and Colleen Camp of *Game of Death* fame. I can remember seeing John, but must have missed Colleen. We also had Kareem Abdul Jabbar appearing in the film *Airplane!* and one or two other Bruce co-stars popping up on TV and other films. And there've been quite a few mentions as well... in *The Professionals* and *Minder* to name but two. One that I unfortunately did miss was what happened recently on *World of Sport* (although members Arthur Stone and Ian Hamilton - to name just two - were much quicker off the mark). The occasion was the appearance in the wrestling of a Japanese martial artist named Sammy Lee. He came on wearing a *Game of Death* tracksuit and underneath he had on the same trunks that Bruce used in *Enter the Dragon*. The commentator remarked that he looked like Bruce (opinions from readers seem to vary on this)... Arthur felt he wasn't copying Bruce, Ian felt he copied his stance. All in the eye of the beholder, I think.

Member Peter Jagger (1087) recently met with Jackie Chan and Ed Parker when they were over (separately) in this country - Jackie to promote his film *The Big Brawl* (see *KFM* 58) and Ed to promote his new book on Elvis Presley. Pete was most impressed with Jackie - although he says there will NEVER be anyone to compare with Bruce; he has, however, been more impressed with Jackie than with anyone else. Ed Parker also said he thought Jackie was doing a very good thing for the martial arts (?) and even though he has not got "the ability" like Bruce, Ed likes the way he puts humour into his films, and "did his own thing." Ed was asked by Pete about the film he took at the Long Beach Tournament, and if there was any chance of the fans seeing it. Ed told Pete that he wasn't going to release it, because it could become commercialised and people could be ripped off. While understanding his reasoning, it's still nevertheless a great disappointment for the fans. One thing I'd like to clear up... Jackie was NOT a stunt man for Bruce Lee, as he has been quoted as saying. If he really said this, then I'm surprised; if he was misquoted, well that happens to all of us. By the way, look elsewhere in the newssheet for a picture of Pete and Jackie.

Back on programs, Tracey Bennett (3039) watched a Sunday one called *Check it Out*; it was for teenagers and showed how young people have made it to the top. There was a picture of Bruce from *Enter the Dragon,* among others, and the commentator said that "these people had taken their own lives because they couldn't stand life anymore." As Tracy says, it just goes to show that they don't know much about Bruce Lee. I'm always amazed that programs go out with researchers doing little or nothing to authenticate what they produce. Stupid remarks like this can cause upset to both family and fans.

Moving on, several more members have taken the initiative and written to various TV stations about the showing of Bruce Lee movies/series... you'll see a couple of the replies, right here in this newssheet. There's not been a lot to cheer about so far, but I get the feeling that, if we keep the pressure up, the tide might soon start to turn. Graham Ellis for instance got a reply from the BBC to say that they were sorry to disappoint him, but regret that they have no plans to show any Bruce Lee films in the foreseeable future; it was signed by one Stella Cundy of the Programme Correspondence Section. I know we are all disappointed with the lack of co-operation from TV and the censors - and other quarters as well - but if you consider just how far the Society and its members have gone since the beginning, I think this should give us the confidence we need to keep on pressing people to make all Bruce Lee material available for everyone to see. When you consider some of the second-rate rubbish dished out on TV and at the cinema, then it becomes more clear the sort of person who sits in the background picking what they think we all want to see. Obviously I'm not asking for Bruce Lee on television ALL the time (although that would be quite okay by me!) - it's just that there ARE so many really good things that could be shown, Bruce among them, that all round it's about time the public had more say on what goes out. I do appreciate that some films (some of Bruce's probably included) simply haven't been released by the film companies for use on television; that, however, is only a small part of the answer.

The TV companies reply...

> *Dear Miss Bennett... thank you for your letter of the 15th August. I regret to inform you that at the time of writing there are no plans for Southern Television to transmit the Bruce Lee television shows you mention in your letter. However, I will pass your request onto our Programme Planning Department for their further consideration.*
>
> *Michael J. Taylor (Publicity Officer)*

> *Dear Mr. Ahluwalia... thank you for your letter of 24th July addressed to Miss Stevens. She has asked me to reply. I am sorry that you are disappointed at not seeing any Bruce Lee films, particularly as we (the BBC) have no plans to show them in the foreseeable future.*
>
> *Sheila Cundy (Programme Correspondence Section)*

THE BRUCE LEE SOCIETY

SPECIAL NOTICE

You will find included with this news sheet, a list of slides and (approx.) 5" x 3" pictures that are at present available from America's World of Bruce Lee organisation. To make things easier for you, I will be handling the actual forwarding of the orders myself so just send details of whatever you want direct to me, c/o 14 Rathbone Place, London WIP IDE. This is just the start of future co-operation between our Society and our American sister organisation.

Something you will NOT find in this news sheet is a cartoon as readers of the last edition will know already of the tragic death of John Bell, the man who kept us so ably supplied with marvellous cartoons. It's a newssheet omission that I'm sure none of us want to see for long. PLEASE, everyone, even if you haven't tried it before, have a go at doing some, and I'll pick out the best for printing.

LETTERS

Dear Pam,

I was glancing through a book called We Don't Mind the Sex It's the Violence *in a London bookshop, written I believe by a lady member of the Board of Film Censors. She lists films from around 1968 to 1978 and mentions that they reviewed* Fist of Fury *in 1976 or 77, when it was requested that the film be given an AA certificate. Now we are in 1980, and Bruce's films are getting shorter. What changed their minds about the certificate rating? I think the whole system could do with a shake up.*

Rick Edwards (1260)

I think we all agree with you on that, Rick. To have kept Bruce's films intact with an adult certificate was, and still is, the only sensible thing; to censor his films and STILL keep an adult certificate shows only stupidity and ignorance on the part of our "guardians." Mind you, I don't believe that in the first place there is anything in Bruce's films to rate the certification they got.

Dear Pam,

If you have the address of this idiot, Bruce Li, or his film producers, I will gladly send them a piece of my mind - no, on second thoughts, I think I'll send a bomb!!! Is there ANYTHING we can do? I really can't stand to see Bruce Lee being degraded... he deserves great recognition, not humiliation.

Cherrilyne Bankes (2863)

Well, as I've said before, we've all got rather strong feelings on Li and his contemporaries; any members wanting to let off steam and share their views with Cherrilyne can reach her at Nottingham.

A RETROSPECTIVE LOOK AT BRUCE LEE MANIA & THE KUNG FU CRAZE OF THE 1970S

Dear Pam,

I recently wrote to Barry Norman (Film '80 and Hollywood Greats) suggesting a series on stars who died young - such as James Dean, and of course Bruce. I gave him a short run-down on Bruce Lee. I got a reply from someone on behalf of Mr. Norman to say "thank you" but they are not planning any more Greats series. However, they will bear my suggestion in mind. I bet they will!

David Moore (1783)

You could be surprised, David - maybe they WILL bear your suggestions in mind. What they do with them, though, is another matter!?!?!

David also tells me that during the program called *Calendar* on 17th of October, Jackie Chan was asked how he was different from Bruce. He replied that, whilst Bruce did straight karate-type punches, he did fancy uppercut/hooking punches. The interviewer then remarked that at the moment Chan is bigger than Bruce in the East, due to Bruce being dead and therefore there were no new films coming out. David wrote to *Calendar* who replied that they could not comment on the accuracy of Jackie's statements, but in no way did they intend to tarnish Bruce's reputation, nor to cause offence to Lee fans and it was certainly not intentional. David also wrote to the *Sun* newspaper, putting them straight on the "stunt man" quote, to which they replied that the article writer was away, but would show him David's letter on his return. Any more info on this from David will of course be passed on.

WARNING

It has come to my notice that several people, including member Kevin Hobbs, have received nothing back for the money they sent to a certain company by the name of Dennis & Co of 58 South Street, Exeter, Devon. Reputable magazines have been carrying advertisements for this company - to the effect that they sell video films but Dennis & Co now appear to have vanished. Anyone who sent money there and has received nothing in return should contact: DC Thomas, Officer-in-Charge, Fraud Squad, Debenham Cornwall Constabulary, Crown Hill Police Station, Budshead Way, Plymouth, Devon (Telephone 0752 701188 ext. 371). PLEASE REMEMBER that even in reputable magazines and books, none of us can be certain that companies advertising are "okay." I can suggest no ideal way of overcoming the problem, but legitimate companies will usually (on request) offer a "cash- on-delivery" service; in other words, you pay for the goods when they arrive at your door.

And, speaking from experience, the sad truth is that companies, just as regularly, get ripped-off by their customers so it really does work both way. So I suppose we just have to learn by experience who can be trusted and who cannot.

SPECIAL MESSAGES & REQUESTS

Andrew Staton (1670) would like to say a special "thank you" to member Dave Langley and his wife for such a great day he had with them - and to wish them a "Happy New Year."

John Wilcock of Birkdale, Southport wants very much to start a martial arts club in his area; he has been studying for several years, including Shotokan Karate, Kenda, Lau Gar Kung Fu, JKD and Wing Chun. His club will meet once or twice a week, with other members who study various arts, from Aikido to Boxing. You can all learn each others' styles. Anyway, no doubt if the club can get started and registered, it could be a good thing. So contact John direct, and give him your ideas and support. He has promised to take full responsibility for the running of it, including accommodation, equipment, and so on. What better offer!

Just to let you know that the Merseyside Martial Arts Shop at 78 Westbourne Road, Birkenhead, Merseyside, England has now closed, (Thanks to Andrew Upton for the information.)

As it's Robert Lee's birthday on 16th December, I shall of course be sending a card and add all our good wishes to him. We'll be seeing him in London again very soon, I'm sure!

Oh - just a message from myself to Ann - have a Happy Birthday on 15th December; the same goes for anyone else having a birthday around Christmas.

While I write this, I've just hear the very sad news that Steve McQueen has died. I really thought he might have pulled it off and come through okay so it's really sad that he didn't make it.

USEFUL ADDRESSES

Graham Ellis (2728) says he bought a fantastic video tape from Moviedrome at 398 Kilburn High Road, London NW6 - containing the *Enter the Dragon* production trailer and film trailer, plus *Way of the Dragon, Fist of Fury* trailers and a complete episode of *The Green Hornet* titled "Silent Gun.".. all for £30. That sounds pretty good to both Graham and myself.

Anyone wanting the single *In Memory of Bruce Lee* by John and Rosalind that was released some years back and is now no longer generally available, will find it at Oldies Unlimited, 6/12 Stafford Street, St. George's, Telford, Shropshire; it costs £1.15 plus 30p p&p.

Back to Graham again, he says *Enter the Dragon* film is now available on video from Carnaby Video of 26 Carnaby Street, London W1V 1PL - priced at £34.95. Also, *Enter the Dragon* on Super 8mm film on 4 x 400' reels (sound) is available from Jef Films Reg'd., Film House, 143 Hickory Hill Circle, Osterville, Ma 02655, USA.

CHUCK NORRIS

David Moore (yet again!) has given me a rundown on Chuck which is useful as several members have enquired about him. Born on 10th March, 1940 in Ryan, Oklahoma; moved to California aged 11 and his first part in films was a small one in *Wrecking Crew* - in which (as we all know) Bruce directed fight scenes. His next film was *Way of the Dragon* and he then co-starred in the one that Bruce turned down, *Yellow Faced Tiger*. From time to time he also appeared in such TV series as *FBI* and *Room 222*. In 1976 he completed a low-budget film *Breaker Breaker* and followed that with *Good Guys Wear Black* (1977), *A Force of One* (1978) and *Octagon* (1980). On high school graduation he joined the Air Force and was posted to Korea in February 1960. He began martial arts training with judo - and broke his shoulder in the second week! Whilst his arm was still mending, he saw people training in Tang Soo Do (now reformed into Tae Kwon Do) and began training in it himself - with his arm still in a sling. Well again, he continued training in both these disciplines and on his return to the States, he was already a Black belt in Tang Soo Do and Brown belt in Judo. He then studied Hap Ki Do for two years and Aikido for three - as well as many other Japanese, Korean and Chinese styles; he also, of course, studied with Bruce. These days, he's married, has two sons and is the owner of no less than 32 schools, all over America.

BARGAIN BASEMENT

Just a quickie from me, Pam: I've got three copies only of *My Way of Kung Fu* LP (bought just before they became generally available) and will sell them at £7.00 each (including post & packing) - which is £1.00 under normal price. The first three people to get me on telephone in the evening after receipt of this news sheet will have the LPs held for them, until receipt of the money. I also have one copy of each of the following: *Screen Magazine* (Japanese) - one dated September 1979, the other undated (but having a picture of Bruce, waist up, yellow *Game of Death* tracksuit, clenched fist forward on one side - on the other, head only, turned sideways, sunglasses and blue background). Both the magazines and the record are brand new, and anyone having purchased these magazines already will know they are full of beautiful pictures, and the quality is excellent. The magazines are available for £6.00 each, including postage - again, first to contact me by phone gets the choice! As I'm going through my Bruce Lee material, I expect other items will pop up... so keep a close eye on the news sheet. It's about time I sorted things out as it's becoming almost impossible to get through the front door - and I'm not kidding!

Kevin Stokes (2624)

Vernon Morgrove (2733)

Peter Jagger (1087) meets with Jackie Chan

verse (and illustration, right) from Keith Thompson (3049)

What is the Tao?
The Tao is

What is Bruce Lee?
Bruce Lee is

He is not dead
For like the Tao
He will never die

Kevin Stokes (2624)

Harry Otty (3084)

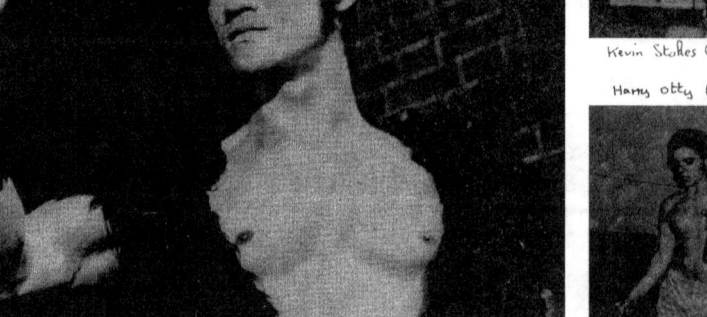

RENEWALS

Members 2804 to 2907 - your second-year membership falls due between now and the end of February. Similarly, members 2531 to 2599 - your third-year is due then as well; and 2171 to 2266 - your fourth-year is now due; and last (but certainly not least!) 1628 to 1828 - it's fifth-year renewal time! Please get those renewals in as quickly and as early as you can... it really does help with the paperwork!

MEMORIAL FLOWERS - JULY 1981

As mentioned previously, each year on the anniversary of Bruce's death the Society will be sending its own tribute to the graveside. Anyone wishing to send a donation to this cause should send it (preferably in the form of a postal order) in an envelope marked "Memorial Flowers" direct to me at London. Sometime nearer the day, I'll hand over the money collected to member Anne French, who has kindly offered to arrange the delivery. There'll be a reminder of this in the next news sheet but, so far as arrangements are concerned, it really would be easier if contributions were to come in as soon as possible.

KFM MAIL ORDER ENQUIRIES

I have to clear up one or two small points. Many members appear to believe that I work for *KFM*, and at their offices. So, of course, I get all sorts of problems to sort out on the lines of, "When will I be receiving my next subscription copy of *KFM*?" and "When is the next issue coming into the shops?," and "Can you send me a convention T-shirt?." Of course, rather than members receiving no reply at all, I then have to send a note back to them explaining that their problem has been forwarded on to *KFM*, which not only means extra delay for you, it also means that the work I'm supposed to do gets delayed as well! Please remember that the only queries to be sent to me are those dealing directly with Society matters and anything connected with *Kung Fu Monthly* should be sent direct to: 14 Rathbone Place, London W1P IDE. I'm sure you'll appreciate that, with only me running the Society, plus the fact that I have a full-time job to do at British Airways, means that I'm kept pretty busy most of the time. I really don't need any more work!!! Ta.

SWOP SHOP

- Andrew Upton (2672), Birkenhead wants cinema posters of all Bruce's films (except *Game of Death*), also any copies of *Film Review* mag that feature Bruce's films (preferably in good condition). Quote prices required please.
- Graham Ellis (2728), 40 Eskdale Road has FOR SALE *Game of Death* tracksuit, medium for £15.00 (plus free to buyer, six glossy B&W Bruce photos, 8" x 6"), 'Indiset' book, £5 (plus free Bruce colour poster from *Fist of Fury*).
- Wayne Denton, Warley has for sale issues *KFM* No. 1-52 (except 12, 43, 44) in mint condition, plus *Game of Death Collector's Edition*, extra copy of *KFM* 4 poster, and *King of Kung Fu* book - all for £30 plus p&p.

- Anne Hunt (1275), Farncombe has for swap: *Combat* Vol. 1 Nos. 1-8, 10, 12, *Inside Kung Fu* Vol. 2 No. 11, *Official Karate* Vol. 6 No. 42, Vol. 7 Nos. 43/46, *Black Belt* Vol. 13 No. 3, *Pictorial Guide of the Martial Arts* by Jim Wilson, *Step By Step Guide to Kung Fu* by Chee Soo, *Secrets of Kung Fu* Vol. 1 No. 4, *Defense Combat* Vol. 1 Nos. 1 and 3, Vol. 2 No. 7, *Karate Illustrated* Vol. 5 Nos. 2, 4, 6, Vol. 6 Nos. 4, 6 (some not in good condition). Want to swap for: *Inside Kung Fu* Vol. 1 Nos.10-12, Vol. 2 No. 1, *The Man Only I Knew* by Linda Lee (USA version). Swap or open to offers.
- Peter Reynolds (2900), Glasgow has for swap: *Life and Tragic Death of Bruce Lee*, and magazines *Kung Fu Master Dragon Fists, King Kung Fu Kak Abdullah Conspiracy* and *Return of the Opium Wars, Manual of Karate* (hardback), WANTS *KFM* 31.
- Edgar Lapada (3009), London. Wants to hear from members with Japanese books to sell - especially *Young Idol Now, Jumbo Screen* magazines etc. Has to swap: will do copies of Bruce's soundtracks (send 3 blank cassettes of 90' each) - or write for details of what will be recorded - plus £5.50, which includes p&p.
- Robert Walker (2565), Clydebank has for sale *Bruce Lee Dragon Sounds Special* and *Enter the Dragon* albums, or swap first album for *Game of Death* album or *Jeet Kune Do: The Art & Philosophy of Bruce Lee*. First person to write will receive Bruce Lee Motion Pictures on paper Vol. 2 and *Official Karate* magazines Jan 1980 & Dec 1979.
- Tim Ussher, Crowborough wants 8mm film projector - cheap/second-hand, any Bruce Lee films.
- Keith Spicer (1960), Kent has for swap *Game of Death* tracksuit in return for any Bruce material.
- Andrew Staton (1670), Leeds has for sale/swap: rare Bruce posters, books & mags. Send SAE to Andrew for list.
- Glynn Darbyshire (2885), Rotherham, has for sale: *Enter the Dragon* on 400ft spool, Super 8mm film, excellent picture/sound quality, contains bottle scene - fine condition, £30.
- Mark James (2880), Nottingham wants any Bruce 8mm sound films - will pay good price.

PEN PALS

- Harry Otty (3084), Liverpool wants pen pal, preferably female/aged around 18, interests music (Elvis but most others too), football, martial arts and Bruce!
- Peter Reynolds (2900), Glasgow wants pen pal, preferably female aged 17-19, interests Bruce, karate, films, sports & music.
- Jimmy Scannell, Wexford, Ireland wants female Chinese Kung Fu fan/or practitioner of Kung Fu, around Jimmy's age of 16.

Lastly, this month there are still a few copies of the much sought after LP by Robert Lee *Ballad of Bruce Lee* (£4.50 inc p&p - Europe £5.50 and rest of the World £6.00). Remember, this is a collector's item because each copy has been personally signed by Robert himself! Also available is a large B&W of Robert & Bruce together - Bruce high in the air! - again signed by Robert so a must for memorabilia collections at £1.20. All cheques and postal orders made out to "Pam Hadden" please. Have a great Christmas and see you in three months! Pam

BRUCE LEE SOCIETY COLUMN
KUNG FU MONTHLY NO. 58

Hi members. As some of you already know, I visited Los Angeles in August, and followed this up with yet another trip in October for a week. During these trips I had the pleasure of meeting again with Brace's mother, Grace, Danny Inosanto, and visiting Norman Borine and Richard Vinson at the World of Bruce Lee Museum, where I have to admit, I spent much of my time! Stand by in *Kung Fu Monthly* for reports on my visits to Danny's Kali Academy, his home, the museum and my meetings with Grace.

The museum is situated just off Hollywood Boulevard, very near to where I'm still hoping to have Bruce's name placed; there's still lots more signatures needed please! If any of you get the chance to go to Los Angeles, you MUST visit the museum. Its unofficial address is No. 1 Hong Kong Alley (a piece of do-it-yourself road-naming that nobody has ever queried!) and it's very close to Vine Street. Apart from the multitude of pictures and photos of Bruce, there are all the personal items that the family has donated. The atmosphere is truly serene and I guarantee you will leave there feeling closer to Bruce than you have ever felt before.

News on the Ed Palmer 8mm Long Beach film. According to member Peter Jagger (1087) he's most reluctant to show it as be doesn't want it copied, commercialised and people ripped-off. His decision is quite understandable, though disappointing. Maybe in time, something can be arranged.

On the subject of "ripping-off", a word of warning to you all. Members have been sending off for videos from a company called "Dennis & Co" in Exeter in Devon. Cheques and postal orders get cashed and that, so far, has been about it! Indeed they now seem to have done the disappearing act. Anybody finding him/herself in this position should immediately contact DC Thomas, Officer-in-Charge, Fraud Squad, Debenham, Cornwall Constabulary, Crown Hill Police Station, Budshead Way, Plymouth, Devon (Telephone 0752 701188. extension 371). Once again, I must plead with you to only send money off to tried and tested sources; otherwise, just make enquiries first.

On the brighter side, I can vouch that you may safely deal with the World of Bruce Lee, with whom the Society and KFM are working closely. Ask for leaflets showing the items on Bruce that they have in stock. Their mail order department keeps itself busy with a steady flow of goodies and it's really worth dropping them a line. But remember two things; it takes nearly a week for an airmail letter to get to the States and whatever you do, make sure you print your name and address CLEARLY. The address to write is: World of Bruce Lee, PO Box 3475, Hollywood, CA 90028, USA.

Lastly for this issue, a reminder that I've still got some personally signed Robert Lee albums available. They are rapidly becoming collector's items, so be quick! Just send £4.50 (includes handling - Europe add extra £1, elsewhere add extra £2) to: Pam Hadden, Bruce Lee Society, 14 Rathbone Place, London W1P 1DE. Make cheques and postal orders payable to Pam Hadden please.

And that's it for now. Back again soon!

- Pam Hadden

BRUCE LEE SOCIETY COLUMN
KUNG FU MONTHLY NO. 59

Hello, and some very interesting news this month that comes via the publicity director of a body calling itself the Cannon Group. It seems that on January 8th 1981, they began a shooting *Enter the Ninja* in the Philippines and Japan. Starring is former Karate World Champion, Mike Stone, and co-starring are Sybil Danning and Sho Kosugi, the all Japan Karate Champion. Sho takes the part of the evil Ninja, against whom Mike makes battle. Now all this sounds very fine and the report even goes to some considerable length in explaining exactly what a ninja is, for the sake of the uninitiated, but do we really need the following statements?

Quote: "(Mike Stone) is in the Guinness Book of World Records for having won 89 straight tournaments without being defeated once, a feat not even Bruce Lee accomplished." Surely it wouldn't have taken too much research on Bruce Lee to have discovered that he would never have been seen dead entering karate tournaments?

And later we get: Quote: "Whoever said Bruce Lee was irreplaceable, hasn't seen Mike Stone. He has the looks, talent, and intense screen presence that will make him a superstar." Need I go on? Now, Mr. Stone might very well make a good film but all this nonsense isn't exactly going to help us enjoy it. WE will be the judge of whether Mike Stone will be able to achieve superstar, let alone Bruce Lee, status. I for one, don't need a press release to tell me how I feel on the matter.

Also, knowing many of you to be admirers of the talent of Elvis Presley, the fact that Mr. Stone was only recently revealing in a Sunday paper the distasteful details of how he "won the heart" of Elvis' wife, Priscilla, is hardly going to make it any easier for him to win OUR hearts. Although, judging by the photos, he might be good looking but that face appears to fit onto a mighty big head!

Anyway, that off my chest, I wish everyone luck with the film; anyone who attempts something new in the world of martial arts movies gets at least my guarded support.

Lastly for this month, in order to get the ball rolling nice and early, I'd like people to start sending in questions NOW for the Questions and Answers session at the upcoming convention. Please write them as briefly as you can and put each question onto a separate sheet of paper. Remember, they should be tasteful (I want no repetition of last year's embarrassment) and, above all, interesting. Send them to: Pam Hadden, Convention Questions, 14 Rathbone Place, London W1P 1DE.

- Pam Hadden

A RETROSPECTIVE LOOK AT BRUCE LEE MANIA & THE KUNG FU CRAZE OF THE 1970S

EDITOR'S NOTES

Throughout the newsletters, there's lots of newspaper and magazine article quoting various peoples' opinions on Bruce Lee. Some are taken out of context and some aren't.

Negative comment made to the media by Jackie Chan, I feel, fall under the former, as Lee is an idol to him. I can't say that I've ever seen an interview where Jackie has anything other than praise for Bruce Lee and you can see from those interviews, how grateful he was for the opportunities afforded to him by his idol. Steve McQueen was an American actor, as well as a student and friend of Bruce Lee, even sending him a card and flowers when he injured his back in 1969.

Martial artist and actor Pat Johnson recalled this story involving Steve McQueen and Bruce Lee when I had dinner with him in 2001:

> Steve McQueen was my best friend up to the time he that he died. He was a student of Bruce Lee for many years and after Bruce became a very famous film star, of course, he no longer taught lessons. So Steve began to train with Chuck Norris and eventually with myself.
>
> After Bruce had passed, Steve told me the story that one day after Bruce had come back from doing a film in Hong Kong, he had called Steve said, "Steve, I've got to get a Porsche. I want to get a Porsche like yours." Now Steve, you have to realize, was a world-class driver. He could have made a living as a Grand Prix driver. He was that good. Anyway, Steve said to Bruce, "Look Bruce, let me take you for ride in my Porsche. It's really a hot car, but if you don't know what you're doing, you can get into a lot of trouble with this thing." So Bruce was all excited, he said, "Okay!" So Steve went and pulled up and picked up Bruce and they went to Mulholland Drive around the San Fernando Valley in LA.
>
> Now Mulholland Drive is a very narrow, very high road on the top of the mountains that surround the San Fernando Valley; very twisty. And if you miss a turn, you're going to go off into the valley. So Bruce and Steve went up to the San Fernando Valley up to the Mulholland Drive to go for the ride. Now Bruce was sitting next to Steve and if you've never been in a Porsche, they have a very deep foot well where your feet goes and a very low seat so you stretch your legs straight out. And Steve was really focused on the road and he said, "Okay Bruce, you ready?" And you hear Bruce say, "Yes! I'm all set. Let's go!" Well Steve took that Porsche through its paces and he was just driving it like crazy. He said, "What do you think of this power, Bruce?" And Bruce said nothing. He heard no noise over there. And Steve says, "Now watch this!" and he goes through the twisting turns and twisting around them and "Isn't that great, Bruce? See how it handles. Now watch this when I slide it!" and Steve would put the thing into a tail slide going right near the edge. "Isn't that great Bruce?" No sound. He twisted the other way, no sound. He says, "Now watch this Bruce. This sucker will do a mean 180."
>
> And Steve just spins it around, a total 180, stops the car and he says, he looks over and says, "Well, what do you think Bruce?" and Bruce isn't there. "Bruce!!" He looks down. Bruce is down in the foot well, covered up and he gets up. I can't use the language that Bruce used. But he said, "McQueen I'll kill you! I'll kill you McQueen! I could kill you!" and Steve, Steve said his eyes opened and he says, Uh-Oh, here is

Bruce Lee, angry, the toughest guy in the world. He's angry and he wants to kill me. So Steve said he took off and started going as fast as he could on the highway. He said, "Bruce, calm down." and Bruce is saying, "Steve, slow down, slow down!" and Steve said, "You won't hit me, will you Bruce?" "No, no." "You won't touch me, will you?" "No, no!" "You won't hurt me, will you?" "No, no." "Just stop the car, stop the car!" So Steve pulled it over, to the side. And Bruce said, "I'd never drive with you again McQueen, never!" That was it, but Bruce then did go out and get his own Porsche.

Yellow Faced Tiger was intended to be a film for Bruce Lee in 1972 after Fist of Fury as the last of the three-picture deal he signed with Raymond Chow in 1971. However, after the success of The Big Boss and Fist of Fury, Lee had a major fall out with director Lo Wei, to a point that police were called. Instead of Yellow Faced Tiger, Lee went on to make Way of the Dragon, taking on writing, directing, producing and acting duties in it. Yellow faced Tiger was released in 1974, directed by Lo Wei and starred Jimmy Wang Yu and Chuck Norris. It was also released under the title, Slaughter in San Francisco.

INTERVIEW WITH GARY DANIELS
From Bruce Lee Fan to Action Movie Star

Gary Daniels (member 2004) is a martial arts actor and former P.K.A. Kickboxing Champion from London. In 1978, along with other members of "The Bruce Lee Society," Gary participated in the amateur film, The Travellers. Over the years, Gary has made a name for himself as one of the leading stars of action movies and has worked with other well respected names including Jackie Chan and Don "The Dragon" Wilson.

How did you become a Bruce Lee fan?

I became a Bruce Lee fan at the age of eight years old. I was enamored by the world of Marvel comic book heroes at that time, using my paper round money for weekly subscriptions to four or five comics every week. So when I was at the cinema to watch the *Airplane* movie - I believe it was - they showed a trailer for next week's release which happened to be *Enter the Dragon*. I will never forget the effect that short trailer had on me and I was totally engaged in the ballistic energy that was Bruce Lee. My Dad, who also became a fan/admirer, sneaked me into a cinema in London to watch *Enter the Dragon* (as they were X-rated at that time) and from that day forward, I was hooked. My life changed and my life's goals had been set.

Do you remember seeing the advert for the Travellers *film mentioned in the Society newsletters? If so, what made you get involved?*

Honestly, I was a very young, shy and introverted boy at the time of the Bruce Lee Society and the *Travellers* gathering so I do not remember seeing the original advert or how I felt about it.

What are your recollections about making the film?

At the time of the *Travellers*, I was living a very introverted life, coming from a broken home where I was drowning in a lifestyle of anger, hate and abuse. Bruce Lee became a guiding light in my life that helped me through a tumultuous time. So that film was a chance to get away from home for a while with my Dad and to be around people with the same interests; martial arts and Bruce Lee. It was a long train journey to Barrow-in-Furness in Cumbria and staying in a B&B, but it was a great time for bonding with my Dad who did not live at home due to his divorce from my Mum.

I have very little recollection of any actual filming but what I do remember is meeting some really good people; Will Johnston, who I am still in contact with today, Andy Hill, a very talented martial artist that was great with Nunchuks and Mick Zameitas and his girlfriend Rosa. Will had a great Bruce Lee collection and actually had a print of the full *Enter the Dragon* film which he screened for us. I was a kid amongst adults and honestly, with hindsight, I didn't really belong in that cast. How do you fit a young boy in a fight film with grown men!? Anyway, there I was. We were a rag-tag bunch

A 15-year-old Gary Daniels takes a break during the filming of the amateur film, The Travellers, *in 1978.*

that really had no experience about film-making and to this day, I have never, ever seen a single frame of film that was shot but it was a fun experience for me.

Did you want to pursue acting as a career prior to making the film?

To be honest, when I saw *Enter the Dragon*, I knew instinctively and intrinsically what I wanted to do for the rest of my life; study martial arts and make movies, both of which I am still doing to this day. At the time of *Travellers*, I was living life unconsciously and was just about getting through life day to day. I was a very young boy, still developing mentally and spiritually, in an environment unsuited for positive growth. Bruce Lee showed me a way out of that lifestyle, he showed me a positive way forward.

Did you have any experiences of speaking with the club president Pam Hadden?

I think that the only time that I briefly met Pam Hadden was when I won a competition through the Bruce Lee Scoiety to win tickets to a press screening of *Game of Death*, which was held in Shaftsbury Avenue in 1978, I believe. This was one of the films first showings before it went on main release.

What was it like being a Bruce Lee fan at that time?

I remember it being a fun, exciting time if you were a Bruce Lee fan. I guess we were the first generation of fans at the time of the Kung fu craze and the Bruce Lee mania of the 70's. There were so many movies, books, novels, pulp fiction, comics, poster magazines and all sorts of memorabilia hitting the stores at that time, anything to cash in on the craze at its height. As I was a boy still in school, I would save any money from my Saturday work or after school jobs, and two or three times a year, I would go to China town in central London. There was a particular shop called "A to Z" which was a small Chinese owned martial arts store that would get all the latest magazines and memorabilia from Hong Kong. I would spend hours looking around secondhand book stores and getting bootlegged videos from a small market stall in Soho and Carnaby Street. At that time, a company called "Simmons International

Promotions" started to bring out some of the best quality books from Japan with full gloss colour pages, as well as putting on conventions where they would bring over members of Bruce Lee's family and students like Dan Inosanto. I remember coming home on the train with plastic bags full of anything I could get with Bruce Lee on the cover or with just a small article inside. Fortunately, my dad would buy books and other items which I couldn't afford and when he had finished reading them, he would pass them on to me and thus, my collection started.

How do you think Bruce Lee's influence on people has changed over the years?

Well, I think that for most people, they were first attracted to Bruce Lee because of his physicality, his charisma and his dynamicism on the screen, but once you researched him, it became more about his martial philosophy and his indomitable spirit in pursuing his life goals. I recently watched the new documentary called *Be Water* and it seems that Bruce Lee is now a poster boy for anti-racism, which fits into the current spiritual shift going on in the world today. You can look at Bruce Lee and see whatever you want to see, whether it is what was on the surface or you can dig deeper and be inspired on a whole different level.

I think it is very important not to treat him like a God that was superior to any one of us but to see him and use his influence as a guide to remind us to look into ourselves and realise that we all have the power to create and improve our own lives, to set, work for and achieve our own highest goals and potential.

A RETROSPECTIVE LOOK AT BRUCE LEE MANIA & THE KUNG FU CRAZE OF THE 1970S

March 1981

HI FOLKS! HERE WE GO WITH NEWS SHEET 19. IT DOESN'T SEEM POSSIBLE THAT ALL THESE MONTHS HAVE GONE SINCE CHRISTMAS ALREADY... AND ALTHOUGH IT'S REALLY A LITTLE LATE, THANKS TO EVERYONE FOR ALL THE SMASHING CARDS I GOT! I COULD PAPER THE HOUSE WITH THEM ALL.

HOLLYWOOD PETITION

I'm glad to say that I've had a much better response of late, to my appeal for signatures. By the way, for new members, we need as many as we can get for a petition that's being sent to the Hollywood Chamber of Commerce - for Bruce's name to be placed by one of the gold stars on Hollywood Boulevard. If YOU haven't contributed as yet, please make a start NOW... send them to me, marked "Hollywood Petition." We still need a lot more. I've had as many as 200 signatures from some members - if all of you could do the same, we'd have enough for half-a-dozen stars!!! Actually, on average, all we need is 14 signatures each - yes, that's all. Yet, I'm sorry to say, the majority of you have still not sent even one. SO COME ON FOR BRUCE'S SAKE!

GENERAL NEWS

Tony Lundberg (2338), one of our Danish members, has a neighbour with the name Bruce - who looks a lot like Bruce Lee, talks Cantonese and practised Kung Fu. His wife is an American

(like Linda) and also has the name Linda! Tony says he had to wonder when he saw their front door (photo shown here)!

Erik Larsen (2376) and Benny Jorgensen (3080) also from Denmark, recently took part in a karate championship - coming second and third respectively. Well done! Next time it'll be first and second.

Still with our Danish Members, Jorgen Miller (2886) says he went to see in London, *Superdragon* and *Clones of Bruce Lee* - expecting to see a load of rubbish. But, surprisingly, *Superdragon* (starring Ron Van Clief) showed a sequence from the *Fist of Unicorn* promotional tour, with genuine bits of Bruce, which Jorgen says was fantastic. In Denmark there is a rip-off film *The True Game of Death!* But it does show fight scenes and the famed balcony scene from *Way of the Dragon* - and again, the *Fist of Unicorn* promo snip! *Way of the Dragon,* by the way, is completely uncensored in Denmark! (Pam here: Anyone like to move with me to Denmark?!).

Can anyone give Jorgen any info on a film called *Flying High* - starring Kareem Abdul Jabbar? He saw it advertised with Chuck Norris' *Good Guys Wear Black*. Jorgen's address is: Kastrup, Denmark.

Paul Smith (1532) sent in the cutting shown here, taken from a sci-fi comic called *Two Thousand AD*. The comic had asked for suggestions for a cast list for a feature film version of one of their great series - entitled *V.C.'s*. One of the characters in the story is Chinese - a martial arts expert called Hen So. There's no guesses who the sender of the article picked for THAT part!

```
THE VCs — JANITORS OF THE UNIVERSE!
Jupe........................................................BURT LANCASTER
Smith.......................................................STEVE McQUEEN
Loon........................................................BURT REYNOLDS
Ringer....................................................DAVID CARRADINE
Dishwasher.............................................ALFRED HITCHCOCK
Computer voice...........................................LEONARD NIMOY
Hen-Sho.........................................................BRUCE LEE
Dwarf Star......................................................YUL BRYNNER
Earthlet Paul Cotterill, Newton-le-Willows. £3 Winner.
```

David Moore (1783) has been studying Chinese horoscopes, and was interested to find the following under Bruce's sign of the Dragon:

> "The Dragon is bursting with health and also represents good fortune. Athletic, and thorough regular exercise will retain youthful composure. Always on the go. Direct, yet incapable of meanness, hypocrisy, scandalmongery or tact/diplomacy. Idealist, perfectionist, refusing to put up with anything but the best; and asks too much of others and himself. Demands a lot, but gives also. Never without admirers - likes to impress. Chatterbox, and sometimes his mouth runs away with him! But however crudely he expresses himself, his opinions are worth listening to and his advice is always good. Enthusiastic to the point of impetuosity - loses temper easily. Gifted, intelligent, tenacious, willing and generous. Whatever his career, be it artistic, religious, military, medical or political, he will shine in it. Other careers suiting Dragons are actor, artist, national hero, and a gangster(!!). Dragons may have casual flirtations. They do, however, thrive on isolation and are self-sufficient. Whatever be-

falls them, they fall on their feet. Super-positive, nothing will keep a Dragon down for long. They are said to wear the horns of destiny. Metal Dragons (Bruce was one) are very strong-willed. Honesty and virtue are paramount virtues to him, and although bright, open and expressive, they are unbending and critical. Action-orientated and combative, he will seek out and motivate those on his own level of intelligence or social standing. He will have little patience with the lazy or foolish. He is, at his best, a magnificent warrior. James Coburn is, and John Lennon was, a Dragon."

David also points out the covering words he found for the Year of the Buffalo (Bull/Ox) - in 1973, when Bruce died: *"Too much work for everyone - we risk working ourselves to death!!"* Thanks David, for a very informative article, which I know members will enjoy reading.

Thanks also to members Anne and Fred Hunt who sent me in a chart which will enable me to tell any member his/her Chinese birth sign. Just drop me a note giving your date of birth, name and membership number - and address to me, together with a SAE and I'll tell you what your sign is. By the way, my sign is the Snake - and Snakes get on very well with Dragons!

Michelle Scully (2919) read David Moore's write up on Chuck Norris in the last news sheet - and has added the following: Chuck's first competition was in Salt Lake City where he drove with three other students... and he was the only one to lose! In 1964 Chuck hit a winning streak and in 1965 won the Californian State Title. In 1966 he won the US Championship, All-American Championship, and National Title. In 1967 he won the International Title and in 1968 he fought and won the World Title.

Andrew Upton (2672) has suggested that at the next convention we read out questions from members/*KFM* readers for the team to answer. I'm quite agreeable to this - just so long as anything unsuitable is removed beforehand as I don't think I shall ever forget the "How did Bruce Lee die?" question that slipped through to Robert. He handled it with great composure but even so, it should never have been asked. Therefore, if YOU have one or more questions to put to the panel, please drop me a card ONLY and don't forget to include your name, address and membership number.

A beautiful picture of Sylvia Lee (Mrs. Robert Lee) - stage name, "Sum Sum".

Andrew also points out that it would be nice to see pictures of winners of competitions and so on. We agree, and all will be remedied this year. As you may by now know, the date of the convention has now been fixed for August 22nd - at London's

Rainbow Theatre in Finsbury Park. And don't forget that I'm interested as always in any constructive ideas you may have to make the day even better than last year. I'm sure there have been times when you've seen something that could be adapted for convention use. There'll be a Swop Shop Corner like we had the first year and, this time, an auction (to raise money for the Society's long discussed Bruce Lee bust). Anything you have that can be donated, please bring it along on the day.

LATE CONVENTION NEWS!

Tickets are going on sale as of now for Britain's third Official Bruce Lee Convention - to be held this year at The Rainbow Theatre, Finsbury Park in London, on August 22nd. Much more detail to follow, but if want to be sure of getting a ticket then, judging by last year, you better book fast!!!

The prices are as follows:

- Single ticket (pre-booked by Society Member) £7.00 Single ticket (for everyone else) £7.50
- Single ticket (on the door for everyone) £9.00
- Five-ticket pack (pre-booked by Society Member) £30.00; five-ticket pack (for everyone else) £32.50

It really does promise to be another monster event, so don't miss it! Just sent your cheque/ postal order (made out to *KFM* please) to: Convention Tickets, *Kung Fu Monthly*, 14 Rathbone Place, London W1P IDE.

USEFUL ADDRESSES

Gilbert Ross (2881) and David Moore (1783) say we can all buy Bruce movies from Mr. P. Johnson of Middlesbrough (or phone after 6pm). He has *Fist of Fury* (uncensored), *Big Boss* (cinema version), *Way of the Dragon* (uncensored), *Enter the Dragon* (uncensored), *Game of Death* (cinema version) - all at £30 each, or any two for £50, or any three for £70. Please DO, however, write first before sending any money, to establish the films are in stock and that everything is in order.

Ernest Bow (2933) gives a collectors' club which sells items on Bruce. The annual sub is £4.95 and the address: BCM, Box No. 281, London WC1V 0XX. Mind you, I personally think that a charge of £4.95 - probably just to receive a mailing list - is pretty steep.

There's a Bruce Lee video for sale from a private collection - telephone after 8pm.

Kung Fu video films for hire/sale - send SAE to P.Y.Tang at 152 Showclough Way, Healey Gardens, Rochdale.

Self-Defense Video Films from W.Ainscough, Bolton - again, WITH CARE!

Sakura Trading Company, 10 Thornbury Road, Isleworth, Middlesex have *Tao of Jeet Kune Do* @ £6.95, *JKD - The Art and Philosophy of Bruce Lee* by Dan Inosanto @ £6.95, *Filipino Martial Arts* by Dan @ £5.90, *Bruce Lee's Fighting Method* (Vols 1-4) @ £3.45. Oriental World at 18A Swan Street, Manchester still have some *Enter*

A RETROSPECTIVE LOOK AT BRUCE LEE MANIA & THE KUNG FU CRAZE OF THE 1970S

the Dragon style fighting gloves at £22.50 plus £1.50 p&p, and *Way of the Dragon* film (colour/super 8/cassette soundtrack) including the nunchaku scene and Norris fight @ £38.70. All the above addresses, by the way, came from David Moore.

From Joseph Chiang (1044) comes the info that W. H. Smith Photographic Dept., 29 Union Street, Birmingham, Warks do portrait paintings from your pictures/photos - write to them for details/leaflets. I've seen some examples and they look excellent and not highly priced. Just imagine having a really nice picture of Bruce, done from a small photo, hanging on the wall!

Joseph also says he got a smashing velvet poster of Bruce from Poster Trading GMBH, Gutleustrasse 154, 6000 Frankfurt Main, Germany. The poster number is JM-3.

For the benefit of new members, I thought I'd mention some of the "regular" shops we have around for Bruce Lee books, magazines, martial arts equipment, etc.:

- Oriental World, 18A Swan Street, Manchester.
- Atoz Martial Arts & Book Shop, 3 Macclesfield Street, London W1.
- For films, Regent Films, PO Box 54, Blackpool.
- Miko Studios, Kennenwestraatweg 35, 1814 GB Alkmaar, Holland.
- Mirage Films, "Delphi," the Street, Swallow-field, Reading RG7 IRE, Berks (Reading 884273).

Keith Thompson (3049) bought a really good bargain in Kung Fu slippers - at £2.85! The shop is Woo Sang, 21 George Street, Manchester. Keith says they also sell good cassettes of Chinese classical and instrumental music. (Pam here - I've got several records of 'modernised' Chinese music - as well as Chinese classical music - and I think a lot of you might enjoy it too. It may not be The Police, Blondie, or even a concerto by Bach, but if you're like me with a taste for all sorts, give it a try.)

Back with David Moore again, a good range of magazines, etc., on Bruce are available from Giko Ltd., 537 Stratford Road, Sparkhill, Warks (tel. 021 773 9247). They also have stuff on Jackie Chan.

SPECIAL MESSAGES/REQUESTS

First off, a good laugh for everyone! Member Joseph Erskine wrote to me to see if I could get hold of a copy of *KFM* 31 (*KFM* themselves are right out). "No problem," I thought... "I'll send him a copy from my collection." Oh dear, what and embarrassment - and a shock - when I looked, I found I didn't have one either!!! ME, without a complete set of *KFM's!* So, TWO copies are now needed. For my part, I'm prepared to swap either a *KFM* 1, 2 or 3 for a copy of 31, BUT ONLY IN PERFECT CONDITION PLEASE. Drop me a line and I'll write back pronto.

Another help - this time from Philip Bell (2506) of Leeds. He's had a leaflet through from the ABC Bradford about the Sunny Films Society who hold all-night film shows of martial arts so can anyone let Philip know the address of the ABC and the phone number? - thanks. I gather they hold quite a few Bruce Lee films.

Michael Cowley of 33 Bellevue Road, Ayr, Scotland is willing to do pencil pictures for members at 50p a time - money returned if not happy. Send SAE for info on sketches, direct to Michael, please.

LETTERS

Dear Pam,

I recently read in the Radio Times *letters page of a lady thanking the BBC for putting on a tribute film for someone called Joyce Grenfell - "after having to wait for over a year." This prompted me to send* Radio Times *a long letter stating that Bruce Lee* fans have waited over seven years - and still no tribute. Whilst I was pleased for the lady in question, how much longer are we, the Bruce Lee fans, to wait for Bruce's well deserved tribute film to be broadcast? Three days later I received a card from the BBC thanking me for my letter and stating that Radio Times had many letters every week and if they didn't publish my letter, it would be passed on to the relevant department. So, Pam, they haven't said they WON'T print it - I'll keep my eyes on the Radio Times' letters page!

Graham Ellis (2728)

Well, Graham, maybe the other fans will also take up reins here and write to the Radio Times and the BBC generally - to keep the ball rolling as much as possible. Come on everyone... let's keep them thinking about us!

Dear Pam,

I keep seeing letters from people who just want to strangle Li, Le, Leon, etc., etc. But the problem isn't as bad as you think! It is bad on video, but I don't think many people are going to waste that sort of money on frauds. Last year I spent two years in Germany - Bruce Lee's name was everywhere, but to them the Le's, Li's and Leon's are all one person... Bruce Lee! I personally never saw a fraud film without "Bruce Lee" written on the advertisements. It seems to me that ALL films have something to do with Bruce! My last week in Germany they had four films of Bruce showing - all almost completely uncut! Even Way of the Dragon had the double nunchaku scene. Another thing... there was a creep called Ti Lung who said Bruce's fighting wasn't real and that he was dead and should be forgotten. The magazine had a PAGE of pictures of Ti and only one small one of Bruce. I think the frauds have done as much for Bruce as the Hunchback did for coathangers!!! They've seriously let him down.

Zahid Jawed (2873)

I was surprised to read Ti Lung's remarks... if he was quoted correctly. He did very well during the Kung Fu "craze" and has made films for quite a few years. I saw him in *Hellfighters of the East* with David Chiang, which is a good film, and to my mind Ti Lung had a good chance of being a pretty popular Kung Fu star in his own right but strangely enough, we didn't hear much of him after that. I've asked Zahid to send me a copy of the article - I'm interested to know what else Ti Lung had to say! And on my next trip to Hong Kong, maybe I might just ask him where HE has retired to and what a shame it is that he never made it in the West!

RENEWALS

Right! Members 2908 to 2972, your second year falls due between now and the end of May; similarly, 2600 to 2697 - your third year is due at this time; members 2267 to 2302 also need to renew their fourth year; and finally, fifth-year members from 1829 to 2021 are due.

THE BRUCE LEE SOCIETY

KFM SUBSCRIPTIONS

Many members STILL write in to me and ask me when their subscription to *KFM* is due - or where they can buy the magazines in their district, etc. Please, I must remind ALL members that, although I run the Society with the backing of *KFM*, I am not in their employ, nor do I work at their offices, or handle subscriptions. All question or problems relating to *KFM* MUST be addressed direct to them at 14 Rathbone Place, London W1P IDE. It's actually taken LONGER for something to go via me!

CHANGES OF ADDRESS

Another thing... will anyone changing their address PLEASE let *KFM* know, if they have a sub to the magazine, and let ME know if they are a Society member. You'd be amazed how many members move house and who then seem to believe I can telepathically discover their new address. It's almost beyond belief! PLEASE LET ME KNOW!!!

PICTURES, CARTOONS, ETC

Right now, I've got so many pictures to use in future news sheets that I've got to call a halt to new ones being sent in! I'll let everyone know when I run short again. (Probably 1982 at this rate!) Any pictures that I promised would be in this sheet, and are not, will appear in June.

MEMORIAL FLOWERS - JULY 1981

I mentioned last time that the Society would be sending its own floral tribute to the graveside of Bruce and for anyone wishing to contribute to send in postal orders in an envelope marked "Memorial Flowers" to me in London (not forgetting to include name and membership number). Well the response was... TWO!!! Yes, two donations were all I got. Maybe you were broke at the time... or "asleep" when reading the news sheet. Whichever, PLEASE don't ignore this very worthy scheme. If you can contribute, PLEASE do it as soon as possible; it takes quite a lot of time and organisation for the flowers to be got to the grave at the right moment.

PEN PALS

Jacqueline McKinney (3082), Derry, Northern Ireland wants male pen pal - any country, around her age of 18 years.
James Flanagan (2824), Oldham wants female Chinese pen pal, or anyone aged between 17-19. Interests are Bruce, keep fit, body-building, sports, reading, Blondie, martial arts. Michael McLaren (2904), Huddersfield wants female pen pal, aged 18/19.

A RETROSPECTIVE LOOK AT BRUCE LEE MANIA & THE KUNG FU CRAZE OF THE 1970S

Julian Midgley (1354) with Danny Inosanto

William Hannon

Member Ann Hunt with wrestler, Sammy Lee

THE BIG BOSS

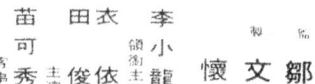

THE BRUCE LEE SOCIETY

SWOP SHOP

- Philip Bell (2506), Leeds, has for sale, legal video cassette of *Enter the Dragon*, uncensored and very good condition. Will accept £50 or swap for tape containing recent recordings of *Police in the East/Police at the Rockapalast* in Germany. Write with offers to Philip, who also has other items to swap.
- John Ruby (2745), Leamington Spa wants *Best of Bruce Lee No. 1* and *Bruce Lee 1940-1973* - will buy or swap, please contact.
- Patrick Hennessy (1771), Dublin, Ireland has for sale or swap for Super 8 sound 400' films: *Fist of Fury* - two 400' colour/silent reels @ £7 per reel. *Game of Death* colour/silent,. 400' @ £7. Bruce trailers etc., colour/ sound @ £10. Lee/Norris fight, colour/silent, 100' - giveaway at £6. *Fistful of Yen* (not Bruce!), 400' colour/silent, £10. Patrick's interests in swap films are modern horror; *The Quiet Man*; old westerns; *The Three Stooges*.
- Tracey Bennett (3039), Washington, Tyne & Wear had all her Bruce items stolen. Can anyone assist with letting her know what duplicate items that they have so that she can get her collection back together again? Thanks!
- Simon Bulley (2738), Peterborough, has for sale *Game of Death* tracksuit - zip back - large, 100% polyester - as new - £12 ono (postage paid, except abroad). Write initially, don't send money. First come, first served basis.
- Bipin Chandra Pandey, Haldwani, India wants *Beginners Guide to Kung Fu* - anyone help? Write to him so he knows we're still alive this side of the world!
- Arthur Stone (1150), Burton-on-Trent wants to know - does anyone own/or have they knowledge of where to get Super 8 movie featuring either James Tien vs Jabbar from *Game of Death* of Bruce vs Chi Hon Joi from the same film? Write to him with any info please.
- John Milne (2046), Glasgow has for sale a few books and magazines on Bruce - write to him for details of these.
- Roy Braithwaite (2509), East Kilbride had for sale 400' colour/sound Super 8 film of *Enter the Dragon* - very good condition, bottle scene and nunchaku scene included - £20; also 100' *Enter the Dragon* trailer, as new for £7.
- Mr. P Chrislakis, Clapton has for sale *KFM's* 2 to 57 inclusive - contact direct.
- Avtar Sohota (3035), Warley has for swaps: *My Martial Arts Training Guide to Jeet Kune Do* plus three glossy B&W autographed photos of Bruce Lee. Wants in exchange *KFM's* 1 and 2. Has for swap *Fighters Monthly* Vol. 1, No. 1 (Bruce Lee The Truth), *Fighters* Dec/April 1980, (Kung Fu & Eric Lee), *KFM's* 24 & 49, *Combat* Vol. 6, No. 11 & Vol. 7, No. 1, *Warriors* Vol. 1 No. 6, *Fighting Arts* Vol. 3 No. 6, plus *Enter the Dragon* Bruce poster and autographed picture of Bruce - all good condition. Wants *Bruce Lee in Action, Unbeatable Bruce Lee*, plus *KFM* 31. Write to Avtar or telephone before ordering to save time if items have gone.
- John Deakin (3090), Liverpool has for sale 400' Super 8 colour/ sound *Game of Death* (includes Lee/Inosanto and Lee/Jabbar fights). Rare/superb quality, £40. Also selling Super 8 colour/sound trailer *Big Boss* and *Enter the Dragon*, each 5' long, or swap for Japanese *Fist of Fury* and *Way of the Dragon* LP's. Write, or phone.
- Suresh Gandhi (1743), Eindhove, Holland has for swap: *Aikido - The Dragon's Gang* sound/ colour 8mm film (2 x 400' reels, German dialogue); wants *Boss 400* 8mm film. Also for swap *Bruce Lee in Action* (Spanish), *Bruce Lee the Little Dragon* (Spanish), *Secret Art* (German). Will swap these for any Japanese Lee book.

- Joseph Erskine (2891), Alloa wants urgently *KFM* No. 31. Please contact with price requested, condition, etc.
- Jorgen Miller (2886), Kastrup, Denmark wants *Bruce Lee - My Martial Arts Training Manual*. Please drop him a line if you can help.
- Ian Hamilton (1213), Sunderland has for sale: colour/silent films - 2 x 400' reels *Big Boss* and 2 x 400' reels *Fist of Fury* - each reel cost £32.50, but will accept £15 each reel; also *Way of the Dragon* with sound cassette - £15; *Game of Death* - £15, *Fist* (poor quality, good action) cost £25, accept £10. Also *Secret Art of Bruce Lee* book - £2.50 plus p&p. (Please add £1 p&p for each film - but give Ian a call first to see what's still available) - phone Tyne & Wear.
- Simon McCall (2897), Leeds wants hardback of *Bruce Lee 1940-1973* in mint/very good condition. Will pay good price.
- Michael McLaren (2904), Huddersfield has for sale... (please write direct for list) - *Kung Fu Monthly* and *Official Karate* magazines. Please send stamp for postage.

ROBERT LEE ALBUM

For the benefit of new members - and for those of you who have been writing in to ask me - the Robert Lee LP *Ballad of Bruce Lee* is still available directly through me. Those of you attending the last convention will have heard such tracks sung by Bruce's brother as *JKD, Parting, Pointing Finger,* and the title song *Ballad of Bruce Lee* (dedicated to his brother). The albums I am selling are all individually signed by Robert himself and the cost is still only £4.60 (including p&p) - Europe £6 and the rest of the world, £6.50. And also still available from me, the black and white photo of Bruce and Robert together, with Bruce doing the amazing flying kick! These are also signed by Robert personally and cost £1.20 to anywhere in the world. ALL postal orders/cheques made payable to PAM HADDEN please (NOT *KFM* in this instance), orders to be sent to London. All monies received, by the way, go direct to Robert and there is no profit being made at either end.

Well folks - that's about it for another news sheet. Don't forget the flower donations and keep the Hollywood petition signatures coming in too! By the way, have any of you realised just how many members have adopted the name "Bruce" as a middle name? There are also quite a few "Bruce-related" addresses such as Lee Close, Bruce Road; there are members with the surname Lee and Saxon; there's

Cumberland Road, Saxon Street - and would you believe we actually have a member called Abdul Jabbar (2488).

Lastly, apologies for the lateness of this news sheet... caused by illness. Bye for now! Peace, Love, Brotherhood! - Pam

BRUCE LEE SOCIETY COLUMN
KUNG FU MONTHLY NO. 60

There's interesting news first of all regarding the BBC and their ill-famed Bruce Lee documentary. Quite a few members seem to have written to the corporation recently, on the basis that it's high time something happened with the programme that was at first promised us and then ended up abandoned on the shelf.

Well, one or two of the replies don't seem to have been such definite "no's" as might have been expected; indeed, "not for a while" seems more the tone now. Don't get too excited by this but it seems to me the pressure we've been bringing to bear might just be starting to pay dividends. That means we must make our campaign even more concerted! If you've already written once, write again! If you've never written to the BBC, DO IT, AND DO IT RIGHT NOW!

Some time ago I mentioned the possibility of commissioning a bust or statue of Bruce Lee. One of the stumbling blocks, however, was that there didn't seem anywhere sensible to put it so that fans would be able to see it easily, while at the same time the work remained safe. The problem would seem to be solved! *KFM's* office in London's Rathbone Place is shortly to be extended, and among other things it will be taking in the shop front underneath. The bust can be placed in the window in complete safety,- to be seen by anyone, day or night!

But it's going to cost money and, to help with this, I've had the following idea. I'd like everyone to donate at least one item of interest. It doesn't have to be to do with Bruce Lee and come the next convention, everything we get in will be auctioned off! Smaller things such as magazines, books, LPs, etc can be sent by post NOW to Pam Hadden. Bigger or more delicate items should, I would suggest, be brought along on the day itself. PLEASE, PLEASE help us in this! A bust or statue will cost a great deal of money (probably a thousand pounds or so) and every little bit will help.

Lastly, anyone with ideas on other ways of helping to raise the cash, please write in immediately. This is my first real attempt at fundraising and members' help would be much appreciated!

- Pam Hadden

BRUCE LEE SOCIETY COLUMN
KUNG FU MONTHLY NO. 61

Marvelous news is that the date of the official convention has now been fixed for August 22nd at London's Rainbow Theatre. The place is absolutely enormous, so let's see if we can't make it 2,000 this time. The final itinerary is still being fixed, but from what I hear, it promises to be another tremendous occasion. Of course, one thing I'll be concentrating on is trying to raise enough cash for the Society to have made the Bruce Lee bust we've been talking about for so long. Now we know there'll be a place for it at the *KFM* headquarters in Rathbone Place, where it can be viewed both day and night. All we have now is the small problem of raising around a thousand pounds! Towards this end, may I repeat what I said last month about sending in contributions to a unique auction that will take place at the convention. Big things (they don't HAVE to be to do with Bruce), please bring with you on the day. Smaller donations (such as books and magazines) can be sent into me direct. I'm delighted to be able to say that one thing we are expecting to show at the convention is part of the celebrated Bruce Lee Museum direct from California. I've been a bit lucky here as I've managed to obtain a very large and illuminated display cabinet which I'm currently in the process of "doing up." It should prove ideal for showing Bruce Lee memorabilia at its very best. The only problem is that it takes about six strong men to lift it!

Lastly for this month, it really seems to me that the Society ought to stage something of its own at the convention in the form of a special stall perhaps, or some sort of display? As you've probably guessed, what I'm actually doing is fishing for ideas! Any flashes of brilliance should be communicated to me directly and believe it or not, August really isn't all that far away.

- Pam Hadden

BRUCE LEE SOCIETY COLUMN
KUNG FU MONTHLY NO. 62

Hi, and the main amazing news this month is, that Robert is definitely coming over this year for the convention. Other delicate negotiations are also in progress for one name in particular and to that end, I expect at the end of June to go jetting off to Los Angeles, to try to push things along a bit. I'm hoping too to get to meet as many of Bruce's friends and relations as possible and partly the idea will be to try to persuade them to say a few words into the tape recorder. If I can get them to do it, I'll give you three guesses where they'll all be played.

I've just been to see a special press showing of the latest Elvis Presley movie. He was half way through making it when he died, so in a way you can see similarities with Bruce and *Game of Death*. But, the really interesting thing is that Presley's last film happens to link quite strongly with the martial arts. Bearing in mind that, for one thing, both Bruce and Elvis were at one time thinking of making a film together, secondly that Presley was quite into the martial arts himself, and thirdly, that a large number of Bruce Lee fans also happen to be pretty keen on Mr. P, well, it seems to me that *KFM* ought to say something on the subject. The editor has been suitably reminded of this fact, so look out for action soon!

I'm sick and tired of the rip-off Bruce Lee bandwagon. I KNOW it's flattering to be imitated, but when businessmen get in on the act and start trying to run conventions, as they are yet again this year, I just wish they would at least come up with some sort of original name. May I please remind all of you that there is only ONE proper convention this year and that is the official one on August 22nd at the Finsbury Park Rainbow Theatre in London. YOU HAVE BEEN WARNED!

- Pam Hadden

EDITOR'S NOTES

Fist of Unicorn was a 1973 Shaw Brothers film directed by Ti Tang and starring Unicorn Chan with the action and fight scenes directed by Bruce Lee, who makes an unintended cameo appearance. Having both been friends since childhood and appearing together in *Way of the Dragon,* Chan asked Lee to choreograph the fight scenes in his new film, which he happily did. Unbeknownst to Lee, the cameras were rolling while Lee rehearsed the actors and stuntman. That footage ended up in the final cut of the film, with the poster advertising Lee's unwitting involvement, having been duped by his one-time friend.

Flying High was an alternative title for the 1980 spoof film *Airplane*, directed by David Zucker, Jim Abrahams and Jerry Zucker, with a cast featuring Leslie Nielsen, Robert Hays, Julie Hagerty and Kareen Abdul-Jabbar.

The *Kung Fu Monthly* Third Bruce Lee Convention is announced for 22nd August 1981. No showings were confirmed.

In this issue, home videos of Bruce Lee's films on VHS and Betamax are getting cheaper in this issue, albeit due to piracy. With the availability of blank tapes and "copy leads," the general public could now freely copy from one tape to another, provided they have two video recorders. In 1981, most genuine videotapes to buy, were around £40. With inflation, that price in 2019, would have been £154. If Mr. P. Johnson from Middlesbrough sells his pirated copies at £30 (£10 under the genuine price), that's the equivalent of someone today paying £115.50 and obtaining a discount of £38.50 from the full price. There were big savings to be had. That's why piracy took off in a big way back in the 1980's, which led to copy protection methods such as Macrovision and later Cinavia being implemented into hardware, software and media.

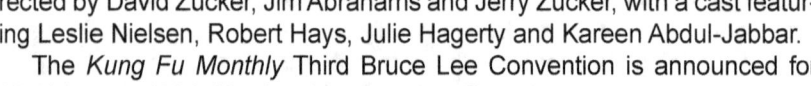
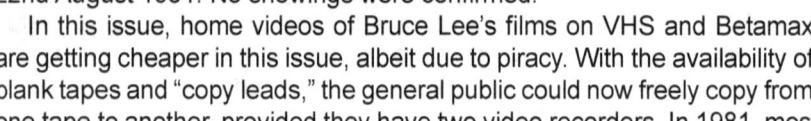

A RETROSPECTIVE LOOK AT BRUCE LEE MANIA & THE KUNG FU CRAZE OF THE 1970S

A FAN'S RECOLLECTIONS
by
Martin Hughes (Member 1695)

Martin Hughes, like most young men in the mid 1970s, was a huge Bruce Lee fan. Martin Hughes and Mark Burns were avid contributors to The Bruce Lee Society in it's early days, scouring various magazines to create merchandise lists with addresses for books, posters, magazines etc. which they would send to Pam Hadden, who in turn, would send to Society members along with their quarterly newsletters. I managed to track Martin down to get some information from him about his involvement with the Bruce Lee scene and Society back in the 70s.

Mark and I got the addresses from imported magazines. We were fairly blessed in living not too far from Birmingham as Cimac used to import stuff from *Black Belt* publishing in the USA and Hong Kong. There was also M&R Chinese Supermarket in Birmingham's Chinatown who had the Hong Kong Jeet Kune Do club poster magazines, which contained fantastic articles and rare photos but with laughable English translations, as well as books.

The odd martial arts magazine used to turn up at the local newsagents too, I think they probably came over the same way that the US comics used to - ship ballast - and that played havoc with continuity and collectability. Being fanatical fans, we used to read every last bit of these things and Mark had this idea and I could write in a linear and legible manner, so we got on with it.

During a visit to London on a school trip in late 1977, we went to the British Museum to see the Egyptology exhibition as it tied in with the RE "O" Levels. Six of us were down there, along with an invited friend. Mark Burns, my friend and fellow Society contributor came, someone else dragged their girlfriend along, with David Hart the RE Master shepherding us about. We had a couple of hours free, so Mark and I worked out the way to The *KFM* Offices at 39 Goodge Street as it didn't look to be too far from the museum and I think we wrote to Pam et al to announce our visit.

For some reason, I expected a pagoda at the very least, rows of typewriters and telex machines, manned by rabid fans like ourselves plus a hotline to Raymond Chow at Concord for the latest on *Game of Death*. Felix Yen and Don Won Ton would beam down from their bamboo thrones and the fair maidens of *KFM* would wait upon us with cups of jasmine tea or some such. Nope.

In reality, it was an alley, some whiffy bins and a doorway with a push button callbox. Not even a brass name plate. This was definitely the address. Was anybody in?

We tried the button. We heard a noise. "*Kung-Fu Monthly?*" we asked. "Er, yeah," came the reply. "It's us! Can we come in? Pam!" we shouted. "Pam's not in. There's nobody here," said the unknown voice. "Er, um. Oh well," we said, but finding that the door was unlocked, we pushed it open and found a long uncarpeted stair case, bare walls and box after box of *KFM's* latest album of Bruce Lee quotes and pictures. I wish that we'd nicked a few boxes now, but we were a fair walk away from the train station and notionally under the supervision of a slightly camp RE teacher.

I'm a long time out of the scene now, but I don't know if Bruce Li ever grew up and found himself. We'd seen a couple of crappy knock-off Bruce Lee flicks (*The Bruce Lee Story* aka *Karado the Hong Kong Cat* and *The Legend of Bruce Lee* – a *Game of Death* knock off), so Mr. Li (in hindsight, probably half-a-dozen different blokes) was the subject of some ridicule amongst the handful of fans from Walsall.

The movie mentioned in the newsletters that we were making was Mark's idea - he was for many years, a spectacular bullshitter.

The Kung-Fu Monthly

BRUCE LEE SOCIETY

President... Pam Hadden

17th January, 1978.

Mr. Martin Hughes,

Membership No. 1695.

Dear Martin,

    Thank you for your letter; I'm sorry to hear you will not be rejoining; however, I am quite appreciative of your reasons. One point, though – I would like to offer you a free year's membership for your assistance with addresses, etc., and also Mark, if you would like to tell him; but it might be you would rather not have another membership, in which case just let me know by return. I would suggest you write direct to my home address on this, not K.F.M.

    I was very sorry to hear you were turned away from the Kung Fu offices - obviously as I do not work there, I was not around to see what was happening. I will mention to the Editor when I go about it, as they usually do not stop members from calling on them; it is very unusual.

    Kind regards,

                  Pamela.

14, Rathbone Place, London W1P 1DE, England.

Above: A reprinted letter from Pam Hadden to Martin Hughes dated 17th January 1978.

SINCE THIS JUNE SHEET HAD NOT (UP TO THE TIME OF WRITING THE SEPTEMBER SHEET) BEEN RETURNED FROM THE PRINTERS, I HAD THEM REMOVE MY CONVENTION WRITE- UP AND REPLACE IT WITH THE "LATE FILM SHOWS" & ADDRESSES INFORMATION AS BELOW WHICH HAD OVERFLOWED FROM THE SEPTEMBER SHEET!!

HOLLYWOOD PETITION

I recently had the pleasure of again visiting Hong Kong and meeting with Robert Lee and Sylvia once more - and just before that, seeing Bruce's mother Grace in Los Angeles. And whilst in Hong Kong, I met with Sheh Kin (Han from *Enter the Dragon*) who, at 69, did not look older than 50. He speaks no English, but luckily I had Robert with me to translate!! Sheh has known Bruce since he was a child - Bruce's father and Sheh Kin appearing together when in the Chinese Opera, and Bruce going along with his father to watch. There'll be more on Sheh Kin soon.

As you will know, plans are in hand for an auction at the next convention - this is to raise money for a bust of Bruce. When I first enquired about doing something like this, my intention was for a full-size statue, but as this would have worked out somewhere in the region of £7-£8,000, the idea has had to be scaled down to a bust. So far, after seeking contributions in the line of unwanted/surplus items on Bruce, the response has been very small. Well, I'll be picking up on that again now - please, PLEASE send in any items you do not require - not necessarily on Bruce - to me at London. All items are being kept QUITE safe with me until the next convention!!

Lenny Franchi (3120) says the following cinemas have late-night Kung Fu film shows: Kilburn State, Edgware Road - Friday and Saturday; ABC Edgware Road - Friday Only; Kilburn Broadway - Friday Only; Bayswater ABC - Friday Only.

Robert Hartsfield (2864) from the US wrote to a local TV station asking for a screening of the series *The Green Hornet*. They answered, however, that they do not have the rights to the film. Bob is now trying the rest of the TV stations and says he'll let us know if he gets any luck. If a showing IS forthcoming, I'll let you all know because many of you DO manage to get over there and might get to see an episode! Who knows...

Stephen Ward (1941) wrote in asking for *Longstreet* to be shown once again on commercial television - their reply: "Thanks for your letter on the late martial artist Bruce Lee. I am afraid we are not inclined to repeat *Longstreet* when there are still first runs available of so many other crime series. As for Kung Fu movies, we are simply not allowed to play them as they are too violent to fit the IBA's various codes. I am sorry we are not able to please you." Signed: Leslie Halliwell, ITV Programme Buyer, Granada Television, 36 Golden Square, London W1R 4AH. Well, that's a laugh! Kung Fu is TOO violent is it? Maybe they've been missing out on some of the TV programmes they've been showing lately. How about writing to Leslie Halliwell with your (polite please) comments.

Unlike the response from the TV people that Stephen received, our member Lenny Franchi (3120) wrote to the *Daily Mirror* about Bruce; not only did they reply to Lenny, they even sent him four photocopies of actual cuttings from their paper. Lenny thought (and so do I) that this was a very nice gesture on their part. (Hey, come on now... don't all go writing to the *Mirror*. I can just see the post they'd receive)!!

On to films, and many members, including James Norman (1908) have written in to say they have seen varied copies of Bruce's films - one week it's *Fist of Fury* hacked to pieces, the next they see one that's absolutely intact! *Enter the Dragon* has had copies with the bottle scene shown, whereas in other copies even the chat scene between Bruce and Braithwaite prior to departure to the island has been chopped! Some members ask "Have the nunchakus been replaced?" when they have seen uncut copies of *Fist of Fury*. The answer is "NO" - not replaced (apparently the censors very rarely replace ANYTHING that's been removed)... it just seems they haven't haven't yet got their scissor-happy hands on all the copies.

Mark Eost (2815) read an interesting article in the Winter 1981 edition of *Official Karate* about a fighting art called Mu Tau, developed from Pankration (the most savage of the Greco-Roman fighting styles) by James Arvanitis. The name Mu Tau means "all powers." Arvanitis emphasizes simplicity, adaptability and economy of motion. "Moreover," the article states, "as Bruce did with Jeet Kune Do, Arvanitis stresses that no two persons will practice the art alike, since we must each develop according to the strengths and weaknesses of his own physiology and mentality. Anyone wishing a photocopy of this article, send me a stamped and self-addressed envelope. I must say, I found it really interesting.

Simon Bulley (2738) says there is a new martial arts book out called *The Ninja*. Simon says this is superior to the Mike Stone ninja film. The new book - a bestseller in the States - is being made into a film by producers Zanuk and Brown (who, you may recall, produced *The Sting, Jaws, French Connection,* and *Butch Cassidy and the Sundance Kid*). Actors being considered for the main part are Robert De Niro, Richard Gere and Roy Schneider. On page 438, reference is made to Bruce thus (on one of the characters, Nicholas, entering a cinema that's showing a Bruce Lee film):

> "The place was almost filled. On screen, Bruce was talking earnestly with a couple of evil-looking Japanese. The audience was noisy, restless for the action sequences. Dialogue they did not appreciate. Nicholas sat back, watching Lee for a time. The years had not diminished his aura - his spirit seemed to leap off the screen, making the most slip-shod productions worth watching. Nicholas recalled the first time they had met - it had been in Hong Kong, ironically, after the period Lee had spent in Hollywood, working as a bit player in films and TV and teaching stars enough of the martial arts to get them by in front of cameras. He was beginning to be somewhat of a star in his own right then. They had taken to each other immediately but time and logistics had worked against them and they had never seen each other again. Lee's death had come as a shock to Nicholas."

I reckon the book, in itself, sounds interesting and the reference to Bruce makes it definitely among my future buys!!!

Keith Spicer (1960) wrote regarding the *KFM* article on Jesse Glover, with special reference to where Jesse states that during practising his judo with Bruce, Bruce asked to be thrown. The result, according to Jesse, was the Little Dragon being thrown with the velocity of a nunchaku in full flight; Jesse stated that he could not believe that Bruce had survived the fall as his head had been aimed at a nearby metal bedpost. This prompted Keith to speculate whether this fall had, perhaps, done more damage than was thought. Could it possibly have been the start of Bruce's headaches, blackouts, etc? I had to admit the remarkable logic in Keith's letter. I wonder if any other members had the same thoughts?

Back to replies from TV stations, and David Moore (1783) got a reply from the BBC when he requested info and showings of the legendary Bruce documentary and repeats of *Ironside*. Here it is: "Thank you for your recent letter. We have made enquiries, and are sorry to have to tell you that the BBC has no plans at present to show a documentary programme about Bruce Lee; neither are his films scheduled for screening in the near future. We do assure you, however, that your interest has been noted, and as programme plans are under regular discussion, it is always possible that new arrangements may be made at a later date. At the moment, though, we regret that we are unable to send you a more hopeful reply." Signed Jane Barrow (Miss), Programme Correspondence Section, BBC. I must say, I do feel that, were more members to write in as David has done, we might just see a happier ending to all our efforts over the years.

David also gave various mentions connected with Bruce. Bruce and Kareem were mentioned in the *Different Strokes* series a few months ago, where a racehorse called Bruslee came third and two horses in another race, Pagoda and Kareem, came first and second. MY favourite that David sent, though, was from a novel *Confessions of a Sport Master*. It says that "The school cook handed out the hardest chops since Bruce Lee"!!!

Still with David (and recapping on info in the last news sheet), it seems that the Elvis film which was being discussed before his untimely death IS going ahead, called *New Gladiators*. Some footage of Elvis doing karate is to be used in the film, but in all probability it will turn out much as Bruce's *Game of Death* did, being nothing like what either star thought it should be! We shall see.

David (again!) has given a list of new martial arts films being planned or already under way, so here they are. *Kill Or Be Killed* (with James Ryan); *Hard Knocks* (with Bill Wallace, retired undefeated World Full Contact Middleweight Champion, and Karyn Turner); *The Dragon Slayer* (with Benny Urquidez, World Full Contact Super Lightweight Champion). Tadashi Yamashita and Byong Yu are to begin filming *The Masters*, written by Stirling Silliphant; Chuck Norris is casting for his new film *An Eye For An Eye*; Fred Weintraub and Paul Heller (of *Enter the Dragon* and *Big Brawl* fame) are planning a new, as yet, untitled film; Jackie Chan is working on an untitled martial arts book.

According to *Fighters* martial arts magazine, at the Chinese New Year, during a Wing Chun Kung Fu demonstration in London by Austin Goh, Eddie Yeoh and Nigel Fan, Bruce appeared on the backdrop and the fans cheered and clapped as if he were there in person; they also showed *Fist of Fury* uncut. As David said - what other celebrity would cause such a reaction, eight years after his death?

Andrew Upton (2672) read an article in *Fighting Stars* dated Summer 1977, concerning *The Silent Flute*. (For fans not familiar with this, Bruce and James Coburn planned to make a film of this - based on Bruce's idea - and discussion took place with Stirling Silliphant. However because of various problems, the idea was eventually shelved. After Bruce's death, the film was finally made, with David Carradine taking on Bruce's part.) The article remarked that Carradine was unsuitable for the part, and Bruce Li should have the role!!! Jon Branam, President of the San Fernando Valley Bruce Lee Fan Club wrote the article - and even tried to get fans to protest at Carradine having the part. Now, much as I was never a Carradine fan, to my mind, anyone suggesting that Li should have the part needs a psychiatrist - and quickly! Anyway, once I saw *The Silent Flute* my opinion of Carradine changed. He did a splendid job of the part. For some strange reason the film never made general release, and fans thus missed a chance to see a film containing a vast helping of the philosophical as well as the fighting side of the martial arts.

I expect, by the way, that many of you have been watching *The Chinese Detective* on TV... what do you think of it? I find his cool, even-tempered attitude, typical of someone whose mind is trained in accepting the various provocations in life - humiliation, frustration, persecution. I enjoy the programme very much.

Member Tony Lundberg (2338) sent the following... his personal feelings on becoming a Bruce Lee fan. It's entitled, *Power of Thought*. "You usually start to LIKE a person - for example, Bruce Lee. Later, you become more concerned about that person, and become maybe a 'fan.' After a while, you start to buy different types of Bruce Lee material; you have a haircut like Bruce, begin to buy the same clothes as Bruce wore. Maybe you then start talking like Bruce - you start to study his martial arts called Jeet Kune Do, and without knowing it, you become a fanatic. Year after year you still study Bruce Lee, and therefore learn more and are more concerned about him; and at last you maybe believe that you are him yourself." And yes - Tony

A RETROSPECTIVE LOOK AT BRUCE LEE MANIA & THE KUNG FU CRAZE OF THE 1970S

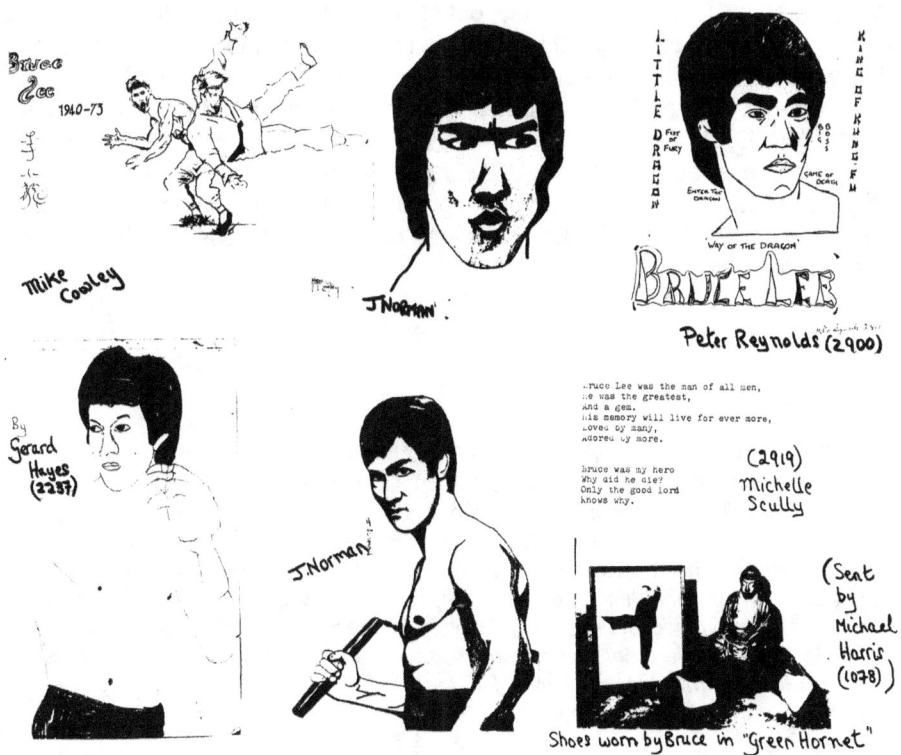

is right; all of us, if we were to admit it honestly, are copying Bruce in some form or another, being influenced by his spirit. That is what being a fan is... you absorb part of that person's image, you project his ways, his ideals, even his lifestyle. Because you BELIEVE in that person - really believe. Bruce, to his true fans, is not a 'passing interest'; he is a way of life - our life - and as such can never leave us.

NEW MARTIAL ARTS FILMS TO WATCH FOR!

Cannonball Run with Jackie Chan. David Moore (1783) says Chuck Norris has signed a five-picture deal with Avco-Embassy - shortly to be released *An Eye for an Eye*. Sho Kosugi (made debut in *Enter the Ninja*) is to star in *Revenge of the Ninja* (Director - Golan; Producer - Globus; Writer David West - Cannon Films Production) - also starring Stephen Hayes (the only non-Japanese authorised to teach Ninjutsu) and Keith Vitali (1980 US National Grand Champion in Karate). Mike Stone will choreograph the fight scenes.

COMPETITION

Well, that's something we've not done for a while, is it?! This time though it's going to be a little different - I think!! Recently, I decided that the space in my home was becoming VERY hard to find - due of course, need I say, to my Bruce Lee items and my personal collections. So I had, out of necessity, to clear my files of copies of letters that I've been sending out to all of you for more time than I care to remember. There were 28 large black files - all filled. How many letters do YOU think I've actually answered since the Society started back in September 1976? I counted every one AND WAS STUNNED!

Have a guess, and send your answer on a postcard marked "Society Letters Competition." I'll be giving an assortment of goodies to the ten members who come nearest the correct figure! Please, postcards only and addressed to: 14 Rathbone Place, London WIP IDE.

LETTERS

Dear Pam,

A rather well-off but boring person I know has a vast library and several video machines, and there are always people eager to crowd into his parties... not to see him, but his films! Looking into his latest batch of videos, I found he had just bought two Warner films - Exorcist *and (you've guessed it)* Enter the Dragon. *My brother and I talked our host into showing this, and sat down with a small group of friends to watch. An amazing thing happened... while it was playing, everyone who passed through the room decided to stop and watch. By the time the real action had begun on Han's island, the room was packed with spectators. It was again real evidence of the Master's mass appeal. I was glad, too, that the spectators saw the complete, uncut version, including bottle fight.*

Simon Bulley (2738)

As yet, I've not acquired a video machine, which is most frustrating as I have two Bruce video cassettes and can't show them! I know that several members now have one and they give shows in their homes, for friends - and like yourself, have discovered that the old Lee pulling power still holds them fast. For those of us who have never met the Master (and I guess that includes just about everyone reading this), we KNOW that force comes across on the screen, but how much better it would have been to have experienced it personally. But, that said, if we can absorb his power from the screen, his philosophy from his books and from those who knew him personally, we have gained something that most people never find in their whole lives.

Dear Pam,

I've just come back from seeing Big Brawl *with Jackie Chan, and had to write. Regarding his fighting ability (if that's what you call it!) it's non-existent. In no way is this man a fighter. Okay, as an acrobat he would be passable, but I read he rates his fighting skills on the same level as Bruce's. He must be living in dreamland! Jackie possesses neither the skill, speed, strength, nor frightening accuracy that Bruce so plainly did. On the screen, Jackie is just the same as every other Kung Fu actor/ fighter, and plainly absent is the sheer animal magnetism of Bruce. It's almost eight* years since Bruce Lee died and no one's come near to equalling him, and I don't believe they ever will.

Molly Cullen (1749)

As I told Molly when I answered her letter, Jackie has been quoted as stating his abilities are something special! I hope he WAS misquoted and did not actually say these things. When I met him, he seemed a very nice, unaffected chap, but of course, since then he's been to the States and his name is spreading so maybe his head's growing too?

MEMORIAL FLOWERS

Up to the time of writing this sheet, I wish to acknowledge, with thanks, the donations received (for the memorial flowers to be sent to Bruce's graveside in July) from the following Members: Phillip Bell, Michael Harris, Mark McAdam, Cherrilyn Bankes and Graham Pugh, Miss R G Heath, Marlene Condy, Jan-Geir Hansen, Gino D'Ambrosio, John Watson, Paul Norris, Richard Gray and Arthur Stone. As much as I appreciate the thoughts of the FEW who have actually answered my call for these flowers to be placed on Bruce's grave, it seems incredible that, with all the members that the Society can now boast, these are the only ones who have made the appropriate action. I know times aren't exactly easy right now, but even so!!!

HOLLYWOOD PETITION

Lots of thanks to all the members who have been sending in the petitions for the Hollywood Chamber of Commerce to place Bruce's name on one of the gold stars on Hollywood Boulevard - keep them coming please. For the benefit of new members, just pop as many signatures as you can in the post to me and help the "World of Bruce Lee" in Hollywood (who are the organisers of the petition) and the Society get Bruce's name on display for all to see. I don't care (on this occasion) who or where the signatures come from - just so long as you don't make headlines in the papers getting them!

And talking about the petition, Marc Willmott (3143) says that when he was collecting signatures, and told people what it was for, many of them were pleased that something was being done at last! So although you may get one or two people who wouldn't sign a petition for anything (probably because they can't write anyway!!!) the majority, you'll find, will. If they don't - well, you can't criticise too much I suppose, because it's a free country. Even so, a good kick in the shins might help (only kidding, honest!)

SPECIAL MESSAGES

Robert Fair (3158) has just bought his first Japanese LP on Bruce, entitled *Bruce Lee Big Special*. It contains various sound sequences/fights from *Way of the Drag-*

THE BRUCE LEE SOCIETY

on. *Enter the Dragon, Fist of Fury, Big Boss* - and he is willing to record for anyone on to cassette - if they'd contact him. His address is c/o Colchester.

Oh, by the way, under "Useful Addresses" - video hire - the Sunny Film and Video Club also show films - Kung Fu of course! - and have a late night showing of these quite frequently. Member Philip Bell (2506) sent the address, and from info he gave, Bruce is very high on the showing list of this club. On May 17th they had *Fist of Fury* - full length and uncut - on May 31st they had the uncut *Way of the Dragon,* and I suggest that interested fans (the club operates from ABC cinemas in Leeds and Bradford) give them a ring to see what's coming up in the future. Naturally I shall expect you all to keep on requesting Bruce's films, again and again, and again...

My thanks to member Paul Haste (2990) who very kindly sent me a copy of *KFM* 31 after my appeal in the last news sheet. It was such an embarrassment to find that I hadn't got one. However, member Joseph Erskine DOES still need a copy, so please, if anyone out there has one, do me a favour and send it off to Joseph (via me at the usual address). My offer still stands of a copy of either *KFM* 1, 2 or 3 for one of these - or if you need anything else, I'll see what I can do!

USEFUL ADDRESSES

Asian World of Martial Arts, 932 Arch St., Philadelphia PA 19107, USA - sell cassette film *The Warrior Within* - tribute to Bruce - starring Chuck, Mike Stone, Moses Powell, Ron Laganoshu, Dan Inosanto - music by Robert Lee. Cost US$59.95. Write first. (E. D. Bow - 2933)

Kung Fu Inc., P.O. Box 29164, Rio Pedros, Puerto Rico 00929, USA - they do a Bruce Lee journal containing photos/penpals/collectors/philosophy/info on meetings & activities from other fan clubs - eight issues per year for US$8. Write direct.

Bruce Lee & Jackie Chan Fan Club, West Book & Trading Co. Inc., 208 Matsusaki, Higashika, Fukuoka, Japan 813 - rare items for sale.

Py Tang, Rochdale sell Bruce videos on VHS/Betamax inc. Cantonese (no subtitles) documentary film on Bruce/Jackie with censored *Game of Death* Lee/Inosanto fight - 90mins - £20 plus £1 p&p. Also Bruce Lee souvenir video showing trailers from *Big Boss, Enter the Dragon, The Green Hornet.* (Andrew Upton - 2672 & John Robinson - 2734)

Madeleine Products, 15 Wallace Ave., Worthing BN11 5RA, W. Sussex, England - sell star cuttings/autobiographies/paperbacks/sheet music & magazines - sometimes on Bruce. Send for their catalogue. Their telephone number is (0903) 503551. (Andrew Upton)

Video Hire; Video Warehouse International Ltd., 329 Hunslet Road, Leeds LS10 1NJ, Yorks. Sunny Film and Video Club, Bristol, Avon - phone 0 27 2 313117.

Record Shop, 1b Mitcham Lane, Steatham, London SW16. Video Sale/Hire (have *Enter* uncensored, new at around £36 - Warners approved, legal copy.)

Bruce Records; "58 Oldies," Dean Street, London W1. They've got a whole section on Bruce... go take a look.

Regent Films, PO Box 54, Blackpool 8mm Films.

Miko Studios, Kennenwestraatweg 35, 1814 GB Alkmaar, Holland do 8mm films.

Giko Ltd., 537 Stratford Road, Sparkhill, Birmingham, Warks (phone 021-773 9247) do Bruce magazines, books, etc. There's a great selection of material here!

FAN CLUBS

Little Dragon Fan Club, A.V. Fraternidad No. 12-56, PO Box 16 's Cod., Postal 3018-A-E1 Tacuya Ealo Java, Venezuela.
World Wide Fan Club, PO Box 29164, Rio Petras, Puerto Rico OOG 2G.
Club Bruce Lee Jeet Kune Do, De Espana Apartado 707, Barcelona, Valencia 234, Spain.

MEMBER'S PICTURES AND DRAWINGS

For the moment I've got rather a pile of these to use in future news sheets - so until further notice, I'm calling a halt to sending any more in.

RENEWALS

Just a reminder to the following: members 2973 to 3056 - your second-year renewal falls due between now and the end of August. Similarly, third-year members 2698 to 2737 - and members 2303 to 2349, your fourth year is due. Also members 2022 to 2084, your fifth year is due. Please get them in as soon as you can, and I look forward to having you with us for another year.

SWOP SHOP

- Robert Hartsfield (2864), Denton, USA has for swap, *World Journal of Martial Arts* magazine - summer '78; *The Man Only I Knew* paperback by Linda (USA); *Fighting Stars* magazines; Bruce personalised pen (ballpoint); assorted good posters plus other items. Wants Bruce records; *KFM* (British); *Life and Tragic Death of Bruce Lee* by Linda.
- Andrew Smithson (1100), has Kent for sale, Betamax video of uncensored *Way of the Dragon* - fantastic action/sound. Will accept £35. Also on Super 8 film, 400' colour - *Way of the Dragon* and *Game of Death,* £10 each.
- Gerard Hayes (2237), Limerick City, Ireland wants videos (or addresses where obtainable) of *Big Boss, Fist of Fury, Way of the Dragon* and *Game of Death.*
- Ian Hamilton (1213), Sunderland, has for sale, Super 8 Sankyo Stereo 800 sound projector with case; also twin speakers (stereo) and accessories - all very good condition. Worth over £400, will accept £150 plus £10 for carriage. Also for sale, 400' colour/silent *Fist of Fury* (good action, poor quality) - £10 plus £1 p&p.
- Lenny Franchi (3120), 6 Croxley Road, London W9 wants video tapes of *Game of Death, Way of the Dragon, Fist of Fury, Big Boss, Enter the Dragon.*
- Mark James (2880), Bulwell wants Bruce Lee films on video - addresses please? Has for sale, all Bruce's fighting scenes on Super 8 colour/sound (German though) from all his films (inc. Inosanto fight). Superb quality. Plus *The Green Hornet* screentest and *The Green Hornet* episode; *Behind the scenes from Enter* and trailers from all films. Will swap for video/sell separately at reasonable prices.

Write or telephone (Nottingham).
- Suresh Gandhi (1743), Eindhoven, Holland has to swap video cassette (VHS) containing all fight scenes from all Bruce's films (uncensored, very good quality). Wants other Bruce material (books, magazines, tapes, video, 8mm film).
- Jayme Rousso (2996), Botafogo, Brazil wants the French book (published by Rene Chateau) called *La Vie et le Mort Tragique de Bruce Lee* - by Linda Lee.

PEN PALS

- Kenneth Dilsuk, St Lucia, West Indies would like, although a non-member, as many pen pals as possible; great Bruce Lee fan but needs more info on him. Make the world a little smaller by writing to him.
- Mr. H. Harry (2291), Durban, South Africa asks for a female Japanese pen pal (he tried once before, but no luck). Can anyone help put him in touch with someone?
- Gerard Hayes (2237), Limerick City, Ireland wants a Chinese/English female pen pal around his age (18-21). Gerard's hobbies are music (rock/country), martial arts, football (Manchester City), movies, etc.
- Robert Hartsfield (2864), Denton, USA would like anyone interested to write to him *re* Bruce on a serious basis - and also to trade. Please write.
- Tony Lundberg (2338), Copenhagen, Denmark wants Chinese male/female pen pals - any age. Interests are Bruce, all martial arts (but especially JKD), Kung Fu movies, Super 8 films, philosophy, Chinese Tai Chi, all kinds of music.

And that's all there's time for this quarter... tune in again soon! *Pam Hadden*

BRUCE LEE SOCIETY COLUMN
KUNG FU MONTHLY NO. 63

It's been quite a while since we had any sort of membership drive for the Bruce Lee Society. It's funny, but I find I get so involved in what we're doing that it's easy to forget there are still any number of people out there especially new Bruce Lee fans who have yet to hear of our great Society. In fact, what I plan to do is work out some campaign for 1982 because it really is time for us to take another giant step forward. I say that because, apart from anything else, it's clear there's now yet another revival of interest in the martial arts and each time that happens, there's always one name that comes out ahead of all the others; of course, Bruce Lee. It's funny the way we seem to get one pretender after another for the throne, and none of them seem to last more than a couple of minutes, at least in terms of real stardom.

If the Society is to succeed the way it has been succeeding over the past few years, it's imperative it continues to attract new blood, thoughts, ideas and enthusiasms; I see changes ahead, but changes for the good.

The suggestion I have to make is this. The Bruce Lee Society is YOUR society, and that means I want to hear from EACH AND EVERY MEMBER what they want to see us doing in 1982. So far, with just a few exceptions, we've been doing the things that we, this end, think are right. Well, it's time everyone else had their say so please don't let me down. Remember, there are two main areas to think about: one, to increase still further the number of fans who could become members of the Bruce Lee Society, and two, to "bend" things (if necessary) so that the Society follows, most exactly, the wishes of the majority of members. Are we doing enough to perpetuate the memory of Bruce Lee? Are there any new avenues to explore in our quest to maintain our number one position in world Bruce Lee affairs?

PLEASE don't just ignore this request. After all, it's probably the most important I've ever made!

- Pam Hadden

EDITOR'S NOTES

Longstreet is another Bruce Lee related item that has never been released in any medium in the UK, joining *Marlowe* and *The Green Hornet*. Created in 1971 by Stirling Silliphant, the series starred James Franciscus as insurance investigator Mike Longstreet. After a bomb kills his wife and leaves him blind, he chooses to pursue and capture his killers, after which he continues his career as an Insurance Investigator, accompanied by his seeing eye dog Pax.

Bruce Lee co-wrote several episodes in the series, starring in four of them; *The Way of the Intercepting Fist, Spell Legacy Like Death, Wednesday's Child*, and *I See, Said the Blind Man*. The full series was released on Region 2 DVD in Japan in 2007 and on Region 1 DVD in the United States in 2017.

Jesse Glover holds the honour of being Bruce Lee's first Gung Fu in the United States. Born in 1935 in Seattle, Washington, Glover met Lee in 1959, practising Judo together, before he began training in Jun Fan Gung Fu, eventually teaching his own style of Non-Classical Gung Fu, which was inspired by what he learned from Lee. Glover has written several books on martial arts including *Bruce Lee: Between Wing Chun and Jeet Kune Do, Bruce Lee's Non-Classical Gung Fu*, and *Non-Classical Gung Fu*. Jesse Gloves passed away in 2012 from cancer, aged 76.

The *Bruce Lee Souvenir* videotape was an early bootleg that appeared in several video rental stores around the country. It was a bootleg in the sense that the footage it contained was not authorised for release by any of the rights holders involved. It consisted of the *Location Hong Kong – The Making of Enter the Dragon* featurette, *Enter the Dragon* trailer, *Return Of The Dragon* trailer, *Fists of Fury* trailer, *The Chinese Connection* trailer, *The Green Hornet* episode "The Silent Gun," *Triple Irons* trailer, *Five Fingers of Death* trailer and *Lady Kung Fu* trailer.

The Chinese Detective was a British drama series, first transmitted by the BBC between 1981 and 1982, running for two series. The series starred British Chinese actor David Yip as detective Sergeant John Ho. He was the first Chinese lead actor in a British television drama series. The series featured traditional police storylines, as well as the prejudice the lead character would face whilst doing his job. Both series were released on DVD in the UK in 2008.

HI MEMBERS - AND WITHOUT FURTHER DELAY, STRAIGHT INTO THE FIRST NEWS SHEET OF THE SIXTH YEAR!!

CONVENTION CANCELLATION

What can I say? I was as stunned as yourselves when I heard that the convention had been cancelled. I'd called *KFM* on 7th August to find out when tickets were going out - and was told the convention was sadly off. Where I could I dropped a line to those members I knew (through letters to me) were coming, especially those from abroad who would be booking plane tickets and accommodation, and those travelling long distances, as I gather at that stage, a letter had not gone out generally from *Kung Fu Monthly*. I know we are all disappointed - but hope we can look forward to one again in the very near future. Any queries on ticket money refunds, future convention date - in fact anything to do with the convention cancellation - should be addressed directly to *KFM* and not myself. As most of you are aware, I don't work for *KFM* nor at their offices, and all the ticket money and requests for tickets are handled by them directly - so to save yourselves time, and me extra work, please deal directly with *KFM* on this.

LATE JUNE NEWS SHEET

You will have noticed that the June sheet is enclosed herewith, and for the delay in getting this to you, may I sincerely apologise. I wrote the sheet and sent it for printing on the 19th May - I received it back just a few days ago! As I seem to be experiencing these absolutely unbelievable delays, I have in future (or until I can guarantee a quick return of the sheets) decided to get these printed elsewhere. And at the same time get the copies of the photos, pictures etc. (which have to be done on a special machine) prepared beforehand myself - as this seems to be where the delay occurs. I feel sure that members would rather receive a news sheet which might be slightly less professional than usual ON TIME than be kept waiting literally months for it so I hope you agree. Hence you will find a considerable improvement in the September sheet getting to you - hope you all noticed!!

MEMORIAL FLOWERS

As most of you know, the Society collected donations for a floral tribute to be placed on Bruce's grave in July - in all, we collected £63 sent by the following members:

Mr. R. Gray (1628), Mr. M. Harris (1078), Mr. M. McAdam (1575), Ms. C. Bankes (2863), Mr. G. Pugh (3052), Ms R. G. Heath (3196), Ms M. Condy (1036), Mr. J. Watson (1933), Mr. Jan- Geir Hansen (3067), Mr. G. D'Ambrosio (1655), Ms. C. Kelleher (3062) and Mr. C. Kelleher, Mr. A. Stone (1150), Mr. P. Norris (2916), Mr. P. Smith (1532), Mr. P. Bell (2506), Mr. N. Wilde (3116), Mr. G. Hansen (2307), Mr. K. Coaker (2511), Mr. J. Elliott (3107), Mr. Y. Jacob (3134), Ms. M. Fernandes (2751), Mrs. A. French (1143), and me!

A pretty good total for 24 people! Anyway, you will see not only the receipt for the flowers ordered - but a letter from the Seattle florists and TWO photographs taken of our tribute at the graveside. It is such a pity that you cannot see this in colour as in the pictures - but maybe if I can get some funds together I can get copies done soon. Anyway, the display looked beautiful, and the message I sent from the Society, together with all the names of the members who donated and a picture of Bruce (which I placed in a polythene cover) can be seen slightly to the left of the bouquet. Thanks

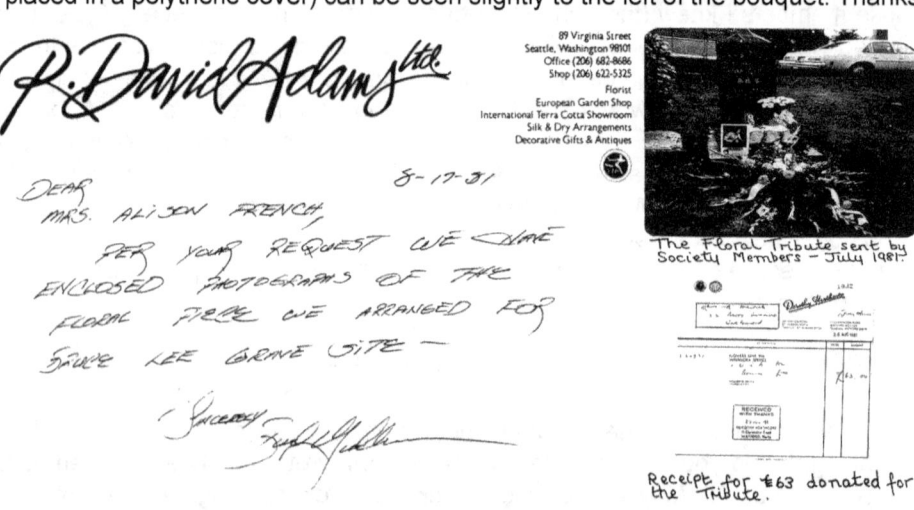

to all of you who donated and VERY SPECIAL THANKS to Alison French, who organised the whole thing on behalf of the Society!

AUCTION ITEMS

My thanks to those members who have sent in items for the convention auction to raise money for a bust of Bruce. If you all agree, I shall hold these until the next gathering. So if any of you have any items, not necessarily on Bruce, don't forget to send them along to me at London, where they are being kept safely in boxes until the day!

HOLLYWOOD PETITION

This is still going, folks! So keep the signatures pouring in, won't you? (For new members, we are sending names to the World of Bruce Lee in Hollywood to get Bruce's name placed by one of the gold stars on Hollywood Boulevard - and we need many, many more signatures - please do your best, as we are all dependant on each other in this venture.

GENERAL NEWS

Member E. D. Bow (2933) says in Russ Abbot's *Saturday Madhouse* a very poor comedy sketch was done on Bruce - he was NOT amused!

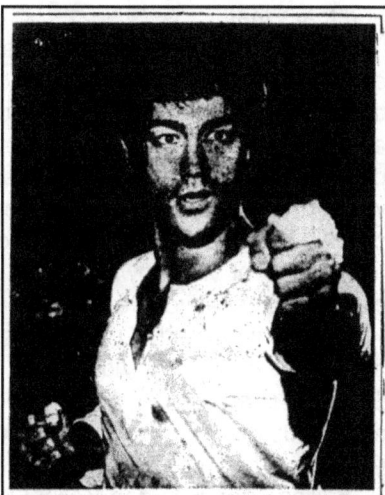

Irreplaceable star: Kung-fu star Bruce Lee, who died eight years ago, had a magic ingredient that made his action-packed thrillers sure box office hits. Hong Kong film industry has been in a slump.

Death of Kung-fu star still haunts Asian films

HONG KONG (Reuter) — The death of Kung-fu superstar Bruce Lee eight years ago is still depressing Hong Kong's once-booming film industry.

No one, it seems, can replace his magic ingredient for action-packed thrillers. Now the local industry is trying for more quality and variety, less blood and gore and instant death.

The budgets are as high or bigger, but movie moguls Sir Run Run Shaw and Raymond Chow are looking to more universal themes and international casts as a way of regaining Hong Kong's foothold in the world movie market.

The problems plaguing the industry are reflected in figures. Hong Kong burst into the market in 1972 with swashbuckling films starring Bruce Lee and setting in motion a boom that rivalled the heyday of Hollywood.

That year, about 130 films were made and output rose to 201 the following year. With Lee's death in 1973, the bubble burst. Last year output dropped to 137.

Chow's company — Golden Harvest International Group — is making a serious attempt to groom Peking Opera performer-turned-actor Jackie Chan as Lee's successor. He has become a household name in Asia but has yet to match Lee's popularity on the international screen.

The top Bruce Lee moneymaker, The Way Of The Dragon, made $1.05 million in 1973, compared with about $2.2 million for the most profitable Jackie Chan film, Young Master.

Productions by the industry before Bruce Lee were aimed at Asian audiences. Now, adding to its woes, the Southeast Asia market is shrinking.

As a Golden Harvest spokesman put it, "Audiences are being more quality-conscious. If we continue to produce quality films the future will be bright indeed."

Darryl Myers (1958) recently went with his girlfriend to see *Friday the 13th* supported by *It Lives Again*. Half way through the last film, the screen burst into action with Bruce! Darryl thought the films had got mixed up (he wasn't complaining!) as it was only on for a minute (underground scene from *Enter the Dragon*) then it went off, but Darryl said it certainly livened up an otherwise terribly boring film!!

Scott Darroch from Canada sent me a cutting recently from his local paper, showing the state of the martial arts' market at the present time in relation to films. I was pleased about the "irreplaceable star" caption - which goes to show that, with all the advertising, promoting, selling and boosting of the so-called "successors" to Bruce Lee, none of them stands a chance - they are just not good enough; and maybe at long last some of the move- makers of martial arts films are realising that, and will stop trying to "replace" Bruce and get on with the job of producing better movies with storylines different to those they keep "pinching" from Bruce. Bruce is irreplaceable, and that's that!!

Andrew Upton (2672) saw an excerpt in Dec. 1978 *Fighting Stars* magazine taken from *Bruce Lee - Incomparable Fighter* by M. Uyehara (a close friend of Bruce, they met in 1968 and he studied under Bruce for a year). It read: "Bruce got infuriated when people boasted they had taught him. Many claimed that but I (Uyehara) don't know of anyone who ever said it to his face. No one dared, because Bruce would quickly dispel it with a challenge to spar or fight. Bruce didn't receive too many praises from top martial artists because he WAS so good - besides, Bruce was not too modest about showing off his ability but he was never reluctant to back up his claims against anyone either."

Back to member E. D. Bow, he sent in a cutting about the *Daily Mirror* Video Club, advertising an *Enter the Dragon* video and a video of the martial arts' group the *Mirror* sponsored here. The *Mirror* Club might be worth joining.

Still on videos, Jorgen Moller (2886) from Denmark hired out a film called *Fist of Fear, Touch of Death*. Of course (even though a picture of Bruce was on the front of the cassette) Jorgen admits to thinking it another rip-off but, as it also mentioned stars such as Fred Williamson and Ron van Clief, he decided to see it anyway (Wise decision!) After a run-down on the stars including Louis Neglis, John "Cyclone" Flood, William "Bill" Lovie, Richard Barrathy and Ron Taganashi, a mention was made of a proposed fight for the Bruce Lee title. Then a brief run-down on Bruce including, to Jorgen's surprise, a scene from *Longstreet*, a snip from *Fist of Fury* where Bruce swings nunchakus in the Japanese academy and some stills. Regrettably, they had dubbed the *Longstreet* clip and Bruce is heard to speak of karate where in the series, he speaks of "Empty your mind, be formless, shapeless, like water etc." Featured then was more martial arts, a scene from *Thunderstorm* (again dubbed silly). This dubbing went on throughout the video, even to where Bruce is supposedly being interviewed and, using shots from various films, he is shown "answering" by a voice being dubbed over the top!! The climax of the video was the fight for the title between Neglia and Flood - with Neglia winning and being crowned as the new Bruce Lee. And that's the end, Jorgen felt (and I agree) that the dubbing was awful, but generally a good video worth fans seeing. Final note from Jorgen, this time on Jackie Chan, is that in Denmark he isn't all that famous.

David Moore (1783) bought the *Enter the Dragon* video and was pleased to find the bottle scene included - he cannot see why this was cut in the first place. He saw *Fist of Fury* at the cinema and was surprised to see the nunchakus still left in, but on seeing *Way of the Dragon* the Lee/Wall fight was cut and the bit where he shoulder-charged the boss into the chair went missing!

Ray Tidswell (1473) also saw *Enter the Dragon* at the cinema with the underground scene cut - and was stunned. So much so that he approached the manager and politely discussed the matter with him. Ray asked why after all these years, when the cinema has been filled to capacity whenever Bruce was shown, did they now show a cut version? The manager said his copy was from America where this scene was cut out; they talked for some time - and the manager, saying that he hoped it was some compensation for the cuts in *Enter the Dragon,* had a special showing for one week of *Big Boss/Game of Death* - which Ray felt, and I must agree, was super of him.

Back to David Moore again, when he recently saw a *Big Boss/Game of Death* double bill, the part where Steiner (Hugh O'Brien) slides his walking stick along the shoulder of the Bruce cardboard cut-out was missing, showing only where the knife is pushed back into the stick. That's one scene I have no objection to seeing removed - and I speak I am sure for many members!! David's cinema are showing quite a few Bruce films lately - mainly due, I am sure, to his polite but determined requests to the manager!!

An article concerning American artist Al Dacascos caught David's eye in *Fighting Arts* Vol. 4 No. 4. He was born in Honolulu of Chinese/Philippino parentage, studied Judo, Jujitsu, Kaju-Kenbo, Sil Lum Pai Kung Fu, Kung Fu, Tai Mantis (combination of Tai Chi Chuan and Praying Mantis) and Escrima. It mentioned a run-in with Bruce, where apparently, David says, after Bruce's fight with Wong Jack Man around 1965, Al was also told to stop teaching non-Chinese or face

a Chinese champion. He refused, beat the champ, and Al's pupils started saying he was better than Bruce. Fighting between Bruce and Al's pupils led to their meeting, but instead of fighting they talked it over and decided their pupils were at fault! They both agreed they each had a good style and left it at that! Several times they trained together exchanging ideas to improve each others' techniques.

Some weeks back I watched the T.V. programme *Quincy* - and it seems I was not alone in spotting the similarity between the episode titled *Touch of Death* and one of the rumours incorrectly surrounding Bruce's death. David Moore (hello again!) and Mark Salter (1792) (Hi! Mark) both wrote to me - it dealt with the murder of an up-and-coming martial arts film star who was (as quoted in the programme) the next

Bruce Lee. There were other similarities to Bruce - such as being an excellent martial artist, keep-fit fanatic, and the mysterious circumstances surrounding his death. The final cause of the star's death in *Quincy* was found to be Dim Mak - delayed death strike (Vibrating Palm) - one of the stories going around was that Bruce died by this technique; it is said that a skilful practitioner of this is able to place his hand, or indeed finger, on the body of another person and, by sending an unfelt "shockwave" through the body can induce death in anything from minutes to months - depending on the part of the body touched and the susceptibility of the person (or part of the body touched) at that time. I must admit

that the programme was well researched, as Mark also pointed out, handled sensibly, and made good viewing. However - on that note - let me assure you that this rumoured story on Bruce IS only a rumour.

Mike Devereux (1061) was recently sent a questionnaire by Sue Kennedy of BBC Enterprises Ltd., 54-58 Uxbridge Road, Ealing, London, W5 2TF, (Telephone: (01) 579 0512), and it asks people to give info under various titles (e.g. sports, music etc.) as to what they would most like to see on BBC TV. Needless to say, under the "Special Interest" section, we all know what Mike will be asking for! If some of you want to do the same thing - why not contact Sue for a copy of the questionnaire and request Bruce (especially the documentary which the BBC have). But it might be wise not to mention Mike's name as to where you got the address - just in case Sue or whoever decides to take revenge!! David (I've heard that name before!) says there is to be a range of martial arts equipment produced using Chuck Norris' name - including karate/full combat uniforms, special stretch-denim jeans and safety equipment, Chuck being very specific about quality and safety in this field. I'll keep you informed of suppliers when I hear on this.

BRUCE LEE NO JOGO DA MORTE
BRUCE LEE -

I recently had the good fortune to be invited by Todd Slaughter (who runs the Official Elvis Presley Fan Club) to see the preview of the new El movie, now released - *This is Elvis*. As many of you know, I am also a keen El fan too, and found the film not only splendidly done with some unbelievably rare shots of El, his family and friends, but so nostalgic as to reduce me to tears in many places - it was a documentary of his

Norman Borine from The World of Bruce Lee - Hollywood.

life, using actors for him as a boy and for the opening shots of "him" entering Gracelands on the night of his death and saying goodnight to his daughter through the door; after that, flashbacks and sequences from his films, stage shows, interviews etc., plus even a snippet of the Beatles thrown in!! The whole film was well put together and enjoyable, and a real tribute to the King of Rock 'n Roll. So why can't someone produce something like this for Bruce - the *King of Kung Fu*? Not the second-rate rubbish produced with some second-rate acting and wicked little innuendos to promote more idiotic rumours surrounding Bruce's life and death, and 'praised' in many cases by sensationalistic publicity-seekers who in reality cannot tell a good martial artist from a Punch-and-Judy doll - we want a well-documented and sensibly produced film so that anyone seeing this will begin to get more of an insight into Bruce. I really cannot understand the long delay in this film being produced - if anyone warrants it, Bruce does.

Thomas Jones (2058) became a fan of Bruce from the first time he saw him on T.V.'s *Cinema* programme about Kung Fu films generally. He admits to splitting his sides laughing, with his brother, at the antics of some "stars" in the programme which were so far-fetched - but when "the legendary Bruce Lee" was introduced (and after thinking "Who the heck is he?") they were transfixed by his face on the screen and his skill and had to find out more about him - so when *Enter the Dragon* was showing locally off they went, to be overwhelmed - with the rest of the tightly packed audience, from young to old, male and female - and became devoted fans from that day!! Thomas also mentioned that when he saw a film on TV called *Once upon a time in the West* starring Charles Bronson, he is sure the music is that used when Bruce searches for Chuck in the Coliseum in *Way of the Dragon*; he's heard the *Big Boss* music in a TV series called *Bluey* and wonders how many other members noticed soundtracks from Bruce's films being used like this?

Shown to the right is a memorial notice from a Seattle newspaper.

Lenny Franchi (3120) paid his own tribute to Bruce on the anniversary of his passing over by burning a candle from mid-day until midnight, surrounded by a pair of nunchakus and a picture. But something quite odd happened to Lenny - he decided to play the James Coburn tribute at three minutes to midnight, and dead on twelve the record stopped and the candle flicked out! It gave Lenny quite a strange feeling as though the Master was there. I know I would have felt the same.

Simon Bulley (2738) has recently got back from a trip to Hong Kong - I'd given him the Golden Harvest address and told him to make himself known to them by writing first, and that I was sure they would show him around the studios. In fact,

Simon was very happy to find them most helpful and friendly, and he was shown around and met some of the many artists and actors I'd met there previously during one of my visits. Simon's account of his time at GH is quite informative and lengthy - in fact it would take up rather a lot of the news sheet in itself! But I think it makes excellent reading - and what I propose doing is to either include the whole article in with the December news sheet OR, if I can persuade *KFM* to put it in their next issue, I will do that. Simon also met Jackie Chan, and found him, as I did, a really nice guy. One thing I can tell you - Jackie himself was disappointed with his *Big Brawl/Cannonball Run* - he had expected complete control over the fight scenes but this had not happened. He feels his next film, *The Protector*, will be big - it is rather like the contemporary police series *Dirty Harry*, set in modern San Francisco, about two rogue cops.

Our member Setudeh Nejad (1419) out in Seattle sent in a cutting showing *Variety Magazine* gross picture ratings during showings a month or so back of various films - a Bruce Lee Festival grossed US $150,000 it's first week and US $115,000 the second. Interesting to note is Jackie's *Cannonball Run* grossed US $2,012,675 which is pretty good, but of course they also have some well-known stars in it too to pull the audiences, such as Farrah Fawcett.

Two references to Bruce in the New York Top 10 Showcase: "Bruce Lee the late martial arts hero" and "Bruce Lee the late Kung Fu great." Seattle University's Language Centre shows a Bruce movie every July - this year it was *Enter the Dragon*.

VIDEO

THE top ten video films this week are:—
1 Alien
2 Damien—Omen II
3 Monty Python & The Holy Grail
4 The Deerhunter
5 Enter The Dragon
6 Straw Dogs
7 Jaws
8 Startrek : The Motion Picture
9 The Omen
10 One Flew Over The Cuckoo's Nest

By courtesy of HMV

LETTERS

Dear Pam,

The sickest news I've heard lately was in the Burton Daily Mail *- the local cinema was showing Bruce Li in* The Dragon Lives *supported by Bruce in* Enter the Dragon *- terrible!*

P.S. I noticed the new Society notepaper "World President" - WOW! Do Ronald Reagan and Maggie Thatcher know about you, Pam?

Arthur Stone (1150)

As I said to Arthur when I wrote to him, it's an insult to have Bruce supporting a Li film - but then, on the other hand, I think that Li needs support, eh? I had to laugh, Arthur, about "World President" - but I reckon I'd do better than old Maggie any day - at least I'd have five days off a year as public holidays in celebration of Bruce!

A RETROSPECTIVE LOOK AT BRUCE LEE MANIA & THE KUNG FU CRAZE OF THE 1970S

Dear Pam,

I recently saw Enter the Dragon *on video and the bottle scene for the first time - can you please tell me, Pam, why the censors removed this sequence? After all I have seen many Western films where people use bottles to smash over someone's head! Yet the censors leave them alone - are they just prejudiced or what?? Surely in this day and age, years after their original release, what harm can these scenes do?*

Neil Wilde (3116)

Neil - we keep getting the same answers, and that is "too violent" - and yes, before you are driven to pulling out your hair in frustration, I too have seen films a hundred times more "violent" than Bruce's left completely untouched. However, I also know that a lot of the missing parts are not necessarily the work of the censors - particularly some of the scenes I've heard are missing. Projectionists are known to snip little bits out here and there - and that is partly why there are such shocking copies around lately. There again, I have known members who are still seeing uncut versions of Bruce's films locally - it just seems unfair that not all his films are intact. I feel too that if I contact the censors and ask why some cinemas show uncut versions whilst others are cut to ribbons, they might JUST go out looking for the good copies - with further disastrous results! Best let sleeping dogs lie, so to speak!!

Dear Pam,

Being in the Forces, I have quite a few foreign friends, and recently one of them showed a movie from the States of Game of Death *- I was over the moon when, for the first time, I saw the Lee/Inosanto battle - was my adrenalin count high! I even got them to show the last reel again containing all three fights - I figure I'm a very lucky person!!*

Shaun Boland (2805)

I hope that eventually everyone can get to see this uncut film - especially those members so far away without easy access to a cinema. It is a super fight - and yes, you ARE lucky!

RENEWALS

Members - a reminder about renewals: 3057-3108 - your second year is due between now and the end of November; also 2738-2803 - your third year; 2350-2530 - your fourth year; 2085- 2170 - your fifth year; and finally 1001-1627 your sixth year is up!! So please - just make sure you pop your renewal off pronto so you are kept in the picture on Bruce!!

ITEMS FOR SALE / BARGAIN BASEMENT

Still available, and a MUST for collectors and new members who have not got this yet, is the Robert Lee L.P. *Ballad of Bruce Lee* containing the title song and such songs as *JKD* and *Parting* - all sung by Bruce's younger brother Robert! Loads more to hear and superbly done. And at an unbelievable bargain price FOR THIS PERSONALLY SIGNED COPY ON THE COVER BY ROBERT HIMSELF!

Price? £4.50 (including postage/packing) in the U.K. (Europe :5.50, rest of the world £6.50).

A black and white PERSONALLY SIGNED BY ROBERT picture of him and Bruce together, with Bruce doing a flying kick over Robert's head! £1.20 (inc. p.&p.) U.K. (Europe £1.40, rest of world £1.50).

Both the record and picture are rare and not to be missed. Cheques/money orders made payable to Pam Hadden, please - and sent to London. All monies for these items go to Robert via me.

So many of you ask about back issues of NEWS SHEETS - so I am now going to make these available to you - from Issue 1 upwards - at a cost of £1.60 for the first 16 issues, which takes you up to and including the June, 1980 edition. If you want copies of the September/December 1980 or the March 1981, these can be ordered at an additional cost of 10p each with the first 16 copies, HOWEVER, ANY INDIVIDUAL NEWS SHEET ORDERED ON IT'S OWN WILL COST 10p plus 14p postage - FROM 3-10 SHEETS WILL STILL COST 10p each plus 20p postage - OR IF YOU ORDER 11 SHEETS OR MORE, STILL 10p each plus 40p postage. (European members/foreign members - please contact me before ordering with your requirements so I can inform you of postage cost beforehand). Cheques/orders made payable to Pam Hadden again as above. All this money will hopefully be going into a Society "kitty" I am starting, for future projects.

SPECIAL MESSAGES & REQUESTS

Congratulations to Paul Wade (1836) and his wife who married on 12th Septem-

THE ROBERT LEE ALBUM!

A Must For Every True Bruce Lee Collector.

In recording this album, Bruce's brother, Robert, paid the finest compliment he could to tne memory of the Master!

His admiration and feeling of loss for the Little Dragon's sad passing have been captured superbly on this fine, top quality LP. Many of the tracks are self-penned, some you may know already. One in fact was co-written by Bruce himself!

The album is not on general release and therefore you're unlikely to find it in many shops. Don't miss out on this unique opportunity – order now while stocks last.

Send £4.35 (includes handling) to:
Robert Lee Album Offer
Kung-Fu Monthly
14 Rathbone Place
London W1P 1DE
(Cheques and postal orders made payable to KFM).

CLUB MEMBER'S PRICE...£4.10.

ber - we wish them good luck for the future, and Paul wanted to say to Kim, through the news sheet, that he loves her very much.

Michelle Scully (2919) does her own headed paper, and is willing to do some for members at 40p for 25 sheets (not including postage). For a sample, drop her a SAE PLUS a 5p stamp to cover her costs and she'll pop a couple of sheets off to you so you see what you get!!

Philip Bell (2506) contacted a company about getting copies of the Bruce Lee JKD Club Yin/Yang emblem made to put on a pullover; as minimum orders are 12 @ £9.95 (around 81p each), Philip wondered if other members would contact him direct if they want one. As Philip has to post emblem to members should they want one, you will have to work out a price with him on this. His address is Leeds.

Has anyone seen/heard of a double *Game of Death* LP? If so, please inform Paul Wade at Hull - he has heard a rumour one is released by Columbia.

Would members inform Caroline Andrew (2939) of any places for info etc. on other stars, especially David Chiang, Fu Sheng, Sonny Chiba. Also Caroline needs held in tracing a film she saw on "Arena" where the comedy here was swinging sausages as nunchakus (she thinks he worked in a restaurant). Caroline's address is Wakefield.

SWOP SHOP

- Avtar Sohota, Warley has for swap only: *My Martial Arts Training Guide to JKD* + three B&W autographed Bruce pictures for *KFM*s 1 & 2 in good condition. Will swap 10 assorted martial arts magazines on Bruce + autographed photo and *Enter the Dragon* poster all good condition for *Bruce Lee in Action* + *KFM* 31. For sale only: Chinese Kung Fu jacket (as Bruce wore) (top quality in black & white detachable collar, sewn in cuffs, four outside pockets, two inside - up to age 17 Chinese size, as new £17 inc. p&p, also good condition Shogun made Karate jacket, fit age 16 Japanese size) - £5.50 inc. p&p + free belt. (Both jackets 100% cotton). Bruce Lee special cassette of trailers/interviews/*Enter the Dragon* documentary/screen tests/*The Green Hornet*/early Bruce in Hong Kong + 8 B&W autographed pictures for £7.25 inc. p&p. Photofile of six greatest stars inc. Bruce/Elvis, also three magazines with Elvis articles + last convention badges & *Enter the Dragon* poster - £3,55 inc. p&p. Write to Avtar before sending items or telephone.
- Vernon Norgrove, Warley has for sale on Bruce: 17 books, two action motion books, 24 posters, 27 B&W photos, two LP's *Enter the Dragon, Game of Death,* one mirror, large velvet framed picture, pair nunchakus £25-£40 ono. Write/telephone Oldbury.
- John Deakin, Liverpool has for sale/swap: Super 8mm colour/sound 20min. *Game of Death* featurette inc. Inosanto and Jabbar fights and film credits - excellent quality - £22, *The Green Hornet* single record - swap for *KFM* 2 or 31, *The Green Hornet* 1960's comic good condition + *Enter the Dragon* LP - swap both for either *Bruce Lee Inedit* or *Tao of JKD*.
- Carl Wallace, Darlington (Tel: Darlington XXXXX) has for sale: New copy *Enter the Dragon* LP - £7.
- Margaret Smith, has for sale: lots of Bruce items - two *Young Idol Now* maga-

zines @ £8 ea, 100 stills - £30, about 50 colour slides - £20, Posters, Chinese magazines - rare/good condition, plus hundreds B&W off-screen shots.
- Wilson McKenna, Airdrie, has for sale: 16mm *The Green Hornet* screen-test USA film, good condition - £10.
- Thomas King, Dunfermline has for swap: *KFM*s 33/34/35, *Dragon* magazines 2-11 inc. & Vol. 2 Nos. 2/3/6/8, *Clash* Vol. 1 3-6 inc, *Fighting Arts* Vol. 2 Nos. 2-4 inc, *Karate & Oriental Arts* No. 53, *Combat* Vol. 1 No. 5, assorted *Clash* posters. Will swap for: original 7"/12" records of any three of following: *Three Wheels on my Wagon* (New Christie Minstrels), *Banner Man* (*Blue Mink/Turn the Beat Around* (Vicki/Sue Robinson), *Rupert* (Jackie Lee), *Massachusetts* (Bee Gees), *Pop Goes the Weasel* (Tony Newley), *I Talk to the Trees* (Clint Eastwood).
- Roy Braithwaite, Westwood has for sale: two mint Bruce Lee *Way of the Dragon* films - both reels 400ft/Super 8mm/sound/German - Reel one covering all fights including nunchakus, Reel two Lee/Norris fight - cost £36 ea. - sell for £28 ea.
- Tim Ussher, Crowborough has for sale: Super 8mm colour/sound films: Bruce trailers, *Fistful of Yen*, *Enter the Dragon* production behind scenes, *Enter the Dragon* film. Non-sound/colour: *Marlowe*, Bruce nunchakus film, *Fist of Fury* reels one & two, *Game of Death*, *Way of the Dragon* plus two good condition projectors.
- Andrew Upton, Birkenhead has for sale (not to be split): *KFM*s 3-38 and Trade Dummy, two flick books, two single 45rpm records *Way of the Dragon*, *Fist of Fury*, *Bruce Lee Revenges*, *Unbeatable Bruce Lee*, *Untold Story*, *Bruce Lee in Action*, *Game of Death*, *JKD* (not Tao), *King of Kung Fu*, *Who Killed Bruce Lee*, *Bruce Lee Nunchakus in Action*, *KFM Scrapbooks 1 & 2*, *Immortal Bruce Lee*, *KFM "GOD" Special*, *Fighting Stars* book - all mint condition - £20 plus £5 p&p.

I'm running out of space, folks - so that's it for this time - had to put some items I could not fit into this sheet on the first page of June sheet whilst it was stuck at printers - anyway, back soon with more info - take care.
PEACE, LOVE, BROTHERHOOD. Pam

EDITOR'S NOTES

The *Kung Fu Monthly* Third Bruce Lee Convention was sadly cancelled, with no reason given at all. Pam had stated in the newsletter that she had called KFM to enquire when tickets were being sent out, only to be told that the event was cancelled. This is corroborated in a letter to Danish member Tony Lundberg dated 8th August 1981, the day after she found out of the cancellation. She wrote, "To say I was shocked is to put it mildly - no one had discussed a possible cancellation with me nor given me to believe that this would be likely to happen. Indeed, *KFM* had not been in contact with me about the format of the convention for many weeks."

As the convention was organised by *KFM*, it was they who held the details of convention-goers, meaning Pam was only able to contact a very few of them with the bad news. She continued, "As you will know, I have nothing whatsoever to do with the sending out of tickets for the convention, nor do I receive the money for this, and as a consequence therefore am unable to contact those people who have written in for tickets to *KFM*, other than yourself who I know (through your letters to me) will be attending - and I felt it my duty to write to you as soon as I possibly could to let you know what had happened. I would appreciate if you could contact anyone who was to travel with you to the convention or that you know was going to attend if you are able, to tell them what has happened. I am contacting *KFM* on Monday to request that they make some sort of announcement informing people of their cancellation, which is their responsibility."

She continued. "My very sincerest apologies for any inconvenience caused to you – but I can assure you it was not of my doing and I knew NOTHING of this until yesterday; even some members, on ringing *KFM* - about their tickets, knew of the cancellation four days before myself, yet I had not been contacted by *KFM*."

Unfortunately, neither *Kung Fu Monthly*, nor the Bruce Lee Society would go on to hold another convention. In later years however, there would be more conventions in the UK. "Bootleg King" Chris Alexis' "Tracking The Dragon" convention featured John Saxon, Howard Williams, and Bob Baker. His 1992 "Tracking The Dragon" convention featured Bruce Lee's daughter Shannon Lee, who only showed up after refusing to appear at a rival convention. The story goes that Shannon was due to attend a convention for the documentary *Death By Misadventure*. However, after landing in London, she called her mother Linda, who informed Shannon that she had just seen the documentary and was appalled by the content. She instructed Shannon not to attend the convention and instead, to get the next flight back home, which would have been the next day. While waiting for the flight, Chris Alexis found out about what had happened and managed to not only organise a last minute convention, but also to convince Shannon to show up as the special guest! Now, anyone that had been to Chris Alexis' conventions will know why he had the nickname of the "Bootleg King." For the uninitiated, Alexis would sell bootleg videos by the hundreds at his conventions. If he had it and could copy it, he'd sell you it. As Shannon was whisked into the convention by Alexis, she noticed huge trestle tables with cloth sheets covering their contents. When she asked what was on the tables, she was told, "Oh, nothing," and taken abruptly to the stage. As soon as she was through the doors, the table cloths were whipped off, to reveal hundreds of bootleg videotapes, which the convention staff proceeded to sell.

The Sunny Film Society at the ABC cinema in Hull was able to show uncut Bruce Lee films as mentioned previously in the book. As the showings were private screenings only for members of a club or society, the usual censorship rules didn't apply. The Sunny Film Society also used the same  loophole to show uncut Bruce Lee films at the ABC cinemas in Leeds and Bradford.

A RETROSPECTIVE LOOK AT BRUCE LEE MANIA & THE KUNG FU CRAZE OF THE 1970S

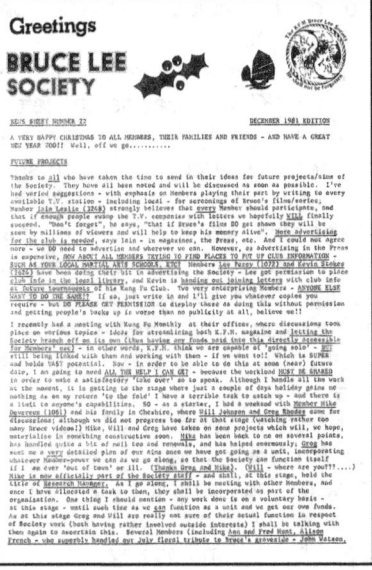

22
December
1981

A VERY HAPPY CHRISTMAS TO ALL MEMBERS, THEIR FAMILIES AND FRIENDS - AND HAVE A GREAT NEW YEAR TOO!! WELL, OFF WE GO...

FUTURE PROJECTS

Thanks to all who have taken the time to send in their ideas for future projects/aims of the Society. They have all been noted and will be discussed as soon as possible. I've had varied suggestions - with emphasis on members playing their part by writing to every available TV station - including local - for screenings of Bruce's films/series.

Member Iain Leslie (3248) strongly believes that every member should participate, and that if enough people swamp the TV companies with letters we hopefully WILL finally succeed. "Don't forget," he says, "that if Bruce's films DO get shown they will be seen by millions of viewers and will help to keep his memory alive." More advertising for the club is needed, says Iain - in magazines, the press, etc. And I could not agree more - we DO need to advertise and wherever we can. However, as advertising in the press is expensive, HOW ABOUT ALL MEMBERS TRYING TO FIND PLACES TO PUT UP CLUB INFORMATION -SUCH AS YOUR LOCAL MARTIAL ARTS SCHOOLS, ETC?

Members Lee Percy (1072) and Kevin Stokes (2624) have been doing their bit in advertising the Society - Lee got permission to place club info in the local library, and Kevin is handing out joining letters with club info at future tournaments of his Kung Fu Club. Two very enterprising members - ANYONE ELSE WANT TO DO THE SAME?? If so, just write in and I'll give you whatever copies you require - but DO

PLEASE GET PERMISSION to display these as doing this without permission and getting people's backs up is worse than no publicity at all, believe me!!

I recently had a meeting with *Kung Fu Monthly* at their offices, where discussions took place on various topics - ideas for streamlining both *KFM* magazine and letting the Society branch off on its own (thus having any funds paid into this directly accessible for members' use) - in other words, *KFM* think we are capable of "going solo" - BUT still being linked with them and working with them - if we want to!! Which is SUPER and holds VAST potential. Now - in order to be able to do this at some (near) future date, I am going to need ALL THE HELP I CAN GET - because the workload MUST BE SHARED in order to make a satisfactory "take over" so to speak. Although I handle all the work at the moment, it is getting to the stage where just a couple of days holiday gains me nothing as on my return "to the fold" I have a terrible task to catch up - and there is a limit to anyone's capabilities.

So, as a starter, I had a weekend with member Mike Devereux (1061) and his family in Cheshire, where Will Johnston and Greg Rhodes came for discussions; although we did not progress too far at that stage (watching rather too many Bruce videos!) Mike, Will and Greg have taken on some projects which will, we hope, materialise in something constructive soon. Mike has been back to me on several points, has handled quite a bit of mail too and renewals, and has helped enormously; Greg has sent me a very detailed plan of our aims once we have got going as a unit, incorporating whatever member-power we can as we go along, so that the Society can function itself if I am ever "out of town" or ill. (Thanks Greg and Mike). (Will - where are you???) Mike is now officially part of the Society staff - and shall, at this stage, hold the title of Research Manager.

As I go along, I shall be meeting with other members, and once I have allocated a task to them, they shall be incorporated as part of the organisation. One thing I should mention - any work done is on a voluntary basis - at this stage - until such time as we can function as a unit and we get our own funds. As at this stage Greg and Will are really not sure of their actual function in respect of Society work (both having rather involved outside interests) I shall be talking with them again to ascertain this.

Several members (including Ann and Fred Hunt, Alison French - who superbly handled our July floral tribute to Bruce's graveside - John Watson, Michelle Scully, Ann Jones, Simon Bulley, Nigel Martin, Arthur Stone - and many more) have all offered their help - and I intend to meet with them as soon as feasibly possible to discuss things in detail and see what assistance each can give to the Society. It will take time - I have handled everything by myself for some years, and now is the time for a team to be formed to give the Society a chance to expand. The only aspect of the club which I did not handle was the ordering of kit items, headed Society paper, etc., and in order to take this over gradually and know the routine, I shall be working closely with Colin at *KFM* to get to know WHO to order from, how to get a satisfactory result (no more delayed news sheets if I go back to a printer in the future!) But this is something which I want someone in the club to handle on my behalf once I know the routine and can explain to them. The sooner the club gets organised, and a team formulated, the better and to start the ball rolling.

MEETING OF LONDON-BASED MEMBERS

I propose having a meeting of members from the London (and closely-surrounding areas) towards the end of January, 1982 - say 23rd or 30th January, on a Saturday early afternoon, somewhere in the West End of London. At this stage, I want a POSTCARD ONLY PLEASE saying if you can attend, and giving your name, membership number and address. When a date is known, you will be notified, giving time, place, etc. - and I will expect a card BACK from you to say if you still intend to come. PLEASE NOTE: Only London/close by members (such as Croydon, Bromley, etc. - anywhere on the close proximity of London) should write in - there WILL BE MEETINGS IN OTHER AREAS LATER. Hopefully, *Kung Fu Monthly* will pay for the hire of a small hall - but we shall have to supply our own foodstuffs. As the meeting will probably take place over a Public House (where else??) food will be available.

FUTURE TRIP TO HONG KONG AND/OR THE U.S.A.

Several members enquired about the possibility of a trip. The main reason for this NOT getting off the ground at this stage is that I personally did not get much response on mentions of this nature in the past. Also, I think I should explain the following: if a trip can be organised, it does not appear (from my findings to date) to be cheap. Obviously, it is dependant upon the amount of people going, as any price quoted will be based on the number of participants at that time - and if, at some future date, several people decide to drop out for any reason, then THEIR portion of the cost will have to be borne by the balance of people remaining. Now you can see just part of the problem. We therefore have to have a guarantee beforehand that ALL seats will be filled. Obviously, we might be able to get a good deal somewhere - but if any of you out there are au fait with the travel trade, have any contacts you can get info from or figures, please let me know. Also, ON A POSTCARD ONLY PLEASE, I would like anyone interested in a trip to inform me: a) The maximum you could afford for fares, hotel and spending money; b) Just how long you would expect to be away (I personally think one week); c) Where you would prefer to go - HONG KONG OR U.S.A. (bearing in mind a combination of both could well be out of our price-range - unless we get a good deal somewhere); d) What you would expect to see; e) What month(s) you would prefer to go. I will not be acknowledging these cards - they will be catalogued, the information kept and used in any plans for any trip organised. I will keep you informed of any progress in this respect in the news sheets.

CONVENTION

I do not have any date from *KFM* re the next convention - but I do not see it coming off personally until the Spring. However, if you have queries or enquiries on this, please call *KFM* direct (Tel: (01) 631 1433) to see when they plan to hold this. Obviously, I do not have the resources to finance such

WHAT age was the film actor Bruce Lee when he died, and when was he born?—Chris Kane, Inchrory Place, Drumchapel, Glasgow.
★★ The star of Kung-Fu movies was 33. He was born in 1940.

THE BRUCE LEE SOCIETY

THIS WINTER BE PROUD TO WEAR THE OFFICAL KUNG-FU MONTHLY SWEAT SHIRT

There's never been another shirt like it! It's warm, it's colourful (deep red and green on winter white) and of course it proclaims the message we all want to hear.

Stocks will be strictly limited so, to be fair, orders will be dealt with on a first come first serve basis. That means, to be absolutely sure of getting your official KFM sweat shirt, you must order NOW!

Just send a cheque or postal order for £8.50 (Society members, £8.00) – that's made out to Kung-Fu Monthly to:-
KFM Sweat Shirt Offer, 14 Rathbone Place, London W1P 1DE

Please state whether you require size small, medium or large and, finally, don't forget to write your name and address CLEARLY!

a venture on my own (at this stage) and organisation on this will HAVE to come from *KFM*. However, I am checking out the possibility of a film festival with the assistance of Golden Harvest in London. When I have more information, I shall let you know, either by news sheet or the Society Section in *Kung Fu Monthly* magazine allocated to us.

NEWS SHEETS

Hope you ALL noticed the fact that the news sheet has gone out on schedule this month!! We are now over one major hurdle and it should not occur again!

SPECIAL MESSAGES

Happy Birthday to Ann Hunt and to all members having birthdays around this time!. Of course, Robert Lee's birthday is on 16th December, too!

Get well wishes go to Eric Canham, recovering after an accident, and Nigel Martin, who was in hospital too. (We are trying to keep members, you two, not lose them!!)

Special thoughts to Wesley Fleming and Patrick Hennessy, too.

Tracey Bennett says a big "Thank you" to the members who so kindly helped her to get a Bruce collection back together again - thanks to Kevin Stokes, Peter Reynolds and Mark Elliott.

RENEWALS

Members - herewith reminders: 3129-3180 - your second year is due between beginning of December and end of February, 1982. The following are also due at this time too: 2804-2907 - third year; 2531-2599 - fourth year; 2171-2266 - fifth year. 1628-1828 - sixth year. I look forward to having you all with us again for the next year!!

AUCTION ITEMS

Although no definite convention date, please still keep the auction items coming in for raising money at a future meeting for the Bruce Lee bust. It doesn't matter if the items are not on Bruce or the martial arts world - anything will be acceptable; send along to me at London, where they are being safely kept until the day!

HOLLYWOOD PETITION

Keep the signatures coming in for the World of Bruce Lee in Hollywood to be able to have Bruce's name placed by a gold star on Hollywood Boulevard - get the signatures ANYWHERE you can.

BARGAIN BASEMENT

Still for sale is the superb Robert Lee L.P. *Ballad of Bruce Lee,* personally signed on the cover by Robert himself!! A real collector's item - and not to be missed! It costs £4.50 (including postage/packaging) in the U.K. (Europe £5.50, rest of the world £6.50). Also, the black and white personally signed by Robert picture showing Bruce doing a flying kick over Robert's head!! Cost £1.20 inc. postage/packing U.K. (Europe £1.40; rest of the world £1.50). All cheques/postal orders payable to Pam Hadden, please, and sent directly to London. All monies for these items go to Robert via me.

If you still want back-issues of the news sheets, it still costs £1.60 from issue 1 up to and including June, 1980. For full details, refer to the last news sheet. Foreign members please contact me first with your requirements so I can inform you of cost with postage, BEFORE sending any money.

GENERAL NEWS

Member Bob Hartsfield (2864) from the U.S.A. is still pursuing the TV stations (see June news sheet) to screen *The Green Hornet.* Still unsuccessful in this venture, he has at least got a screening of *Marlowe,* which he reckons is better than nothing! Also (lucky devil!) on their Cable TV they have a regular showing of Bruce's films, and the programme director states that Kung Fu films are their most requested. Bob also has an almost complete set of picture cards from *The Green Hornet* which he managed to pick up - and is on behalf of the Society trying to see how suitable copies can be made at a reasonable price for sale to members. More on that next issue, hopefully. They are very unique.

David Dixon (1650) recommends a film called *Martial Arts* which he bought for his projector. At first, he was unsure of its content, but took the word of the salesman that

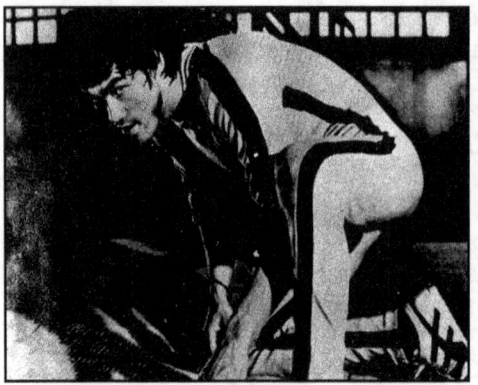

Bruce was on it - and David was glad he did!! It contained trailers for *Big Boss, Fist of Fury, Way of the Dragon, Enter the Dragon* (under American titles), together with *Triple Irons* (*New One Armed Swordsman*), *Lightning Swords of Death, Five Fingers of Death* (*King Boxer?*) and *Lady Kung Fu* (*Hapkido*). As David says: "The Americans don't really have censorship so all Bruce's films are shown as originally intended - WHOLE! (Take note, Mr. Ferman (Secretary of the British Board of Film Censors), says David!) I am sure that the non-Bruce films mentioned above will interest many Kung Fu fanatics too!

Iain Leslie (3248) recently bought *Game of Death* from Py Tang (see "Useful Addresses"). Although the film was not the best of quality, to see the complete UNCENSORED LEE/INOSANTO fight was, he said, truly amazing - an unbelievable fight!! It cost him £23 plus £1 postage/packing plus £5 for life membership to the video club. Incidentally, he timed the fight scenes as follows: Hapkido fight - two min, 32 seconds/Lee-Inosanto fight - three mins, 17 seconds/Lee-Jabbar fight - four mins, 55 seconds - total 10 mins, 4 secs! As Iain says, Danny Inosanto was quoted as giving a total of 28 minutes of fight scenes being filmed - so where are the other 18 minutes? (Pam here - I was informed when visiting Golden Harvest in Hong Kong that there was, in fact, more footage "in the can" - including an outside fight scene; as to where it is now, or what is intended doing with it, that remains to be seen. We know it is not being used for *Tower of Death* as this "epic" will incorporate footage edited from Bruce's films before going to the scissor-happy censors!

Still on timings of fights, those from *Way of the Dragon* were checked by Douglas Banks (2839) - and the total, including the Coliseum fight, came to just 6 1/2 mins. And the censors say they do not cut out much! Douglas also found an old cinema programme with an article on Bruce which, although the facts were a little mixed - Douglas thought in this case they were a little cute!

Back to Iain, and the letter he received from Granada Television *re* his request for a showing of the *Green Hornet*. Again, as with the BBC, another complete blank, but we won't give up! Why not drop a line to Granada Television and back Iain up on his request??

Still with Iain, after writing in to me stating they NEVER show Bruce movies in his area, he recently had both *Way of the Dragon/Fist*

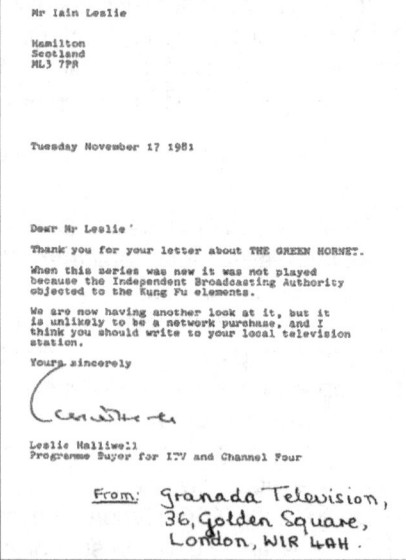

of Fury showing - but so VERY badly censored. However, he said the audiences still seemed to love the films, and as always they were good entertainment - censored or not.

In comparison, Stephen Ward (1941) belongs to the KC Film Club (Life Membership 25p then £2.25 admission fee to films thereafter), which shows Kung Fu films. The Club goes all over the country, although Stephen's is based at Slough, Berks, (see "Useful Addresses"). They show Bruce regularly and recently had the complete uncut *Way of the Dragon* - the place was packed and full of tension and anticipation. KC Club promised Stephen more Bruce films - members should contact them and see where their nearest club is. THAT's the *Way of the Dragon* to see the *The Big Boss* in action!!

Peter Reynolds (2900) got to see *Enter the Dragon* recently paired with *Black Belt Jones* (Jim Kelly). However, if you see the advertisement, it gives the star of Jim's film as Bruce! Talk about conning people!! No wonder there are many people around that think every Kung Fu film out must have Bruce in it - and are seeing on many occasions just a load of absolute 23rd-rate rubbish! Take the Li films - and the times they are advertised with Bruce Lee's name alongside! I suppose as long as the cinema managers get the money from the people, they don't really care how they get them into the cinema. If any members see a film advertised that blatantly states the Little Dragon is starring in it, and he isn't, PLEASE SEND THE NAME AND ADDRESS OF THE CINEMA, THE FILM DETAILS, AND THE DATE SHOWING, so that I can pass the info to Golden Harvest. This representation must STOP. NOW!

On the opposite front, one thing I am in favour of - if they HAVE to show censored versions of Bruce's films - is to let people know this before entering the cinema - and I have to give full marks to the ABC Cinema in Wigan who DID state that fact on their advert. And although it was put as the second feature (which I do not agree with), at least it was teamed with a decent film starring Clint Eastwood - *The Enforcer*. (Cutting sent by Thomas Jones - 2058).

Thomas also says that in an interview with Bruce's barber in an old *Fighting Stars* magazine, (his name is Joe Torrenueva), he says he also taught Bruce to cut hair!! So, says Thomas, it seems Bruce was also a hairdresser of sorts!! Tom seems to have a few things in common with Bruce - Tom's birth sign is Pisces (double Yin-Yang sign); he's a keen disco-dancer born in 1958 (Bruce won the Cha-Cha Championship in 1958); Tom's friend is Danny - Bruce's close friend was Danny Inosanto; Tom and Bruce both loved art at school; Tom's brother sings/plays guitar, as does Robert, Bruce's brother. And Tom used to go fishing with his father for eels - spelt backwards that is LEE! Enough said!

David Moore (1783) tells me (on reading an article) that the producers of *The Big Brawl* (Jackie Chan) were looking for a special knife-type weapon for the film - the original script called for brass knuckles with a blade poking out each end, to be used by Ron Max (who played the villain Leggetti). Stunt-Coordinator Pat Johnson felt this weapon lacked martial arts' flair and impact and suggested replacing it with a pair of Filipino Balisongs (butterfly knives), and obviously, for the instructor, he chose Danny Inosanto! Danny taught Ron, and although the producers thought Danny might have to double for Ron in the scene, it was a credit to Danny's skills with the knives - and as a teacher - that Ron performed the sequence in the movie himself. Incidentally, David goes on, Dan arranged a balisong sequence for the movie *The Killer Elite* starring James Caan. But the knife scene, unfortunately, landed up on the cutting room floor. What a terrible waste, says David - and I wholeheartedly agree. Danny is a SUPERB martial artist - and a modest, gentle man who deserves MUCH more publicity than he gets - much, much more. I hope that Danny will be part of any future meetings that the Society will have. It certainly is my intention that he shall.

Dan Inosanto

David's other snippet - Yip Man's son was in Britain on second July for a trip - but no other information is available on that. Anyone hear anything??

It seems that our "friend" Bruce Li (La Shao Lung/Roy Lee Lung etc.) has now popped up in India! He is featured in a film called *Katilon Ke Katil* meaning "Murder of the Biggest Murderer." It seems, however, that he has not made much impression with our Indian member, V. S. Narayanan, who cannot see why Li was ever billed as the duplicate of Bruce. For one, says our member, he does not even have the stern face of the Master that sent a shiver down the spine of his opponent!

It seems that feelings on Mr. Li are pretty universal - although with due respect everyone has a different opinion, to which they are entitled. (Anyone wishing a copy of the article on the film, drop me a stamped and self-addressed envelope and I'll send you one).

For all those wide-awake members watching out for tunes from Bruce's films being used, on 21 October, the TV programme *Starburst* had a magician and one of his magic tricks was to play as backing music, *Enter the Dragon*. Needless to say, myself and other members "conjured" up all sorts of visions when roused by THAT tune ! And Desmond O'Reilly (3068) heard *Fist of Fury* being played on a programme called *Flight of the Doves* - it quite amazed him but certainly excited the scenes! His local pirate radio station also had Bruce's screams introducing an advert and managed to get *Dragon Power* played at a local disco when the DJ saw and enquired about his Society badges!! Desmond said the music on the speakers was FANTASTIC! (I remember forgetting to turn down the volume on my player after putting the record on once - and nearly breaking all records - and my neck! - getting to the volume control - Pam).

Simon Bulley saw the *Big Boss/Game of Death* double-bill recently, which ran for a whole week at the cinema - everyone enjoyed themselves immensely - and the showing was a great improvement on a previous Bruce double-bill when it was only put on for one night!! The cinema has since learned the error or their judgment on that occasion! Re film mistakes, Simon mentioned one he noticed in *Game of Death* - although the 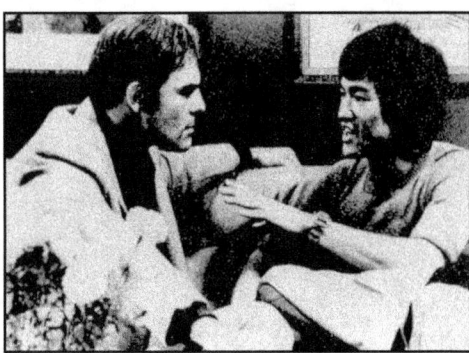 warehouse fight and the break in by "Bruce" into the restaurant took place at night, when he fought Jabbar and Jabbar's elbow breaks the square window it is broad daylight! Then it reverts back to night when Dr. Land tries to escape across the roof! Some continuity! Simon admits to seeing Bruce Li recently, and found him not as bad as he was led to believe. He feels that Li does a lot towards giving Bruce Lee's films a mythical quality, and that no danger to Bruce's legend is in sight so long as Li does not try to pass himself off as Bruce Lee. (Pam here; but that is JUST what is happening - especially when it comes to advertising. How many times do we SEE Bruce Lee's actual face superimposed onto cinema posters, and videos, and magazines, when he is not even in the film concerned - and people not in the know are conned into believing this is the real thing!! It is not so much what Li does - but the way that he and the companies behind him go about it! They ride on the Lee bandwagon! - AND THAT I CANNOT ACCEPT - and nor can other fans).

PEN PALS

Michael Clark (3048), Alfreton, wants Chinese female pen pal anywhere. Interests (of course!) Bruce, and Gung Fu, Chinese culture - aged 16 to 25

Bob Hartsfield (2864), Denton, USA wants Chinese/Japanese pen pals to write to and trade with.

HELP/ASSISTANCE NEEDED

JORGEN MOLLER (Kastrup, Denmark) was interested to know more about Bruce's weight- training, his techniques, etc., the systems he used - what about all you fanatics getting in touch with Jorgen and discussing it??

Glynn Darbyshire, Rotherham asks why, during the scene in *Enter the Dragon* where O'Hara opens the door and Bruce tells him "Outside" is Bruce supporting himself with a chair when balancing on one leg - a feat which Glynn reckons Bruce could do quite well without support?? Anyone any logical explanation (apart from it being something which was written into the film for no specific reason by the director/producer?)

Stephen King, Glasgow asks the waist/chest size of Bruce during *Enter the Dragon* filming, and his waist size when he started training in 1959. Also, what exercises he did to develop his back muscles.

LETTERS

Dear Pam,

I feel we're going through another martial arts boom - not as big as 1974 but nevertheless a move forward all the same, with the TV Kung Fu series repeat and the advent of ninja films, which might spark of the general public's adrenalin and get the BBC Bruce documentary shown. There's always hope, and if we, the fans, are relentless and keep writing, our efforts will surely pay off. I've written - and I'll let you know my progress.

Shaun Boland (2805)

Although a Bruce documentary exists, for some reason the BBC are now denying this! In fact, not only did members Paul Smith (1532) and Jon Sly get negative replies but Paul had his supporting petition returned to him. They do, however, suggest Paul contacts the IBA about the documentary (buck passing?) and give the address. So please, members, why not write to the IBA and mention that the BBC suggested you do this, asking for the documentary? (That should put a hornet in the nest - sorry about that pun! However, on the hopeful side, Paul received an answer to his enquiry to Minicards (they do albums with stickers on sports personalities) - and they are initially interested. In fact, if you all put pen to paper and WRITE to Minicards, I feel we could be seeing that album shortly. I shall write - please back Paul and I up on this venture! We alll need each other's support - it is the ONLY WAY TO GET THINGS DONE. I'm a fan too, and I'd also like to see new things on Bruce. So come on, please write!

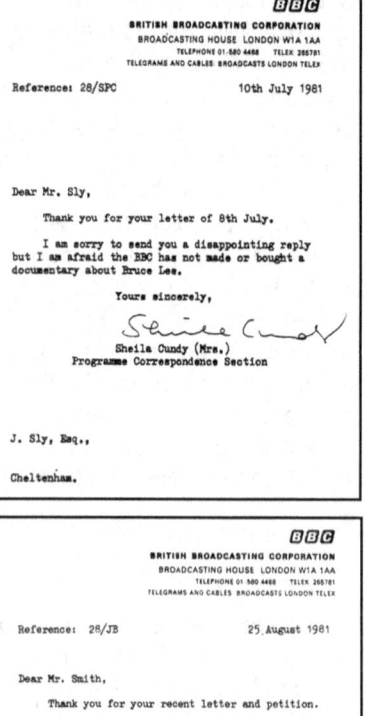

346

Dear Pam,

As you know, I'm a great Jackie Chan fan - even more so after meeting him. Although I cannot see anyone beating Bruce - he is the best - why do people keep comparing them? As Jackie said: "Bruce is Bruce, Jackie is Jackie."

Peter Jagger (1087)

As you said, Peter - the comparisons regrettably are inevitable. You are not alone, though in your views - Members Caroline Andrews and Kin Tong Liu (2939/3223) are ardent fans! (Want their addresses??) Caroline says Jackie is an up-and-coming young star - she also believes all artists should be judged in their own right. Tong says he's pretty brilliant, smooth, beautiful and skilful! (Pam here: Part of the trouble is that Jackie was quoted to have said he was better than Bruce - and if he DID say that, then it is he who is making comparisons. However, having met Jackie in his earlier days, he seemed a very nice guy.)

David Smith (3304) admits Jackie is good, although nowhere near as good as Bruce! But David says Jackie could show some other martial artists a thing or two! But regarding Bruce Li, says David - having seen *Fist of Fury Part II* describing Li as the "new martial arts master," he suggests Mr. Li should be informed he is a poor imitation of the real thing and should not try to take over the title, as he is not worthy.

Well - I think that is enough on Jackie and Bruce Li, and we'll close the issue. Everyone has their own opinion, and this should be respected.

Dear Pam,

Having seen Enter the Dragon *after it's "operation," the underground scene is completely cut and of course the film just does not now make sense - here's what happens: Bruce, after climbing down the rope, eliminating first one then two guys and moving to the operations room with his friend cobra tucked in the bag, he rudely awakens the snake and, after throwing him into the room and getting rid of the guards, sends his message and makes for the lift - eliminating some people on the way. When people pour from the lifts (and the action should start!) Bruce runs straight into a trap! Then China's answer to J. R. Ewing utters the immortal words: "The battle with the Guards was magnificent; your skill is extraordinary!" WHAT BATTLE?!! The only battle was in waking the snake! Ruined my night, that did!*

David Dixon (1650)

David - I laughed so much over your remarks - especially the J. R. Ewing bit! Still, it is upsetting to see such cuts - but despite that fact you still gave us all a good laugh!

NEW FILMS
(Info via David Moore - 1783)

- *Force Five* - Benny Urquidez, Joe Lewis, Bong Soo Han, Sonny Barnes, Ron Haydon, Richard Norton and Pamela Huntington - Summer 1982 release.
- *Shinobi* - Eric Lee, Tadashi Yamashita and Karen Shepherd - currently filming in Japan.
- *An Eye for an Eye* - Chuck Norris - Summer release in the States.
- Also planned for Chuck - *The Jade Jungle* - to be filmed in Hong Kong and Macau for MGM around now.
- Sterling Silliphant putting final touches to *The Masters*.
- Jackie Chan readying for new Golden Harvest film *The Protector*.
- Toshiro Mifune planning to star in *The Equals* (rumoured budget $15 million).
- Eric Lee just finished *Weapons of Death* in San Francisco with Nancy Lee, Bob Ramos, Gary Huey, Gina Lau, Ralph Castellanos and Gerald Okamura (brilliant weapons expert) with spectacular fight to the death at film end.

OTHER MARTIAL ARTISTS
(Info from David Moore)

Agimiro Gonzalez, martial arts master born El Tucuyo, Venezuela. Trained in arts at age 13; after few years travelled to capital of Caracas and studied under Chinese/Indian masters; studied Yoga/appeared in films and TV. Founded Shaolin Chi Kuoshu Society of Venezuela, and also the Little Dragon Club.

SWOP SHOP

- Simon Bulley, Peterborough has or sale: *KFM* 41 @ 40p/*KFM* 30 @ 50p - buy both and get a free B&W picture of Bruce from *Game of Death*. Also for sale and/ or swap for Bruce items - *Game of Death* tracksuit good condition. Price negotiable. Write to Simon with offers.
- David Willett, Newark has for sale: *Bruce Lee's Fighting Method* vols.1-4, *Kickboxing Muay Thai* - Stockma, *Dynamic Kicks* - Chang Lee, *Ninja* - Adam, *Secrets of Shaolin Temple Boxing* - Robert Smith, *Know Karate-Do* - Bryn Williams, *Takami-yama: The World of Sumo* - Wheeler, *Farewell My Friend* - Uyehara, *Secret Art of Bruce Lee* - KFM, *Bruce Lee JKD* magazines. vols. 1-10, *Bruce Lee Revenges, Unknowns in Martial Arts Learning, Bruce Lee The Fighting Spirit, Bruce Lee in Game of Death, Bruce Lee Game of Death Extract Edition, Reminiscence of Bruce Lee, His Privacy & Anecdotes, Studies on JKD, Secret of JKD & Kung Fu, Nunchakus in Action, Black Belt's Best of Bruce Lee No. 2, Who Killed Bruce Lee, Bruce Lee in Action, Secret Art of Bruce Lee,* 22 pictures of Bruce, pair of Bong Sau gloves, closed finger karate sparring gloves. Write for prices of items individually or preferably selling the lot for £25 to Society member.
- Lenny Franchi, London has for swap: *Game of Death/Enter* (with nunchakus sequence) videos for copies of any *Way of the Dragon, The Big Boss,* and *Fist of Fury* video OR SELL FOR £20 each inc. p&p.
- Peter Jagger, Birmingham says his friend has model of GH car for swap and Peter has *Green Hornet Annual* for swap. High prices paid for *Fighters Monthly* Vol. 1 No. 12, *Best of Bruce Lee* No. 1, *Farewell to the Dragon, Kung Fu Superstars, Wisdom of Bruce Lee, Films of Filming* (Bruce on cover), *Deadly Hands of Kung Fu* Nos. 2, 3, 7, 27, *Enter* front of house stills. Will consider above items for the car/annual.
- Michael Clark, Alfreton has or sale: Super 8 colour/sound films *Enter* (inc. bottle scene) 20mins. long - £20 ono & GH - 2 x 400ft reels (30 minutes running time) - £25 ono. If interested please ring Michael on Sundays between 10 am and 1 pm - Alfreton XXXXXX. Wants: Mint condition *Game of Death* Japanese soundtrack - your price paid.
- Tony Lundberg, Copenhagen, Denmark - wants original newspapers/photocopies of articles on Bruce's death. Contact him with offers and/or price/swaps.
- Peter Reynolds, Glasgow has for swap/sale: 10 karate hardback books - wants *Bruce Lee 1940-1973* and/or *Secret Art of Bruce Lee* or sell karate books for £10 (list available from Peter).
- Philip Bell, Leeds has for sale: *Way of the Dragon, The Big Boss, Fist of Fury, Enter the Dragon,* and *Game of Death* uncensored very good condition films at £40 each. Also, GH Screentest plus trailers of all Bruce's films very good condition - accept £35. Rare collectors' item: Bruce's childhood films *Kid Cheung, Orphan* etc., again will accept £35 very good condition. Will consider swap for any Police or Beatles' video - and if anyone can assist with where to get these videos will send them free Bruce Lee poster.
- Seisuke Suzuki, Shizuoka, Japan has for swap: Japanese/Chinese magazines on Bruce Lee. Wants: *Best of Bruce Lee, Power of Bruce Lee,* any magazines on Bruce Lee worldwide. Please send him details direct.
- Avtar Sohota, Warley has for swap/sale: *Game Of Death* soundtrack inc. Lee/ Inosanto fight. Wants: *KFM* No. 1, *Bruce Lee in Action* in good condition. For

swap: *Enter the Dragon* soundtrack; Wants: *KFM* 2 & 31 in good condition.
- Tom Lavery, Portadown, Northern Ireland wants: *Longstreet, Green Hornet, Marlowe* on VHS videotape. Also Press books from all films on Bruce Lee/cinema posters from all except *Game of Death*/8"xlO" colour cinema stills.
- David Moore, Wakefield wants (or details of where to get): *Bruce Lee the Incomparable Fighter* by M. Uyehara. (Pam here: so do I - please let me know also).

USEFUL ADDRESSES

- KC Kung Fu Film Club, Plant Theatre, Fulcrum Entertainment Centre, Slough, Berks. - late night Kung Fu film shows Fridays - uncut - lots of Bruce!
- Andy's Record Shop - for Bruce Lee videos on hire at £2 per day, along with £40 refundable deposit on return of the video (info from Simon Bulley) Copies of ninja book mentioned last news sheet - try Woolworths, John Menzies or larger Boots stores. Publisher: Granada Publishing Ltd., 36 Golden Square, London, WIR 4AH. Price £1.95. (Info from David Moore).
- Cimac Martial Arts, 606 Stratford Rd., Sparkhill, Birmingham, BII 4AP - cut price books and offering bumper pack of Bruce Lee magazines at @4.99 + p&p (should be over £11) for Xmas. Free poster with every order.
- Karate and Oriental Arts, 838 Fulham Rd, London, SW6. - lots of Bruce Lee mags inc. *Fighting Method* Vol. 1-4/*Tao of JKD*/Bruce Lee by Jesse Glover/*Inside Kung Fu* back-issues at 75p ea. vol. 4 Nos. 9/10 inc. Elvis article; Vol. 5 No. 7 *Game of Death* feature and Vol. 7 No. 1 with Dan Inosanto.
- Fantastic Films magazine recommended (Neil McLean) for info on ALL Bruce Lee videos (under American titles).
- Merrion Superstore, Merrion Centre, Leeds (Nr. Highlander Pub) - super martial arts stock inc. punch bags, nunchakus, tracksuits (*Game Of Death* type) etc. and Bruce Lee magazines from Hong Kong (also on Jackie); *KFM's* 1/2 etc.
- Cinevisual Inc., 2067 Broadway, New York 10023, USA. Sell Kung Fu videos - for US$60, two for US$100 inc. American Bruce Lee films. Each film two hours long.
- Empire Publications, 35830 Cumberland Way, S.E. Enumclaw, Washington 98022, USA - sell pencil drawings exquisitely reproduced - 17"x22r' - for framing - US$14.95. Write for details, (info from Bob Harsfield)

Well - I'm fast (again!) running out of space. Have a really great Christmas - see you soon! Oh - if buying videos from the States, please be careful and check first that it is suitable for use on your machine, warns David Moore (1783). SEE YOU. Pam

---

Bruce Lee Society Research Manager Mike Devereux

Pam and I talked over at length as to what my "role" could be defined as and ultimately we came up with research manager. Pam was being overwhelmed with the workload so in essence I was doing my bit to try to take some of the weight off her. We planned the first convention together and on the day that it took place emotions were running high. She put so much into getting it right and the numbers that turned up that day, from all over the world, astounded us! We went to LBC radio to do a spot to promote the convention and got advertisements out into the newspapers!

The 70's were a crazy time for lots of different reasons but there are two things that are monumental in my life, Bruce Lee and Pamela Hadden. They both impacted me in such a deep way and I'll always be grateful to have known them both!

BRUCE LEE SOCIETY COLUMN
KUNG FU MONTHLY NO. 64

First of all there's great news on the book front! For literally years now, I've been badgering away to get *Wisdom of Bruce Lee* released in this country. So far, all most members have seen of it, have been the miserable few paperback copies that floated over from America. Considering it was originally a British publication, I thought that a pretty poor show! I won't go into the reasons WHY that happened as I think they're well known enough by now. All I'm going to say is that, at last, it's coming!

According to the powers-that-be at *KFM*, plans are now well advanced for 'Wisdom' and two other publications that were originally only available on short supply, to be re-printed later this year. I say re-printed; in fact, certainly in the case of *Wisdom*, it's going to be a case of a new look as well! I think that news is great. And what's more, I'm told if these sell well, there's a lot more goodies in the pipeline! Sounds to me we all better buy two copies each just to make sure!

I wrote last time about the need for you all to take the initiative and to tell me just what YOU want out of the Bruce Lee Society, now and into the future. Well, letters are already starting to roll in and the more, the merrier please! But, in addition to that, certain more fundamental plans are being laid which could have an equally dramatic effect on us. It looks as though we may soon be putting ourselves on a stronger and more permanent footing. In short, the plan is to make the Society a self-supporting organisation in its own right.

If all this comes about, it should bode well for all of us. We've been singing the praises for Bruce Lee over quite a few years now, and people outside the Society take us very seriously indeed. It's probably no bad thing if we all dust off the cobwebs and take OURSELVES rather more seriously too! Stand by for more news on what could be a very exciting new year.

– Pam Hadden

EDITOR'S NOTES

Pat Johnson at the Bruce and Brandon Lee Association's 2001 "Fury of the Dragons"

Pat Johnson was born in 1939 in Niagara Falls, New York. He began training in Tang Soo Do in 1963, while stationed in South Korea with the US Army, gaining his Black Belt in just thirteen months. After leaving the Army, Johnson met and formed an association with Chuck Norris, rising to the rank of chief instructor at Norris' school in Sherman Oaks in 1968. That same year, he formulated the penalty-point system still used in karate tournaments.

From 1968 to 1973, Johnson was captain of the undefeated Chuck Norris black belt competition team, winning 33 consecutive titles.

In 1971, he became the National Tang Soo Do

champion. In 1973, Johnson was cast as a villain in Bruce Lee's completed film, *Enter the Dragon,* as an enforcer for the mob, sent to collect a debt from John Saxon's Roper on the golf course.

In 1984, Johnson served as stunt co-ordinator on the film *The Karate Kid.* Johnson also featured in the movie as the head referee at the All Valley Karate Tournament. He was one of only two cast members who knew any martial arts before shooting began, with the other being Darryl Vidal who was featured in the Semi-Final contest against Johnny Lawrence. Vidal invented the famous Crane Kick that Daniel LaRusso uses to win the tournament.

Johnson would later choreograph the fight scenes for the 1990 film, *Showdown in Little Tokyo* starring Dolph Lundgren and Brandon Lee.

One of Johnson's most famous students was Steve McQueen, whom he personally trained, becoming good friends. When McQueen would check into hotels with "lady friends" in the 1970's, he would do so under the name of "Pat Johnson."

Black Belt Jones was a 1974 blaxploitation martial arts film directed by Robert Clouse starring Jim Kelly and Gloria Hendry. It was Kelly's first starring role after *Enter the Dragon* and the filmmakers wanted to capitalise on it's success. Kelly stars as Back Belt Jones, who fights the Mafia and a local drug dealer who is threatening a friend's Karate dojo.

Released to mixed reviews, the film's main criticism surrounded Kelly's poor impersonation of Bruce Lee. In years that followed, the film gained a formidable cult following. The film has only been released on home video once in the UK; in 1983 on VHS and Betamax.

Seisuke Suzuki is a name well known amongst collectors of Bruce Lee memorabilia. He has released two books in Japan on Bruce Lee collectables, each containing hundreds of colour photos of books, magazines, posters, videotapes, LP records, CDs, Bruce's personal belongings etc. The books were titled *Super Bruce Lee Collection* Vol. 1 and Vol. 2. Both books are currently out of print.

Even though people knew the difference between the VHS and Betamax system of home video cassettes, they weren't aware of the different PAL or NTSC TV systems that these players used. PAL was used in the UK and much of Europe (France used the SECAM system) while NTSC was used in the USA and Asia. An NTSC tape wouldn't play on a PAL system and vice versa. In later years, many PAL video recorders and then DVD players would allow "NTSC Playback" which was a "'quasi" playback system with the NTSC to PAL conversion taking place "on the fly." Unfortunately, PAL to NTSC conversion couldn't be done in the same way and could only be done via a full digital conversion. The conversion these days is much simpler using a computer and basic video conversion software.

A RETROSPECTIVE LOOK AT BRUCE LEE MANIA & THE KUNG FU CRAZE OF THE 1970S

23 March 1982

HI THERE - AND I EXPECT YOU ALL NOTICED (WHO COULDN'T?) THE CHANGED FORMAT OF THE FRONT OF THE NEWS SHEET - A SUGGESTION OF MIKE DEVEREUX, THE SOCIETY'S (NEW!) RESEARCH MANAGER! HE THOUGHT A "NEW LOOK" IN PREPARATION FOR THE SOCIETY EVENTUALLY "GOING SOLO" WAS A STEP IN THE RIGHT DIRECTION, AND I'M INCLINED TO AGREE!! MIKE HAS ALSO PRODUCED THE FANTASTIC LIST OF VIDEOS ENCLOSED WITH THIS SHEET - HE'S PUT A LOT OF WORK INTO THIS, AND I FEEL IT'S AN EXCELLENT PIECE OF WORK!

FIRSTLY, NOW - LET ME THANK YOU ALL FOR THE LOVELY CHRISTMAS CARDS - HOPE YOUR NEW YEAR IS TURNING OUT WELL, AND THAT THE BAD WEATHER IS BEHIND US FOR GOOD! TALKING ABOUT BAD WEATHER...

MEETING OF LONDON-BASED MEMBERS AND FUTURE MEETINGS

One could call this the meeting that never was! Because that's about the size of it! Maybe it was the fault of the weather - but then again maybe the apathetic reaction I've somehow got used to receiving over the years of running the club is the reason. Anyway, apart from members of the Society who I knew would come anyway, I received TWO letters from members generally in and around the London area who wished to meet up and discuss future aims of the Society as suggested in the last news sheet. I have to admit I was disappointed - but as I said, it isn't the first time that I've tried to get something started only to come up against a brick wall. I'm glad that the lack of enthusiasm is not felt by all Society members. Although I anticipate meetings in other areas, I am not making any date in this news sheet. Maybe it's about time I put some of the responsibility to members themselves to arrange things - so what I would like is: For all of you to get in touch with Members near you, and check out who would be interested in getting together at some future date - where to meet, how many of you could make it - just to see what potential exists for my making a special journey to that area. Then, if I hear BRIEFLY from one member in each particular area (you decide who!) of his/her findings - date(s), venue etc., and anticipated attendance figure - I can then view the overall situation and make arrangements to suit. If I find that several areas can be combined, I shall put area representatives in touch so that they can liaise among themselves and get final figures etc. and suggested mutually convenient meeting places (such as a training hall). The meeting(s), however, would HAVE to take place on a Saturday - we've all got jobs or whatever to attend during the week. Any hiring fee for halls, etc. - please mention this in your notes to me. It's now up to you - if you want the meetings, you'll respond. I shall only visit the areas who show they WANT a meeting - which I think is fair enough.

As mentioned, Mike Devereux (1061) is now part of the organisation - as he gets into the swing of things, I shall be handing other projects to various members where I feel they can assist. So far the Society "official" staff is Mike and I - and already I must admit that it is a relief to feel a little of the "load" is now shared in answering letters and general ideas.

Among the numerous offers of assistance is one from Anthony Boswell (2570) who has a home computer and hopes to get a printer as well soon, which could help enormously with storing/retrieving data etc. We shall be meeting shortly on this. Also being studied is Greg Rhodes' plan of future aims of the club - but obviously, first things first! I won't go into more details at present - but as things progress, I shall tell you through the news sheet and, where I find I need further assistance in certain fields. I will request your help.

FUTURE TRIP TO HONG KONG AND/OR U.S.A.

Again, the response to the mention in the last sheet was small - in fact, only four members (despite the many enquiries I had received previously) took the trouble to write in giving estimates of their expected total outlay for a trip, to assist me on costing same. Obviously, with such a small response, no reasonably cheap holiday could be anticipated, but for the few who wrote to me, let me say that if we can get together for a Hong Kong/U.S.A. trip ourselves, we shall do so. One member, Dawn Squires (3280) who responded, also took the initiative to check out a local travel agent, who said (as I already told you all) that the more who go, the cheaper the trip. All I can now say is - I shall STILL investigate and come back with any good news I get - but if I get a small group together, it is no good then everyone wanting to "climb aboard"! Let's see what happens.

Martin Schell (1819)

Martin Schell (1819)

Martin Schell (1819)

GENERAL NEWS

Maria Fernandes (2751), one of our Brazilian members, is in contact with the French Bruce Lee Fan Club, and has heard - to her great joy and mine - that ALL the Bruce rip-off films have been withdrawn UNDER FRENCH LAW - they cannot be shown as starring Bruce Lee if it is not a real Bruce film! Man behind the action there, it seems, is Rene Chateau, who produced the French super book publications *Inedit*, *La Vie et la Mort Tragique de Bruce Lee* (Linda's book in French) and *La Legende de Petit Dragon* (*Legend of the Little Dragon*). It seems Rene has a certain amount of "pull" in France.

Maria also says that the *The Green Hornet* is being shown in Sao Paulo for the second re-run, and that re-runs of *The Big Boss*, *Fist of Fury* and *Way of the Dragon* will soon be showing at local cinemas UNCUT! All in all, I feel we in England get a very poor deal compared with fans abroad. Comments on Bruce's punch which Maria has read: "It was reckoned that Bruce's power-to-weight ratio was phenomenal. I have heard that he could give a punch of 350lbs per square inch, although his own weight was only 140lbs! This really was a great accomplishment. It is considered that a good karate punch achieves approximately 100lbs per square inch!" (Josh Hernandes).

Another snippet from Maria (in regard to Bruce's friend James Lee): "Apart from a Gung Fu man, James was a welder, and made some headgear he wanted Bruce to test. Bruce told James he did not think it a good idea to test the gear whilst James was wearing it, but James insisted and Bruce finally gave it a try. (In an earlier test the mask had withstood blows from a small sledgehammer, but Bruce decided not to punch the mask with full force). It turned out a wise move on Bruce's part because his punch caved in the mask until it was pressing into James's face! The mask was made from heavy steel rods, and the way that it collapsed convinced Bruce that he had reached a level of punching power that could never be fully directed towards another human being unless he were trying to kill him. I still feel the only people who fully understood the depth of Bruce's skills are those who have stood before his fists and feet. All of the film in the world isn't worth a live demonstration of how helpless anyone was when they worked out with Bruce." (Jesse Glover).

On to Simon Bulley (2738) - he asks if members know the link between Bruce and David Carradine apart from the Kung Fu series? Answer: John Carradine, David's father and noted actor for many years, appeared in the "Alias the Scarf" episode of the *The Green Hornet* and also in *Kung Fu* as the blind preacher, Serenity Johnson.

Simon's local cinema is soon to show *Big Boss 2* (Please note: NOT a Bruce Lee movie) - advertised as "More thrilling than *Way of the Dragon*; exciting like *Fist of Fury*," and, as Simon says: "Starring Bruce (Li) somebody (you know what I mean!)" and he'd be surprised if it served up a tenth of what it's advertising - (so would I.)

Simon has yet to see the Adam Ant video with Adam impersonating Bruce - many fans have seen it, and it appears to be quite good. (By the way, there's a cutting of Adam's get-up, courtesy

From: Ann & Fred Hunt and Gino D'Ambrosio

of Ann Hunt, Fred Hunt and Gino D'Ambrosio).

Finally from Simon - recently he saw a splendid video *Bruce Lee Souvenir* which is a compilation of material previously available on Super 8mm film. It shows the making of *Enter the Dragon*, American *Enter the Dragon* trailer, American trailer for *Return of the Dragon* (*Way of the Dragon*) with super clips from the double-nunchaku scenes and Bob Wall, Wong In Sik and Chuck Norris fights. All followed by American trailers from *Big Boss/Fist of Fury* with action scenes - music changed from the *Fist of Fury* theme to the *2001: Space Odyssey* music (*Also Sprach Zaruthustra*). And finally on the video - an episode of the *The Green Hornet* called "The Silent Gun."

Michelle Scully

David Moore (1783) has done a list of places where Bruce items are available - and listed the items, too! - as well as a list of martial arts films released in 1981 - and these lists are included with this sheet. This is a worthwhile project on David's part - which I am sure you all appreciate, as I do. Also, David says Chuck Norris's film *An Eye for an Eye* is on release in the States, co-starring Mako (*Big Brawl, Incredible Hulk*) who is also a real-life black belt. Filmed in San Francisco, Chuck plays an undercover "cop" fighting a dope-smuggling ring, and sets out to break this after his partner and girlfriend are killed. David says Chuck's films improve each time. Also spotted by David - another error by the *Combat* magazine - this time, in their December 1981 issue No. 35, they show a photo of James Tien in *Big Boss* with the caption "Bruce Lee in a scene from *Big Boss*!" David cannot understand how a so-called established magazine like that can make such terribly stupid mistakes! He has written to them to tell them.

Gino D'Ambrosio (1655)

Ernest Bow (2933) asks you all to watch out in the *Evening News* for adverts about Bruce Lee Film Spectaculars run by Sunny

THE BRUCE LEE SOCIETY

Films (previous newssheets) - a private film club who seem very keen on Bruce! A few months back they had an all-night spectacular showing full-length versions of *Fist of Fury, Way of the Dragon* and *Game of Death* - not to be missed!

Thomas Jones (2058) pointed out an error in *KFM* "Quickies Corner" where reader R. Symes said John Lennon numbered Bruce as one of his body-guards, but Tom says there seems to be a mix-up as Phil Spector (Lennon's friend and musician in his own right) had grown unpredictable and almost para-noid and was reputed to carry a gun in his waistband and to have numbered Bruce among his bodyguards! (Odd! I!) Anyway - this info in book called *John Lennon, the Life and Legend*, page 54, a *Sunday Times* special tribute.

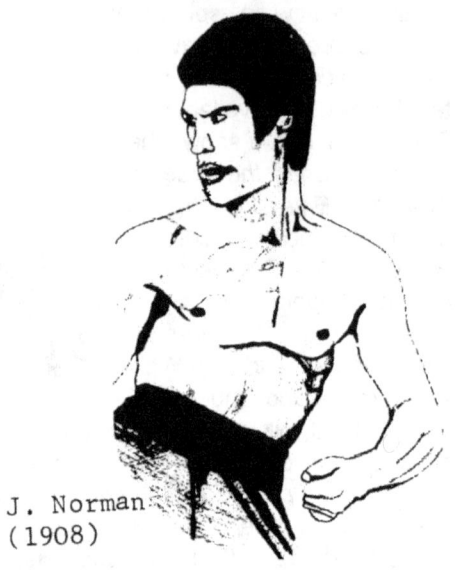

J. Norman (1908)

Off to Iain Leslie (3248) - he writes regularly to various TV stations to get Bruce films shown - having written to the Independent Broadcasting Authority (70 Brompton Road, London, SW3 1EY - Tel: 584 7011) - he received the reply shown. Personally, their reply sounds "favourable," as indeed they are considering *The Green Hornet* - maybe more letters from members could at last prompt this organisation into a showing of the series - I'd love to see the replies you receive, so please DO write to the IBA pressing for *Green Hornet* to be shown, and let them see what sort of fans Bruce has. And as Iain also wrote to Scottish TV (Cowcaddens, Glasgow G2 3PR, Scotland) but found they had not been offered the series yet from America, maybe a few '"chasing" letters from US could get them contacting the States direct. We MUST get something shown on TV soon - but only if we ALL PULL TOGETHER! Iain also says he finds it unbelievable that the BBC can re-run the Chinese adventure series *Water Margin* and also *Kung Fu* - with many violent fight scenes which (for some reason) they find acceptable - and yet they cannot show such as *The Green Hornet* or Bruce's films which far surpass any of the repeats and would probably have such a rating as to astound even them.

Still with Tom - both he and I watched the movie *The Yakuza* (which fellow-member David Moore (1783) has tried to get shown for some time) starring Robert Mitchum, about the Japanese Mafia. A superb film - with first-class action towards the end by the Japanese star Takakura Ken using a Samurai sword, with Mitchum somewhat in the shade. Throughout the film, the culture and traditions of the Oriental way of life was prevalent, lending authenticity to, and clarifying actions throughout, the film. Well worth watching if it comes your way. Tom also says he has heard the *Fist of Fury* music at the beginning of the Stanley Baker film *Robbery* - he was quite astounded. Of course, though I watched the film, I HAD to be doing something else at the start of this, would you believe.

A RETROSPECTIVE LOOK AT BRUCE LEE MANIA & THE KUNG FU CRAZE OF THE 1970S

On to David Moore again - he read in a recent paper about a 72-year-old man attacked by muggers who let fly with a punch to one youth's mouth and they ran off. "You can tell how hard he hit the lad," says David, "because the old gentleman had to go to hospital to have his hand seen to which was cut when he punched the youth." The main thing to catch David's eye was the caption to the article - "Fist of Fury - battling Joe Studden!" Bet the youths don't go picking on any "frail" elderly people too soon in the future, says David!'

Neil Wilde (3116) (in giving suggestions on future Society projects) suggested photo-novels on Bruce's films, which is a sound idea. Now if anyone of you out there has any knowledge of, or experience in,

> SF/af   23rd December, 1981
>
> Iain Leslie Esq.,
>
> Hamilton, ML3 7PR,
> Scotland.
>
> Dear Mr. Leslie,
>
>   Thank you for your recent letter. I am afraid that I have been unable to trace any information on a Bruce Lee documentary - this may well exist, but ITV are not planning to screen such a programme.
>
>   Mr. Leslie Halliwell, the buyer of foreign programmes on behalf of ITV, informs me that the series "Green Hornets" is under consideration; as yet, however, there are no definate plans for purchasing.
>
>   Yours sincerely,
>
>   Susun Fewell, (Miss)
>   Information Assistant

this type of "project"' - please let me know. If several of you feel able to tackle this together - those of you with writing experience able to "precis" down a film script to caption frame blow-ups from the film with the storyline/dialogue - then drop me a line. I'll work on it from there. I'm sure I have quite a few "expert" writers out there - so come on, why not get your own project going for the club??

From:
Shahad Setudeh
Nejad
(1419)

Carl Jones (2121) saw *Force Five* (Director: Robert Clouse/Producer: Fred Weintraub) starring Joe Lewis - says Carl: "To put it mildly it's the most blatant *Enter the Dragon* rip-off, including Braithwaite interview, secret island run by an Oriental drug-king, karate-suited guards - the whole works!" Mel Novak ("Stick" in *Game of Death*) has a small part, as does Pat ("It's the dough, Roper") Johnson, wearing virtually the same clothes and uttering almost the same lines! Carl says the martial arts scenes are lousy - see it at your peril!

Bob Hartsfield (2864) of Denton, U.S.A., has now a price to have the *Green Hornet* picture cards (almost a complete set) reproduced for members - mentioned last news sheet. He did a lot of checking out, and has come up with a cost (per set, colour on card and laminated, including postage/handling) of US$17.00 (about £7-£8). Bob might be able to get them cheaper, depending on how many write to him. So - I for one am getting a set! And I know that you will all be clambering to get pen to paper and write off to Bob to order these rare sets. BUT DO NOT SEND HIM ANY MONEY YET - write first with your name, address and membership Number - and let Bob take it from there. He will get back to you when he knows how many sets to order, and if he can get the cost down, and the time it will take to produce. I've heard about, but never had a chance to get, the *The Green Hornet* cards. Thanks, Bob!

THE BRUCE LEE SOCIETY

Seisuke Suzuki (3269)

Neil McLean (3303) and Robert Lee

N. B. Dennis

RENEWALS

The following members fall due for renewal from now until the end of May: 3158-3218 (second year); 2908-2972 (third year); 2600-2697 (fourth year); 2267-2302 (fifth year); 1829-2021 (sixth year).

ADDRESS CHANGES

Members changing their address MUST let me know in good time so that items do not go astray. If you have a *KFM* subscription - then let them know separately, as I do not handle this or work at their offices - or indeed, work FOR them! Several members have recently asked about items not received - and just happening in the same letter to mention, casually, that they had moved from their previous address. Obviously, if they do not tell me beforehand, the items ordered are sent straight to the address on file - come on, be fair! I'm not telepathic!! Also - ANYONE HAVING DIFFICULTY OBTAINING *KFM* OR GENERAL ENQUIRIES ON THIS, PLEASE WRITE TO THEM DIRECT AT 14 RATHBONE PLACE, LONDON, WIP IDE, and for those out-of-the way places who cannot get copies, why not take out a sub with *KFM* and solve your problems??

MEMORIAL FLOWERS - JULY 1982

It doesn't seem possible, but yes! It's one year since I placed the first contribution request for a Society memorial floral tribute to Bruce's graveside. The response was only 24 people from the whole of the Society - can you believe that? Yet we collected £63 which gave a superb tribute to Bruce's memory. And the flowers (organised by our own Alison French, your fellow member) were

---

New York
Burt Reynolds, Angie Dickinson, producer Howard Koch, director Irvin Kershner, and international film mogul Raymond Chow have been named winners of the major National Association of Theatre Owners Awards for 1980. Honors will be presented at the NATO Awards banquet to be held October 22 at the Hyatt Regency Hotel in New Orleans, it was announced by A. Alan Friedberg, president of the organization which represents more than 8000 motion picture theatres in the United States.

"Showmanship is proving more than ever in this period of national recession to be the most reliable tool available to the film exhibition industry," Friedberg observed. "For that reason the 'Showman Of The Year' award to Chow takes on special significance. With his very first film, 'Enter The Dragon,' Chow and his Golden Harvest Productions introduced the most recent and one of the most lucrative genres, the martial arts film.

"This was enhanced by his subsequent series of films with Bruce Lee and Jackie Chan, star of Chow's upcoming Warner Bros. release, 'The Big Brawl.'" Other films made by Chow's company this year include "The Cannonball Run" and the Charles Bronson-Lee Marvin starrer "Death Hunt."

From: Shahad Setudeh Nejad (1419)

placed with the names of all those who donated at the graveside - a picture and the receipt from the florist reprinted in the September 1981 sheet for information. So now come on - EVERYONE - please; just send in your donation - NO MATTER HOW SMALL - it doesn't matter, really! Although I keep a record of names of those donating (for the list to the graveside) and a running total of the amount (so that anyone if they want can see what has happened to the money), the amount of the donation is unimportant - but the number of people donating IS of significance, in that this year I want the list overflowing so that the American fans can see our loyalty even though we are unable to be there. I appreciate and understand that for some people even a small amount would be difficult - especially with the all-round financial situation we face - but please, if you can, something small. I will stipulate, though - there is no limit to how small the donation, but I will ask that no donation go above £2 from any one member. Send donations to "Memorial Flowers," c/o London. (not forgetting to include your name/membership number for list), to reach me by the end of June VERY, VERY LATEST! It takes several weeks to organise. A list of names will be published in the September news sheet, together with the receipt from the florist.

TRIPLE BOOK OFFER

Bruce Lee King of Kung-Fu — the original and still one of the greatest. It's packed with photographs and essential information.
Who Killed Bruce Lee — a written and photographic study of the anti-life forces that beset this century's greatest kung-fu master.
The 2nd Sensational Bruce Lee Scrapbook — produced in response to enormous demand and a sequel to the original KFM Scrapbook. Once again, it's full of rare and interesting photographs and information.

Price for each book is £1.25 (includes handling). Price for all three together is £3.00 (also includes handling). Just send cheques/postal order (made out to KFM please to: Triple Book Offer, Kung-Fu Monthly, 14 Rathbone Place, London W1P 1DE.

BRUCE'S MUM, GRACE LI - A PRESENT FOR HER??

I'd dearly love to give her a present from Society members - such as a piece of English China or the like. Wouldn't it be nice for her to receive something from us - after all the pleasure her son has given us? I think so - shall we do it? After all, we might also be able to have it engraved. Or even a piece of silverware engraved? If you are keen to contribute - send me a POSTCARD ONLY with name and number and amount you wish to donate -again, keep within your own personal budget. Get the cards to me within four weeks/six weeks of receipt of this sheet - when I know how much contributed, I (or someone who might get delegated!!) will then drop letters to all who sent postcards, giving suggestion as to what we think we will purchase at the price pledged - and asking for the money pledged by each member to be then sent to the Society. As to what we shall have engraved - if we can buy some silverware - give your brief wording when you send your postcard. I know of silversmiths around London who do SUPERB engraving - but until I know how much we shall have, I cannot price accordingly.

SOCIETY WRITE UP/JOINING LETTERS

Anyone wishing to put up information sheets about the Society in their local clubs/training halls etc. - please let me know and I'll send some, together with joining letters. So far, despite my mentioning this last sheet, I've only had a response from Kin Tong Liu (3223) - apart from the two members who suggested the idea, Lee Percy and Kevin Stokes! Nice to know you are all awake out there - are you???? Come on - the more members we get, the bigger we get, the more we can do!

MORE USEFUL ADDRESSES

Glynn Darbyshire (2885) says the following LP's (or double-LP where stated) are available from Flyover Records (15 Queen Caroline Street, London, W6. Tel: 01-748 1595): *World of Bruce Lee* (double), *Big Boss, Fist of Fury, Way of the Dragon, Game of Death, Tower of Death*. All single LP's cost £8.99 (except *Tower* which costs £9.49) plus 50p post/packing; double LP's cost £14.99 plus £1 p&p. (Thanks, Glynn).

SPECIAL MESSAGES/INFO/REQUESTS

Congratulations to Knud-Erik Larsen (2376) on recently winning a Bronze Medal in the Danish Karate Championship in Randers, Denmark.

David Niedzailek (1021) recently joined the Py Tang Video Club (previous news sheets). He is well satisfied with this. Having, however, had varied remarks from members on this club - ranging from the quality of the films supplied being "poor" to "excellent" - it seems that as (as David says) the club is very keen to help Bruce Lee fans, your best bet would be to write direct to Py Tang if the films supplied are bad, saying you are dissatisfied, and asking for his comments - I feel sure, judging from the service he has given in the past, that he will be only too happy to exchange any 'bad' films. He has far too much to lose by getting a bad reputation - I think he is fair (Address: Rochdale).

Pam here - anyone know where I can get hold of a copy of *Starburst* magazine No. 41? Ta!

LETTERS

Dear Pam,

Is it true that while Kareem Abdul Jabbar was making Game of Death, *his family in America were shot, and when he himself went back, he also was shot?? Also, I read an article on a great martial artist called Wang Ziping, a renowned Wushu ex-*

pert. He died in the same year as Bruce - was there any connection between them?

Kin Tong Liu (3223)

Well, I can't answer Tong's questions - can anyone else? If so, write to him direct at Liverpool. By the way, Tong sent the complete article on Wang - I found it interesting reading, so if members want a copy send me a SAE with a note and I'll post off to you. (Pam)

Dear Pam,

I'm writing this having just seen Game of Death II (Tower of Death). *I entered the cinema a little apprehensive (due to the many rip-off films about, saying Bruce is in them when really his name is just used to pull in the crowds). My brief views of the film? The Bruce clips were worth seeing (even though none of Bruce fighting opponents). The remainder of the film contained martial arts action that was interesting, exciting and mostly realistic - I'd recommend the film for the Bruce clips at the beginning and the action, although the story was not good.*

Peter Jagger (1087)

I've yet to see the film, Peter. I've not even seen it advertised! However, a couple of other members appear to have been also lucky. If anyone hears of it coming around the London area, please drop me a line. (Pam).

By the way - I spotted Colleen Camp (*Game of Death*) in a film on TV the other week called *Lady of the House* - she played Rosette, one of the "ladies" in a bordello.

Dear Pam,

I don't know if a programme That's Hollywood *is shown on TV in England, but if it is look out for the episode on comic strip heroes, as there is a small scene shown of Bruce in* The Green Hornet. *I've written to R.T.E. (the Irish TV station) here twice on showing Bruce's films - they never even replied. You think the TV stations in England are bad, but at least you get a reply!! Censoring here is as bad as England, but it makes me really angry that if they have to do it, why don't they do it right! Their cuts are changing the whole continuity of the storyline. Is it this bad over in England?*

Connie and Conor Kelleher (3062)

I'm afraid so - it seems immaterial to the censors whether the story is ruined, they must "preserve" their rights to hack away where they please, regardless of the consequences to the audiences. Videos seem to be also subject to censorship, I have now found, although at first we thought they had "escaped." (Pam).

Dear Pam,

My collection on Bruce is growing, I'm pleased to say. However, I get remarks from acquaintances such as "Don't you think you're going too far with Bruce Lee?" but I don't care - how can you explain to these crackpots who cannot see the sheer beauty of Bruce Lee? It's not just his Kung Fu I like - it's his being on that cinema screen. As long as I'm breathing on this Earth, Bruce Lee lives on!! I will always love, respect and admire the man - the Little Dragon!

Thomas Jones (2058)

And that's what makes fans, Thomas. Mind you - with some people, it is just a passing "fad" where they swap idols every few months. They are not true fans - they are as fickle as the wind and never really get a deep emotional feeling for the person they "for the moment" admire. A real fan, like yourself, will always feel the same over the years - the person may be in the background of the news, but is always in the foreground of ones emotions. (Pam).

SOCIETY BACK-ISSUE NEWS SHEETS & HOLLYWOOD PETITION

Keep sending in the petition names - and for more on this see Mike's comments on the video list of how to get a free copy of the *Enter the Dragon* video for the person sending the most signatures!

ROBERT LEE LP OFFER

Still available is the superb Robert L.P. *Ballad of Bruce Lee,* personally signed - and costing £4.50 (inc. posting/packaging) in the U.K., (Europe £5.50, rest of the world £6.50). Postal orders/cheques payable to Pam Hadden, London. For news sheet back issues, tell me what ones you want, and I'll write back with total cost for you to remit to me. All issues available.

LATE SNIPPET OF NEWS

I received a cutting from one of our U.S.A. members Shahad Setudeh Nejad (1419), which was undated but I believe was not too far back in time stating as follows: "Biggest shocker this summer is the arrest of Director Lo Wei, charged with conspiracy to commit criminal intimidation. Lo's arrest came after detectives launched the biggest anti-Triad operation in Hong Kong since 1956. Lo directed the first Bruce Lee movie."

You've Waited Long Enough, At Last...

THE "GAME OF DEATH" SUIT OFFER!

Yes, KFM has finally located some excellent reproductions of Bruce Lee's amazing YELLOW AND BLACK, ONE-PIECE TRACK SUIT. Snug fitting and comfortable, we are anticipating an enormous response to our offer for this rare and unique garment.

ORDER YOURS TODAY!
Normal price... £19.00

Special 'discount' Society members price... £16.00
(both prices include full handling)

When ordering, please stipulate the size you require:-
Small, Medium or Large

Rush your P.O./Cheque (made out to KFM) to:-
KFM Suit Offer
14 Rathbone Place
London W1P 1DE
(Please allow at least 4 weeks for delivery).

I'd be very interested if any member (Shahad??) can give me the date that this article was printed - would be very pleased to hear from you. The article was in *Variety* magazine and written by Mel Tobias.

SWOP SHOP

- Tony Lundberg, Copenhagen, Denmark has for swap: Loads newspaper articles on Elvis throughout his life and after his death. Wants: newspaper articles on Bruce's death, book *Dear Bruce Lee*, Oriental magazines on Bruce.
- Peter Jagger, Birmingham - his friend has *KFM* 1 to sell - offers to Peter's address please.
- John Rogers, Basildon as for sale: Japanese soundtrack albums of *Big Boss, Fist of Fury, Way of the Dragon* @ £7 each or all three for £18. perfect condition. (cost £10 each). Wooden nunchakus - £3, various books, magazines very cheap - SAE for details.
- Mirjana Vicelarevic, Hegotin, Yugoslavia wants: copy of either *Life & Tragic Death of Bruce Lee* or *Bruce Lee - The Man Only I Knew* - by Linda Lee (same book, different titles with the latter containing "flick action" pics). Please contact Mirjana if you have, know where to get.
- Floyd Osborne, Nuneaton wants: *KFM*'s 1-3, 12, 13, 31-33, plus *Game of Death* collectors' edition, *Wisdom of Bruce Lee, Unbeatable Bruce Lee, Farewell my Friend, Bruce Lee The Incomparable Fighter, Tribute to Bruce Lee,* Black Belt's *Best of Bruce Lee* Nos. 1 & 2, *Book of Kung Fu* - will pay original price or double.
- Takeshi Hasegawa, Aichiken, Japan has for swap: Japanese, Chinese magazines; 24 Japanese Bruce Lee Fan Club Bulletins, *Enter the Dragon* comics, *Game of Death II* pamphlet, record, poster, movie records LP's and pamphlet - all good condition. Wants: *My Martial Arts Guide to JKD, Best of Bruce Lee* Nos. 1 & 2, *KFMs* 1, 2, 31-33, *Dragon, Fighters,* and *Combat* magazines with Bruce Lee covers published in Italy, France, Germany, Spain, Denmark etc.
- Kin Tong Liu, Liverpool has for sale: video of *Big Boss* (quality not brilliant but watchable) - will sell for £15. Shows all last fights inc. one where he breaks promise not to fight; three consecutive kicks and short punches; also *Enter the Dragon* tape in good condition for £15, with underground, bottle scenes etc. (VHS). Write first.
- Ernest Bow, Basingstoke has for swap: videos - *Big Boss, Bruce Lee The Superstar from Hong Kong,* Bruce Lee & Jackie Chan - *Great Dragons from Hong Kong, Bruce Lee Kung Fu Superstars* - swap for four issues of martial arts movies or LP *Dragon Sounds Special*.
- Ian Hamilton, Sunderland has for sale: *KFM Scrapbook* No. 2 60p; *Secret Art* - £1; Super 8mm colour/silent *Fist of Fury* (poor quality, good action) - £10.
- Paul Wade, Hull has for sale: *Untold Story* - £1; *World of Bruce Lee* - £4.50; *King of Kung Fu* - £1; *Best of Bruce Lee* No. 2 - £1; *Martial Arts Movies Special* - £1. Also: Super 8mm colour, sound films - *Enter the Dragon* - 3 x 400ft - £52; *Green Hornet* - 600ft - £21; Trailers to *Boss, Fist of Fury, Way of the Dragon* - one reel - £13. All excellent condition & prices inc. p&p.
- Mark Salter, Sheffield has for sale: (offers please!) - *KFM* 1 (USA edition), *KFM* 3, *Life & Tragic Death of Bruce Lee* paperback, *Enter the Dragon* paperback by Mike Roote, *Bruce Lee Untold Story* (signed by Grace Li), *Kung Fu Cinema of Vengeance, Chinese Gung Fu* by Bruce Lee.

THE BRUCE LEE SOCIETY

- Douglas Banks, Stoke-on-Trent has for sale: Betamax video recordings - trailers of all five Bruce Lee films with best fight scenes, behind scenes of *Enter the Dragon,* complete *The Green Hornet* episode "Silent Gun." Write to Douglas with offers.
- Avtar Sohota, Warley has for sale: videos (poor quality but watchable) at blank-tape prices - so if you're not satisfied with content you can wipe clean, re-use the video-tape again, and have lost nothing price-wise. They are: *Fist of Fury* (cut) - £9.95; *Way of the Dragon* (uncut) - £12; *Fist of Fury, Big Boss* on one cassette (cut) - £14; *Game of Death* (my best print.) - £15 (cut).

PEN PALS

Andrew Upton (2672) aged 18 wants male pen pal around same age. He likes all Martial Arts (especially Shotokan Karate - he's a green belt); films; personalities' real names. Address: Birkenhead.

Conor Kelleher, Macroom, Ireland wants Chinese male, female pen pal - interests are Bruce, Martial Arts, Chinese culture, reading, natural history and animals.

MARTIAL ARTS VIDEO LISTS

Hi members! Mike Devereux your Research Manager here with my first effort at trying to bring to you news and information that I hope will please everyone! To start off with, for a long time now, I've been very interested in video and I thought that it would be a good idea to put a list of martial arts films that are available on video together, so that those members who are interested in the fight films other than Bruce's famous flicks, would have a good idea of what is available. The list is in no specific order, but where possible, I have tried to give the length, format available, and distributor of each film. Happy viewing to you all!

P.S. You will find the key to the distributors initials at the end if the list, along with addresses.

- *Bruce and Dragon Fist...* Bruce Le — VHS & BETA. — 85mins — £34.95 IVC
- *The Angry Dragon...* Cheung Kik — VHS & BETA. — 73mins — £34.50 VID
- *Two in Black Belt...* Chok Chow Cheung — VHS & BETA. — 90mins — £29.90 VCL
- *Black Dragon Revenges the Death of Bruce Lee...* — VHS & BETA. — 90mins — £39.95 INO
- *Bruce & Shaolin Kung Fu...* Bruce Le — VHS & BETA. — 85mins — £34.95 ICV
- *Treasure of Bruce Lee...* Bruce Le — VHS & BETA. — 85mins — £34.95 ICV
- *Hero of Shanghai...* Kuan Tai Chen — VHS & BETA. — 85mins — £34.95 ICV
- *The Tiger Strikes Again...* Bruce Li — VHS & BETA. — 85mins — £39.95 INO
- *Bruce Lee against the Supermen...* Bruce Li — VHS & BETA. — 80mins — £39.95 INO
- *Bruce's Fingers...* Chan Wai Man — VHS & BETA. — 91mins — £39.95 INT
- *Bruce Lee The Man The Myth...* Bruce Li — VHS & BETA. — 91mins — £39.95 DAV
- *The Clutch of Power...* Chan Sing — VHS & BETA. — 90mins — £29.90 VCL
- *Hero of the Time...* Tan Tao-Liang — VHS & BETA. — 85mins — £34.95 ICV

A RETROSPECTIVE LOOK AT BRUCE LEE MANIA & THE KUNG FU CRAZE OF THE 1970S

- *The Invincible Iron Palm...* Chin Hsiang-Ling — VHS & BETA. — 70mins £19.95 VIP
- *Deadly Chase for Justice...* Chan Wai Min — VHS & BETA. — 85mins £34.95 ICV
- *The Dragon Dies Hard...* Bruce Li — VHS & BETA. — 77mins £39.95 INO
- *The Dragon Lives Again...* Bruce Li — VHS & BETA. — 90mins £29.90 VCL
- *Duel with the Devils...* Tan Tao-Liang — VHS & BETA. — 85mins £34.95 ICV
- *Invincible Super Chan...* Han Shian Chin — VHS & BETA. — 90mins £39.95 INO
- *The Iron Monkey...* Chen Kuan-Tai — VHS & BETA. — 85mins £34.95 ICV
- *Jaws of the Dragon...* Jimmy Nam — VHS & BETA. — 92mins £39.95 MNT
- *Lady Karate...* Chia Lin — VHS & BETA. — 86mins £34.95 ICV
- *Marvellous stunts of Kung Fu...* — VHS & BETA. — 85mins £34.95 ICV
- *18 Riders for Justice...* Chen Sheng — VHS & BETA. — 85mins £34.95 ICV
- *Exit the Dragon Enter the Tiger...* Bruce Li — VHS & BETA. — 84mins £39.95 INO
- *Fearless Young Boxer...* Peter Chen — VHS & BETA. — 83mins £34.95 ICV
- *The Fierce One...* Jimmy Nam — VHS & BETA. — 84mins £34.95 ICV
- *Fist of Fury 2...* Bruce Li — VHS & BETA. — 95mins £39.95 HOK
- *Five Kung Fu Daredevils...* Lo Lieh — VHS & BETA. — 85mins £34.95 ICV
- *Godfather of Hong Kong...* Tien Peng — VHS & BETA. — 89mins £39.95 INT
- *General Stone...* Tan Tao-Liang — VHS & BETA. — 90mins £29.90 VCL
- *Match of Dragon and Tiger...* Yue Tin Lung — VHS & BETA. — 87mins £39.95 INO
- *Men on the Hour...* Lo Lieh — VHS & BETA. — 85mins £34.95 ICV
- *The Real Bruce Lee...* Bruce Lee & Dragon Lee — VHS & BETA. — 120mins £39.95 INT
- *Return of Bruce...* Bruce Le — VHS & BETA. — 85mins £34.95 ICV
- *Mysterious Heroes...* Carter Wong — VHS & BETA. — 90mins £29.90 VCL
- *Return of Fist of Fury...* Bruce Le — VHS & BETA. — 84mins £34.95 ICV
- *Shaolin Iron Finger...* Huang Chia Daa — VHS & BETA. — 85mins £34.95 ICV
- *Return of the Dragon...* Yue Tin Lung — VHS & BETA. — 90mins £39.95 INO
- *Super Dragon...* Ron Van Chief. — VHS & BETA. — 90mins £39.95 HOK
- *Snake in the Monkey's Shadow...* John Chan — VHS & BETA. — 85mins £39.95 INO
- *Shaolin Kung Fu Master...* Wong Tao — VHS & BETA. — 85mins £34.95 ICV
- *Shaolin Master and the Kid...* Yueh Hua — VHS & BETA. — 85mins £34.95 ICV

ICV - Inter-continental Video, 147 Wardour Street, London, W1.
VID - Videx Video, 14 Palmsrston Road, Sutton, Surrey.
VCL - VCL Services Ltd, 58 Parker Street, London WC2.
IKO - Inter-ocean, 29 Great Pulteney Street, London W1.
INT - Intervision Video, Unit 1, McKay Trading Est, Kensal Rd, London W10.
VIP - Vipco, 9 Sentinel House, Sentinel Sq, Brent Street, London NW4.
DAV - Derann Audio Video, High Street, Dudley, West Midlands.
MNT - Mountain video, 45 New Oxford Street, London WC1.
HOK - Hokushin, 2 Ambleside Avenue, London, SW16.

ENTER THE DRAGON - BRUCE LEE

The original uncut film from Warner Home Video. Marketed by WEA Records Ltd, P.O. Box 59, Alperton Lane, Wembley, Middlesex, HA0 1FJ. Also available from all good video stores for £34.95.

8MM FILMS

All members interested in 8mm film of Bruce Lee, please note: Apart from, the trailers and other great goodies that are on the market, you can obtain the full films of *Big Boss, Fist of Fury, Way of the Dragon* and *Game of Death,* all on 4 x 400ft reels, and perfect picture reproduction. They are very slightly edited so as to keep as much action in there as possible. They are available in this country, for about £50 for one reel and don't forget, there are four reels to one film. If you want to save money and get the films for about £35 inc p&p, then write to the following address for details:- B.V. V/H Van De Kleut's, Handelsbureau, Top Film, Amsterdam, Westerkade 19, Holland. This company has taken over Miko Studio and are very reliable.

THE HOLLYWOOD PETITION

If you are a true devoted fan of Bruce lee, then you. MUST want to see his name go on one of the gold stars that line up along Hollywood Boulevard. To do this as you all know, we need an awful lot of signatures to get the wheels turning! Those of you who have contributed so far have done a marvellous job, and we cannot thank you enough! But we still need more! To add incentive, The Bruce Lee Society is making this offer: Between now and the next news sheet, whoever can send in to Pam the most signatures, will receive absolutely FREE, a copy of *Enter the Dragon* on video (VHS format). The quality of the video is excellent and cannot be beaten! I wonder which of you out there will get it? See the next news sheet for the result!

That's it from me for now! Since writing this sheet, *The Big Boss* and *Fist of Fury* have been released by the Rank Organisation but more on that next time.

Remember, the spirit of Bruce Lee lives on! Mike Devereaux - Research Manager.

USEFUL ADDRESSES
Courtesy of David Moore (1783)

BOOKS AND MAGAZINES

Sakura Trading Company, 10 Thornbury Road, Isleworth, TW7 4HG.
A Guide to Martial Arts Training with Equipment by Dan Inosanto - £6.45, *Bruce Lee's Fighting Method* - Vols. 1-4 - £3.45 each vol, *Tao of Jeet Kune Do* by Bruce Lee - £6.95, *JKD - Art and Philosophy of Bruce Lee* by Dan Inosanto £6.95, *Filipino Martial Arts* by Dan Inosanto - £5.90, *Martial Arts Movies* (magazine) - £1.95, *Bruce Lee Untold Story* (magazine) - £1.95. Many more magazines, books, and martial

arts equipment. Postage costs: Orders costing up to £1.00 (30p postage), £3.00 (60p), £25.00 (95p).

Bruce Lee Collectors Club, 537 Stratford Road, Sparkhill, Birmingham, B11 4LP.
Annual Membership: £4.95 - includes a catalogue of items to buy (books, magazines, etc,) concerning Bruce, sold at discount prices to members, quarterly newsletter, sew-on patch and a yearly membership card.

Giko Ltd, 537 Stratford Road, Sparkhill, Birmingham, B11 4LP.
World of Bruce Lee (book) - £6.95 + 60p postage (Contributions by Linda Lee, Norman Borine, Dan Lee, Dan Inosanto, Jim Lau and others. Many new photos.), *Bruce Lee Memorial Magazines* Nos.1-12 inclusive. Many martial arts, magazines, books and equipment.

Cimac Martial Arts Wear Ltd, 606 Stratford Road, Sparkhill, Birmingham, B11 4AP.
Bruce Lee Memorial Magazines Nos.1-12, *Bruce Lee Combats, Bruce Lee - Nunchakus in Action, Bruce Lee Revenges.* Many more magazines, books, and martial arts equipment.

Karate & Oriental Arts, 638 Fulham Road, London, SW6.
Bruce Lee Martial Arts Phenomenon (magazine) £1.50, *Bruce Lee Memorial Magazines* Nos.1-12 £1.20 each inc p&p (Buy three or more £1.00 each inc p&p.), *Bruce Lee in Action* £1.50, *Bruce Lee Combat* £1.50, *Bruce Lee Revenges* £1.50, *Bruce Lee Immortal Dragon* £1.50, *Bruce Lee - Fighting Spirit* £1.50, *Bruce Lee Game of Death Extract Edition* £1.75, *In the Steps of Bruce Lee* £ 1.50.
Many back issues of *Inside Kung Fu* magazine @ 75p each including: Vol. 4 Nos. 9/10 (Elvis and Karate), Vol. 5 No. 7 (*Game of Death* Special), Vol. 5 No. 10 (Ed Parker), Vol. 7 No. 1 (Dan Inosanto). Back issues of USA magazines *Black Belt, Official Karate,* and *Defense Combat* 75p each. Back issues of *Karate & Oriental Arts* magazines @ 50p each including Nos. 64, 65, 67, 69 (featuring Bruce Lee) and 76, 77 (featuring *Game of Death*). *Bruce Lee* by Jesse Glover (Book) £4.00. Many other good martial arts books available too.

FILM AND VIDEO

Oriental World, 18A Swan Street, Manchester
Way of the Dragon Super 8mm colour/silent with cassette (includes nunchaku scene/ coliseum fight) £38.70, *Game of Death* Super 8mm Colour/Silent (includes Dan Inosanto scene and Kareem fight) £38.70, *Enter the Dragon* Super 8mm Production Film (*Robins Nest* documentary) colour/silent - £21.55, *Enter the Dragon* Super 8mm colour/sound Trailer £11.55 + 50p p&p, *Big Boss* Super 8mm colour/sound trailer £11.55 + 50p p&p, *Enter the Dragon* Super 8mm colour/sound 20 mins/400ft. £44.70, *Big Boss, Fist of Fury, Way of the Dragon* and *Game of Death* complete uncensored (Each film in four reels, each 20 minutes) £50.50 per reel inc p&p or £195 each complete film inc p&p. Good quality/German dialogue. *Enter the Dragon* style sparring gloves - medium/large £22.50 + £1.50 p&p.

THE BRUCE LEE SOCIETY

Mirror Video Club, Room 325, Daily Mirror, *Holborn Circus, London, EC1P 1DQ.*
Life Membership - £5. Discount on video films for members. In stock: *Enter the Dragon*. Also video cassette of martial arts touring team from the People's Republic of China who toured UK in 1981. (one hour long). Membership price £25.50, Non-membership price £29.50.

J. Hasted, 20 Southwell Grove Road, Leytonstone, London, E11.
Has *Fist of Fury* and *Game of Death*, and *Enter the Ninja* videos £31 each including p&p. Many other films on video.

Tang Video Club, 152 Shawclough Way, Healey Gardens, Rochdale, OL12 6EE.
Enter the Dragon, Way of the Dragon, Fist of Fury, Big Boss, Game of Death on video cassette. Different versions available including censored, uncensored and also uncensored with slow motion addition. Many other films including Chuck Norris and Jackie Chan.

SIP, 17 Tottenham Court Road, London, W1.
Magazines, books, posters, photos, postcards and paper-cuttings on Bruce Lee. Also video films on VHS, Betamax and Philips systems. *Enter the Dragon* deluxe colour box £45, Normal plain box £40, *Green Hornet* and early Bruce Lee (whole episode of *Green Hornet* titled "Silent Gun" plus Bruce Lee's early films). Deluxe £45, plain £40, *Fist of Fury* (All fights complete and short comedy scenes edited) deluxe £45, plain £40, Bruce Lee video ("Green Hornet Screen Test" in black and white, trailers of all Bruce's films and *Enter the Dragon* Production Film (*Robins Nest* documentary) deluxe £45, plain £40. Also has *Game of Death, Big Boss* and "Kato" video films.

Book Century Martial Arts Supply, 3034 Del View, Del City, Oklahoma 75115, U.S.A.
Chuck Norris Karate System (book) 200 pages, 650 instructional photos, US$9.50 (£4.00) money order made out to "Fitness Media." Write first to check availability and postage cost from USA. Also Chuck Norris Fan Club, 142 So. 18th Maywood, Illinois 60153, USA.

Videotime, 132 Kirkgate, Wakefield, West Yorkshire.
Many video films available. Write for information.

Land of Video Ltd, 20/21 Tottenham Court Road, London, W1P 9RA.
Land of Video sell the newly-released Rank *The Big Boss* and *Fist of Fury* videos at £44.95 each in excellent quality (I've seen them!). If you are unable to call personally, they will mail them to you at extra cost of £1 in the UK/Ireland and £2 anywhere else in the world, to be added to the cost of each video ordered. The titles are available on VHS, Betamax, and V2000, so state which is required when ordering and give your name and address clearly. They also state that *Way of the Dragon* and *Game of Death* are due to be released in about one month's time.

MARTIAL ARTS MOVIE RELEASES DURING 1982
Courtesy of David Moore (1783)

The Last Adventure
Stars: Eric Lee, with Gini Lau, Ralph Cagtellanos, Lanai Lee, Steve Labounty, Alan Gin, Gerald Okamura. Director: Paul Kyriazi. Fight Choreography: Eric Lee and Sid Campbell.

Revenge of the Bushido Blade
Stars: Leo Fong with Cameron Mitchell, Marwin Roberts.

Big Brawl (US - *Battlecreek Brawl*)
Stars: Jackie Chan, with Jose Ferrer, Mako, Ron Max, Kristine de Bell. Director: Robert Clouse. Producer: Fred Weintraub. Music: Lalo Schifrin. A Golden Harvest/Warner Bros Production.

The Octagon
Stars: Chuck Norris with Lee van Clief, Art Hindle, Tadashi Yaraashita, Karen Carlson, Carol Bagdasarian. Director: Eric Karson. Producer: Joel Freeman. Music: Dick Halligan. Screenplay: Leigh Chapman. Executive Producers: Michael Leone, Alan Beckin.

Kill or Be Killed III
Stars: James Ryan

The Masters
Stars: Tadeshi Yamasbita and Byong Yu. Screenplay: Stirling Silliphant.

Hard Knocks
Stars: Bill Wallace and Karyn Turner. Script: Don and Judy Quine.

Enter the Ninja
Stars: Franco Nero and Susan George with Christopher George, Alex Courtney, Sho Kosugi. Director: Menshem Golan. Producers: Judd Eernara and Yoram Globus. Writers: Judd Bernard and Menahem Golan. Music: Laurin Rinder and W. Michael Lewis. Fight Choreography: Mike Stone. A Cannon Group Inc. and First City Films Production.

The Golden Killer
Stars: Carter Wong.

Shinobi
Stars: Eric Lee with Karyn Shepherd, Tadashi Yamashite.

Revenge Of The Ninja
Stars: Sho Kosugi with Stephen Hayes, Keith Vitali. Director: Menahem Golan. Fight Choreography: Mike Stone.

THE BRUCE LEE SOCIETY

The Falcon's Claw
Stars: Eric lee

Force Five
Stars: Joe Lewis, Benny Urquidez, Richard Norton, Sonny Barnes, Pamela Huntingdon with Bong Soo Han, Ron Haydon. Director: Robert Clouse. Producer: Fred Weintraub.

The Protector
Stars: Jackie Chan. Producer: Raymond Chow.
A Golden Harvest Production.

The Equals
Stars: Toshiro Mifune. CBS Theatrical Films Production.
(US $15million Budget)

Shogun
Stars: Richard Chamberlain, Toshiro Mifune, Yoke Shimada. Director: Jerry London. Producer/Writer: Eric Bercovici. Music: Maurice Jarre. NBC TV America (Film version - 2 1/2 hours. Longer TV version six hours - US $22 million Budget - Currently showing on BBC TV)

Kill and Kill Again
Stars: James Ryan with Ken Campu, Norman Robinson, Bill Flynn, Stan Schmidt, Anneline Kriel. Producer: Igor Kantor.

Weapons of Death
Stars: Eric Lee (formerly released as *The Last Adventurer*).

An Eye For an Eye
Stars: Chuck Norris with Mako. Fight Choreograghy: Chuck Norris and Aaron Norris. An Avco Embassy Picture.

STAFF NEWS

An addition to the Society staff: John Watson is now about to take on the title "General Manager" and he is, at the moment, trying to research out suitable places so that we can ask *KFM* to now put on either a convention or a film show. Bear in mind though, until we go solo, they still hold the money!

A thought to end the newsletter (from the opening lines of the *Water Margin* series which Simon Bulley feels describes the relationship between Bruce and the Society):

"The ancients have taught us not to loathe the snake because he has no horns, for he may grow up to become a dragon. So may one just man become an army."

See you soon - Pam

BRUCE LEE SOCIETY COLUMN
KUNG FU MONTHLY NO. 65

Hi everyone. Well, as I promised last time, things really are starting to move for the Society. The powers-that-be at *KFM* control, have confirmed that they'd be delighted to see the Bruce Lee Society become gradually self-supporting. They're going to be offering all the help and advice they can, but at the same time they realise that it's essential for the Society to be able to find its own feet. There comes a time for any organisation of this kind, when too much spoon-feeding starts to cut down on the effectiveness. After all, Bruce Lee never asked anyone else to run his show for him!

It's also, of course, quite a dangerous time for us. Should members fail to rise to the challenge that presents itself to us, no longer will we be able to rely on somebody else to "bail us out". Therefore, to get the ball rolling, probably by the time you read this, there will already have been a meeting of interested London members. I will have been looking for ideas, offers of help and business expertise, and the opinion of everyone as regards to the kind of Society they'd like to be part of in the years to come. Let's hope things worked out as well as planned!

And depending on how well the above went, the idea is to continue this same momentum all over the country. Therefore what I'm asking for NOW is that any person in any part of the British Isles who feels they are at all good at organising things, would they PLEASE get in touch with me so we can discuss what the chances are in their particular area. Include a telephone number if at all possible.

Once I have a reasonable list of areas in which to set up meetings, then I'll co-ordinate all of them in such a way that I shall be able to visit them all personally. That way, the result should be a really well planned campaign, organised on a national scale.

In the meantime, anyone who wishes they had gone to the London meeting but who couldn't make it, or who didn't hear about it in time, please get in touch and let me know, as briefly as you can, just what kind of involvement you see yourself being able to make.

Lastly for this month, one proposal that's constantly being thrown up is the one to have an ongoing series of film shows all over the country, run by the Society. I certainly see this as an ideal way of arousing local interest and I'm actually taking steps at this moment to see whether it might be possible. More on that, no doubt, in the next newsletter.

And for anyone who wants to drop me a line, the address is: c/o 14 Rathbone Place, London W1P 1DE.

- Pam Hadden

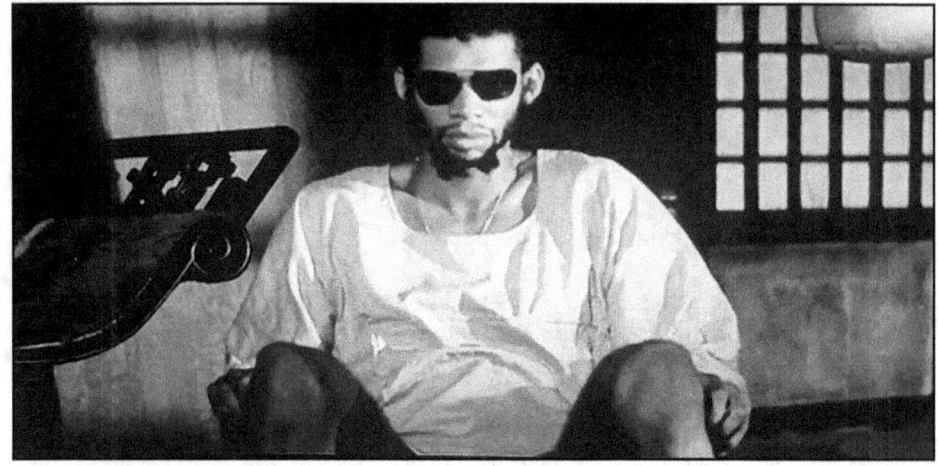

EDITOR'S NOTES

The shooting of Kareem Abdul-Jabbar's family that was referred to was 1973 Hanafi Muslim massacre, which took place on 18th January 1973, but his immediate family were not involved. Two adults and a child were shot to death, four other children ranging in age from nine days to ten years old were drowned and two others were severely injured. The murder took place in Washington, DC, at a house purchased for a group of Hanafi Muslims to use as the "Hanafi American Mussulman's Rifle and Pistol Club." The property was purchased and donated by Kareem Abdul-Jabbar, then a Milwaukee Bucks basketball player.

Wang Zi-Ping was a Chinese martial artist and practitioner of traditional medicine from Cangzhou, Hebei Province in China. Born is 1881, he served as the leader of the Shaolin Kung Fu division of the Martial Arts Institute in 1928 and was also the vice chairman of the Chinese Wu Shu Association. Wang was famed for his mastery of Chaquan, Huaquan, Pao Chuan, Bajiquan, and T'ai Chi Chuan, as well as being a master of Wu Shu. He died in 1973, aged 92.

Game of Death 2, released in places as *Tower of Death* teased Bruce Lee fans with trailer featuring then-unseen *Enter the Dragon* footage. When the film was released, the only new footage was of Lee's character from *Enter The Dragon* talking to the Abbott played by Roy Chiao, which is now in the 25th Anniversary cut of *Enter the Dragon* and footage of Lee exploring his room upon arriving on Han's island in the same film.

The film's premise is that Bruce Lee's character from the 1978 rewrite of *Game of Death* Bobby Lo, is murdered and his brother, Billy Lo, sets off for revenge and the truth. There is a different version of the film that exists however, which removed all of the Bruce Lee footage and subplot and features an entirely new plot and alternative footage. This version of the film was released on VHS in Korea in 1981 and hasn't been released anywhere since.

A RETROSPECTIVE LOOK AT BRUCE LEE MANIA & THE KUNG FU CRAZE OF THE 1970S

24
June
1982

HELLO, MEMBERS - IT SEEMS LIKE JUST A COUPLE OF WEEKS AGO THAT I WROTE THE MARCH NEWS SHEET, AND YET HERE AGAIN I'M OFF WITH THE JUNE ONE! WE'LL SOON BE COMING UP TO THE SEVENTH YEAR OF THE SOCIETY, WHICH ALSO SEEMS INCREDIBLE, DOESN'T IT?? I'VE BEEN TOLD WE ARE AMONG THE LONGEST-RUNNING FAN CLUBS AROUND - WHICH CAN'T BE BAD! BEFORE I BEGIN THE SHEET, I'D JUST LIKE TO DRAW YOUR SPECIAL ATTENTION TO THE HEADINGS "MEMORIAL FLOWERS" AND "GRACE'S PRESENT" - PLEASE DO READ AND RESPOND - ALL YOUR HELP IS NEEDED AS A SOCIETY MEMBER AND FELLOW FAN!!

LOCALISED MEETINGS

I've heard NOTHING from any members about localised meetings (last two news sheets). Maybe you are all still in hibernation from the bad winter - so come on, wake up, and let's hear something from you!!

FUTURE TRIP - HONG KONG AND/OR U.S.A.

I've had a letter from an agent who is looking at small-party trips, and trying to see if he can give me a costing on this - small party trips being the only thing we can consider at this stage due to the poor response from members. One thing I WILL mention - if members DO wish to join any future prospective trip that might get going, they CAN include friends and family to travel with them at whatever the price might be. Anyway, if a reasonable price can be obtained for the fare, I shall then check with a friend in Hong Kong on accommodation, and also Seattle/Los Angeles, and for any other expenses which would be necessary for coaches, etc. Bear in mind - this sort of thing is new to me too on an organisation basis, and the whole project takes a great deal of arranging.

MEMORIAL FLOWERS - 20TH JULY 1982

Since I placed the request for donations to the floral tribute (to go to Bruce's graveside for the second year running) in the last news sheet, I have had contributions from 29 members which has brought in some £56 sterling plus two donations in foreign currency yet to be converted. So - for all those members wishing to contribute who have not yet done so (and I DO understand that some members have waited until nearer the time to donate but WAS surprised at only receiving so few contributions so far from the whole club) - PLEASE - do send a little something for the flowers, no matter how small, as we want to do something special for the grave. There is no limit to how small the donation - but I will ask that no donation go above £2 from any one member. Send donations to Pam Hadden, Memorial Flowers, London, (not forgetting to include your name and membership number for the list to be sent to the grave) TO REACH ME BY THE END OF JUNE - VERY VERY LATEST!! It takes several weeks to organise, and this will, as last year, be ably handled by member Alison French once I have all donations to hand and passed the total to her. As mentioned last sheet, a list of donators will be published in the September news sheet, together with the receipt from the florist.

GRACE'S PRESENT

As mentioned in the last sheet, it was thought a lovely idea to send a present to Bruce's mum - and I requested members to send in their names/Society numbers to me stating what amount they would wish to donate (no money just yet, please, just what you CAN send when the time comes). Well, this project will now MOST DEFINITELY BE GOING AHEAD - so far I have had around £52 pledged, but I'D STILL LIKE TO HEAR FROM ALL MEMBERS WHO HAVE NOT PLEDGED A DONATION - PLEASE, THE AMOUNT YOU PLEDGE IS IMMATERIAL BUT THE THOUGHT IS IMPORTANT!! I feel a piece of silver would be ideal and other members seem to agree - it would be lasting and a reminder of our thoughts on Bruce. And after receiving various words from members as to what would be suitable for engraving on this silverware, I have decided on what I consider to be a simple yet so apt suggestion from member Ian Fawcett (2918) which is: "HE WAS A SON TO YOU - HE WAS A SUN TO US" I hope you all agree. All postcards pledging a donation should be sent to me by 7th August latest (Address as above); after that date, I shall be "calling in the money." Whatever chosen will be accompanied by the names of those who donated - it's a pity that it cannot be something which has the name of nearly EVERYONE in the Society against it! - but feel it only fair at this stage - unless I get a stupendous onslaught of donation pledges! - that the names of the donators only be sent with the present - do you agree?? In the September news sheet I shall give the final total obtained, what silverware shall be sent, and just how and when it shall be presented to Grace. I hope this meets with approval from you all.

WORLD OF BRUCE LEE - REQUEST FOR HELP

I've heard from my good friend Norman Borine (who runs the above organisation) that they have now moved from their Hollywood address back to Eagle Rock, their original location!! I have just dropped him a line to see what items he might have for sale - and hope to have some positive details for the next news sheet. HOWEVER - ONE IMPORTANT THING I MUST ASK - it seems Norman has a lot of things planned for the future, which will also incorporating working with the Society more - and for a publicity campaign he needs COPIES OF ANY GOOD PHOTOGRAPHS TAKEN OF HIMSELF, DANNY INOSANTO OR THE SHOW GENERALLY DURING THE VISIT HE MADE TO LONDON IN JUNE, 1980, AT WESTMINSTER CENTRAL HALL. All the copies of various photos Norman had were recently stolen, and he says if anyone can help, he would be most grateful and very happy to send them the cost of the pictures. If anyone can let me have them at London, together with the price, if any, you require, I shall then mail them to Norman with your names/addresses. ONLY GOOD PICTURES SUITABLE FOR PRINTING, PLEASE. Many, many thanks from Norman and myself.

GENERAL NEWS

Firstly, it seems everyone liked the cover of the last news sheet designed by Mike (Research Manager) Devereux. The video list he produced, and the movie and useful addresses list from David Moore, also went down EXTREMELY WELL! For the future, I've decided that wherever possible I'll be giving write-ups submitted by members on martial arts films and videos in detail, so we can get to know just what we are likely to be seeing! So do drop me a line with your comments on anything you see and, if we have not researched it already, I'll put your comments into a news sheet.

You will see that I've started the ball rolling this sheet with a couple of write-ups from members, as well as an interview with Stirling Silliphant sent in by Maria Fernandes, two articles on how people feel on Bruce, a poem and a member's meeting with Robert Lee and Dan Inosanto (see separate sheets). From now on, any interesting articles on Bruce will be printed in full - and anything you feel would be printable please let me know. Any specific pointers on Bruce's philosophy/quotes would be of interest, too, that you might think merit printing.

I'm still streamlining the kit - with a new-type plastic membership card being done, something like an Access/Barclaycard. This will run for the duration of membership - thus eliminating the need to send a separate one each year. All members holding a cardboard membership card will receive a plastic one as and when they renew their membership.

There will be one standard kit which will last for one year - this being sent to new and renewing members alike throughout the year, and the kit changed for the following year, and so on. This will then cut down my having to send out (as at present) six different batches of items, pictures etc. (And soon to be seven when the seventh year starts!) The badges as at present will remain part of the kit, and will not change. Anyway, more on this when it is completed!!

Ian Clarke, Anne Hunt, Gino D'Ambrosio, Nicholas Coleman, Shahid Saleem and many others, sent in a cutting stating that Albert Goldman (who wrote the controversial book *Elvis*) plans one on Bruce. Says Ian: "Goldman believed Bruce died under mysterious circumstances - other notables thinking along the same vein being Danny Inosanto and Ed Parker. Their opinions should be listened to." I wish Mr. Goldman all the luck in the world - he's going to need it!!

Lee's life on the line

AUTHOR ALBERT GOLDMAN, whose book on Elvis Presley earned him a reputation as a character assassin, is now turning his laser-like attention to Bruce Lee.

But he assures me from Hong Kong that he is not planning to chop the Kung Fu hero down to size.

Bewildered and hurt by public reaction to his Elvis book he says: "I was a great admirer of Lee and in any case I am not a put-down merchant.

"Bruce Lee is said to have died from the after effects of taking aspirin. Yet at 32 he had the body of an 18 year old super athlete. There's something wrong there and I intend to get at the truth."

Hold tight, fans!

Ian also states, "Just as interesting is the latest news of Director Lo Wei's arrest following his involvement with the Triads - the Chinese equivalent of the Mafia (see March news sheet for cutting). Lo Wei and Lee did not exactly like each other, and it's possible Lo Wei had a hand in Lee's early death. He could have been slipped one of the poisons which is undetectable in the body after 48 hours, as no known satisfactory conclusion came about from the autopsy. Triads could silence anyone knowing the truth - after all, the Hong Kong police are the most corrupt in the world, and these are the people who investigated Lee's death. Is there then any wonder that, after nine years, we still do not know the truth?"

Well, personally I feel that if Mr. Goldman IS able to get at the truth - and not go speculating and adding more comments to the many that abound about Bruce's death - it might settle the matter once and for all. My concern is that the family - who, after all, are the ones to be considered - may be put through yet again another lot of publicity on unfounded speculation submitted by a man who, in my opinion, is like many others - out to "feather his own nest" at the expense of whoever it takes - at whatever the cost. There was too much rubbish put out about Bruce - as with ANY superstar who tragically dies at a young age, such as James Dean etc. - and I do not necessarily wish Mr. Goldman "luck" - I WISH HIM CAUTION!

On another note, David Moore (1783) saw *Magnum Force* with Clint Eastwood on TV, and found the music played whilst Eastwood and two

Glynn Darbyshire (2885)

crooked cops were running around inside a ship was the same as the music in *Enter the Dragon* where Bruce creeps past the guards on his first night-time prowl. (Both films having the music score done by Lalo Schifrin). David also says that a month or two ago, *Combat* mag had an article by writer Chris Welling where Bruce is supposed to have said his skills were down to camera tricks and special effects!!! David wrote a VERY irate letter to *Combat* and Mr. Welling to put them straight, and the letter was printed in the April 1982 issue of that magazine. (Pam here: *Combat* is noted for messing up articles/pictures on Bruce! Some of their mistakes have been unbelievable - even (as mentioned in a previous news sheet) to printing a picture of Bruce and a Chinese actress friend and saying it was Bruce and his WIFE!!

Still with music, Satvinder Singh (3321) says that the programme *Star Sound Extra* (Radio 2 plays record requests every Monday night at 1030. On 15th March they played *Fist of Fury,* and Bruce was also briefly mentioned on *Film 82* a little while back.

Member Paul Corrigan (1711) is in contact by radio with people worldwide - and is now going to act as Overseas Liaison Officer in getting pen pals and info whenever possible. He will "spread the word of the Society to many foreign countries" - so as soon as I get anything from Paul, I'll be giving it to you!!

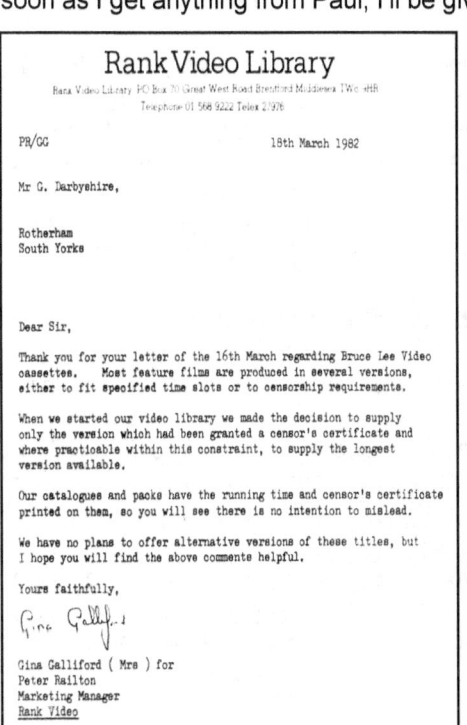

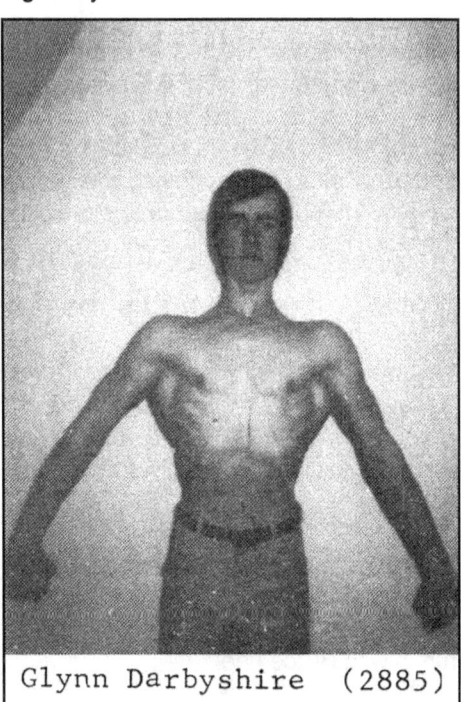

Glynn Darbyshire (2885)

You'll also notice in the sheet member Glynn Darbyshire's drawing and instructions in a defence against a full swing - if any other members wish to send in a good structural drawing with instructions in the same format as Glynn's, I will consider this for future news sheets maybe a special move which has worked for yourself and which you might wish to pass on to other members! Glynn also wrote to Rank Video Library concerning the cutting of the videos on Bruce - and you will see their reply which is self-explanatory - but still does not justify what has been done!!!!

Graham Jukes (3318) recently wrote to Central TV (Midlands area) to get Bruce's films showing on TV - they replied and said at the moment they have no intention of showing these, but Graham's letter had been passed to their films schedules office which means maybe at a future date they could be shown on the new Channel 4.

Our one and only Icelandic member, Hilmar Gudsteinsson, went to see Jackie Chan recently - he says he knows that people keep saying Jackie is trying to copy Bruce, but thinks these remarks are unfair. Hilmar thinks Jackie a fairly good fighter and actor where films are concerned, and quotes the words of DAN INOSANTO from *FIGHTING STARS* - April 1982 - "I enjoy watching Jackie Chan - he isn't the fighter Bruce was, but I enjoy his moves. He has a different style. A lot of people try to copy Bruce but not Jackie; he's sort of a comedian acrobat!!" And in the same issue, ERIC LEE says: "I feel that the legend created by the late Bruce Lee is still very much with us today and will continue to grow with time. No matter who you are, or how different your style, people will always compare you with him but that is to be expected. Bruce opened the door and made it possible. He will live forever in our hearts."

Shahid Saleem (3293) has the following comment to make on getting the *The Green Hornet* shown on TV - he says we should get a sponsor with a large amount of money to put in and then ask the TV people if they could put it on by the money we give them!! Well - it's a nice idea Shahid, but things just don't always work like that. And, although money counts for a lot - and there is the old saying that "money talks" - I do not think that in this case it would have much effect. Still, if we can find that RICH SPONSOR!!!- any members with very rich IN-LAWS????

AL DACASCOS REMEMBERS BRUCE LEE

Graham Jukes thought members might be interested in this article he saw on Al Dacascos - "An excellent martial artist" says Graham - which appeared in *Fighting Arts* magazine Vol. 4 No. 4 - so it is printed in its entirely in this news sheet - hope you all enjoy it!! (Personally, though, after reading the article, I'd say Al fancies himself rather!).

Anything interesting happen to you when you first started teaching in San Francisco?

Yes. I had a run-in with some of the local Chinese kung fu people and almost a run in with Bruce Lee.

Bruce Lee?

Yes, Bruce's school was only about six or seven miles away from mine. We were in the Oakland area. His was on Broadway and mine was on East 14th Street. Well how it got started was the fault of our students both mine and his they were each saying that their teacher was the best, that I was better than him, that he was better than me; you know the sort of thing. Well even while this was going on, circumstances made Bruce and I sort of natural allies. You're probably familiar with the story of Bruce's fight with the Kung Fu teacher Wong Jack Man? Well anyway to cut it short, four or five Chinese guys from San Francisco's China Town went to Bruce's school. I think it was in 1965 and told him he had to close his school down because he was teaching Caucasians and that he should only teach Chinese. They made a lot of noise and Wong Jack Man was the one who had been chosen to challenge him. He incidentally was also one of my teachers who taught my wife Malia and I some forms but I didn't get to know anything about this until after I had a similar incident happen to me. Anyway, Bruce got real angry at this and they fought and of course Bruce won, in fact that fight was a turning point for Bruce in his way of thinking and training because even though he won, he practically ran out of steam and he realised that condition was very important, also not just aggressiveness but that's a different story.

My turn for a visit came about a year and a half after that - a different group of Chinese, but the same story They just came in and said, "We're from San Francisco" I said, "Yeah and..?" They said. "You're only half Chinese and you're teaching whites - you're only supposed to teach Kung Fu to Chinese." I told them that my teacher had given me permission to teach whomever I liked. When that didn't cut any ice I got angry and said something like "What the has it got to do with you people anyway?" Then one of them says, "Lets have a friendly match - you and me and if you lose, you must close down your school." When he said that, my ears just got hot, I said "Yeah, okay, lets go." Most of my students were in the changing rooms but a few came out to watch. Now I was so mad by this time, I was really itching to go. So as soon as he salutes, I just went right at him. Normally you step back into your stance, but I just went "wham!" I blasted him in the face, I elbowed him, took him down and just kept on going into him and he was yelling at me in Chinese to stop. The rest of them wanted to come in on it then, so I jumped up and I said. "Come on you bastards, come on," but they said they didn't want any problems so they got him up and they all left.

Now after I'd cooled down, I got worried, I thought, "Oh, what have I done now?" They're going to come down on me with the whole Chinese Tongs or something. So I got my students together and I told them, "I think maybe we're going to have some problems." They just said, "Okay we're ready." There were a lot of Filipinos, Chinese, Mexicans and so on amongst them - all hot blooded people, you see, and they were all behind me.

For a while, nothing was heard but I was suspicious of anyone I saw that was more slant-eyed than me. A couple of months later one of my visitors came round and said, "Hey, we made a mistake. Your teacher told us not to antagonise you. We didn't know you had connections with our association."

I had one other run-in with some Chinese after that, when a few students and I had gone to Chinatown to watch the New Year Festival. A group of young militant Chinese, members of a new Tong group attacked us and we ended up putting eight of them in hospital. The papers the next day reported it as a gang fight but word soon got around that it was us who were responsible and our reputation grew some more. Some of my students then began spouting off even more that I was better than Bruce. So it was heating up between our schools and, things came to a head after one of my students - who had only eight months training, fought and beat one of Bruce's students - who had been with him for two years - at a party they were at. They had argued and ended up going to it in the back yard.

Apparently what had happened was that Bruce's guy had come in using a typical Wing Chun technique but the way we worked was to feint to draw an opponent to come in on us straight and then we'd switch and come in from the side. Now the Wing Chun guy wasn't prepared for that, you see. I was familiar with some Southern Preying Mantis style which is similar to Wing Chun, so I kind of knew the principles of how they came in, and I had taught my students how to fight against them.

Now up to this time, Bruce and I had still not met each other but, I was friendly with one of his assistant instructors, James Lee - I used to go to his house and we'd discuss techniques and so on. Also, as I said, because of our similar run-ins with the Chinese, both of our groups were sort of the outcasts there.

Anyway, I finally met Bruce in Los Angeles at one of the International Karate Championships. I went up to him and said "Look Bruce, as you know, some of my students and some of your students have been saying things about who is better and so forth." He just said. "Don't pay attention to that. It's not the instructors who make problems, it's the students." I said, "Well I'm sure glad to hear that. I thought maybe you were pissed off with me and was ready to go at it!" And he said, "No. Al. I got nothing against you - you've got a good style. I've got a good style and that's the way we feel about it."

After that we met on several occasions and discussed things. He was impressed with some of my leg techniques, and I was impressed with some of his hand techniques. Bruce wasn't really a kicker then; he was more of a puncher at that time. He didn't really develop his kicking techniques until around '67/'68. We never did any formal working out together it was more like, "Okay, what would you do in this situation? Do you think that this technique or this way is better than that way?" And we'd often talk about Chinese philosophy, just what you'd call rapping sessions. Our wives and children became very close friends and Linda Lee would send her kids up to Denver, Colorado, when we moved there, to go skiing with us and our kids would go to Los Angeles to stay with them sometimes. But Bruce and I never got that close or saw that much of each other because we were always too busy with our respective things - he was off developing his movie career and I was going off in another direction. But we always maintained a lot of respect for each other.

SPECIAL MESSAGES & REQUESTS

A special message (which regrettably arrived too late for the last sheet) comes from Stephen Fothergill to his fiancé, Christine - they have been engaged for one year on 24th February and she also celebrated her 20th birthday on 29th March. All good wishes to Christine and also to them both for the future.

Any members knowing of classes in Cantonese in the Leicester area, please drop a line direct to Anthony Ivison, Leicester. In fact - anyone speaking Cantonese might like to write to Anthony anyway and give him a few pointers!!

I'd like to wish "Good Luck" to Knud-Erik Larsen who takes part in the Denmark v. Germany National Karate Championships to be held in Randers.

BRUCE'S BOOK LIST

During one of my visits to Los Angeles, Danny Inosanto was so very kind during a visit to his home to make for me various photocopies of original writings he had on Bruce - among these a list of books owned by Bruce in his own handwriting! There were 288 listed - rather a lot to list in one go, so in this and every following news sheet (until complete) I will be giving the title, author and year printed of around ten at a time. There are about 20 or so written in Chinese, so obviously I'll leave these out until such time as I might get them translated. Anyway, here are the first titles:-

Karate - Nishiyama (1959)
This Is Karate - Mas Oyama (1965)
Vital Karate - Mas Oyama (1967)
The Manual of Karate - E.J, Harrison (1959)
The Way of Karate - Mattson (1963)
Tengue of Karate - Augustin De Mille (1962)

What Is Karate? - Mas Oyama (1958)
What Is Karate? - Mas Oyama (1963) revised
Karate By Picture - H. O. Plee (1962)
Kongau (Korean Karate) - M. Y. Woo (1964)
Karate - John Kuhl (1965)
Mas Oyama's Karate - B. Lowe (1964)

More next time, folks!!

USEFUL ADDRESS

Mark Salter (1792) says Giko Ltd., of 537 Stratford Road, Sparkhill, Birmingham BII 4LP - Telephone (021) 773 9247/8 - has the following videos: *Game of Death* - time approx. Two hrs. VHS - £45. *Way of the Dragon* - time approx. Two hrs. VHS E120 - £45. *Fist of Fury* plus Bruce Lee feature - time approx. Two hrs. VHS - £45. *Enter the Dragon* (Warner video) - time approx. 86 mins. VHS Beta - £47.95. *Enter the Dragon* - full screen feature plus fight sequences in wide screen action (no action cut-off) - fight scenes 25 mins. - £45. *Bruce Lee Special* (screen tests, trailers, *The Green Hornet* episode "The Silent Gun," early Bruce in Hong Kong) - VHS E120 - £45. *Green Hornet* ("Kato and the Blow-pipe Killings"; "Kato and the Out-of-Space Invaders"; "Kato and the Chinatown Connection") - time approx. 75 mins. E120 - £45. (Thanks Mark!!)

SOCIETY LETTERS COMPETITION - JUNE 1981

I asked members to write in to me giving the amount of letters they thought I'd answered since the Society first started. I truthfully had such a poor response to this competition -in fact to ANY competition I have run in the past! - and I thought I'd let you know I had TWO ANSWERS! (Yes, I'm disgusted, too!) So is it any wonder that I completely forgot about any winners' names! Well, it seemed a little unfair really to pick just one of the two (most welcome) replies I received - even though their answers were way of the track! - so I declare Michael Harris and Avtar Sohota joint winners. Michael gave the answer of 40,000 and Avtar 28,000 - the actual figure was 19,742 - which I thought was high enough, but after reading what Michael and Avtar put down I feel like hiding away!!!! Well - by copy of this news sheet I am asking that MICHAEL AND AVTAR CONTACT ME BY LETTER TO SAY IF THERE IS ANY SPECIAL ITEM OR ITEMS THEY ARE AFTER - AND IF SO, I WILL TRY TO SEND WHAT THEY REQUIRE. If I cannot help on this - then I shall pick out a batch of goodies for them. I look forward to hearing from you both!!

HOLLYWOOD PETITION
WINNER OF FREE VIDEO OF ENTER THE DRAGON

Following on Mike Devereux' offer in the last news sheet (which was a marvellous gesture on his behalf!) that the person sending in the most signatures between the March and June news sheets would receive a free copy of *Enter the Dragon* if they sent in the most signatures to get Bruce's name placed against a gold star on Hollywood Boulevard, I'm pleased to announce that the winner is: MICHAEL HANNAH

(3333) by a VERY WIDE MARGIN - IN FACT, HE SENT IN OVER 4,400 (yes, you read it right!) SIGNATURES. Mike will be sending him his copy of *Enter the Dragon* very shortly!! Well done, Michael! And don't forget, we still need MORE, MORE, MORE signatures to go to the World of Bruce Lee so that we get this achieved!!

LETTERS

Dear Pam,

It's really good to see there are still people around who love Bruce as I do. Bruce really changed my life. Where I train in Coventry, people love it when I talk about Bruce, although when I first joined the instructors didn't like it. But now they understand and when I bring books to the club (Bruce Lee of course!) they gather around and enjoy them. Now a lot of the people in the club are into the greatest fighter ever - BRUCE! They also want to join the Society, so please send me some joining letters. I'd also like to join any future trip to Hong Kong/U.S.A. It's a shame you had so little response from the members - I hope they pull themselves together out there and decide just what they want out of the Society. It's a great thing that the Society is doing so COME ON you members, use the Society - that's what it's there for. I hope you all will!

Owen Wint (3285)

Thanks for your nice comments, Owen - and I hope that the Society can in the future do much more with the help of it's members. I must admit - sometimes I wonder what is expected of the club - and sometimes I get very disheartened at the lack of enthusiasm, which sometimes then dampens my own.

Dear Pam,

For some time I've thought that the voices of Keye Luke (Master Po in the *Kung Fu* TV series) and Sheh Kien ("Han" in *Enter the Dragon*) were similar. Re-reading the June 81 sheet, and that Sheh Kien cannot speak English, I compared my *Enter the Dragon* video and the video I have from an episode of *Kung Fu* and have concluded that the old man in *Enter the Dragon* who tells Bruce how his sister died and the voice of Sheh Kien and Master Po are the same. Anyone know the answer for sure??

David Moore (1783)

Yes - when I met Sheh Kien, Robert Lee acted as interpreter for us both! I don't know the answer - anyone else??

RENEWALS

The following members fall due to renew from now until the end of August: 3219-3270 (second year); 2973-3056 (third year); 2698-2737 (fourth year); 2303-2349 (fifth year); 2022-2084 (sixth year). I look forward to having you with us for another year.

WILLPOWER

I wonder how each of us would treat that phrase in relation to ourselves and our future achievements? Bruce put down his own personal aims (made his own personal "code of practice") which he adhered to, under headings of "Willpower," "Emotion," "Reason," "Imagination," "Memory," "Subconscious Mind," "Conscience," and "Adversity" - having

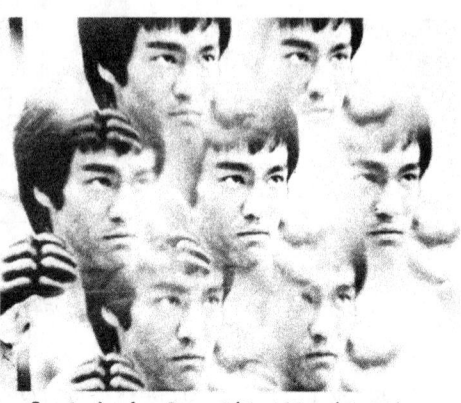

Sent in by Des O'Reilly (3068) - picture taken by his dad with special lens

first defined just what each of these things meant to him. Maybe from what he wrote we can obtain an insight into our own standards which we need to set in order to achieve self-discipline - so for this sheet, here is what Bruce said under "Willpower": "RECOGNIZING THAT THE POWER OF WILL IS THE SUPREME COURT OVER ALL OTHER DEPARTMENTS OF MY MIND, I WILL EXERCISE IT DAILY, WHEN I NEED THE URGE TO ACTION FOR ANY PURPOSE; AND I WILL FORM HABITS DESIGNED TO BRING THE POWER OF MY WILL INTO ACTION AT LEAST ONCE DAILY."

In the next news sheet - "EMOTION."

ROBERT LEE LP & SOCIETY BACK-ISSUES OF NEWS SHEETS

Still available is the SUPERB Robert Lee LP *Ballad of Bruce Lee,* personally signed - and still costing £4.50 (inc. posting/packing) in the U.K., (Europe £5.50, rest of the world £6.50). Postal orders/cheques payable to Pam Hadden, London. For news sheet back-issues, tell me what ones you want, and I'll write back with total cost for you to remit to me. All issues available.

PEN PALS

Anthony Ivison (3308), Leicester wants a Chinese girl pen pal aged 16-20, living anywhere.

Glynn Darbyshire (2885)

SWOP SHOP

- John Kemp, Bristol has for sale: VHS videos *Marlowe* and guest appearance of Bruce as "Kato" in three *Batman* episodes - Excellent Quality - £20 each.
- Mr. R. Coppen, Suffolk wants: *KFMs* 1-3, 12, 31-33, *Bruce Lee The Man Only I Knew*, KFM 1974 *Bruce Lee Scrapbook*, *Bruce Lee's Non-Classical Gung Fu* - high prices paid - immaculate condition only please.
- Tom Lavery, Portadown, Northern Ireland wants: copy of poster shown in September '79 news sheet, *Popster Magazine* No. 23, hardback book *1940-73*, press books for all Bruce Lee's films, *Man Only I Knew*, video of *Film 78* - Barry Norman reviewing *Game of Death*, back-issues of *Deadly Hands of Kung Fu*, set of front of house still from *Enter the Dragon*.
- Jeff Woods, Bristol wants: *Tao of JKD*, *Art and Philosophy of Bruce Lee*, *Secret Art of Bruce Lee*.
- Christopher Bell, Ipswich has for quick sale: Brand New *Enter the Dragon* video Betamax - cost £43.99 but sell for £32. (Selling only because Chris was made redundant and unable now to rent video machine).
- Lee O'Neill, Omagh, Northern Ireland wants: *KFMs* 2, 3, 11-14 inc., 26, 28, 30-33 inc., 36 & 44. Also *Way of the Dragon*, *Big Boss*, *Fist of Fury*, *Enter the Dragon* singles & any LP's/cassettes on Bruce Lee.
- Nigel Brookes, Leek asks can anyone let him know where to get copy of 7" single *Dragon Power*?
- Mick Bargota, Tipton, wants: *KFM's* 45-49 inc. and 60 onwards. Also T-shirts, badges, stickers on Bruce Lee.
- Robert Walker, Clydebank has for sale/swap: *KFM's* 5, 59, 25, *Bruce Lee Inedit* & *La Legende du Petit Dragon* (French), *Bruce Lee Motion Pictures on Paper*, Bruce Lee *Game of Death* tracksuit, *Bruce Lee Dragon Sounds Special*, *Enter the Dragon*, and *My Way of Gung Fu* LP's, first convention mug, single *In Memory of Bruce Lee* (John & Rosalind), *Bruce Lee Fighting Methods Advanced Techniques*, *Dragon* posters 1 & 2, *Super Kung Fu* (*KFM*), second *Bruce Lee Scrapbook*. Wants: any martial arts protective gear, gloves, weapons etc. and anything on Bruce Lee or Kung Fu.
- Dave Cansick, 30 Bland Rd., Leicester has for sale: 30 books/magazines inc. *Green Hornet* annual, *Wisdom of Bruce Lee*, 20 posters, 40 different photos, 20 LP's, 20 singles inc. *In Memory of Bruce Lee* - ring Leicester or write.
- Paul Norris, Bolton has for sale: Super 8mm films - 400ft *Way of the Dragon* & sound cassette, *Fist of Fury* parts 1 & 2 (silent 400ft ea.), 400ft *Game of Death* (silent) - £15 ea., 500ft film containing *Green Hornet* screen test, the *Big Boss*, *Enter the Dragon*, *Game of Death* trailers, behind the scenes on *Enter the Dragon* - will accept £25. Wants: *Way of the Dragon* & *Game of Death* on video.
- Michael Tsang, Belfast, Northern Ireland has for swap/sale, all very good condition - Book/ cassette on *A Guide to Cantonese* and also *A Guide to Mandarin* by Y.C Yuen - Mandarin - £18; Cantonese - £15, (inc. P&P). Wants (or offers): *Tower of Death*, *Ballad of Bruce Lee* LP's & *World of Bruce Lee* double-LP.
- Mark James, Bulwell has for sale: 10 x 400ft Super 8mm colour/silent films from *Big Boss*, *Fist of Fury*, *Way of the Dragon*, *Game of Death* - superb quality/sound - German dialogue - price £21 each inc. p&p. Videos: price £25 ea. inc. p&p - uncut *Fist of Fury*, *Way of the Dragon*, also *Fearless Hyena* & Bruce Lee/Jackie Chan Special from Hong Kong - all reasonable quality.

- Vincent Norgrove, Warley has for sale: three photos Roger Moore - £3.50, seven of Jackie Chan B&W & three colour photos - £7, two books on Jackie Chan - £4, two booklets on Jackie Chan (Big Brawl & Young Master) - 50p ea., four news sheets & one badge - 50p. Will sell or settle for swaps on Bruce.

HOW I MET ROBERT AND DANNY
By member Neil McLean (3303)

I'd like to tell you of how I came to meet Robert, Bruce's brother, and Danny Inosanto.

I was talking to some Bruce followers at this hall, when all of a sudden some of the security men (who treated everyone nicely, actually), asked us if we would do them a favour as there were some young girls who had got through to backstage and were looking for Robert and Danny. They asked if we would help them find the girls so I said, "Sure," as it was fairly early. Wandering around backstage for quite some time, I suddenly heard a cracking sound of sticks in this room, so being my curious self, I opened the door and "G.O.D" (get it? What a sight!), it was Danny and his student going through their warm-up with their Escrima sticks.

Neil McLean (3301) and Dan Inosanto

I just stood there with my mouth wide open as I could not believe it! Then Dan said: "Yes?" and I mentioned (stuttering all the time), "Hello, I'm Neil McLean and I'm from Scotland. I came down here to see you but I NEVER thought like this!" Dan just laughed and said, "Well, aren't you going to say something?" Just then I started to function and asked: "Was Bruce so fast?" Dan replied, "Well, you've been watching me and I haven't a tenth of the speed of Bruce" I said, "Yes, and you were moving like a blur yourself!" Dan laughed, and said that as they were just practicing with the sticks at that moment, they were not as fast as they would be at the show that afternoon, as they had to go through the movements again and again - as the weapons can hurt if one gets hit. Noticing the camera I was holding, Dan asked if I wanted a picture of the two of us together, and when I nodded, Dan turned and said: "Robert - here, take this picture will you?" I turned, and to my surprise there was Bruce's brother! He must have been sitting behind watching us all the time! He said "Sure" and took the picture. Dan then said he had to practice and walked away laughing with his student, because I never replied, but just stood there looking at Robert.

Obviously, I do not remember everything we talked about, but I do distinctly remember saying to him that I could not believe I was there talking to him. Robert said: "You sure are, Neil, I can assure you!!" I asked what it was like being Bruce's brother, and he said, "Just the same as anyone else who had a brother. You see, having grown up with him through our younger days, I saw nothing in him which was different to anybody else's brother."

I asked what Bruce was like as a young boy, and Robert said, laughing: "Always fighting! You know, I saved us a lot of beatings in those days because he was always wanting to pick a fight and I didn't! So I had to talk our way out of it." I asked: "Why do you say "beatings?" and Robert said: "You should have seen the numbers he would pick on!" I also asked when Bruce became famous in Robert's eyes, and he said that although everyone knew of his "bit" parts in programmes but over in Hong Kong, he was not really made famous until he became the assistant in *The Green Hornet* and then he mentioned to them of some of the names he was teaching over in the States! I finally asked: "And what was it like when *Big Boss* was shown?" to which Robert replied: "Amazing! He just changed overnight into a hero for everyone and an idol!" Dan returned and took a picture of Robert and I. Dan then had to practice and Robert also to do his speech, but on departing, Robert said to me that it was great talking to me. WOW! I just walked out of there and thought about what had happened!

Guess who??!!?

STIRLING SILLIPHANT INTERVIEW FROM *KICK* MAGAZINE
From member Maria Fernandes in Brazil

"How did you first hear about Bruce Lee?"

I was at one of those instantly "forget-the-name-of-the-host" Hollywood parties. Bruce had been invited to Las Vegas by Vic Damone, the singer. Vic had been very interested in Oriental martial arts but was somewhat sceptical about its effectiveness as a form of combat. "A good tough street fighter," he insisted, "could always beat a karate man, especially an Asian, because Asians were smaller, thinner and just basically could not stand up to a big, tough American street brawler." At the time, Vic employed the services of two huge armed bodyguards, one of whom held contempt for martial artists in general. Bruce studied the situation and arrived at a way of proving the effectiveness of martial arts without getting anyone hurt. "I'll tell you what we can do," Bruce said. "Put one bodyguard in front of the door - when I come through the door" - he explained to the bodyguard - "stop me if you can." The other bodyguard Bruce placed about five feet behind the first man, and told him to put a cigarette in his mouth - "Let's assume that the cigarette represents your holstered gun" - he continued. "Vic, when I come through the door, I want you to begin counting to five. By the count of five, I will be past the first bodyguard and will have knocked the cigarette from the mouth of the second bodyguard - the cigarette is equivalent to his gun. When he sees me come through the door, he should try to take it out of his mouth before I kick it out. Now - I'm at a disadvantage because I'm telling you all this in advance. If I succeed, then would you buy it as an acceptable example of what martial arts can do?" Everyone said: "Sure; Oh Boy! Yeah!" - Bruce then left the room. Meanwhile, Vic said to his bodyguards: "Look, I don't want you to hurt him, 'cause he's small and he's Chinese. But I don't mind if one or both of you knock him on his ass! Give him a good shot, and let's settle this matter once and for all." So - everyone waiting, right? Suddenly, there's a loud wrenching explosion; not only does the door fly open, but it's torn completely from the wall! Bruce kicked the son-of-a-bitch right off its hinges!! The door slams the first bodyguard so hard he's knocked violently out of the way with the door jammed in his face. Two seconds later - no more - the cigarette flies past the second bodyguard's nose Bruce had kicked it from his mouth while he stood there, frozen in place. Bruce turned and looked at Damone who, eyes wide, was saying: "Holy Shit!!"

TRIVIA DEPARTMENT
From member Simon Bulley (2738)

Did you know that Gig Young and Dan Inosanto appeared in two films together? Both were in *The Killer Elite* (1975) and three years later in *Game of Death*.

Mako is the only Oriental film star to have appeared with all three of the martial arts movie stars who have "made it" in the West. He appeared with Bruce in "The Preying Mantis" episode of the series *Green Hornet* (1966), Jackie Chan in *Big Brawl* (1980) and with Chuck Norris in *An Eye for an Eye* (1982). Speaking of *An Eye for an Eye*, the film review magazine *Cinema* gives the film a very bad write-up. However, it says of Chuck: "He appeared with the legendary Bruce Lee in *Way of the Dragon* - remember?"

A blow for the side of copyright has been struck with the release of the video *The Black Dragon Avenges the Death of Bruce Lee*. All mentions of the name "Lee" have been erased from the soundtrack and he is described only as Bruce throughout the film, though it is obvious the last name has been purposely scrubbed. I wonder what the story behind that is?

Bruce was mentioned several times in a recent *About Anglia* report on a local Karate club. One instructor commented that youths who wanted to become "Bruce Lee in a week" soon left the club. A young black fighter said that he only joined the club after his mother had seen *Enter the Dragon* and convinced him that martial arts were THE thing to do!

FILM SNIPPETS
Members' Reviews of Kung Fu and Other Martial Arts Films

I went to see a Kung Fu double-bill the other day - *The Clones of Bruce Lee* and *Super Dragon*. The first film - although a main feature - was abysmal. The acting, fighting and dubbing were universally awful and the three lookalikes were so bad that they made me long for Bruce Li (whose *Lama Avenger* film I praised in my last letter). The only interesting aspects to the film were a showing of the *Unicorn Palm* wrap party footage with Bruce Lee, the large role given to Jon Benn (last seen as the gang boss in *Way of the Dragon*), and the return of the still-enormous Yang Sze, famous as "Bolo" in *Enter the Dragon*. *Super Dragon* on the other hand is a terrific film. The difference between well-choreographed fight scenes and speeded up dancing has never been more clearly shown than it is when you compare the "action" of *Clones of Bruce Lee* to the combat in *Super Dragon*. The movie stars Jason Pai Pau, a fine Chinese actor/martial artist, and Ron van Clief, ex-karate champion. It was filmed in the Philippines and the director, Tommy Lee Chun, makes good use of Filipino sets and landscapes. The story, though by no means original, is clearly told and provides a solid framework for some excellent set pieces. Surprisingly, a lot of weapons-work (no nunchakus) is intact in the cinema release. For a glance at how a good kung fu film can be made WITHOUT Bruce, I advise all fans to ignore the misuse of Lee's name in *Clones of Bruce Lee* and just see *Super Dragon*. It's worth the admission fee all by itself.

I hope no one will think that recommendation means I'm putting down Bruce, because I'm sure he'd rather his followers went to see good, original martial arts cinema, rather than be misled by his name being in large letters on inferior rubbish.

Simon Bulley (2738)

VIDEO SNIPPETS
Members' Write-Ups on Various Films Seen on Video

Recently seen on a couple of friends' video:

The GOOD: Uncut versions of *Game of Death* and *Way of the Dragon* (excellent), *The Real Bruce Lee* (Great for 20 minutes of early Bruce but the other hour-and-a-half was hilarious - "See Dragon Lee fly and kick villains in the head at the same time!"), *Breaker Breaker* with Chuck Norris starring (Actually, this was on the boring side and not half so good as his *Force of One* but having said that, the fight scenes did make up for it).

And now to the BAD! Another movie by Joe Lewis, *Jaguar Lives*. Again, the fighting was lousy and the plot uncomprehendable! The bore of the year!

And the UGLY! *Bruce Lee: The Man, The Myth* set out with good intentions and impressed me in parts (early Wing Chun training especially), and the attention to detail was really great - the actual *Big Boss* sets, the same actors from *Big Boss*, "Bruce" directing scenes at the Rome Fountain, and what looked like the actual *Enter the Dragon* set. However, Bruce Li's fighting scenes were wildly exaggerated and near the end - the May 1973, collapse (of Bruce) was staged in a room resembling the interior of the starship Enterprise, leading us to believe that Bruce used more electronic equipment than Mr. Spock!

Carl Jones (2121)

Received from Py Tang Video Club was *Big Boss, Game of Death* and *Way of the Dragon* complete and uncensored. I must admit - I was amazed at *Way of the*

Dragon. I knew of course about the nunchaku battle being cut out from the cinema version, but did you know there was a further nunchaku fight in the restaurant? Bruce threw his darts, which became the signal for the waiters to attack, and Bruce to start swinging yet again. I've never even seen photos of the fight scene let alone knew it existed.

I also found practically every fight scene in the film was different - it was almost like seeing a brand-new Bruce Lee film! I never before realised just how much the censors had chopped out - even the Lee/Norris fight was almost twice as long as the "British" version. I always thought it strange that Bruce - who made "flowing like water" his life's philosophy, could turn out such a jerky-looking film on his directorial debut. Now I see that the film does indeed flow like water - a very moving experience!

One film I do not recommend ANYONE buying is *Fist of Fear, Touch of Death* - it's supposed to contain authentic interviews taken from his *Longstreet* days, but I found the "interviews" to be entirely phoney. The makers took shots of Bruce from *Longstreet* and inserted their own people as interviewers and made it appear as though Bruce was answering. The result is badly done, wrong voice, and the lips in no way match the words. They have Bruce contributing his success to some phoney ancestor and they even have a lengthy slice of his childhood film *Thunderstorm* masquerading as some old home-movie. Original dialogue has been erased and dubbed over the top, with Bruce even calling his older brother "Jack" instead of "Peter." Definitely a film to warn the fans about!

Arthur Stone (1150)

CHARISMA
Written by Enrico Cocozza
(A friend of member Iain Leslie)

This is a word too easily applied to individuals with strong personalities. It should not be used too freely. What does it mean? What is charisma? We are told that charisma is "a spiritual power given by God." It is a "personal quality or gift that enables individuals to impress or influence many of his fellows." The word is derived from "Charis" (one of the three Greek Charities or Graces - Aglaia, Euphrosyne and Thalia) and Charis was the Goddess of whatever imparts graciousness to life. If we carefully consider these definitions and origins of the word we may, hopefully, come to some conclusions.

I think the key in the true application of the word lies in the phrase "imparting graciousness." A person endowed with the gift of true charisma is a giver. The person having charisma glows with the gift of a divine power and when his mind and body are fully charged with it his positive aura can be experienced and we can grow spiritually by being in communion with him. Did Bruce Lee really have charisma in this sense? Yes, but not only when he practised the martial arts. He possessed it above all in his quiet moments of meditation when universal truths, using him as their vehicle, were given utterance from his lips, and in those moments when he was guiding those who came to learn from him. Is it not significant that his mother's name was Grace? He was born of Grace, and was endowed with Grace and I use the word in the sense of divine influence.

I feel he was of the race of the Gods and this explains why he was called to leave this life at the early age of 32. For at that age, in a sublime, private moment, he must have looked upon the face of the ultimate truth and recognised the divine pattern in which he played a significant part. That moment had nothing to do with his material achievements, even in his artistic fulfilment in his films. His striving for perfection in the martial arts went side by side with the growing of his spiritual side and, just as he finally achieved perfection on the physical plane, so his soul reached the ultimate stage of blissful nirvana. And nirvana implies the cessation of individual existence when the individual must rejoin the countless particles of the divine force. His death was not a death - it was merely a passing into the ultimate state where he is a god. And he had come from that same place.

Light cannot be experienced without darkness, the positive cannot exist without the negative. This explains the apparently sordid aspects of his brief life, the rumbustious, fiery side of him that found expression when he was so young in street fighting, his utter inability to bear defeat in any form, his apparent susceptibility and sensitivity to beauty that led him occasionally astray. These aspects made him human. Without them - a god we may never have recognised as a fellow human being. Whether the memory of Bruce is proliferated or not is of no great consequence when we consider, as his great friend James Coburn said, "He completed himself with his own death - the circle was rejoined." The important thing for us is that we were given the privilege of becoming part of his circle by submitting to his genuine charisma and by thus loving him.

MY THOUGHTS ON BRUCE
Member Setudeh Nejad (1419)

Today, after nearly nine years, I have come to believe that Bruce was not understood here or there. People see Jeet Kune Do as Bruce Lee's style, which is not so. They do not see the JKD as a school of thought that does not necessarily concern martial arts or fighting. People don't understand martial arts' ideas, at least most of them don't and don't try to understand why these were created. It is not enough to praise Bruce Lee and only praise him. Jeet Kune Do is misunderstood and neglected and this is a loss of legacy to the only thing that keeps Bruce Lee's legend live.

P.S. Ask the members what do they see in *Enter the Dragon* that they do not see in other martial arts films? A friend of mine who does not know anything about martial arts told me that when he sees *Enter the Dragon*, he feels different and good for a while and a strange feeling remains in him, but he does not know the reason for it. Anyone else in Britain or elsewhere that feels the same must try to find the reasons as I did, and then he can truly live. Today, I no longer put Bruce Lee posters in my room and no longer praise Lee for his fighting but for his art and wonderful thoughts that gave me the opportunity of practicing Zen and Taoism which are the origins of Jeet Kune Do. What I have said is a MUST to everyone considering himself/herself a Lee fan or follower.

"The Tao which is spoken is not eternal Tao." - Lao Tzu

POETS CORNER
By Conor Kelleher
(Brother to member Connie Kelleher)

Here's some words to remember Bruce Lee - the greatest man the world will ever see.

Although it has been some years since he past, his legend lives on and forever will last.
When we think back to the life that he led, it hardly seems possible Bruce Lee is dead.
But when he appears like a fury on screen, the thoughts of his death fade away like a dream.
Bruce Lee spent his life striving for perfection - he never stopped to take a break, always stayed in action.
When he stopped fighting his mind turned to thinking on the life we're meant to live and the purpose of our living.
So how could we forget him, a man we love well - a man with our deep respect who has no equal.
A man who was strong, swift, gentle and loving and tender - this was Bruce Lee - the man we shall always remember!

Well - that about wraps it up for this issue - regrettably, I've no more space - see you all. - Pam

EDITOR'S NOTES

Albert Goldman, born on 15th April 1927 in Dormont, Pennsylvania, was an American author, writing primarily on culture and personalities of the American entertainment industry. Goldman first achieved success in 1974 with the book, *Ladies and Gentlemen – Lenny Bruce!!* which, while being mostly positive in it's appraisal of Bruce's talents, it was criticised by Bruce's friends for allegedly distorting his character.

In 1981, Goldman released his biography *Elvis*, considered by many to be one of the most controversial books ever written about Elvis Presley.

It was on the back of this book that rumours began circulating that Goldman was writing a biography about Bruce Lee, and considering his previous track record, there was much speculation in regards to what it would contain. In the end, Goldman didn't release a book about Bruce Lee, but he did write a very unflattering a two-part article for Penthouse magazine which was published in January and February of 1983. After the article on Bruce Lee, Goldman wrote a controversial book in 1988 about Beatles musician John Lennon, titled *The Lives of John Lennon*, followed by a second book on Elvis Presley in 1990, titled, *Elvis: The Last 24 Hours*.

Albert Goldman passed away from a heart attack on 28th March 1994. He was 66 years old.

Al Dacascos, born 6th September 1942 in Honolulu, Hawaii is a martial arts practitioner of Won Hop Kuen Do, his own unique style of Kajukenbo.

An eighth degree Black Belt, Dacascos has won over 200 championships and appeared on just as many martial arts magazine covers over the years. In 1977 he was inducted into the *Black Belt* Hall of Fame as Instructor of the Year and again in 1992 by *Inside Kung fu* magazine. Al Dacascos was the first Kung fu practitioner to compete in the American martial arts tournament circuit. Always been a visionary, and he has achieved his dream of creating a network of schools and five generations of black belts to reflect his style.

The *Fighting Arts* article reprinted in issue 24 is corroborated in Linda Lee's 1975 book, *Bruce Lee: The Man Only I Knew*.

His son is martial artist and well-known actor Mark Dacascos, star of, *Only the Strong, Drive, Brotherhood of the Wolf, Hawaii Five-0, Iron Chef America, John Wick 3, and Showdown in Manilla,* the latter marking his directorial debut with his father choreographing the fight scene. I spoke to Mark some time ago about the incident mentioned in the article:

> My father opened up his own martial arts school in San Francisco and like Bruce, had begun teaching Caucasians. He was threatened in a similar way that Bruce was and also had to take similar action as he did.  The Chinese clan then tried to create bad blood between my father and Bruce, spreading rumours that each was calling the other down. They circulated the story that my father claimed that he taught Bruce everything he knew, in the hope that both men would lose their tempers and put each other out of business. When my father approached Bruce at the Long Beach International Tournament in California and pointed out that he had never called him down, Bruce slapped him on the back, told him to forget it and they shook hands.
>
> My mother Malia and Linda Lee became friends, just after Bruce passed away, when Linda went on a world tour in memory of Bruce Lee. One of the producers of the tour asked my mother, who was one of the top female competitors on the martial arts circuit in America, and my father, who was a top ten fighter and one of the only Kung Fu guys to compete in tournaments at that time, to go on this tour with Linda and they became good friends.
>
> After Bruce Lee passed away, Linda, knowing that Bruce respected my father's art and skill, championed my father for the role of Bruce Lee in a biographical movie back in the 70's, but the movie never got made but my father was Linda's first choice. The movie was made 20 years later when my friend Jason Scott Lee played Bruce Lee. Linda wrote a book  called Bruce Lee: The Man Only I Knew. At the beginning, in the acknowledgements, she thanked two martial artists; Jhoon Rhee and Al Dacascos – Bruce's "fellow martial artists." That made me so excited and so happy. I'm like a million martial artists who have been so inspired by Bruce Lee. Bruce Lee, Jackie Chan, Jet Li, my father, my mother – those were my martial arts heroes when I was growing up. Bruce Lee was the first Asian guy that I saw kick butt on the screen and today, he's still one of my heroes.

Details of Bruce Lee's vast book collection first appear from issue 24, but only in small batches. If you want a comprehensive list (though not complete), you may wish to purchase James Bishop's fantastic book, *Bruce Lee: Dynamic Becoming.*

As mentioned before, Keye Luke played Charlie Chan's *Number One Son*, Kato in *The Green Hornet* serials, Master Po opposite David Carradine in *Kung Fu,* and provided the dubbing for Mr. Han's voice in *Enter the Dragon.*

Shieh Kien, the actor who played Han in *Enter the Dragon* could not speak English. The producers of the film attempted to have him record his own dialogue, to no success, so they had Keye Luke dub Shih Kien's voice on the film's soundtrack.

Video cassettes were still relatively new in 1982. In a 1982 Boots Christmas catalogue offered a "Ferguson Videostar" VHS recorder for £599 (£2129 in 2019). The average wage in 1982 was £500 a month, making the cost to purchase a VHS recorder more than a month's salary. With the high cost of purchasing a video recorder, many opted to rent one, whether for a day, a weekend, a week or a month.

JOIN THE BRUCE LEE SOCIETY
And stand to win a "chance-in-a-lifetime" prize!

The KFM Warehouseman recently discovered just a few RARE COPIES OF THE 'BRUCE LEE SCRAPBOOK'!!!

25 of these valuable and sought-after editions we're looking forward to passing on to you, the KFM readers — and here's how.

The names and addresses of all those who join the BRUCE LEE SOCIETY from NOW, for the next two months, will be put into a hat — and from that, the 25 lucky winners will be chosen.

Yes, it's as simple as that. A £3.25 subscription to the world's most exclusive and successful Little Dragon club guarantees YOU the chance of winning what most collectors would give their eye teeth for. . .a KFM 'BRUCE LEE SCRAPBOOK'!

Remember, apart from all the goodies — like badges, stickers and exclusive photos — that the Society gives to its members, at the helm there's Pam Hadden, who over the past few years has devoted just about all her spare time towards spreading the word of the Master, Bruce Lee -- the Legacy that He gave to us. She deserves YOUR support!

Join the Society — and stand the chance of winning a FREE 'Scrapbook' by posting off immediately a £3.25 cheque/PO to: The Bruce Lee Society, 14 Rathbone Place, London W1P 1DE.

PS. . .don't worry, present Society members, **your** chance is coming in the next News Sheet.

A RETROSPECTIVE LOOK AT BRUCE LEE MANIA & THE KUNG FU CRAZE OF THE 1970S

25
September
1982

WELCOME TO THE SEPTEMBER NEWS SHEET - AND THE START OF THE SEVENTH SOCIETY YEAR! I HOPE THAT WE CAN ACHIEVE GOOD THINGS FOR THE FUTURE - AND WITH YOUR HELP, I AM SURE WE CAN AND AS A GOOD END TO THE SIXTH YEAR, I'LL GO STRAIGHT ON TO...

MEMORIAL FLOWERS
Tribute sent to Bruce's graveside in Seattle - 20 July 1982

What can I say??? I was SO pleased at the response this year - by the time I'd listed and added up the money, we got a GRAND TOTAL OF £145 sterling! It was good to get a positive response, and to know that the tribute would be SPLENDID! All monies, plus a list of contributors' names surrounding Bruce's picture (in similar format to the front page of the news sheet - it DID look rather nice) were sent to Alison French to make the arrangements with the florist, as she did last year. The name-list was to be placed with the flowers by the graveside. Pictures have been taken by the florist - and although I had hoped to have them for the September sheet so we could all see what the flowers looked like, when received these will have to be shown in December. In the meantime, I will get copies of what pictures we receive so that members might purchase these for their collection.

I feel (and I am sure you will agree) the florist has done a SUPERB job and you will see from the pictures, that the flowers have been arranged, as was suggested to him, in the form of the YIN AND YANG SYMBOL - beautifully done in red/yellow carnations surrounded by white with contrasting arrows in red and yellow mixed with white. The florist also surrounded our picture/name list in red carnations like a frame; the centre of the symbol had a white ribbon with "BRUCE" on, and two streamers ran from the symbol - one in red, one in white, saying "HE SHALL NOT BE FORGOTTEN" and "FROM THE BRUCE LEE SOCIETY."

You will see from the copy of the florist's letter to Alison reprinted below that our flowers were the first to be placed at the graveside - with the exception of one solitary beautiful red rose (I wonder from whom that was??) behind our tribute and on the actual grave.

Member Alison French, of course, kindly arranged the sending of the money and dealing with the actual florist for the flowers (well done, Alison, for all your efforts!) and I know you would all wish to say a big "thank you" to her for her efforts on our behalf.

The receipt for the money I collected and which Alison paid into her bank for transfer to the Seattle florist is shown below - for the total amount of £145 collected.

Shown above - letter from the Seattle florist about our tribute

Receipt from Lloyds Bank for £145 less £4.16 their commission of £4.16 - total of £140.84 converted at rate 1.725 US$ = US$242.95 sent to florist.

Now - as so many of you asked about copies of the actual photos for your files - I am making these available to you at a cost of 60p each or £1 for both copies (to include postage). If, however, you live overseas, please add an extra 15p whether you order one or both pictures. I also have copies of the floral tribute from last year, too - again (two pictures), prices as above. If you require ALL FOUR PICTURES, please send £1.80 (members abroad - £2) which will include postage/packing. They are lovely pictures, and in one picture from last year you get a distance shot from the graveside with a group of people standing beside it near our flowers (photos approximately 3" x 4").

The following were the contributors to the floral tribute: Alison French, Michael Harris, Michael Hannah, Chik Liak Tan, Arthur Stone, John Cook, Brenda Williams, Gino D'Ambrosio, David Rodman, Inge Hutama, Graham Hardie, Diane Webb, Mark Peters, Thomas Jones, Susan Pietzyk, Lee O'Neill, Jeffrey Woods, Caroline Newitt, Lee Percy, Mustafa Abdi, Robert Young, Pauline Bouckley, Hugh Lagan, Jonathan

Westley, Alex Corsini, Greg Rhodes, Steven Mather, Molly Cullen, Niels Larsen, Duncan Smith, Ian Hamilton, John Aspinall, T. Law, Cary Dean, Iain Leslie, Martin Holmes, Ken Wright, Gary Woods, Mark James, Niels Bjerre, Clive Ramsbottom, Ian Fawcett, Alan Thompson, Richard Baczyk, Nicholas Coleman, Glynn Darbyshire, Paul Kabrna, Ann and Fred Hunt, Ronald Gray, Gregory Hansen, Paul Short, Susan Cuff, Paul Norris, John Rutter, Cherrilyne and Graham Pugh, Paul Corrigan, Jackie McArdle, G. Evans, John Conville, Michael Day, David Scott, John Rogers, Barry Latcham, Maria Fernandes, Connie and Conor Kelleher, Duncan Lee Baker, Pam.

Pictures of the floral tribute sent to Bruce's grave - 1982 (Apologies for darkness of printing on this occasion)

Browsing through some of my notes from various trips, I came across the following martial arts' terms which I thought might be of some interest:

SEE FOO (SIFU) - Instructor; SEA HING - your Senior/Older Brother; SEA DAI - your Junior/ Younger Brother; SEA JO - Founder of the style and system; SEA BAK - Instructor's Senior; SEE SOOK - Instructor's Junior; SEA GUNG - Grandfather - your Instructor's Instructor; JEET DA - stop hit; HOU JEET TEK - back stopkick; JIK JEET - straight stop-kick; O'OU JEET - hook stopkick; JUK JEET - side stopkick; CH'UNG CHUIE - vertical fist; BIU JEE - finger jab; JEET TEK - foot obstruction/stopkick; TAN DA - right stop-hit with side cover; WQANG PAK DA - right stop-hit with crosshand cover; LOY HA PAK DA -right stop-hit with low inside cover; OUY HA PAK DA - right stop-hit with low outside cover.

GRACE'S PRESENT

So far, I am pleased to say you have pledged around £100 (with foreign money to convert, I do not know the exact figure until this has been sent in, and converted into sterling by the Bank). Anyway - NOW IS THE TIME TO SEND IN YOUR DONATIONS THAT WERE PLEDGED.

Address them to me at London - PLEASE, NOT *KFM* OFFICES as the money could be paid straight into their account and it takes time and delays matters if this happens. I have the names of those who have pledged amounts - and now await your contributions. (Those of you unfamiliar with this project - we are going to buy a gift of possibly silver to send to Grace, Bruce's mum, to be engraved with the words: "A SON TO YOU; A SUN TO US" - (courtesy of suggestion by member Ian Fawcett) - from the Society. So if you wish to be a part of this project, just drop your contribution - as small or as high as you want - (together with your name, society number and address) along to me at the above address. From now until the December news sheet I will collect together the money, check out and buy the present, and then we shall decide on when to present the gift to Grace).

GENERAL NEWS

I am now getting so many different reports on the content of the various Bruce videos released by Rank that I am completely at a loss as to the original format of these. It would seem that some copies contain scenes missing from copies bought elsewhere in the country - which makes me wonder what is happening. We know that, when the censors cut scenes from copies of films for release, these films can yet again be cut by local authorities in the various parts of the country who might not like a certain scene - or who have been forced to remove parts from the films due to complaints from the local police on the behaviour of people who had seen certain scenes and been influenced by them - but surely that cannot be the case with videos? Or can it? I would, however, have imagined that censoring on these would be done at source - by Ranks themselves - on the instructions of the censors; and that this would be the only censoring done. Which, if so, does not account for the variety of copies going around. (Or maybe the odd uncut copy just gets through now and again.)

Letter from Rank to Ricahrd Baczyk saying that althought there were some cuts in Way of the Dragon *they hoped that most of the scenes he wished to see were preserved for him! Some chance!!*

Over to member Tim Ussher who, in February, went to Hong Kong and visited Golden Harvest - and was thrilled to be given a pair of green nunchakus which they state were used by Bruce to practice with offset. Also shown on the outside of these nunchakus are another pair which Tim had specially made as a replica to those from *Enter the Dragon*. Tim has made a very nice offer to members, too - if you want copies of any pictures he took in Hong Kong (for those unable to go themselves) he can do a set of 30 photos (to include film locations of *Game of Death* and *Enter the Dragon,* Queen Elizabeth Hospital and ward, Bruce's homes as a boy and film star, and Bruce's dressing room, props and film viewing room, dubbing room, editing room etc., at Golden Harvest). The cost for the set would be £10. Contact Tim at Crowborough, Sussex.

World of Sport recently presented the Basketball Final between the Los Angeles Lakers and the Philadelphia 76'ers, and David Moore noticed Kareem Abdul Jabbar was as usual playing with Lakers - who won. With someone as tall as Kareem they have the advantage to start, I feel! Although he didn't do too well in *Game of Death* against Bruce!

David also saw a recent episode of *Chicago Story* TV series, where two cops are patrolling in a car and are asking each other questions on television "cop" shows. One asked: "Remember *Longstreet*? Who was the self-defense expert in the series?" His partner answered (quite correctly!) "Bruce Lee."

Still with David - Benny Urquidez (World Super Lightweight Full Contact Champion) and his brother Ruben, and Chuck Norris and his brother Aaron have been sworn in as special deputy marshals for the county of Riverside, State of California.

Also, through a friend, David learnt that a Bruce Lee film was shown in the People's Republic of China (Mainland China) for the first time and the young people went CRAZY in the streets smashing tiles and things. He asks if either myself or any other members heard about it. I haven't but have you?? Sadly, this behaviour is yet another example of what the censors use for the reasons they cut Bruce's films so badly - why DO people carry on like this and (through their misguided actions which they think shows their admiration for Bruce) give more "fuel" to the censors' remarks and therefore ruin any chance we might have of having Bruce's films shown intact in the future?

Mistake spotted by David on the cover of the *Enter the Dragon* video - it states the running time is 86 minutes yet when he timed it he found it ran for 94 minutes (whose complaining?).

On to Owen Wint's article in the last news sheet about the interest he has created among his fellow-students in his martial arts club, David says similar things happened to him at his club where, if any argument or discussion starts on Bruce, they always go to David and ask him about it, such as: "How tall was he?" - "He started in karate, didn't he?" He's even been asked: "How did he die - he shot himself, didn't he?" (can you believe that??) When David cleared out some spare books, magazines etc., he took them around to the club - and they went like hot-cakes.

Still with David - he recently saw a book called *Movies on Video* by Roy Pickard; browsing through, he saw that Bruce's films *Enter the Dragon, Fist of Fury* and *Big Boss* were mentioned, but as Mr. Pickard put them down, calling them "boring, Kung Fu codswallop" etc., needless to say, said David: "I did NOT buy the book!." He did, however, buy *The Manual of Martial Arts* (£6.75) by black American Ron Van Clief. It is quite a good book with instructions from Karate, Kung Fu, Tae Kwon Do and Aiki-Jitsu. Ron mentions Bruce a few times, having met him in the early 1960's when Bruce introduced him to Wing Chun (some of the punching techniques in the book are similar to Wing Chun). Says Ron: "I will always remember Bruce - he was a friend and martial-arts brother." When he is stressing to stick to the essentials when defending yourself, Ron recalls when Bruce once told him: "Simplicity is the key to true martial arts application." One comment that confused David, however, was when Ron says he visited Shaw Brothers' studio in Hong Kong and met Bruce's mentor (?) - Director Chiang Cheh - who was responsible for *Big Boss* and *Fist of Fury* (?) - David says: "I thought Lo Wei was the director of these films - funny how a Shaw Brothers' director can take the credit, isn't it??" At the back of the book under the section for the "University of Martial Arts Hall of Fame 1965-81" are some entries David thought of interest: 1965 Superstar Award: Ed Parker. 1966 Martial Arts Author Award (for his book *Kempo Karate*): Ed Parker. 1967 Martial Arts Author Award (for his book *Chinese Gung Fu*):- Bruce Lee. 1967 Best Fighter: Chuck Norris. 1969 Best Demonstration: Bruce Lee. 1971 Superstar Award: Chuck Norris. 1972 Best Demonstration: Bruce Lee. 1973 Martial Arts Author Award (for his book *Arnis and Escrima*): Dan Inosanto. 1975 Superstar Award: David Carradine. 1976 Sensei (Master) of the Year: Ed Parker. 1977 Sensei of the Year: Chuck Norris. 1980 Superstar Award: Chuck Norris. 1981 Superstar Award: Chuck Norris. All round, says David, a good martial arts book.

Another book, *Comprehensive Asian Fighting Arts* by Draeger and Smith dealt with various martial arts styles worldwide, with a section on Kung Fu masters - one being Huo Tuan Chia, the master poisoned in *Fist of Fury*. Knowing that the film was based on a true story, I read the information on Huo with interest; apparently he was a Master of Mi Tsung I, a style which uses both "soft" and "hard" techniques and changes so abruptly and often that the opponent cannot build a defense or mount an offensive against it. This style suited Bruce's Jeet Kune Do in its use of both soft and hard and confusing tactics - and David says he feels that Bruce knew this and it was one of the reasons he chose the story.

Maria Fernandes, our Brazilian member, and Shahab Setudeh Nejad, in Seattle, have both told me of the Bruce Lee comic strip cartoon *The Legend of Bruce Lee* currently showing in the *Los Angeles Times* and which has been offered by that syndicate to some 1,400 newspapers who have the option of running the strip. Based on Bruce, his life-style and philosophy, it has the full backing (thank goodness!) and blessing of Linda Lee - so we know that anything done in this vein will be of a tasteful nature and a fitting tribute to Bruce. As Linda said: "I know it is something that Bruce would have liked. It is unique, and rather flattering for his name to be honoured in such a way. The character in the strip would be just like any role he would have played in a movie as an actor." In many ways, the strip has a movie-flavour in both tone and acting. But Linda pointed out one major difference between the comic strip and dozens of martial arts films that have invoked Bruce Lee's memory through a variety of look-alikes and similar name-spellings. "You know" she continues, "There have been so many lousy movies released in the past where ac-

The Dragon is back!

The legend of Bruce Lee lives on in the comic pages of The Seattle Times beginning Sunday May 23 and daily May 24.

His life, his work and his mastery of martial arts are unveiled through the series. Karate technique and Jeet Kune Do philosophy combine for fast-action plots tempered by Lee's eternal journey toward enlightenment. It's entertaining . . . educational inspiring. Don't miss it!

In the comic pages of

The Seattle Times

Sent by Shahab Setudeh Nejad

tors have impersonated Bruce or played off his name and done similar things that they have become rip-offs. Here is a chance for Bruce Lee fans to see him in something new without it being an exploitive film that he doesn't even appear in."

In fact, the creators of the strip have gone out of their way to ensure both the accuracy and integrity of the character - the strip's writer, Sharman DiVono, is not only a martial artist but has also contacted Linda on many occasions to ask such questions as "What would Bruce have done?" or "What would Bruce have thought?" in a particular situation. Books that the strip will draw teachings and writings from are: Bruce's *Tao of Jeet Kune Do*; *Zen and the Martial Arts* by Joe Hyams; *Hagakure - The Book of the Samurai* by Tsunetomo Yamamoto; *Bruce Lee's Fighting Method* by Bruce and M. Uyehara; *Jeet Kune Do - The Art and Philosophy of Bruce Lee* by Dan Inosanto; and *Bushido The Warrior's Code* by Inazo Nitobe.

Back to David Moore - he read in *Fighters* magazine that veteran artist Chuck Sullivan spoke well of Bruce, saying they had met a few times and spoke briefly. Chuck went on to say: "Even as a kid, at that time he tried to dispel the myths in the art. He tried really hard to show that there is no magic and that it is all just learning, hard work and more hard work. It's the old 1% inspiration and 99% perspiration. And that's what he was into at the time, and he developed it to such a high degree that it looked almost like magic when he did it." This was in the early 60's when Bruce was only in his early to mid-twenties and hadn't begun his really intensive training. After reading something like that, says David, you really appreciate how good Bruce was before his death.

In a book *The Karate Dojo* by P. Urban (says David) I came across a piece which I immediately connected with Bruce concerning Ch'i, the internal energy practised by many martial artists: "A person who consciously or unconsciously allows his Ch'i development complete freedom of flow seems to charge the air around him with electricity; the moment such a person enters a room, a dynamic presence is felt, and all eyes turn towards him." (Pam here: Yes, even on screen that "presence" comes over to us - so just imagine, can you, what it must have been like to have met Bruce and absorbed such energy from him and to have felt the effect of this?)

David Moore here - I'm very interested in the paranormal. In Issue 66 of the *Unexplained* magazine was an article on numerology - prediction of the future and finding out a persons character by taking his/her name - and any change in name/nickname used throughout life - and by using the Hebrew system of numbers instead of stars, arriving at a single number for each of those names. By using "Bruce Lee," "Li Jun Fan1," "Li Yuen Kam," and "Little Dragon," I came up with the numbers 4, 3, 1 and 6 respectively - and the following overall picture of Bruce as follows: No. 4 - dependable, down-to-earth, born organiser, fair, meticulous to detail, subject to sudden irrational rages/depressions that seem extraordinary in people who are usually models of calmness. (four traditionally regarded by numerologists as the number of ill-luck). Often people whose number is four pay dearly for any success they achieve in life. No. 3 - extrovert, intelligent, creative, witty. Generally make friends easily and seem to succeed at anything they turn their hand to. Proud, ambitious, and leisure-loving. No. 1 - Dominant and a leader. Usually pioneers, inventors, designers. But often put their plans into practice with little regard for the way they will affect people most directly involved. Tend to dominate everyone they meet. Rarely have close friends and are sometimes, despite their confident appearance, very lonely people. No. 6 - Happy, tranquil, well-balanced and home-loving. Affectionate, loyal, sincere and conscientious. No uncreative; many are successful in the performing arts.

FILM SNIPPETS
Members' Reviews of Kung Fu and other Martial Arts films

I went to see *Sharkey's Machine* with Burt Reynolds, and was surprised to see Dan Inosanto make an appearance as one of the Chin Brothers - two Oriental hit-men. In one scene, Dan, armed with a knife, waves it menacingly in the same fashion as bad-guy Leggetti in *Big Brawl*. (As I told Pam some time ago, Dan trained the actor Ron Max who played Leggetti to use the Balisong knives so it wasn't surprising Dan looked so effective with them.) It was great to see Dan in a straight non-martial arts film. It shows how highly his skills are appreciated in the film business. (David Moore)

It's nice to see a top actor working with top martial artists - firstly in the film *Cannonball Run* with Burt Reynolds and Jackie Chan; and then, in Burt's new film *Sharkey's Machine* to my surprise none other than Bruce's number-one student, Dan Inosanto. He played a part similar to Bruce's first major film *Marlowe*. He's a hood and appears in two separate parts, first where they beat up and kill a drug dealer informer using sword sticks, and next when Dan is beating up and knocking out Burt. Dan does some fancy handwork with a flick-knife before cutting off two of Burt's fingers. But unfortunately, like Bruce, he gets killed by Burt with a speargun then gets kicked off a boat. (Eric Canham)

I recently rented *The Octagon* on video starring Chuck Norris, and I can certainly recommend it. The plot revolves around a vicious training camp for ninjas, and although the story is somewhat confusing and short in action in the early stages, the last 20 minutes or so make up for it - it's packed with some great fight scenes as Chuck battles it out with the Ninjas (who are armed with Sai swords, etc.) before confronting the evil ninja leader (played by Tadashi Yamashita - a great US weapons expert) in a Kama battle. (Carl Jones)

I recently saw *The Challenge* (formerly *The Equals*) starring Toshiro Mifune, and I must say it was very good. It combined the traditional practise of the martial arts with good action and an exciting climax. Well worth a visit to your cinema AND it is on with a good short film about Japanese martial arts which helps you to understand the main film better. The only complaint was that the scene which was shown on *Film 82* of a contest between a man and a woman, with the woman winning, wasn't in. Co-stars Scott Glenn, Shago Shimada, Atsuo Nakamura (Lin Chung in the TV series *Water Margin*?), Sab Shiraono, Calvin Jung and Donna Kei Benz.

Member Maria Fernandes was FURIOUS when she heard about Chris Welling's remarks on Bruce's skills being down to "camera tricks and special effects" - in fact she will be writing to *Combat* magazine where the article appeared just to say how mad she is - and how misguided they are. And to back up her facts on Bruce's skills, she quotes the following comments made by fellow-martial artists and people who had seen Bruce in action, to quote but a very small example, which shows just how high Bruce's skill as a martial artist rated:

> "I don't know how Bruce does it. He moves so fast - before you could even get set, before you could even do anything, he's always on top of you! He amazed me with his quickness!" (Jhoon Rhee)

> "Only later Ryan (O'Neill) would admit he was hit and kicked more than 100 times in 15 seconds!"

> "Bruce could move eight feet in three-quarters of a second and could jab at your eyes and withdraw his hand in just one-tenth of a second!" (Mito Uyehara)

> "Bruce moved so fast that if we shot him at regular speed during the fight scenes everything would have been a blur!" (Mrs. Margaret Curtis Walters - Bruce's English teacher at the University of Washington)

> "He moved so fast they couldn't catch him on the films, so he had to stylize it - it then became an exhibition more than anything else in the films ... He was so fast with the nunchakus that sometimes even the slow-motion camera couldn't catch them!" (Taky Kimura)

> "Afterward, Bruce told me to block his punches. Those punches were so fast that I couldn't block any of them!" (Hayward Nishioka)

> "You were pulled, pushed, twisted and kicked all in a matter of seconds. His speed was literally unbelievable. He could hit you before you could even see him do it. He had to slow down for the camera in his pictures as well as allow for reaction time from the stuntmen or actors!" (Herb Jackson)

> "Suppose a guy did a technique that you didn't see? How are you going to score something like that? All I saw was a mean blur from Bruce. It lasted only about two seconds and the opponent was out. I found later that he was in the hospital!" (Ronald Kealoha - Bruce's first Hawaiian student in America)

Pam here: I wonder if *Combat* have the decency to print Maria'a letter - and admit how stupid Chris Welling has made them look for printing such utter rubbish in the first place? Keep your eyes open for me - and let me know if you see any further comments from them in their magazine! Ta!

SO FAR I've had no response to my request for pictures for the World of Bruce Lee who needed photographs of the show held in London in June 1980 at Westminster Central Hall. Please, if you can help, let me know.

Carl Jones says he would be interested to read a detailed review of *Game Of Death II* and so would I, so can anyone oblige with this for the December news sheet??? Thanks!

One of our long-standing members, John Aspinall (1527) recently moved to Australia for a year, and I think it might be nice if he heard a few words from fellow-members here, and maybe he can tell you what's going on Bruce-wise that direction!

(Address: Manly, New South Wales, Australia). Also, notified by John, is the death of Hironiro Ohtsuka, Grand-Master of Wado Ryu, in which style John received his Black Belt. Hironiro died on 29th January, 1982, aged 90. He was 10th Dan Mejun, and John says the martial arts, especially Karate, will be at a tremendous loss.

CHAMPION'S CLOSE-UP
DANIEL LEE

Mention the name *Bruce Lee* to any martial artist and you are likely to meet with a host of varied responses and reactions. The man, his style and his career remain very much a mystery today. One man, however, who knew Lee, studied his style of jeet kune do and has seen through the clouds that envelop his mythic image is Daniel Lee.

Born in China, raised in Shanghai, Daniel Lee began his career in the martial arts as a classic-style boxer. In his early youth he showed the moxie and tenacity that propelled him to the top in boxing competition. Soon, however, he realized that something was missing—the thrill of victory was only temporary despite an illustrious record. After arriving in the United States, Lee began studying other forms in the martial arts. His search for something deeper, to counter the fighter's spirit that lived within him, led him down a student's trail that eventually culminated with his study of jeet kune do with Bruce Lee. For the former pugilist it proved to be the perfect blend of philosophical rhetoric backed by physical skills.

Today, Daniel Lee continues to lead a very active life—both within the arts and outside them. Professionally, he works as a senior research engineer at the Jet Propulsion Laboratories in Pasadena, California, (the aeronautics lab that was involved in the photo research of Saturn and Jupiter last fall) and continues his interest in the martial arts by teaching tai chi chuan and jeet kune do.

His thoughts follow:

FS: Why did you begin studying jeet kune do with Bruce Lee?

LEE: I was studying the martial arts with Dan Inosanto and was just in the process of getting my black belt in kempo karate. While studying with Dan, I had just seen Bruce in a demonstration in Long Beach—his lightning speed and clear-cut philosophy really impressed me; I wanted very much to study with him. That was the first time he appeared in L.A. I liked the simplicity, the crisp movements, his philosophical approach. It was the first time I had seen someone put philosophy into action; I had seen philosophers and martial artists, but never the two together.

FS: Was the style that markedly different from the one you were studying?

LEE: Yes. I had learned over 100 ways of countering a right punch. I was so bogged down in techniques. But I found that using these techniques in freestyle nothing worked. When you do techniques, someone throws a punch and you go through a whole beautiful routine while he or she just stays there. In reality, that person would react and everything you'd planned and scripted would fall apart. That was very frustrating.

FS: There are no step-by-step fights.

LEE: No, just spontaneous reaction. Bruce Lee said, "Use no way as the way; use no limit as the limit." He was advocating a personal search for the right technique rather than drills. My training had been very ritualistic and I thought that was the way. Boundaries are set by those forms, by the structures, telling you how to fight. Bruce said that a real fight was outside those boundaries. Also, jeet kune do seems to adapt to the hands of a boxer, and I was a boxer in China.

FS: You've made an interesting transition, though. You've gone from two very physical arts—boxing and jeet kune do, as well as the others—to tai chi. Why?

LEE: Tai chi was to me like Chinese culture, an art rooted in the philosophy of the Tao. When I was boxing, I pretty much ignored it, but when I came to this country I realized how much I had missed. One hopefully reaches a stage where one needs to tie the martial arts and philosophy together. I was already a champion boxer, but it reached a point where it was meaningless. They call you champ, but the insecurity sets in; people are challenging your championship. It becomes a duty rather than enjoyment. I was searching for something deeper, something self-satisfying, for personal growth and more peace of mind and tranquility.

FS: Many fighters never reach that point. They always have to fight so that by the time they are 35 or 40, they just can't step down—they're always in the ring. They have no connection between what they did physically and their mental state.

LEE: With so much fighting, it influenced my consciousness. When you encounter little things you immediately want to fight. You have a very hostile attitude towards people. To master others requires force; to master yourself requires strength. I wanted strength. Not so much discipline and controlling my temper, but how to be gentle. Tai chi had that quality, that softness and pliability of strength. I had always pursued hard strength, but hardness is a disciple of death; pliability is the disciple of life. That's what Lao Tze said.

FS: After you briefly began tai chi in China, you then came here and again picked up with the martial arts. From kempo to jeet kune do. Another contradiction, perhaps. Jeet kune do is a fighting system, isn't it?

LEE: Just like tai chi—the symbol is the yin and yang—it is softness and hardness. Unity consists of two complimentary forces. Tai chi has to be soft because of its training method. To learn to be soft and yielding, to be rooted yet compliant, takes discipline. Many of the JKD principles are the same. JKD *is* more aggressive, but the applicable techniques are very different from what I learned before. It's a circular movement. I find no conflicting training, but rather it expands my consciousness. It involves circular motion, conserving energy, rebounding back rather than straight-line motion, which exhausts energy. JKD also uses your opponent's force. Tai chi is to achieve peace within yourself through discipline.

FS: Then what is jeet kune do?

LEE: JKD is sort of an extension of tai chi, but it is not a style. Bruce said that any style sets a boundary, remember that. He explored all different disciplines and he saw no reason for limiting yourself to one area. For example, boxing is good because it develops the hand; but it has rules where you can't backfist, you can't kick, thus it develops only one portion of your body. Judo is only effective once you grab someone and bodies make contact. But the most efficient way is totality.

FS: Would you call JKD a fighting system then?

LEE: It literally means the way of intercepting the fist. The word "do" or "dao" appears in many arts, where it means technique. But in jeet kune do it means central concept, or the way, or philosophy. And the central theme is that there are no limits or boundaries, no beginning or end. Bruce Lee used jeet kune do for lack of a better name.

FS: People are anxious to pin a style down. So, was it a style, a system or what?

LEE: He said it was a concept—a concept to explore. His technique was rooted in wing chun (kung fu), which also has its limitations. But Bruce dared to step out of its bounds and question its validity, very rare for an Oriental fighter.

FS: What would you tell a student today if they asked what martial arts style they should study?

LEE: It depends on their temperament. All the martial arts are good. The arts should be a form of personal development and exploration. You should, however, go beyond the bounds of your art, as Bruce said, and be free from them. So a fighting system has to be based on your own research, you need your own creativity. You need to ask yourself if it is working for you. You have to absorb what is useful for you and adapt it to your body, and discard the rest. The arts should be dynamic, incorporating your own experience and continually expanding. ✯

POETS CORNER

From Alison French - this first poem being about the scene from *Big Boss* - Bruce sits by the water: All his family are dead (or so he thinks) and his mind goes back to how things had been just a few days before:

> By the river you are sitting - hunched up, looking into space. Eyes sad, face etched in thought and in grief. Where is your mind? Lost in pictures; in memories on the screen of lost time. You gaze into nothingness, hands together as you remember. Your handsomeness is heightened by your pain at the losses you have suffered. You held them dear but they are dead and your mind turns, turns to revenge. Anger takes over as you realise what you must do.

And now - a touching poem from Ann Hunt:

> When I am sad and lonely, and everything goes wrong, I seem to hear you whisper: "Cheer up - and carry on." Each time I see your photograph, you smile and seem to say: "Don't cry - I'm only sleeping." We trust in God to meet one day.

Enter the Dragon CINEMA QUIZ
By Karen Shaub & Sent In By Greg Rhodes

1. Who wrote the screenplay for *Enter the Dragon*?
2. Who wrote the novelization?
3. Who played Bruce's opponent in the opening scene?
4. How often does Han hold his tournament?
5. What is the name of the stewardess found floating in the harbour?
6. Name the actress who played Mei Ling.
7. How many of Han's daughters are we shown?
8. What is the name of the girl who speaks to Bruce in the caverns and where is she from?
9. Name the well-known martial artist who hits Bob Wall with boards in Braithewaite's film.
10. Name the 3 real-life martial artists who Roper beats up on the golf course.
11. What is the loan shark's name?
12. How much money and interest does Roper owe?
13. When does Roper's loan come due?
14. In a flashback sequence Williams goes to a Kenpo school, name the 2 famous black-belts he sees there.
15. How many sugar lumps does Braithewaite take?
16. How much time elapses before arrival of Lee's message & Braitewaite's receipt of it.
17. To whom does Braithewaite want to talk when he makes his phone call?
18. Who plays Braithewaite?
19. The last line Bruce speaks is "You have offended my family and you have offended the Shaolin temple." What is Bruce's next-to-last line?
20. Other than fists, feet & other natural equipment, what weapons does Bruce utilise?
21. Han strikes Lee with blades several times during the final confrontation. How many?
22. Which one of Han's hands is missing?
23. What colour are the eyes of Han's cat?
24. What does Han say we are all born knowing?
25. During the fight with Williams, one of Han's girls can be seen with a word written on her face in reverse. What is the word?

Answers in December, folks!

SPECIAL HELP AND REQUESTS

As most of you know, I have been attempting to streamline the kit to keep costs down and to decrease paperwork, thus making it easier to run the club when I take this over myself. One project was a new plastic membership card, something on the lines of Access/Barclaycard, that would fit into pockets etc. Once a member received this on joining, it would then not involve the sending of a new one every year - thus timesaving and money saving. I had been given a rough quote of 12p to 15p each, maximum cost, so imagine my surprise, no - horror was more the word, after telling you all the cards would be done shortly, to find the firm now wanted 47p each. So obviously, if I went ahead with these, that would NOT be keeping costs down and indeed would mean putting up prices, which is not my intention. SO - I NEED YOUR HELP - URGENTLY! If any members know of, or work for a company who could produce such cards (they do not need raised surfaces for lettering as with Access cards etc., but will be completely flat), then PLEASE, PLEASE LET ME KNOW NOW. I will take it from there. I have all the artwork prepared, so that now I just need the supplier!! If I cannot get one - then I shall have to find an alternative type of card. ANYONE HAVE ANY IDEAS AS TO TYPE/STYLE/ MATERIAL FOR THIS???? I would VERY MUCH WELCOME your suggestions and help at this stage. In the meantime, old-type cards will be sent out.

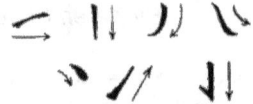

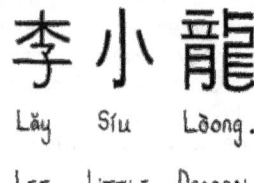

Courtesy of Paul Corrigan

NEW FILM INFO
From David Moore

In the making is a film *They Call Me Bruce* starring Johnny Yune (which may be the same as the spoof film starring Johnny Yu). Co-stars Margaux Hemingway, Gene Lebell and Pamela Huntington (of *Force Five*).

Joe Lewis, former Karate and full-contact champion, is to star with Stuart Whitman and Gene Lebell in a film called *Magnum Thrust*.

Revenge of the Ninja, which has had its hold-ups, is finally scheduled to begin filming.

AN APOLOGY

Last news sheet I gave some info from David Moore that *Combat* magazine article-writer Chris Welling had stated "Bruce had told me his skills were down to camera tricks and special effects." Actually (and David put me straight on this!) it was Welling himself that had said he thought Bruce's skills were down to tricks! And not only THAT mistake - but David says the article mentioning "Al Tabasco" should in fact have read "Al Dacoscas," who is an excellent martial artist experienced in different Kung Fu styles, karate, judo, kempo and Filipino stick fighting. *[Editor's Note: In this book, the name was corrected by myself in the previous issue. Pam unfortunately got the name wrong on this occasion too, as it should have read "Al Dacascos."]*

...AND A WARNING
From David Niedzailek (1021)

FLYOVER RECORDS in London have gone into liquidation - and David warns members NOT to send any money to this company for records thinking it is still trading; David lost £10 - and hopes that he can prevent any other members doing the same. (THANKS, DAVID!)

BRUCE'S BOOK LIST (Part II)

Following on the last news sheet, here's the second selection of books from the 288 owned by Bruce! (courtesy of Dan Inosanto who kindly gave me a copy of the list from Bruce's own handwritten notes which he possesses). Many members will have some of the books - and many of you will now be trying to obtain others! It certainly would be an achievement to be able to obtain all, or nearly all, of the books in the complete list - and it might even give some of you more ardent fans something of a challenge to achieve this! Mind you - I would think that some books are now nearly impossible to find - but who knows?? There are many second-hand bookshops around (from whence I have obtained many rare books in the past) who will be worth visiting. Anyway - here are another selection....

Kenpo Karate - Ed Parker (1960)
Secrets of Chinese Karate - Ed Parker (1963)
Kempo - Waraki Hara (1967)
Fighting Arts of the Orient - James Yimm Lee (1958)
Chinese Gung Fu - Bruce Lee (1963)
Fighting Arts of the Orient (Revised) - James Yimm Lee
Chinese Karate Kung Fu - T.Y. Wong (1961)
Tai-Chi Chuan - Cheng Man Chin (1958)

Tai-Chi For Health - Edward Maisel (1963)
Modern Karate Kung Fu (Part A) - James Lee (1958)
Tai-Chi Chuan - It's Effects and Practical Application - Yeerning K. Chen
Modern Karate Kung Fu (Part B) - James Lee (1962)
The Secret Arts of Chinese Leg Manoeuvres - Lee Ying Hing (1962)
Modern Karate Kung Fu (Book 1 Part A) by James Lee (1963)

More next time!

"EMOTION"

Last time, I gave you Bruce's own personal definition of the word 'WILLPOWER' in relation to his own aims - this time, as promised, his writing under the heading "EMOTION":

"REALISING THAT MY EMOTIONS ARE BOTH POSITIVE AND NEGATIVE I WILL FORM DAILY HABITS WHICH WILL ENCOURAGE THE DEVELOPMENT

THE BRUCE LEE SOCIETY

OF THE POSITIVE EMOTIONS, AND AID ME IN CONVERTING THE NEGATIVE EMOTIONS INTO SOME FORM OF USEFUL ACTION."

LETTERS

Dear Pam,

Let me give you some martial arts info here in India. Recently I saw a movie titled The Cobra. It is a direct lift from Enter the Dragon - the set-up and the story are the same. The hero's name is Ardhendra-Bose who actually models for the famous textile company "Bombay Dying." He is a freak at martial arts! Also recently we had an International Tournament at Indore City between Singapore and India.

Rajiv Gaikwar (3354)

Well, Rajiv - it seems that the rip-off artists are not only in Hong Kong! Jumping on the Bruce Lee bandwagon seems to be a worldwide-activity! Thanks for your letter, Rajiv.

Dear Pam,

Please could you print in the news sheet any details you might have of the next convention; and I know I speak on behalf of ALL Bruce Lee fans in saying a convention is very important as it gets everybody together as well as meeting old friends and making new ones.

Duncan Smith (1456)

I am entirely in agreement with you, Duncan - and from the enquiries I receive it seems a unanimous opinion. I have enquired to KFM (who as you know hold ALL funds in respect of such conventions, including ticket monies - not myself!) to see when the next convention might be held - it was intimated that plans were in the pipeline, but so far, regrettably, I have been unable to find anything definite. So what I now suggest is this - WHY NOT ALL WRITE IN TO KFM to the MANAGING DIRECTOR to ask when they plan to hold the next convention. I feel sure that, when Felix Dennis there sees just how keen you all are to "get the show moving again," plans will be forthcoming to organise the much-needed meetings!! Don't forget - my one voice ALONE doesn't count for much - after all, it is for EVERYONE that the conventions are held - so EVERYONE should

KFM is delighted to announce the arrival of Back Issue Bonanza No.6. Now at last, readers who missed out on some of the more recent editions have got a chance to 'plug the gaps'!

BONANZA 5.   Issues 18, 19, 20, 21 and 22
BONANZA 6.   Issues 23, 24, 25, 26 and 27

Each of the above BONANZAS is on offer for £1.20. In the years to come, your back copies of Kung-Fu Monthly will become sought after items and complete sets will be valuable. Don't miss out on this chance to update your collection – Send your cheque or postal order off immediately to:

Back Issue Bonanza 5/6
Kung-Fu Monthly
14 Rathbone Place
London W.1.
CLUB MEMBER'S PRICE, £1.00 ONLY
(Please allow at least 4 weeks for delivery).

try to get the event going!! Don't you agree?? Maybe because you HAVE NOT BEEN WRITING *KFM* feel there is no urgency to put a show on. Come on now - let them see JUST HOW KEEN YOU ARE - PLEASE!!

And the following letter comes from John Aspinall, recently moved to Australia:

Dear Pam,

Fist of Fury and Way of the Dragon will be showing in a small picture studio in the City - it will be interesting to see how many show up. I'll be taking some mates along to see Bruce to initiate them into the spirit of Bruce, because they haven't see him yet!! The fools! And another point - about a month back I watched a martial arts film with a friend who does not do any martial arts - and I have never been so embarrassed watching a movie in my whole life - my friend thought it was hilarious! The film was American and called Kill and Kill Again with James Ryan. To any martial artist it was an insult. If that is what the general public believe artists do then we'll become laughing stocks plus it so embarrassingly resembled Enter the Dragon in parts it's a wonder I sat and watched the whole film!

John Aspinall

I've had very similar embarrassing moments when people have seen this type of rubbish and, unknowingly, thought that all martial arts films were in the same vein - including Bruce's. I've soon put them right and on occasions taken them to see Bruce - to their enlightenment. But for the small minority who "see the light" there are many thousands more who have yet to find the truth!!

Dear Pam,

Recently some friends and I went to see two Sonny Chiba films (one of my favourite artists!) - called Kung Fu Street Fighter and Blood of the Dragon - and we all had a good time and enjoyed the films, and went home happy - that is until I read an article on Chuck Norris in the June Film Review I'd just bought, concerning his film An Eye For An Eye. The article said that many artists had been hailed as successors to Bruce Lee, naming Lo Lieh, David Chiang, Jim Kelly, Wang Yu and Jackie Chan, but that all had proved mere shadows next to the martial arts king. (True!) It then went on to say: "Then Chuck Norris came along. Not only has he equalled the Oriental master, but has surpassed him in popularity"!! Sure, Chuck Norris is good! He wouldn't have been seven times Karate champ if he wasn't! But reading that bit of paper left me incensed. How the Hell anyone can say Norris EQUALLED Bruce Lee is beyond my comprehension, but to go so far as to say he SURPASSED Bruce Lee in popularity took the biscuit. Never in my short years have I read such complete and utter rubbish! Okay, some Westerners are not at all bad at the sport and I'll even watch their films. But in my opinion no one looks half as good as the Orientals, no matter how hard they try. They just do not have the talent, the grace of movement or the style! Don't think I am biased, because believe me I am not. I am white myself but give me a Chinese Martial Artist any day - just compare them! BRUCE LEE WAS AND ALWAYS WILL BE THE BEST!

Caroline Andrew (2939)

THE BRUCE LEE SOCIETY

Well, Caroline - I feel that on many points you have spoken for the majority of fans as regards the comparison of Chuck and Bruce. I like and admire Chuck - both as an artist and as a very modest person - but the comments in that article are ridiculous. What do other members feel about it - have you any comments on Caroline's letter - or the article??

Dear Pam,

I've just seen two Sonny Chiba films and in the first film *Kung Fu Street Fighter*, a guy comes at Sonny with a pair of nunchakus. I thought the censors had banned them and other weapons from martial arts films, or is it just Bruce's films?!? I also saw them for a few seconds in *Revenge of the Dragon* (again with Sonny) and another scene was shown with a girl plunging a sai fighting dagger into the top of a man's head. This was AFTER the censors "ban the weapons" rule so that IS going on? This is surely a blatant bias against Bruce. Could you tell me the address of Mr. Ferman and his bunch of slash-happy butchers (the censors) as I feel like writing to them to ask them about this.

David Moore (1783)

VERY happy to oblige with the address, David - and I hope other members will back you up with this matter: British Board of Film Censors (Secretary: Mr. Ferman) - Soho Square, London, W1. It also seems strange that, on television which is FAR more easier for youngsters and anyone to see, violence is prevalent - and they've even shown nunchakus. Like you say, David - it seems that Bruce has had more than his fair share of cutting all round!

USEFUL ADDRESSES

From Ann and Fred Hunt, who are keen fans of the *Monkey* and *Water Margin* TV series, they thought fellow fans would like the address of the TV company who brought these out: Nippon TV Network Corp., International Relations Section, 14 Niban-Cho, Chiyoda-ku, Tokyo 120, Japan. After writing to say how much they liked the programmes, they were pleased to get not only a reply from Nippon but a picture of the *Water Margin* cast as well!!

Courtesy of Glynn Darbyshire

Member Mustafa Abdi (3292) recommends his Wing Chun Kung Fu master, Victor Kan, whose Gym is at 9, Earlham Street, London WC2 (Just of Cambridge Circus between Tottenham Court Road and Leicester Square Tube Station on the opposite side of the road). Telephone: (01) 240 0017. Open 3-10 p.m. Mondays and Wednesdays. Beginners and all grades welcome.

David Niedzailek recommends Py Tang for a video-film documentary on Bruce/Jackie Chan - quality good although, David says, not as good as other Py Tang videos - and exclusive to the Py Tang Club (which you must join for a life-membership of £5 in order to obtain videos from them). Bruce footage contains some rare film of Bruce from a HKTV show breaking a board; inside and outside Bruce's house in Kowloon and his training equipment (which the interviewer tries out!); footage of Bruce's funeral and clips from *Big Boss, Fist of Fury, Way of the Dragon, Enter the Dragon* and *Game of Death* (with the whole Bruce/Dan fight but not the Bruce/Kareem fight although you see a shot of them staring at each other). There's also a demonstration by a Kung Fu student doing JKD, as well as lots of talking (regrettably

The Official Kung-Fu Monthly Back Issues Binder is already selling a storm! At last dedicated readers are able to keep their rare KFM copies in ABSOLUTELY PERFECT CONDITION.

This smart black binder is silver-embossed with the world famous Kung-Fu Monthly Emblem and makes a superb addition to anyone's bookcase.

STAY AHEAD!! If you haven't ordered yours yet (or maybe the first is getting a little full!) send immediately, a £2.75 cheque/postal order to:
KFM Binder Offer
14 Rathbone Place
London W1P 1DE

Special Society Member's Price... only £2.50
(Please allow at least 4 weeks for delivery)

in Chinese). The Jackie Chan footage has an interview with Fred Weintraub/Robert Clouse about Jackie with clips from his films. David says he likes what he sees of Jackie and, although he's not a serious Kung Fu artist, he's very good at what he does - especially acrobatics. Cost of the tape £29 including post and package; runs for 84 minutes - well worth the money (VHS/Betamax format)!

SWOP SHOP

- David Willett, 41, Balderton has for sale: copy of *Tao of Jeet Kune Do* by Bruce Lee (softback) - £3.
- Robert Walker, Clydebank, Dumbartonshire has or sale/swap for any Karate gear: *Game of Death* tracksuit - £6, *Fist of Fury,, Enter the Dragon, My Way of Kung Fu* single-LPs, *Who Killed Bruce Lee*, second *Scrapbook, Fighting Method Advanced Techniques/Legend of Bruce Lee* (paperback) by Alex B. Block, *Exciting Cinema Kung Fu 1974 Special Issue*, first convention mug, *Motion Pictures on Paper*, plus Bruce Lee posters and *KFM*.
- Andrew Upton, Birkenhead has for sale: *KFM's* 3-12, 14-18, 20-22, 24, 26-30, 32, 33, 35, 36, 38-40, 42-44, 46-49 and spare No. 5, *Bruce Lee King of Kung Fu, Unbeatable Bruce Lee, Bruce Lee Fighting Spirit, Black Belt's Best of Bruce Lee No. 27, Game of Death Extract Edition, Bruce Lee in Game of Death, Immortal Dragon, Bruce Lee in Action, Who Killed Bruce Lee, Unknowns in Martial Arts Learning, Bruce Lee Reminiscence, Bruce Lee the Untold Story, Bruce Lee Scrapbooks* 1 and 2, *Privacy and Anecdotes, Bruce Lee Revenges*, 45's records *Dragon Power* and James Coburn Flexidisc tribute, *Way of the Dragon* poster magazines, *KFM* trade dummy, Kung Fu ("All you ever wanted to know about Bruce Lee King of the Kung Fu movies" on cover, *KFM Game of Death* special, *Kung Fu*. £25 plus £5 p&p.
- Carl Jones, St. Helens has for sale: (all prices inc. p&p) - double-LP *Enter the Dragon* - £8.50, single-LP *Enter the Dragon* (music only) - £2, *Dragon Power* 12" single - £l.25, Bruce Lee interview cassette - £2, Bruce Lee *Inedit* - £3.50/*Film Bulletin* July '73 (colour *Enter the Dragon* issue) - very rare - £3.50/*Best of Bruce Lee* No. 2 - E1.25, Bruce Lee colour calendar - 1980 - £1, *Fighting Stars* (Bruce issue) - £1, *Deadly Hands of Kung Fu* Nos. 26 & 28, *Fighting Arts* (Dan Inosanto issue), *Bruce Lee & JKD* magazines Nos. 1-12, *KFM* 3; *Bruce Lee King of Kung Fu, Music & Video* (Bruce Lee issue) - all at 75p each. Alternatively: will trade above for VHS video on Bruce; also wanted: cassette of *Game 2* soundtrack and anything on *Game 2*.
- R. Brown, Blackpool has for sale: Bruce Lee records (mint); 12 Single & Double-LP's; 12 7" & E.P.'s, 1 12, *Game of Death* & *Enter the Dragon*, Double-LP); *Way of the Dragon* etc. - lots more. Also beautiful pictures of Bruce Lee on albums, 7", 12." Plus *Big Boss, Fist of Fury, Enter the Dragon* and "behind the scenes" on *Enter the Dragon, Big Boss, The Green Hornet* videos. All Bruce Lee at his best.
- Paul Short, Sheffield wants: English version of *Game of Death* poster.
- Niels Bjerre, truer, Denmark aants: copy of *Life & Tragic Death of Bruce Lee* by Linda Lee. Please quote price wanted.
- David Moore, Wakefield has for Sale: Size 4 (5ft 4in-5ft-8in) Black Kung Fu wrap over jacket worn only twice - £5.

A RETROSPECTIVE LOOK AT BRUCE LEE MANIA & THE KUNG FU CRAZE OF THE 1970S

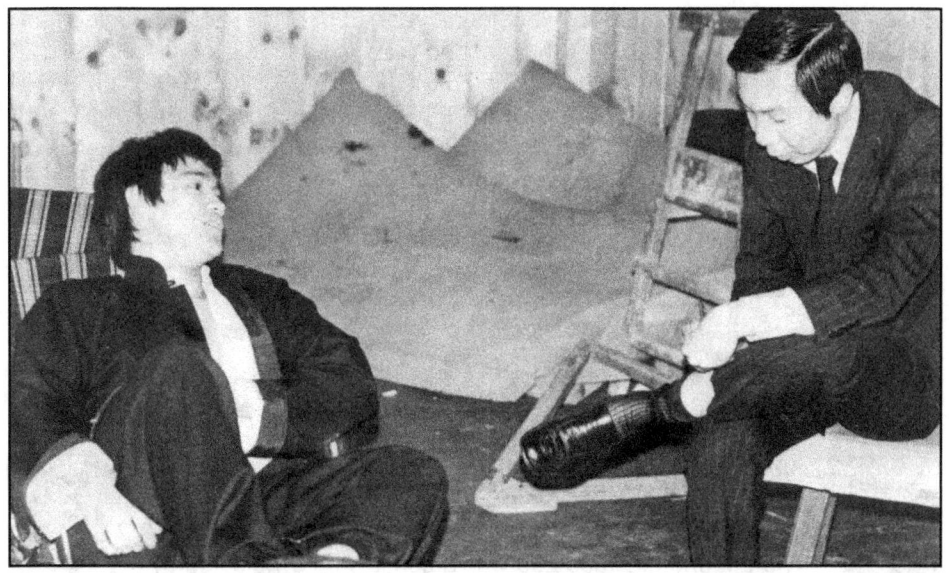

- Paul Shephard, Birmingham has for sale: large amount of Bruce Lee material (inc. *KFM's* 1- 50 plus one binder, *Game of Death* Special *KFM*, cinema posters to *Big Boss, Fist of Fury, Enter the Dragon, Game of Death,* many Chinese books (rare pictures); English/Chinese versions of Bruce Lee JKD Club of Hong Kong books, large posters of Bruce Lee and few paperback books, Double-LP *Enter the Dragon* & *Bruce Lee Big Special* - many, many more items. Write to Paul for full list - whole collection for £60 -but will sell separately.
- Alexander Dow, Aberdeen has for swap: very large collection of Bruce Lee/martial arts material inc. many rarities. Wants: complete collection of Bruce Lee films on Super 8 (4x400ft reels) with *Enter the Dragon* in English & rest in German. Send SAE for complete list of items available.
- Robert Opie, Larkhall has for Sale: *Fist of Fury, Way of the Dragon, Enter the Dragon* VHS videos - unused -(bought Betamax machine after buying videos) - *Way of the Dragon* complete, all fights, English with Dutch subtitles, bonus extra - credits from USA print showing title *Return of Dragon* - £39.95 plus £1 p&p, *Enter the Dragon* complete, all fights, English sound - bonus extra: fights repeated on last 30 mins. with less cut-off on large action scenes (running time 2 hrs.) - £35, *Fist of Fury* - all fights intact, complete feature, English with Dutch subtitles - £39.95. All films in smart deluxe box with Bruce Lee in action on cover - p&p £1 extra per cassette.
- Ernest Bow, Basingstoke has for swap: newspaper cuttings of Elvis' death plus two magazines (one in pieces) and one paperback book *My Life with Elvis*; wants any Bruce Lee poster magazines and newspaper cuttings on his death.

RENEWALS

A reminder about renewals. Members 1001-1627 - your seventh year is due between now and the end of November; similarly 2085-2170 - your sixth year; 2350-

2530 - your fifth year; 2738-2803 - your fourth year; 3057-3108 - your third year; and last (but not least!) - 3271-3304 - your second year!

FINALLY - before I close - A SINCERE APOLOGY TO THOSE OF YOU WHO WERE WAITING RATHER A LONG TIME FOR YOUR ROBERT LEE LP's TO BE SENT - DUE TO PROLONGED HEALTH PROBLEMS WITH MY MOTHER, WHICH EVENTUALLY NECESSITATED A DASH TO HOSPITAL, SOCIETY MATTERS UNFORTUNATELY HAD TO TAKE SECOND-PLACE. GLAD TO SAY MUM'S ON THE MEND - AND I AM BACK IN FULL SWING AGAIN! THANKS FOR YOUR PATIENCE. See you all in December. PEACE, LOVE, BROTHERHOOD.

Pam

EDITOR'S NOTES

Kung Fu Street Fighter aka *The Street Fighter* was a film starring Sonny Chiba, released in 1976 with 13 seconds of cuts from its BBFC submitted running time of 86 minutes 29 second.

The Legend of Bruce Lee was a comic strip syndicated by the *Los Angeles Times Syndicate* in 1982. Written by Sharman DiVono and illustrated by Fran Matera, the comic strip debuted on 23rd May 1982. Very few newspapers in the United States opted to carry it and by September the strip was cancelled. In 1984, *The Legend of Bruce Lee* was collected into a two-issue magazine series by American comic book retailer Nostalgia World.

26
December
1982

HELLO, MEMBERS! WELCOME TO THE DECEMBER NEWS SHEET - BUT BEFORE I GO ANY FURTHER I'D LIKE TO WISH ALL OF YOU A SUPER CHRISTMAS AND NEW YEAR - AND HOPE THAT 1983 BRINGS EVERYONE GOOD LUCK AND HAPPINESS - AND THAT WE AS A CLUB CAN ACHIEVE SOME OF THE THINGS WE NEED!

GRACE'S PRESENT

The donations pledged have been coming in rapidly - but there are still a few outstanding amounts. Could all members who have NOT sent in their money, please let me have it soonest or if you are unable to send it for any reason, please do drop me a line; or it holds the whole project up. (Anyone wishing to donate toward a present for Bruce's mum, please send your amount with your name and membership number to me where it will be placed with the money I hold. I will give members until the end of January, 1983, AT THE VERY LATEST to send their money - after that I will be moving ahead on the purchase of the item and to decide how best for it to be presented to Grace. Obviously - the more we collect the more we can do - so please, do join us!

FUTURE CONVENTION/MEETING

I receive so many enquiries (understandably!) about another convention, and like yourselves I want to see this come about SOON! But please do remember, that I do not personally hold any Society funds (membership fees, renewals etc.) nor any ticket money already paid to *KFM*. As most of you know, although I run the Society with the backing of *KFM*, I do not work for them nor at their offices, and all my mail comes to me at home via their offices after they have extracted all monies. SO - to get this long-awaited convention on the road again, what you must ALL DO NOW - IS WRITE TO Mr. Felix Dennis, managing director of Bunch Books (*KFM*), and ask him to please try to do something soon - and especially in view of the fact that next July is the 10th anniversary of Bruce's death - so that all members/fans of Bruce can get together at this most important time. Understand - I cannot stand alone on this - you must make your views known to *KFM* direct, too - that is the only way we can get something done!!! Write yourself - get friends to write in, too - bring this next convention about! And why not send in your own petitions for this direct to Felix?? Come on, folks - what about it??

GENERAL NEWS

I know that many, many members have written to TV stations in an effort to get something shown on Bruce - so far without success. So imagine the delight of many fans to find that Central TV has started showing (as from 31st October) episodes of *Green Hornet* (see list of all 26 episodes below):

1. The Silent Gun, 2. Give 'Em Enough Rope, 3. Programmed for Death, 4. Crime Wave, 5. The Frog is a Deadly Weapon, 6. Eat, Drink, and Be Dead, 7. Beautiful Dreamer - Part 1, 8. Beautiful Dreamer - Part 2, 9. The Ray Is for Killing, 10. The Praying Mantis, 11. The Hunters and the Hunted, 12. Deadline for Death, 13. The Secret of Sally Bell, 14. Freeway to Death, 15. May the Best Man Lose, 16. Seek, Stalk and Destroy, 17. Corpse of the Year - Part 1, 18. Corpse of the Year - Part 2, 19. Bad Bet on 459-Silent, 20. Ace in the Hole, 21. Trouble for Prince Charming, 22. Alias "The Scarf," 23. Hornet, Save Thyself, 24. Invasion from Outer Space - Part 1, 25. Invasion from Outer Space - Part 2, 26. The Hornet and the Firefly. *[EDITOR'S NOTE: Not shown were two crossover episodes from the series* Batman. *These episodes are, "A Piece of the Action" and "Batman's Satisfaction."]*

Radio Television Eire (RTE) stations 1 and 2 in Ireland are now showing *Longstreet*!!! The episodes to watch for with Bruce are: "The Way of the Intercepting Fist," "Wednesday's Child," "Spell Legacy Like Death" and "I See Said the Blind Man." So all you lucky fans having this rare opportunity to see Bruce - get watching that TV and catching him on film in some unique footage! And for you video freaks - you don't know how lucky you are, so don't miss out!

And still on the subject of TV Channels - Ian Willis wrote to Yorkshire TV and Channel 4 to see if they might do something soon on Bruce. You will see from the copies of the replies that Yorkshire have sent their usual-worded "put off" letter - but, luck indeed! Channel 4 are, as I see it, a VERY GOOD PROSPECT, and I think we might stand a chance of some success. In fact, I'd even go so far as to say an excellent chance, especially in view of the showing today by this Channel of *The Valiant Ones* (please see my closing remarks at end of sheet) which is a Chinese but English-dubbed film from Golden Harvest. SO - I AM ENLISTING YOUR

A RETROSPECTIVE LOOK AT BRUCE LEE MANIA & THE KUNG FU CRAZE OF THE 1970S

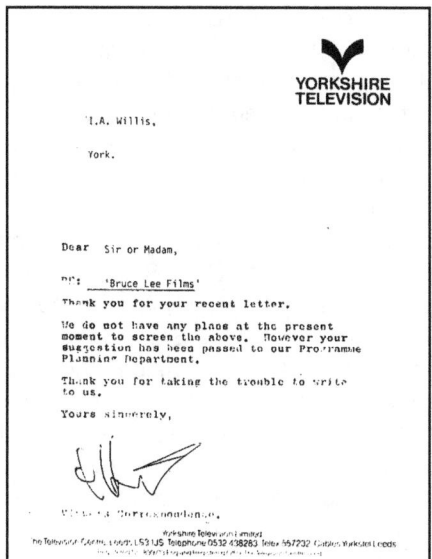

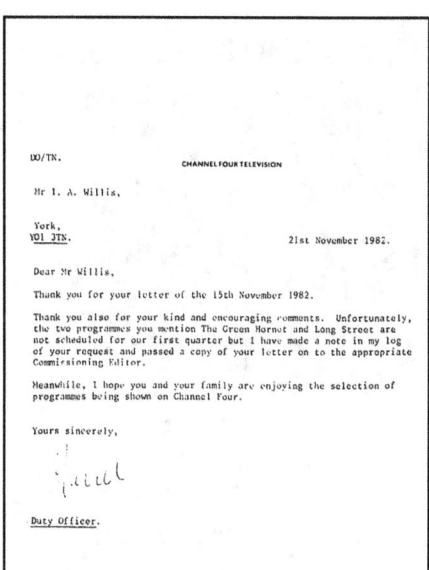

SUPPORT - TO BACK UP IAN'S LETTER AND MINE WHICH I HAVE JUST SENT TO CHANNEL 4 (address under "Useful Addresses" heading) asking that they be more adventurous (as indeed they are at present) than the other archaic TV stations whose "stick in the mud" attitude and little tin God comments drive us all to desperation, and show Bruce's TV series *The Green Hornet* and *Longstreet*, together with his films, and also *Marlowe* with James Garner where he has a small (but Oh! so noticeable!) part. I am sure that if enough of us write to Channel 4 - even get your friends to sign your letter as well - we will achieve something with them!! PLEASE - DON'T LET YOURSELVES AND ME DOWN! LET'S TRY HARD, SHALL WE???? Bruce deserves that from us all. I think we will pull it off this time!!

Michael Harris has given a run-down of *The Tower of Death* LP - he states that firstly the album suffers the same fate as *Game of Death* in that the album has duplicated some tracks, but on the whole it is quite good. The cover shows Bruce in a scene from *Enter the Dragon* where the Monk tells Bruce about the death of his sister; the back-cover shows scenes from the film. The insert sheet again shows *Enter the Dragon* scenes with Bruce. The tracks are shown here and the album number is VIP-28022 on the Victor Label:

SIDE ONE

1. Alone in the night (vocal) 4:08
2. (as above) but piano solo/dialogue 2:49
3. The Challenge (sound effect/dialogue) 6:23
4. Letter to my brother & dialogue 6:21
5. Fallen Heroes (instrumental) & sound effect 4:30

SIDE 2

1. Fallen Heroes (piano solo) 3:00
2. Revenge & dialogue 5:41
3. Alone in the night (instrumental) 4:31
4. Go to Hell & sound effect 4:48
5. Fallen Heroes (vocal) 4:18

THE BRUCE LEE SOCIETY

REVIEWS

Tang Lung agilely avoids the blade of Huang Cheng-li's sword in the final moments of the film.

Tower of Death

Wu See-yuen, director. Yuen Ho-ping, martial arts choreography. Cast includes Bruce Lee, Tang Lung (Kim Tai-chung), Huang Cheng-li, Roy Horan, Li Hai-sheng, Chang Cheng-wu, Roy Chaio. A Raymond Chow Production for Golden Harvest.

When the long-awaited *Game of Death* was released, Bruce Lee fans were dismayed to see how a story unlike his original concept was fabricated to incorporate the 20 minutes of actual footage Bruce Lee had completed before he died. They were unhappy with the way anonymous look-alikes were used in the rest of the film and the way close-ups of Bruce Lee from his various films were inserted to substitute for the stand-ins. Rumors circulated that Golden Harvest was withholding other incomplete scenes from *Game of Death*, for a sequel. That long-awaited sequel was made, with very little publicity, this time by the veteran Chinese actor film team of Wu See-yuen and Yuen Ho-ping, who gave us *Snake in the Eagle's Shadow*, *Drunk Monkey in the Tiger's Eye*, *The Server Rivals* and other memorable films. This sequel was titled *Tower of Death*, and in some ways is closer to Bruce Lee's original concept for *Game of Death* but with a few twists.

There is actual Bruce Lee footage included in this film, but none of it is from the unfinished *Game of Death*. Most of the footage consists of scenes from *Enter the Dragon* which ended up on the cutting room floor. The rest is made up of scenes taken directly from the final print of *Enter the Dragon* and close-ups from his other films used as inserts as was done in *Game of Death*. As none of the Bruce Lee footage involves any fighting, all of the film's fight scenes are evenly staged with Tang Lung (Kim Tai-chung), who doubled for Lee in *Game of Death* also.

The scenes with the real Bruce Lee include: Bruce with the old Shaolin monk (Roy Chaio), a scene which appeared in the Chinese version of *Enter the Dragon* but was cut from the English version; Bruce entering and inspecting his room for the first time in Han's fortress; Bruce conversing with Mei Ling in his room; Bruce in tears speaking to his butler about his sister's death; Bruce exercising in his room; and Bruce drinking tea with Braithewaite. These scenes are spliced in with footage of his double, Tang Lung, and dubbed with all new dialogue.

The Bruce Lee footage lasts only for the first half hour of this 90-minute film and none of it is action. The filmmakers were wise not to try to make another whole film with this patchwork method. The character portrayed by Bruce Lee is Li Chen-chiang (Billy Lo in the English version), who dies early in the film so that his brother, Li Chen-kuo (Bobby Lo in the English version), portrayed by Tang Lung, must investigate and avenge his brother's death.

On the other hand, the few new scenes of Bruce Lee were interesting to see even though the dialogue has been changed. This may be the only chance fans have to see these outtakes from *Enter the Dragon*, and for completists, this may be worth the price of admission. As long as fans know what to expect, they will not be disappointed.

The film opens with a montage of Bruce Lee writing his book on jeet kune do and Huang Cheng-li practicing with his wooden sword. The two of them are friends and both are top fighters subject to challenge. Chin Ku (Huang Cheng-li) is challenged at his home and Bruce motions to let him easily dispatches his opponent. Cheng Chiang (Bruce Lee) then goes to a temple where he talks to the old monk about his brother, who needs motivation to practice his lessons harder. Chen Chiang sends his brother his book on jeet kune do to study. Chin Ku dies mysteriously and Lee goes to Tokyo to investigate. He is attacked in a Japanese nightclub and the fighting spills out onto the streets of Tokyo. At the funeral, Chin Ku's coffin is stolen by a helicopter and Lee is killed while trying to prevent the theft.

Lee's brother, Chen Kuo (Tang Lung), goes to Tokyo to investigate his death, which leads him first to the Castle of Death and then to the Tower of Death, built underground by a king centuries ago. Chin Kuo infiltrates the Tower of Death and fights his way through a gauntlet of killers including Li Hai-sheng, and finally confronts Chin Ku. Having faked his death to smuggle some drugs in his coffin, Chin had to kill Lee to prevent exposure. Chen Kuo avenges his brother after a long battle to the death.

The plot is fairly simple and allows for lots of action, well choreographed by Yuen Ho-ping. The highlights include Chen Chiang's fight on the streets of Tokyo and all of Chen Kuo's fights as he infiltrates the Tower of Death. The fights in Tokyo are supposed to be Bruce Lee in action but although he's tried to imitate Lee's style, Yuen has added too much acrobatics to the fighting for it to be authentic jeet kune do. They've even added the Bruce Lee fighting yells to try to fool the audience. Chen Kuo battles the guards (including Yuen Hsio-yi in a bit part) in the Tower of Death, a muscle man in a leopard skin, traverses an electrified corridor, fights a monk (Li Hai-sheng) who wields a staff tipped at one end by a sickle and an axe at the other, and finally confronts Chin Ku, who attacks with his sword. The last half hour of the film is almost non-stop action, fast paced and well choreographed. Yuen should be congratulated for his visually stunning choreography which makes this film a winner.

Tang Lung is the star of this film, playing both Bruce Lee's role and his own. He is a very good martial artist and does a fine job in both parts, as he did in his fights in *Game of Death*. His Bruce Lee impersonation is better than that of either of the two actors who have made a living doing it, Ho Trung tao (Bruce LI) and Huang Kin-lung (Bruce Lo), being more subdued and controlled in his actions. He is gather slender and the director tried to cover this up by putting him in a baggy shirt, right after his fight fitting one is torn from him just before he enters the Tower of Death. He executes most of his stunts with precision and speed but he obviously was not up to all the acrobatic stunts required of him by Yuen Ho-ping, since actor Yuen Biao was used as his stunt double in all the more grueling acrobatic scenes. Yuen Biao also doubled for Lee in some scenes of *Game of Death*. He is a co-student of Jackie Chan's and has been making films for Golden Harvest *(Knockabout, The Young Master, Dreadnought)* as well as being a martial arts choreographer in Samo Hung's "Hung Action Group." Tang Lung, with a little help from Yuen Biao, gives us a dazzling display of martial arts action that will leave you panting.

Kudos to Huang Cheng-li and Li Hai-sheng, for providing strong opposition for Tang Lung to fight. Both are known for their villainous portrayals in numerous films and they do not disappoint the audience with their admirable performances. *Tower of Death* may not have been made with the best of intentions but it is an exciting, action-packed film, which I recommend without reservation.

Victor L. Lim

'GAME' Review from 'Martial Arts Movies' - April 82 (from Carl Jones

---

Still with *Tower of Death - (Game of Death II)*, Carl Jones sent in the review of the film from the US magazine *Martial Arts Movies* (April 1982), which is reprinted for members here. As I have not yet seen the film, it gives me some idea what I'm missing - or not missing, as the case may be.

Our Indonesian member, Inge Hutama, sent an extract from the *Dear Bruce Lee* book (O'Hara Publications - 1980) - showing two touching letters from fans of Bruce and how his teachings and guidance has helped them, and expressing their sadness at his loss but how they have gained from his ideals. (See separate sheet). If anyone knows where I can purchase a perfect copy of this book, I would welcome a note - Pam.

Now on to a not-so-nice subject - Vic Charles! Several members, including David Moore, Barry Latcham, Anthony Ivison and David Edwards, have written to me, infuriated by the article in *Sunday Magazine* (given with *News of the World*) dated 17th October, 1982. The article, by Paula Yates, starts by stating Charles is "Britain's third Dan World Champion Karate Star" (as Anthony Ivison put it - "Chumpion" not "Champion") and member David Edwards says: "This for a start gives the wrong impression about his skill as he is only concerned with the sport aspect of karate i.e. point scoring techniques, and weighing 14 stone he would not be in the same category as any Japanese opposition." A point strongly backed up by the other members mentioned. During the interview, Vic had the audacity to say (quote): "It was the Bruce Lee boom which, in a certain way, encouraged me. THERE'S NOTHING WRONG WITH BRUCE LEE, BUT HE WAS ONLY AN ACTOR - HE DID A BIT OF MARTIAL ARTS AND HE WAS GOOD ON FILM BUT ANYONE CAN KILL SIX GUYS AND LOOK GOOD ON FILM!!!!"

Oh! Mr. Charles - have YOU made some enemies! You misguided, stupid, ignorant little upstart! Needless to say, Anthony, the two Da-

A RETROSPECTIVE LOOK AT BRUCE LEE MANIA & THE KUNG FU CRAZE OF THE 1970S

Dear Bruce,

You've come to mean so very much to me over the past six years that it is very difficult for me to know where to begin this letter. I could say that you have given me purpose and direction that I have lacked all my life. I could tell you that you've helped me find the courage to at least try and express my thoughts and my feelings, indeed my very self, and the hell with what anyone else thinks about my efforts.

I could tell you many things, but now that I think about it, the most important thing you've given me was the opportunity to meet friends. I know that doesn't sound like much, but believe me it is very important to a classic introvert like me. And the people I met through you are special almost beyond words. I have found that Bruce Lee fans, as a group, are the most honest, sincere, intelligent and sensitive people I have ever encountered, qualities I admire, qualities that I have often found to be lacking in many people today.

Whether they come to you equipped with these traits fully developed or whether study of your life and your philosophy made latent traits bloom is unimportant, for those traits are there and that is all that counts in the end.

I discovered you at the beginning of what was to become both the most lonely, God-awful miserable period of my then 26 years, and at the same time the most wonderful. After I found that I was no longer content just to sit in a lumpy seat in some rundown theater that smelled of God knows-what and marvel at your intensity, I began to become more active as a fan, began to reach out, began to develop contacts with these also-lone strangers who were to become my best and truest friends at a time when friendship was the thing I needed most.

Self discovery, Bruce, is the most beautiful yet painful experience any human being can ever have. And with your example behind me, and the cheerleader-like encouragement of those cherished friends, I am beginning to make those first steps toward self-discovery and growth. How odd that your life officially "ended" at the age of 32, and that my own (after six years of gathering up the courage) is finally beginning at the same age!

Oh Bruce, you'll never know how much you have done for so many of us. Thank you.

Love,
Karen Shaub
St. Petersburg, FL.

> Time has a way of passing by all too quickly, but when you live with a memory that has left such an impact on the world, the days, months and years become insignificant. Has it really been six years since you left us?

> How odd that your life officially "ended" at the age of 32, and that my own (after six years of gathering courage) is finally beginning at the same age! Oh Bruce, you'll never know how much you have done for so many of us.

HE STILL LIVES

Dear Bruce,

I wish this letter was being written for your eyes alone. It should mean that you were still with us, reading your fan mail and reveling in the success that is so rightly yours.

Time has a way of passing by all too quickly, but when you live with a memory that has left such an impact on the world, the days, months and years become insignificant. Has it really been six years since you left us? You wouldn't think so when you look at the martial arts magazines on sale today and still see your face on the covers.

This past month, while once again watching *Enter the Dragon* for the umpteenth time, I tried to remember what my life was like before you came on the scene.

I honestly can't recall living without the excitement of finding one of your movies playing in a nearby theatre or mulling through numerous bookstores and discovering another article devoted to you or a new poster catching you in action or at leisure. Your very existence has given me endless hours of enjoyment, thanks to your willingness to share yourself through your acting, your writing, your teachings.

Last year, I found myself needing to find a way to express my thanks and respect to you, finally an idea came to mind. For our vacation, my husband and I planned a sort of pilgrimage to an area where you had spent part of your life. We decided on the Los Angeles area. Four months before we left, I researched every book and magazine in my collection, hunting for names and addresses of people and places that were important to you. We arrived in Los Angeles well prepared.

Bruce, I felt your presence immediately as our plane landed. Yes, even the airport was an emotional experience for me, thinking of how frequently you must have flown to and from Los Angeles. Our travels took us to your small school on College Street in Chinatown—how close I felt there! We walked for miles on Wilshire Boulevard toward where you lived for a short period of time, visited the various studios where you worked and even got to spend an afternoon at the world's only museum dedicated to you. For each day of our vacation, you were there with us; the sensation was too overwhelming for me to describe. The only way I can sum up my feelings during those two weeks is to tell you that the five and one-half hour return trip home was the unhappiest I have ever experienced. I didn't want to leave all those places and people that had been part of your life. Only one thing would have made our trip more perfect—seeing you. Our future trips will include San Francisco and Seattle as a continuation of our pilgrimage. Perhaps some day, I'll even be lucky enough to visit Hong Kong. Wherever you have been, I wish to be there too.

In closing, Bruce, I want to thank you for sharing my thoughts and feelings with me. I know in my heart that we are all part of one another and when one of us departs before his time, it is the responsibility of the rest of us to carry on his life and ideals. This is our way of showing our love and respect to you. This is what I strive to do each day of my life.

Sincerely,
Chris Avitabile
Yonkers, NY

'Dear Bruce Lee' letters from the O'Hara Publication of the same name (courtesy Inge Hutama).

---

vid's, Barry and myself were FUMING over this stupid load of rubbish. How the *Sunday Magazine* could print such a blatant falsehood like that is unbelievable. SO - I am POSITIVE all of you want to write to the magazine and put them in their place, so here's the address - I'D PERSONALLY LIKE TO SEE YOU ALL GIVE THEM A PIECE OF YOUR MIND ON THIS OCCASION - I'M WITH YOU ALL THE WAY! At least let the magazine know how stupid it looks for printing such an article and making themselves a laughing-stock for being so misinformed. As Barry said: "VIC CHARLES SHOULD KEEP HIS BIG MOUTH SHUT." And David Moore says that after he saw Vic win the Superstars award, he became a fan of his - but not any more!! (*Sunday Magazine*, 18 Ogle Street, London, WIP 7LG).

On to better things - David Edwards says *Video Viewer* (November 1982) had a two-page article on Bruce; they pointed out one or two minor faults in his films, but apart from that they are all in favour of Bruce. The article ended with the words: "IN ALL HIS FILMS, THOUGH, THE SINGLE FEATURE WHICH SET THEM APART FROM THE HUNDREDS OF IMITATORS IS THE SHEER POWER OF BRUCE LEE'S PHYSICAL SCREEN PRESENCE, A RARE AND SADLY SHORT-LIVED GIFT." (*Sunday Magazine* - take note.)

Still with David and also member Arthur Stone – *The Professionals* had a scene recently where Lewis Collins, confronted by an opponent in a half-hearted karate-stance, says: "Even Bruce Lee cannot deflect bullets." Another mention came in the *9 to 5* TV series when Rita Moreno tries to persuade Rachel Dennison to work in China, and says: "What do you think of Bruce Lee films?" (Pam here - wonder what her answer was??!?) In *Different Strokes* a bully comes out with the words: "What have we here - another Bruce Lee?"

David Moore read an article in the *Sun* newspaper on the John Blake page concerning rumours that Elvis is still alive and that he did a deal with the CIA who arranged his disappearance so he could live below his Graceland Mansion in a maze of underground tunnels and rooms to recover from a serious illness and one fan claims that he spoke to Elvis on a train in Canada. David wrote to Mr. Blake and told him of similar rumours that had sprung up after Bruce's death; that 'it was only a publicity stunt for his new film *Game of Death,* "that he was in trouble with the Chinese Triad gang and gone into hiding," "he had been poisoned by jealous kung fu or karate masters or even ninja assassins," "drugs overdose," "that he had shot himself!" Mr. Blake said he will try to use the info in the future but, said David, it is now a month and nothing!!

Jonathan Westley - whilst watching the *Charlie Chan* film on BBC2 recently - was surprised to see that Kung Fu's Master Po, Keye Luke, was playing the part of Chan's son - and Jonathan said he was even more surprised (*KFM* 69) to find that Keye Luke was Kato in 15 chapters of "The Green Hornet Strikes Again." Says Jonathan - "I think we owe Mr. Luke a lot."

News now from Shahab Setudeh Nejad, our member in Seattle, to say that the *Legend of Bruce Lee* cartoon has ceased suddenly from the *Seattle Times* and without completion. On enquiring, Shahab was told: "The contract for it had ended." Says Shahab, "Such is the American way of doing things!" Shahab was kind enough to send me most of the cartoon cuttings from the papers, which I hope, copyright permitting, to produce in future news sheets in some format.

Also from Shahab - Chuck Norris was recently in a programme called *P.M. Northwest*, which he unfortunately missed! Also to be reproduced as soon as space allows, are Shahab's personal writings on Bruce.

Although very disappointing on the newspaper cartoon score, It seems that a cartoon film is on the way! Preliminary drawings have been done (says member Eric Canham) and a budget of US $1 million agreed. It will take about 12 months to complete and will be 80/90 minutes long. If it is successful, it may also be made into a 26 half-hour TV series!!

Paul Corrigan has a deep interest in the Chinese language, so much so that he has been learning it for some time, and because he knows that many fans would like to have a little knowledge and learn some signs, he has kindly started to send in special articles for your info. Our sincerest thanks, Paul - and keep them coming in! (Pam here: I am now going to have a little practice; but it does look hard, doesn't it??? HELP!) Anyone wanting larger copies of this, drop me a line and enclose postage.

Still with Paul - you will see a short extract from the book he is writing called *Jig Saw Philosophy*. I'd be interested to see more, Paul!

I also hear from member Arthur Stone that he and fellow member Simon Bulley have been working on a photonovel, with Arthur designing layouts and Simon supplying the words. "It is looking good at this stage," says Arthur! More on these projects in the future.

ELEMENTARY CHINESE BY MEMBER PAUL CORRIGAN (1711).

CHINESE CHARACTERS consist of several component parts. Each component, when standing by itself, is also a character in its own right. The components of Chinese characters are composed of a number of strokes. In writing Chinese, most of these basic strokes start from left to right and from top to bottom. Chinese characters are written in a progressive stroke order.

The rules of stroke order in writing Chinese can be found in the character yǒng (Mandarin), or wíng (Cantonese), meaning "everlasting". This character consists of five strokes and includes the eight fundamental points required in writing Chinese:

The written Chinese language is a much more demanding task than the spoken. It will take at least two years of full-time study to learn to read Chinese newspapers or magazines. But, if you don't fancy putting in so much time and effort, you can still have a lot of fun learning some Kung Fu terminology:

手 saú, hand.   腳 keùk, foot.   拳 k'uén, fist.

截 tsit (Jeet), intercepting.   拳 k'uén (Kune), fist.   道 tò (Do), path, road, way. = J.K.D.

In other words, J.K.D. is pronounced Jeet Kune Do and means – THE WAY OF THE INTERCEPTING FIST...

Until next time, here are a few more interesting Chinese Characters to be going on with:

豹 p'aaù, leopard.   虎 foó, tiger.   鶴 hók, crane.

馬 mǎ, horse.   刀 doū, knife, sword.   熊 hùng, bear.

鷹 yìng, eagle.   鹿 lúk, deer.   狗 kaú, dog.

A SHORT EXTRACT FROM MY BOOK, JIG - SAW PHILOSOPHY:

Martial Arts have made great strides during the past few years. Since the sad death of the famous Bruce Lee we have learned more than even optimists would have believed possible; and it is also true that the Martial Arts have become a part of our everyday lives.
    What I have attempted to do here, is give not only exponents of the Martial Arts something to think about, but something for every human being to reflect upon. Inevitably, much has been left out and much more has been glossed over; but I hope that what is written may be of interest to those who read it.
    My sincere thanks are due to the publishers and Pan for their help...

The reason why rivers and seas receive the homage of a hundred streams, is that they keep below them. Thus, they are able to reign over the mountain streams.
    If you wish to be above men, put yourself below them. If you wish to be before them, stand behind them. Thus, though your place be above men, they do not feel your weight; though your place be before them, they do not count it an injury.
    If you can't be a highway, then just be a trail, if you can't be the sun, be a star. It isn't by the size that you win or you fail - Be the best of whatever you are!
    Stop being concerned about what other people think about you. Watch what you are thinking about other people.
    Be not concerned that a man does not know of you; be concerned that you do not know of him.
    Worry not that no one knows you; seek to be worth knowing.

Paul Corrigan

(1711).

    Cary Dean says he is intrigued by the way Bruce's shoes keep changing around in *Game of Death* not only from white with red-and-blue stripes, but also two different pairs of yellow shoes with varying stripes! Bruce vs. Danny - type "A" yellow shoe, Hapkido fight - type "B," type "A" again during the Jabbar fight, but to confuse the whole thing there are stills of Bruce fighting Jabbar minus blue tunic! Cary asks how many others have noticed it and have any of you spotted anything similar in other of his films?
    I've just been lucky enough to have been sent the *The Silent Flute* film script by member Andrew Staton, which is super!! And a most generous offer from Andrew - if other members would like a copy he would send this at a cost of £1.50. He can also offer a complete photo-story of Bruce's life (he sent me a few examples and they are excellent) - ten sheets in all at a total cost of £1 the ten, plus also he can offer a *Bruce Lee in Action* photosheet for 50p, and copies of the *Regulations of Bruce's Jun Fan Institute* - a copy of which was given by Roy Hollingsworth whilst Andrew was visiting Taky Kimura in Seattle. In Bruce's neatest handwriting, it costs £1 per copy. (All these prices include post and packing - but for members living abroad, please drop a note to Andrew first to see if extra postage is needed). A most generous offer by Andrew, and one which I am sure most of you will wish to take up!! Thanks, Andrew. (Address: Leeds).

RENEWALS

Members - herewith reminders about your renewals: 3304 to 3322 - your second year falls between now and the end of February, 1983; similarly, 3109-3157 - your third; 2804-2907 - fourth year; 2531-2599 - fifth year; 2171-2276 - sixth year; and 1628-1828 - your seventh year. Please send it in to me.

MEMORIAL FLOWERS - PICTURES

These pictures are still available from me at London with the two pictures from this year PLUS the two from last year costing £1.80, or if you just want this year's pictures, the two are £1.00. They are quite lovely.

USEFUL ADDRESSES/INTERESTING ITEMS

For the many members wishing to write to various organisations concerning Bruce, here are some of interest:

- Golden Communications (Overseas) Ltd., (Golden Harvest - London), 47, Greek Street, London, WIV 5LQ.
- British Board of Film Censors, Soho Square, London, W.I.
- Channel 4 TV, 60 Charlotte Street, London, WIP 2AX. (Telephone: (01) 631 4444)
- Golden Harvest International Ltd., 8, Hammer Hill Road, K0WL00N, Hong Kong.
- Rank Video Library, P.O. Box 70, Great West Road, BRENTFORD, TW8 9HR, Middlesex., England. (Telephone: (01) 568 9222)

BRUCE LEE ENDS THE ROCKY TRILOGY
From: Gino D'Ambrosio

Jonathan Westley says that Giko Ltd. (537 Stratford Road, Sparkhill, Birmingham BIT 4LP - telephone (021) 773 9247/8) are offering 7 17" x 22" drawings showing various dynamic poses of Bruce in action. They are £2.45 each plus 50P postage or £18.95 for all seven including postage and packing. Also a JKD medallion in yellow/red with black background and a smart tracksuit jacket with the Yin and Yang sign on the back and the words "Bruce Lee - JKD" around the symbol. Price - £14.95 plus £1 post and packing - medallion £1.95 plus 30p post. Jonathan recently bought a book called *Yin and Yang* (Pam here: I've got a copy and it is very interesting) - which explains all about balance and harmony and harmlessness/non-violence, also Taoism in different religions. Price: £3.50. (Published by Aquarian Press). Also by the same author (J. G. Cooper): *Taoism*. Another book he acquired is *Dynamic Nunchaku Training* by H. Ramazwa which he found interesting, and says it "is nice to see the Japanese side of things." It would make a great Christmas present, he says! Clive Ramsbottom tells me that Py Tang now have in stock 10 feature films from the *Green Hornet* - good quality (English) at £30 each. (Pam here: Py Tang is now a Society member).

BRUCE'S BOOK LIST (Part III)

Here is another selection of Bruce's books taken from his original list in the possession of Dan Inosanto:

Body and Mind in Harmony - S. Delga (1961)
Secrets of Judo - J. Watamabe (1960) *Practical Karate Vol. 1-6* - Nakayama/Draeger (1963-1966)
Cannon of Judo - Kyugo Mifume (1956)
Illustrated Kodakan Judo - Mifume (1955)
Judo For Young Men - Otaki/ Draeger (1965)
Judo Training Method - Oshikawa/Draeger (1966)

A Guide to Judo Grappling Techniques - R. W. Smith (1965)
Secrets of Shaolin Temple Boxing - R. W. Smith *(1964)*
The Hand is My Sword (Karate) - Robert A. Trias (1959)
Pa-Kua - Chinese Boxing - R. W. Smith (1967)

More next time!

REASON

Having given Bruce's own definitions under "WILL POWER" and "EMOTION," we go onward to "REASON": "RECOGNISING THAT BOTH MY POSITIVE AND NEGATIVE EMOTIONS MAY BE DANGEROUS IF THEY ARE NOT CONTROLLED AND GUIDED TO DESIRABLE ENDS, I WILL SUBMIT ALL MY DESIRES, AIMS AND PURPOSES TO MY FACULTY OF REASON, AND I WILL BE GUIDED BY IT IN GIVING EXPRESSION TO THESE."

VIDEO INFO

Enter the Ninja has just been released on video - it's an official release.

FILMS INFORMATION

Referring back to the September news sheet where David Moore learnt through a friend of a Bruce Lee film shown in mainland China, over which the fans went mad, member Anthony Ivison tells me that the film shown was called *Shaolin* and not, in fact, one of Bruce's films. Thanks for the snippet, Anthony - and over to David to sort out his friend for giving him duff information!

Now back to our regular film-buff David - there is now a date of June, 1983, for the start of the filming of *Revenge of the Ninja* in Los Angeles and the Philippines (starring Sho Kosugi, Keith Vitali and Stephen Hayes, who is the only non-Japanese authorised to teach proper Ninjutsu - the art of the ninja). Hayes has also worked as adviser for the film and mini-TV series *Shogun* (Pam here: What a SUPER series that was!) starring Richard Chamberlain and Toshiro Mifune.

Also mentioned by David is the fact that Chuck Norris has, since 1981, been a free agent in the film world, having fulfilled his three-picture deal with American Cinema. His first independent film was *An Eye for an Eye* - when released in America, it grossed in New York alone $1 million in its first week, topping all other releases. Which prompted David to wonder why we did not hear of this in film magazines and newspapers - strange! Although David does point out the possibility of a bias against martial arts films as a reason. Could be....

Chuck has signed a six-picture deal with MGM - and his first film for them was *Jade Jungle* with a budget of between $7-8 million. Between *Eye* and *Jungle* he made *Silent Run* playing a Texas Sheriff called Dan Stevens who has to stop a genetically-engineered maniac (something similar to those Harrison Ford had to track in *Blade Runner*), who is murdering people. This sci-fi horror/martial arts movie had a budget of $4-5 million and is the first film Chuck has co-produced through his own company - Top Kick Productions. Released in April in the US and now on release here in the UK. *Silent Run* also stars Brian Libby (as the maniac), Toni Kalem as Chuck's girlfriend, Ron Silver, Steven Keats, William Finley and Stephen Furst, and is an "X" Certificate.

Chuck's brother Aaron (stunt co-ordinator for *Silent Run* and *Jade Jungle*) has signed to star in his own film *Raider Stone*.

Dan Inosanto (after *Sharkey's Machine*) has signed to star in *Skirmish* - a film dealing with the Filipino martial art of Escrima. Filming began in August - and as a matter of interest, says David, the word *Escrima* means "skirmish" and the term was given to the Filipino art by the Spanish who took over the Philippine Islands because they did not think of it as much of a fighting art - a "skirmish." The term Escrima stuck to this day. However, when the Spanish conquistadors realised just how deadly the art really was, they banned its practice with a death penalty to anyone caught breaking the ban. But that did not stop the Filipinos! (I'm glad to say - Pam)

POEMS

From Ann & Fred Hunt - in memory of Bruce's 42nd birthday:-

Bruce - Today we would have loved to have you here, on this your 42nd birthday.
But God took you to his garden to share it with him.
But times change many things - but not the memory that this day brings!

PEN PAL

Paul Corrigan, ardent CB radio fanatic spreading the word of Bruce, has asked me to get a Society pen pal(s) for Kerstin Beckmann, Baden-Wurttemburg, West Germany - she's 18, and apart from Bruce, her interests are: Foreign Languages (speaking German, French, Spanish and English), reading, music and travelling. So I'm sure she'd welcome members worldwide - so get writing, folks!

ENTER THE DRAGON CINEMA QUIZ
(September News Sheet)

Purely for your personal amusement one evening, I popped the quiz into the last sheet; now, here are the answers overleaf, so you can just see how well you did - or otherwise. Bet there were a lot of you surrounded by books, magazines and video machines trying to get the answers!!

Answers: 1. Michael Allin, 2. Michael Roote, 3. Hung Kim-Bo, 4. Every three years, 5. Mary King, 6. Betty Chung, 7. Six, 8. Sharon from California, 9. Tadashi Yamashita, 10. Pat Johnson, Darnell Garcia and Mike Bissell, 11. Freddy, 12. "175 big ones" - $175,000, 13. Monday the 15th, 14. Steve Saunders and Donnie Williams, 15. In his scene with Lee he drinks it black, no sugar; later he has tea with two lumps, 16. A half-an-hour, 17. A colonel, 18. Geoffrey Weeks, 19. "Boards don't hit back," 20. Bo, sticks, nunchaku, and (yes, it does count) the cobra, 21. Five. Once on each cheek, once across the abdomen, once across the back and once across the chest, 22. The right, 23. Blue, 24. "We are all ready to win, just as we are born knowing only life," 25. Love (Hope you enjoyed it, folks!)

LETTERS

Dear Pam,

I went to Giko recently and saw a couple of young lads (no more than 15) buying Bruce Lee artefacts. they must have been about six when the Bruce craze was in full swing. I find it amazing that Bruce is still as strong today as he ever was in crown pulling.

Shaun Boland (2805)

Yes, Shaun - it's a good feeling to see that Bruce is now reaching the young people - let us hope that they are still able to have the opportunity to see the better copies of his films, and not the completely desecrated ones now left by the censors!

Dear Pam,

Some months ago I wrote to the BBC TV Programme Record Breakers *to ask if there is a record for the person with the fastest punch and kick, and to consider Bruce and Muhammed Ali for the punch record and Bruce and Bill Wallace for the kick (Bill, former World Full-Contact Champion, who is said to have had his kicks timed at 60mph). In May the BBC replied saying they did not know of such records, but would pass my enquiries on to* The Guinness Book of Records. *In late August I received a letter from Colin Smith, correspondence editor for the book, and as you will see from these letters, it looks like there will never be any such records, I'm afraid!*

David Moore (1783)

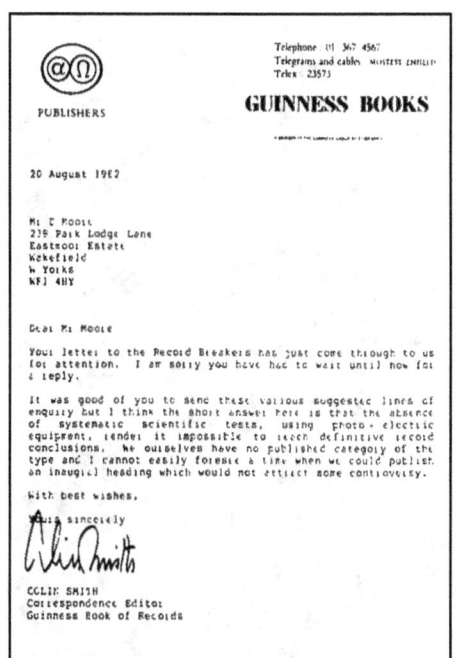
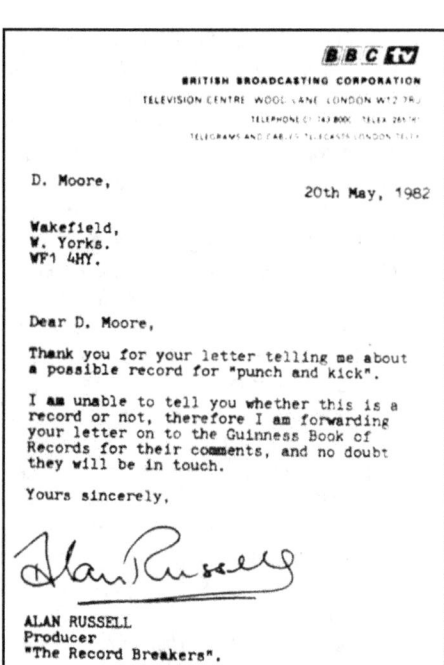

It certainly was an original idea of yours but unfortunate that there is nothing we can do further on this. Still, I would not think there is any doubt in the minds of those who have seen Bruce, or known him, and been aware of his skills, as to his speed and ability - but it WOULD have been nice to see his name in there as a record-breaker. It seems such a shame that someone as talented as Bruce should not have something written about him in an official or recognised document/book.

Dear Pam,

One of my flatmates went for a weeks holiday up to Queensland's Gold Coast surfers' paradise, and told me that he turned on the TV and Lo! and behold! One of Bruce's films (judging by his comments Enter the Dragon*) was just beginning. Lucky devil! Wish they would screen it down here in Sydney - although at the moment* Enter the Dragon *IS playing in the City along with* Mad Max 2.

John Aspinall (1527)

I wish the same here, John - and thanks for the cutting on *Game of Death 2*.

Dear Pam,

I enjoyed the series Fame *- it is fascinating watching other people's egos, their ups and downs, the very well-choreographed dance scenes - it has a good "get up and go" feel. Now what does Bruce have to do with a series like* Fame? *Let me say "the ego." Because I'm sure that if Bruce were still alive he would not be into martial* arts films today. Bruce loved acting and the fame and to expand as an actor. He'd have loved to act in a movie such as the dramatic heart-stopping Fitz Carraldo which starred Klaus Kinski or The Man Who Fell to Earth with Bowie - a man who is characteristically unique, always one step ahead. He took the brave step on to a wooden stage on Broadway not to sing or dance but to act straightforward presentation of a character in front of a theatre-wise audience - not takes or retakes - a daunting task for even the most hardened cinematic actor. Bowie took the part with grace and guts but still says he's no actor!! Now this is what Bruce wanted - to stand in front of the camera - not to do kung fu but to act. Bruce Lee did not make the history of Kung Fu films - he IS the history of Kung Fu films! He never got the chance to really act. If only he could have made a few more movies - played a part as a crazed bizarre movie that is cinema. I'm sure, Pam, you will understand what point I am trying to make. Bruce wanted to be the best martial artist in the world, used films to get himself understood. Being a complete perfectionist hung on films, I believe he would have taken any part that looked good by the throat and wrung it dry! Then he would have been pleased with himself. Bruce is the one who had a real gift - Jeet Kune Do - but did not act it out.

Gino D'Ambrosio (1655)

Well, Gino, I agree that Bruce would, indeed, have changed his direction had he not passed over - but although he loved acting I personally feel he would have gone into some deep and philosophical, meaning, films - the storyline was there in *The Silent Flute* although regrettably not many of you have seen it - to project his feelings in the arts even further; I still feel that his art would be uppermost and take first place - even to filming - and that he would have gone more into directing than taking the part eventually. What do other members think??

SPECIAL REQUESTS
HELP WANTED/EMERGENCY CORNER - PLEASE HELP!

Anthony Ivison (Leicester) wants to know from fellow members of any instructor or club doing Monkey Style Kung Fu in and around the Leicester area - and even up to 100 miles away! (Now that is what I call KEEN!!) So please - if anyone can assist, please drop a line to Anthony at his address.

A RETROSPECTIVE LOOK AT BRUCE LEE MANIA & THE KUNG FU CRAZE OF THE 1970S

John Rogers and his wife have been trying to trace some friends very hard; they used to work with them, and have exhausted all methods possible so far by themselves. Can all members especially those in the Bristol area) please do a bit of searching for our friends here, and let John know (Basildon) if you have ANY info as to the whereabouts of the following: Amparo Pantoja (originally from Colombia); Romila Sowambur (from Mauritius); and Tracey Poeton - last heard of in Bristol).

If anyone knows of any companies doing Bruce LP's by mail order, please let Don Quinn know. (Dublin, Ireland). Or maybe one of you reliable members might offer to buy them if he sends the money to you plus postage?? Why not write and offer your help. It would be a nice gesture for those fans who are unable to obtain such records.

And help needed for Kevin Hobbs (Leominster) as to whether any of you know if the video cassette *The Warrior Within* (shown on cutting reproduced here from an American magazine) is available near you, and if so where, please. I'd also be interested to have the address for printing next sheet.

Anthony Ivison wants a copy of *Chinese Gung Fu*. Can anyone help?? I've sold all the copies I had so cannot assist him.

From: Kevin Hobbs

ROBERT LEE LP's

Don't forget I still have copies of this rare tribute to Bruce by his brother Robert Lee at a cost of £4.50 UK addresses (£6 Europe and £7.50 countries abroad.) A rare collector's item so do not miss it. Write with postal orders/cheques to me at London.

BACK-ISSUE NEWS SHEETS

If you require any of these, drop me a line with the issues you require, and I will tell you cost.

SWOP SHOP

- Andrew Staton, Leeds has for sale: The following Japanese items (prices include p&p): *Bruce Lee in Fist of Fury* (rare Japanese book) - £6, *King of Kung Fu* (rare book) - £4, *Bruce Lee and Jackie Chan* book - £10, *Bruce Lee Deluxe Movie Book* - £10. Also following English books, magazines: *Too Young to Die* - £6 (has Bruce article), *Between Wing Chun and JKD* - £4, *Jackie Chan the Martial Artist*

- £2, American *KFM* 1 - £4, *KFM* Trade Dummy No. 1 - £6, *KFM's* 3, 5, 64 - 60p each, *Game of Death* Press Book - £4, No. 14 Bruce Special - *Deadly Hands of Kung Fu* - £3, *Martial Arts Movies* - £2, records and tapes: *Dragon Power* single (picture sleeve) - £2, *Enter the Dragon* single - £2, *Bruce Lee & Friends* compilation tape - £1. Also Bruce Key Ring - £1.50, *Bruce Flick Book* - £2, Brass Bruce Lee Belt buckles - £3 each.
- Duncan Lee Baker, Bournemouth wants: Bruce souvenir mug showing his face, Bruce sports and shoulder bags (red, blue or green), *Beginners Guide to Kung Fu*, *Book of Kung Fu*, posters (Bruce kicking his way through a door, painted by Jeff Cummings, dragon poster with purple background, *Enter the Dragon* stance, with green dragon behind with tail around Bruce's leg). Also would like to hear from members of places to get Bruce material.
- Anthony Ivison, Leicester can anyone help him obtain a copy of *Chinese Gung Fu* by Bruce Lee? Please drop him a line.
- Tom Lavery, Portadown, Northern Ireland will pay £20 for each episode of *Longstreet* showing Bruce - providing they are good quality recordings on VHS tape. Or will swap them for: *Film Review* with Bruce, *Game of Death* article, *KFMs* - 50 issues inc. 2, 3, 31, 32, 33. Many rare photocopies of articles on Bruce (early 1970's), 50 *Way of the Dragon* 35mm frame slides.
- Lee O'Neill, Omagh, Northern Ireland wants urgently *KFMs* 2, 3, 14, 30-37, 44 - please help. Also single records of all films and *Green Hornet* & *Dragon Power* single.
- Mustafa Abdi, London wants: *Black Belt's Best of Bruce Lee No. 1* - swap for any Bruce Lee uncut video films (VHS, Beta). Also has Bruce Lee documentary film and another special - contact for info - £25 each film inc. p&p, also wants: Japanese *Green Hornet* annual.
- Takeshi Hasegawa, Aichi, Japan has for swap: *Game of Death 2* video tapes, Japanese stickers, photos, magazines Wants: magazines, movie posters, photos worldwide.
- Lee Stanley, Sheldon has for sale (write with offers for what required and Lee will answer) - *Kung Fu Monthly* folder, *KFM* 1, B&W Trade Dummy, *KFMs* 1-66 (doubles 3-10, 28, 47 & 50), 2 *KFM Game of Death Special Collectors Edition*, 1 copy each *Bruce Lee JKD* magazines 1, 4, & 7, *Best of Bruce Lee 2*, *Combat* Vol. 1 No. 5 1975 (with Bruce), *Karate* Jan-Feb No. 76 (*Game of Death*), *Bruce Lee King of Kung Fu* by Felix Dennis & Don Ayteo, *Fighting Spirit*, *Immortal Dragon*, *Studies in JKD*, *Combats*, *Bruce Lee In the Big Boss*, *Secret of JKD & Kung Fu*, *Privacy & Anecdotes*, *Game of Death*, *Reminiscence of Bruce Lee*, *Memorial Special Collectors Edition*, *His Unknown in Martial Arts Learning*, *Game of Death Extract Edition*, *Bruce Lee In Action* (*KFM* Collectors Edition), *Who Killed Bruce Lee?*, *Unbeatable Bruce Lee*, *Karate* - Mar-Apr '82 No. 95, *Fighters Monthly* (with Bruce) Vol. 1 Nos. 3 & 5.
- Bob Hartsfield, Denton, USA has for sale: USA *Tao of Jeet Kune Do* (Bruce Lee), *Unbeatable Bruce Lee* (Hard Back) USA, *King of Kung Fu*, *Bruce Lee's Fighting Method Basic Training* (USA), *Tao of Wing Chun Do* Vol. 2 (USA), Posters - three *Enter the Dragon*, one *Fist of Fury*.
- Kevin Hobbs, 21 Pump Piece, Leominster, Herefs. HR6 8PN, Eng: Wants: *The Big Boss*, *Fist of Fury*, *Way of the Dragon*, *Game of Death* on 8mm or video - write with details.
- Paul Shepherd, Birmingham has for sale: two complete sets *KFM* 1- 50 (one set in binder), all *KFM* "Special" items i.e. *Game of Death* etc., cinema posters

A RETROSPECTIVE LOOK AT BRUCE LEE MANIA & THE KUNG FU CRAZE OF THE 1970S

to all films except *Way of the Dragon* Chinese books, Chinese, English versions magazines from JKD Club of Hong Kong, large posters, paperback books, double stereo LPs - lots more. Write for full list to Paul, lot for £60 but will split if necessary.

Before closing, I must praise the *Shogun* Japanese series which is superb! Richard Chamberlain, Toshiro Mifune and Yoko Shimada portrayed their parts beautifully - I'd be happy to hear what our Japanese members think.

Also enjoyable was to see Dan Inosanto in *Killer Elite* on BBC2 - I just wish there had been more of him.

Finally - Channel 4 showed *Valiant Ones* and I spotted such actors as Chan Fu Yee (mesmerised by Bruce in the underground scene from *Enter the Dragon*, the Monk from *Enter the Dragon* who spoke of Bruce's sister and one of the Japanese from *Fist of Fury*. It makes me feel Channel 4 ARE the people to keep chasing.

You share the characteristics of one of the 12 animals in the Chinese lunar calendar. Find the year of your birth in this table and see which animal it is.

Cockerel	1897	1909	1921	1933	1945	1957	1969	1981
Dog	1898	1910	1922	1934	1946	1958	1970	
Pig	1899	1911	1923	1935	1947	1959	1971	
Rat	1900	1912	1924	1936	1948	1960	1972	
Ox	1901	1913	1925	1937	1949	1961	1973	
Tiger	1902	1914	1926	1938	1950	1962	1974	
Rabbit	1903	1915	1927	1939	1951	1963	1975	
Dragon	1904	1916	1928	1940	1952	1964	1976	
Snake	1905	1917	1929	1941	1953	1965	1977	
Horse	1906	1918	1930	1942	1954	1966	1978	
Ram	1907	1919	1931	1943	1955	1967	1979	
Monkey	1908	1920	1932	1944	1956	1968	1980	

Finally - reprinted here is a copy of the Chinese Lunar Calendar. Next year is the "Year of the Pig." Look at the chart to find your own sign. Pam

EDITOR'S NOTES

Issue 26 mentions that the *Seattle Times* cartoon strip was suddenly dropped for apparently no reason but there were talks of an animated movie with an agreed budget of $1million. It appears that the project was sadly never completed. Baring Manga and Anime, there have been some kid-targeted martial arts animations over the years including *Chinese Gods, Chuck Norris' Karate Komandos, Teenage Mutant Ninja Turtles,* and *Jackie Chan Adventures.*

Video view-in

KUNG FU star Bruce Lee has been dead for over five years. Now Rank Video are releasing his last film, (The Way Of The Dragon,) and a cartoon, with Lee as an Eastern Superman, is in production.

ADRIAN HODGES

Skirmish was a 1981 film directed by John Steven Soet and starring Jackson Bostwick, Kija Manhare and Dan Inosanto. After her sister is killed in a fight, Janet (Kija Manhare) sets out to investigate her sister's death using her skills in escrima. Janet teams up with Sheriff Lon Walker (Jackson Bostwick) who has already been investigating a series of martial arts related murders by the maniacal Teak. The film's climax features the spectacular battle against Teak's premier henchman Julio Montoya (Dan Inosanto). Sadly, it appears that the film has never had a home video release.

A RETROSPECTIVE LOOK AT BRUCE LEE MANIA & THE KUNG FU CRAZE OF THE 1970S

27
March
1983

WE'RE AWAY WITH THE SPRING NEWS SHEET - AND ALTHOUGH IT'S HARD TO BELIEVE, THE TIME HAS AGAIN COME AROUND TO START THE BALL ROLLING WITH OUR ANNUAL TRIBUTE.

MEMORIAL FLOWERS - JULY 1983

For the third year running, the Society will be sending a floral tribute to Bruce's graveside at Lake View Cemetery, Seattle. The first year we collected £63; last year £145 - which was super! - and this year - BEING THE 10TH ANNIVERSARY OF BRUCE'S DEATH - I really want to see a fantastic response. Many of you have sent for the pictures of the flowers for both years so you know what lovely tributes they were. Now in order to get everything organised as smoothly as possible, please - come on! - do send in a donation - no matter how small - to make this the best tribute ever. Send your cheque/postal order (made payable to Pam Hadden ONLY, please - NOT *KFM*) in an envelope marked "Memorial Tribute" - to London. Remember - I keep a list of names (which will be placed by the graveside), amounts received, and a running total to keep the records straight; I then pay the total into my account and immediately send a cheque for that figure to member Alison French - who has so superbly handled the matter in the last two years. Once we have decided on what the flowers should look like, Alison takes over the project, liaising direct with the florist in Seattle. It all takes time, so money should be sent to me by the last week in June - THE VERY, VERY LATEST DATE. (Any cheques/postal orders made payable to *KFM* will, regrettably, have to be returned to the person sending this for reissue - sorry, but there are too many problems otherwise, and just not the time to sort them out).

I'd also welcome - when sending your donation - ideas on what YOU feel the flowers should look like; we considered a dragon - but believe this would be an impossible task for the florist and any suggestions would be helpful. Maybe "Bruce - 1940-1973" - your comments, please.

Fan's lament - written after seeing a video of *Way of the Dragon* and finding it slashed to ribbons:

> *Do you see what they've done to your movies, Bruce?*
> *Do you see how they've cut them to shreds?*
> *Do you see all your art destroyed by fools?*
> *I wonder what's inside their heads?*
> *It can't be much if they just cannot see*
> *The beauty and skill in your "style."*
> *All REAL Bruce fans understand and respect;*
> *The "clowns" who misuse you are vile!*
> *Their hooliganism spoils things for the rest -*
> *They're why "Do-Gooders" continue to hack.*
> *It seems so unfair to people who care,*
> *So - PLEASE - give us ALL film of Bruce back!*
> *(Alison French - 17.12.82.)*

> *Ten years have passed since that sad day.*
> *The one we loved was called away.*
> *We did not say a last good-bye -*
> *For you were gone,*
> *And God only knows why!*
> *(Ann Hunt - "We miss you, Bruce")*

GRACE'S PRESENT

I have now received £99.15 - a little shorter than was pledged, as it should have been over £130 (pledgers - where HAS your donation gone?) As mentioned before, silverware has been decided upon (with engraving from the Society etc.) - and then the item presented to Grace, hopefully by my making the trip to Los Angeles for this. Regrettably, the item I had in mind to purchase (calculated on the pledged money!) I am now unable to get - so I will purchase what I feel suitable. Final details will be given in the June sheet, when all will be revealed! (If any members who have not contributed wish to do so, I will give you until mid-April to get it to me, as I shall be buying the present then, so come on, do help, and send to me at the above address marking the envelope "Grace's Gift."

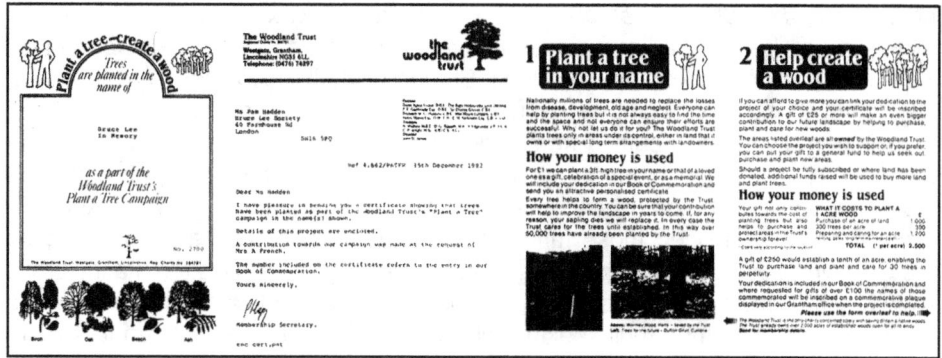

PLANT A TREE - CREATE A WOOD
The Woodland Trust

Alison French surprised, and delighted me, by having a tree planted by the Woodland Trust (at a cost of £1) in the wording "Bruce Lee - In Memory" which is entered in their Book of Commemoration; and I also received a certificate to that effect. It seems that anyone can do this in the name of your choice. And for £25, you can name the Woodland Project where you want your money to go (in either Cumbria, Devon, Gloucestershire, Sussex or Lincolnshire, or to a General Fund for future projects), again listed in the Book of Commemoration and a certificate sent. But if £100 is sent, not only does the contributor receive a certificate and have a listing in the book, but the actual commemoration is included on a plaque in the offices of the Woodland Trust for all to see! So I thought; What if EVERY member sent in a donation and, after say six months, I gave you the figure we had collected and, if short, we aimed at reaching the £100 target? Wouldn't that be something to have Woodland named after Bruce? I think that is something he would have liked! On a separate sheet, you will see a copy of the Woodland Trust's letter to me, the certificate, and the leaflet sent by the trust giving all details. I think it would be a lovely idea - so if you care to "create a wood" with me, start sending in your money now - and get your friends/relatives to do it too - if not in the name of Bruce at least in the interests of conservation to keep our countryside alive!

GENERAL NEWS

Member Setudeh Nejad, our member who left England to study at Seattle University, has written to say he was in Japan for a while researching for a book he wishes to write on comparative cultures, and whilst there he was delighted to find numerous mentions of Bruce on TV, newspapers and magazines. "Lee's image," he says "is still very much alive, popular and on the front page." Since his arrival into Japan, two Bruce Lee movies (and also Jackie Chan) have been shown; one commentator on TV mentioned Bruce's name three times before a movie, and although Setudeh does not speak Japanese, he says he obviously recognised the words "Bruce Lee'" when said!! Programmes mention Bruce; and some weeks back a joint Japanese-Chinese production - *The Shaolin Temple* - has been a hit in Tokyo. Famous shopping districts such as "Ginza" had magazines with excellent photos of Bruce, although they were not fan or martial arts publications. Setudeh said he also saw *Tower of Death* with footage which he had never seen before and it WAS Bruce himself!

Setudeh also sent a cutting from *Newsweek* magazine (he is now back in Seattle), which is entitled "Young Fu: The Junior League" commenting on children's martial arts in the States. It says: "Teenage males have been trying out Kung Fu since Bruce Lee flashed those furious fists 13 years ago. These days, however, they're being upstaged by boys and girls as young as three. Unlike the macho craze launched by Lee's so-called "chop-socky" movies, the current karate kick owes more to self-preservation than thrill-seeking. Many parents enrol their children to armour them against a violent society - to enable them to protect themselves. But kiddie karate also has its drawbacks and detractors. Young bones, Doctors say, cannot withstand repeated blows, youngsters become unduly fearful or suffer nightmares etc. Lessons are a relative bargain - but parents should shop very selectively: "You don't want Mr. Bad-Ass Bruce Lee teaching your kids" warns John Stewart, executive editor of *Inside Kung Fu* magazine. "Look for a human being." Well - I am not sure just what Mr. "Bad-Ass" John Stewart is trying to do but I think he would be better advised to start seeking out these good schools from the bad and making the names and addresses available to the parents, instead of coming out with "silly little comments" fit only for children's ears. If you too feel strongly about it, drop both *Newsweek* magazine and *Inside Kung Fu* magazine a line - Pam.

David Moore tells me that the California Martial Arts Academy opened last summer in Los Angeles, and among the list of celebrities who appeared as guest instructors were: Stephen Hayes - Ninjutsu (adviser on the TV series *Shogun* and the only non-Japanese authorised to teach authentic Ninjutsu); Bill Wallace - full-contact Karate (retired World Middleweight Champion); Dan Inosanto - Kali and Escrima Filipino martial arts and one of Bruce's best and closest friends; Jesse Glover - non-Classical Gung Fu and one of Bruce's earliest pupils; Tim Tackett - Kali, boxing and JKD; Larry Hartsell - JKD. David also says that November 1982 *Official Karate* mag (which has been running for around ten years) incredibly had several mistakes in that issue. They said Bruce died on July 14 1973 - "On 13 July 1973 Bruce was a seemingly healthy and happy young man... the next day he was dead." *Return of The Dragon* (*Way of the Dragon*) was dated 1973, and JKD was translated as "Fist Intercepting Way." They also said that after he was noticed at the Long Beach Tournament, it was not long before he was starring in a movie with the help of Jay Sebring (hairdresser to the stars) and William Dozier, TV Producer. "What movie?" asks David, "as *Green Hornet* was a TV series and Bruce certainly did not 'star' in *Marlowe*." (Mind you, David - many people use the term "star" loosely to denote an appearance of a person in a film, so they COULD be just using this figuratively. Also - when I've seen *Marlowe* at the cinema, most people leave after Bruce goes over the balcony - so he seems to have been considered the "star" anyway. - Pam)

David also wrote to *Revue* magazine as they did an article on Elvis on his birthday, and David hoped they would do one on Bruce. However, they only put a mention in their Diary Page saying Bruce was born on 27 November. But it was a mention, says David - and next year, who knows?

I supplied the censors' address last sheet, so David wrote to Mr. Ferman about the seemingly dual standards of censorship, pointing out the use of nunchakus and various other weapons in Sonny Chiba films etc., yet Bruce's movies are axed to bits. He went on about films which received "X" certificates and should possibly only receive an "AA" such as Chuck's *An Eye For An Eye*. The battle scenes in *Conan The Barbarian* were very realistic, including the chopping-off of a man's head showing the falling body and bloody neck in clear view. It got an "AA," yet Bruce's films are cut and receive an "X." He pointed out that if other stars' films (such as Burt Reynolds, Clint Eastwood, etc.) were censored as much as Bruce's, there would be an outcry. David is awaiting a reply from Mr. Ferman.

Jonathan Westley also wrote to the censors to say he saw a recent horror film where a man was attacked and hacked to death in the most gory way with a pair of shears. The censors' argument has always been that "people can make and use nunchakus shown in Bruce's films" (but I suppose they DON'T in Sonny Chiba films???...Pam) and Jonathan quite rightly points out (as I did when I met Mr. Ferman) that it is a damn sight easier to get hold of a pair of shears and use them than to obtain a pair of nunchakus.

Regarding the *Way of the Dragon* video - another pointer Jonathan made was that if - as the censors say - Bruce's side-stamp kick to Chuck's leg followed by some dazzling combination punches to his chest were considered "horrific" (?) and not suitable to be shown to the public, then why - WHY - are they allowed in the credits?? (Indeed why, Jonathan - the censors really have never had any answers for this, have they??)

Back to an article in a past news sheet on the Chinese horoscope, Jonathan has a book which states under "Dragon": Bursting with health; an idealist and perfectionist; refuses to put up with anything less and makes him ask too much of himself and others. Demands a lot, but gives a lot too. People listen to him and his influence is considerable. Over-proud, enthusiastic to the point of impetuosity; loses his temper easily; gifted; intelligent, tenacious; willing and generous. Can do anything - whether his career is religious, military, medical or political, he's going to shine - he will be a success.

Niels Bjerre recently saw the film *Butterfly* starring Orson Welles and James Franciscus of *Longstreet* fame. We do not see much of James these days - I wonder if this was a recent film and just what he is doing with himself? Anyone have any news? - Pam.

David Niedzailek says he is disgusted (as are other members) with the Rank Video *Way of the Dragon* - it is cut to ribbons and by doing this they are playing right into the hands of the video pirates. However, Py Tang (who is now a member) does supply the videos uncut - and members who buy from him urge others to do the same - he will also be getting the *Longstreet* series in soon.

Maria Fernandes from Brazil was rather put out by *Film Review's* article stating, "Chuck Norris not only equalled Bruce but has surpassed him in popularity." Says Maria, "How many films has Chuck done - but how many did Bruce have the chance to do? How many people are working on Chuck's promotion/publicity - yet how many people worked against Bruce when he tried alone, bar hands, to break into Hollywood? How many years has Chuck been living - how many years though did Bruce have to do everything he had in mind before death took him away from us? Even so - how many people around the world have Chuck posters in their rooms and how many have Bruce's?" (Well, I get Maria's points and in some ways agree, but I like and admire Chuck very much. He cannot be held responsible for what *Film Review* has printed and in all honesty, Chuck is very popular and a good martial artist. Bruce stood out on his own; we all know that and I do not think we can compare. Bruce went beyond a martial artist - that is what we must all understand. He encompassed so much more. He was aware - understood life. And, quoting from Maria's letter to me, Chuck once said: "I told myself - I have won the International Championship of karate - if I cannot win over Bruce I am not a hero at all. But after a long conversation with Bruce, I knew that he could defeat me at any moment. I see this not through actual comparison but his demonstration. I knew he was superior. After conversation, I admired him wholeheartedly. For I have not seen anyone who can win over him, and no-one like him knows so thoroughly about life. No matter in which aspect, he can be my teacher." On Hong Kong TV, both Bob Wall and Chuck Norris recognised Bruce as their teacher before two-million spectators. Again from Chuck: "Bruce was a very ego-guy - confident of his ability and knowledge, which some people didn't like. Bruce, I feel, wanted to be the strongest man in the world - and I think he was!! He was always striving to learn - he was creative. It amazed me, his inventiveness. It's a shame that a great martial artist like Bruce had to leave us so soon but I feel he accomplished more in his lifetime than most people would accomplish in 70 or 80 years and I think he lived a full life." I think that sums up Chuck's admiration and respect for Bruce very nicely, don't you? A tribute from a very nice guy! – Pam.

David Edwards tuned in to the *Green Hornet* on Central TV - "It was brilliant to see Bruce in fight scenes other than in his films, the fights being of a totally different type than those in the movies - therefore they offer a whole 'new' area to enjoy. Mind you, the reception was poor and it was like watching TV through a snowstorm!" David states that his New Year's resolution was to write to Channel 4, ITV and the BBC to try to get Bruce's films/series shown "I only hope," he says, "that other members stir themselves into action on this." (SO DO I, DAVID - IT CAN MAKE ALL THE DIFFERENCE, BELIEVE ME! So please - DO keep writing to the TV stations - I think they might be weakening, especially Channel 4! People such as David and Paul Das have had encouraging replies - not the usual "fobbing-off" letters - so let's all help the cause along - PLEASE!! With Bruce's 10th Anniversary coming up - it would be nice to have something as a tribute around that time, such as a film, or two, or three?

Still with David Edwards, he saw an article about Sugar Ray Leonard in *Playboy* (June 1982). As a fan of Sugar Ray, David was surprised (and delighted) when he read the following comments from the boxer: "One of the guys who influenced me the most wasn't a boxer - I always loved the cat-like reflexes and artistry of Bruce Lee, and I wanted to do in boxing what he was able to do in karate. I started watching his movies before he was really popular in *Enter the Dragon* and I patterned myself after him in a lot of ways. For example - to start with I liked the fact that Lee was always in control and very confident. He'd lay back and be a gentleman and he wasn't

Regulations Of The Jun Fan Institute

1) Do not get involve in situations that will jeopardize the reputation of our Institute. Exercise your better judgement.

2) Student will be immediately expelled for teaching our method without permission.

3) Treat your instructor with great respect and listen to his advice. Always address your instructor formally and consult him when in doubt regarding the program and/or regulations of the Institute.

4) Each student must carry his current quarterly card for inspection upon request. This card will indicate your authenticity as a Jun Fan member. Observe the date of expiration; membership will terminate without renewal.

5) Be punctual for classes and always report your absence to your instructor.

6) Smoking is not allowed inside this Institute.

7) Bow before and after practice. If you are late to class, wait at the door till your instructor acknowledges you for salutation. Whenever two students practice together, they should bow to each other. Observe the difference between student to student bowing and student to instructor bowing.

8) No unnecessary talking during instruction.

Failure to follow the above regulations will be subject to dismissal.

Jun Fan Institute Regulations in Bruce's writing (sent in by Andrew Staton)

really outspoken, but all along he knew that whenever he wanted to he could kick any guy's butt!! He had lightning reflexes and he could move and think and just pick his opponent apart. In a sense my left jab comes from him; my hands are still not as strong as I want them to be, and after watching Lee I became much more precise about landing my jabs on an opponent's nose or between his eyes. I also got some moves - both offensive and defensive - from him. For instance, he'd let a punch come within a fraction of an inch of his face and then he'd slip it and pop a guy! Lee was an artist and - like him - I try to go beyond the fundamentals of my sport. I want the public to actually see a knockout in the making, starting from the moment I begin setting up an opponent, start picking my shots and then - pow! - finish him off..." So, (says David) he's not just an excellent boxer but a Bruce fan as well!!

Still with David, there was a two-page article in *Look In* magazine (the *Junior TV Times* magazine) with a quarter-page picture of Bruce and the following words: "Next time you see a Bruce Lee look-a-like kicking his way out of trouble in a film, spare a thought for the ancient Chinese (that's Bruce martial-arts movie King, on the left)..." So the article presumes that the little kids reading the article know of Bruce, which is flattering. (And indeed, very good advice and super to know that at least ONE magazine seems to be aware of the rip-offs simulating Bruce - Pam).

Another article about Joe Lewis (*Inside Kung Fu* magazine) quotes him as saying: "As a personality I feel Bruce was kind of a fantasy-type character. He demonstrated a tremendous amount of external physical efficiency, and he came across as if he were hard both externally and internally - I don't think anyone will every be as great as Bruce, or that anyone can take his place. Like Elvis - there was one, and only one."

In a Jason Lau - Pa Kua instructor - interview (*Inside Kung Fu*) he said: "Bruce Lee pointed out things that some could not accept. For one he said that the forms had limitations. I look at it this way - Bruce was a young man who wasn't practiced in the old school of Kung Fu. He practiced by doing - he used his mind. He hurried himself, improved himself. He would learn some skill quite well in a short period of time. He was smart. Then he got involved with movies and did not have much time to

```
THE COMPLETE BRUCE LEE ROUTINE (Sent by V. S. Narayan)
Fitness (Sequence A. Monday, Wednesday, Friday)
        1. Skipping  2. Good morning exercise (loved jogging)  3. Catch stretch  4. Jumping
        Jacks  5. Squats without weights  6. High Kicks
    (Sequence B. Tuesday, Thursday, Saturday)
        1. Groin stretch  2.Side leg raise  3. Jumping squat  4. Shoulder circling
        5. Alternate splits  6. Leg stretch
Forearm/Waist Sequence A, Wednesday, Friday)
        1. Waist twisting  2. Palm up curl  3. Roman chair  4. Knee drawing  5. Side bends
        with dumbbells  6. Palm down curl
    (Sequence B, Tuesday, Thursday, Saturday)
        1. Leg raises  2. Reverse curl  3. Sit up twist  4. Leverage bar twist  5. Alternate
        leg raise  6. Wrist roller
Power Training (Every day)
        1. Press lockout  2. Press start  3. Rise on toes  4. Upright rowing  5. Squat
        6. Shrug  7. Deadlift  8. Quarter squat  9. Frog kick.
(Bruce ran up to at least 45 minutes a day, starting with easy jogging and building up to
sprinting. Also did similar on stationary bicycle or cycled on the open road. Training for
power he opened with a press with a slight difference. Instead of pressing all the way from
shoulders to arms length overhead he would take the bar overhead, lower it a couple of inches,
then press it out. He repeated this 10 times before lowering bar to his chest and then perform-
ing 10 repeats of the press start. With heavy bar across shoulders, he would perform a rise
on toes 20 repeats/Sometimes varied this by holding bar behind his legs/Upright rowing, keeping
elbows well up and bringing the bar up under chin/Squat, going all the way down with medium·
weight/Shoulder shrugs holding bar in front of legs/Deadlift, sometimes with bar in front of
him but more usually in straddle position/Quarter squats working up to really heavy poundages/
frog kicks.)
```

keep up his martial arts training. You can push yourself too hard, which I think he did. It's a shame he didn't follow through with a good instructor. He learned Wing Chun for a while, then jumped into a few other forms, then formed a new style. He didn't call it a style; instead he told people it was a form. Old timers call him a rebel - I call him smart. But the smart guy killed himself."

Seen recently by myself and David on TV - the underground scene from *Enter the Dragon* in the Roman Polanski film *The Tenant* when two actors were at the cinema.

Also for those members who asked, here is the complete Bruce routine of training sent to me by member V. S. Narayan from India. I know it will be of great assistance to many members who have not seen it before.

Member John Maidment, who is also the director of the Filipino Martial Arts Association, sent me a letter which makes interesting reading, so I have reproduced it in full for you all. It would seem all other countries are luckier than us in getting Bruce shown on TV, radio, etc!!

Jonathan Westley read an article in the November issue of *Official Karate* which included several mistakes, but he was touched by the following: "Today Linda has finally built a new life on the tears of the last

Filipino Martial Arts Association

March 1, 1983

John Maidment * Director *
Dennis J. White * President *

Promoting Health, Physical Fitness; and the Martial Arts of the Philippines

BRUCE LEE SOCIETY
c/o Pam
40 Farmhouse Road
London, England
SW16 5BQ

Dear Pam,

I am sorry to have taken so long to write this letter but I trust the information will be able to printed in the summer edition of your news sheet.

I am a second-stage student of Dan Inosanto, currently enrolled in Nursing school - upon graduation I plan to move to California to train full time with Dan.

I thought that you would like to let your readers know that this year in Newfoundland we are planning to commemorate Bruce's passing by way of TV, radio, printed media and public demonstrations of Gung Fu to inform people that his memory his still strong with many of us - we intend to inform the unknowing as to his impact on the martial arts and west-east cultural exchange. I hope to be able to let people aware of the fact that Bruce was a real human being; not a god or superman; but a real person, a caring father & husband and a highly devoted martial artist - it was his determination to succeed that made him the best, but I know that many people still have an inflated & unrealistic fax fantasy of him.

In honor of his birthday this past November, a local cinema ran a double feature: Fists of Fury (The Big Boss) & Chinese Connection (Fist of Fury) to sold out audiences for 3 weeks!: So I know that his screen appeal is still just as strong as in the seventies; and I'm sure that it will be remain strong for many more years.

I would like to let you know that "The Warrior Within" contains No footage of Bruce other than clips from his funeral and a movie still. The rest is just general martial arts (but good) and a commentary by Bruce's mother and brother as well as by Dan Inosanto; plus about 4 minutes of the Kali Academy's class - taken around 1979.

We are currently running our own local TV show (on Cable) and feature a three minute spot at the end of each show of a reading from The Tao of Jeet Kune Do, which has gained favorable response so far. It has been that particular TV show that has helped to promote our system/non-system the most since I began spreading the arts in 1978.

It is hoped that we will be able to sponsor a trip to Newfounldand by either Dan or Richard Bustillo or Ted Lucaylucay (both senior students of Dan's) sometime this year or possibly send myself and three students to California for training. It is very important to renew our training and since distance is a big factor we purchased a Video Tape Recorder plus some Kali/JKD training tapes which were produced by Guro Ted Lucaylucay and are using them as reference sources.

If any of the Society members would like to contact me (especially if planning a trip here) please feel free to do so.

All the best to the Society and I hope that I will be able to contribute more to it than it will give me in return.

Yours in the spirit of Kali, and Bruce,

John Maidment (#3127)
Director - Filipino Martial Arts Association

FILIPINO KALI: Eskrima/Arnis Sikaran KICKBOXING; Lee JunFan GungFu/Boxing

P.O. Box 848 · Mt Pearl · Newfoundland · Canada · A1N 3C8

one. She has her children, and her memories, but behind her, in a guarding combat pose, stands a shadowy, misty figure in the accepted Kung Fu stance – watching over her and the family forever - just as forever his fans will cheer him on in dark theatres in all four corners of the world where Bruce, for all eternity, continues to fight evil." (Much as I feel the magazine was sincere, I think the above sounds just a little too slushy for my taste - Pam).

Jonathan, a keen disco-dancer, said he intended, in a recent competition, to wear his *Game of Death* suit and to use plastic nunchakus to add something different! (How did he do, I wonder? Let me know, Jonathan!)

Also are the Jun Fan Institute Regulations in Bruce's neatest handwriting (referred to in the December news sheet) sent in by Andrew Staton, and which item is something which every fan should hold a copy of in their collection on Bruce! (Please remember if you have any interesting snippets to send me a copy for the news sheets!)

Paul Corrigan got together a condensed list of Bruce sayings - all 50 of them!! I will not be able to print them all in one go, so shall reproduce one page (in Paul's own writing as it's so neat!) every news sheet until you have them all. The first eight are shown here. (Thanks Paul).

> **The Wisdom of Bruce.** Collected by Paul Corrigan.
>
> 1. Self-education makes great men.
> 2. A man is born to achieve great things if he has the strength to conquer himself.
> 3. You can acquire a lot in life, if you are prepared to give up a lot to get it.
> 4. It's not what you give, it's the way you give it.
> 5. Those who are unaware they are walking in darkness will never seek the light.
> 6. You must learn defeat. Like most people you want to learn to win. To learn to die is to be liberated from it. When tomorrow comes, you must learn to die and be liberated by it.
> 7. Youth is the time to study wisdom, old age is the time to practise it.
> 8. To a mind that is still, the whole universe surrenders.

Dan Inosanto had an interview in *Fighting Stars* magazine which deserves printing in full. From this you will get to see just how he and Bruce became such good friends, and how they both, in their way, taught something to each other, and Dan says his relationship with Bruce was "very special" to him. Having met Dan, I can say he is one of the most gentle, sincere, aware, modest and talented people I have ever met - nothing is too much for him and he will go out of his way - no matter how busy - to help anyone. A truly lovely guy.

LETTERS

Dear Pam,

Karate & Oriental Arts UK *bi-monthly magazine had a special 100th edition and on their introduction page they covered the karate and martial arts' scene in Britain since their first issue in 1966. Under the heading "1970" they say: "Bruce Lee erupted, shadowed by Carradine's* Kung Fu *series, on the unsuspecting Western world." How can they say that with cinema queues for Bruce's films, such as* Fist of Fury, *going down streets, around corners and out of sight. And many people went off* Kung Fu *when they found out Carradine could not actually do the art. Of course I am going to drop a line to* Karate & Oriental Arts*!!*

(David Moore)

A RETROSPECTIVE LOOK AT BRUCE LEE MANIA & THE KUNG FU CRAZE OF THE 1970S

Dan Inosanto has appeared in, and/or been an advisor to, several movies involving the martial arts—Game of Death, Battlecreek Brawl, and most recently, Sharkey's Machine starring Burt Reynolds. He also holds down a full-time position teaching history and physical education to junior high school students.

But those pursuits are all secondary to his real aim in life, the driving force within him to spread the concepts of jeet kune do as laid out by the late Bruce Lee.

Inosanto spent six years with Lee as one of his disciples. He has been called Lee's prodigy, although Inosanto himself is far too humble to accept that honorable title, warranted or not.

The fact is, however, that nobody in the world today works as hard as Inosanto at imparting the many ideas and philosophies inherent in Lee's jeet kune do. He does so not only as an instructor at his Filipino Martial Arts Studio in Torrance, California, but also by traveling worldwide, conducting seminars and demonstrations. He is, in a word, dedicated.

Nobody alive understands the concepts behind jeet kune do like Inosanto does. Perhaps nobody can put them to work quite as well as he does either. How does this expert martial artist explain the meaning of jeet kune do, the style that is really no style? How does he feel about the status of the martial arts community today? How does this educator-actor-technician feel about his own life as a martial artist?

Dan Inosanto answers those questions and more as the subject of this issue's Champion's Close-up:

FS: A lot of people seem to misunderstand jeet kune do. What exactly is it? What isn't it?

INOSANTO: Jeet kune do is really not a style, it's a level of understanding. It's hard to explain, but basically that's what it is. It's nothing a person can belong to or be a member of. It's not a combination of different styles, even though many people think so.

FS: If it's not a style or a combination of styles, what is it?

INOSANTO: Jeet kune do is merely a name used to free ourselves. I hope to free my followers from clinging to the style, pattern, or mold. There is no series of rules or classification of techniques which constitutes a so-called jeet kune do system. To begin with, there is no such thing as a system or method of fighting, although there are some progressive approaches to training. It is like putting a pot of water in wrapping paper and trying to shape it structurally. People try to say JKD is a composite style because of the philosophy... To fully under one must transcend into the reality that it is not for or against, but is simply an organic tool. A good jeet kune do man rests on intuition. The key word is direct intuition. He's saying a style should never be like a bible. Principles can be broken or violated. In short, that's what it is. It's not a style, it's a level of understanding of martial arts. It is like the word relaxation. The essence is relaxation, but there are many forms. Some guy might take his vacation in the Bahamas and another takes it in Hawaii. Another goes to the mountains. Another guy goes to the beach. Who's to say which is better? If you understand that, you understand the roots. And the roots are relaxation, not the beach or the mountains. Basically, that is what jeet kune do is.

FS: Is that what Bruce Lee meant when he said, "No one way is the way?"

INOSANTO: Yeah, using no way as the way. Many people have a way—the shotokan, the Japanese way, the Chinese way, the Korean way. Bruce was saying use no way as the way. There is no limitation or structure. No limit is a limit. You see, when a boxer tries to solve his problems, he must use his boxing skills in the context of boxing. When a karate man must solve his problems, whatever his style is, he must be free to adapt to whatever they are. The object is to be free. It's a higher level of freedom.

FS: Some have considered you to be Bruce Lee's prodigy? Do you feel that is an accurate assessment of yourself?

INOSANTO: I don't think so. He had a heck of a lot of guys who could have been. I was just fortunate to be around at the time. He passed on a lot of things to me. He helped me grow. But it would be incorrect to say I was his prodigy. Let me say he spent a lot of time with me and I learned a whole lot of things from him and am able to grow from what he taught me. There were a lot of people he was close to. Everyone had a different relationship with him, and I had that one section of a relationship with him that made it very special for me.

FS: He taught you many things, but didn't you teach him certain areas of the martial arts?

INOSANTO: I shared with him. I shared with him a little bit about single stick fighting. And I shared the nunchaku with him. He took that to another level. I think that is where his genius was. Most people are bound by tradition. If you can accept the past tradition, you can reach a further height—take it to another level.

FS: How can you measure the ability of a martial artist?

INOSANTO: Everyone has a different measurement they use to judge a martial artist. Some people use tournaments as their measurement. That's how they measure progress. Some people measure it by the amount of knowledge they've accumulated. But the measurement of a good martial artist is his self-perfection of movement. Some of the best martial artists you never hear about; they won't be in a magazine, although they are very good. I know from my own experience that there are a whole lot of good martial artists nobody even knows about. They are simply very low key.

FS: You don't seem to place much emphasis on tournament competition. Why?

INOSANTO: It's all a matter of what you want to pursue. You need to determine where you are. If I want tournament competition, then by all means, enter. But it is not really one of our goals. You sometimes get confined in the tournament structure. It's hard to explain. Everyone has a different goal. Everyone uses a different platform to grow by. Some people need tournaments to grow by, others do not. The more tournaments you enter doesn't mean the more you're going to get better. Before I met Bruce, I thought I'd enter as many tournaments as I could and just get better and better. But that wasn't necessarily true. It's like music or poetry; Bruce thought they were vehicles to grow by. Tournaments are a form of expression, that's what Bruce taught us. Around 1967 or 1968, Bruce had a number of good competitors who could have done well in the national tournaments—a high number of them. But tourney success was not an important aspect of his philosophy. A lot of people with big tournament reputations who came to learn from Bruce were not as good as his other students.

FS: When did you quit competing at tournaments?

INOSANTO: I quit when I saw from Bruce that it wasn't the way to go. The last tournament I entered was in 1965. I took a second in the black belt division at the U.S. Karate Championships. I remember bringing back this trophy and showing it to Bruce and he said it wasn't worth much. I didn't quite believe him in those days, but I'm a firm believer now. Talking to an outsider, it's hard to explain, but people who have joined ... they understand now. There are a lot of things you can't cover in a tournament and it shouldn't be the only goal. I remember one time a student of mine placed first at a tournament and came back and the other students wiped him out. Yet on that day at the tournament, he won. Tournaments are a measurement, but not a complete measurement. There are many factors involved.

FS: How about your movie career? Anything on the horizon?

INOSANTO: Well, I don't really know. If a part comes along and I have the opportunity, I'll take it. But I really don't go out of my way to look for a part. Most of the parts I have gotten people have just come around and asked me. I'm not taking any acting lessons. But if a part comes up, it might be fun to do.

FS: Do you have an idea as to what would be the ideal movie role for you to play?

INOSANTO: I really don't know. I would like to push a film that uses Filipino martial arts. I might have a chance to do it.

FS: How do you feel about martial arts movies? Have they progressed or regressed in your opinion?

INOSANTO: I think they've made progress. I think Bruce's movies set a standard for others to either surpass or fall below. Some movies have been pretty good either from a fighting aspect or because of the plot. I've seen a lot of movies where I've liked the story line. These people are just expressing it their way. I enjoy watching Jackie Chan. He isn't the fighter that Bruce was, but I enjoy his movies. He has a different style. A lot of people try to copy Bruce, but not Jackie Chan. He's sort of a comedian acrobat.

Article by Dan Inosanto
(sent by Maria Fernandes)

Many of Bruce's fans (myself included) felt the *Kung Fu* series was given too much publicity in relation to Bruce's art - the series itself was, I thought, pretty good in its own right -but to compare Carradine, an actor and (at that time) a non-martial artist taking a part, to Bruce - a martial artist who took his art seriously, is ridiculous;

however - we all know that magazines/newspapers/and people usually amass all and sundry into the one pot and, regardless of quality, popularity and talents, they are all classed under the one heading. And with *Kung Fu* being shown weekly on TV to thousands, that of course became known to more people, initially.

> Dear Pam,
>
> I'm getting ruffled with all the Bruce/Jackie Chan comparison - there is no similarity in style or acting. Jackie is primarily involved in comedy films whereas Bruce, as we all know, was always acting in all-action fighting films, if we ignore his earlier ventures before Big Boss. Bruce was unsurpassed in his art on screen and off; Jackie is unmatched in his style also. What I mean is that the styles practiced by both these artists are totally different/contrasting in all respects - therefore it is unjust and unfair to compare two such true artists in the same category when in reality no such category exists which includes them. Bruce films are historical monuments in cinematic martial arts - he introduced the "mystic" of the arts to the media, who in general were plain, ignorant and narrow-minded. Indeed, there will never be anyone like Bruce in the history of martial arts. HE IS and always will be KING. Jackie Chan is no newcomer to the brigade - his many films, though not classics, are plain, well-made action/comedy films - his style perhaps unorthodox, but not the same boring techniques used by some artists. (Chuck Norris wins this category for his spinning back-kicks). Jackie should be taken for himself and not compared to Bruce - he beats the living daylights out of other contemporary artists in his field. Keep the lunging back-fists, turning side-kicks and double knuckle-punches and give me Bruce and Jackie any day! Thanks for letting me sound off, Pam.
>
> (William Sung)

I also personally feel no comparison should be made between Bruce or any other artists - he was unique, and there is no getting away from that fact; he was an enigma - something which many people, even now, cannot accept; that is a strange fact of life - if you do not understand it - scoff at it, pretend it is not there or does not exist, or, as has happened in many cases, kill it. They will never accept what their narrow-minded ignorance cannot understand - nor do they wish to understand. (Pam)

> Dear Pam,
>
> Here and Now *is a programme about Asians etc. in Britain. Recently they filmed a programme about Lau Kung Fu School, with Master Yah talking about Kung Fu and showing my Sifu, Nick Swarmi, sparring. Several people practicing mentioned Bruce in that he brought the art to the West. Also in my local paper there was an article were people complained that the* The Green Hornet *series is screened too early, with a picture of Bruce.*
>
> (Satvinder Singh)

Thanks for the info, Satvinder. Maybe if you care to drop me the address of your school I can print it next news sheet for interested members. Regarding *The Green*

Hornet - At least some people are getting to see it, which is more than we in London can say.

> Dear Pam,
>
> In recent magazines I found an article on the female equivalent of Vic Charles, called Susan Smith. (Playboy's *Playmate Sept 81*). She states she practices karate and is a brown belt but it's clear also that she is not interested in the martial arts and this is just one of a number of sports she does "for the challenge" and to improve mind/body. Although no expert, she says: "Lots of people get their karate notion from Bruce Lee/Chuck Norris films, and a lot of that stuff is flashy trick photography. When going for your black belt there are no camera angles - you recite the poem of perseverance and fight your way out of a corner. You don't walk away thinking you've passed - it's not simple cheap thrill action, it's discipline." So in other words, in her eyes, Bruce/Chuck rely on camera angles while SHE does the "real thing." She discusses Bruce/Chuck as though not real artists - or maybe I got the wrong impression.
>
> (David Edwards)

Well - we seem to be having a real bout of Bruce "knockers" lately. Obviously, Ms. Smith must have some talents in the arts to become a brown belt, but that in itself does not make her an authority - nor has she done her homework on Bruce and Chuck, being completely unaware of their talents. And like passing your driving test, when you get your belts it shows you have reached a certain level of achievement - and from then on you are continually absorbing/learning - it is a never-ending road which "passing the test" allows you and qualifies you to take. So, Ms. Smith, you've still got a long, long way to go!

And now I hope members will allow me a little self-indulgence in printing the following from David Edwards:

> "Finally I'd like to praise the Society. Before I joined I thought the only benefits were discounts on books, etc., etc., and that you just wore a badge to show you were a Bruce fan. I thought the newsletter would be a couple of sheets with pen pals and odd bits of info and petitions. Now I've joined I can't wait for the excellent newsletter to arrive - crammed with all sorts of info - and everyone seems to help each other out with memorabilia, addresses etc. I will stay with the Society for as long as it goes on - which is hopefully for ever!"

Thanks, David, and to the other members who frequently write in with similar comments; running the Society single-handed is hard work

- and this letter was a shot in the arm for me! Luckily I've had many offers of help - and because it has become far too much for one person - especially with my own full-time job at British Airways - some of these members will be getting a response from me with letters to answer, etc. very soon! Which will assist the Society too in time.

THE BRUCE LEE SOCIETY

RENEWALS

The following members fall due for renewal from now until end May; 3323-3354 (second year); 3158-3218 (third); 2908-2972 (fourth); 2600-2697 (fifth); 2267-2302 (sixth); 1829-2021 (seventh).

HELP REQUESTED PLEASE

Alan Hall (Ashington) would be extremely grateful for addresses from members as to where he can obtain uncensored Bruce videos on Betamax format - any help greatly appreciated! (I've already put him in touch with Py Tang!)

GREEN HORNET CARS

Some FANTASTIC news - so many members have written to me in the past asking about where to get the Corgi model cars from this series, and when I let it be known I had one I was inundated with offers to sell at prices ranging from £10 to £100! Well - I've still got it - and it's NOT for sale! But member Andrew Staton has a friend who has managed to get copies of this unique car - all original. And this car is so rare - to my knowledge it has not been on sale in this country for about 12 years! The cost of the car is £14 - and Andrew asks that you write to him initially about this, and he will put you in touch with his friend - his address is Leeds. I certainly never expected to hear of this car being available again, I can tell you!

BRUCE'S BOOK LIST
(PART IV)

More from the list of Bruce's collection:

Weight Training For Championship Judo – Draeger/Inokuma (1966)
The Sport of Judo - Kobayashi/Sharp (1957)
Technique of Judo - Takagaki/Sharp (1957)
Judo in Action - Kazuzo Kudo (1967)
My Study of Judo - G. Koizume (1960)
Judo - The Basic Technical Principles & Exercises - Koizume (1958)

Demonstration of Throws - TP Leggett (1963)
Demonstration of Gentleness - Jigor/Kano (TP Leggett) (1964)
Championship Judo - TP Leggett (1964)
Judo Combination Techniques - T. Kawamura (1960)
What is Judo - Kodakan (1947)
What is Judo (Revised) - Kodakan (1956)

IMAGINATION

Here is Bruce's definition of "imagination" - which he most certainly did not lack!! "RECOGNISING THE NEED FOR SOUND PLANS AND IDEAS FOR THE ATTAINMENT OF MY DESIRES, I WILL DEVELOP MY IMAGINATION BY CALLING UPON IT DAILY FOR HELP IN THE FORMATION OF MY PLANS."

USEFUL ADDRESSES
(from David Moore)

Try the following for magazines/books/martial arts equipment:

- Samurai Sports, 246 Wednesbury Rd., Pleck, Walsall, Staffs., England.
- Oriental World, 18a Swan Street, Manchester, Lancs., England. Battle Orders, 8c George Street, Hailsham, E. Sussex.
- Martial Arts International, 92 Fargosford Street, Coventry, W. Midlands, England.
- Bushido Martial Arts Co., 63 Sheaf Street, Sheffield, England.
- GIKO LTD., 537 Stratford Rd., Sparkhill, Birmingham B11 4LP, W. Midlands, England.
- Cimac Martial Arts Wear Ltd., 606 Stratford Rd., Sparkhill, Birmingham BII 4AP., England.
- Karate & Oriental Arts, 638 Fulham Road, London, SW6., England. Sakura Trading Co., 10 Thombury Rd., Isleworth TW7 4HG, Middlesex.

FILM NEWS

Leo Fong is to star in an action/adventure film *Kill Point*. Leo is an excellent martial artist who has studied and written books on many styles of Kung Fu. This isn't his first film - he starred in *Manila Gold, Bamboo Trap*, and *The Last Reunion*. (David Moore)

VIDEO INFORMATION
(Courtesy of David Edwards)

Recently watched a video entitled *Slaughter* which I believed to be a horror movie as the cover showed a man's head, eyes bulging, with a chain around his throat. Discovered, however, it was a martial arts film (Golden Harvest/directed by Lo Wei) starring Chuck Norris, who plays a bad guy. An enjoyable plot - a modern-day version of *Big Boss* - fight scenes plentiful, a cross between Hong Kong "chop-suey" and the sort seen in Chuck's later scenes - a new film to me, and pleasant to watch. *The Man From Hong Kong* video (Raymond Chow film - I personally enjoyed when first released - Pam) stars Jimmy Wang Yu as a Hong Kong police inspector sent to Australia to extradite a drug-smuggler (Samo Hung from *Enter the Dragon*) but who starts to track down the whole gang led by George Lazenby. Two good parts are the restaurant fight and the way he gets his revenge. *Enter The Streetfighter* (Sonny Chiba - who Mas Oyama says is superior to Bruce) has an unclear plot (maybe I was just too slow) but lots of fight scenes, most of which were very good. During one fight Sonny adopts the JKD "ready" stance shown in *Tao of Jeet Kune Do*. Some scenes are gory - throats ripped out, eyes poked in and a knife stuck in one man's eye. The cover says: "Sonny is the natural successor to Bruce" and Bruce is also mentioned in the first minute of the film. Whilst I do not think we will ever have a real successor to Bruce, Sonny Chiba is one of the best runners-up.

THE BRUCE LEE SOCIETY

Some interesting books from David:	Price		Store
POWER KICKING - Leo Fong	£4.95	inc. post/packing	Samurai Sports
POWER TRAINING IN KUNG FU AND KARATE - Ron Marchin/Leo Fong	£5.50	inc. " "	" "
WINNING TOURNAMENT KARATE - Chuck Norris	£3.60	inc. " "	" "
DYNAMIC KICKS - Chong Lee	£3.75	inc. " "	" "
'DEAR BRUCE LEE'	£4.45	(plus rates as given)*	Sakura Trading Co.
DYNAMIC NUNCHAKU TRAINING - Kanazawa	£5.95	" " " "	" "
WING CHUN KUNG FU - J. Yim Lee (Technical Editor - Bruce Lee)	£4.45	" " " "	" "
TREATING MARTIAL ARTS' INJURIES - Dennis R. Burke M.D.	£3.95	" " " "	" "
FILIPINO MARTIAL ARTS - Dan Inosanto	£5.95	" " " "	" "
BRUCE LEE'S FIGHTING METHOD - Vol.1-4	£3.95 ea.	" " " "	" "
TAO OF JEET KUNE DO -	£6.95	" " " "	" "
BRUCE LEE - THE UNTOLD STORY -	£1.95	" " " "	" "
WORLD OF BRUCE LEE -	£6.95	inc. post/packing	Karate & Oriental Arts
BRUCE LEE PHOTO ALBUM -	£3.95	inc. " "	" "
KARATE & ORIENTAL ARTS MAG) NOS. 69 & 77 FEATURE BRUCE)	65p each inc. "	"	" "
MARTIAL ARTS MOVIES MAG) £1.25 each OR FROM JAN.82 ONWARDS) £18.50 per year			" "
Good poster of JACKY CHAN FROM 'SNAKE IN THE EAGLE'S SHADOW' -	£2.50	inc. " "	" "
INJURIES IN COMBAT SPORTS - Dr. Greg McLatchie	£6.60	inc. " "	Offoxpress, 59 Lakeside, Oxford OX2 8JQ Oxford, England.

WARNING WHEN BUYING VIDEOS
(David Moore)

Be very careful, when sending to AMERICA for videos, as not all U.S. tapes fit British machines; they MUST be marked "PAL" no matter what format you have (VHS/BETA etc.) BE CAREFUL. (And thanks, David, for telling us! - Pam)

ROBERT LEE LP/BACK ISSUE NEWS SHEETS

Please drop me a line if you require to know anything about cost of this fabulous L.P. and for any back-issue news sheets you might require. (DON'T miss out on the record - it's a really super tribute and beautifully sung by Bruce's brother!

SWOP SHOP

- Brad Walker, Lancaster, U.S.A. has for swap: lots of Bruce Lee items - books, magazines, posters, films etc. too numerous to list! Write to him for list. Wants: ANY non-U.S. books/magazines with Bruce on cover worldwide and ANYTHING ELSE! including Bruce Lee Treasure kit offered with early *KFM*, Bruce Lee mug/poster/T-shirt offered *KFM* 3.
- John Milne, North Carbrain has for sale, Bruce Lee original framed painting 21" x 26" - cost £50, offers please, *Green Hornet* "Silent Gun" super 8 colour/sound 2 x 400 ft reels - £20 ono plus p&p, Motion pictures on paper Vol. 1 - £1+p&p, Bruce Lee Japanese book - £6.50, *Bruce Lee Deluxe* Japanese book - £8.50, *Martial Arts Training Guide to JKD* - £5 ono plus p&p, *KFM Game of Death* - £2+p&p, *1940-1973* hardback book - £3+p&p, *Bruce Lee Extra* - £4+p&p, first *Bruce Lee Scrapbook* - £3+p&p.

- Julian Midgley, Perry Barr, wants: *Dragon* poster magazine nos. 8 & 11, *Legend of Bruce Lee* paperback, *Enter Film Bulletin*, *KFM Game of Death Special*, *Superstars of Kung Fu* by *KFM*, *Scrapbook '75* (red cover), *Bruce Lee The Man Only I Knew*, plus any foreign material especially Japanese/American etc, Good prices paid.
- David Mills, Kingstanding has for sale: first *Bruce Lee Scrapbook*, second *Scrapbook*, *JKD* magazines 1-12, *Motion Pictures on Paper*, *Who Killed Bruce Lee*, *Chinese Gung Fu* and many, many more books/magazines, super 8mm films (inc. Lee/Inosanto *Game of Death* fight). Write for more info.
- Stephen Chan, Portadown, Northern Ireland has for sale/swaps considered: all Bruce Lee videos uncensored, Bruce Lee/Jackie Chan documentary, Chuck Norris *Eye for an Eye* and *Silent Rage* - all VHS - £25 each inc.p&p.
- Paul Das, Middlesbrough wants: Film posters to *Big Boss, Fist of Fury, Enter the Dragon* and any books on the films apart from *Enter the Dragon*, also any other items like super 8mm films. Good prices paid.
- Stephen King, Glasgow has for sale: three Bruce Lee films - *Way of the Dragon* (length 350ft/22mins), *Enter the Dragon Behind the Scenes*, *Game of Death* (350ft/22mins) - all colour/sound except *Way of the Dragon* which has sound cassette, Super 8mm. Write with offers.
- Lee O'Neill, Omagh, Northern Ireland wants: *Green Hornet* magazines/books - good prices paid - write with info.
- Claudio Luce, Burton-on-Trent: This non-member has kindly offered his *KFM* collection - 36 inc. and 9-55 inc. all for £20.
- Kevin Hobbs, Leominster wants: outtakes from Bruce's films on 8mm/video - write giving details.
- Tim Ussher, Crowborough: Regrettably forced to sell collection - please write for details/prices - he has vast collection too big to mention here!!

Well, we've run out of space, just a couple of final things; My thanks to all who wrote with addresses where to buy *Dear Bruce Lee*, and special thanks to Greg Rhodes who sent me a copy as a present! Very much appreciated, Greg.

David Niedzailek sent in a slogan for the Society: "THE BRUCE LEE SOCIETY - You Know It Makes Sense!" (Thanks, David!)

STOP PRESS

I've had to re-juggle and retype this page to squash things up a bit to get this info in!! Had a call from my good friend Eddy Pumer - there is a project in the pipeline now that could be SENSATIONAL!! Can say no more, except PLEASE KEEP WRITING TO CHANNEL 4 ABOUT BRUCE - PLEASE, I CANNOT EMPHASIZE HOW VERY VERY IMPORTANT THIS NOW IS - IF PROJECT COMES OFF YOU WILL ALL BE THRILLED!!!!!!

EDITOR'S NOTES

In past issues of the newsletters, TV stations had deemed *The Green Hornet* too violent to be shown on TV. When Merlin Entertainment released their *Green Hornet* VHS in 1994 containing the episodes, "The Frog is a Deadly Weapon," "The Silent Gun" and "Programmed for Death," the BBFC passed the work with a PG (Parental Guidance' certificate. When Revelation released the 1974 feature film *The Green Hornet* and the 1976 feature film *Fury of the Dragon* on VHS and DVD in 2008, the BBFC passed them with a PG and a 12 certificate respectively. In issue 83, TV stations had begun to show the series, with Central TV being mentioned, though as one member states, some members of the public were writing to their local newspapers to say that they still deemed it to violent to be shown so early. Though it doesn't give a screening time, in issue 28, Martin Hughes from Birmingham (who would probably be receiving Central TV), mentioned that *The Green Hornet* was being shown at 9.30am on a Sunday morning.

The film *Slaughter* mentioned, is the 1974 film *Yellow Faced Tiger* aka *Slaughter in San Francisco*, starring Jimmy Wang Yu and Chuck Norris, mentioned earlier in this book.

A RETROSPECTIVE LOOK AT BRUCE LEE MANIA & THE KUNG FU CRAZE OF THE 1970S

28
June
1983

WITH THIS, THE JUNE 1983 NEWS SHEET, WE ARE ALMOST AT THE 10TH ANNIVERSARY OF BRUCE LEE'S PASSING - IN HIS MEMORY, JOIN US NOW IN SHOWING YOUR RESPECT FOR THIS INCREDIBLE MAN - A GENIUS WHO, IN HIS SHORT LIFESPAN, WAS TO INFLUENCE PEOPLE WORLDWIDE WITH HIS DETERMINATION, PHILOSOPHY AND LIFESTYLE, AND WHO HAS SET THE PATH FOR FREE-THINKING AND SELF-DEVELOPMENT IN ALL FORMS OF THE MARTIAL ARTS - HIS LEGACY REMAINS WITH US FOR ALL TIME, AND IS CARRIED ON THROUGH HIS FANS EVERYWHERE; HAD HE LIVED, THERE WOULD HAVE BEEN NO BOUNDS TO HIS ACHIEVEMENTS. SO PLEASE, REMEMBER...

MEMORIAL FLOWERS - JULY 1983

Thanks to all members who have already sent in their contributions for the floral tribute to Bruce's graveside at Lake View Cemetery, Seattle. But now an URGENT plea to all those who have still not contributed and wish to. So far we have fallen rather short of last year's figure - which is a dreadful disappointment and surprising, especially with this being the 10th Anniversary. So please - send me your donation NOW - BY RETURN OF POST - cheques/postal orders made payable to Pam Hadden ONLY at London. Time is VERY SHORT - and the occasion very important, so please do help.

GRACE'S PRESENT

You will be pleased to know that since my last sheet, we achieved a grand total of £130 for Grace's present. After looking at many, many items in silver, and other things too, I finally purchased what I thought was a personal and suitable gift. This was: A SOLID SILVER (HALLMARKED) JEWELLERY/TRINKET BOX - HINGED TOP, PLAIN SIDED AND WITH THE LID HAVING A PLAIN CENTRAL OVAL FOR A SMALL AMOUNT OF ENGRAVING - PATTERNED EDGING TO THE LID; AND THREE ORNATE LITTLE FEET TO THE UNDERSIDE OF THE BOX.

The cost for this was £115; the balance of the money (plus extra which I will add) will pay for the engraving on the box. The lid will contain the words (in the small oval): "TO GRACE"; the remainder of the engraving will be placed around the sides of the base to say: "From the Bruce Lee Society" on one line, and below: "Bruce - A Son to you - A Sun to us" - (these last words being a shortened version of those suggested by Ian Fawcett, and which I do not think could be replaced by anything which could have had more meaning and yet be so complete - absolutely beautiful). A picture (or pictures) will be taken of the present and produced next time - and I now intend to make arrangements to meet with Grace and present this to her. Pictures will be taken, and her comments duly printed in the very near future. I hope that you are pleased with what has been purchased - I felt that this present was more in keeping with something especially for her to use - she is a super lady who loves all Bruce's fans and is thrilled at how devoted they remain over the years. I know she will be thrilled. Thank you all for your contributions!

PLANT A TREE - CREATE A WOOD
The Woodland Trust

So far, after the March news sheet, I've had £10 towards this project. I'll keep this and wait for further contributions so that I can send the total amount to the trust to have trees commemorated in Bruce's name (remember, £25 gets the Society and Bruce listed in the Commemoration Book and a certificate - £100 gets a certificate, listing in the book AND a plaque displayed in the offices of the trust for all to see permanently!) So not only would we be planting trees in Bruce's name, but also planting them for future generations! I look forward to receiving what you can manage....

GENERAL INFORMATION

Barry Latcham sent in a cutting on Chuck Norris (shown opposite) which was shown in the August 1980 *Film Review*; Chuck speaks well of Bruce, as he always does. But the interviewer states that Chuck choreographed the final battle in *Way of the Dragon* - both Barry and I were curious to know how that remark was made, when it was Bruce in fact who had done the direction on this.

> "I'd not forgotten that Chuck Norris appeared with Bruce Lee in *Return Of The Dragon* and had actually choreographed the climactic karate battle. I asked him what kind of a man Bruce really was.
>
> "Bruce Lee was completely dedicated," Chuck answered sincerely. "He was a dynamic, confident individual and wonderful to work with. Bruce had two goals — to be renowned as a martial artist and to succeed as an actor. I'm happy that he was able to achieve both goals during his short life."

A RETROSPECTIVE LOOK AT BRUCE LEE MANIA & THE KUNG FU CRAZE OF THE 1970S

Also sent in by Barry was the reply he got from Channel 4 on enquiring about the showing of Bruce's films - much the same as other replies received! But they are weakening, I feel....

Still with Channel 4, it would appear that someone there needs a lesson in just who Bruce Lee is (see their letter to Carl Jones). It certainly is news to me that Bruce made *A Touch of Zen* and *The Valiant Ones* - he kept that very hidden over the years!! Yes, Channel 4! We would certainly have been MOST pleased to hear you were showing Bruce Lee films - and such a shame you do not even know the difference! (DO drop them a line on their mistake - I most certainly shall!)

Seen by several members - Kareem Abdul Jabbar in an episode of *Different Strokes* as a school teacher (Yorkshire TV 13th April). (Pam here: Doesn't he now do a TV advert also - anyone else see it and remember what it is?)

Ernest Bow says he read an article in *Real Kung Fu* (Vol. 2 No. 2) on Yasuaki Kurata, where it seems he has met Bruce on many occasions and expressed admiration for the late superstar. Bruce, to Kurata, is: "A perfectionist in the making of action films, who always knew what to do perfectly in posing any movement in a fighting scene." Ernest also gave me the following write-up on *Enter the Dragon* from the *Video At Home* magazine 1982 - "The Legendary Bruce Lee. Unknown in 1971. Two years later an International cult hero - and star of the biggest martial arts epic ever filmed. Whatever 'Star Quality' may be, Bruce Lee had it.." (Warner *Enter the Dragon* Video Number R031009).

Again from Ernest, an article in *Time Out* (December 10-16 1982) on Bruce in *Way of the Dragon* and *Enter the Dragon* by Tony Rayns, refers to him as "spending his teens as a delinquent and child-actor in Cantonese movies, dying glamorously young; has since been endlessly imitated and impersonated, but his narcissism(?), physical self-assurance and film presence have not been equalled. *Way of the Dragon,* which he nominally wrote and directed himself, wasn't intended for export, and most of it, especially the "carry-on" style comedy in some scenes, is primitive film-making by any standards in the world. *Enter the Dragon* was a low-budget re-hash of the island scenes from the Bond movie *You only live Twice.* American Director Robert Clouse gets everything wrong - he doesn't even manage to show Lee's body full-length." (Presumably that last remark that Mr. Rayns did not actually see the whole of *Enter the Dragon* - he certainly could not have seen the beginning fight scene - if that wasn't showing Bruce in full-shot then I certainly do not know what was. - Pam) Anyway, I think that a somewhat "strange" write-up for *Enter the Dragon* - and the "narcissism" remark on Bruce is going just a little too far in any one's judgement. Okay - Bruce was certainly guilty of an ego - what person with any form of talent doesn't to a certain extent? - but to infer that Bruce was so in love with himself as to be 'narcissistic' is absolute rubbish. A tinge of JEALOUSY, perhaps, Mr. Rayns?

Andrew Upton recently wrote to *Sunday Magazine* suggesting they write an article about Bruce for the issue including 20th July - they replied: "Thank you very much for your letter and the information about Bruce Lee. This was very interesting and we will keep it in mind when we plan the July issue. We hope you will continue to enjoy *Sunday Magazine.* Andrew says: "Sounds promising - it really is about time Bruce received the media attention that he so much deserves." (Pam here: Yes, it DID sound promising, so why not write in to support Andrew's request to *Sunday Magazine*? If you need the address, I am sure Andrew will oblige if you send him a stamped and self-addressed envelope to Birkenhead and ask him for this.)

Andrew Staton has great news - *The Silent Flute* is going to be shown on ITV on a station-to-station basis. So it is up to members to write to their local stations and find out when it is going to be shown in their region. (See Granada TV's letter). Do write to the TV people - and if you see it advertised as to be shown in your area, let me know, PLEASE. Thanks.

Also sent in by Andrew - an article written by Clive James in the *Observer* of 20th February 1983. Although I may not agree with all he says in this article, Clive's typical "try-to-get-you-going" phraseology makes fairly interesting reading.

Although I hate to admit it - I've missed every episode of the very popular *Way of the Warrior* series on TV (see article courtesy of Laurie Towey), which has been covering various aspects of the martial arts. I've been so busy trying to catch up on work that I just didn't get around to seeing TV - and could REAL-

---

GRANADA TELEVISION LIMITED

36 Golden Square London W1R 4AH
Telephone 01 734 8080, Telex 27937

Mr Andrew J Staton
Leeds
Yorkshire

23 March 1983

Dear Mr Staton

Thank you for your letter regarding THE SILENT FLUTE. This film is available for scheduling by ITV companies on a station by station basis and will, no doubt, be played by Yorkshire Television in due course. Perhaps you should address your enquiry to them direct.

Yours sincerely

Jeremy Houlton
Deputy Programme Buyer

LY kick myself as I've just found out that Dan Inosanto was on last week's episode on the Filipino art of Eskrima! (To have missed Dan is a disgrace - has anyone got the episodes on video? I'd LOVE to see them - please let me know if you have - Pam.) Such a shame, though, that this series could not have devoted one complete episode to Bruce?? It seems (says member Julian Midgley) that the book from which the series was taken contains a whole chapter on Bruce - so why not the series?

And says Jonathan Westley: "Well done to the BBC for their splendid series, the *Way of the Warrior* (whose theme sounds like the music to *Fist of Fury*). In the book accompanying the programme (which has been named the best martial arts book ever by the book reviewer in *Combat* magazine) there is an article on Bruce which writes strongly in his favour - although Jeet Kune Do is defined as 'the way of the exploding fist.'" Years ago when Kung Fu was the craze the BBC showed a film on Chinese Gung Fu with a man working out on a wooden dummy, a scene from a Kung Fu film and how they made the fake sound effects - I shall write to see if it can be repeated.

On the funnier side, does anyone remember when the Goodies invented "Ekythump" using black pudding as Kali sticks? Jonathan also says he recently bought a book in a second-hand shop called *The Japanese Fighting Arts*, which briefly describes and explains the principles of Karate, Aikido, Kendo and Judo. Under Judo, the instructor says: "It takes a combination of all the combat arts to acquire a complete defence. The ideal would

CLIVE JAMES
Wit of the East

The first of an occasional series on aspects of contemporary culture high and low.

WHEN Oscar Wilde was in his full, brief flower, any witty remark, whoever made it, was immediately attributed to him. Later on the same thing happened to Dorothy Parker. Like the practitioner of no other literary genre, the great wit is assumed to incarnate his gift, leaving room for no one else. While he lives, he is not one among many: he is alone. When he dies, there is a tense wait for the birth of such another.

But what if a great wit were to be born, live out his short life, and pass away unappreciated? By the nature of his talent, it couldn't happen. The news about Bruce Lee was bound to come out sooner or later. Perhaps it was his very fame as a Kung-Fu film star that overshadowed his genius for comedy.

Bruce, before his death at 32, was worshipped world-wide as the young man who brought the Chinese martial arts into the twentieth century and the international arena. With his handsome face distorted by the blood-curdling cry of *kiai*, Bruce would kick the pistol from the hand of any assailant not smart enough to realise that the chief advantage conferred by fire-arms is their ability to kill from a distance. Now Bruce sleeps, but his fame is greater than ever. In Britain there is vast interest in the details of his life, methods and philosophy: yet further evidence for the theory that mass culture is not imposed from above, like defoliant, but grows spontaneously from below, like jungle. On the surface, the British reading public is interested in Salman Rushdie's living-room and the forthcoming novels of Lisa St Aubin de Terán. Deeper down, however, where the sales are in the millions instead of mere thousands, the people who buy books for love are interested in Bruce Lee.

'The Power of Bruce Lee,' 'The Secret Art of Bruce Lee,' 'Bruce Lee's Last Interview'—these are the volumes that sell straight off the van. It is a market in which there is no division between pundit and common reader. All readers are pundits, and collectively they have decided that Bruce Lee was not only the foremost modern philosopher of Kung-Fu, but the most penetrating wit ever to come out of the East.

The forty-third issue of *Kung-Fu Monthly* carries a cover-story entitled THE WIT OF BRUCE LEE, OUTRAGEOUS HUMOURIST! You won't need to be told about this if you are subscribing to *Kung-Fu Monthly* already. It is statistically likely that you are: no precise figures are available, but estimates indicate that Lambeth Palace is almost the only prominent address in Britain not receiving KFM 12 times a year.

If by some slim chance, however, you are not already a subscriber, now is the time to place your order and thus make yourself eligible for a discount on the Bruce Lee one-piece track-suit offer. 'You've waited long enough . . . Yes, KFM has finally located some excellent reproductions of Bruce Lee's amazing YELLOW AND BLACK, ONE-PIECE TRACK SUIT. Snug-fitting and comfortable, we are anticipating an enormous response to our offer for this rare and unique garment.'

It will be seen that KFM's command of grammar is not always exact. But the master himself was perfect in this

respect as in all others. For Bruce, language was just another form of expression, like kicking people in the head. He gazed with narrowed eyes into the deep secrets of human laughter, mastered them, and turned them to explosive use, like his feet which kicked not just 'at' an opponent, but 'through' him, as in *taneshiwari*, or Breaking Techniques. His tongue was like a third foot.

'Which is not to say that his foot was in his mouth. Nevertheless, perhaps because the language of the body was even more international than Chinese or English, he seems to have favoured mime as the vehicle for his outrageous humour. 'Once, whilst being chased by a gang of thugs through the back streets of Hong Kong,' KFM recounts, 'he managed to get a little way ahead—and then pulled off a neat little stunt.

'He leapt onto a nearby roof, stripped down to his under-

Lee: His tongue was like a third foot.

pants and sat meditating in the cross-legged position. When the heavies arrived he screwed up his face and squinted to such a degree that they failed to recognise him. When asked by the police if he'd seen anybody come by in the last few minutes he nodded — and pointed in another direction. They dispappeared in hot pursuit!'

The Bruce Lee one-piece track suit was a functional item of equipment, since if you kick people all day for a living the strain on the crotch of your trousers is immense. (Though not as immense as the strain on the crotch of your opponent's trousers, if, emulating Bruce, you 'execute the roundhouse kick to the exposed groin.')

This question of split trousers became the occasion of outrageous humour for the high-spirited Bruce, known to his disciples as the Little Dragon. 'One day while on the set of " Big Boss," ' says KFM, ' the Little Dragon was talking to support actress, Nora Miao. In a serious voice he asked her, " What do Kung-Fu fighters have more than anyone else ? " Nora, and one or two other people around, decided that it was obviously an important question, so they thought long and hard. Eventually they gave up and asked him what it was. He replied, " More torn trousers" — and promptly produced a pair with an enormous gaping rip in them. It was a good joke, and everyone laughed.'

Like all true wits, Bruce seldom repeated himself. He used an idea a second time only if he could make it more humorous. (In KFM the word is sometimes spelt ' humerous,' probably in homage to Bruce's strongly developed upper arm.) His famous Japanese telephone-engineer disguise is a case in point. 'In "Fist of Fury," who could ever forget Bruce's Japanese telephone-engineer, disguise? Once more, many Western audiences may have missed the absurdity of a Chinese actor disguising himself as a Jap. Out East, it had them rolling in the isles!'

Readers should not jump to the conclusion that 'isles' is a misprint for 'aisles.' Around Hong Kong there are many small islands whose inhabitants, after a long day manufacturing toys for export, ask for nothing more than to watch Bruce Lee bewilder the enemy with a mixture of roundhouse kicks, blows with the extended knuckle and humerous impersonations. But the important point is that the Japanese telephone-engineer disguise is not allowed to rest there. Dining out with friends in Hong Kong, Bruce brings the routine to perfection.

'Eating out,' laughs KFM, 'frequently gave the Little Dragon the opportunity to turn on the hilarity. One day he accidentally knocked out one of his contact lenses. The other people at the table were worried he might flare up at this embarrassing incident. The Master, however, saw the funny side of it and, quickly he donned a pair of heavy, shell-rimmed glasses. At once he seemed transformed into the famed Japanese telephone-engineer disguise—the table rocked with the joke.'

Most of the great wits have had to rehearse their ad libs. Even Byron wrote better than he spoke. Sheridan was the only one who had it to burn. But perhaps Bruce Lee was his equal as a wit, and his superior as a free spirit. To purchase Drury Lane, Sheridan reputedly sold his wife's favours to the Prince of Wales, and ever afterwards was careful not to offend his grand connections. Bruce, secure in the love of an audience larger than Charlie Chaplin's, could be as shocking as he wished.

'One of the best remembered scenes,' says KFM, ' has to be in " Way of the Dragon," where a customer visits the toilet, only to discover the Little Dragon standing on the seat. His knees are bent and he's poised over the basin ready to take his trousers down! Though the impact of the joke was a little lost on the West, for Eastern audiences it was hilarious. Well they could appreciate the difficulties encountered by a Chinesemen brought up with very different toilet facilities to those normally used in our part of the world.'

This shaft of wit might have been lost if someone had not seen it as his duty to interpret Bruce Lee's outrageous humour for an Occidental audience. But someone did. Culture is more robust than we tend to imagine. Creativity arises spontaneously and scholarship along with it. There is something encouraging about the way Bruce Lee's permanent significance as a wit has emerged from his temporary fame as the man who revolutionised the martial arts. The martial arts will be revolutionised again, but the wit of Bruce Lee endures—an important contribution to the world culture which has become a reality in our time.

KUNG FU	JUDO	KENDO	KARATE
Bruce Lee popularised this unarmed combat involving kicking and striking.	Japanese grappling sport. Involves throws arm locks and hold downs.	Mediaeval sword-fighting of the samurai. Fighters use bamboo staves.	Developed in Japan in the 1920s. It involves punching, kicking and striking.

Oriental ways for warriors

SPORTS halls all over Britain echo to the thuds, grunts and gasps of a quarter of a million people practising martial arts.

Fuelled by Emma Peel's leather-clad antics in The Avengers on TV in the Sixties and Bruce Lee's Kung Fu films in the Seventies, Oriental combat has overtaken in popularity the traditional European fighting sports of boxing, wrestling and fencing.

It all began quietly enough 65 years ago when a judo school opened in Pimlico, London.

Today there is a bewildering choice of 73 organisations offering more than 30 Oriental styles of keeping fit through the skills of attack and defence.

The list reads like the menu in a Chinese restaurant. It ranges from Tae-Kwon-Do, Korea's answer to karate and kung fu, to T'ai-Chi-Chuan, meaning supreme ultimate fist, which is practised by old people as a slow, rhythmic exercise.

Others have romantic names — such as Ai-kido, meaning way of harmony — but, in fact, a method of locking an opponent's joints and throwing him.

On Wednesday a

MARTIAL ARTS

BBC-TV series, The Way of the Warrior, examines development of the sports from their origins with a fifth century Buddhist monk in China.

It spread to Japan and the Japanese exported their skills with such vigour that Britain now has 1,000 clubs and thousands of schools teaching judo. Britain has produced three current world champions.

And in karate Britain is the only country to have beaten Japan twice at its own game.

John Goodbody

be a judo man who boxes and does karate for the kicking techniques." Also in the book *Logan's Run* on which the film was based, there is a referral to training in combat: "Each culture has evolved a method of personal combat. From Japan, Ju Jitsu; from China, Kempo and Karate; from France, Sarate; from Greece, boxing and wrestling. The finest points from each art were combined." Jonathan asks: "So do you think they were getting a little idea of Jeet Kune Do?" (It would certainly seem that the writer was, like Bruce, a free-thinker and practitioner of a more personalised and less restricting form of art - Pam).

On the subject of videos - Carl Jones wrote to Rank Video Library about the censoring of Bruce's films - and it seems, judging by their letter, that the problem still lies with the censors direct in the material they supply to Rank's for production. I can understand Rank's point - if they do not have the complete material to start, it is impossible to give a really satisfactory product.

John Maidment, in Canada, who runs the Filipino Martial Arts Association (see contact under "Martial Arts Addresses" section) says the club is holding a memorial tribute to Bruce on 16th July at a local shopping mall, featuring three live performances of Kali, Wing Chun, Lee Jun Fan and

A RETROSPECTIVE LOOK AT BRUCE LEE MANIA & THE KUNG FU CRAZE OF THE 1970S

kickboxing, plus continuous displays of posters/books/magazines on Bruce and slide/ audio tape presentations and tapes of Bruce's films, plus *The Warrior Within*. They are also dedicating all demonstrations given in July/ August to Bruce's memory, including demos on 27th/28th July and an annual summer tour of the province of Newfoundland (about 500 miles away to their furthest demo.) Super stuff, John - I only wish that all Society members could join in with you there. (Which puts us somewhat to shame - what happened to our convention, *Kung Fu Monthly*? Let me have the Society kitty and see what I can do - certainly something, at least. Any of you bother to WRITE to *KFM* recently - OR ARE YOU GOING TO LEAVE IT COMPLETELY FOR ME TO KEEP CHASING? DROP A LINE TO: COLIN JAMES, *Kung Fu Monthly*, 14, RATHBONE PLACE, LONDON, WIP 1DE, ENGLAND - TELL HIM YOU WANT A CONVENTION - OR A FILM SHOW - SOON!

Kevin Hobbs wrote to Golden Harvest in London to ask if they had any outtakes from Bruce's films (clippings where the scenes went wrong). Their reply - in the negative - is shown here, so that seems to answer THAT little question. Or does it? I seem to remember another member writing to me stating that GOLDEN HARVEST in Hong Kong had said (on the enquiry as to whether there was any footage on Bruce still available in the "vaults") that "regrettably no - there was no more footage available ONLY FILM WHERE THE SCENES HAD GONE WRONG." (If that member reads this - please confirm back to me again, would you?) It would appear that Golden Harvest - as well as myself! - get confused sometimes.

Last news sheet, Jonathan Westley - a keen disco dancer - said he was going to wear his *Game of Death* tracksuit in a dance competition, and I asked him to let me know how it went. "Well," he says "I did not do so well in the freestyle - I had one recall in the partner dances and the team I was in with four girls (trust you, Jonathan! - Pam) came fourth in our age group. I did not (as originally intended) use my nunchakus in the dancing in case I hit someone accidentally but I did use them in a recent disco exam for my second Gold Bar and danced to *Dragon Power* with the nunchaku sounds. I got a 'Highly Commended' from a very strict examiner who just happens to do karate so he might have appreciated the idea. I also got my silver in Latin dancing and am experimenting to do the 'Sticking Hands' from Wing Chun and putting it with the Cha-Cha (which Bruce did once, much to the annoyance of Master Yip Man!) Anyhow, I enjoy my training (much helped by the weight- training schedule in the last news sheet) and am coming up with new ideas!"

Well - I'll say one thing for Jonathan - he's not lacking in imagination; what about a flying sidekick thrown in next time? Or the somersault which Bruce did during the tournament in *Enter the Dragon* against O'Hara? (Actually, the somersault I believe is one of the major moves in the new dance craze in America with the pavement dancers - it seems very much based on martial arts' techniques - very martial arts "Orientated"!! (There's a joke there, somewhere!)

The condensed list of Bruce Lee sayings (the first eight appeared in the last sheet) from Paul Corrigan were popular - and as promised, the next batch are printed here. (Thanks again, Paul).

I've heard that the Albert Goldman book on Bruce (he did the very controversial one on Elvis after his death) is coming along. Exactly what the content, or how much questionable material is involved - seems to be unknown at this stage, however, sources have it that the usual type of Goldman "dirt" will be thrown around. (Anyone finding any cuttings or seeing anything on the release of this book, please let me know). I'll keep you up-to-date on this as I hear.

Another little snippet from Laurie Towey the ABC Sheffield (Sunny Film Society) presented an all-night martial arts spectacular on third April - *An Eye for an Eye* (Chuck), *Tower of Death* (Bruce), *Martial Club* - (voted best Kung Fu Film 1981), *Thundering Mantis*. (Thanks for the info, Laurie.)

9. Nobody is born with knowledge.

10. Patience is not passive, on the contrary it is concentrated strength.

11. If you love life, don't waste time, for time is what life is made up of.

12. To strive actively to achieve some goal gives your life meaning and substance.

13. Our main business is not to see what lies dimly at a distance, but to do what lies clearly at hand.

14. If you make an ass of yourself, there will always be someone ready to ride on you.

15. Knowledge will give you power, but character respect.

16. If you think a thing is impossible, you'll make it impossible.

17. Mistakes are always forgivable, if one has the courage to admit them.

John Aspinall, who moved to Australia, has sent me a very interesting article from *People Magazine* dated 30th May 1983. Purported to be about one of Bruce's "closest friends," William Cheung, it states that Cheung believes Bruce was murdered, and in a film he is co-producing, he is prepared to "name names." "I know how Bruce died and I know what caused his death - and who was behind it." If you want to know what else he has to say - turn to the separate sheet enclosed and read on I pass no comment. But I WOULD like yours.

A RETROSPECTIVE LOOK AT BRUCE LEE MANIA & THE KUNG FU CRAZE OF THE 1970S

Bruce Lee, right, wipes out a baddie in one of his films. He sometimes believed he was as invulnerable as the characters he played.

THE MURDER OF BRUCE LEE

Bill Cheung fighting to get the real story of his friend Bruce Lee's death on to the screen. He believes Lee (right) met a sinister end at odds with the death by misadventure finding of the Hong Kong inquest.

TEN YEARS after his sensational death in Hong Kong, adopted city of his celluloid dreams, the memory of Bruce Lee is still as vibrant as a kung fu kick from the indestructible character he played in a string of violent cult movies.

The golden idol of the martial arts continues to inspire adoration and posthumous imitation. And beyond the grave continues speculation that Bruce Lee, nicknamed the Little Dragon, met a sinister end at odds with the "death by misadventure" finding of an inquest.

The whole Bruce Lee saga is being resurrected by one of his closest friends. William Cheung, himself an acclaimed kung fu exponent and maths-economics graduate of the Australian National University, is convinced Lee was murdered.

"I know how Bruce died and I know what caused his death and I know who was behind it," Cheung states boldly. He is working these notions into a feature film which, though fictional, is patently based on his murder theory and the life of Bruce Lee.

"Fiction may sometimes reveal truths not possible in any other way. Those who look beneath the surface may find the answer to the riddle of Bruce Lee's tragic death," says Cheung, the co-scriptwriter on the movie. If the script sticks to the synopsis, fans of Bruce Lee and kung fu are in for triple-X lashings of violence, spectacular fights, steamy love

'I know how Bruce died — and who killed him'

scenes, and a Chinese James Bond who meets the dastardly end that Cheung imagines of his friend.

The similarities between this fictional character and martial artist Lee are eerie. In Cheung's treatment, the film becomes a carbon copy of Bruce Lee's death.

Lee died on July 20, 1973, in the apartment of his mistress, Betty Ting Pei. He was 32, wealthy, apparently healthy, in his acting prime after the success of five films like Enter The Dragon, produced by Raymond Chow's Golden Harvest Productions.

Two months earlier, he had been rushed to hospital after an attack of convulsions. Tests showed a swelling of the brain which doctors treated with the drug manitol.

Recovered, Lee rang Cheung four days before his death to tell him he had reached some decisions about his career which were going to upset a lot of people. He would say more when he met up with Bill in Australia en route to America.

Lee good naturedly challenged Cheung to a kung fu contest in Australia, and before hanging up spoke keenly of meeting the Aussie James Bond, George Lazenby, for dinner at Hong Kong's Miramar Hotel.

Lee didn't make the dinner date. He had gone to bed that afternoon in Betty's flat, complaining of pounding headaches for which he took aspirin before lapsing into a coma.

Hong Kong, which could be described as five million people treading a rumour mill, refused to believe its hero hadn't been done in. Black theories flourished ... it was the triads, the ruthless Chinese mafia; it was kung fu traditionalists angered by Lee's disregard for their shibboleths (once he said caustically that black belts were only good for holding pants up); some even contended that he faked his own death.

The September inquest recorded nothing so fanciful. Dr Robert Teare, professor of forensic medicine at London University and a veteran of 90,000 autopsies, concluded that Lee died from an acute cerebral oedema (fluid discharge) caused by hypersensitivity to aspirin — death by misadventure.

Partly correct, Cheung reckons. He insists that Lee was given a drug that doctors had forbidden because of fatal allergic results. And that the fatal dose was deliberately induced.

He has amassed an impressive catalogue of evidence to support his contention. After gumshoeing around Hong Kong on and off after Bruce's death, a publisher urged him to write a book that would "leave nothing out". The book came out, all right — full of gaps.

The pages about his investigations were mysteriously lost or stolen from the publisher. These missing sections pinpointed Cheung's murder suspects. Undeterred, he kept playing Chinese detective. In Hong Kong, people

'He seemed to realise that someone was out to get him'

acting for an influential film investor tried to bribe him with a ritzy flat and a girl on tap if he'd lay off. A few days later he was attacked in an alley.

"It was a hint to silence me," Cheung maintains. "If I ever had any doubts about my suspicions they were quickly dispelled by these tactics."

He is adamant that the villainous triads did not kill Lee. "They regarded him as a sort of hero and as long as he said nothing and left them alone he was in no danger from them. They even laid off pressuring a girlfriend of his who owed them thousands for gambling debts

"Actually, Bruce told me he had a warning note slipped into his pocket by triads, during our last phone conversation. I could tell from his voice that he was anxious for his safety."

Cheung said the only other person he had ever mentioned this phone call to was Bruce's mother Grace Lee in San Francisco. "Even now I can't tell you everything. But it was clear he was in trouble and he seemed to realise that someone was out to get him."

Why? Money, Cheung suggests strongly. Bruce had been offered to name his own price to make movies in the US instead of Hong Kong.

"You must understand that Bruce's change of plans and that American trip meant some people would have been ruined if he'd lived. Millions of dollars were involved."

Grace Lee began to share Cheung's suspicions after a delay of more than two weeks in shipping Bruce's body to the US. Cheung says the delay was deliberate, to eliminate all traces of the drug that killed him.

"I also discovered that the girl who owed the triad gambling syndicate money had the debt paid by a mystery benefactor within 24 hours of Bruce's death. I also know she was being paid to inform on him."

The tenacious Bill Cheung, who used to teach unarmed combat to US Pacific Fleet personnel before setting up his Melbourne kung fu school, survived too many vicious street brawls with Bruce to back away this late in the day. He plans to finish the movie by next year. By why has he waited until now?

"Let's just say that a certain, once very powerful and wealthy individual is no longer in circulation," he said with typical oriental inscrutability.

Courtesy of John Bastow and Shaun Boland, the following from *Combat* magazine "Newsline":

> Kung Fu - Wing Chun Master Simon Lau is to feature in an anatomy programme soon to be screened on Channel 4. The programme deals with the way the body's parts function and Simon's input covers the use of muscles and their operation. Much of the format is top secret but we can tell you that it will be spectacular in the extreme." The programme producers have adopted a most unusual approach and one which is sure to appeal to the Bruce Lee fans and martial-artists in the audience. Simon also features large in the forthcoming BBC series dealing with the origin of the martial arts (*Way of the Warrior* already mentioned - Pam). After reviewing all the major schools in Hong Kong and Taiwan, the BBC researchers returned to North London having decided that the best Kung Fu is to be found there of all places!
>
> Also on the box is Lau Gar Jeremy Yau, who's recent documentary on Central TV received wide acclaim. It certainly appears as though telly is waking up to the martial arts and there are plans to produce a definitive self-defence series in the pipeline. The producer responsible for the project is currently visiting martial arts clubs of all types in order to evaluate first-hand the various self-defence options available. John also mentioned that his close friend, Asif Abbas, was a student of Praying Mantis Kung Fu under David Brown, a Ju-Jitsu expert, and Asif proved its superiority over John's Shotokan Karate in several brief "encounters" at school. John says he has already studied a combination of martial arts with Mr. Brown, and feels he will now continue under him.

(Pam here: I've got several members who study Shotokan Karate and who are excellent at this. Again, we are back to Bruce's ideals, that not every style or move is suitable to everyone else, so what might bring the best out for one may be restricting for another person).

And Shaun says: "Congratulations should go out to the Great Britain Karate Team for winning the World Championships, proving that British martial artists are a force to be reckoned with. Also, a point to note is that Karate and Taekwondo are on the agenda for the next Olympics. With all this publicity and more to come, people will delve back into the roots and along the line they will come across Bruce Lee!! Well, let them judge for themselves, but I advise you that within the next few years you'll have to open a new Bruce Lee Society for the, '...*and I thought Bruce Lee was only a movie star-type people.*'" (Shaun - believe me, I am getting them already! - Pam)

FILM POLL

Barry Latcham says we ought to have a film poll to see which is the most popular of Bruce's films - and as I am so busy, he has offered to run this. So - what's your most favourite of his films? Just drop a postcard showing your preference for *Enter the Dragon, Fist of Fury, Big Boss, Way of the Dragon, Game of Death* in the order 1 to 5. Post this to Barry at Co. Durham, (PLEASE - DO NOT SEND DIRECT TO PAM) with a brief, and I do mean BRIEF!, reason why you picked your first choice. He wants the cards by the end of July so he can sort them out before I write my September news sheet. This is NOT a competition - just a poll. Personally, I had great difficulty in voting for my favourite Bruce movie, but Barry is making me give my vote too, so I'll have to get a decision very soon! Even Society presidents cannot opt out of this one!

VIDEO INFORMATION

Py Tang, our member who runs a video club, wants me to tell you he now has the four episodes of *Longstreet* containing Bruce - "Way of the Intercepting Fist" (training with Longstreet - James Franciscus - most of the way), "Spell Legacy Like Death" (training at the beginning), "Wednesday's Child" (real action at the end - Lee vs knife man) and "I See Said The Blind Man" (Lee remains quiet). Peter says each episode plays about 45 minutes - so all four episodes go very nicely onto a three-hour cassette. Write to him direct at Rochdale for further details and price.

And Andrew Upton says he recently bought the uncensored *Way of the Dragon* from Py Tang "to see the incredible nunchaku scene it was worth every single penny. I thoroughly recommend it. My only criticism was that it seems to be a normal English copy and a foreign (probably Dutch) copy edited in for the fight scenes." (Pam here: Well, as long as the copy is good, and all the fights are there in entirety, I reckon all members would be happy to see it no matter whether is was made up of 20 different film-parts!!)

Iain Leslie says that Jackie Chan's *Big Brawl* is now released by Guild Home Video - it is entertaining, better than many other Kung Fu films flooding the market.

Wilson McKennan has been told by Rank Video that *The Silent Flute* was to be released at the end of May 1983.

ROBERT LEE LP/BACK ISSUE NEWS SHEETS

If you are a new member and have not yet got your copy of the superb LP by Bruce's brother Robert - which is a tribute to the Little Dragon and called *Ballad of Bruce Lee* - then drop me a line on this; the cost of the record is £4 plus postage - and I can tell you the postage cost when you write. All records are personally signed by Robert on the front cover - that in itself is a fantastic rarity without the beautifully-sung LP - so don't hesitate, get those pens moving!

Also available - large black and white photograph of Bruce doing a leap over Robert's head - also signed by Robert! Cost £1 plus postage - drop me a line. And not forgetting - all copies of Society news sheets are still here if you want them - write to me giving details of which ones you require and I'll tell you cost plus postage. (Remember - do enclose a stamped and self addressed envelope for a reply).

GREEN HORNET (BLACK BEAUTY) CAR

Further to the last news sheet, just to tell you that Andrew Staton has given me the address from where you can now obtain this VERY RARE model car from the *Green Hornet* series. As I have mentioned before, this car has been off the market for several years, and is indeed an opportunity NOT to be missed by any Bruce Lee fan - please write to: Mr. D. Rankin, London. The cost is £15 - but initially he needs to know how many people want them before he goes abroad to purchase them. Drop him a line DIRECT before sending any money.

For those martial artists living in and around Leeds, Andrew sends the following martial arts addresses: (more needed by Pam, please, so send them in).

Wing Chun School - original Yip Man style (Sifu was taught by Sam Kwok, who learned from Yip Chun, son of Yip Man (and we all know who he taught!!) Address: Yip Chun Martial Arts Association, St. George's Activity Centre, Great George Street, Leeds 1. Wing Chun Kung Fu - Fast, Effective Chinese Self Defence System. Thursdays: 7pm to 9pm.

John Maidment, whose letter I printed last news sheet wants any members/fans of Bruce to write to his Association in Canada - he and his pupils in the school he runs would be delighted to hear from you. Here's the address: Filipino Martial Arts Association, P.O. Box 848, Mount Pearl, Newfoundland, Canada AlN 3C8.

HELP WITH ADDRESSES

James Blore, Nottingham wants addresses of ANY Kung Fu classes in the Nottingham area - mainly of the Shaolin Kung Fu or Ju Jitsu styles.

Kevin Leayy, Hitchin wishes to know of any Kung Fu Clubs in and around the Stevenage, Hitchin or Letchworthareas.

Drop them a line direct - and thanks!

LETTERS

Dear Pam,

Reading through KFM every now and again, watching what's happening with the Society and videos of Bruce etc., I've recently been reminded what a positive influence Bruce has been on my life, and I'm also very aware of the fact that he has been dead for almost ten years and the interest in him goes on, more people becoming fans through videos and the local re-screening of the The Green Hornet. *A word or two about this series - this has now ended and I'm not holding out much hope for a further series. Sunday mornings at 9.30 does not attract a large audience. The programmes themselves are fairly cheap and badly acted, filled with bit-part actors never seen again. Bruce and his part at the end where he manages to get a kick or two in are definitely the best parts of the entire programme.*

Some plots are original, but defies belief as it all takes place in a movie backlot atmosphere. Organised crime in the series only happens in this claustrophobic, edge-of-the-desert town. One is also treated to lots of warehouse/ tiny airport/people's front yards (large yards, though!) scenes. Some of my friends have videoed episodes, and may be willing to swap or sell, if you think this is a good idea.

Martin Hughes

I'm sure that there are members who'd be very glad to obtain copies of these episodes, Martin - and if so, I suggest they drop me a SAE with a note enquiring about this. I'll then collect together and pass on to you. And like yourself (and other fans) it would seem that Yorkshire TV are in agreement

about the only good thing in the series being Bruce - (see their letter courtesy of Andrew Staton). They are also against the violence, which they take more seriously than the 'Batman' series; Okay - maybe they are right there - but there are STILL more violent things being shown on TV - for children and at children's viewing time - than any Bruce series OR film - yet they (the TV people) have so far (and I do state "So far"!) not relented and shown a Bruce film; so stupid!

> 15th December 1982
>
> Andrew J. Staton, Esq.,
> Leeds
>
> **YORKSHIRE TELEVISION**
>
> Dear Mr Staton,
>
> Thank you for your most persuasive letter about 'The Green Hornet'.
>
> It is a series I have viewed twice and which simply is not what could be called remarkably good. If it did not have Bruce Lee in it, the series would, I am sure, have been long forgotten. The problem quite simply seems to lie in the amount of violence within each programme which is on a more serious level than the clashes in 'Batman'. This brings forth the consideration about suitability for children and then frankly whether, if shown at a later time, the series would be too childish for adults.
>
> We have, therefore, thought a great deal following previous requests. I can only look at the reaction in other areas and take another long look at our attitude towards the series although at the present time I do not believe our view will radically change.
>
> Thank you for writing. Sorry the reply could not be more encouraging.
>
> Yours sincerely
>
> Ken Bellini
> Head of Programme Purchasing

Dear Pam,

With it being 10 years now since Bruce's death, I still feel very close to the man. Over the past 18 months Bruce has been a source of strength and encouragement to me, and although he is gone his spirit lives deep within us and is renewed with each new person who sees his ideas. So I would be happy to donate to Bruce's flowers and enclose a cheque. I've also enclosed a Yin/Yang brooch for you - it changes colour with the temperature. It is unique. I sent one to Selina Scott of Breakfast Time *and received a lovely photo and "Thank you" card saying she will be wearing it. (It reminded me of the* Breakfast Time *symbol of the sun). If any Society members want one, please contact me enclosing a stamped and self-addressed envelope and £2.50 and I will send them one.*

Jonathan Westley - Colchester

Jonathan, I was DELIGHTED with the brooch - and I can confirm to other members that the same day I got it I was fascinated, and just sat firstly holding it in my hands, then blowing on it, then putting in different places - I even stuck my tongue out and placed it on that!! (Well, we've all got funny habits!) And the colours ranged from black/deep blue; black/pink; black/turquoise; deep blue/green; light/dark green, and many, many more - it's smashing! A little smaller than the Society brooch, it contains a safety clip. Very neat and can be worn by anyone anytime - in fact, I've worn it every day since! I'm sure, like me, anyone getting one will be delighted. Make nice presents, too!

Dear Pam,

Remember in one of my last letters I said I'd seen Way of the Dragon *at the cinema with the double-nunchaku scene? Well, last week I rented* Way of the Dragon *on Star video, and was disgusted that the alley scene was cut out completely and other segments. It's ridiculous to cut videos - after all, they are for home viewing anyway, and the worst of it was I had some mates around and kept telling them to watch for this fantastic scene! And then they cut the flaming thing out. It was disgusting!*

John Aspinall in Australia

I can understand not only your frustration but your embarrassment at having built this up to your friends and then found it missing. It amazes me that films such as Bruce's are cut, yet pornographic films can be bought by anyone anywhere anytime. Freedom of choice? Only if the choice is left to the censors or other "authorised" bodies.

Dear Pam,

I wonder how many people can honestly say their lives have been greatly changed by someone they've never met? My life has been influenced by Bruce over nine years now - as I matured I learnt to respect his ability, dedication - and that throughout life there will obviously be obstacles - but if you want to succeed dedication and perseverance are the keys. Bruce left a message to us all - however it is interpreted does not matter as long as your path through life is made much easier and successful. I cannot really tell you why I wrote this - I just picked up my pen and wrote. One must have faith in oneself, say what you think, dare for success. Bruce did - that is why he succeeded in life.

Shaun Boland

And on that note, members - with the words of Shaun and Jonathan - I will close the letters section; We have all been affected by Bruce - we must all make of ourselves what we can. On this, the 10th anniversary of his passing - "Peace, Bruce." Your fans are with you always.

FOREIGN FAN CLUBS

Member Aluizio de Oliveira Jr. has written asking that I print the address of his Club in Brazil - it is: The Bruce Lee Association, Caixa Postal 496, 38100-Uberaba-MG, BRAZIL. (They, like ourselves, aim to promote the work, art and life of Bruce and to keep contact with Bruce Lee fans worldwide - please drop him a line).

PEN PALS

- Dawn McCrae, Glasgow wants pen pals anywhere.
- Ernest Bow, Basingstoke wants American pals (come on, America, give them some names!!)

BRUCE'S BOOK LIST
(PART V)

More book titles from Bruce's vast collection:

Judo: Appendix Aikido - Kenji Tomiki (1961)
The Complete Seven Katas of Judo - Kawaishi (1957)
The Handbook of Judo - Lebell/Coughran (1962)
Judo - Bowen, Hodkinson (1963)
Judo - M. Feldenkrais (1958)

Judo - Sadaki Nakatayashi (1965)
Contest Judo - C. Yerkow (1961)
Judo Throws: Counters - E. Dominy (1956)
Modern Judo (Complete Manual) - C. Yerkow (1943)
Judo - E. J. Harrison (1952)
Judo - E. Dominy (1958)

More next time - and thanks for the letters of appreciation for this list which was made available to me by Bruce's friend and fellow-martial artist Dan Inosanto, when I was in Los Angeles visiting his home and one of his academies.

MEMORY

Having given Bruce's definitions of willpower, emotion, reason and imagination, we now go on to his views on "Memory": "RECOGNIZING THE VALUE OF

AN ALERT MEMORY, I WILL ENCOURAGE MINE TO BECOME ALERT BY TAKING CARE TO IMPRESS IT CLEARLY WITH ALL THOUGHTS I WISH TO RECALL, AND BY ASSOCIATING THOSE THOUGHTS WITH RELATED SUBJECTS WHICH I MAY CALL TO MIND FREQUENTLY."
Next time - "Subconscious Mind."

RENEWALS

The following members fall due to renew from now until the end of August: 3354-3394 (second yr); 3219-3270 (third); 2973-3056 (fourth); 2698-273 (fifth); 2303-2349 (sixth); 2022-2084 (seventh).

SWOP SHOP

- Mr. M. Tsang, Belfast has for sale/swap: *Enter the Dragon* double-LP, *Fist* soundtrack LP, *Game of Death* soundtrack LP, *Dragon Sounds Special* LP, Bruce Lee *Game of Death* colour, silent film, *Enter the Dragon* colour, sound 8mm projector. Send SAE for details of prices, give your swap offers.
- Jim Storey Jr., Belfast has for sale: Bruce Lee Scrapbook, *Popster* magazines. Nos. 23, 26, *Deadly Hands of Kung Fu* No. 14 on Bruce Lee, *Life and Tragic Death of Bruce Lee, Legend of Bruce Lee* by Alex Block.
- Lee O'Neill, Omagh urgently needs (please help) *KFMs* 1, 2, 14, 31, 32, 45.
- Mark Salter, Sheffield has for sale/swap: two copies (one signed by Grace Lee) of *Untold Story*, Dan Inosanto picture (autographed), *KFM. Scrapbooks* 1, 2, 12" *Dragon Power* single (new), *Who Killed Bruce Lee?, Bruce Lee In Action, Game of Death Special Collectors' Edition, Enter the Dragon* Japanese double-LP, *Bruce Lee Game of Death, Unbeatable Bruce Lee, Secret Art, Power of Bruce Lee, Life and Tragic Death of Bruce Lee, The Man Only I Knew, Enter the Dragon* paperback, *Beginners' Guide to Kung Fu, Circle of Iron* paperback (*Silent Flute*), *Bruce Lee 1940-73* hardback, *King of Kung Fu, Best of Bruce Lee No. 2, My Martial Arts Training Guide to JKD, Game of Death* press release, *Kung Fu Cinema of Vengeance, Unknown in Martial Arts Learning, Bruce Lee in Game of Death, Bruce Lee Revenges, Studies in JKD, Privacy & Anecdotes, Secrets of JKD & Kung Fu, Nunchakus in Action, Fighting Spirit, Reminiscences of Bruce Lee, Game of Death Extract Edition, Immortal Dragon, Combat, Superstar from Hong Kong, Memorial Special, Bruce Lee in Big Boss, Warrior from Shaolin, Martial Arts Phenomenon, Mystery of Bruce Lee, Last Interview* cassette, all *KFMs*, other martial arts magazines i.e. *Black Belt, Fighters Monthly*, etc., Michael England, Oldham wants: Rare items on Bruce - please send details, price.
- Kamiljit Khaira, Birmingham ants: *KFMs* 1, 2, 12, 13, 14, 31, 32, 33, *Beginners Guide to Kung Fu, Book of Kung Fu, Game of Death* book.
- Michael Clark, Alfreton has for sale: *Enter the Dragon* uncensored 400ft 8mm 20min film - £11 inc. p&p - write to him first before sending money, he asks.
- Carl Jones, St. Helens has for sale/swap for Bruce Lee, Jackie Chan, Jimmy Wang Yu videos VHS OR back issues of *Martial Arts Movies* (uncrossed postal orders only if cash) - Japanese material: *Roadshow* July '78 (*Game of Death* issue) - £1.50, *Roadshow* Sept '79 (sixth anniversary of Bruce Lee's death) £3 + £1.50 p&p, *Motion Picture Times (Game of Death)* April '78) £3 + £1 p&p, *Young*

Idol Now (rare) £3 + £1 p&p, *Story of Chinese Gods* (Lee cartoon movie magazine - £1 + 50p p&p, *Fist of Fury* pressbook photocopy - £1 + 50p p&p, cuttings pack of photocopies, ads, stickers, stationery, pencil box etc. - £2 + 50p p&p, *Game of Death* cinema poster £2 + 50p p&p, Rare Bruce Lee *Way of the Dragon* poster - £1 + 50p p&p, *Star Cinema* pamphlet (pictures + B&W poster - £1 + £50p p&p. Other material - *JKD* magazines 1-12 - 50p + 50p p&p, *JKD Luxury Magazines* - £1+ 50p p&p, *Bruce Lee Untold Story* £1 + 50p p&p, *KFM* 3 - £1.25, *KFM* 6 - 75p, *Dragon* Nos. 2, 4 - £1.25 each, *Popster* No. 23 £1.25, *Kung Fu Annual* (Carradine & Lee) - £2 + 50p p&p.

- Julian Midgley, Birmingham has for sale: *Life & Tragic Death* £1.50, *Power of Bruce Lee* £1, *KFM Game of Death* £1, *Bruce Lee Stars in Game of Death* poster £1, *Secret Art* hardback £2, *Untold Story* £1, *Martial Arts Guide to JKD* £4, *Unbeatable Bruce Lee* £1, *Who Killed Bruce Lee*? £1.50.
- Kevin Hobbs, Leominster has for sale: 8mm colour, German sound films *Fist of Fury, Big Boss* - 4x400ft reels each film.

OKAY, FOLKS - I'm going over to the separate sheet enclosed to finish up with my final bits and pieces - BUT REMEMBER - MEMORIAL FLOWERS, WOODLAND TRUST AND WRITE TO CHANNEL 4 - PLEASE! Pam

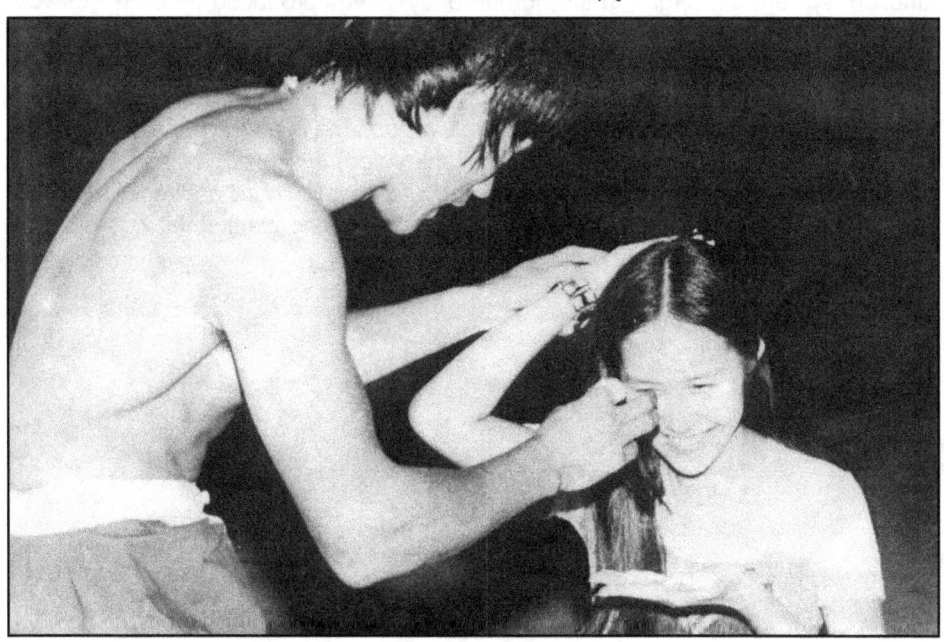

EDITOR'S NOTES

The Kareem Abdul-Jabbar adverts mentioned by Pam could have been several. Around that time, he was advertising, amongst other, "Atari" and "Nestle Crunch."

As stated earlier in the book, Albert Goldman didn't release

a book about Bruce Lee, instead writing a two-part article for *Penthouse* magazine which was published in January and February of 1983.

William Cheung, born October 1940 in Kowloon, Hong Kong is a Wing Chun practitioner and the current grandmaster of his Wing Chun lineage, Traditional Wing Chun or TWC. After witnessing the legendary Ip Man defeat a challenger, Cheung became his student, living with his master for three years before leaving Hong Kong. Whilst living with Ip Man, Cheung introduced his friend of six years, a 15 year old boy by the name of Bruce Lee to Ip Man to also become a student. Cheung and Lee both became involved in street fights but after seriously wounding a Triad leader in 1957, Cheung and his family emigrated to Australia, where in 1973, he began to teach Traditional Wing Chun professionally in Melbourne. Two years after  Cheung moved to Australia, Bruce Lee was sent to the the United States by his father Lee Hoi Chuen for the same reason. William Cheung resides in Victoria, Australia today.

The series that Simon Lam was taking part in was called *The Living Body* and was a 26-part series running from 1984 and covering every major function, system and organ in the human body. It was produced by Goldcrest Films and Television and was released on VHS in 1985, followed by Laserdisc some years later.

Py Tang supplied tapes of varying quality during the 1980s. In issue 28 of the newsletters, it's noted that their *Way of the Dragon* tape is an English version of the film (most probably the 1982 X certified Rank video) which appeared to have the double- nunchakus scene edited in from a Dutch copy. There are reports that Py Tang would also edit in footage from Super 8 to "fill in the blanks" if it was needed, resulting in noticeable quality drops when they did so.

29
September
1983

HI MEMBERS! WELCOME TO THE START OF THE SOCIETY'S 8TH YEAR! YOU ALL KNEW THAT I WAS GOING TO LOS ANGELES TO PRESENT GRACE LEE, BRUCE'S MOTHER, WITH THE GIFT FROM THE SOCIETY MEMBERS, AND NOW I SHALL TELL YOU ABOUT THAT BUT FIRST WOULD LIKE TO DRAW YOUR ATTENTION TO THE 'SPECIAL ITEMS' HEADING LATER, AS I MANAGED TO BRING BACK A VERY LIMITED SUPPLY OF RARE ITEMS, SO OFF WE GO...

LOS ANGELES 1983 - OUR GIFT TO GRACE

As anyone preparing for a trip knows, chaos reigns prior to departure - and with myself, there was no exception. The lovely silver jewel box purchased by the Society for Grace, neatly wrapped in cloth and inside its box, was safely tucked inside my bag. I ran through my check-list of things to do and take - which of course as always was incomplete. When satisfied that I had everything necessary, I set off for the airport and, with plenty of time to spare checked-in and boarded my flight to L.A.

I'd already telephoned ahead and found to my delight that not only was Grace at home, but that Robert, Bruce's singing/acting brother was currently staying with her during a period away from Hong Kong. Robert, being the nice guy that he is, offered to meet me at Los Angeles airport, and on arrival there, knowing just what Customs Control in that area of the world is like and how long it can take to get through, made sure I was one of the first from the plane and down into the Passenger Arrivals section. At Customs, I declared the gift and was cleared, and, after tripping over someone's suitcase and nearly pushing some unsuspecting gent onto the baggage conveyor belt, and then getting bowled over by some child playing racing cars with a trolley, I expected further trouble collecting my case afterwards, but none occurred, so was very delighted to find that I was out into the main building in under 15 minutes (which for L.A. MUST be a record!) And imagine just how I felt to see not only Robert waiting for me (an experience which every lady should have!) but to find that Grace too was with him. They are such terrific people, and when you consider that they had travelled many miles to the airport to meet me, and are very busy people, you can understand just how nice they are and how welcome I was made to feel.

After our preliminary chats, we set off in Robert's car for Arcadia - a suburb in L.A. where Grace and Robert live. The journey takes about an hour, and during the trip Robert pointed out various sights, and also mentioned that L.A. was in deep preparation for the Olympic Games which are to be held there in 1984 - and the racing track near to their home will be a hive of activity as this is where the races etc. will be run. The airport itself, which has been in a state of half-erected and bubble-shaped buildings over the last four years that I can remember, is now moving fast ahead with construction to facilitate the amount of people who will pass through this busy airport during the Olympics. And hotels are "sprucing-up" in readiness for the business they will be afforded during that time. During our drive, we stopped off to meet a good doctor friend of Robert and Grace, Dave, who treated Grace when she had a fall and cut her head a little while back, which required stitches. She is quite well now, and since that time, Robert, Grace and Dave have remained firm friends.

Grace, holding box, with Robert and Pam

We made arrangements to meet up for dinner, and then set off to get me booked into the Ramada Inn Hotel about 10 minutes walk from the Lee house. Once I had settled myself in, we all went over to Grace's home, and it was then that I told her that the Society members had bought her a present which I had with me. Robert, of course, already knew about this before I went to L.A., but it was a great surprise to Grace: I took the blue box containing the silver jewellery box from my bag, and said: "Grace, this is from the Society members, we wanted it to be something personal for yourself, but in memory of Bruce. We hope you like it - it comes with all our love." I think the only way I can describe Grace's reaction when she opened the box was - she was absolutely delighted! She read the words: "To Grace - from the Bruce Lee Society, London - Bruce: A Son to you - A Sun to us" - and was quite overcome, and said that the box was "Ab-

Grace, Robert and Pam outside Grace's home

solutely beautiful," and added; "It is a lovely gift - and I shall always treasure it; it will always be on display in my home. Please - thank everyone for thinking of me in this way." We took some photos, and you can see a picture of Grace, Robert and I where she is holding the box. You can also see a picture of the box close-up - it really is quite lovely, and it seemed that it was just the right present! Robert too was delighted - he is, obviously, very close to Grace, and it pleased him  that we had remembered her in this way. Anyway, she is a super lady, and I hope it gives her much pleasure. It certainly gave us pleasure to present it to her, I know.

Robert is currently in the process of opening a Cocktail Lounge in Little Tokyo, Los Angeles - around October/November, it is anticipated. I'll let you know when, and if any of you are in that area, I am sure you would love to drop by and see Robert - he will, of course, do some singing there, as well as employing other artists such as a pianist, and I reckon it will do very well! When in L.A., I met a friend of his who plays piano - and sings just like Engelbert Humperdinck! It is quite possible he will work with Robert in some capacity. Robert chatted generally about his life at the moment - he is not only opening the lounge but runs a company specialising in organising shows, etc. which is also doing well, and is based in Hong Kong. Grace and Robert also plan to move from their present accommodation in Arcadia to their larger house nearby, overlooked by the San Bernardino mountains, which I gather also has a rather nice swimming pool! Robert says that next time I come over, I can go swimming every day!! Sounds great - and I think I'd better get some swimming practise in, otherwise I reckon Robert will be spending much of his valuable time hauling me out of the pool!! (Who knows, girls - if I play my cards right I might even get the kiss-of-life!!)

During my trip, I spent the whole time in the company of Grace and Robert, meeting their friends at their favourite restaurants, Chinese, Japanese and Indonesian, at the Tennis Club to which Robert belongs, just watching TV at Grace's home, or shopping, etc. Invariably, we all kept pretty late hours! We also went to some clubs where we relaxed and listened to singers in the company of friends.

Although Robert's singing/acting career has mostly been in Hong Kong, he is recognised in most of the places we went to in L.A. He also gets his fair share of adoration from the ladies, too!! One incident particularly amused me at a lounge we went to - on leaving the premises, a young, attractive Oriental lady passed her telephone number over to Robert! Needless to say, there were many comments on that!

Hot-shot Robert in action!!

Robert anticipates that he will be doing a further record later on when he finds time between his other commitments; his hobbies, apart from tennis, as mentioned, include shooting pistol and rifle on many of the ranges around L.A. He is also a qualified instructor in the use of firearms, and owns a small and impressive collection of guns, including one belonging to Bruce, which are kept in an armoury nearby. Seeing my interest in the weapons, Robert asked if I might like to try my hand at shooting on a range (patrolled by the police and quite legal, of course) in the mountains. I certainly did not need further prompting and, in the company of Grace, Robert, Dave and two other friends, set off for the San Bernardino's - about an hour's drive - and the views there were magnificent! The range itself is what appears to be a dried-up river-bed with small hillocks either side, and cans, bottles and other targets all around, and cans hanging from trees on the hillside. I have ALWAYS wanted to shoot since I can remember, but like many things just never got around to it; so, with Robert's very safety-conscious instruction on the handling and loading of the guns, he took each of us in turn to try our hand at the various guns he had brought; when I succeeded in hitting some of the targets, I think I amazed myself more than anyone!! And I loved every minute of it! Robert reckoned I should try to join a club in England - I said I would have to check it out, but rules here are much more stringent about the use of firearms. The guns I tried included various calibres - a Ruger, a Colt and a Magnum .357, together with a .22 rifle, and once you have got the initial idea of how to handle the guns safely and behave in a responsible manner, then how you progress after that is (literally!) in your own hands! We spent an enjoyable hour or so in this fashion, then returned down the mountain - and back to earth! With a strong feeling that, having taken the initiative, this was something you could do again and again!! Since my return to London, I have found and joined a shooting club - both pistol and rifle - and am thoroughly enjoying the break from my usual routine and doing something which, in all honesty, I find extremely relaxing!!

Grace in a relaxed mood at home

It seems that Brandon, who is now 18, hopes to go soon to take drama/acting classes, and that this sort of career seems to be strongly on the cards for him. Whether he will endeavour to "follow in the footsteps of Bruce" is as yet unknown - we shall see but he, like Bruce, is a very individual person. He will make up his own mind on his future aims. He is fairly tall now at about 5'10" - and very much like Bruce in ways and looks. Shannon, now 14, is a very pretty girl - I saw a picture of them both, and they are two quite stunning teenagers! (Yes - before you write - I AM trying to get a copy of a picture to show!) Brandon has been driving a car now for about two years, I believe - and comes to see Grace regularly and take her out. As I get more info, I shall pass it on to you all.

Norman Borine of the World of Bruce Lee came to meet me during my trip - he sadly regrets the closure of the Museum in Hollywood, but does say that he aims, at some future date, to get this reopened. Meanwhile, he has offices and a mail order section back in his old premises at Eagle Rock outside L.A. He is still handling the collection of names for the petition for Bruce's name to be placed on Hollywood Boulevard, and when I asked him how this was progressing, he said that the people who organise the placing of names were now looking at this. He said he will keep my informed further as and when he hears anything.

He has been given the sole rights by Linda Lee to have a medallion produced which is a replica of the one worn by Bruce, which are now in stock and I have obtained a VERY LIMITED SUPPLY OF THESE AT A SPECIAL PRICE - (see under 'SPECIAL ITEMS') - EACH A NUMBERED COPY!! Also - A FEW COPIES OF A RARE HAWAIIAN MAGAZINE. Norman and I shall be working on getting hold of other items for members on a regular basis now - so keep watching the news sheets!

Of course, Dan Inosanto is, as usual, a very busy man so I did not get to meet up with him this trip as he was away filming, so hope that we shall get together the next time I'm there. As you know, he has been teaching Brandon the martial arts for some time, so if Brandon does make any films in this field he is more than adept at doing the job properly, with the guidance he had from Bruce as a lad and then with Dan as his teacher in later years, a man for whom Bruce's philosophy and way of life was second-nature as one of his closest and most trusted friends.

When I finally left Los Angeles after a splendid and very happy six days, I was very sad, but shall be going back as soon as I can get leave and the Society workload subsides somewhat (now THAT will be the day!!)

GENERAL INFORMATION

David Edwards says that the martial arts have been featured a few times lately on TV, apart from the *Way of the Warrior* series. On BBC2 there was a feature on Master "Toddy," the well-known Thai Boxer from Manchester on the local News Programme *Granada Report*. Also on *Just Amazing*, Austin Goh, Nigel Fan, and Eddie Yeoh of the Wing Chun Ying Woo Kwoon gave a demonstration of breaking and Chi similar to the one given by the Wushu troupe of China a few years back. Also in an episode of *T. J. Hooker*, someone used a balisong butterfly knife which escrimadors such as Dan Inosanto use. They also use PR-24 batons on *Hooker* which were developed from the Japanese Tonfa.

Still with TV, several months ago on the *Private Benjamin* series Bruce was mentioned because the episode was about self-defence. David also says that in the May issue of *Video Review* there is a three-page feature on Bruce titled "Bruce Lee - The Leaping Legend," giving a detailed description of his life/films and ending with: "Bruce Lee was a capable actor and introduced to the West the power and beauty that the martial arts can be, the true fusion of strength and philosophy. He was a legend."

One good thing on nunchakus, though, comes from Barry Latcham, who says there was a clip of Bruce on the programme CBTV, and although only lasting a few seconds, it showed the opening nunchakus fight from *Fist of Fury*. This was shown in connection with Raymond Chow who is the top film producer in the world. Says Barry: "It is the first clip or mention of Bruce I have seen on TV since *Marlowe*. Barry also wonders if anyone noticed the preview of BBC2's new *American* series, introduced by Jonathan King - where among the preview sites was a cinema showing a Bruce Double bill of *Chinese Connection* (*Fist of Fury*) and *Fists of Fury* (*Big Boss*).

Again, in this month's magazine *Video*, there is an article on Bruce by Martin

Coxhead. (The same one mentioned by David Edwards above, it sounds - Pam). Although he made the odd mistake, the article was good, says Barry, and Mr. Coxhead shared the same opinion as Barry in that the *Clones of Bruce Lee* was tasteless, and ends the review with the words that: "Bruce Lee was a legend."

Still no joy, it appears, with Channel 4 as far as showing any Bruce footage; David Hall, brother of member Alan Hall, and member Jonathan Westley, each had a negative reply from them stating, "There were no plans to show either of Bruce's series - *Longstreet* or *The Green Hornet*. Again, member Michael Clark wrote to them, and they answered in similar vein but stating that "his request has been noted and passed to the department concerned."

Still with the TV companies, Susan Crane wrote to the IBA and the BBC about Bruce's films/series; her reply from the IBA was as for Channel 4, and the BBC state "they have no films under licence at present and that not all films are available to them for various reasons, usually copyright, or because ITV have acquired them."

On to the British Board of Film Censors - Jonathan wrote to them, and chased them up when he got no reply! They eventually came up with the letter shown opposite - I thought it was interesting enough to print, as it contradicted what had been said previously by the video distributors, who had stated that the films were censored on the instructions of the British Board of Film Censors! It now comes to the stage of asking who's bluffing who on this?!

Jonathan also says that Giko have a new quarterly magazine called *Self-Defence International* - the first issue came out a few months back and had some great articles on Bruce. One was an appreciation of *Enter the Dragon* and brought out some facts on the versions being shown of this film. Jonathan had never seen the part where Bruce met the high priest just after the opening fight scene, and for those of you who also have not seen this, the words exchanged between the monk and Bruce were as follows:

The monk says, "I have seen that your technique has risen beyond mere technique. I hope that you have united your mind and heart, and developed to the highest state - can you explain it?"

Bruce replies, "That is found in turning the technique into a formless state. Besides, when you face your enemy, what do you feel? In my eyes there is no enemy." "Why?" asks the monk. Bruce replies: "It's because the word is abstract." "Abstract?"

BRITISH BOARD of FILM CENSORS
3 Soho Square, London W1V 5DE
President: THE RT. HON. THE LORD HARLECH K.C.M.G.

Secretary: James Ferman   KRP/JK

Telephone: 01-437 2677/8
Telegrams: CENSOFILM, PHONE, LONDON   6th June 1983

Mr Jonathan Westley
Colchester
Essex

Dear Mr Westley

Thank you for your letter about the videos of the Bruce Lee films.

I regret that you did not receive a reply to your earlier letter but the Boards workload has increased considerably with the Amendment to the Cinematograph Act.

Although it is anticipated that the Board will be viewing video tapes distributed by companies belonging to the British Videogram Association this has so far not happened, so any tapes that you have of Bruce Lee films have not been seen by the Board.

Yours sincerely

K R Penry
Assistant Secretary

- the monk is confused. "I feel that combat" says Bruce, "is only a game, but I play it seriously. To be a true martial artist one must not be confined by the form. Instead, one should mix and assimilate martial arts so that one can use it freely. When your opponent expands, you should contract. But when your opponent retreats, you should attack him while he is not prepared. This is taking retreat as a way to advance and taking advance as a way to retreat. When I am in an absolutely favourable condition, I will attack subconsciously and certainly I can beat down my opponent."

Jonathan says that this gives him an even greater insight into Bruce's personal thinking. Giko goes on to point out one or two ideas that would have helped *Enter the Dragon* to be a much more presentable film - comparing Bruce's minor part to John Saxon's, and saying that the fight between Su Lin and the rapists could have been better, that the introduction to the tournament fighting could have been more exciting instead of "two old men clashing poles, then straight into the Parsons vs. Williams fight." Says Giko - "all the extras seem to be of the same build/height." (Jonathan reckons that's because they got a job-lot of karate suits in one size!)

Jonathan personally reckons the plot could have been improved by Williams being kept alive - and Roper, Williams and Bruce being thrown into prison all together. Next day, they are led into the courtyard to face Bolo. Roper/Williams both fail to defeat him - but of course Lee does the job. The guards attack, and the all-out battle ensues. "I also think," says Jonathan, "that O'Hara should have known that Su Lin was Bruce's sister before they fought." Some worthy comments there, I feel.

Still with Jonathan, he says that after seeing *The Silent Flute* he reckons it is one of the best he has even seen; although the fighting is not spectacular, it has tremendous spiritual qualities, and shows Carradine in much greater depth to the character in *Kung Fu*. Jonathan also liked the film *Silent Rage* with Chuck Norris - "A lot of good action and adventure, and a very believable plot - an extremely good film." However, Jonathan got very mad recently when seeing the poster advertising the Johnny Yune film *They Call Me Bruce*, which said: "With a little practise anyone can be as good as Bruce Lee." Jonathan's comments cannot be printed, I'm afraid - but I agree with them wholeheartedly.

On to David Moore - seen in the June 1976 issue of *Official Karate* magazine, an article giving comments by Ron Duncan; he talks of giving up performing weapons demonstrations because "he has not had the recognition he feels he deserves." He also goes on about how "Black martial artists are not regarded as highly as they should be (which David - and I - do not really think is true when you look at black Americans Ron Van Clief and Moses Powell) and the media has distorted the use of weapons." Duncan particularly picks out Bruce: "The fellow, namely Bruce Lee, has been the main culprit, and I hold him guilty. He has destroyed the martial arts with that nonsense of his on the screen, with his strutting arrogance. The martial arts did not begin and end with Bruce Lee. I'm tired of his name being shoved down my throat!." David says, "How CAN Duncan say that? Bruce's weapons techniques were practical, not too flashy but with just enough showmanship to entertain his audience. Didn't Bruce eventually surpass Dan Inosanto in speed and skill? - and Dan is regarded as a Master in the Filipino Arts. And surely most of the martial artists studying weapons today do so as a result of seeing Bruce's films? "Of course," says David, "Mr. Duncan felt he was brave enough to make this statement nearly three years after Bruce's death (when the magazine was printed). Where was he prior to 1973?" (Pam here: In all honesty, Bruce too had to contend with a certain amount of prejudice - but he did not sit there complaining about how Eastern martial artists were not given as much notoriety as those from the West - he went out and FOUGHT FOR IT. I'm glad to say that among my friends there are martial artists from ALL nationalities, creeds and colours - including black - who were not in agreement with Mr. Duncan's remarks: the general opinion was that he has a VERY large chip on his shoulder - maybe over the years he has now overcome this. Bruce was the originator of the breakdown in many prejudices which seem to surround us these days - I'd be interested to hear from ALL members on the above comments.')

Still with David, another back-issue of *Official Karate* (September 1979) says that Aaron Norris (Chuck's brother) taught Karate to actor Kurt Russell for the U.S. TV film *Elvis - The Movie* shown around Christmas 1981. Unfortunately the Karate sequences finished up on the cutting-room floor, leaving only two VERY brief scenes of Kurt as Elvis practising. The magazine states that, seeing as Karate was such an important part of El's life, it's too bad there was not more shown.

David also says that *Unexplained Magazine* (dealing with the paranormal and anything that is "strange") had an article in issue 121 on the "Death Touch" (also known as Delayed Death Strike/Vibrating Palm/Dim Mak). This included the rumour that Bruce was killed in this way, but also DID put the record straight and gave the true reason for his death. "In the East," they state, "any unexpected death of a notable person can provoke rumours of a Dim Mak assassination. The untimely death of the martial arts Superstar Bruce Lee in July 1973 had precisely this effect." A photo of Bruce's funeral was also shown, with the comments: "Mourners crowd around the coffin at a Hong Kong funeral. Their grief is for the Superstar Bruce Lee, the hero of numerous Kung Fu films. He probably died from a freak reaction to a tranquilliser - but many fans think their hero has been killed by a delayed death touch from some unknown rival."

Also recently seen by David in the *News of the World*, was an article on British film director Michael Winner (*Death Wish* fame) and his battle with the censors on his new film *Wicked Lady* where the censors wished to cut a scene with Faye Dunaway/Marina Sirtis fighting with whips. Winner objected, invited 50 film-makers/journalists to watch the film and not one thought any cuts were needed if given an 18 certificate. Faced with such weighty opinion, the censors backed down. "I wish," says David, "that something like that could be done with Bruce's films." (Pam here: I know that nothing can be done now to reverse the censors' cuts but when discussing such things with Mr. Ferman (Secretary of the Board) some time back, he said that once a film is cut they do NOT replace these parts, and as David says, it's a pity that there was not something done from the beginning.)

David recently heard that on the ITV programme *CBTV Channel 14*, Raymond Chow was mentioned as a prolific film producer who had not received recognition (Run Run Shaw, the other big Hong Kong Producer, had been made a "Sir"). Mention was made of Chow's "new star" - although no name was given. The best part of the show was a clip of Bruce using nunchakus from *Fist of Fury*.

Member John Milne says that Chuck Norris was in Glasgow recently on TV's *Scotland Today* (25th August) to promote his new film *Lone Wolf McQuade*. (See also under "FILMS").

In a special edition of *Photoplay Magazine* under "Star Interviews" it said: "Curiously enough, the biggest cult hero in the 70's was an Oriental, Bruce Lee - an expert in the arts who taught styles of self-defence to a number of Hollywood celebrities in the 60's. When the spectacular visual appeal of the arts dawned on film-makers, he transferred his skills to the big screen in *Big Boss, Fist of Fury* and *Way of the Dragon*. By the time *Enter the Dragon* came in 1973, the likeable young star had unexpectedly and mysteriously died, resulting in fan hysteria on a scale unseen since Valentino and Dean. Exploitive material followed - the worst of which was a film called *Bruce Lee - Game of Death*, concocted around just three minutes of unseen Lee footage." Says David: "*Game of Death* was not made to exploit Bruce - it's worth watching for the genuine footage, and as anyone knows this lasts longer than the three minutes stated."

The 1982 "Miss Olympia," Rachel McLish, says in *Muscle And Fitness* magazine: "I'm taking martial arts lessons from Byong Yu, who taught Bruce Lee." Says David: "Byong was a successful tournament fighter between 1970-73, and may well have worked with Bruce, but of course he was not Bruce's teacher."

Christ Quinten (Brian Tilsley of *Coronation Street*) says he would like to make martial arts films like those of the late Bruce Lee."

Recently, in *Hill Street Blues* a "junkie" fancied himself as a martial artist when high on drugs - lashing out at passers-by, he was approached by a police officer who said: "Hey Bruce Lee - what're you doing?"

On 20th July (Steve Wright's Radio 1 programme) David heard mention of Bruce's death on that day in 1973. And on the *Rockford Files* recently, John Saxon (Roper in *Enter the Dragon*) played a bad guy, fighting using the martial arts, but eventually was defeated by James Garner - not using the arts, however, even though he studied this under Bruce.

And recently on Channel 4, a group of women were asked who their fantasy male was - one replied: "Bruce Lee."

Amjid Majid saw in the *Scottish Evening Times* ("Back File" section) the following: "Bruce Lee, a Chinese-American actor specialising in Kung Fu roles, died in hospital after being found ill at home. He was 33." Amjid did not like the comment that Bruce "specialised in Kung Fu roles," as though Bruce was just an actor and nothing more; also, he was not found ill at home but in Betty Ting Pei's apartment, and died aged 32.

In the last news sheet, I mentioned about Kevin Hobbs writing to Golden Harvest (London) about outtakes from Bruce's films, where they replied that there were no such clips where the scenes went wrong on either video or 8mm. I remembered someone had written to me stating that Golden Harvest in Hong Kong HAD confirmed such material existed and member Paul Das has confirmed to me that it was he that received such a reply which is now reprinted for your info. As I said before; There's a lack of communication between Golden Harvest branches somewhere.

Ian Fawcett gives more info on the *Chinese Gung Fu* programme mentioned in the last sheet which was a series of half-hour documentaries on "dangerous jobs" called The Risk Business. This episode featured actors/actresses from Shaw Brothers' Studios, Hong Kong, and showed Shi Szu/David Chiang and various film clips etc., shooting on location, dubbing etc. - and although Bruce was mentioned, no clips of his films were shown. As far as Ian knows, this particular programme was not again shown, although the series was repeated. (Thanks, Ian, for filling us in on this).

Last sheet I mentioned the anatomy programme on TV to feature Wing Chun Master Simon Lau. It would seem, however, that member Mark McStea was not at all happy with the way Mr. Lau's Manchester club was run when he joined it, with Mark saying that Mr. Lau stopped arriving on time, and the lessons were not extended to allow for this. A beginners' class was joined into their class, thus cutting down their advanced classes and Mark was charged a further £10 when he lost his membership card (£10 being initially paid to join the club!) All in all, very unsatisfactory and with attendance dropping rapidly, the club eventually closed.

On a more pleasant note, Mark recently bought a Green Hornet annual at a book fair, and although it contained no Bruce photos other than the inside cover, some of the drawings are excellent. He also bought some copies of TV Tornado, a comic from 1967 featuring the Green Hornet comic strip from issue six - one copy stating "He is a real-life karate black-belt and practises an advance form of Jiu Jitsu called Gung Fu."

More Bruce Lee sayings as complied by Paul Corrigan.

MEMORIAL FLOWERS - 1983

This must have been the best display yet! As you can see by the three photographs the florist did us (and Bruce) proud! The actual coloured pictures are beautiful - and if you want copies of all three, this will be £2 (UK/Eire members); £2.20 (Europe) and £2.50 (Overseas). Should

GOLDEN COMMUNICATIONS COMPANY LIMITED

Ref. No. GC-83-103   10 February, 1983

Mr. P.A. Das
Middlesborough
Cleveland
England

Dear Mr. Das,

Thank you for your interests in Bruce Lee and his films.

To answer your queries, we only have some out-takes, and trims of Bruce's footage left in our studio here.

I also regret that advertising materials for our films are only available to established film distributors with whom we have a current distribution contract for the film in question.

Perhaps the enclosed photograph will find a place in your collection of memorabilia.

Yours sincerely,
GOLDEN COMMUNICATIONS CO., LTD.

LINDA TSE
Advertising/Publicity Department

16. If you don't want to slip up tomorrow, speak the truth today.

17. If you want to do your duty properly, you should do just a little more than that.

20. Only knowledge that is used sticks in your mind.

21. Our Universe is not only more mysterious than we imagine, it is more mysterious than we can imagine.

22. One great cause of failure is lack of concentration.

23. A wise man can learn more from a foolish question, than a fool can learn from a wise answer.

24. Character is to the soul what outward appearance is to the body.

25. Pessimism blunts the tools you need to succeed.

26. Optimism is a faith that leads to success.

you require copies of the floral tribute for 1982 and/or 1981 - do drop me a line and I will give you the cost) PLEASE MAKE ALL CHEQUES/ POSTAL ORDERS PAYABLE TO PAM HADDEN ONLY, PLEASE - NOT "THE BRUCE LEE SOCIETY/ KFM". And I'd like to thank ALL of those people who contributed to these lovely flowers; a copy of the bankers draft for the total amount of £118 (converted to dollars of US$182.02) is shown so you know just where your money went. This was sent to the credit of the florist, David Adams Ltd., in Seattle. And a 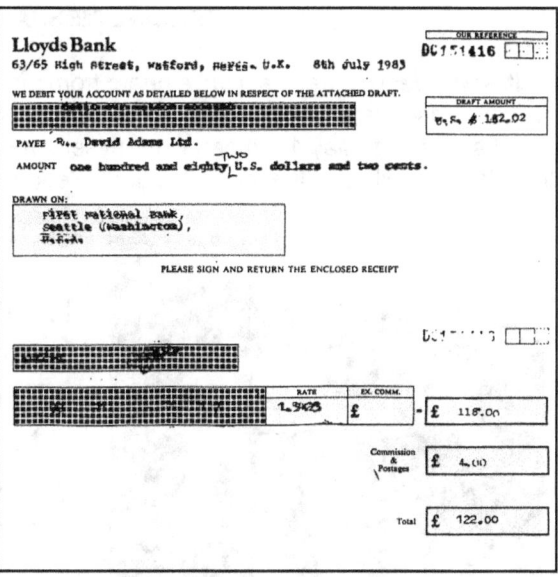 remark from someone who saw the flowers: "They stood out like a blaze of colour and people felt the need, from a distance, to go and see the tribute. They looked beautiful." (And a big "Thank You" to member Alison French for handling this for us all.) And the following were contributors: Nicholas Coleman, Michael Holmes, Wilson McKennan, Inge Hutama, Kay Parsons, Fess Parker, Susan Crane, Ken Wright, David Mills, Michael Harris, Norah Thornthwaite, Molly Cullen, Jonathan Westley, Paul Kelly, Peter Tang, Michael Clark, Susan Pietrzyk, Gary Robertson, John Maidment, Michael Day, Dermot Doherty, Barry Latcham, Shaune Bridgwood, Timothy Street, Paul Dean, Duncan Lee Baker, Iain Leslie, David Proctor, Mrs. Proctor, Lee Bryson, Stephen Downs, Pauline Bouckley, Arthur Stone, Ann and Fred Hunt, Neil Wilde, Keith Watson, John Pratt, B. J. Williams, John Watson, Alison French, Pam.

RENEWALS

Just to remind members about their renewals: members 1001-1627 - your eighth year is due between now and the end of November; likewise 2085-2170 - your seventh year; 2350-2530 - sixth year; 2738-2803 - fifth year; 3057-3108 - fourth year; 3271-3304 - third year; 3395-3435 - second year.

SPECIAL MESSAGES

It is with deep regret that I have heard from member Frank Salmon of the death of his very close friend and devoted Bruce Lee fan, Stuart Garland. Tragically, he died whilst swimming. May 1, on behalf of myself and all members, pass on our sympathies to his family and friends at this time. Peace, Stuart.

Member Frank Salmon (right) with his closest friend, Stuart Garland, just before Stuart's tragic death

BRUCE'S BOOK LIST
PART VI

Here are the next titles from Bruce's personal book collection:

Higher Judo: Ground Work - M. Feldenkrais (1952)
A Complete Guide to Judo - R. W. Smith (1958)
The Manual of Judo - E. J. Harrison (1952)
Judo: the Budokwai - British Judo Association (1957)
Techniques of Self-Defense - Ching Nam Lee (1963)
Judo and Judo-Do - Hubert Klingerstorff (1953)
My Method of Self-Defense - Kawaishi (1957)
Defend Yourself With Judo - A. D. Harrington (1962)
Judo, Self-Taught in Pictures - Hubert Klingerstorff (1952)
Bushido, The Soul of Japan - Inazo Nitobe (1899)
Book of Self-Defense - Honor Blackman (1965)

SUBCONSCIOUS MIND

The following is Bruce's definition of the above relative to himself: "RECOGNISING THE INFLUENCE OF MY SUBCONSCIOUS MIND OVER MY POWER OF WILL, I SHALL TAKE CARE TO SUBMIT TO IT A CLEAR AND DEFINITE PICTURE OF MY MAJOR PURPOSE IN LIFE AND ALL MINOR PURPOSES LEADING TO MY MAJOR PURPOSE. AND I SHALL KEEP THIS PICTURE CONSTANTLY BEFORE MY SUBCONSCIOUS MIND BY REPEATING IT DAILY."

SPECIAL ITEMS

I am delighted that I have had the opportunity, during my trip to L.A., to obtain from Norman Borine a very limited number (50) of the numbered commemorative issue of the medallions he has reproduced - with the sanction of Linda Lee - which is a faithful reproduction of Bruce's own solid-gold creation. Mind you - the ones I offer are NOT solid gold! (that would cost you a fortune!) but they ARE 22-carat gold-plated, each with its own individual number and - reminding us of Bruce's basic philosophy in life - bearing the inscription, in both English and Chinese: "Using no way as way; haying no limitation as limitation." Numbered editions (there are only 500 of these to be done) will be selling in Birmingham for around £15 each - and I am happy to be able to say that I am selling these, including a gold-plated 24" chain, and a card of authenticity, depicting Bruce at the front, and bearing the number of the medallion sent, at a cost of £11 each, including postage. I am sure they will be snapped up - so, to register your name for one of these, send me a CHEQUE/POSTAL ORDER MADE OUT TO PAM HADDEN ONLY, PLEASE. When I have the 50 marked as sold, I shall then despatch the money to Norman who will forward these medallions to me. This will probably take about six weeks to reach me and forward to yourselves. Anyone who is unlucky enough not to be in time to register for a medallion will have his/her money returned immediately.

I was also lucky enough to obtain eight copies only of a unique and rare Hawaiian newspaper magazine called *Hawaii's Kung Fu and Other Martial Arts* dated June 1974, in memory of Bruce. These 40-page magazines are in mint condition - front cover in mauve/white, remainder in black/white, almost entirely devoted to Bruce with articles/interviews with Linda Lee, Taky Kimura, Margaret Walters (former Student Advisor at the University of Washington) and Walter Riley, Dean of that University; articles on Kung Fu/Tai Chi Chuan/ Tae Kwon Do. It is a rare opportunity to obtain such an item. And to be fair, as there are only eight, I shall reserve two of these for overseas members, bearing in mind that they do not always get the news sheet as quickly as other members and thus miss out on the opportunity. (And for members abroad sending for ANY items from the Society, I shall have to ask that in future you send me currency equivalent to the Sterling amount asked for, as I am having terrible problems in getting cheques etc. in such currencies as Rupees. African Rands, put through my account.) And the cost of this rare magazine (including postage) is £10 - write quickly to save missing out on this - they won't take long going.

And anyone who has not yet bought the Robert Lee *Ballad of Bruce Lee* LP, drop me a line for cost and postage. The same goes for back-issue news sheet - tell me what ones you want, and I'll give you the cost.

FILM POLL

Here's the result of the film poll organised by member Barry Latcham last sheet to find out how Bruce's films rated in order of popularity from 1-5. As Barry only got replies from a few people, his idea on another poll to see what was Bruce's greatest fight sequence has been abandoned. Comments as to why a fan picked a film as

No. 1 are given also.

		'ENTER'	'GAME'	'FIST'	'BOSS'	'WAY'
		2	5	1	3	4
Arthur Stone:	"Incredible display of animal aggression"					
Amjid Majid:	"Fantastic double-nunchakus scene"	2	3	4	5	1
Paul Short:	"Lee/Norris fight must be the greatest ever filmed"	2	5	3	4	1
N. Green:	"Spectacular Lee/Norris fight; have yet to see the uncut version"	2	5	3	4	1
Nicholas Coleman:	"Superb fight sequences by the Great Bruce - with the guards, weapons etc."	1	5	2	4	3
Alison French:	"Very professional; and Bruce looks fantastic in his suit at the grave"	1	5	3	4	2
Peter Tang:	-	2	1	4	5	3
Barry's:	-	2	3	1	5	4
Pam's:	"The only film which gave Bruce the professional back-up needed to place his talents where they were meant to be - at the top. Good support - action in keeping with a professional like Bruce".	1	5	2	3	4

RESULT: first *Enter the Dragon,* second *Way of the Dragon,* third *Fist of Fury,* fourth *Big Boss,* fifth *Game of Death.*

And thanks to Barry for handling this poll.

VIDEOS

David Edwards says there have been several films (written by Stirling Silliphant) released on video recently, including *The Wild Bunch, Earthquake, and Black Belt Jones.* Despite the fact that Jim Kelly (for which *Fighting Stars* magazine criticised him) ripped off Bruce by copying his noises, stances and expressions, mainly at the beginning and end of the film, in one part practically copying the underground scene from *Enter the Dragon,* the film is above average and very enjoyable. "It's a pity," says David "that Kelly copies Bruce, as he has the skill to become a martial arts star in his own right."

The Silent Flute is due for release now - David hopes the fight scenes are somewhat better than the amateurish mess seen in *Kung Fu* and that Carradine does not let down Bruce's ideals. (Pam here: I've seen *The Silent Flute* when it was previewed - I thoroughly enjoyed it, and to be honest, Carradine handled his parts well - the fight scenes were good, and the whole thing worth watching. I would be interested to see what happens to it on video!! However, I found it mainly worth watching for the philosophical aspects it put over - and this, in conjunction with the fighting, was ideal to me).

Susan Crane has bought *Fist of Fear, Touch of Death* which she says is "smashing - some lovely fight sequences of when Bruce was young. Quite a controversial film."

Elvis - The Movie (see under "General News") is now released on video showing, albeit brief, scenes with Kurt Russell as Elvis practising Karate. Kurt's portrayal, says David Moore, is the best he has seen and he doesn't make a caricature of Elvis like his impersonators do, instead, he plays it straight. The singing voice is by Ronnie McDowal.

Peter Tang (see "Useful Addresses") has ALL Bruce's films uncut, including *Green Hornet, Longstreet* series and Jeff Ebdy says he has just received a tape from Peter called *Nunchakus Special* containing sequences from many films with all the Bruce footage such as double-nunchakus from *Way of the Dragon* and Bruce vs. Dan in *Game of Death,* which he says is excellent. Also available - *Game of Death II* - Peter is the only person to be selling this.

Rank Video have released *Drunken Master, Snake in the Eagle's Shadow* (Jackie Chan) plus four instructional tapes: *Never Cry Rape, The Art of High Impact Kicking, Shaolin Kung Fu,* and *The Science of In-Fighting*, with the latter being presented by Wong Shun Leung, who of course taught Bruce with Yip Man. David says another tape *Death Machines*, is not worth watching - "There's not much action and it's corny and unexciting."

NEW FILM INFORMATION
From David Edwards

Lone Wolf McQuade, Chuck Norris's new film, co-stars David Carradine who fought against the films release in court because his contract stipulated he was not to kill the film's heroine (Barbara Carrera); and that he did not want to be beaten by Chuck because it ruins his reputation as a star "possessed of boundless courage and physically and spiritually indomitable." Says David: "Who's he kidding?" (In the final print, he IS beaten by Chuck!) Co-stars are Leon Isaac Kennedy of *Penitentiary I and II* and *Body and Soul*. Still on *Wolf,* Steve Roskruge read in *Star* of 16th July that Carradine put two points to the company: a) he did not want to punch a woman in the face etc., etc. and b) did not want to look second best.

USEFUL ADDRESSES

Susan Cuff says she obtained 12 photos of Bruce, all very good, from: J. Ellis, 156 Pullman Court, Streatham Hill, London, SW2 4SE but write to this address before sending money.

And for those members not yet aware of member Peter Tang who runs a video club, he can supply ALL Bruce's films and series, uncut, so write to him with complete confidence. His address: 152 Shawclough Way, Healey Gdns., Rochdale OL12 6EE.

David Edwards recommends the martial arts shop he goes to: Samurai Martial Arts Centre, 75 Victoria Street, Liverpool.

David, and also Jonathan Westley, both recommend Giko Ltd. (537 Stratford Road, Sparkhill, Birmingham B5 7EP) for their new magazine called *Warrior* devoted to Bruce, and a book called *Bruce Lee - The Elusive Dragon* which tells of films Bruce might have made in comic-strip form - just published, this costs £2.95 plus 75p post/packing.

As there is also a new book out shortly by Dan Inosanto called *Absorb What is Useful* - members might like to check this out too. Giko also sell Maple Escrima Sticks (£8.95 + 75p) in black/red or black/yellow stripes, as Bruce used in *Game of*

Death; sponge nunchakus (*Enter the Dragon* design) in black/yellow 12"/14" length. (£3.95 + 75p). Dragon Shurikens (eight points) with "good luck" symbol - £2.95 + 50p - but members do need a martial arts commission licence for this last item. Also many new books/weapons on sale too. Write to Giko for their catalogue which costs £l.

CONGRATULATIONS

Welcome additions to two families!! Paul Wade wants to thank his wife Kim for giving birth to a beautiful daughter, Nicola. And Ian Kirk and his wife deserve congrats too on the birth of their son - named after Bruce, of course!!

PEN PALS

Laurie Towey wants English/American pen pal (female) around his age of 18-25.

SWOP SHOP

- Dennis P. Nutter, Leeds has for sale: Bruce Lee videos - *Big Boss* £25; uncensored *Game of Death* (Lee/Inosanto fight) - £35. Write direct.
- David Phillips, Hawkshead has for sale: two Bruce Lee films: *Way of the Dragon* 350ft, 22 mins, colour + sound cassette, *Enter Behind The Scenes Trailer* 100ft, Super 8mm. Write with offers.
- Paul Wade, Hull has for sale: *Deadly Hands of Kung Fu* Sept.75 - £1, 2 Chinese Bruce Lee magazines £1.50 both, *Bruce Lee King of Kung Fu* £1, *World of Bruce Lee* £3, *Dear Bruce Lee* £1.50 - all excellent condition, prices inc. p&p. OR will sell lot for £6.50 inc. p&p.
- Kevin Carter, Keighley has for swap: *Bruce Lee Farewell My Friend* (excellent condition). Wants: *KFM's* 31, 32 or 1, 2, 3 or posters, books, magazines on Sylvester Stallone in *Rocky*.
- Duncan Lee Baker, Bournemouth wants: 7" *Dragon Power* single - send him address, or if can supply yourself the cost.
- Keith Graham, Edinburgh has for sale large collection of Bruce Lee items - books, magazines, *KFM*s, records. Over £100 in records alone - EVERYTHING for £150. Drop him a line direct.
- Pardip Kumar, Birmingham has for sale/swap: *Book The World's Greatest Movie Stars and their Films* - including Bruce Lee. *Cult Films* (including *Enter the Dragon*). Both books £10 each or will swap for any Bruce Lee items of *Game of Death, Enter the Dragon,* and other Bruce Lee items.
- Barry Latcham, Crook has for swap: *Zombie Flesheaters* uncut video - excellent condition. Wants: *Big Boss* (Rank) in original box and excellent condition, Betamax,
- Tim Ussher, Crowborough has for sale: An extremely large Bruce Lee collection - many rare items - write to him for details.
- Alec Joyce, Hayes has for sale (All excellent condition, sold as a whole or separate): Bruce Lee items: (books): *Enter the Dragon, Bruce Lee Lives, Chinese Gung Fu, Bruce Lee Fighting Method* vols. 1, 2 & 4, *Reminiscences of Bruce Lee, Superstar of Hong Kong, Game of Death, Bruce Lee - His Unknown in Martial*

Arts Learning, Bruce Lee Combats, The Fighting Spirit, Bruce Lee King of Kung Fu, Tao of JKD, Power of Bruce Lee, Who Killed Bruce Lee, KFM magazines 3-70 plus binder, *Kung Fu* magazines *Bruce Lee 1940-1973, Bruce Lee Untold Story, Secret Art of Bruce Lee, Bruce Lee's Game of Death, Bruce Lee Stars in Game of Death*; numerous posters, pictures; (Tapes): *Bruce Lee & Friends, The Last Interview, Enter the Dragon* (soundtrack).

- Paul Das, Middlesbrough has for sale as a whole (but numbered groups considered separately) - all items mint: *KFM's* 1-75 plus all *Special Editions*, LP's: *Boss, Fist, Way, Enter* (double LP), *Game, Tower, Enter* (music), *Dragon Power* 12" single, cassettes (sixteen) many rare items, *Memorial Posters* 1-12 including photos, *Bruce Lee Fighting Method* 1-4, *Secret Art of Bruce Lee, Bruce Lee 1940-1973, Tao of JKD* hardback, *Bruce Lee Untold Story, Who Killed Bruce Lee?, Bruce Lee In Action, Unbeatable Bruce Lee, Power of Bruce Lee, Bruce Lee King of Kung Fu, Scrapbooks* 1 & 2, Set of 15 JKD Hong Kong Fan Club books, photos, paperbacks - *Man Only I Knew, Life and Tragic Death of Bruce Lee, Enter the Dragon Cinema Posters, Way, Game,* Set of four magazines - *Nunchakus in Action, Privacy & Anecdotes, Studies on JKD, Secret Art of JKD*, three volumes of *Flick Books*, six sheets of stickers, one scarf, two homemade scrapbooks, Set of 20 Chinese magazines on Bruce plus one English book, Various photos, posters (not good condition) and bits and bobs, like nunchakus. Whole lot for £200 plus P&P.
- Mark McStea, Wythenshawe has for sale set of front of house stills (as shown outside cinemas) - colour, mint, rare - £12.50.

HELP NEEDED, PLEASE

David Edwards (Northwich) would like any members knowing from where he can obtain Jesse Glover's second and third books - *Bruce Lee's Non-Classical Gung Fu* and *Non-Classical Gung Fu* to write to him with this info.

LETTERS

Dear Pam,

By looking at views on nunchakus by the media/Censors it seems like they just try to ignore them in the hope they won't encourage violence in young people. Then why do Granada TV show an episode of Magnum on Monday 25th July at peak viewing time with nunchaku in? The scene shows Magnum and a friend being knocked down by a nunchaku-wielding man. Anyone, of any age, could be watching this and yet the censors do no allow the nunchakus into Bruce's films even though they carry an "X" certificate, (which I personally think is stupid) and are watched in the privacy of people's homes on video or in the cinema. Why show them on TV and yet not in Bruce's films? It all seems crazy to me.

(John Curley)

Agreed, John - this point has been raised many times, but as our long-standing members know, we seem to be up against illogical reasoning on this score. Every point you make has been made with the censors - but to no avail. It seems that the only way to obtain Bruce's films AS THEY WERE MEANT TO BE SHOWN is to purchase certain videos - and of course our member Peter Tang can supply all uncensored copies as already stated.

Dear Pam,

I've been a Bruce fan for nine years; it was because of him, that at 13, I started training in Wado-Ryu Karate; because of him I took up Tae Kwon Do for three years, passing six belts (four away from black); because of Bruce I now study Lau Gung Fu, and for as long as I can remember trained my mind and body everyday that I can, going jogging/weight-training/Gung Fu etc. I do not drink or smoke - all because of Bruce. And because of Bruce, I plan to go to Hong Kong - as a means of saying "Thank you." Bruce taught me a lot - so I thought, this being the 10th anniversary of his tragic death, I'd like to do something, so after donating to the floral tribute and Grace's present, I'd now like to donate £5 to the very worthwhile "Plant a Tree" campaign - it's the least I can do. And I think that: Bruce would have supported such a venture also. So thanks, Bruce - thanks a hell of a lot! And keep up the good work with the Society, Pam. Must go and write to Channel 4 now!

(Michael Clark)

I know that your feelings, Michael, are felt by all who have been reached by Bruce and his lifestyle; it is something we all feel as part of our daily routine now - I can't describe my feelings the first time I watched Bruce, but really, I don't have to, because you ALL know that incredible exhilaration and yet feeling of completely being drained of any energy after watching his performances, hearing his views whether in interviews or through the voices of his many friends and colleagues - how DOES one really describe how you feel when you speak on Bruce? Only his fans can really knew. And it's a great feeling, isn't it?

ALBERT GOLDMAN'S BOOK ON BRUCE

Although I had heard that this book (as controversial no doubt as the one he wrote on Elvis') had been released in the States, when I was there I found NOTHING on this, even though I checked with several stores. Anyone seen or heard anything further on this, please????

Well - time to close now. More next time:. Take care - Peace, Love, Brotherhood.

Pam

EDITOR'S NOTES

As stated in this issue, Norman Borine's "World of Bruce Lee" museum has unfortunately closed.

Pam said that she had learned through Grace and Robert Lee, that Dan Inosanto was training Brandon, and that Brandon was thinking about following in his father's footsteps. As we all know Brandon did follow in his father's footsteps but wasn't interested in becoming a copy of him or living in his shadow. Brandon took on a few martial arts-related projects because the opportunity was there for him and it was a ladder to where he wanted to be as an actor and as an individual.

In his early career, he even played Kwai Chang Caine's (David Carradine) son in *Kung Fu: The Movie*, a feature film update on the TV series of the previous decade in which Bruce Lee was rejected for due to looking "too Chinese."

He continued his action movie mantra in Hong Kong with *Legacy of Rage* opposite Bruce's old foe Bolo Yeung, before shooting *Laser Mission* in Australia, both of which saw mediocre sales. He returned to the United States to film the buddy cop movie *Showdown in Little Tokyo* with Dolph Lundgren and Tia Carrere. Plagued with post production issues, Warner Brothers gave it a limited theatrical release in the US and in most countries the film went straight to video.

After *Showdown in Little Tokyo*, Lee was cast in the lead role of the Fox action film, *Rapid Fire*. The film received mixed reviews but critics praised Lee's performance and charisma. His biggest project to date was the role of Eric Draven in Alex Proyas' film adaptation of the graphic novel *The Crow*.  Sadly, this would be Lee's final movie. On 31st March 1993, whilst filming a scene for *The Crow*, a gun, supposedly loaded with a blank cartridge, fired a projectile at Lee, who immediate collapsed upon impact. He was rushed to New Hanover Regional Medical Center in Wilmington, Carolina, where after six hours, despite all attempts to save his life, he passed away from his injuries. He was just 28 years old. A private funeral took place three days later, where attendees included Kiefer Sutherland, Lou Diamond Phillips, Steven Seagal, David Carradine, Jeff Imada and Dan Inosanto. He was buried next to his father Bruce in Lake View Cemetery in Seattle, Washington, in a plot intended for his mother Linda.  His headstone inscription is a quote from one of Brandon's favourite books, *The Sheltering Sky* by Paul Bowles and reads:

> "Because we don't know when we will die, we get to think of life as an inexhaustible well. Yet everything happens only a certain number of times, and a very small number really. How many more times will you remember a certain afternoon of your childhood, an afternoon that is so deeply a part of your being that you can't even conceive of your life without it? Perhaps four or five times more, perhaps not even that. How many more times will you watch the full moon rise? Perhaps twenty. And yet it all seems limitless." For Brandon and Eliza. Ever Joined in True Love's Beauty.

After Brandon's death, film distributors saw a huge surge in sales of his films; mediocre releases suddenly hit rental and sales charts. His final film, *The Crow* was completed with the permission of Brandon's family, including his fiancé Eliza Hutton and was released on 13th May 1994 to critical acclaim, garnering a cult following.

As with *The Kentucky Fried Movie* a few years prior, as soon as someone appears to be pretending to be or look like Bruce Lee, the fans went into meltdown with rage. *They Call Me Bruce* was no exception. The 1982 film was an American action comedy, directed by Elliott Hong, and starred Johnny Yune and Margaux Hemingway.  The title was a reference to that Johnny Yune's character was referred to as "Bruce" throughout the film due to his resemblance to Bruce Lee and probably to the racial stereotype that "all Asians look alike."

The Risk Business was a BBC TV series, presented by Michael Rodd, Judith Hann and Kieran Prendiville, which ran from 1977 to 1981. It followed a similar format to *Tomorrow's World* and *Horizon*.

Fist of Fear, Touch of Death, also known as *The Dragon and the Cobra*, was a 1980 Bruceploitation martial arts film set at the 1979 World Karate Championships at Madison Square Garden, where the "successor" to Bruce Lee would be determined. Made seven years after Bruce Lee's death, any footage which featured him was taken from his earlier films or television appearances.

Wong Shun Leung, born 8th May 1935 in British Hong Kong was a Wing Chun martial artist, student of Yip Man and teacher of Bruce Lee. Stemming from his fascination with the stories of legendary Wing Chun practitioners, Wong sought out a Wing Chun teacher, eventually being taken by friends of his older brother, to meet Yip Man. Wong joined the Wing Chun group and eventually came to assist Yip with teaching his students, with one of those students being Bruce Lee. After Lee achieved film superstardom, Yip Man told Wong Shun Leung, "Without your guidance and encouragement, Bruce Lee wouldn't be having such achievement."

Wong was scheduled to attend a screen test for *Game of Death* on the set of *Enter the Dragon* after Bruce Lee had finished shooting the film and was working on dubbing in June 1973. A photograph showing the screen test exists of Lee, Raymond Chow and Wong on the "Han's Trophy Room" set of *Enter the Dragon*. There is also brief footage of the screen test in the 1973 documentary *The Man and the Legend* which shows Lee throw a punch at Wong to gauge how the latter would respond to a film punch.

Wong later confirmed the screen test, stating, "About two months before Bruce Lee died, he called me up and wanted me to participate in the making of *Game of Death*. He had also invited me to the studio to attend a screen test. I did not promise to act in the film, yet I still went to attend the screen test to please him. [The screen test] was for *Game of Death*, but I declined because I thought that the moves of Wing Chun style wouldn't look good on film. I think the Wing Chun method is ugly for movies but very good and very logical for real fighting."

After Lee's death, Wong took a role in the film, *Legend of Bruce Lee*, in which he played the role of himself, as an instructor at Yip Man's school who first met a teenager named Lee in the 1950s. In the 1980s, he released his first and only instructional video, titled, *Wing Chun: The Science of In-Fighting*.

Wong Shun Leung passed away on 28th January 1997, aged 61. Posthumously, Wong Shun Leung was commemorated in two recent documentary films by renowned Bruce Lee historian and author, John Little; *Wong Shun Leung: The King of Talking Hands* and *The Art of Wong Shun Leung: A Ving Tsun Journey*.

A RETROSPECTIVE LOOK AT BRUCE LEE MANIA & THE KUNG FU CRAZE OF THE 1970S

30
December
1983

WELCOME TO THE DECEMBER NEWS SHEET - AND MY THANKS TO ALL THOSE MEMBERS WHO HAVE SENT IN GOOD WISHES AND CHRISTMAS CARDS. A HAPPY NEW YEAR TO YOU ALL.

MEMORIAL FLOWERS - JULY 1984

Once again the time has come for the Society to think about its floral tribute to be sent to Bruce's graveside in Seattle; I know that this is usually mentioned in the March sheet, but find that people tend to leave sending their money until the last minute, causing some minor problems. To alleviate this, I am bringing the whole project forward to give everyone concerned a chance to handle their part in good time. We have been sending flowers now for three years, and last year's display was, I think, quite exceptional. The flowers really stood out brilliantly, and showed the American fans that Bruce is remembered worldwide, and that he remains in our hearts always. So please, do start to send in your donations early - NO MATTER HOW SMALL THEY MAY BE - so that we can get this organised as soon as possible and give the florist in Seattle time to do something equal to - if not better than! - 1983. All cheques/postal orders should be made payable to Pam Hadden ONLY, please - (NOT *KFM* or "The Society," as this causes unbelievable problems, and if incorrectly made out will regrettably have to be returned to the sender for reissue) and send in an envelope marked "MEMORIAL TRIBUTE" to London. I keep a list of contributors' names (which will be placed by the graveside), amounts received, and a running total to keep the records straight, pay the total amount into my account and immediately send a cheque for that figure to member Alison French who handles this important project. We then liaise on what the flowers should look like, and then Alison takes over the project, dealing with the florist direct, and sending them the money. Obviously, this all takes time - so please, get your donations in as quickly as possible - BUT IN ANY EVENT BY THE 8TH JUNE 1984 AT THE VERY, VERY LATEST. So come on, folks - please do not delay - let's make this a superb tribute to Bruce!

PLANT A TREE - CREATE A WOOD
The Woodland Trust

In the March, 1983, news sheet I mentioned the above project and said I would give it six months to see how much money we could collect to have trees planted in the name of "'Bruce Lee" for which we would receive a certificate and a listing in the Book of Commemoration held by the trust; well, I've given it almost one year - and have received just £19. I shall give until the end of April for further donations and then shall send whatever amount has been collected to the trust, printing a copy of the certificate in due course. I had hoped that we would have reached the £100 mark (because that would have meant that the actual commemoration would not only have been entered in the Book but also displayed on a plaque in the offices of the trust for all to see!), but at £19 we are a long, long way short, regrettably. It is a worthy cause, as each £1 donated plants a young tree, and ensures that our woodland is preserved for future generations. With the way that our countryside is being threatened, it is nice to be able to help to keep this, and honour the name of Bruce Lee at the same time.

GENERAL NEWS

Member Diane Webb was recently browsing through her local library when she came across a copy of *Cult Films* by Danny Peury. The book fell open at the *Enter the Dragon* section - "Which goes to show," Diane says, "that it is a popular film!" The book reviews and comments on 100 films, and on the whole, the author is quite flattering in his comments about Bruce: "It just so happened that the most charismatic sexual film personality of the period was working in the Kung Fu genre... Lee's physical capabilities seem impossible - his fight with O'Hara is particularly stunning... Most significantly *Enter the Dragon* stars the finest action-hero in cinema history in one of his few roles: the one and only Bruce Lee at his remarkable best." The writer also refers to "the incomparable Bruce Lee."

Gary Robertson recently saw the film *The Shootist* during Christmas - and spotted Hugh O'Brien from *Game of Death*.

Over Christmas was a film called *Maserati and Brain* which had two Chinese brothers using nunchakus and a samurai sword. (Pam here; again - why can this be allowed - especially when children are at home for the holidays - and yet the censors cut Bruce's films and say it is to protect the young from copying the use of such weapons as nunchakus? It just goes to show how UTTERLY ABSURD this country's censorship is. Why one set of rules for Bruce - and another set for everyone else?)

Michael Day says that in edition number three of *Self-Defence International*,

A RETROSPECTIVE LOOK AT BRUCE LEE MANIA & THE KUNG FU CRAZE OF THE 1970S

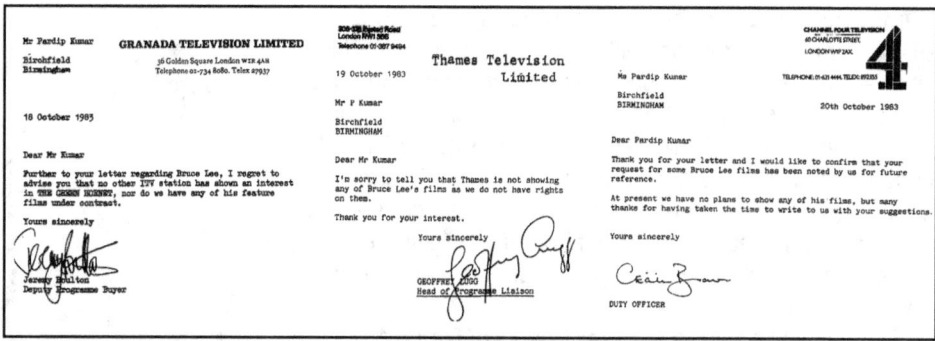

there's a three-page article on *The Green Hornet*, including two action-shots of Bruce from the series.

Pardip Kumar has written to Thames Television, Granada Television and Channel Four Television asking about the showing of Bruce's films/series; again, like other members, they do not seem to be doing anything in this field. I do make the plea that members write to as many stations as they can - the big companies and the small - to see what can be done to show Bruce's films and series.

Pardip also wrote to TV South West (Derry's Cross, Plymouth PL1 2SP, Devon, England) asking if they plan to screen any Kung Fu films but their reply was negative, although it is possible that they might do so at some future date. He also chased up Central TV about screening *Green Hornet* (currently being shown on Saturdays at 9.30 a.m.) at a more suitable time, also emphasizing that this series should be shown on a national basis as it is unfair to all other Bruce fans to have it so restricted.

Pardip enclosed a leaflet on Equagesic tablets (which Bruce took for a headache prior to his death). Pardip says he thought other members might be interested in this. It says that HYPERSENSITIVITY may rarely occur with Meprobamate or Aspirin - as we all know, Bruce was one of these rare cases.

Still with Pardip, on a recent Clive James show a Chinese man was seen banging nails into a piece of wood. When he had finished, Clive said: "Bruce Lee built a whole house that way!!"

And referring to John Curley's remarks (last sheet) about the use of nunchakus on TV yet censored from Bruce's films,

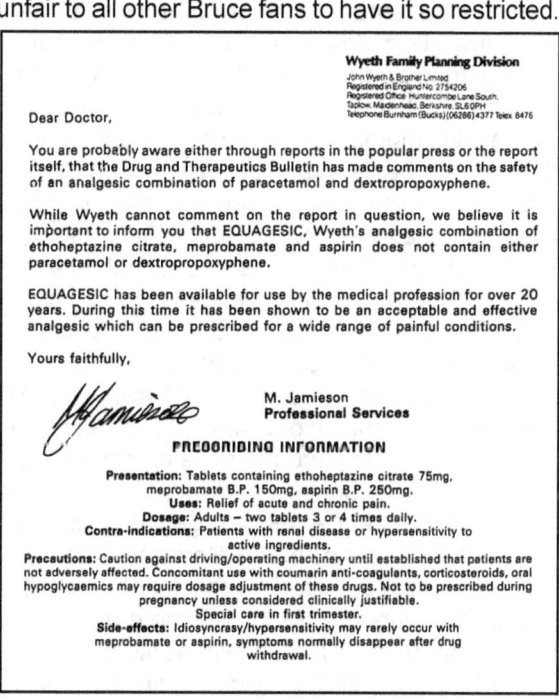

Pardip agrees since he saw a programme (Houston, BBC) where Houston was attacked by a man using flick knives, swords, Escrima sticks and nunchakus. And this was at 7 p.m. when anybody, even young children, could be watching. Why show them on TV and not in Bruce's films if they are considered as such a bad influence? "I think," says Pardip, "the censors should use sense, not scissors when treating Bruce's films." (I can assure you, all us fans are with you, Pardip - yet still the censors snip away. - Pam).

Duncan Baker wrote to Peter Powell of Radio 1 about the anniversary of Bruce's death and Peter read out the following over the air: "I've got a letter from Duncan Lee Baker from Bournemouth. He mentions the fact that Bruce Lee died 10 years ago today. Duncan is part of a Kung Fu club, and also a regular reader of many magazines including *Kung Fu Monthly*. He just wants to express his best wishes to everybody who is involved in Kung Fu in Britain and also to be remembering Bruce Lee's death. So I'd like to do that for you; a very interesting letter actually from Duncan - thank you for it."

Peter Tang, who runs the video club, has a word of warning to members: "Do please be careful when watching videos of *Game of Death*. I sell the uncensored version of this including the Bruce/Dan nunchaku sequence in excellent quality, and take the opportunity to express one point I feel very strongly about personally. American, German and 8mm films of *Game of Death* are all dubbed with pathetic cries from Bruce/Dan, downgrading the whole fight and spoiling the sound effect. I call this first-degree murder to kill off Bruce's achievements by dubbing it like this, and for what reason? These versions not only destroy Bruce's skills but give a false impression of him; members having not heard the original would be misled into thinking of Bruce at a lower level and believe it. Apart from my own club members, nobody has heard the original, and I shudder to think how Bruce fans of the Western world are cheated. Please remind members that if they can only watch the dubbed version, they must have reservations and do not think of Bruce as the way they hear him." Thanks, Peter - I am sure members will make note of this important fact.

Dermot Doherty mentions the Jackie Chan Fan Club, but warns: "When I wrote to Golden Harvest, I received back a photocopied letter dated August 1982 consisting of lots of sweet words but it was awful! I also got order forms for the club, where one year's membership costs US $34 (around £22!?), which is pretty expensive!! The benefits for this are merely a bi-monthly news letter and membership card. All products such as photos or posters have to be bought, unlike the Society, where at the renewal of membership you get interesting things and photos. All in all I think the Jackie Chan club is a rip-off." (Pam here; Well, it DOES sound expensive, and at that price, they should include a badge or photograph at least! Has anyone else seen the cost for this club advertised elsewhere?)

Thomas Vickers has thrown some light on the Albert Goldman book (which I heard had been written by this man, but could not obtain any copies during my

American trip). "Living in the States," says Thomas, "I keep up with all the American publications and information on Bruce. The only thing Mr. Goldman wrote was a two-page article in *Penthouse* magazine, during January/February 1983. It was informative, but Mr. Goldman was very opinionated in writing it, making Bruce sound like a drug addict and a fake. I personally disliked the article very much. Anyone wishing to read it should write to *Penthouse* to get the back-issues. As far as I know, there is no future plan for an entire book about Bruce by this man." (Pam here: When I first heard about this book, it seemed that Goldman was doing research for a book on Bruce, therefore I'd presume that the above articles might be the forerunner to that book. I will still keep my eyes and ears open just in case, and trust that members will do the same and let me know of anything they hear. P.S. Thanks, Thomas.)

David Moore recently saw *Ten to Midnight* starring Charles Bronson as a cop hunting the killer of young women. The suspect is supposed to be a karate expert, and has a Bruce Lee *Dragon* poster (as advertised in early *KFM* magazines) on a wall in his apartment.

In *Combat* (June 1983), David says there was an article by Bey Logan where he mentioned Bruce and Dan Inosanto as experts on nunchakus in films (particularly Bruce's films), and the dreadful censorship to British film showings (particularly the weapons in Bruce's films!) "It was," says David, "a very good article indeed so well done, Bey Logan!!"

Again from David, he recently read a book on Randolf Turpin, the coloured British boxer who reached the top, won the world title and plummetted to the bottom again. There was a quote in the book which not only suited Turpin's life but David feels was relevant to Bruce's short but packed life: "TO ALL THE SENSUAL WORLD PROCLAIM - ONE CROWDED HOUR OF GLORIOUS LIFE IS WORTH AN AGE WITHOUT A NAME!"

In another book called *Toughen Up - The Chuck Norris Fitness System* by Chuck/Wilmer Ames (£4.95), there are exercises aimed not just at the martial artist but anyone who wishes to lose some inches or make him/herself than little bit fitter. Excellent book for anyone interested. (Pam here; Can you let me know where to buy, David - thanks.) The book also gives some info on Chuck's background/film career, and shows just how successful his films have been - *Good Guys Wear Black* made US$19 million in its first year, *A Force of One* grossed $25 million and *An Eye for an Eye* grossed $1 million in its first week in New York alone, topping all other releases! Why do we never hear anything about this in the press/cinema magazines? It seems to me film critics do not take martial arts films seriously enough in comparison to *Rocky*-type films etc.

Black Belt magazine has been printing ballot forms for their *Black Belt Hall Of Fame 1983* (not to be confused with the list printed in September 1983 news sheet under the University of Martial Arts Hall of Fame). David has given a short selection of past awards which were printed next to the ballot forms, in which he thinks members might be interested: (from 1968-1982): "Man of the Year" 1974 - Bruce Lee, 1976 - Ed Parker, 1977 - Chuck Norris, 1978 - Bill Wallace. "Competitor of the Year" - 1968 - Chuck Norris, 1971 - Mike Stone, 1973 - Bill Wallace, 1975 - Joe Lewis, 1977 - Bill Wallace. "Instructor of the Year" - 1975 - Chuck, 1977 - Al Dacascos (friend of Bruce), 1979 - Ed Parker. Others, Jujitsu - 1969 - Wally Jay (friend of Bruce), Jeet Kune Do - 1972 - Bruce Lee, 1977 - Dan Inosanto. Editor's Award: 1979 - *Karate Illustrated* USA magazine - Jhoon Rhee (friend of Bruce, Tae Kwon Do master and Angela Mao's co-star in *When Tae Kwon Do Strikes*). 1979 - *Fighting Stars* magazine - Chuck Norris. David says to note that Norris/Stone and Lewis all had "special" instruction from Bruce and went on to be America's (if not the World's) top three fighters in competition in the 1960's to the mid-1970's.

On writing to Yorkshire TV asking about the *Green Hornet* series, pointing out that this was no worse fight-wise than the two karate episodes of the cops series *CHiPs*, he also enquired about *Longstreet*, and other non-Bruce martial-arts related episodes such as *CHiPS*, *Magnum*, *Quincy*, *Men of the Dragon*, and if they would be showing *Silent Flute*. "Got a reply!" says David. "Incredible that after three years of writing to them they answered! Unfortunately, they say they do not have any programmes/films in this vein, and it is difficult to tell at present whether they will do so in the near future; but they will certainly keep my suggestions in mind although they make no promises."

After watching the excellent *Way of the Warrior* series, David wrote to Howard Reid, the producer, at the BBC to compliment him, and ask if there was to be a second series. His reply was that he was currently working on a possible series, so maybe if other members write, they can get the BBC to see just how interested we are, especially mentioning Bruce, of course!!

David has also compiled a film list which he thought might interest you all; it is quite long so will be split into suitable parts, the first list being films of Leo Fong, Jim Kelly and Ron Van Clief of America. David says he hasn't included EVERY film they've made, but tried to use those not so well-known. (Next sheet, we shall have some rarer films of Sonny Chiba (Japan), Wang Yu (Hong Kong) and a short section of other stars.)

BBC
BRITISH BROADCASTING CORPORATION
BROADCASTING HOUSE WHITELADIES ROAD BRISTOL BS8 2LR
TELEPHONE & TELEGRAMS BRISTOL 732211
TELEX 265781 BSA

HR/LDH

8 August 1983

D Moore Esq

Wakefield
W. Yorks.

Dear Mr Moore

Thank you very much for your recent letter. I am glad that you found the series so interesting.

Unfortunately, the TV world works so slowly that we do not yet know whether we will be able to use our extra footage for videos, or whether there will be a follow-up series. I have, however, already begun to work on a possible series, and agree with you that all the arts which you mention should be included. Whether or not the BBC will decide to make more films on the martial arts remains to be seen.

I will let you know if there are any further developments about video programmes.

Yours sincerely

Howard Reid

Dr Howard Reid

Leo Fong: *The Bamboo Trap, Manila Gold, The System, The Tiger's Revenge* (formerly titled *Enforcer from Death Row* with Charlie Davao), *The Outside Man, The Last Reunion* with Cameron Mitchell and Chanda Romero (A Koinonia-Pelifilm picture), *Revenge of the Bushido Blade* with Cameron Mitchell and Marwin Roberts.

Jim Kelly: *The Black Foo Dang Master* (martial arts choreography by Ron Van

A RETROSPECTIVE LOOK AT BRUCE LEE MANIA & THE KUNG FU CRAZE OF THE 1970S

Clief), *Take a Hard Ride* with Jim Brown and Lee Van Clief, *Hot Potato* with Irene Tsu (produced by Fred Weintraub and Paul Heller), *Black Samurai, Truck Turner, Black Belt Jones* with Gloria Hendry (directed by Robert Clouse and produced by Fred Weintraub and Paul Heller), *Three the Hard Way* with Jim Brown and Fred Williamson, *Bamboo Gods and Iron Men, Golden Needles* with Joe Don Baker (directed by Robert Clouse and produced by Weintraub and Heller - Sequoia Productions).

Ron Van Clief: *Super Weapon* with Charles Bonet (directed by H. Scarpelli, J. Sotos and produced by Serafin Karalexis), *Black Dragon's Revenge* (also known as *The Black Dragon Revenges the Death of Bruce Lee*) with Charles Bonet, Jason Pai Piau (directed by Tommy Lo Chung - produced by Serafin Karalexis), *Enter the Three Dragons* with John Saxon and Dragon Lee, *Super Dragon* with Jason Pai Piau (directed by Tommy Lo Chung and produced by Joseph Estrada).

Thomas Jones wrote to me some time back about Phil Spector "who numbered Bruce Lee as one of his bodyguards!" (see previous news sheets). Thomas since read in *TV Times* that this man started to get into films and it said "he helped to finance Kung Fu film-star Bruce Lee's *Enter the Dragon*!? Says Thomas: "That's news to me, Pam! (And to me, Tom - I think this guy is a bit of an odd-bod myself. Anyone else throw any light on this? - Pam) Tom also says that he recently fell badly and hit his face. He got home, but on the next day when he could not eat he was rushed to hospital, x-rayed, and had to wait around for several hours - during which time he occupied himself by reading a *Kung Fu Monthly*. He says that during the hours that went by, Bruce was with him, and helped him through. He later found he had broken a bone in his jaw - not very pleasant, and glad to know he is now on the mend.

One of our longest-standing members, Arthur Stone, has now become a professional writer, and has already had a couple of scripts published in the *Eagle*, a series called *Werewolf* (sold but not yet printed), and right now he's working on the artwork for a horror tale set in the jungle. You might remember that he wrote several long stories in the past, as well as a film script. I am sure we all wish him much luck in his future career in whatever projects he tackles.

Pardip Kumar recently saw a play (part of a series of short stories by Faruk Dondy on TV) which was about Kung Fu. In one particular part, some kids were watching a film with a projector, and Pardip noticed this was none other than Bruce Lee in *Fist of Fury*.

Also in Redditch, Bruce Lee fans were treated to a tremendous triple bill of *Fist of Fury, Big Boss* and *Way of the Dragon* - it was really great, he says!

In the book *Marathon Man*, says Andrew Upton, he was amazed at the following on page 46: "Chen decided to use his nunchakus - an honourable weapon, ancient as air - two hard wooden sticks connected by wire or leather if you liked. Chen liked wire. He was a master with the nunchakus - to the Caucasian world, the strangeness of the weapon lent it an aura of fear; 'Noonchuck,' the whites called it. 'Never let Chen get his noonchuck on you.' Then came the kung fu movie craze, and Bruce Lee used the nunchakus and, before Chen's horrified eyes, the sacred thing became a toy for delinquents across the globe - they were becoming common. COMMON! It was humiliating. Chen went to all the Bruce Lee movies and writhed."

THE BRUCE LEE SOCIETY

In a magazine that Andrew buys called *Joy of Knowledge* is a fact-index building up into an encyclopedia. He eagerly awaited the entry for "Lee" and this is it: "LEE; Bruce (1940-1973) - Chinese-American film actor. Won little recognition until he starred in a number of Hong Kong Kung Fu films such as *Fist of Fury* (1973) and *Enter the Dragon* (1973). His karate skills and ferocious snarl made him a cult hero."

SPECIAL REQUESTS/ HELP NEEDED

Rajinder Chumber of Birmingham wishes to obtain *KFM's* 12, 13 & 14 - can anyone assist? Write to him direct please.

Mr. J. Malone (Lincoln) and Mr. R. Armstrong (Belfast, Northern Ireland) would like members to write to him direct, giving addresses where they can obtain LP's of Bruce Lee soundtracks - or maybe someone could tape these for them? Drop them a line folks.

27. A fat belly cannot believe that such a thing as hunger exists.

28. Knowing is not enough — We must apply. Willing is not enough — We must do.

29. He who wants to succeed, should learn how to fight, to strive and to suffer.

30. If you spend too much time thinking about a thing, you'll never get it done.

31. If you do the thing you fear, the death of fear is certain.

32. Showing off is the fool's idea of glory.

33. How easy to die! How hard to live!

34. A good teacher protects his pupils from his own influence.

35. True refinement seeks simplicity.

USEFUL ADDRESSES

For members' information, the address of the Jackie Chan Fan Club is: A6 - 16F Hankow Centre, 47 Peking Road, Kowloon, Hong Kong.(But please see comments on this under "General News").

Kamiljit Khaira has given the following Kung Fu school address: Lau Kung Fu, 16 Temple Passage, Birmingham - taught by Master Yam.

The address of the Bruce Lee Association (run by member Aluizio de Oliveira Jnr.) would welcome anyone wishing to join and they also want someone in England to act as their correspondence to inform them of any information or events relative to Bruce so why not drop him a line folks?? (Address: Caixa Postal 496, 38100 - Uberaba - MG, Brazil.)

And another club (run by Yuvaraaj Thaker) wants members to write to them as he buys, sells and swaps items on Bruce. He would welcome hearing from you too, at his address: Bruce Lee Memorial Fan Club, "Nandanvan," Flat No. 18, 269 opposite L.T.M.G. Nurses Quarters, Sion (W), Bombay 400002, India.

Another club starting up is run by Saul Chipunza (No. 1 Hawthorn Drive, Lochinvar, Harare, Zimbabwe) and he'd be delighted to hear from you! (especially with a view to obtaining items etc.) Get those pens working!

Giko Ltd. (537 Stratford Road, Sparkhill, Birmingham B11 4LP) have the following: Bruce Lee JKD tracksuit jacket only - nylon/light blue/two navy stripes on shoulder/Bruce JKD symbol on back/white zip-up front/two zip-up pockets - small/medium/large; £14.95 plus £1 post/packing. Bruce JKD medallion - enamelled red/yellow JKD insignia on black background/gold chain and trim - £1.95 plus 30p p&p. Back issues of *Self-Defence International* magazines (possibly the only British magazine on a par with America's *Black Belt* magazine for quality) - £1.95 plus 60p p&p - Vol. 1 Nos. 1, 2, 3 each. Giko catalogues: £1 inc. p&p.

COLLECTION TO GIVE AWAY!!

Lee Percy needs room at home, so his vast collection HAS to go! And he has made the sensational offer to members that he will give this away free of charge as long as the person will collect the items from him. What an offer! So if you want the items, and are also prepared to collect, drop him a line; he will collect all names together, draw out a winner, and then contact that person to collect. Thanks, Lee, for your VERY generous gesture - I am sure you will be inundated with requests! (Ilford, Essex).

VIDEO INFORMATION

Peter Tang (our member who runs the very successful video club) has given the following list of videos he sells unobtainable elsewhere: *The Secret Rivals* (John Lu/Wang Tao) - English, *New Secret Rivals* (John Lu - Chinese/subtitles, *Laughing Hyena* (Jackie Chan) - Chinese/subtitles, *Bruce Lee - The Man, The Myth* (uncensored) (Bruce Li) with nunchakus - English.

Michael Harris, Kevin Carter, Pauline Bouckley, Dave Midgley, Iain Leslie and Pardip Kumar (to name but a few!) also tell me Peter has *Fury of the Dragon* which runs for 1 1/2 hours containing three episodes of *Green Hornet*. This costs £25 plus £1 p&p, and Michael says he was pleasantly surprised by the content. Excellent quality/sound/colour. Write direct to Peter at Rochdale.

David Moore also mentioned *Fury of the Dragon* obtainable from Entertainment on Video. He says this has four episodes of Bruce (as opposed to Peter's three). Says David: "It was nice to see early footage of Bruce in action, except for two things: some of the fighting takes place in semi-darkness so it is hard to make out what is happening and secondly, there wasn't enough of Bruce for me!"

David says that *The Challenge* starring Toshiro Mifune, Scott Glen, Atsua Nakamura and Donna Kei Benz is available on CBS/Fox Label. Excellent film directed by John Frankenheimer and possibly the most polished martial arts movie ever filmed, about the struggle between two Japanese brothers who both wish to own two Samurai swords called "the Equals." Nakamura plays the bad brother running a giant business/criminal empire and Mifune the good brother heading a martial arts school keeping up the traditional Japanese fighting styles - Kenjutsu (art of the sword), Kyujutsu (archery), Shuriken (throwing stars) and Aikijutsu (a jujutsu style which was the forerunner of the modern Aikido). The climatic sequence where

Mifune storms his brother's modern building complex, using traditional martial arts against modern weapons, is brilliant. This film is a must!

According to David, *Silent Flute* is now on release by Rank Video with David Carradine and Jeff Cooper. (Everyone must know this was the film Bruce, James Coburn and Sterling Silliphant were going to make around 1969 but the plan fell through at that time). "Well, Carradine finally got around all the obstacles thrown against him and I must  say he has made a very good film, playing the four parts Bruce intended for himself, with Jeff playing Coburn's part. Whilst Carradine is not an 'expert,' he is better at fighting than in the Kung Fu series. From what I have read on *Flute* from magazines and books, I think Carradine has captured Bruce's ideas and the spirit of the project very well indeed! I thoroughly enjoyed it and could not see why it wasn't released nationally, instead of just in London."

David also says, "*Snake In The Eagle's Shadow* (Rank) is the second Jackie Chan film I've seen and I enjoyed it very much. The comedy/martial arts are excellent and now I cannot wait to see Jackie's *Drunken Master* also by Rank. *Battlecreek Brawl* (Guild Home Video) starring Jackie is already on release. Although a good film, Jackie seemed restricted - he later said he wasn't allowed much say in the filming/fight scenes - and seems much more at home in *Snake*."

Finally, *Sharkey's Machine* (Warner Bros.) starring Burt Reynolds is a good film, and also worth a mention purely because Dan Inosanto makes two very short appearances as one of the Chin Brothers Oriental "hit men." Though Dan is killed off like Bruce in *Marlowe,* it was good to see him in a serious non-martial arts film also. Hollywood must recognise Dan for his skills, having worked on *Killer Elite, Big Brawl, Sharkey's Machine*, and is now to star in his own film on Filipino fighting arts called *Skirmish*.

Pardip Kumar saw the video *True Game of Death* with Bruce Lei. Although the film showed a bit of Bruce to start, the old familiar rip-off then began. The print was appalling as was the dubbing. The only good thing was the video case with a great Bruce picture - which of course insinuated this video was a genuine Bruce Lee one - "Remember," says Pardip, "that it's not what's outside the video that matters but what's on the inside."

Iain Leslie tells of the release of *Dragon Lord* (Guild Home Video) starring Jackie - and Iain says that Jackie can inject new life into the martial arts film industry so let's wish him luck as he's not a bad fellow at all!!

RENEWALS

A reminder to members about renewals: members 1628-1828 - your eighth year falls due between end December/beginning March. Likewise - 2171-2276 (seventh year); 2531-2599 (sixth year); 2804-2907 (fifth year); 3109-3157 (fourth year); 3304-3322 (third year); 3436-3477 (second year). I look forward to hearing from you.

SPECIAL ITEMS
BACK ISSUE NEWS SHEETS/ROBERT LEE LP's
BLACK AND WHITE PHOTO OF ROBERT AND BRUCE

Should you require any of the above, drop me a line with your requirements and I will give you a price plus postage. Bruce fans - you MUST obtain the Robert LP as this is a rare and very collectable item NOT to be missed!

DANISH CONVENTION REPORT

Member Tony Lundberg from Denmark organised a Bruce Lee convention there in October, and from all accounts it went extremely well! Here's Tony's write-up about this:

"1983 was a special year for hundreds of Bruce fans in Denmark who went to see our very first convention held on 30th October at the Vetserbro Ungdomsgard. There was a wonderful feeling there, which makes you feel warm and happy inside, and a little proud because you know it is YOU who have collected hundreds together at the very same place, who are all there for the very same reason - and then you can feel the spirit of Bruce Lee walking around the people at the convention. We showed *Fist of Fury, Behind The Scenes of Enter the Dragon, The Green Hornet Screen Test,* two American trailers of *Game of Death* and *Enter the Dragon.* There were lots of words spoken about Bruce - also a successful quiz with eight people, four on two teams, with 32 questions. The death of Bruce was a very serious matter - we spoke and explained very carefully how he died, and behind the speaker was a large screen showing newspaper articles from the day after Lee's death. Philosophy was read - during which time shadowplay of two fighters in combat showed on the screen - it was very nice. There were two breaks where fans could go and eat and drink, and of course buy some of the great Bruce Lee items. We also held a Bruce Lee 'imitation' contest - it was very funny and extraordinary. Then some speakers spoke some very fine poetry about Bruce. The convention was from 2.30 p.m. until 9.30 p.m. - and I am sure it was a very fine success! (Thank Goodness.)"

(Thanks, Tony, for the run-down, and congratulations on your first convention. I hope there are many more to come!) And I gather, too, that *Game of Death Part 2* was released on 31st October in Denmark - it was given a very good write-up by the press, but still did not run for more than nine days - Tony was not impressed with the film!!

CONSCIENCE

Here is Bruce's own definition in relation to his own ideals: *"Recognizing that my emotions often err in their over-enthusiasm, and my faculty of reason often is without the warmth of feeling that is necessary to enable me to combine justice with mercy in my judgments, I will encourage my conscience to guide me as to what is right and what is wrong, but I will never set aside the verdicts it renders, no matter what may be the cost of carrying them out."*

THE BRUCE LEE SOCIETY

BRUCE'S BOOK LIST - PART VII

Herewith a further range of book titles from Bruce's personal collection:

Vital Karate - Masatatau Oyama (1967)
Kempo Self Defense - Naraki Hara (1967)
Aikido - Kisshomaru Uyeshiba (1963)
Aikido - Koichi Tohei (1961)
What Is Aikido? - Koichi Tohei (1962)
Aikido In Daily Life - Koichi Tohei (1966)
The Techniques of Aikido - Thomas H. Makiyama (1960)
This is Kendo - Sasamuri, Warner (1964)
The Womanly Art of Self-Defense - C. W. Krone Jr. (1967)
The Fine Art Of Ju Jitsu - Watho, Beldam (1906)
What Is Self-Defense? (Kenpo Jujitsu) - J. M. Mitosi (1953)
Kill Or Get Killed - Col. Rex Applegate (1961)
Guerilla Self-Defense - G. F. Jowett (1943)
Self-Defense - Eric Dominy (1957)
American Judo Illustrated - A. H. Farrar (1945)
Fighting Arts Of The World - J. F. Gilbey (1963)

SWOP SHOP

- Thomas Vickers, Toledo, U.S.A. has many extra items in his Bruce Lee collection which he is willing to trade to other fans. Write to him direct for info.
- Aluizio De Oliveira Jr., (Bruce Lee Association), Uberaba, Brazil wants English records of Demis Roussos - can anyone help him? Write direct please.
- Jesbir Kumar, Birmingham has for sale/or swap considered: All *KFM*s (apart from couple) - £35. Write for details first – Don't send money!
- Tim Ussher, Crowborough has for sale: many, many Bruce Lee items too numerous to list. Write to Tim for list/prices.
- Dennis Nutter, Leeds has for sale Bruce Lee special tape featuring all fighting scenes from Bruce Lee films inc. double nunchakus/uncut Coliseum fight from *Way of the Dragon,* Lee vs. Inosanto fight from *Game of Death,* Bruce Lee original screen test and lots more - running time two hours - £40; also *Game of Death* £25; *Bruce Lee Souvenir* - £15.
- Mark Salisbury, Tunbridge Wells has enormous Bruce Lee collection inc. *KFM*s 3-34, first *Scrapbook, Game of Death* magazine, albums (*Enter/Fist/Boss/Dragon Power*) and posters. Send SAE for more info direct to Mark.
- Pardip Kumar, Birmingham has for sale/swap considered: three-hour VHS cassette - slow-motion *The Big Boss, Fist of Fury, Way of the Dragon* nunchaku fight (music only); clips from "Preying Mantis" episode; clips of Lee from *Longstreet, Marlowe,* Lee on HKTV breaking boards, funeral, clips from all films, plus *Green Hornet* screen test/trailers from all films and *Green Hornet*/cameras in Lee's house. Sell for £25 or swaps considered. Also all Bruce Lee videos uncut at £25 each and *Real Bruce Lee* at £15 or swap.
- Lee O'Neill, Omagh, Northern Ireland wants *KFM*s No. 1 & 2 - will pay VERY high price in mint condition - it's important to Lee! - write direct.

WELL - out of space, folks! For those of you who are waiting to see their letters in print, or information, watch for the March news sheet!!.
Peace, brotherhood, and...

Love - Pam Hadden

ENDINGS AND REFLECTIONS

After seven years and 30 issues, The Bruce Lee Society news sheet #30 was the last news sheet to be issued and marked an abrupt end to the Bruce Lee Society. Without word, without warning, it just stopped. No, "Goodbye." No, "Thanks for the memories." Nothing.

There has never been a completely clear explanation of why the Bruce Lee Society ended, but former member Andrew Staton offered some insight into the financial and editorial factors that may have contributed to its dissolution. "I am not really sure of the complete reasons, but I did meet Bruce Sawford, editor of *Kung Fu Monthly*, at Bunch Books in London shortly before it ceased publication. He said that the owners felt that the magazine had done its run and wanted to concentrate on new, more popular and fashionable magazines. When I spoke to Pam, she said it was hard to get money out of Bunch Books (the owners of *Kung Fu Monthly*) to pay for sundries such as new badges and general materials to run the club. She was using her own money to run the Society which, even though she was generous, there had to be a limit."

Andrew Hadden, Pamela Hadden's son, says it was Pamela's passion for Bruce Lee that made her overlook, for many years, the personal financial hardship of running the Society. "My mom used to talk about the Society with my grandmother. She would tell her how there's quite a lot of work in it and my grandmother would come out with a perfectly practical point, being an Irish woman: 'So, how much are you actually getting paid for all this then?' She thought my mum was completely mad for doing it for nothing. My mum did it because, like most people who do it, they're enthusiasts and it's their thing and they actually enjoy doing it. So, I can well understand why she did it for nothing. My mum's full-time job was as a secretary for British Airways and she didn't have a hugely glamorous or exciting life."

The all-consuming commitment to Bruce Lee and his fans was also clearly a factor in the Bruce Lee Society's demise. Pam Hadden's stewardship of the Society took a significant toll on her, and she was quite ill by the time the Society closed. "At the end of the society, my mum was about 42 years old," said Andrew Hadden. "She was practically a middle-aged woman and running the club took a lot of hard work. I don't think the level of enthusiasm was there anymore. There were still lots of Bruce Lee fans and actually coping with all the fan mail that she got just tired her out. I just think that she had had enough."

Fan mail was not the only manner in which Bruce Lee

The "Home" of The Bruce Lee Society from 1976 to 1983. All newsletters, membership packs and other correspondence were sent from this mid-terraced house in London. Photo by Google from April 2019.

fans reached Pam. They would ring her on the telephone at all hours of the day and night. "I was kind of the answering machine," recalled Pam's son. "I always answered the phone and vetted the calls. I could filter out the bad calls by just saying sorry, she's out, she's on holiday or whatever. I was always the answering machine unless I was out, then she had to answer the phone herself."

"Pam was so dedicated to running the Bruce Lee Society that she suffered badly," said Staton. "Most fans are happy with whatever a club offers by way of information and events. However, there is a small minority that has so little in life that their need for knowledge on Bruce Lee (or any of their other interests) becomes an obsession for them. If you do not feed that obsession, you become a target. Pam warned me about these fans. She regretted giving her home phone number out to some of them as they would ring her home at all hours and, if she didn't give them the answers they wanted, they'd give her a load of abuse down the phone! You could see she was tired, and her nerves were really bad."

Occasionally, members would step in to help Pam. Alison French took on the task of organizing an annual floral tribute commemorating Bruce on the date he passed and bought with donations from Society members. "I had been sending flowers myself via a friend who lived in Canada for some years, but she moved back to the UK. So, I asked Pam about doing a joint contribution. We had been talking and writing on a regular basis at that time and she thought it was a good idea, so I took it on."

Left to Right: Andrew Hadden, Pam Hadden, Fred Hunt, and Terri Freestone.

"The Society itself was amazing; organising those huge conventions, all the interesting and artistic people who contributed, but Pam mainly did everything herself," said French. "You could tell Pam had so much to do with the Society and just to get a newsletter out every three months and arrange everything else she did must have put her under a lot of stress. However, I don't remember that side coming over to me. She was always fine when we met and very helpful when I came to one convention at seven-months pregnant and couldn't find a seat. It was really busy but she got them to put me up in the projection room."

French recalled another example of Pam Hadden's kindness. "She was very friendly and thoughtful. I just found again the piece of tree from the garden outside of Bruce's house that Pam sent me after her trip to Hong Kong. She was always nice to me and told me to phone her whenever I wanted."

There were also issues impacting Pam Hadden's life that were unrelated to the Bruce Lee Society. Her job at British Airways was tremendously taxing, and she ultimately left it a few years after the Society ended. There were also health issues, physical and mental, that began plaguing Pam Hadden in the 1980s. On 13th June

1991, less than two months shy of her 50th birthday, Pam Hadden joined her idol Bruce Lee in death following a brave battle with breast cancer. She is buried in Streatham Park Cemetery in London SW16.

When contacted for this book, Bruce Lee's brother Robert Lee offered some recollections of his friend Pam. "Ms. Pamela Hadden was a very nice, friendly, honest, and warm person," said Lee. "She always had a bright and wonderful smile on her face. I greatly respect her dedication and hard work towards the

Pam Hadden, Robert Lee, and Will Johnston rehearse on stage at the 1980 convention.

Bruce Lee Society during the years when she was actively involved. I was deeply saddened to find out, after her passing, that she had a terminal illness. She even made a point, before her death, to air freight me back all the *Ballad of Bruce Lee* albums that I left in her possession after my appearance at the Bruce Lee convention."

Pam Hadden served the Bruce Lee fans well over the seven years that the Bruce Lee Society was active. Managing the Society newsletter, receiving and responding to tens of thousands of letters, and (at the same time) maintaining a full-time job, was a feat in itself and one of which Bruce Lee himself would have been proud. In 2011, Felix Dennis, publisher of *Kung Fu Monthly*, recalled Pam Hadden's exceptional commitment to The Bruce Lee Society. "Pam Hadden was a wonderful president of The Bruce Lee Society which was founded at *Kung Fu Monthly*," said Dennis. "Quite simply, Pam worshipped the ground that Bruce Lee walked on and did more than anyone to keep Bruce Lee's memory alive – not to mention answering hundreds of letters from members of the Society personally."

"She died too young," said Alison French. "She was always trying help others but had too many balls to juggle at times."

"Pam Hadden is the unsung hero of Bruce Lee fandom," added Andrew Staton. "I think the newsletters that Pam wrote and compiled were, along with *Kung Fu Monthly*, integral in feeding the eager public's need for information on the legacy of Bruce Lee in the Seventies. Without Pam, the tapestry of nostalgia on Bruce Lee at that period in time would not have been as rich. I hope this book reminds fans to always pay tribute to this tenacious lady and her thankless work to keep the memory of Bruce Lee alive."

THE BRUCE LEE SOCIETY, PAM HADDEN, AND ME
By Tony Lundberg (member 2338)

Back in 1973, when I was nine years old, I was visiting a Chinese friend of mine, who introduced me to Bruce Lee by showing me a Chinese Kung Fu magazine, which featured a piece on Bruce Lee. I still remember the picture and the impact it did to me; Bruce Lee was standing in white shorts, making this beautiful sidekick. He was topless, and stood there rank and majestic, tanned and muscular. I was so impressed by the way he looked, and thought to myself, "One day, I will be like him."

I asked my friend, if I could buy this magazine from him, and he sold me that very picture from the magazine, which he had cut out. I paid him twice the value of the magazine, but I didn't care; I just had to have it and I still have it, 47 years later.

So I asked a lot of questions about Bruce Lee, because I wanted to know everything. I asked around to see if anybody knew anything about this Chinese dude, and thank God, I came across the Chinese community, who knew all about Bruce Lee, and here I got all the information and the stories that I needed.

Overnight Bruce Lee changed my life and I became a huge fan, collector, and later, a Bruce Lee historian. I have collected Bruce Lee memorabilia ever since and now have one of the biggest private Bruce Lee collections in the world, containing over ten thousand items. I am one of the only people in the world to have made over one hundred projects about Bruce Lee., including quizzes, film festivals, exhibitions, movies, tv shows, radio shows, conventions, tributes, books, poems, magazines, articles, annual meetings, wax figure petition etc.

I heard about The Bruce Lee Secret Society by some pen pals of mine, and decided to know much more, about this "mystic" club. I thought back then, that the name "Secret Society" sounded so cool, so mysterious, and that was very appealing to me.

Needing to know much more about this club, I asked all my friends if they had heard anything about this Chinese Kung Fu dude called Bruce Lee but they just looked at me like I was from a distanced planet, and said "WHO?!?" Then I asked them if they had heard about this great Bruce Lee fan club, called The Bruce Lee Secret Society, but without saying anything, they just look at one another, turned their eyes around and left, like I had the plague.

I next went to all the newspapers stands in Copenhagen and asked them the same questions but again, nobody knew anything about Bruce Lee. So I asked at the newspaper stands if I could look through their German and British martial arts magazines to see if I could find anything about this mystic and secret society.

One day, whilst looking through those magazines and long after my first introduction to Master Lee, I saw an advertisement for The Bruce Lee Society and thought I would love to join them by becoming a member and maybe help them out as much as I could, which I did many times throughout the years.

Around 1977, at the age of 15, I began writing to Pam Hadden, the then president of The Bruce Lee Secret Society. I asked her about anything; about Bruce Lee, his family, new publications, other fan clubs etc. Pam, for me, was a sweet, humble, and lovely lady, a great and trustworthy woman, and such a great friend, who I love and miss very much. She was the most hardworking woman I have ever met. She had a full time job at British Airways and spent all her spare time and holidays working like crazy to keep her Bruce Lee club running.

Anne Hunt (1275; right) with Pam Hadden (centre) at the first convention.

She was so nice to me in every way, and helped me out by giving me a lot of great and secret information about the Bruce Lee community, free Bruce Lee merchandise, such as books, old newsletters, Bruce Lee magazines, posters, the *Kung Fu Monthly* magazines, the *KFM* binders, stickers, the treasure kit, badges, stickers, etc. for the help I gave her throughout the years.

We use to write one another for many years, exchanging news from our respective countries about daily living and news about Bruce Lee. She use to tell me a lot of secrets about what she had heard from the Lee family, information which was never published and was not going to be published ever.

Pam meant the world to me in those years, so I kept my word and have never told anybody the secrets Pam told me because a word is a bond, and I loved Pam for her dedication, the person she was, and for all her hard work so I will take a lot of secrets with me to the grave. I owe it to Pam, the Lee family and most of all, to Bruce Lee.

Over the years we discussed various subjects, and I told her what I thought about specific issues, topics, upcoming projects, the fan club and the people around her. I told her many times that she had to be careful about whom she was talking to and working with because of the knowledge she was sharing with me, about her work with the fan club, and the people around her.

At that time, I was also chosen to be the country representative for many other fan clubs in England and other countries in Denmark so I knew all the bullshit that were going on between the clubs but I stayed loyal to Pam through the years and asked her if she wanted me to stop working for them like I worked for her. She said no because she felt that my work was so important and if I kept her updated about

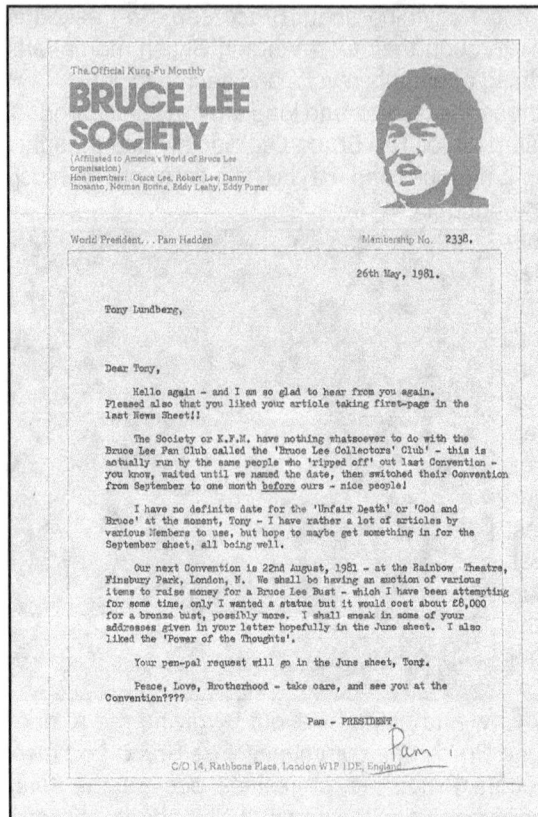

what was going on, that would be great. I kept her informed but I never turned my back on anybody, staying as neutral as I could, because the work came first, and my friendship with Pam meant the world to me.

We spent a lot of time discussing new ideas I had for The Bruce Lee Society and in general. She used to write to me about her ideas for the Society, asking me for advice and so on. We kept on writing to one another for several years, even after the club sadly ended the way it did.

Pam did not leave or stop the Bruce Lee Society, it stopped her; she was just worn out. Let me rephrase that; the Society, the people around her like The *Kung Fu Monthly*, the S.I.P, The Bruce Lee Collectors Club, etc. did not leave much time for Pam to be herself and have a normal social life. The way I see it is that she was forced out. Pam was working like crazy for British Airways, spending 12-13 hours there at times, which was so stressful for her. Then she'd spend all her recreational time on the Bruce Lee Society. When she decided to leave it all behind, she was totally worn out. She got so sick, physically and mentally, that she was hospitalised for a long time and she never recovered from that.

Pam's downfall started in 1981, when The Bruce Lee Collectors Club waited to announce their Bruce Lee convention, which they did after The Bruce Lee Society had announced the date for their The *Kung Fu Monthly* convention. So a rotten trick was pulled when The Bruce Lee Collectors Club announced that they had decided to schedule their convention for the month before The *Kung Fu Monthly* one, which turned everything upside down, for Pam and her society. From then on, she could not trust anybody in the same circle. She sent me a letter about it on the 26th May 1981, writing:

> "The Society or KFM *have nothing whatsoever to do with the Bruce Lee Fan Club called the 'Bruce Lee Collectors' Club' - this is actually run by the same people who ripped off our last convention - you know, waited until we named the date, then switched their convention from September to one month before ours - nice people!"*

A RETROSPECTIVE LOOK AT BRUCE LEE MANIA & THE KUNG FU CRAZE OF THE 1970S

She wrote to me again on the 6th August 1981, where she mentioned that she was no longer angry at The Bruce Lee Collectors Club, only at their behaviour:

> "Well, I'm not so angry on the club anymore, only their behaviour in the past, using their proper name of SIP, and trying to ruin our convention. Apart from that, and the high prices they used to charge, I'm not bothered, and certainly do not wish to influence anyone else in that respect. They do sell items on Bruce - maybe even rare ones, I don't know - but I am glad when more things are made available to members; no, I'm not mad, as long as they play the game properly and compete, but not try to ruin."

It seems to me that a lot of projects Pam was involved in were not healthy for her, because the people behind those projects weren't professional enough and couldn't back it up, leaving Pam with a lot of pressure and responsibility. *Kung Fu Monthly* didn't tell her and others close to her, that they were cancelling projects she was involved with. They lied to her face, and were in my opinion, backstabbing her big time, trying to ruin and hurt her, which I think, they finally did.

That's one of the main reasons that Pam pulled the plug and quietly went away. She didn't want to be reminded of anything that had anything to do with The Bruce Lee Society or *Kung Fu Monthly* so she refused to talk about or answer anything concerning those, or the people that were connected to any of it and I respected her for that, because it nearly killed her.

If she ever did want to talk or write about it, I supported her in any way I could and answered her back in a manner she could cope and rely on.

In my opinion, her work of keeping the Bruce Lee name alive, and the people she was working with, which she trusted with her life, were the same people who made her so sick, so she had to be hospitalised for a long time, after which, she was forced away from her beloved Bruce Lee fan club, and had no choice but to close it down. Pam never recovered from that, and got cancer later on. She was never the same person after that.

From what I understand, I was the very last Bruce Lee fan, and the only one she wrote to

> Date the 13th of Nov. 86.
>
> Dear Tony,
>
> Hope this short note finds your correct address - This is Pam Hadden - ex-President of the B.L.S. just dropping you a line to wish you well - my apologies for not dropping you a line sooner but I have been keeping away from any commitments as far as letter writing was concerned - I was pretty sick just after the Society closed with all the pressures, and I'm afraid I could not cope with anything other than day to day routine. I hope you are well. If you wish to drop me a line, please do - but please - no questions on Bruce or the Society closure - just let me know how you are & what's happening your end!!
>
> Regards - Pam

> 15/12/88
>
> *Christmas greetings and best wishes for the New Year.*
>
> To Tony – have a good Christmas to you and your girlfriend!
> Pamela (Hadden)

until the very end. My last mail from her was a card for Christmas 1988. After that, I never heard from her again, which made me so sad for years to come, but it also made me feel so angry because of all the hypocrites in the Bruce Lee community that were close to her, pretending to be her confident, should have been there for her. Instead they took advantage of her kindness, weaknesses and vulnerability. She didn't deserve that.

I still have all of her letters, Christmas cards, birthday cards and all of the rare Bruce Lee material she gave me throughout the years, which I treasure with all my heart and it's material I will never sell or trade with anyone. Respect, peace, and love, Pam.... For being such a lovely giving woman and for your outstanding work for keeping Bruce Lee's name alive. I am proud to call myself your friend forever.

Tony Lundberg
September 2020

All letters and photographs in this section appear courtesy of Tony Lundberg and are kindly used with permission.

EPILOGUE: AFTER THE BRUCE LEE SOCIETY

Throughout the tenure of The Bruce Lee Society, other fan clubs were up and running too. One of those fan clubs was The Bruce Lee Collector's Club which was originally run by the late Bruce Lee fan Roy Plant who voluntarily managed the club on behalf of Cimac and Giko martial arts entrepreneur Tim Ward in Birmingham.

In 1985, two years after the Bruce Lee Society folded, Pam Hadden contacted Tim Ward to see if he would be willing to take on the club to run alongside his Bruce Lee's Collector's Club, which he agreed to do. At the time, Ward had handed the management of the club over to Andrew Staton, who elected to merge it with the Bruce Lee Society. "I went down to London and met Pam for the day," said Andrew. "She was a great lady; so kind and understanding, full of stories and she wished me luck continuing the club in a new format."

Andrew Staton, along with several people including fellow Bruce Lee Society and *Kung Fu Monthly* contributors Will Johnston and Greg Rhodes, would run The Bruce Lee Collector's Club for several years before evolving into The Bruce Lee Association. "When Tim left Giko, Greg, Will, and myself changed the name to the Bruce Lee Association, so that, under Greg's suggestion, the magazine would be called *BLAM (Bruce Lee Association Magazine)* and the cover artwork was done by Will's brother, James.

In respect to Brandon Lee after his tragic death in 1993, the club changed its name again - this time to The Bruce and Brandon Lee Association (BBLA) and re-

The BBLA team with Van Williams at the Kato Show convention in 2002.

named its magazine, *Dragon Tracks*.

The next few years were a mixture of joy and sorrow for the Bruce and Brandon Lee Association, Andrew Staton, and some of the team. "There was a point after this that I was voted onto the Bruce Lee Educational Foundation board thanks to John Little, and we became the British leg of this official organisation," said Staton. "However, within a year, the foundation folded and a new legal team took over the name and likeness rights of Bruce Lee. The new legal team was hard on clubs that had been keeping the legacy of Bruce Lee alive all these years. Therefore, it was with some regret I had to close The Bruce and Brandon Lee Association." The British martial arts magazine *Martial Arts Illustrated* provided a lifeline for the club for a time. "Thanks to a regular column in magazines such as *Martial Arts Illustrated*, *Impact*, and more recently, *World of Martial Arts*, we were able to carry on in some capacity and keep fans informed on Bruce Lee news, reviews and interviews under the guise of different titles; the latest one being the *Jun Fan Journal*," said Staton.

Though the Bruce and Brandon Lee Association doesn't exist as a "club" anymore, and *Martial Arts Illustrated* and *Impact* have both ceased publication, BBLA staff members continue to write about Bruce Lee and Brandon Lee for several magazines including *World of Martial Arts, Black Belt,* and many more.

Bruce Lee continues to be an inspiration for people from all over the world, regardless of geographic location, language, race, or religious beliefs. Numerous documentaries have been made about his life and so will many more in the future. An innovator in his lifetime, almost 50 years after his passing, Bruce Lee is still regarded by many as the greatest martial artist of all time.

THE BRUCE LEE SOCIETY MEMBERSHIP

Here is a list of members and membership numbers collected from the newsletters, *Kung Fu Monthly* and from the members lists that Pam Hadden sent to members. Sadly, the list is only 20% complete. Should you wish to see a more up-to-date list or contribute to the list, please visit https://www.bruceleesociety.co.uk/memberlist

"Under the skies, under the heavens, there is but one family." — Bruce Lee

(1007) Eileen & Joey Green
(1009) John Rogers
(1011) C. Carruthers
(1013) Keith Mandley
(1016) M Campion
(1019) Kevin Walker
(1021) David Niedzailek
(1023) Alexander Martin
(1024) N.J. Savage
(1029) Andrea McLean
(1030) Brett Morgan
(1032) Gary Chedgzoy
(1033) Kevin Hobbs
(1036) Marlene Condy
(1040) Soong Ken Ma
(1044) Joseph Chiang
(1048) Brian Cuffe
(1051) Chris Morgan
(1056) Will Johnston
(1061) Mike Devereux
(1064) Derek Crane
(1068) David Frase
(1069) David Ryder
(1072) Lee Percy
(1073) Diane Webb
(1078) Michael Harris
(1081) Mark Freeth
(1087) Peter Jagger
(1090) Ann Fitzgerald
(1099) M Haycock
(1104) Stephen Hill
(1109) Alan Mount
(1116) John Stuart
(1120) B Haria
(1127) Jeff Millington
(1134) N Kumar
(1138) Peter Love
(1143) Alison French
(1144) P Mansell
(1148) Andrew Barratt
(1150) Arthur Stone
(1151) David Montagu
(1156) Steven Willard
(1160) P Brown
(1164) Paul Short

(1167) James Hynes
(1177) G. Hudson
(1188) David Leeming
(1189) Ralph Canswick
(1191) Stephen Hatcher
(1194) Kate Feeney
(1195) Kay Drummond
(1199) Paul Mason
(1202) Robert Connelly
(1213) Ian Hamilton
(1214) Ian Grant
(1217) B Langston
(1218) Hugh Lagan
(1226) L J Turner
(1232) Eric Holden
(1238) David Fieldhouse
(1249) Paul Collins
(1251) Andrew Timberland
(1259) Robin Blades
(1260) Rick Edwards
(1266) M Percival
(1270) R Dale
(1271) S Bearsmore
(1272) Joe Woods
(1275) Anne and Fred Hunt
(1278) S Gostage
(1293) M Yates
(1296) C.R.N. Kellaway
(1301) Deborah Pledge
(1311) Tim Stephens
(1314) Cary Dean
(1322) Mick Bargota
(1328) Tony Thompson
(1330) S. Jolley
(1336) P R Brown
(1337) T Sira
(1338) Brian Fletcher
(1339) J.W. Cook
(1353) Brian Rusk
(1354) Julian Midgley
(1359) Nigel Martin
(1360) Graham Hughes
(1363) Michael Butler
(1367) J Spence
(1378) Brian Beaumont

(1380) Rajinder Jutlla
(1381) Graham Jenkinson
(1382) Gerard McNamara
(1383) John R. Bell
(1385) Michael Sanderson
(1386) Karen Bird
(1403) J Sim
(1407) N. Allwood
(1410) Joyce Tompkins
(1413) Helen Cook
(1419) Shahab Setudeh Nejad
(1423) Richard McColl
(1432) Trevor Bayles
(1433) Derek Walton
(1440) David Coe
(1443) Andy Hill
(1445) Chris Bowman
(1446) Peter Ward
(1456) Duncan Smith
(1469) Stephen Leigh
(1473) Ray Tidswell
(1477) Danny Wilde
(1478) William Luke
(1494) Adam Davies
(1496) Paul Davies
(1497) T.McEniry
(1498) Gerald Rae
(1511) S.S. Green
(1521) David Anthony
(1527) John Aspinall
(1528) Stephen Bogle
(1530) Anthony Jackson
(1532) Paul Smith
(1535) John Corns
(1537) M Marchant
(1541) Keith Milner
(1543) Joseph Hartley
(1550) Audrey Slade
(1554) Steven Walpole
(1559) John Scott
(1563) Eileen O'Connell
(1565) Dennis Cartwright
(1567) Glynn Barker
(1573) Michael Adams
(1575) M. McAdam

(1577) Andrew Southern
(1578) Kevin Hunt
(1582) Burker Ali
(1583) Freddie Furnival
(1585) Peter Stride
(1598) Peter Barnacle
(1621) Paul Brosnan
(1622) Ronald Porter
(1628) R. Gray
(1634) S Chapman
(1636) Peter Stubbs
(1638) Richard Miller
(1640) Michael Wyldbore
(1645) George McFarlane
(1649) James Wilson
(1650) David Dixon
(1655) Gino D'Ambrosio
(1658) Harminder Singh Rana
(1662) Tom Surgenor
(1663) Kieran O'Neill
(1668) D M Darby
(1670) Andrew Staton
(1674) Arthur Crosthwaite
(1675) David Colville
(1680) Paul Nayman
(1681) Kathy Parsons
(1686) Michael Werkowski
(1687) Mark Burns
(1688) Geordie Nokes
(1690) A. Lindsay
(1695) Martin Hughes
(1696) Mick Zamiteas
(1701) Michael Day
(1708) Christopher Navas
(1709) Crysia Zwiryk
(1711) Paul Corrigan
(1712) Martin Frampton
(1713) Paul Rogers
(1715) Anthony Clarke
(1717) Paul Ashton
(1718) Paul Ruiz
(1721) Peter Willetts
(1724) James Ruddy
(1728) H. Craig
(1729) John Kemp

(1735) Shane Phipps
(1739) Kevin Houlihan
(1743) Suresh Gandhi
(1747) John Chater
(1749) Molly Cullen
(1752) David C. King
(1755) Michael Hodson
(1763) Shiela Boardman
(1771) Patrick Hennessy
(1772) Ronald McVeigh
(1776) David Atkinson
(1783) David Moore
(1788) P Wright
(1789) Richard Robert Green
(1792) Mark Salter
(1793) Peter Thomas
(1797) Raghuir Kandola
(1799) Pete Broad
(1800) Conrad O'Connor
(1810) Ian Camilleri
(1815) Jeffrey Proctor
(1819) Martin Schell
(1823) A J Billings
(1828) Al Briers
(1834) Patricia Davies
(1836) Paul Wade
(1844) Fred Stuffin
(1854) David Short
(1856) David Hare
(1865) S Powell
(1874) Richard Zincke
(1877) David Ridge
(1885) Kevin Taylor
(1889) John Okane
(1890) Brian Beck
(1891) Ian Milner
(1897) Terry Barrett
(1900) Anthony A Woodcock
(1904) Tom Wheeler
(1905) George Tseu
(1908) James Norman
(1911) David Cresswell
(1912) Thomas Tong
(1922) S A C Franklin
(1924) Trevor Livett

(1927) Rajendra Chandarana
(1931) A.Smyth
(1933) John Watson
(1935) Wesley Fleming
(1939) R.S. Richardson
(1940) Eric Henderson
(1941) Stephen Ward
(1943) Margaret Smith
(1944) Derek Hamer
(1945) Keith Graham
(1947) William Longson
(1951) Sean Andrew McCarthy
(1956) Colm Quinn
(1956) John Black
(1958) Darryl Myers
(1959) Gary Ainge
(1960) Keith Spicer
(1963) D Attwell
(1976) James McKeown
(1978) Gino Crane
(1987) Ramesh Krishnaswamy
(2000) David Casey
(2003) Edward Brian Whittaker
(2004) Gary Daniels
(2005) Stephen Hale
(2009) Angela Davenport
(2025) Dave Goodwin
(2026) David Evans
(2033) Kathryn Wray
(2034) Pier Cocozza
(2035) S Plant
(2037) P Glynn
(2038) Muhammad Hussain
(2039) David Lee
(2040) M. Lockwood
(2041) Ian Venson
(2042) Keith Gurden
(2043) Timothy Diamond
(2044) Lyn Warwick
(2045) N Genge
(2046) John Milne
(2047) Wayne Denfny
(2048) David Willett
(2049) Tina Maltby
(2050) Howard Broomhead

THE BRUCE LEE SOCIETY

(2051) Ronnie Baker
(2054) Martin French
(2055) Graham Lawson
(2056) S Williams
(2057) David Scott
(2058) Thomas Jones
(2059) K Slack
(2060) Gerard O'Brien
(2061) Hans Duggal
(2062) Steve Flumley
(2063) Danis van der Merwe
(2064) Zamir Ahmed
(2065) Julius Fernandez
(2066) Neil Marshall
(2067) Zahid Akhtar
(2068) F J Autin
(2069) Robert Pascoe
(2070) Sunil Sharma
(2071) Allan Wood
(2072) Neville Cachia
(2073) Andrew Robinson
(2074) Michael Minnis
(2075) Phillip Rendall
(2076) Keith O'Hara
(2077) Ian Stones
(2078) Fraser Reid
(2079) Prakash Menta
(2080) Kenneth Hill
(2081) Ronald Dyson
(2082) Steve Durkin
(2083) Nicky Wilson
(2084) F Jenkinson
(2085) Carl Hempsey
(2086) Aidan Connolly
(2087) Robert Bowden
(2088) P J Blount
(2089) P Pang
(2090) F Higginbottom
(2091) Mary Rennie
(2092) John Tandon
(2093) Archie Watson
(2094) G Chandler
(2095) James Williamson
(2096) Craig Jones
(2097) Andrew Booth

(2098) M Ripley
(2099) S Holmes
(2100) L Perry
(2101) David Brough
(2102) Alex Micallef
(2103) Pai Bansal
(2104) Martyn Oliver
(2105) A. Delgoda
(2106) Susan Pietrzyk
(2108) S Lawton
(2109) John Hill
(2111) A Gee
(2112) M Snowden
(2113) P Randerson
(2114) Amrat Vakharia
(2115) Josephine Binns
(2116) Nicholas Hodge
(2117) Islam Giny
(2118) Ebrahim Janat
(2119) T. Cape
(2120) K A Judd
(2121) Carl Jones
(2122) Andrew Aylett
(2123) Philip Neale
(2124) Tony Williamson
(2125) Heinrich Damsgaard
(2126) P Hand
(2127) T Jinney
(2128) Ayyaz Siddiq
(2129) Kath Thomas
(2130) Pte. Peacock
(2131) Tpr. Imrie
(2132) Kishan Chand
(2133) Ka Lam
(2134) Allan MacDonald
(2137) K F Yap
(2138) Steven Aris
(2140) Philip Gerreyn
(2141) P J Batkins
(2142) P Dickins
(2143) M Sharp
(2144) Duncan Edwards
(2146) Antwan Lombarts
(2147) P N Whittington
(2148) Richard Chiira

A RETROSPECTIVE LOOK AT BRUCE LEE MANIA & THE KUNG FU CRAZE OF THE 1970S

(2149) Yim Fai Lo
(2150) D C Clarke
(2151) Bruce Heller
(2152) A McCabe
(2153) Alan James
(2155) Paul Cottington
(2156) John Harvey
(2157) Navrat Sihra
(2158) A Smaith
(2159) Robin Coote
(2160) Allan Fallow
(2161) Ronnie Heller
(2162) Neil Baldwin
(2163) Valda Johnson
(2164) Alan Watson
(2165) N Fern
(2166) M Murray
(2167) Paul Mountain
(2172) Don Clift
(2186) Gary Stubbs
(2187) Andrew Clarke
(2196) John Latto
(2199) Alex Buttigieg
(2200) Yael Shelach
(2202) Stephen Whiteley
(2203) Laura Bagguley
(2206) Paul Bocking
(2208) Anthony King
(2213) Willem Uroegh
(2230) Wayne Jones
(2237) Gerard Hayes
(2238) Anthony Leong
(2241) S.Collingwood
(2243) T.G.Symons
(2256) Gary Anderson
(2262) James ter Beek
(2278) M.Nicolle
(2287) Martyn Lewis
(2290) Stephen Roberts
(2291) H. Harry
(2294) Sean Daly
(2299) Alison Pickard
(2306) Dale Bennett
(2307) G. Hansen
(2313) Paul Das

(2314) Roy Stannard
(2315) Lee Squires
(2319) Melanie Ogden
(2320) Lorraine Rawson
(2324) Gary Nash
(2325) Neil Devine
(2326) Carl Humpage
(2331) Paul McKenna
(2337) John Richardson
(2338) Tony Lundberg
(2340) Mark Gardener
(2344) G.A. Skipper
(2346) Paul Marks
(2351) Linda Diver
(2352) Colin Lindell
(2360) Sharon Hill
(2368) Chris Cadman
(2371) J McGeachy
(2376) Erik Larsen
(2377) Colin Joelson
(2378) A. Burns
(2388) William Black
(2424) P. Inglesfield
(2434) Malcolm Taylor
(2444) Keith Emberton
(2445) Ian McNaughton
(2462) David Henderson
(2487) David Rawson
(2488) Abdul Jabbar
(2495) Munir Shaffi
(2506) Phillip Bell
(2509) Roy Braithwaite
(2511) K. Coaker
(2546) Mohammed Afzal
(2561) W. Wilkinson
(2565) Robert Walker
(2567) Steven Robertson
(2570) Tony Boswell
(2585) David Thomas
(2599) Elvis Whetton
(2599) Jayne Coupe
(2602) Graham Waggett
(2607) Tony Harrington
(2610) Tricia Irvine
(2618) N.Kavanagh

THE BRUCE LEE SOCIETY

(2619) Graeme Warwick
(2624) Kevin Stokes
(2631) Alan Cousins
(2637) Gillian Wood
(2643) Robert Chamberlain
(2660) Steve Palmer
(2670) Michael Roakes
(2672) Andrew Upton
(2673) Mark Tyler
(2688) Shaune Bridgwood
(2692) Raj Sahni
(2694) Phillip Lai
(2699) K. Spicer
(2701) Alan Appleton
(2708) Colin Quinton
(2715) William Ross
(2720) Andrew Waite
(2728) Graham Ellis
(2734) John Robinson
(2738) Simon Bulley
(2745) John Ruby
(2751) Maria Fernandes
(2759) Andy Curtis
(2768) Bryan Bath
(2782) Ann Jones
(2805) Shaun Boland
(2818) Shane James
(2824) James Flanagan
(2839) Douglas Banks
(2863) Cherrilyne Bankes
(2864) Robert Hartsfield
(2873) Zahid Jawed
(2880) Mark James
(2881) Gilbert Ross
(2885) Glynn Darbyshire
(2886) Jorgen Muller
(2891) Joseph Erskine
(2897) Simon McCall

(2900) Peter Reynolds
(2904) Michael McLaren
(2916) P. Norris
(2918) Ian Fawcett
(2919) Michelle Scully
(2933) Ernest Bow
(2939) Caroline Andrew
(2990) Paul Haste
(2996) Jayme Rousso
(3009) Edgar Lapada
(3034) L.K. Stanley
(3035) Avtar Sohota
(3039) Tracey Bennett
(3048) Michael Clark
(3049) Keith Thompson
(3052) G. Pugh
(3062) Connie & Conor Kelleher
(3067) Jan-Geir Hansen
(3080) Benny Jorgensen
(3082) Jacqueline McKinney
(3084) Harry Otty
(3090) John Deakin
(3107) J. Elliott
(3116) Neil Wilde
(3120) Lenny Franchi
(3134) Y. Jacob
(3158) Robert Fair
(3196) R. G. Heath
(3223) Kin Tong Liu
(3248) Iain Leslie
(3285) Owen Wint
(3293) Shahid Saleem
(3303) Neil McLean
(3304) David Smith
(3308) Anthony Ivison
(3318) Graham Jukes
(3321) Satvinder Singh
(3354) Rajiv Gaikwar

A RETROSPECTIVE LOOK AT BRUCE LEE MANIA & THE KUNG FU CRAZE OF THE 1970S

THE K.F.M. BRUCE LEE SOCIETY

EPHEMERA

THE BRUCE LEE SOCIETY

BRUCE LEE — THE VITAL STATISTICS

BORN:	November 27 1940 in San Francisco's Chinese Hospital
FATHER:	Li Hoi Chun (died February 1965)
MOTHER:	Grace Li
BROTHERS/SISTERS:	Bruce was born the 4th of 5 children. His brothers and sisters were Agnes, Phoebe, Peter and Robert.
WIFE:	Linda Emery
CHILDREN:	Two. One Son, Brandon and one daughter Shannon.
DIED:	July 20th. 1973 in Hong Kong's Queen Elizabeth Hospital.
HEIGHT:	5'7½"
WEIGHT:	140 lbs.
ASTROLOGICAL SIGN:	Sagittarius.
EDUCATION:	Several schools in Hong Kong before enrolling in St. Francis Xaviers College. Following that, visited USA to attend Edison Vocational High School and finally majored in philosophy at Seattle, Washington University for three years, although he never completed his course.
RESIDENT:	Cities in which Bruce lived for any length of time include: San Francisco, Hong Kong, Los Angeles, Seattle, Oakland, and finally Kowloon Tong in Hong Kong.
FILMS:	Tears of *San Francisco* (made when Bruce was still a tiny baby). This was followed by a number of Cantonese movies in which Bruce starred as a young child, made in Hong Kong, including *Kid Cheung*, *Birth of a Boy*, *Orphan Ah Sam* and The *Long and Winding Road*. In the 1960's, in the USA Bruce starred in several TV series including *The Green Hornet* and *Long Street*. He also made guest appearances on other TV shows including *Ironside*, *Blondie*, *Here comes the Brides* and *Batman*. He co-starred with James Garner in the MGM film *Marlowe* and finally returned to Hong Kong where he made the following kung-fu movies. *The Big Boss* and *Fist of Fury* for Golden Harvest, *Way of the Dragon* for Concorde and *Enter the Dragon* for Warner Brothers and Concorde jointly. Bruce had begun shooting *Game of Death*, but had not completed the film when he died.
MARTIAL ART:	As a boy in Hong Kong he learned Tai Chi Chu'an and aged 13 he undertook Wing Chun Kung-Fu under Yip Man, a respected and revered master of the art. Later Bruce developed his own style of Kung-Fu which he termed Jeet Kune Do (literal translation: The Intercepting Fist). In the USA he founded three Jun Fan schools of Kung-Fu in Seattle, Oakland and Los Angeles which attracted many pupils, several of them famous (Steve McQueen, James Garner etc). He closed these schools following his return to Hong Kong. In 1972 he was awarded a place in *Black Belt* magazine's 'Hall of Fame'.

Above: Vital Statistics Sheet (Front)

A RETROSPECTIVE LOOK AT BRUCE LEE MANIA & THE KUNG FU CRAZE OF THE 1970S

WHAT THE STARS SAY —
A BREAKDOWN OF BRUCE LEE'S OWN BIRTH CHART

Bruce Lee was born in San Francisco in the early hours of the morning of the 27th November 1940.

The Sun in the first house gives a desire to be appreciated for oneself alone. there may be a conscious effort to dominate any situation. First house suns indicate strong wills, abundant vitality and great self awareness. The subject is ambitious, working hard in order to achieve personal distinction in the eyes of the world. They must feel themselves to be persons of importance and distinction.

The Sun in trine with Pluto gives highly evolved powers of concentration and will, insight into situations and the ability to make the most efficient use of energy and resources. There is often an interest in systems of spiritual self-development. This aspect gives energy in creative self-expression.

The moon in the twelfth house means that moods and emotional responses are strongly affected by the unconscious and past experiences. There may be a reluctance to communicate feelings. Also indicated are secret love affairs, neurotic tendencies and loneliness.

The Moon in Scorpio gives strong emotions that are based on wilful desire. There is a tendency towards brooding and desire for revenge. The subject may be preoccupied by sex, his problems frequently having a sexual basis. Fantasy and dreams play an important part in his life. There is an inner pressure to keep pushing forward. There is a danger of turning to drugs or alcohol or promiscuity in order to release pent up feelings.

The Moon in conjunction with Mercury brings an awareness of his personal emotional nature and responses. The subject is sensitive to other people's opinion of him. Feelings may overrule the reason. Domestic and family affairs are of great important to him.

The Moon in conjunction with Venus brings a highly emotional response to beauty and harmony that is often manifested in artistic ability. The subject is sensitive, affectionate and self indulgent.

The Moon in opposition to Jupiter shows a tendency to get carried away by benevolent impulses and a possibility of extravagance and waste. Kindness may be indiscriminate and lacking in wisdom.

The Moon is opposition to Saturn shows a tendency to emotional depressions caused perhaps by clinging to worn out relationships and family ties. May give a stiff formal manner that makes it hard for the subject to respond to people in a natural way.

The Moon square to Pluto shows an intense emotional nature that generates a psychic field that can make others (especially women) feel uneasy. There may be a desire to forget the past or to destroy ties that confine. The subject is annoyed by small and petty details becoming impatient if events move too slowly.

Mercury in the first house makes the subject quick-witted and adaptable and keenly self-analytical. There is an enquiring restless mind. Actions and self-awareness are based on logic and reasoning.

Mercury in Scorpio gives an intuitive mind. Things and events are seen accurately but not necessarily charitably. A determined mind gives the strength to surmount obstacles that many would find impossible. The subject may be sharp tongued. With the Sun in Sagittarius and the Moon in Scorpio there may be a visionary disposition. People feel he 'knows more than he cares to tell'. He makes a dangerous opponent.

Mercury in opposition to Saturn makes the subject somewhat defensive and suspicious, prone to depression and anxiety with a tendency to look on the dark side. Nervous and respiratory disorders are possible. The subject tends to rigid self-discipline and mental loneliness.

Mercury in opposition to Uranus gives eccentric opinions, sometimes tactlessness, arrogance and conceit. The subject considers himself especially gifted. There is considerable nervous tension and addiction to the unusual and unconventional.

Venus in the twelfth house can indicate clandestine romances, platonic affairs or a life of sacrificial service. Personal comforts and desires may be discarded. There is a love of quiet and solitude, some social shyness and compassion. Artistic inspiration from the unconscious. The subject requires a practical direction for effort that gives meaning to life.

Venus in opposition to Jupiter makes the subject spoiled and too involved with meaningless social activity. Martial problems may centre around matters of religion. The subject likes to be the centre of attention.

Venus in opposition to Saturn brings frustration of joy, beauty and happiness in the subject's life. Often indicates an unhappy marriage where the partner is unresponsive (or older than the subject).

Mars in Scorpio shows powerful emotions and desires that give relentless courage and thoroughness in the execution of intentions. The subject is resourceful, energetic and courageous in difficult situations. There is a powerful sex drive. The subject is secretive and may hold grudges. A tendency to try dominate others emotionally.

Mars in opposition to Jupiter brings extravagant tendencies and aggression. The subject is restless with a desire for travel and adventure. Prone to boasting and exaggerating his own importance.

Mars square to Pluto. This can be a dangerous aspect because it forces the subject to use force to gain his desires. Can result in an exalted form of courage. The subject may desire to perform some spectacular deed from egotism. This aspect can indicate an early death.

Above: Vital Statistics Sheet (Reverse)

THE BRUCE LEE SOCIETY

THE BRUCE LEE SECRET SOCIETY
39 Goodge Street, London W.1.

Rules and Regulations

1) This card represents one year's membership to the Bruce Lee Secret Society (BLSS). For details of annual renewal, see the back cover.

2) This card is your own personal property. It is not to be sold, lent or exchanged to another who is not a current member of the BLSS.

3) The BLSS reserves the right to refuse membership or to expel any person whose actions are seen to be detrimental to the name of the Society.

4) The BLSS reserves the right to at any time instigate closure of the society with suitable refund where deemed appropriate.

5) Of the £2.95 subscription fee, £1.50 shall cover the Society Kit currently on offer to new or renewing members. This shall be sent once a year soon after receipt of subscription. The remaining £1.45 covers costs and overheads and also ensures receipt of the quarterly news sheet.

6) From time to time the Society shall make special mail-order offers available to its members. When ordering these it is essential that membership numbers be included with all names and addresses. (This also applies to KFM offers where a special reduction in price to Society members is in operation).

I............................ do hereby agree to adhere by the rules and regulations of the Bruce Lee Secret Society. I also promise in the name of Bruce Lee to honour the Kung-Fu Code and never to bring the club into disrepute. Finally, I shall undertake the task of keeping alive the name of the world's greatest ever martial artist, Bruce Lee — the Little Dragon.

Signed ....

Date of Expiry

To ensure that you retain the same membership number, please arrange for your annual subscription to reach us within one week of the above expiry date. To renew, return this card, along with £2.95, to the Bruce Lee Secret Society, Kung-Fu Monthly, 39 Goodge Street, London W1P 1FD.

Above: First-Year Membership Card 1976/77

A RETROSPECTIVE LOOK AT BRUCE LEE MANIA & THE KUNG FU CRAZE OF THE 1970S

BRUCE LEE

KFM Bruce Lee Society — He shall not be forgotten

2nd year

The K.F.M.

BRUCE LEE SOCIETY

No.

THE BRUCE LEE SOCIETY
14 Rathbone Place, London W1

Rules and Regulations

1) This card represents one year's membership to the Bruce Lee Society (BLS). For details of annual renewal, see the next page.

2) This card is your own personal property. It is not to be sold, lent or exchanged to another who is not a current member of the BLS.

3) The BLS reserves the right to refuse membership or to expel any person whose actions are seen to be detrimental to the name of the Society.

4) The BLS reserves the right to at any time instigate closure of the Society with suitable refund where deemed appropriate.

5) Of the £3.25 subscription fee, £1.75 shall cover the Society kit currently on offer to new or renewing members. This shall be sent once a year, soon after receipt of the subscription. The remaining £1.50 covers costs and overheads and also ensures receipt of the Quarterly News Sheet.

6) From time to time the Society shall make special mail-order offers available to its members. When ordering these it is essential that membership numbers be included with all names and addresses. (This also applies to KFM offers where a special reduction in price to Society members is in operation).

I, ...
do hereby agree to adhere by the rules and regulations of the Bruce Lee Society. I also promise in the name of Bruce Lee to honour the Kung-Fu Code and never bring the club into disrepute. Finally, I shall undertake the task of keeping alive the name of the world's greatest ever martial artist, Bruce Lee — the Little Dragon.

Signed, ...

Date of Expiry

To ensure that you retain the same membership number, please arrange for your annual subscription to reach us within one week of the above expiry date. To renew, return this card, along with £3.25, to the KFM Bruce Lee Society, Kung-Fu Monthly, 14 Rathbone Place, London W1P 1DE.

Above: Second-Year Membership Card 1977/78

THE BRUCE LEE SOCIETY

The K.F.M.

BRUCE LEE SECRET SOCIETY

This is to certify that

_____

has been accepted this day

_____

as a full, bona fide member of
The Kung-Fu Monthly
BRUCE LEE SECRET SOCIETY

I do hereby agree to be bound by the Kung-Fu Code of Honour.

Signature of member _____

Signature of President _____*P.P.Fadden*_____

THE KFM BRUCE LEE SECRET SOCIETY – 39 GOODGE STREET, LONDON W1P 1FD

Above: First-Year Membership Certificate 1976/77

A RETROSPECTIVE LOOK AT BRUCE LEE MANIA & THE KUNG FU CRAZE OF THE 1970S

The K.F.M.

BRUCE LEE SOCIETY
2nd year

This is to certify that

_____

has this day

_____

completed one full years membership of
The Kung-Fu Monthly
BRUCE LEE SOCIETY

I do hereby agree to be bound by the Kung-Fu Code of Honour

Signature of member _____

Signature of President _____ P.P.Hodden _____

THE K.F.M. BRUCE LEE SOCIETY, 14 RATHBONE PLACE, LONDON

Above: Second-Year Membership Card 1977/78

THE BRUCE LEE SOCIETY
Goes From Strength To Strength!

In the Summer of 1976, there was no Society. The President of the Bruce Lee Fan Club had recently resigned her post and closed down the movement. Immediately, Kung-Fu Monthly found itself innundated with pleas from its readers that a new club be formed to celebrate the memory of the late Master. The message was clear... to help satisfy the needs of Little Dragon fans everywhere, something had to be done – and done quickly!

From that small beginning grew one of the largest and most successful appreciation societies ever known. Kung-Fu Monthly magazine, being the only remaining publication to hold true to the memory of Bruce Lee, was a natural to act as the foundation for such a club. Then as now, KFM has been proud to confirm its cherished position as number one martial arts magazine in the world – and its support of the greatest-ever exponent of kung-fu has long been legendary.

But who to be Society President? Fate took a hand and directed towards us probably the two most able candidates around. Pam and Carmella seized the reins with undisguised relish and kung-fu history had begun.

The path has been stony – the direction often not clear. But always, there's been one thing the Bruce Lee Society has been able to count on. *The unswerving loyalty of the most enthusiastic membership any club has ever had!* The tough, unstinting work put in by Pam and Carmella (who later, sadly had to leave us) is, I am certain, remembered with gratitude by every single member who has ever written in to the club. No letter has been ignored, no question has been left unanswered where help has been possible.

And still the movement strides ahead! Already a sister Society exists in the United States and many more are planned around the countries of Europe. The name of Bruce Lee CANNOT and WILL NOT be forgotten – all of us must make sure of that! It will take time, dedication and, above all, great effort, but I know I can count on every single one of you to do what must be done. The lessons we have to learn from the Master – his revelations and his sayings – shall serve as a guide to us all. Let's make sure we do not shirk our duty, for the word must continue to be spread.

To salute YOUR one full year's membership, The Bruce Lee Society offers a brand new pack, consisting of the special 2nd year membership card and scroll (coloured red), more rare photos of the Master and, most importantly of all, a unique 2nd year SOLID METAL BADGE/BROOCH finished in GOLD and BLACK! The design is beautiful and its importance, unmistakable.

Please remember the renewal fee is just £3.25 and in order that you retain your current membership number, I must ask that you send in your cheque/postal orders as soon as you can! I hardly need remind you of the value for money being offered. *A regular 3-monthly News Sheet – a full feature in every issue of Kung-Fu monthly* – a guarantee that ALL your letters to Pam, the President, will be answered in full – the Swop Shop, Pen-Pals, Competitions, endless new facts & information – reductions on KFM mail order goods. The list is enormous... what other club has ever offered as much?

May I thank you for your support over the last year – may you long continue to remain with us.

Felix Yen – Editor of Kung-Fu Monthly & Chief Honorary Member of the Bruce Lee Society.

RENEWAL INFORMATION
Please send this slip, along with £3.25 (cheques/postal orders made out to Kung-Fu Monthly) to:
The Bruce Lee Society
Subscription Renewals
14 Rathbone Place
London W1P 1DE

Name
_____

Address
_____

_____

Present Membership Number
_____

Above: Second-Year Renewal Form 1977/78

A RETROSPECTIVE LOOK AT BRUCE LEE MANIA & THE KUNG FU CRAZE OF THE 1970S

The Kung-Fu Monthly
BRUCE LEE SECRET SOCIETY
39 Goodge Street, London W.1.

The KFM Bruce Lee Secret Society — He shall not be forgotten

Now is your chance to join the one and only BRUCE LEE SECRET SOCIETY!

You'll get pictures, information, a club badge and sticker, a membership scroll, a regular column in each and every edition of the fantastic Kung-Fu Monthly, plus a superb three-monthly News Sheet. On top of it all there's a swop shop and, coming soon, a comprehensive kung-fu mail order book list, featuring in particular, Bruce Lee the greatest martial artist the world has ever known.

IT'S GREAT VALUE FOR MONEY!!

Send just £2.95 to the above address... I promise you won't be disappointed!

Joint Presidents ... Pam Hadden, Carmella Rapa

Above: Bruce Lee Secret Society Advertisement Flyer (1976)

THE BRUCE LEE SOCIETY

THE BRUCE LEE SECRET SOCIETY.

HI — it's Jenny Lee here and am I happy to be writing these few words! Thanks largely to a lot of persuasion from you, the KFM readers, I am delighted to announce the grand opening of the *Bruce Lee Secret Society*. Yes, your own Kung-Fu Monthly is taking up the reins along with Pam Hadden and Carmella Rapa (who will be joint presidents of the club). They'll handle all the letter writing and day-to-day running of things ... good luck Pam and Carmella, I know you're going to need it! OK, I've said my piece so it's back to the mail bags for me. Over to you ...

Thanks for the intro' Jenny — we couldn't have done it better ourselves! Because we've got so much to tell you, I hope you'll forgive us if we itemise everything — that way we'll be able to squeeze more in.

1) On application you'll receive your membership card and a number, plus the fabulous *Society Kit*, containing your very own official certificate of membership (for framing), a *Bruce Lee Secret Society* badge and sticker, an autographed Bruce Lee pic and *four incredible photos of the Little Dragon in action that we promise have never been published in the world before!* All this plus news, views, facts and info — what a great package!

2) Then, once every three months, we'll post to you the quarterly Society news sheet — brim full of the latest chit-chat, letters, pen-pals, club offers and much more.

3) In every single issue of KFM you'll find your very own *Bruce Lee Secret Society* corner ... we'll be handling that!

4) All members will soon be able to get a discount on most KFM mail order offers.

5) On top of all that, there'll be lots of special Bruce Lee mail order products exclusively on offer to club members.

6) We are very sorry, but we have to point out that there is NO connection whatsoever between this and the previous Bruce Lee Fan Club. Regretfully therefore, we shall not be able to enter into any correspondence in regard to problems arising from its closure.

7) Sorry again! ... but we do really have to restrict membership to the United Kingdom only.

8) Finally, may we say here and now that we shall *not* be replying to letters that come without stamped addressed envelopes — you have been warned!

So there it is — what a great line-up and all for an annual subcription of only £2.95 — not bad eh?

Judging by the mail deluge that comes in through Jenny's door we think we have a fair idea of what we are letting ourselves in for — it's a good thing we're gluttons for punishment! But remember, if you've got any bright ideas on what you'd like to see in your club, don't hesitate to write ... we promise you ALL letters will be answered. And by the way, don't forget that's exactly what it is — your club. After all, what's a club without members? The old Bruce Lee Fan Club apparently had around five thousand members when it closed ... let's see if we can double it — and keep open! DON'T DELAY
Just send your £2.95 to:
The Bruce Lee Secret Society
Kung-Fu Monthly
39 Goodge Street
London W1P 1FD

(Cheques/Postal orders made out to Kung-Fu Monthly please.)

We'll get your Society Kit and membership card off to you as quickly as possibly. See you soon — *Pam and Carmella.*

Above: Full Page Advertisement in *Kung Fu Monthly* No. 22

A RETROSPECTIVE LOOK AT BRUCE LEE MANIA & THE KUNG FU CRAZE OF THE 1970S

THOUGH THE MASTER IS GONE

Yes, sad to say the Master *has* gone but that does not mean he will be forgotten — far from it! *The Bruce Lee Secret Society* is devoted to the memory of the Master. We are governed by his teachings, his sayings, his way of life. Though the Little Dragon himself is no longer here to lead the way, the great gift that he left with us and the example of excellence he set, lives on in our hearts and minds.

And when you become accepted as a member, just take a look at what you're entitled to get:

* A personal *membership card* — to carry with you always!

* The absolutely unique *badge* and *sticker* — available ONLY to members — plus photos, a biography and a fact sheet.

* Your very own *membership scroll*, tastefully designed for mounting and displaying.

* A superb THREE-MONTHLY *News Sheet...* full of gossip, rumours, secrets, fan's comments, pix, pen pals, competitions, a swop shop and much, much more.

* A regular page in Kung-Fu Monthly, the world's greatest ever martial arts magazine — not to mention great money saving reductions on all the KFM mail order goods.

* A guarantee that ALL your letters will be answered and wherever possible, all your problems solved!

Remember, the only way you can be absolutely certain of having a share in the great movement which the Master has created is to become a part of the *Bruce Lee Secret Society*.

NO OTHER FAN CLUB HAS EVER OFFERED AS MUCH... and yet, unbelievably, all this can be yours for ONLY £3.25. That's right, and new members are ALWAYS welcome, so don't just think about it, MAKE SURE you join right now — you'll never regret it!

Send immediately your £3.25 cheque or postal order to:

The Bruce Lee Secret Society
39 Goodge Street
London W1P 1FD

The K.F.M.

BRUCE LEE SECRET SOCIETY

Above: Full Page Advertisement in *Kung Fu Monthly* No. 28

MEMBERSHIP BADGES

Above: First to Eighth-Year Pin Badges

Secret Society Badge

Secret Society Vinyl Sticker

Above: Bruce Lee Society Scarf

Above: Bruce Lee Society Paper Stickers
Below: 1976 Christmas Card (A5 Folded Once)

"He Shall Not Be Forgotten!"

THE KFM BRUCE LEE SECRET SOCIETY – 39 GOODGE STREET, LONDON W1P 1FD

The Kung-Fu Monthly
BRUCE LEE SECRET SOCIETY
wishes all its members a
VERY HAPPY CHRISTMAS

Joint Presidents ...
Pam Hadden, Carmella Rapa

Above: 1977 Christmas Card (A4 Folded Twice)

Left:
Full Page Advertisement in *Kung Fu Monthly* No. 21

> *DRAMATIC NEWS!*
> KFM is planning to start its own **Bruce Lee fan club!** Hold on ... don't write in yet. Full details in KFM No.21.

Above:
Small Advertisement in *Kung Fu Monthly* No. 20

A RETROSPECTIVE LOOK AT BRUCE LEE MANIA & THE KUNG FU CRAZE OF THE 1970S

FULL WEBSITE LINKS TO QR CODES

VIDEO LINKS

http://bruceleesociety.co.uk/1	Location Hong Kong The Making of Enter the Dragon
http://bruceleesociety.co.uk/2	Bruce Lee Souvenir Video
http://bruceleesociety.co.uk/3	The Kung Fu Years
http://bruceleesociety.co.uk/4	Bruce Lee: A Warrior's Journey Trailer
http://bruceleesociety.co.uk/5	Bruce Lee in GOD. Trailer 1
http://bruceleesociety.co.uk/6	Bruce Lee in GOD. Trailer 2
http://bruceleesociety.co.uk/7	Bruce Lee: Number One Son Screen Test 1965 BW
http://bruceleesociety.co.uk/8	Bruce Lee: The Man and The Legend Trailer
http://bruceleesociety.co.uk/9	Jesse Glovers Tour of Bruce Lees Seattle
http://bruceleesociety.co.uk/10	The Green Hornet Black Beauty Featurette
http://bruceleesociety.co.uk/11	Half a Loaf of Kung Fu Trailer
http://bruceleesociety.co.uk/12	The Real Bruce Lee Trailer
http://bruceleesociety.co.uk/13	Bruce Lee 1965 Number One Son Screen Test (Colour)
http://bruceleesociety.co.uk/14	1983 Nestle Crunch Commercial With Kareem Abdul-Jabbar
http://bruceleesociety.co.uk/15	ABC Longstreet 1971 TV Promo
http://bruceleesociety.co.uk/16	Airplane Trailer
http://bruceleesociety.co.uk/17	Al Dacascos in Denver 1973
http://bruceleesociety.co.uk/18	Atari Commercial With Pele, Andretti and Kareem Abdul Jabbar
http://bruceleesociety.co.uk/19	Bette Rogge interviews Keye Luke
http://bruceleesociety.co.uk/20	Bill 'Superfoot' Wallace vs Joe Lewis
http://bruceleesociety.co.uk/21	Black Belt Jones 1974 Official Trailer
http://bruceleesociety.co.uk/22	Bruce Lee Tower of Death Game of Death 2 Trailer
http://bruceleesociety.co.uk/23	Bruce Lee Kato vs Robin - Batman TV Show 1967
http://bruceleesociety.co.uk/24	Enter the Dragon Abbott Scene
http://bruceleesociety.co.uk/25	Bruce Lee Birthday Party World of Bruce Lee Museum 1981
http://bruceleesociety.co.uk/26	Bruce Lee vs Ji Han Jae (Game of Death) Clip
http://bruceleesociety.co.uk/27	Bruce Lee scenes in Fist of Unicorn aka The Unicorn Palm
http://bruceleesociety.co.uk/28	The Big Boss 1971 Movie Trailer Rejected 35mm English Version
http://bruceleesociety.co.uk/29	Bruce Lee Tracking The Dragon Birmingham Convention 1990
http://bruceleesociety.co.uk/30	Bruce Lee - The Orphan 1959
http://bruceleesociety.co.uk/31	Bruce's Deadly Fingers Trailer
http://bruceleesociety.co.uk/32	Chinese Detective Trailer (1982)
http://bruceleesociety.co.uk/33	Chuck Norris Karate Kommandos 1986 Official Trailer
http://bruceleesociety.co.uk/34	Elvis Presley - New Gladiators
http://bruceleesociety.co.uk/35	Fist of Fear Touch of Death Trailer
http://bruceleesociety.co.uk/36	Fist of Unicorn Trailer
http://bruceleesociety.co.uk/37	Gary Daniels Fight Scenes
http://bruceleesociety.co.uk/38	Goodbye Bruce Lee Trailer 2
http://bruceleesociety.co.uk/39	Goodbye Bruce Lee Trailer
http://bruceleesociety.co.uk/40	Grandmaster Wang Zi Ping
http://bruceleesociety.co.uk/41	Green Hornet Strikes Again 1941 Clip
http://bruceleesociety.co.uk/42	Hot Potato 1976 Trailer
http://bruceleesociety.co.uk/43	In Conversation with John Saxon Enter the Dragon
http://bruceleesociety.co.uk/44	Interview with Grandmaster William Cheung
http://bruceleesociety.co.uk/45	Jackie Chan Adventures Season 1 Trailer
http://bruceleesociety.co.uk/46	Jackie Chan Talking About Bruce Lee
http://bruceleesociety.co.uk/47	Ji Han Jae Remembers Bruce Lee
http://bruceleesociety.co.uk/48	JKD Band Dragon Power 1979
http://bruceleesociety.co.uk/49	King Dragon The World of Bruce Lee Trailer
http://bruceleesociety.co.uk/50	Kung Fu Killers Trailer
http://bruceleesociety.co.uk/51	Legend of Bruce Lee Thai Boxer

http://bruceleesociety.co.uk/52	Lost Interview with Bruce Lee Mentor William Cheung
http://bruceleesociety.co.uk/53	Interview with Bruce Lee Mentor William Cheung
http://bruceleesociety.co.uk/54	*Martial Arts Today TV* James Demile
http://bruceleesociety.co.uk/55	*Monkey* TV Series Opening Song
http://bruceleesociety.co.uk/56	Kareem Abdul Jabbar On Bruce Lee's Training
http://bruceleesociety.co.uk/57	Kareem Abdul Jabbar Atari Ad
http://bruceleesociety.co.uk/58	Joe Lewis On Bruce Lee and Kickboxing
http://bruceleesociety.co.uk/59	*Chinese Gods* Clip
http://bruceleesociety.co.uk/60	Pat Johnson Clip from 2016
http://bruceleesociety.co.uk/61	Playing *The Silent Flute* David Carradine Documentary
http://bruceleesociety.co.uk/62	Remembering Bruce Lee Pat Johnson
http://bruceleesociety.co.uk/63	Ruby Chow Documentary
http://bruceleesociety.co.uk/64	*Slaughter in San Francisco* 1974 Trailer
http://bruceleesociety.co.uk/65	*Teenage Mutant Ninja Turtles* 1987 Series DVD Preview
http://bruceleesociety.co.uk/66	The Amazing Kung Fu Eddie Hamill Highlights
http://bruceleesociety.co.uk/67	*The Brown Hornet* Clip
http://bruceleesociety.co.uk/68	*The Iron-Fisted Monk* 1977 Trailer
http://bruceleesociety.co.uk/69	*The Kentucky Fried Movie* Trailer
http://bruceleesociety.co.uk/70	*The Real Bruce* Lee Trailer
http://bruceleesociety.co.uk/71	*The Silent Flute* UK Trailer
http://bruceleesociety.co.uk/72	*The Street Fighter* Collection Trailer
http://bruceleesociety.co.uk/73	*The Water Margin* 1972 - Original HK Theatrical Trailer
http://bruceleesociety.co.uk/74	*They Call Me Bruce* Trailer
http://bruceleesociety.co.uk/75	*Three the Hard Way* 1974 Trailer
http://bruceleesociety.co.uk/76	*Wong Shun Leung The King of Talking Hands* Trailer
http://bruceleesociety.co.uk/77	William Cheung on Meeting Bruce Lee
http://bruceleesociety.co.uk/78	*Fist of Fury* Original Theatrical Trailer
http://bruceleesociety.co.uk/79	*The Big Boss* Original 35mm Title Sequence
http://bruceleesociety.co.uk/80	*The Big Boss* Original Theatrical Trailer
http://bruceleesociety.co.uk/81	*The Big Boss* HK Promotional Trailer
http://bruceleesociety.co.uk/82	*Way of the Dragon* Original Theatrical Trailer
http://bruceleesociety.co.uk/83	*Way of the Dragon* UK 70s Trailer
http://bruceleesociety.co.uk/84	*Way of the Dragon* UK 70s TV Spot 1
http://bruceleesociety.co.uk/85	*Way of the Dragon* UK 70s TV Spot 2
http://bruceleesociety.co.uk/86	*Enter the Dragon* Original Theatrical Trailer 1
http://bruceleesociety.co.uk/87	*Enter the Dragon* Original Theatrical Trailer 2
http://bruceleesociety.co.uk/88	*Enter the Dragon* Extended Theatrical Trailer 1
http://bruceleesociety.co.uk/89	*Enter the Dragon* Extended Theatrical Trailer 2
http://bruceleesociety.co.uk/90	*Game of Death* Original Theatrical Trailer
http://bruceleesociety.co.uk/91	*Game of Death* Greenhouse Fight
http://bruceleesociety.co.uk/92	*Game of Death* Alternate Ending
http://bruceleesociety.co.uk/93	*Game of Death* Alternate Title Sequence
http://bruceleesociety.co.uk/94	*The Green Hornet & Fury of the Dragon* (Trailers)
http://bruceleesociety.co.uk/95	*Bruce Lee The Legend* Trailer
http://bruceleesociety.co.uk/96	*Bruce Lee The Man & The Legend* Trailer
http://bruceleesociety.co.uk/97	*Enter the Dragon* Chinese Trailer
http://bruceleesociety.co.uk/98	*Number One Son Screen Test* BW Excellent Quality
http://bruceleesociety.co.uk/99	Brandon Lee Interview 1992
http://bruceleesociety.co.uk/100	Jackie Chan Action Reel *Top Fighter*
http://bruceleesociety.co.uk/101	*The Life & Legend of Bob Wall* Trailer
http://bruceleesociety.co.uk/102	James Coburn Interview
http://bruceleesociety.co.uk/103	*Marlowe* Trailer
http://bruceleesociety.co.uk/104	Twelve Weeks in Hong Kong Photo Film
http://bruceleesociety.co.uk/105	*The Karate Kid Beyond The Form*
http://bruceleesociety.co.uk/106	*The Karate Kid Fight Choreography*
http://bruceleesociety.co.uk/107	*Bruce Lee His Life and Loves* Nora Miao

A RETROSPECTIVE LOOK AT BRUCE LEE MANIA & THE KUNG FU CRAZE OF THE 1970S

http://bruceleesociety.co.uk/108	*Celebrity Relics*
http://bruceleesociety.co.uk/109	*The Big Boss* 8mm Trailer
http://bruceleesociety.co.uk/110	*Bruce Lee The Man The Myth* Trailer
http://bruceleesociety.co.uk/111	*Exit the Dragon Enter the Tiger* Trailer
http://bruceleesociety.co.uk/112	*Bruce Lee Fights Back from the Grave* Trailer
http://bruceleesociety.co.uk/113	Bruce Li Interview
http://bruceleesociety.co.uk/114	*Kill Bill Vol. 1* Trailer
http://bruceleesociety.co.uk/115	*Kill Bill Vol. 2* Trailer
http://bruceleesociety.co.uk/116	*Once Upon a Time in... Holllywood* Clip
http://bruceleesociety.co.uk/117	*The Wrecking Crew* Clip
http://bruceleesociety.co.uk/118	*Curse of the Dragon* Clip
http://bruceleesociety.co.uk/119	*Dragon - The Bruce Lee Story* (Featurette)
http://bruceleesociety.co.uk/120	Tracking The Dragon 1994 with Taky Kimura
http://bruceleesociety.co.uk/121	*Cutting Edge #46: Enter the Dragon*
http://bruceleesociety.co.uk/122	*LMF - 1127* Music Video
http://bruceleesociety.co.uk/123	*The One Armed Swordsman* Trailer
http://bruceleesociety.co.uk/124	*The Man From Hong Kong* Trailer
http://bruceleesociety.co.uk/125	*The One Armed Boxer* Trailer
http://bruceleesociety.co.uk/gd	Glynn Darbyshire Figure Collection
http://bruceleesociety.co.uk/bridge	*Building the Bridge: The 2000 Bruce Lee Philosophy Lectures In Ireland* documentary

STORE LINKS

https://amzn.to/3iOuj9C	*King Dragon* Book on Amazon
https://amzn.to/2Czv1bn	Jim Kelly on Amazon
https://amzn.to/3iP4BlC	*Kentucky Fried Movie* on Amazon
http://bruceleesociety.co.uk/kfkvod	*Kung Fu Killers* on Amazon
https://amzn.to/2EeUmHW	*Bruce Lee & I* (Ji Han Jae) DVD on Amazon
https://amzn.to/3awFvVp	*Dragon Power* on Amazon
http://bruceleesociety.co.uk/blingod	*Bruce Lee in G.O.D.* on Amazon
https://amzn.to/3aybyEC	*Bruce Lee: A Warrior's Journey* DVD on Amazon
https://amzn.to/3g4XrYk	*Bruce Lee: A Warrior's Journey* Book on Amazon
https://amzn.to/3iP4giF	Gary Daniels on Amazon
https://amzn.to/2E7Ty7R	Joe Lewis on Amazon
http://bruceleesociety.co.uk/demiledvd	James Demile DVD on Amazon
https://amzn.to/310UeF0	*Immortal Dragon* DVD on Amazon
https://amzn.to/313GcCP	*The Lost Interview* on Amazon
https://amzn.to/2E6ilcu	*The Real Bruce Lee* on Amazon
https://amzn.to/311tfJu	Jackie Chan on Amazon
https://amzn.to/3g56Jna	*Bruce Lee Biography* by Robert Clouse on Amazon
https://amzn.to/2Edx31b	*Bruce Lee The Untold Story* on Amazon
https://amzn.to/315Eq46	*Goodbye Bruce Lee* on Amazon
https://amzn.to/3kLNAdE	*Bruce's Deadly Fingers* on Amazon
https://amzn.to/2PWa39l	*Iron Fisted Monk* on Amazon
https://amzn.to/311eXZu	*Bruce Lee; The Man & The Legend* on Amazon
https://amzn.to/3h4cpix	*New Gladiators* on Amazon
https://amzn.to/2PWSGWt	*Slaughter in San Francisco* on Amazon
https://amzn.to/2Q23KSe	*Fist of Unicorn* on Amazon
https://amzn.to/3fZSGzj	*Airplane* on Amazon
https://amzn.to/3g4VMSx	*Longstreet* on Amazon
https://amzn.to/3g63qw4	Jesse Glover Books on Amazon
https://amzn.to/2CzU0LH	*Chinese Detective* on Amazon
http://bruceleesociety.co.uk/todlink	*Tower of Death* VHS to DVD Transfer Link
https://amzn.to/3av8N77	*Legend of Bruce Lee* on Amazon

THE BRUCE LEE SOCIETY

https://amzn.to/3iOV121	*Bruce Lee: Dynamic Becoming* on Amazon
https://amzn.to/3hhZOsB	*Streetfighter Collection* on Amazon
https://amzn.to/3g55pkz	*Chinese Gods* on Amazon
https://amzn.to/3ayE0GA	*Jackie Chan Adventures* on Amazon
https://amzn.to/311oO1s	*Teenage Mutant Ninja Turtles* on Amazon
https://amzn.to/3g55Mvt	*Karate Kommandos* on Amazon
https://amzn.to/3kRFq3x	*Green Hornet* 1974 Film on Amazon
https://amzn.to/3g9cm3L	*Fist of Fear Touch of Death* on Amazon
https://amzn.to/3axIcGz	*They Call Me Bruce* on Amazon
https://amzn.to/3gcwqTf	*Science of In-Fighting* on Amazon
http://bruceleesociety.co.uk/wsldocs	Wong Shun Leung Documentaries on Amazon
https://amzn.to/3hkj5cP	Bruce Li on Amazon
https://amzn.to/2E6WPF3	*Kill Bill* on Amazon
https://amzn.to/3hjiF6w	*Game of Death* on Amazon
https://amzn.to/2Yp986o	*Silent Flute* on Amazon
https://amzn.to/3hpSvio	Bruce Lee: *The Man and The Legend* on Amazon
https://amzn.to/2Eri97x	Seisuke Suzuki Book on Amazon
https://amzn.to/2QtyonP	Mark Dacascos on Amazon
https://amzn.to/3l8sgPE	Brandon Lee on Amazon
https://amzn.to/2EaKeQN	*Making of Enter the Dragon* by Robert Clouse on Amazon

DOWNLOADS & BOOK LINKS

https://bruceleesociety.co.uk/penthouse1983.pdf 1983	*Penthouse* Article by Albert Goldman

OTHER BOOKS IN THE DRAGON LIBRARY SERIES

The Art of Boxing and Manual of Training: The Deluxe Edition
by William Edwards

Bruce Lee: Dynamic Becoming
by James Bishop

Out-Fighting Or Long-Range Boxing: The Deluxe Edition
by Jim Driscoll

Ringcraft: The Deluxe Edition
by Jim Driscoll

Scientific Boxing: The Deluxe Edition
by James J. Corbett

The Straight Left and How to Cultivate It: The Deluxe Edition
by Jim Driscoll

The Text Book of Boxing: The Deluxe Edition
by Jim Driscoll

www.ingramcontent.com/pod-product-compliance
Lightning Source LLC
Chambersburg PA
CBHW070255240426
43661CB00057B/2560